Heidegger's Philosophy of Being

Heidegger's Philosophy of Being

A CRITICAL INTERPRETATION

HERMAN PHILIPSE

PRINCETON UNIVERSITY PRESS

PRINCETON, NEW JERSEY

Library of Congress Cataloging-in-Publication Data

Philipse, Herman.
Heidegger's philosophy of being : a critical interpretation / Herman Philipse.
p. cm.
Includes bibliographical references and index.
ISBN 0-691-00117-0 (cloth : alk. paper). — ISBN 0-691-00119-7 (pbk. : alk. paper)
1. Heidegger, Martin, 1889–1976—Contributions in ontology. 2. Ontology. I. Title.
B3279.H49P48 1998 111—DC21 98-34876

This book has been composed in Times Roman

Princeton University Press books are printed on acid-free paper and meet the guidelines for
permanence and durability of the Committee on Production Guidelines for Book
Longevity of the Council on Library Resources

http://pup.princeton.edu

Printed in the United States of America

10 9 8 7 6 5 4 3 2 1

10 9 8 7 6 5 4 3 2
(pbk)

TO HENDRICKJE

The real community of man, in the midst of all the self-contradictory simulacra of community, is the community of those who seek the truth, of the potential knowers, that is, in principle, of all men to the extent that they desire to know. But in fact this includes only a few.

Allan Bloom, *The Closing of the American Mind*

CONTENTS

PHILOSOPHERS seek to acquire not only knowledge but also wisdom, as Voltaire tells us in his *Dictionnaire philosophique*. This holds undisputedly for the greatest philosophers of ancient Greece, Plato and Aristotle, and for the Christian thinkers in the medieval tradition. They all believed that knowledge and wisdom are closely related. No logical gap yawns between the scientific system of the world of Plato or Aristotle, for instance, and the idea of human sapience they advocated. The latter follows from the former, since their teleological worldviews imply an account of the *telos* or sense of human existence.

However, since the scientific revolution in the seventeenth century, which substituted a mechanical view of the world for the old, teleological one, the connection between knowledge and wisdom in Western culture has become more and more problematic. Unlike the mainstream Greco-Judeo-Christian tradition, modern science teaches that man is not the center and purpose of the universe. Mankind is but an accidental outcome of an aimless evolution of matter, and will sooner or later be crushed by cosmic processes. If this is what science teaches us, one might feel, like young Ludwig Wittgenstein, that even when all possible scientific questions have been answered, the problems of life remain completely untouched.[1]

The modern tension between knowledge and wisdom causes a centrifugal tendency in philosophy itself. Some philosophers consider scientific integrity as the highest philosophical virtue. In their eyes, to voice one's opinions on human wisdom and the "meaning of existence" is a symptom of bad taste in intellectual matters. Others stress the sterility and irrelevance of scientific philosophy for life, and seek to revitalize the discipline by linking it to the arts, or by an attempt to find inspiration in alien cultures or in earlier stages of Western civilization, in which science and wisdom were still closely intertwined. This rift in modern philosophy explains in part the fierce and contradictory responses to the work of a philosopher who is, according to many scholars on the Continent, the greatest thinker of the twentieth century: Martin Heidegger.

In *Sein und Zeit* (1927, *Being and Time*), Heidegger's first major publication, which caused his celebrity overnight and radically transformed the continental philosophical scene, there is an intimate connection between the epistemic program of a fundamental ontology and a specific ideal of an authentic human life (*eigentliche Existenz*). As Heidegger stresses in the final paragraph of section 62, his fundamental ontology presupposes the existential ideal, and he says that presupposing it is a positive necessity.[2] Because of this connection between philosophical knowledge and wisdom, between *Wissenschaft* and an ideal of human life, Heidegger squarely belongs to the great philosophical tradition of the West. Yet this very connection accounts for the critique of scientifically minded philosophers such as Husserl, who reproached Heidegger for having written a book which is, though unmistakably of genius, thoroughly unscientific.³ It also explains the fascination *Sein und Zeit* exerts on ever new generations of readers.

I vividly remember the impact *Sein und Zeit* made on me when I read it for the first time, about a quarter of a century ago, during my years as an undergraduate. Whereas Heidegger's elaborate ontological characterization of human existence as being-in-the-world purported to liberate philosophy from the dusty epistemological problems over which I had agonized to no avail, his existential ideal of an authentic life, inciting one to a passionate "freedom toward death," seemed to justify and aggrandize my personal history as a young man who tried to break free from the limitations of his background, and who took irresponsible risks during reckless mountaineering tours. Here finally was a philosopher for whom philosophy meant more than an intellectual game concerned with artificial problems such as the problem of the external world, a philosopher who tried to intensify life itself. As Heidegger said at the end of the *Disputatio* with Ernst Cassirer in Davos (1929), philosophy has the task of kicking man out of the lazy attitude in which he merely uses the works of the mind, and of throwing him back, as it were, into the harshness of his destiny.⁴ What attracted me to *Sein und Zeit*, apart from the dazzling phenomenological analyses of human existence, were what seemed to be a sober-minded and yet heroic acceptance of human finiteness, the absence of any attempt to reconcile oneself to one's mortality by postulating a transcendent realm, and the glorification of individual independence.

Shortly afterwards, however, doubts overcame me as to whether my interpretation of *Sein und Zeit* had been correct. I had read the celebrated "question of being," which Heidegger raises in the introduction to the book, as a question concerned with the meaning of human existence. Accordingly, the central thesis of *Sein und Zeit*, that *time* is the horizon of each and every "understanding of being," seemed a natural one: if human existence is essentially finite, we have to find its meaning within the horizon of the limited time of our life, and not in an imaginary eternal realm. Yet I got the impression that Heidegger's later writings refuted this atheist and existentialist interpretation of the question of being.⁵ Already in *Was ist Metaphysik?* (*What Is Metaphysics?*), the inaugural lecture of 1929, Heidegger wrote that *being* itself (*das Sein selbst*) reveals itself in human existence (*Dasein*), when Dasein transcends itself, exposing itself in nothingness.⁶ According to the postscript of 1943, human thought should obey and listen to "the voice of being."⁷ What disturbed me was not only the fact that these and similar phrases echo traditional theological sayings, but also and particularly the contempt for logic and rationality Heidegger expressed in the lecture. Was his not a deeply theological mind, which wanted to "break" the power of reason and to "resolve the idea of logic in a turbulence of more original questioning" concerning being and nothingness?⁸ What else was this than the traditional *sacrificium intellectus* in order to reach God in faith? And how is one to interpret Heidegger's question of being, if the word "being" refers both to human existence and to a mysterious nonentity, called "being" in a participial sense, which reveals and conceals itself and to whose voice the thinker has to listen? What is Heidegger's relation to traditional monotheistic theology?

In the course of time, other questions were added to these. Heidegger is often called a master of philosophical questioning. Pupils such as Hannah Arendt and Hans-Georg Gadamer testify how in his seminars Heidegger was able to restore the great philosophical texts of the past to their original expressive power, and how he inspired his students to question the seeming philosophical self-evidences of the present. However, there is one type of question Heidegger rarely asks and apparently considers philosophically irrelevant: biographical questions about the philosophers whose works he endeavors to elucidate. The laconic phrase with which Heidegger began a lecture course on Aristotle the first of May 1924, that Aristotle "was born, worked, and died," functions as an annulment of Aristotle's tragic and interesting life, as if the lives of philosophers do not matter at all for the interpretation of their works.[9] Now this may be true of philosophers such as Frege, whose writings barely give us a reason to consider his life story. But what about Heidegger himself, who advocated a specific existential attitude in *Sein und Zeit*, and whose work is deeply rooted in the *Lebensphilosophie* (philosophy of life) of Kierkegaard, Dilthey, and Nietzsche, according to which one's philosophical convictions express one's life as it is shaped by physiological, historical, political, religious, or social conditions?[10]

On this issue philosophers—Jaspers, Löwith, and Habermas are among the notable exceptions—often have been naïve, while journalists like Paul Hühnerfeld, sociologists such as Christian Graf von Krockow, and historians such as Hugo Ott, have taught us to ask the proper and improper questions about Heidegger's life, and to hear the political resonances concealed in Heidegger's texts. No wonder that these questions focus on Heidegger's Nazism, even though Heidegger's adherence to Hitler is not the only, and perhaps not even the most important biographical fact relevant to the interpretation of his works. Discussions of Heidegger's involvement with the National Socialist movement have come in at least three waves: the first directly after the war, when Heidegger was deprived of his professorial rights on 19 January 1946; the second after the publication of the *Einführung in die Metaphysik* (*An Introduction to Metaphysics*) in 1953, which occasioned the young student Jürgen Habermas, writing in the *Frankfurter Allgemeine Zeitung* of 25 July 1953, to raise the question as to whether Heidegger's later philosophy did not declare National Socialism innocent of its crimes; and the third after the new publication in 1983 of Heidegger's rectoral address of 27 May 1933, accompanied by Heidegger's own official version of the events of 1933–34, and edited by Heidegger's son Hermann Heidegger.[11] This publication triggered Hugo Ott's historical investigations into Heidegger's life, because Ott was asked to review the pamphlet, which was, as he ironically observes, a "contribution to the fiftieth anniversary of Hitler's rise to power."[12] The third wave has not stopped yet, and especially after Victor Farias's study on Heidegger and Nazism appeared in 1987, it tends to swamp all other Heidegger scholarship.

I do not intend to add another book to this ever-growing stream. Yet questions regarding the relation between Heidegger's work and his life cannot be ignored by those who want to understand his philosophy. Certainly, the texts are the only and final authority where interpretation is concerned, but one cannot decide in advance which contexts will be relevant to interpreting these texts. Should one study the philosophical tradition only? Should one draw in great religious writers, such as Luther and Eckhart? Should one also study the cultural and political situation in Germany after the Great War and Heidegger's personal life in order to grasp the meaning of his teachings? There can be no a priori ban on any of these directions of research.

Heidegger suggests in the pamphlet published in 1983 that he renounced his adherence to National Socialism in the spring of 1934. However, according to Karl Löwith, Heidegger expressed his loyalty to Hitler during a conversation in Rome in 1936, and agreed that his political involvement was based on his philosophy, especially on his notion of historicity.[13] What, then, is the relation between Heidegger's philosophy and his political stance? The task of the historian will be to unearth the facts on the basis of testimonies and of documents which, for a large part, still are locked up in archives. Such a fact is the case of the prominent chemist Hermann Staudinger, who was denounced by Heidegger, as Hugo Ott discovered.[14] But if the historian finds texts neglected by the philosopher, texts in which Heidegger says, for instance, that "the *Führer* himself and alone *is* the present and future German reality and its law," what is the significance of such texts for Heidegger's philosophical thought?[15] Doesn't the fact that in this example the verb "is" is italicized indicate that there is a relation between this text and Heidegger's question of being, as Ott suggests? What is this relation? Do Heidegger's political texts move at the periphery of his thought, or do they occupy its very center?

In order to answer these and similar questions, a philosophical interpretation of Heidegger's oeuvre is needed that distinguishes the essential from the accidental, the center from the periphery, the fundamental structures from the incidental details. To develop such an interpretation is the first major objective of this book.

Initially, it may seem easy to find the center of Heidegger's thought. For Heidegger endorsed a conception of philosophy that might be called monogamous, or, less kindly, monomaniac. According to Heidegger, a philosopher should merely think one thought, or ask only one question. This one question, at least in Heidegger's own case, is the celebrated *question of being*, and my interpretation of Heidegger's philosophy focuses on the question of being. However, as soon as one tries to concentrate on the question of being, one will get the feeling that, to paraphrase Nicholas of Cusa, the center and the periphery of Heidegger's philosophy coincide. It is hard to determine what Heidegger's question of being amounts to, and its meaning seems both to manifest and to conceal itself in the most peripheral details of his texts.

More specifically, the interpreter of Heidegger's question of being has to face a great number of nearly insuperable difficulties. One is that Heidegger understood his thought as a *Denkweg* (path of thought) and compared this road to *Holzwege* (forest trails), which may lead to nowhere. Between 1930 and 1940, a *Kehre* (turn) occurred in the path of Heidegger's thought, and the second part of *Sein und Zeit* was never published. Much later, in 1953, Heidegger added a preface to the seventh edition of *Sein und Zeit*, in which he said that nevertheless "the road it [*Sein und Zeit*] has taken remains even today a necessary one, if our Dasein is to be stirred by the question of being."[16] Was Heidegger stirred by one and the same question in *Sein und Zeit* and in the later works, as he suggests in 1953? Or did *Sein und Zeit* turn out to be a dead end, so that the question of being in the later works is not precisely the same question as the one in the earlier book?

Other difficulties stem from the sheer bulk and the textual nature of Heidegger's works. To begin with, the edition of the collected works (*Gesamtausgabe*) will amount to about one hundred volumes of an average of four hundred pages each. Heidegger did not want the edition to be a critical one in the usual philological sense. He ruled, for instance, that later additions should be incorporated into the original texts without notice. This fact should render the scrupulous scholar extremely cautious about using it.[17] Second, Heidegger wrote texts of a great variety of philosophical genres. Whereas the published part of *Sein und Zeit* is a systematic treatise in the grand German philosophical style, with a pretension so high as Germany had not seen since Hegel's *Phänomenologie des Geistes* (*Phenomenology of the Spirit*), the later works are mostly modest and short: essays, talks, letters, dialogues, and lectures. What explains this change in the genre of Heidegger's publications? Is it somehow related to the turn in his thought? In the third place, Heidegger developed the question of being often in a dialogue with other philosophers, from Anaximander to Kant and Nietzsche, and with poets such as Rilke, Hölderlin, and Trakl, a dialogue disguised as an interpretation. As a consequence, Heidegger's thought is characterized by a special elusiveness, because in his *Erörterungen* (elucidations) his own intentions and those of the philosopher or the poet he tries to elucidate merge imperceptibly into each other. In fact, one has to know the works of the philosophers and poets interpreted by Heidegger as least as well as Heidegger himself did in order to be able to distill the Heideggerian essence out of these texts. Fourth, Heidegger cannot be accused of explaining clearly and unambiguously what he means by "the question of being" and by many other key expressions in his works. As Paul Edwards says, "Heidegger and his followers appear to operate on the principle that, if it is repeated often enough, even the most nebulous locutions will become familiar and *seem* to be intelligible."[18] Add to this the great variety of interpretations of Heidegger's question of being in the existing literature, and the fact that quite often Heidegger's German is difficult, if not impossible, to translate, and one will understand the degree of overconfidence, or of derangement, which one must possess in order to intend what I want to do: to add one more book to the existing literature on Heidegger.

There can be only one justification for such an undertaking: that the interpretation proposed is new, at least to some extent, that it is clearer than the existing interpretations, at least at some substantial points, and that it is historically correct, however problematic these notions of clarity and correctness will be according to followers of Heidegger. At best, an interpretation of Heidegger's question of being should also explain why there are so many conflicting interpretations of this question, and it should explain, and not merely state, some of the difficulties noted above, such as that of the relative untranslatability of Heidegger's works. These indeed are the merits I am claiming for my book.

In calling my interpretation *critical*, I mean three things. First, I insist on a traditional distinction between two kinds of interpretation, applicative and objective, historical, or critical ones (see § 5, below), a distinction that is obfuscated by authors such as Gadamer and Heidegger. I am aiming at an interpretation of the second, critical and purely historical kind. Second, I claim that only an interpretation of this critical nature is a legitimate basis for making up one's mind about the truth of Heidegger's philosophy, at least to the extent that his philosophy purports to be true. In other words, such an interpretation should be the basis for a critique of Heidegger's thought. However, as I said before, Heidegger's philosophy not only aspired to truth or knowledge; it also and even more aspired to wisdom, to acquiring a specific "fundamental attitude." As in the case of Pascal, for instance, this attitude can only be obtained on the basis of an *Entscheidung* (decision), which Heidegger's thought is meant to induce. If this is the case, the proper reaction to Heidegger's writings is not only to try to understand them; it is also to try to make the decision Heidegger wants us to make, or, perhaps, to make the opposite decision. The Greek word for a decision is *krisis*, and my interpretation is in the third place critical in the sense that it is meant to induce a decision regarding Heidegger's question of being. Inducing such a decision is the second major objective of this book.

My earlier critical publications on Heidegger gave rise to an interesting type of response. Colleagues whose work is deeply inspired by Heidegger asked me, not without a certain degree of hostility: Why don't you leave Heidegger alone, if you are so critical? An astonishing reaction: as if it is not legitimate to study the works of a philosopher unless one entirely agrees with what he says. Hugo Ott reports a similar response to his attempts to discover the historical truth about Heidegger's past, a truth that is sometimes at variance with what Heidegger himself wanted us to believe. Ott's attempt to maintain his mental independence was at once catalogued as an attack on Heidegger's philosophy by an enemy, as a sacrilege that made Freiburg into "an unholy place."[19] These reactions are symptomatic of two features of Heideggerian thought that make the attempt to understand and assess it into an exciting intellectual and personal challenge: first, the fact that Heidegger is not so much concerned with purely intellectual puzzles as with fundamental human attitudes and deep moral choices; and second, the fact that it seems to be difficult to keep one's independence and intellectual integrity when one immerses oneself in Heidegger's writings, difficult to such an extent that a more or less independent mind is perceived as a menace by some followers of Heidegger.

I have tried to write a lucid and relatively short book, and to avoid the dreary habit of many authors on Heidegger to offer endless paraphrases and summaries instead of a substantial interpretation. For those who know Heidegger's texts well, I hope to be provocative. For those who do not know Heidegger's works at all, I aim at making them more easily accessible. There is one thing an interpretation of a great philosopher should never pretend to be: a substitute for reading the original texts. I will argue that, for specific reasons pertaining to the nature of Heidegger's thought and to his highly innovative use of the resources of the German language, it is impossible to translate his texts without destroying their structure, their power, their magic. This is why I decided to quote Heidegger in German in the notes, even though this might be felt as an impoliteness to English and American readers. Quotes in the main text are in English, but where I seem to translate Heidegger, I intend merely to paraphrase him. All paraphrases and translations are mine, unless indicated otherwise.[20]

The structure of the book is as follows. In the introductory first chapter I offer a number of reasons as to why an interpretation of Heidegger's question of being is still needed and why it is difficult to give one. I summarize several main themes from *Sein und Zeit* in order to show why Heidegger's work is relevant to issues all philosophers, analytic and naturalist philosophers included, are trying to deal with. Furthermore, I state six of the problems that an interpretation of Heidegger's question of being has to solve, and I explain what kind of interpretation I intend to provide.

In chapters 2 and 3, I develop my interpretation of Heidegger's question of being, using the method of resolution and composition. Chapter 2 is analytical; it specifies five aspects of or strands in the question of being, which each determine a different meaning of Heidegger's question. Indeed, it is the central thesis of my interpretation that Heidegger's question of being has four or five very different meanings or "leitmotifs," as I call them. In the synthetical third chapter, I attempt to show how these leitmotifs hang together, and I try to solve a number of specific problems, such as the problem of the untranslatability of Heidegger's texts, the problem of the turn, the problem of the unity of Heidegger's *Denkweg*, the problem of Heidegger's involvement with Hitler, and problems inherent in Heidegger's relation to Nietzsche. I hold that reading Heidegger's works resembles listening to Wagner's overtures. Different leitmotifs are interwoven in the texts, and one will not understand the question of being unless one analyzes these distinct themes and their complicated interweavings.

Chapter 4 is critical. On the basis of my interpretation, I assess the fundamental structures or leitmotifs of Heidegger's thought. Such an assessment of the work of a great philosopher will rarely lead to total adherence, nor to total rejection. It must be critical in the sense that the attempt is made to separate the valid from the invalid, the true from the false, the fruitful from the sterile. There is a tendency among Heidegger's disciples to claim that a critical assessment of Heidegger's thought is impossible, because, it is suggested, it would be impossible both to understand what Heidegger wants to say and simultaneously to be critical of what he says. Analytical philosophers will retort that this is nothing but a rhetorical strategy of immunization. However, in the final part of section 17, which is a short study of Heidegger's rhetoric, I purport to show that such rhetorical stratagems are not mere rhetoric: they are rooted in the fundamental structures of Heidegger's thought.

ACKNOWLEDGMENTS

VARIOUS institutions, audiences, friends, and students offered me assistance and support while I was writing this book. After my long years as a dean of the faculty, the University of Leiden generously allowed me the research time needed in order to complete a book of this size. In spite of the fact that Dutch universities do not have a sabbatical system, I was able to spend a leave of six months as a visiting fellow at Princeton University in the spring of 1995 and a shorter leave as a guest of St. John's College, Oxford, in the spring of 1996. I am grateful to Bas Van Fraassen for inviting me to Princeton and to Peter Hacker for sponsoring my stay in St. John's. In January 1996, Jean François Courtine kindly allowed me to use the phenomenological library of the Ecole Normale Supérieure at the Rue d'Ulm in Paris, enabling me to study with efficiency the French literature on Heidegger.

Drafts of this book were used as lectures at the universities of Leiden, Oxford, and Edinburgh, all in 1996, and I benefited from the ensuing discussions. Peter Hacker took the trouble to read and comment on my entire manuscript, and I greatly profited from his sharp-witted mind. Parts of the manuscript were read by Han Adriaanse (University of Leiden), Michael Inwood (Trinity College, Oxford), Menno Lievers (University of Utrecht), Wouter Oudemans (University of Leiden), Thomas Pavel (Princeton University), Lambertus M. de Rijk (Universities of Leiden and Limburg), C. J. M. Sicking (University of Leiden), Barry Smith (State University of New York at Buffalo), Fritz Stern (Columbia University), Bas van Fraassen (Princeton University), and Ad Verbrugge (University of Leiden). I am much obliged for their criticisms and encouragements. During the spring of 1996, I used my manuscript as the main text for an advanced seminar on Heidegger at the University of Leiden, and many of my theses were fiercely discussed by my students. Especially helpful were comments by Nicole Bodewes and Wybo Houkes. Lastly, I wish to thank the referees of Princeton University Press for their generous and stimulating comments on the penultimate draft.

Heidegger's Philosophy of Being

Introduction

HEIDEGGER WAS a master of the Socratic method. During his lectures, he often tried to confuse his listeners as much as possible in order to destroy their preconceptions and to encourage an open-minded discussion of a topic.[1] In this introductory chapter, I proceed likewise. My main objective is to expound the problem of interpreting Heidegger's question of being in its full and baffling complexity. To those who expect an easygoing introduction to Heidegger's thought, this may seem to be a superfluous deviation. However, we are well advised to fathom the profundity of the difficulties before embarking on a Herculean project, and in order to arouse a thirst for knowledge, we must make our ignorance manifest. I also provide background information on Heidegger's oeuvre, especially *Sein und Zeit*, and I discuss Heidegger's notion of interpretation.

There are many interpretations of Heidegger's question of being in the extensive secondary literature. Let me quote at random and by way of a sample a few recent American authors. It has been suggested that the meaning of the question of being, and indeed the meaning of the word "being" as Heidegger uses it, are relatively clear. We have to remember, Hubert Dreyfus writes in his commentary on *Sein und Zeit*, that "what Heidegger has in mind when he talks about being is the intelligibility correlative with our everyday background practices."[2] According to another exegesis, developed by Thomas Sheehan, Heidegger's expression "being itself" refers to "the analogically unified meaning of Being which is instantiated in all cases of the Being of this or that."[3] Michael Zimmerman defends yet a third interpretation. He holds that Heidegger defined "being" as "the history-shaping ways in which entities reveal themselves."[4] And Mark Okrent argues in *Heidegger's Pragmatism* that the question of being is a transcendental question; it supposedly is concerned with the pragmatic conditions under which an entity shows up for us *as* a being of a certain kind.[5]

Although these readings reveal important aspects of the Heideggerian notion of being, they all remain problematic. The existing interpretations of Heidegger's question of being do not account for a great number of Heidegger's texts,[6] or are too abstract to be really informative,[7] or, finally, are in fact nothing but summaries of the various stations of Heidegger's *Denkweg*.[8] The very fact that there are many different and incompatible interpretations of the question of being points to the problematic nature of this question, and, indeed, to the problematic nature of any attempt to interpret it. What explains the divergence among the various interpretations? Why is it so difficult to reach agreement on the meaning of

Heidegger's question? Is it possible to give an adequate interpretation of the question of being at all?

In this chapter, I first discuss two fundamental difficulties that seem to stand in the way of any attempt to interpret Heidegger's question of being. The first difficulty pertains to the fact that the question of being appears to be hidden, or concealed, or somehow essentially inaccessible (§ 1). The second stems from Heidegger's view on logic (§ 2).

Interpreting Heidegger's question is not only difficult; it is also necessary in order to unravel the mysteries contained in Heidegger's masterpiece *Sein und Zeit*, of which I give a synopsis in section 3. This book is considered by many as one of the great classical texts of twentieth-century philosophy, and it raises problems that are vital to philosophers of all persuasions. Focusing on the introduction to *Sein und Zeit*, in which Heidegger unfolds his question of being, I then state six problems that an interpretation of the question of being has to solve. These problems are contained in the text, even though sometimes one needs to scrutinize it to discover them, and one is advised to read Heidegger's introduction to *Sein und Zeit* along with my comments (§ 4). Of these problems, the sixth and final problem is the most important one: What is the relation between Heidegger's question of being and his revolutionary analysis of human existence in *Sein und Zeit*? Why did Heidegger think that he had to develop an ontology of human existence in order to be able to raise the question of being properly?

Heidegger held specific views on interpretation, and he may be considered as the founder of a new school of interpretation theorists, to which belong authors such as Gadamer and Derrida. Should an interpretation of Heidegger's thought be internal in the sense that it aims at conforming to Heidegger's own views on interpretation? We have a choice here, and many types of interpretation of Heidegger's philosophy are conceivable, internal and external ones. I argue that we should not conform to Heidegger's own notion of an interpretation or elucidation (*Erörterung*) in order to be as fair to Heidegger's intentions as one can be (§ 5).

§ 1. HEIDEGGER *ABSCONDITUS*

If we want to assign a starting point to the way of Heidegger's thought (*Denkweg*), it seems to be most appropriate to single out an event that took place in 1907, the year of Heidegger's eighteenth birthday.[9] In that year Dr. Conrad Gröber, the later archbishop of Freiburg, who was born in Meßkirch like Heidegger and had been rector of the Konradihaus in Konstanz where young Martin lived during his time at the *Gymnasium*, gave Heidegger a copy of Franz Brentano's dissertation, *On the Manifold Sense of Being in Aristotle*.[10] Looking back on his life, Heidegger wrote that this book incited him to raise the question of being.[11] Clearly, Heidegger wants us to interpret his philosophical journey as starting from Brentano and

Aristotle. What, then, are the contents of Brentano's dissertation, and how could the dissertation give rise to Heidegger's question of being? In this first section, I give a provisional answer to these questions. As the reader will see, however, the answer leads us into difficulties that may seem insuperable.

In his concise book of 220 pages Brentano attempted to solve the traditional interpretative problems of Aristotle's doctrine of being. The introduction explains why, according to Aristotle, the question of being is the first and most fundamental question a philosopher should investigate. Being (*to on*), says Aristotle, is the primary thing our mind conceives, because it is the most universal and the most fundamental to thought.[12] Furthermore, (first) philosophy is defined as the study of being as such (*to on hei on*), which establishes the first principles of the sciences.[13] Finally, the more abstract a word is, the easier we are misled by its equivocations, so that we do well to analyze the meaning of "to be." For these reasons, Aristotle in his *Metaphysics* investigates only one question, what is being, and he holds that this question is fundamental to the sciences.[14]

However, as Brentano argues in his first chapter, this unique question does admit of a multiplicity of answers, because according to Aristotle "being" is said in many ways (*pollachōs*).[15] In fact, Aristotle even recognizes various distinctions among the ways in which "being" is used. Of these, the distinction between four ways of saying "being," which Aristotle mentions in book V.7 of his *Metaphysics* (1026a: 33), is the most basic one. The four ways are: (1) *kata sumbebēkos* (what something is said to be incidentally), (2) "being" in the sense of being true, (3) "being" in the sense of being potentially or being actually, and (4) "being" as it is said in the ten categories. Accordingly, Brentano discusses Aristotle's analysis of each of these senses of "being" respectively in the remaining chapters 2, 3, 4, and 5 of his book.

For readers who are not familiar with Aristotle's *Metaphysics*, I come back to it below, and try to explain clearly why, according to Aristotle, the question of being is the fundamental question of philosophy (see § 7). At this point, I do not assume any familiarity with Brentano or with Aristotle, nor, of course, with Aristotle's question of being. Even without understanding Aristotle we may draw some conclusions concerning Heidegger's question of being. Why did Brentano's dissertation give rise to Heidegger's question? Heidegger learned from Brentano's dissertation, it seems, that the philosopher has to answer one and only one question, the question of being. Furthermore, he learned that this question is more fundamental than the problems of the special sciences, and that, in fact, it is the most fundamental question a human being can ask. Should we conclude that Heidegger's question of being is identical with Aristotle's question of being, and that the reason Heidegger wanted to raise it anew was simply that he was not satisfied by Aristotle's solution to the problem of being?

This is at least what Heidegger suggests when he explains with hindsight how Brentano's dissertation motivated his philosophical journey. In "Mein Weg in die Phänomenologie" (*My Way into Phenomenology*) Heidegger expresses his question of being as follows: "if being is said in many ways, what then is the leading and fundamental meaning? What does to be mean?"[16] It seems that Heidegger was not satisfied with Aristotle's answer for the following reason. Although Aristotle analyzed different meanings of "being," he did not discover the one leading and fundamental sense (*Sinn*) from which the other meanings are somehow derived. If so, Heidegger's question of being is identical with, and yet more focused than Aristotle's: it aims at discovering one fundamental sense that underlies the other senses of "to be." This provisional interpretation is confirmed by section 3 of *Sein und Zeit*, where Heidegger says that we have to elucidate the sense of being *tout court* in order to be able to construct the various possible modes of being.[17]

Let us provisionally adopt as an interpretative hypothesis the assumption that Heidegger's question of being aimed at finding the one and fundamental sense of "to be," from which the others can be derived, even though we do not yet grasp at all what this obscure formula means. A clear expression and articulation of the fundamental sense of "to be" would then provide the answer to Heidegger's question of being. Do we find such an answer in Heidegger's writings? If this is what we expect, we will be disappointed. Our disillusionment comes in phases, when we read somewhat superficially *Sein und Zeit* and the later works.

A first reason for worry is contained in the second half of section 5 of *Sein und Zeit*. In this section, Heidegger elucidates the provisional aim of the book, which is to show that time, or temporality, functions as the "horizon" of all understanding of being.[18] Heidegger argues that philosophers of the past used a notion of time as an implicit background for understanding being, because they distinguished the temporal being of nature and history from the atemporal being of numbers and geometrical relations. But was the traditional conception of time a fundamental one? It is a central thesis of *Sein und Zeit* that the proper notion of time or temporality, which must function as a horizon of understanding being, should be developed on the basis of an interpretation of the temporality of human existence (*Dasein*). In the third paragraph of section 5, Heidegger concludes that "the question of the meaning of being will first be concretely answered by the exposition of the problematic of temporality."[19]

But what form will such a concrete answer have? Will it consist in a clear and unambiguous articulation of the one and fundamental sense of "being," which Aristotle failed to find, expressed in one or more propositions? This is what Heidegger denies in the next paragraph of section 5: "Because *being* cannot be grasped except by taking time into consideration, the answer to the question of being cannot lie in any blind and isolated proposition." He concludes the paragraph by specifying the positive form an answer to the question of being will have: "according to its most proper sense, the answer gives us an indication for concrete ontological research, that it must begin its investigative questioning [*untersuchenden Fragen*] within the horizon we have laid bare; and this is all that the answer tells us."[20]

Our first disappointment, then, is this: Heidegger's answer to the question of being consists in an indication as to how we should start our ontological query. In other words, the answer to the question of being will merely teach us how to ask the question of being properly. We now understand, apparently, why Heidegger concludes the published part of *Sein und Zeit* by saying that the book is only a *way*, a way to the clarification of the fundamental ontological question, a way that we must seek and *follow*.[21] For only if we have followed the way of *Sein und Zeit*, Heidegger seems to tell us, are we able to ask the real question of being and to conduct our ontological investigation in the right manner.

So far, so good, the reader will observe. As soon as we have learned to ask the question of being properly, will we then not be able to answer this question and to express clearly the one and fundamental sense of "being" or of "to be" that Heidegger was looking for? Heidegger's procedure seems to be a traditional one in philosophy, which is inevitable because philosophical questions rarely are clear as they stand, so that a clarification of the question has to be the first stage in a philosophical inquiry. What we now expect is that Heidegger, having clarified the meaning of the question of being in *Sein und Zeit*, proceeds to answer the question in his later works. In this expectation we will be disappointed as well.

There are a great number of texts in the later works in which Heidegger suggests that we cannot provide an answer to the question of being at all. In *Gelassenheit* (*Resignation*, 1959), he intimates that thinking in the proper sense requires resignation. "We should do nothing, but wait," says the teacher in the short dialogue that is meant as an elucidation of this notion of thinking.[22] More than twenty years earlier Heidegger propounded a similar view in lectures he gave in the summer term of 1935, which were published in 1953 as *Einführung in die Metaphysik* (*An Introduction to Metaphysics*). At the end of this text, he stresses that in the context of philosophical reflection (*Besinnung*), the title *Sein und Zeit* does not refer to a book but to what is assigned to us (*das Aufgegebene*). "That which is properly assigned to us is something we do not know and which, to the extent that we know it *really* [*echt*], to wit *as* assigned to us, we always know it only *in our questioning*." And he concludes: "To be able to question means: to be able to wait, even a life long."[23] Thinking in the sense of the later Heidegger seems to be a specific kind of questioning, that is, of asking the question of being, and asking this question is equivalent to a specific kind of waiting. According to the later Heidegger, then, the question of being is not a question we should attempt to answer. It is a question we should learn to ask properly and with resignation. To quote Heidegger's celebrated phrase in "Die Frage nach der Technik" (*The Question Concerning Technology*), "questioning is the piety of thinking."[24]

In view of these and similar texts, we will perhaps cease to expect that Heidegger provides an answer to the question of being. What he seems to aim at is rather to induce his readers to adopt the right kind of questioning attitude. Asking the question of being is nothing but adopting this attitude. But is it at least clear what this attitude consists in? Did Heidegger succeed in clarifying the meaning of the question of being?

Quite often in the later works Heidegger suggests that he did not—and perhaps even could not—succeed in doing so. According to the introduction (1949) to the inaugural lecture *Was ist Metaphysik?* (1929), the philosophical community passed over the question of being with the self-assurance of a somnambulist. This is not due to a misunderstanding of *Sein und Zeit*, caused by unclear writing or careless reading. Heidegger rather claims that inattention to the question of being is due to the fact that we are "abandoned by being."[25] In 1969, during the only television interview Heidegger ever gave, the then eighty-year-old thinker stressed once more that the question of being was not yet understood. Again he did not attribute this lack of understanding to careless reading of his texts, but to the fact that being had concealed itself, that it had withdrawn in our time.[26] Were Heidegger alive today, I imagine that he would not express himself differently. We may safely assume that, according to Heidegger, we do not understand the question of being that he wanted to raise, and this will be our third disappointment.[27]

Let me summarize and conclude. In texts such as "Mein Weg in die Phänomenologie" Heidegger endorses Aristotle's conviction that the question of being is the basic and only question of philosophy. It seems that he wanted to raise this question anew because he was not satisfied with Aristotle's answer. In particular, he wanted to grasp the fundamental sense of "being" from which the other senses are derived. What we expect on the basis of these texts is that the meaning of Heidegger's question of being is identical to the meaning of Aristotle's question of being, and that Heidegger provides a new answer to this question. But this expectation is disappointed in three ways. First, *Sein und Zeit* merely aims at a clarification of the question of being, not at answering it. Second, many later texts suggest that we are not able to answer the question of being. Finally, Heidegger repeatedly affirms that we simply do not understand the question of being. Yet the question of being is said to be the most crucial question a human being can ask.

Sober-minded readers will conclude that we had better leave Heidegger alone. What are we to think of a philosopher who raises pompously and ponderously an allegedly central question of philosophy, and ends up by telling us that we cannot answer—indeed, cannot even understand—this question? However, in view of Heidegger's profound influence on contemporary philosophy, the mysteriousness of the question of being may arouse our curiosity. How can Heidegger claim to be able to raise a question that nobody understands? How are we to interpret Heidegger's statement that our ignorance of the question of being is due to the fact that being conceals or withdraws itself? These claims seem to be alien to the atmosphere of Aristotle's thought, from which Heidegger allegedly derived his question of being.

One might think that the concealed nature of Heidegger's question of being stands in the way of an attempt to interpret this question. No doubt Heidegger's repeated assertion that we do not understand the question of being complicates its interpretation. Nevertheless, I do not conclude that interpretation is impossible. On the contrary, the very fact that we do not understand the question of being, even according to Heidegger himself, makes an attempt at interpretation more urgent than ever. If Heidegger suggests that we cannot understand his question in principle, we should not be discouraged. This suggestion may be taken simply to be yet another feature of Heidegger's question of being, a feature that an interpretation of the question of being should be able to explain. I call this feature the *concealment* of the question of being. To the extent that the name "Heidegger" stands for the unique question that the bearer of the name wanted to raise, we might speak of *Heidegger absconditus*.[28]

§ 2. HEIDEGGER ON LOGIC

Apart from the concealment of the question of being, there is another difficulty that seems to block from the outset any attempt at interpreting Heidegger's question of being. This difficulty is raised by Heidegger's pronouncements on logic in *Was ist Metaphysik?* and elsewhere.[29] Let me expound the difficulty by a partial analysis of *Was ist Metaphysik?*

In this inaugural lecture, which Heidegger gave at the University of Freiburg on 24 July 1929, he did not talk about metaphysics, as the title might suggest, but elucidated (*erörtern*) a metaphysical question, in order that metaphysics might "present itself" to us.[30] At first sight, this question is concerned with "the Nothing" or with "nothingness" (*das Nichts*). But because Heidegger in a sense endorses Hegel's pronouncement from the first book of the *Wissenschaft der Logik* (*Science of Logic*), that "pure being and pure nothingness are the same," the question raised in the lecture is equivalent to the question of being itself.[31] Heidegger unfolds the question in the first part of the lecture, elaborates it in the second part, and answers it in the third part. Characteristically, he says that we have already obtained the answer that is essential for our purposes, if we take heed that the question concerning the Nothing remains actually posed. This allegedly requires that we actively complete the transformation of man into his Da-sein, a transformation that every instance of *Angst* occasions in us.[32]

According to Heidegger, the dominance of intellect and logic has to be "broken" in order that we may raise the question concerning being and nothingness.[33] A brief summary of the first part of Heidegger's lecture will show why he thinks that this is the case. In this first part Heidegger unfolds the question of the Nothing. He starts with two observations on metaphysical questions in general: these questions are always concerned with the totality (*das Ganze*) of metaphysics, and they somehow call into question the questioner himself. The latter observation leads

Heidegger to a succinct analysis of science—in the broad sense of the German *Wissenschaften*—because his inaugural lecture is addressed to the scientific community of the University of Freiburg. How is the scientist called into question by metaphysics? What Heidegger wants to show in part 1 is that science essentially implies or suggests the metaphysical question of nothingness.

Heidegger says in 1929 that science is characterized by a specific relation (*Bezug*) to the world, by an attitude (*Haltung*) in which we freely choose to let things speak for themselves, and by the fact that in science one being, namely, man, "breaks into the totality of beings" (*Einbruch*) in such a manner that being "breaks open" and "is restored to what and how it is."[34] In all three respects, *Bezug*, *Haltung*, and *Einbruch*, the scientist is concerned with beings and with nothing else. Heidegger repeats the phrase "and with nothing else" six times in different variations in order to prepare his conclusion: that when the scientist tries to say what he is up to, he inevitably speaks of something else, namely, the Nothing, or nothingness (*das Nichts*). It follows that in reflecting on science we cannot avoid the metaphysical question: What about the Nothing?[35]

Is this a sound argument? Rudolf Carnap criticized Heidegger's *Was ist Metaphysik?* in his 1931 essay on "The Elimination of Metaphysics through Logical Analysis of Language."[36] According to Carnap, metaphysical discourse is not true or false: it is meaningless and consists largely of pseudosentences, even though it often appears to make sense. Pseudosentences may be generated in two ways. The metaphysician might use a word in a manner that seems to be meaningful, although in fact he has emptied the word of all signification. This has happened, Carnap says, in the case of the word "God," which was originally used with reference to—or in forming empirical hypotheses about the causes of—phenomena such as the plague, thunder, and lightning, but which lost its empirical meaning in the later development of religion. Second, the metaphysician might form sentences that violate logical syntax, even though they are correct according to the rules of ordinary grammar. Carnap criticizes the first type of pseudosentence on the basis of his verification principle, whereas in the second case logical analysis of language will reveal that metaphysical discourse is meaningless.[37]

It is important to distinguish these two sources of meaninglessness, for even if one rejects the verification principle, one still has to admit that violations of logical grammar may generate meaningless pseudosentences. This is precisely what seems to have happened in the first part of *Was ist Metaphysik?* In the premise of Heidegger's argument, that science is concerned with beings *and with nothing else*, the word "nothing" expresses a negation and an object-variable. It means: there is not something that science is concerned with, except beings.[38] But in his conclusion Heidegger mistakes this expression of a negation and an object-variable for a definite description, as if there were something, namely, *nothingness* or the Nothing, about which we might ask meaningful questions. Clearly, then, Heidegger's conclusion does not follow from his premise, and it is meaningless because it violates the rules of logical syntax.

Does this settle the matter of Heidegger's question of being and nothingness? Should we conclude that it is a pseudoquestion? We are tempted to do so. Yet this would be rash, for Heidegger seems to have anticipated Carnap's critique, albeit in an informal way.[39] In the second part of the lecture, Heidegger admits that his question of nothingness is paradoxical. The question presupposes that there is something whose nature we might investigate. Of this something it is then said that it is nothing. But is this not a contradiction? Indeed, Heidegger explicitly admits that raising the question of nothingness violates the principle of noncontradiction. "The commonly cited fundamental rule of all thought, the principle of noncontradiction, universal 'logic,' crushes the question."[40]

Heidegger adds, however, that this violation knocks out the question of nothingness only if we accept the presupposition that logic is the highest authority concerning nothingness, and that "nothing" is derived from "not," from the negation.[41] He goes on to argue in the second and third parts of the lecture that things are the other way around. Negation, he claims, is derived from (an experience of) the Nothing. There is a fundamental experience (*Grunderfahrung*) or fundamental mood (*Grundstimmung*) of *Angst*, and in *Angst* we experience the Nothing, because in this experience everything, the totality of beings, becomes indifferent to us and slips away from us. *Angst* reveals nothingness, and nothingness is more fundamental than negation, since "the Nothing itself nots," Heidegger claims.[42] Moreover, he contends that from the experience of nothingness in *Angst* originates the original openness of being (*das Seiende*) as such: that it is being and not nothing.[43] This is why Dasein (Heidegger's term for human existence) is being exposed in nothingness, and why nothingness is the condition of the possibility of beings being manifest to us.[44] If this is so, the experience of the Nothing in *Angst* is more fundamental than science, because science presupposes that beings are manifest. In the third part of his lecture, Heidegger concludes that because "negation is based on the *not* [*das Nicht*], which originates from the *notting* of the Nothing [*das Nichten des Nichts*]," the "power of the intellect in the field of inquiry into nothingness and being is shattered," and that this "decides the destiny of the authority of logic in philosophy. The very idea of logic disintegrates in the whirl of a more original questioning."[45]

The reader will wonder what Heidegger intends to say by all of this, and he will probably conclude with Carnap that *Was ist Metaphysik?* is an incomprehensible and even meaningless text. I assume that after having read my book, the reader will be able to decide for himself, on the basis of my interpretation, whether he agrees with Heidegger that the authority of the intellect has to be destroyed. This introductory chapter of my book aims at raising questions and arousing wonder, and I will not state my interpretation of *Was ist Metaphysik?* and similar texts in the present section. However, even without fully understanding what is happening in Heidegger's inaugural lecture, we may distinguish two strands in his pronouncements on logic, which he himself does not keep apart.

The first is the idea, which Heidegger inherited from Husserl, that logical constants such as "and," "or," and "not" are referring expressions, which derive their meaning from (an experience of) the referent. This notion was common in the first quarter of this century, and probably Wittgenstein was the first philosopher to reject it, in the *Tractatus*.[46] If this idea is correct, logic stands in need of a philosophical foundation, as Husserl argued in his *Logische Untersuchungen* (*Logical Investigations*).[47] Such a foundation would consist *inter alia* in a description of the referents of logical constants, from which their meanings would be derived. Following Hume, Husserl calls the experience of the referents the "origin" (*Ursprung*) of meanings. Against this background, Heidegger's inaugural lecture might be read as an original contribution to foundational research in logic: he argues that the meaning of the logical constant "not" is derived from, or rooted in, an experience of nothingness in *Angst*.[48] This theory is fanciful, but it is not much more so than Russell's view that the meaning of the word "or" originates from the coexistence of two incompatible motor impulses in our nervous system, neither of which is strong enough to overcome the other.[49]

According to this first strand in *Was ist Metaphysik?* there is no reason to doubt the validity of logic, and the "more original questioning" is nothing but the quest for a foundation of logic. But if this first strand were the only one, Heidegger's violent condemnation of logic, and the idea that the authority of logic and of reason has to be destroyed, would be irrelevant and inappropriate. We must conclude that there is a second strand in Heidegger's pronouncements on logic, apart from the attempt to ground logic on something else, and that this second strand is in conflict with the first. According to this second strand, raising the very question of being and nothingness is *incompatible* with the most fundamental logical principle, the principle of noncontradiction. We saw that Heidegger himself stresses the incompatibility and that he accepts it. This is why, if he nevertheless wants to ask the question of nothingness, the authority of logic has to be destroyed. But what happens if the authority of logic, and more in particular the principle of noncontradiction, is abolished?

Much of Heidegger's early work is inspired by Aristotle. We will be tempted to say, however, that there is one chapter in Aristotle's *Metaphysics*, the fourth chapter of book IV, which Heidegger did not sufficiently take to heart. In this chapter, Aristotle tries to refute those philosophers who deny the principle of noncontradiction, confronting them with a dilemma. Either they implicitly accept the principle, even though they officially reject it, or they will not be able to use language at all. For on the one hand it is not possible to deny the principle of noncontradiction unless one at the same time presupposes its validity, because to deny it is to state that something is not true. How can one assert sincerely that something is not true if one really thinks that it is true at the same time? The very speech act of denying involves the principle of noncontradiction. In other words, what one *means* by saying that something is not true is that it is *not* also and at the same time true. On the other hand, it is equally impossible to give up the principle of noncontradiction implicitly, for instance, by using language without applying it, because as soon as one allows that simultaneously and in the same respect a statement might be true of a thing and not true of that thing, this statement loses its sense. As a consequence, each and every meaningful use of language involves the principle of noncontradiction. If one wants to give it up implicitly, one cannot but keep silent.[50]

Should we not conclude that we must accept the principle of noncontradiction and forget about the question of being, if at least we have to choose between the question of being and the principle? How can one take seriously a philosopher who claims to reject a principle without which meaningful discourse is impossible? Even merely pretending that one rejects the principle of noncontradiction seems to be an absurd and irresponsible act. Suppose that you are mistakenly accused of murder, and that you refute the accusation by producing evidence that contradicts it. Yet you may be sentenced to death if the jury and the judges pretend to reject the principle of noncontradiction. From a more philosophical perspective, one might point out that Heidegger's expression "the authority of logic" (*die Herrschaft der "Logik"*) is misleading, as if the rules of logic were an external authority that one might shake off. Rules of logic are not like the laws of taxation, which one may try to dodge. They are rather like rules of grammar: if one does not stick to them, one will end up producing meaningless noises or empty marks. There seems to be no point at all, then, in attempting to interpret the question of being, if raising this question really violates the principle of noncontradiction.

In his book on Heidegger's critique of logic, Thomas Fay argues that we should interpret Heidegger's invectives against logic as polemical statements, aimed at those who defend on logical grounds the thesis that metaphysics is nonsensical. This thesis was indeed propounded by Wittgenstein in the *Tractatus*, and members of the Vienna Circle such as Carnap endorsed it.[51] But what does Fay mean when he stresses that Heidegger's invectives against logic must be evaluated as polemical statements? Is this to suggest that one should not take them literally, and that raising the question of being does not really violate the principle of noncontradiction? Fay in fact denies this, writing that we should "eschew the path of a too facile concordism," and that "if one takes logic as it has traditionally been understood . . . , one is forced to say that it is incompatible with Heidegger's way of thought."[52]

It seems inevitable to draw the conclusion that Heidegger's question of being and nothingness is nonsensical because it is ruled out by the principle of noncontradiction. If so, any attempt at an interpretation of the question is misguided, because there are no meaningful interpretations of nonsensical questions. Shouldn't one commit to the flames all writings in which such interpretations are proposed?

I would not have written the present book if I endorsed these conclusions without qualification. Let me provisionally indicate how one might try to avoid them. Admittedly, the way Heidegger introduces the question of nothingness in the first part of *Was ist Metaphysik?* is illegitimate, because it violates logical grammar. But, one might ask, does Heidegger not ostensively define the word *Nichts* (nothingness) in the second part? Should we not apply the principle of charity and assume that Heidegger meant *Nichts* from the outset in the sense given by his ostensive definition, so that his introduction of the question of nothingness is needlessly misleading? On the basis of this interpretation, we might perhaps discover that there still is a meaning to the thesis of the incompatibility of logic and the question of nothingness, and that this incompatibility is such that it does not rule out the question of being.

In a crucial passage in part 2 of *Was ist Metaphysik?* Heidegger says that there is a basic demand (*Grunderfordernis*) for the possible advancing of the question of nothingness, namely, that the Nothing "must be *given* beforehand" and that "we must be able to *encounter* it."[53] According to Heidegger, we experience the Nothing in the fundamental mood (*Grundstimmung*) of *Angst*. If we want to apply the principle of charity, the term "nothingness" or "the Nothing" as Heidegger uses it should not be taken as a symptom of misunderstanding logical grammar, but as ostensively defined in *Angst*. According to this interpretation, "nothingness" simply means or refers to what we experience in *Angst*. What, then, do we experience in *Angst*?

Both in *Sein und Zeit* (§ 40) and at the end of the second part of *Was ist Metaphysik?* Heidegger gives an elaborate phenomenological description of this experience. According to *Sein und Zeit*, what we experience in *Angst* is that the meaningful world, in which Dasein leads its day-to-day life, sinks away into meaninglessness. Everything becomes insignificant. This is why *Angst* is not fear of a specific entity in the world. No particular thing is the object of *Angst*, and in this sense, *Angst* reveals no-thing or nothing.[54] But because of the very fact that in *Angst* all particular things become insignificant, *Angst* would annul what Heidegger calls *Verfallen*—the alleged fact that we flee from ourselves into worldly occupations—and it brings us back to ourselves as contingent and finite beings-in-the-world, that is, it reveals in an obtrusive way the very phenomenon of *world* and of *Dasein* (see § 3, below). It follows that "nothingness" in Heidegger's sense refers to a positive phenomenon, the phenomenon that all things become insignificant in *Angst*. Moreover, Heidegger pretends that the experience of nothingness (*das Nichts*) is a prerequisite for thematically experiencing being (*Sein*) in the sense of our being-in-the-world as such. This is why according to *Was ist Metaphysik?* the Nothing and being belong together.[55]

If this is the correct interpretation of the term "nothingness" in *Was ist Metaphysik?* Carnap's critique of the lecture is uncharitable, because Heidegger defines the term ostensively by reference to *Angst*. It seems, however, that on this assumption it becomes difficult to understand why Heidegger thought that raising the question of being and nothingness is incompatible with logic. If Heidegger's term "nothing" is used in a sense very different from the way it is used in ordinary language and in logic, there is no incompatibility between his question of nothingness and the principle of noncontradiction. What, then, explains Heidegger's calumnies against logic?[56]

An analogy between *Was ist Metaphysik?* and Wittgenstein's *Tractatus* may point the way to a possible answer. According to the *Tractatus*, logic defines the bounds of what it makes sense to say. Furthermore, all statements describe possible facts, and the totality of facts is the world. It follows that logic defines the totality of possibilities in the world, given the totality of objects. But if the world consists of facts, the sense of the world, that which makes the world valuable to us, must lie outside the world.[57] Wittgenstein concludes that the significance of the world and of life transcends the bounds of sense. It cannot be expressed in language and lies, therefore, beyond logic. Nevertheless, there is such a significance. Wittgenstein calls it the mystical.

One might suggest that Heidegger could mean something similar when he says that raising the question of nothingness is incompatible with logic. For the question of nothingness and of being is concerned with the significance (*Sinn*) of being. This question cannot be raised as long as we remain within the bounds of logic in Wittgenstein's sense, that is, as long as we merely try to formulate statements about things or events in the world, where the world is conceived of as a meaningless multiplicity of facts.[58] This might be one of the reasons why Heidegger says in *Sein und Zeit* that the answer to the question of being cannot be expressed in a set of propositions, and, indeed, that it cannot be formulated at all.

At this point, I am only suggesting the possibility of an interpretation. We wondered whether Heidegger's liquidation of logic justifies a disqualification of Heidegger as a philosopher and whether it renders superfluous the attempt to interpret his question of being. We now see that we need an interpretation of the question of being in order to grasp the precise meaning of Heidegger's liquidation of logic. Surely this reason for trying to interpret the question of being is a scanty one. More convincing reasons are to be found in Heidegger's masterpiece, *Sein und Zeit*.

§ 3. THE PHILOSOPHY OF *SEIN UND ZEIT*

If Heidegger had not published *Sein und Zeit*, he would not have ranked as one of the greatest philosophers of the twentieth century. None of Heidegger's other works equals *Sein und Zeit* in scope, analytical depth, philosophical nerve, and conceptual creativity. The later writings in part derive their significance from their relation to *Sein und Zeit*, and, indeed, as Heidegger wrote in the preface to its seventh edition (1953), the road that *Sein und Zeit* has taken "remains even today a necessary one, if our Dasein is to be stirred by the question of being."[59] In other words, it is impossible to understand the question of being in the later works if one has not studied *Sein und Zeit* first. In this section I try to arouse the reader's interest in Heidegger's question of being by means of a brief summary of *Sein und Zeit*, Heidegger's first major philosophical publication.[60] Why study *Sein und Zeit*?[61] Let me begin by saying some words about its composition.

According to the original plan of the book, which Heidegger discloses in its eighth section, *Sein und Zeit* was to consist of an introduction and six divisions (*Abschnitte*), divided into two parts of three divisions each. Heidegger published merely one-third of the work: the introduction and the first two divisions of part 1.[62] One might say that part 1 is predominantly systematic or constructive, and that part 2 was meant to be historical and destructive. We will see presently why, according to Heidegger, *Sein und Zeit* had to consist of a constructive and a destructive component. In the unpublished part 2 Heidegger wanted to deconstruct the history of ontology, taking the problem of temporality as a guiding principle. Its three divisions were to be concerned with Kant, Descartes, and Aristotle, respectively. The material on Kant was published separately in 1929 as *Kant und das Problem der Metaphysik* (*Kant and the Problem of Metaphysics*) and one might read this book in order to get an idea of what Heidegger meant by notions such as *Destruktion* (historical de[con]struction) and *Wiederholung* (retrieval) of traditional philosophical problems and programs.

As far as the unpublished third division of part 1 is concerned, it is crucial to note that its title, *Zeit und Sein* (*Time and Being*), is an inversion of the title of the work as a whole. We may conclude that this third division was meant to perform a pivotal function, but we grope in the dark as to its precise contents.[63] Thirty-five years after the publication of *Sein und Zeit*, on 31 January 1962, Heidegger held a conference under the title of the unpublished third division, *Zeit und Sein*. However, as he says in *Zur Sache des Denkens* (*Concerning the Topic of Thinking*), the volume in which this conference was published, the conference does not fit in with *Sein und Zeit*, even though it is still concerned with the same question, the question of being.[64] Heidegger adds that the publication of *Sein und Zeit* had been broken off after the second division of part 1 because at the time he was not up to the task of elaborating the theme *Zeit und Sein*.[65]

In reading the published fragment of *Sein und Zeit*—from now on I will often use the title *Sein und Zeit* to refer to this fragment only—it is important to keep in mind the original plan of the book and to remember that four of its six divisions were never published. But of course its fame rests on what was published, especially on divisions 1 and 2 of part 1. In these divisions Heidegger develops his "fundamental ontology," that is, his ontology of human existence. It is above all this ontology that profoundly transformed the European philosophical scene in the second and third quarters of the twentieth century, even though the influence of Heidegger's later thought took over during the 1960s and 1970s.[66] Without Heidegger's fundamental ontology of human existence, books such as Sartre's *L'Être et le Néant* (*Being and Nothingness*), Merleau-Ponty's *Phénoménologie de la Perception* (*Phenomenology of Perception*), Emmanuel Levinas's *Totalité et Infini* (*Totality and Infinity*), and Gadamer's *Wahrheit und Methode* (*Truth and Method*) could not have been written. Perhaps it is true that these authors neglected the main question of *Sein und Zeit*, the question of being, which Heidegger unfolds in the introduction to the book (I will discuss some aspects of the introduction in the next section). Nevertheless, what impressed the first generations of readers of *Sein und Zeit* was the fundamental ontology of human existence (*Dasein*) in divisions 1 and 2, and this ontology remains Heidegger's most striking achievement. For this reason I will now briefly discuss some of its main themes.

Heidegger inherited from Husserl and Scheler the notion that the factual, empirical sciences must be underpinned by a priori ontologies, which are concerned with the fundamental concepts or with the essence of types or regions of being, such as history, nature, space, life, Dasein, language, and the like.[67] Accordingly, Heidegger distinguishes between an *ontical* or factual level and an ontological level of analysis of Dasein. He severely criticizes some of the philosophers who influenced him most in *Sein und Zeit*, such as Kierkegaard and Dilthey, for having moved merely on the ontical, empirical-psychological, or edifying plane, and for not providing us with an ontology of human existence.[68] An ontology of human life or Dasein should aim at essential, a priori generality, and not merely at the empirical generalities discovered by anthropology, psychology, or biology.[69] As Heidegger says, the structures of Dasein he wants to exhibit are "not just any accidental structures, but essential ones which, in every mode of being that Dasein in fact may realize, persist as determinative for the character of its being."[70] This implies that we do not know these essential structures by means of empirical-theoretical generalizations and empirical investigations into diverse cultures; we know them on the basis of a generalization that is ontological and a priori.[71] Heidegger claims that the essential structures of Dasein somehow are the "conditions of possibility" for all ontical or factual manifestations of human life.[72] Taken together they constitute the "fundamental constitution of being" of Dasein.[73] In *Sein und Zeit*, Heidegger often uses the term "being" ([*das*] *Sein*) for such a constitution of being, whereas "a being" (*ein Seiendes*) refers to an entity that has a specific constitution of being. Put into this terminology, ontology aims at analyzing being, that is, the constitution of being of entities, whereas ontical analysis describes the empirical properties and merely contingent characteristics of entities. In the case of human existence, the ontology of Dasein analyzes the fundamental constitution of being that we humans have, whereas history, sociology, and psychology move at the ontical level: they describe diverse factual manifestations of human life.[74]

Heidegger barely discusses the crucial methodological or epistemological question as to how we are able to obtain a priori general knowledge of the basic structures of human existence. We cannot derive it from knowledge of our biological substratum, for instance, because biology is an empirical science.[75] Yet it is quite clear what he would have answered. Dasein is able to obtain general knowledge of the essential structures of its constitution of being because it pertains to this ontological constitution that it *already grasps* its own constitution. In other words, Dasein has understanding not only of its ontical possibilities, but also of its essential constitution of being (*Seinsverständnis*).[76] If this is the case, Heidegger assumes, Dasein will be able to articulate conceptually its understanding of its essential constitution of being, that is, to develop an ontology of itself, independently of empirical research on the varieties of human life and culture.[77] Because we allegedly possess this possibility, Heidegger says that Dasein *is* ontological.[78] Unfortunately, in giving this answer Heidegger assumes what is to be explained, to wit, how it is possible to understand the essence of being human without doing ample empirical research in anthropology.

According to Heidegger, we cannot characterize the essence of our constitution of being as a static content or *what*, because it is not the case that we simply obtain as a fact does, or occur as an event, or are extant as a stone or a plant. We *are* not simply, but we have to be our being, that is, we have to realize our life as our own and to define ourselves while doing so. What we will be like is a result of the way in which we live out our existence, and this result cannot be static, for we have to construct and reconstruct our life all the time. The essence of Dasein lies in its existence, as Heidegger says.[79] This is why the word "Dasein" does not designate an entity with a static nature; rather, it expresses the dynamic mode of being of beings like ourselves.[80] Heidegger redefines the traditional term "existence" as a technical term for our constitution of being: we ek-sist in the sense that we have to effectuate our being. Having to construct our life, we are always ahead of ourselves, anticipating future possibilities. For the same reason, the word "essence" in the context of *Sein und Zeit* receives a more dynamic sense than in traditional philosophy, a shift of meaning that is facilitated by the fact that the German *Wesen* can also be used as a verb. What Heidegger wants to characterize in *Sein und Zeit* is the way we perform our life (one of his pet words in this connection is *Vollzug*). He purports to show that we can only properly understand this way on the basis of an acceptance of the finite time structure inherent in our Dasein. In other words, *finite time or temporality has to be the horizon of understanding the structure of our existence*. This is the first main thesis of *Sein und Zeit*, a fairly trivial one.[81]

However, accepting our temporal finiteness implies confronting death, and Heidegger claims that really confronting death is impossible without *Angst*. Because of the terrifying nature of *Angst*, he says, we have the tendency to flee from it and to engage frantically in worldly affairs. We try to hide our finiteness from ourselves, and to make ourselves feel at ease in everyday life. The tendency to flee from finiteness, as revealed in *Angst*, and to flee from it into worldly occupations is what Heidegger calls *Verfallen*, the "falling" of Dasein. Even though we implicitly understand our own being, we allegedly try to escape from self-understanding and from accepting our condition as it is.

Accordingly, Heidegger contends that Dasein is faced with a fundamental choice: the choice between being oneself (*eigentlich*, authentic) and fleeing from oneself (being *uneigentlich*, inauthentic). It may seem that the choice between inauthenticity and authenticity is merely a choice at the ontical level. It appears to be concerned with the question of how we want to live out our existence. But in fact the choice has ontological and epistemological implications. How can we interpret the constitution of our being ontologically as it really is, if we flee from this very constitution of being in our actual life? While fleeing from it, we will inevitably misinterpret our constitution of being. We now understand why according to *Sein und Zeit* living up to the ideal of authentic life, at least during some exceptional moments, is a prerequisite for developing an adequate ontology of existence. As Heidegger says in section 62, an adequate ontology of human existence would be impossible without a specific ontical ideal, the ideal of being authentically oneself. A particular mode of being, authentic existence, is a necessary condition for being able to obtain a specific kind of knowledge, ontological knowledge of Dasein. This intimate connection between an ideal of authentic life and the prospect of obtaining knowledge of the deep structures of existence makes *Sein und Zeit* such an exciting book. Philosophy ceases to be merely an academic endeavor. It presupposes an authentic experience of life and Heidegger intimates that it may lead to a more authentic life.

Heidegger's view of humans as self-interpreting and self-misinterpreting beings raises two questions, which he wanted to answer respectively in the first and the second parts of *Sein und Zeit*. First, what is the authentic interpretation of Dasein, the interpretation that reveals Dasein as it really is? Heidegger deals with the first question in the published fragment of *Sein und Zeit*. What makes this fragment especially gripping is Heidegger's claim that he is the first philosopher who consistently develops an authentic ontological interpretation of human existence.

The unpublished part 2 of *Sein und Zeit* was meant to discuss the second question: How does Dasein interpret its own existence and the world from within its inauthentic mode of existence, its falling? According to Heidegger, *the entire philosophical and scientific tradition from Plato and Aristotle on remains within an inauthentic self-interpretation* because it tries to understand human existence on the model of another type of entity. The philosophical and scientific tradition conceives of human existence in terms of the same set of ontological categories (substance, property, state, and the like) that it also applies to animals, inanimate objects, and artifacts. According to Heidegger, we overlook the ontological deep structures of human existence as long as we apply this set of categories to it. Dasein has the tendency to understand itself on the model of things in the world, as if, whenever Dasein reflects upon itself, these things cast their reflections on it. But by understanding itself in terms of worldly things, Heidegger claims, Dasein misunderstands itself, and the temptation to understand itself in this manner is part of Dasein's flight from itself, its falling.[82] This is a very radical claim, and it is the second main thesis of *Sein und Zeit*. Let me briefly explore some of its implications.

First, if the entire philosophical and scientific tradition of the West is based on an inauthentic misunderstanding of Dasein, Heidegger will have to develop a radically new set of categories to capture the deep structures of human existence. In order to distinguish these new categories from the traditional ones, such as substance, for instance, Heidegger calls them *Existenziale* (existentialia). The distinction between the ontological and the ontical level of analysis, if applied to human existence, becomes the distinction between the existential level and the existentiell level.[83] Because Heidegger claims that he is the first to develop a set of existentialia, he also has to invent a philosophical terminology to express these existentialia. His attempt to do so makes for difficult reading. Heidegger introduces convoluted technical terms such as *Alltäglichkeit* (everydayness), *Befindlichkeit* (finding-oneself-in-a-situation), *Erschlossenheit* (disclosedness), *Faktizität* (facticity), *Ganzseinkönnen* (potentiality-for-being-a-whole), *Geschichtlichkeit* (historicality), *Gewesenheit* (the-character-of-having-been), *Jemeinigkeit* (mineness), *Gelichtetheit* (clearedness), *Schon-sein-bei* (being-already-alongside), *Seinkönnen* (potentiality-for-being), *Sein-zum-Tode* (being-toward-death), *das Woraufhin* (the upon-which), *Zuhandenheit* (readiness-to-hand), and the like. Yet this is another reason why *Sein und Zeit* is such an exciting book: even though Heidegger in developing his existentialia draws on many sources, such as Aristotle, St. Paul, St. Augustine, Eckhart, Luther, Pascal, Hegel, Kierkegaard, Count Yorck von Wartenburg, and Dilthey, his ontology of human existence is one of the most original philosophical ventures of this century.

The second implication of the radical claims that we tend to misinterpret our ontological constitution and that the entire history of philosophy and of the human sciences consists mainly of a series of misinterpretations, is that we will not be able to develop adequate existentialia unless we simultaneously criticize the traditional interpretations, which allegedly obscure the deep structures of human existence. Accordingly, the construction of new categories (existentialia) has to be coupled with a destruction of traditional conceptual structures, as Heidegger argues in sections 5 and 6 of *Sein und Zeit*. This explains the global organization of the book. The first, constructive part has to be followed by a second, destructive part. Ideally, construction and destruction should go hand in hand, and Heidegger in fact anticipates quite often in part 1 the destructions of part 2, because he cannot develop his existentialia without showing why the traditional categories are inadequate. Conversely, the philosophical point of Heidegger's destructions, such as his *Kant und das Problem der Metaphysik*, cannot be grasped without at least some of his constructive insights.

I have naïvely translated Heidegger's term *Destruktion* by "destruction," and indeed this is what the word means. Much ink has been spilled to argue that this translation is misleading, and that we should prefer the term "deconstruction." However, Heidegger chose his terminology with care. *Sein und Zeit* is a revolutionary book, and like all revolutionaries, Heidegger wanted to destroy the tradition and make a new start. As we will see later, it is no accident that Heidegger borrowed the term *Destruktion* from Luther, who used it in connection with his attempt to dismantle the tradition of the Schools which, according to him, had perverted original Christianity by conceptualizing it in terms of Greek philosophy.[84] There is no harm at all in using the word "destruction" as long as one clearly sees what is required, according to the Heidegger of *Sein und Zeit*: to "destroy" a conceptual tradition and what is achieved by doing so.

Heidegger claims that in the course of our intellectual tradition its basic concepts have become entirely natural and inconspicuous to us. We use these concepts unwittingly, without paying attention to the original sources from which they were genuinely drawn in the past.[85] With a Husserlian term, we might say that traditional concepts are "sedimentations" of past conceptual life, so that a tradition not only transfers concepts of the past but also conceals their nature. As Heidegger says, what a tradition transmits is often made so inaccessible that it becomes concealed.[86] In order to destroy a conceptual tradition, then, we should first explicitly reappropriate it. More particularly, we must uncover the original sources of our traditional concepts. Like Hume and Husserl, Heidegger assumes in *Sein und Zeit* that concepts must somehow be derived from some kind of experience.[87] Allegedly, the experiential origin or "source" of the basic concepts of our philosophical tradition has long been forgotten, and it has been concealed by layer upon layer of interpretation. Reappropriating the tradition means that we reconstruct the experiences that once gave rise to the basic concepts of philosophy.[88]

The example of the Aristotelian notion of a substance as a *concretum* of matter and form will illustrate what Heidegger means. One might argue, and in fact it has been argued quite often, that the traditional concepts of matter and form originated from the domain of artifacts, because in producing an artifact, we form matter.[89] Aristotle then generalized these concepts into categories which, he claimed, would hold for all beings, that is, for beings as such. This generalization is the move that Heidegger objects to.[90] He assumes, like Husserl and the Neo-Kantians, that each major domain or type of being has its own basic constitution of being, so that we should develop a proper set of basic concepts for each domain. As a consequence, a deconstruction of traditional concepts, that is, a reconstruction of the experiences from which these concepts were once derived, may amount to a destruction: the deconstruction shows that the traditional concepts have a much more limited scope than is generally assumed.

Heidegger concludes that his "destruction is . . . far from having the *negative* sense of shaking off the ontological tradition." On the contrary, it would show the positive possibilities of that tradition, "and this always means keeping it within its *limits*."[91] However, this passage is misleading and even disingenuous, for by the very act of showing the limited scope of ontological concepts such as matter and form, one destroys the ontological tradition that claimed universal validity for these concepts. The fact that destruction requires that one uncover the experiential origin of traditional concepts, and that it in this sense shows their "positive possibilities," does not at all imply that Heidegger's destruction of the tradition is not a real destruction. As I said, the word "deconstruction" should not be preferred, although I will use it as an equivalent for purely stylistic reasons. Derrida, who made the term popular, does not share the Husserlian view of basic concepts as originating in experiences that Heidegger endorsed in *Sein und Zeit*. As a consequence, Derrida's notion of deconstruction is entirely different from Heidegger's concept of destruction, and one should not confuse the two. Nor should one confuse Heidegger's notion of destruction with his later idea of a *Verwindung* (coping with, mourning for) the tradition of metaphysics.

I come now to a third implication of Heidegger's second main thesis in *Sein und Zeit*, the thesis that it is impossible to understand Dasein authentically in terms of the traditional ontological categories. This third implication is that Heidegger's thesis amounts to a radical variety of antinaturalism. Philosophical naturalism, in the widest possible sense, is the doctrine that in order to explain the structures of human existence, we have to use the scientific worldview as the background of our explanation and to regard ourselves as products of biological evolution. According to the naturalist, no other worldview is a reasonable option, given what we know in fields such as elementary particle physics, cosmology, organic chemistry, genetics, and evolutionary biology.[92] There are many varieties of naturalism. A scientistic naturalist claims that all valid explanations are of the type developed in mathematical physics, and that the usual explanations provided by psychology, history, or economics must be either reduced to, or eliminated in favor of, natural science explanations. A more moderate naturalist will hold that many structures of human existence "supervene" on biological structures without being reducible to them. It has been argued, for instance, that human consciousness is in part a product of social structures, especially the rule-governed structure of language, and that for this reason the mind cannot be reduced to, or significantly explained by reference to, structures of and causal processes in the brain only. There are many kinds of nonreductive naturalism, as contemporary philosophy shows.

According to a weak interpretation of Heidegger's second main thesis, Heidegger is merely an antireductionist. He is supposed to be claiming that we cannot use the categories of biology or of traditional ontology in interpreting the fundamental structures of human existence because these structures supervene on, and cannot be reduced to, their biological basis. If this is what he means, Heidegger is not necessarily an antinaturalist in the most radical sense; he might reject scientistic naturalism and yet be a more moderate naturalist himself. However, I will argue in this book that in fact Heidegger defends a much stronger thesis, a thesis that is incompatible with all varieties of philosophical naturalism. Such a stronger interpretation is also borne out by the details of Heidegger's philosophical development. As Kisiel suggests, Heidegger's earliest lectures were already "motivated by the desperate struggle to salvage meaning against the scientific worldview."[93]

Thus far, I have concentrated on the most fundamental theses and on the philosophical pretensions of *Sein und Zeit*. Let me now round off this section by discussing the two published divisions of part 1 in some detail. There can be no question of summing up the existential analyses in these divisions. Heidegger develops his new categories of Dasein (existentialia) by means of elaborate descriptions, and the existentialia are mutually dependent, so that they form a complex conceptual network. Furthermore, in order to construct his new conceptual framework, Heidegger constantly has to be on his guard to prevent contamination of the existentialia by the traditional ontological categories, such as body and mind, which have become our habitual vehicles of self-interpretation. No brief summary of Heidegger's analyses can do justice to the complexity of his conceptual structures, and summaries will be easily misunderstood, because the reader will tend to interpret them in terms of his habitual ontological framework, the very framework Heidegger wants to destroy. In section 18 I provide a detailed analysis of two notions that are central in *Sein und Zeit*, the notions of *das Man* (the One, the They, or Everyman) and *Sein-zum-Tode* (being-toward-death).

According to Dreyfus's recent commentary on *Sein und Zeit*, division 1 is the most original and most important section of that book.[94] This cannot have been Heidegger's own view because, as its title says, division 1 is merely a preparatory fundamental analysis of Dasein. Indeed, the analysis of the finite temporality of Dasein, which is the objective of Heidegger's fundamental ontology, is to be found in division 2. We might say that in division 1 Heidegger gives a preliminary and static sketch of the existential structure of Dasein, focusing on its average everyday mode of existence, whereas in division 2 the analysis of temporality and of authentic being-toward-death explains how this structure hangs together and why our existence is characterized by the dynamic existential that Heidegger calls *Sorge* (care or concern). Nevertheless, there is an explanation for Dreyfus's preference for division 1. This division relates more clearly than division 2 to traditional preoccupations of analytic philosophy and to a central theme of traditional epistemology. One of Heidegger's aims in division 1 was to undermine a conception of philosophy that prevailed around the turn of the century, the conception of first philosophy as epistemology. In order to introduce division 1 of *Sein und Zeit*, it is useful to digress briefly and explain the conception of philosophy Heidegger wanted to refute.

Modern epistemology originated in the scientific revolution of the seventeenth century.[95] The problem of the external world, which was to become the main epistemological problem in the second half of the nineteenth century, arose as a consequence of the ontological aspect of the scientific revolution. Seventeenth-century philosophers and scientists substituted a corpuscular ontology for Aristotelian hylemorphism. In order to avoid the circular explanations of Aristotelian science, it was postulated that the theoretical corpuscular mechanisms, by which empirical phenomena such as sound, color, and heat were to be explained, would lack these "secondary qualities" as they appear to the observer.[96] It seemed to follow, however, that macroscopic objects, which were thought to be aggregates of corpuscles, must also lack secondary qualities. How can a macroscopic object that is composed of colorless particles be really colored itself? The seventeenth-century physicists and philosophers concluded, misleadingly, that the material world is very different from the way we perceive it to be: it is a purely material multiplicity without colors, sounds, temperatures, and other secondary qualities. Physics was supposed to have refuted the commonsense conception of the universe.

The new corpuscular ontology had drastic implications for the theory of perception, and it eventually led to the problem of the external world. First, the original *explananda* of corpuscular physics, phenomena such as color and sound, had to be conceived of as subjective impressions in the mind, caused by physical mechanisms, for it was thought that they could not be real physical phenomena. Second, because these phenomena nevertheless seem to be perceived *as* existing in the world, perception had to consist of an unconscious projection of impressions into external reality. This projective theory of perception was then generalized to all contents of perception. According to modern philosopher-scientists, from Descartes and Berkeley to Kant, Helmholtz, Husserl, and Freud, the world as we perceive it—the phenomenal world, in Kant's terminology—is nothing but a projection by the mind. The projective theory of perception directly implies the problem of the existence of the external, physical world: if the world we perceive is a projection of the mind, how can we know that there is a real physical world that causes the impressions and that exists *an sich* (in itself), independently of the perceiving mind?

Rationalists such as Descartes and Leibniz could easily defuse the problem, because they claimed to possess an extraperceptual access to physical reality. The problem of the external world became a central worry for empiricists, since it seemed to invalidate the only source of knowledge that empiricists acknowledge. In periods of scientific advance, which refuted the a prioristic convictions of the rationalists and corroborated empiricism, the problem of the external world paradoxically tended to become the central problem of philosophy. This happened both in the eighteenth century and in the second half of the nineteenth century. During the latter period, philosophers gradually reached the conclusion that epistemology must be the basic philosophical discipline because it deals with the problem of the external world. Epistemology had to replace metaphysics as first philosophy because it deals with a fundamental presupposition of all sciences, the presupposition that there is a material world independent of the knowing mind. Eduard von Hartmann, Edmund Husserl, and many Neo-Kantians explicitly defined epistemology as first philosophy.

It is this conception of philosophy that Heidegger attempts to refute in the first division of *Sein und Zeit*. Heidegger agreed with logical positivists such as Carnap that the epistemological problem of the external world is a pseudoproblem, but he disagreed with them about its diagnosis.[97] Whereas Carnap thought that the problem is spurious because it cannot be decided by empirical and scientific means, Heidegger argues in section 43a of *Sein und Zeit* that its spuriousness is caused by the fact that Dasein and its relation to the world were conceived of on the model of objects and external relations in the world, that is, in the way science had conceived of them since Antiquity. If one thinks of Dasein as an entity in the world, and of the world as a collection of things to which Dasein is merely externally related, then it seems possible that Dasein might exist without the world.[98] According to Heidegger, however, this very conception is due to the falling of Dasein, and the problem of the external world will disappear as soon as one begins to understand Dasein and the world properly. Whereas Carnap blamed the epistemological problem for not being sufficiently scientific, Heidegger rejected epistemology because its problems arise only within a scientific conception of the world. Such a conception is inadequate, he argued, because it misunderstands the constitution of being of Dasein and of the world. As the epistemological tradition is based on mistaken assumptions about our and the world's *being*, the question of being, and not epistemology, has to be elevated to the status of first philosophy. Moreover, because the problem of the external world is raised within a scientific conception of the world and of ourselves, we have to restrict the scope of science in order to eliminate this problem.

How, then, does Dasein relate to the world according to division 1 of *Sein und Zeit*, and how should we specify its *being*? With a term borrowed from Bradley and Wittgenstein, we might say that according to Heidegger Dasein and the world are *internally related*. World is a constitutive structure of Dasein.[99] Accordingly, Heidegger says that all existentialia of Dasein must be understood on the basis of the fundamental ontological structure of being-in-the-world (SZ, § 12). The primary phenomenon of the world is not a meaningless totality of things or of facts, but a "meaningful" structure of mutually referring means, resources, and human institutions, such as tools, houses, roads, libraries, cities, woods, fields, and the like. This meaningful world-structure ultimately refers to a "for-the-sake-of-which" that is rooted in Dasein, because Dasein exists for the sake of itself (§§ 14–18). Furthermore, being *in* the world is not an external relation of two entities, one of which is located inside the other, but it primarily means dwelling and cultivating, working and being at home in an environment. The spatiality proper to Dasein consists in the fact that Dasein always finds itself in situations that open up possibilities of action and manipulation. Dasein and world are internally related, then, because it is impossible to conceive of Dasein without taking into account its everyday world, and it is impossible to conceive of the world as a meaningful referential structure without considering Dasein. However, if Dasein and world are internally related, it is nonsensical to raise the traditional question of epistemology as to whether Dasein does perhaps exist without the world. The problem of the external world could only arise on the basis of an abstract and inadequate picture of the world as a meaningless multiplicity of entities, a picture that is the product of Dasein's falling. At least this is what Heidegger claims.

Heidegger initially defines Dasein as that entity "whose being is in each case *mine*." Dasein is always concerned with itself.[100] It has to effectuate its being, so that its essence (*Wesen*) consists in the fact that it has to be. In other words, its essence must be understood on the basis of existence, and its existence is in each case mine. Heidegger coins the existentiale *Jemeinigkeit* (mineness) to express this characteristic of our mode of being (§ 9).

In view of this definition of Dasein as in each case mine, it may come as a surprise that according to Heidegger you and I are not the real actors of our daily existence-in-the-world. The one who leads everyday life, Heidegger claims, is what he calls *das Man* (the They, the One, the Anyone Self, or Everyman, §§ 25–27).[101] Like the world, Everyman is an existential structure of Dasein, because the world that opens up in daily existence does not derive its meaning from you or from me, as philosophers of consciousness such as Husserl had argued; it already has the meanings that They take it to have. World as meaningful structure is impossible without the others, of past and present generations, and because basically we always live, act, and think as Everyman lives, acts and thinks, Heidegger says that in our daily existence we stand in subjection to the indefinite other or to Everyman (*das Man*). Our being has been taken away by the Others.[102]

On further consideration, then, Heidegger's claim that Everyman is the real subject of our average daily being-in-the-world seems to be inherently plausible. We are born into a specific culture, acquire a particular language, and live in a world that has been shaped by past generations. The cultural matrix into which we are "thrown" by being born of parents who happen to belong to a particular culture, nationality, class, and profession is partly constitutive of our personal identity, of our "self." As a consequence, it is inevitable that all our more personal ways of living out our life move within and are based on these shared and impersonal forms of life that open up the possibilities of structuring our life which in fact we have, so that our being-in-the-world is fundamentally shared and impersonal. In Heidegger's words, "out of this [average, everyday] kind of being—and back to it again—is all existing, such as it is."[103]

As soon as we have accepted the idea that the One or Everyman is the subject of our average daily life, we will be confronted by a second surprise. If the One is the inevitable basis of all our more personal endeavors, because it partly constitutes our identity, why does Heidegger identify the One with inauthentic existence?[104] Heidegger's description of Everyman or the One is punctuated with negative connotations. He says, for instance, that because in using public transport or in reading newspapers we are like everyone else, our Dasein "completely dissolves into the mode of being of 'the others,' " and that in this inconspicuous way, "the real dictatorship of the One is unfolded."[105] He also says that the One deprives particular Dasein of its responsibility,[106] and that individual Dasein is dispersed (*zerstreut*) into Everyman, so that it must free itself from it in order to find itself.[107] Furthermore, he argues in sections 35–38 that Dasein-as-Everyman is disclosed to itself in *Gerede* (idle talk), *Neugier* (superficial curiosity), and *Zweideutigkeit* (ambiguity), and that being so disclosed constitutes the falling of Dasein.[108]

It seems that in the expression *das Man* Heidegger mixes up two different although connected notions. This fact explains a persistent contradiction or tension in *Sein und Zeit*: Heidegger on the one hand stresses that we cannot free ourselves from the One or Everyman, and on the other hand claims that we have to liberate ourselves from it in order to become authentic. The first of these notions captures the insight that our personal existence would be impossible without a shared cultural background or form of life that partly constitutes our identity. It would be absurd to say, however, that this background deprives us of our responsibility, because, on the contrary, the very phenomenon of responsibility is impossible without such a background. We learn to be responsible for ourselves within the matrix of our culture. The second notion is that of what is sometimes called the dictatorship of public opinion, or the terror of mediocrity, which Heidegger associates, like Kierkegaard and Nietzsche, with democracy and reading daily newspapers. There is a connection between the second notion and the first. The dictatorship of Everyman might be seen as a conservative, unimaginative, narrow-minded, and conformist way of endorsing a common cultural background, in which one identifies oneself entirely with traditional stereotyped roles. But the two notions are not identical. One cannot free oneself from one's cultural background, even though one might move into a different one, but one might try to escape from the dictatorship of public opinion by gradually becoming more independent and by realizing that one is more or less free to define one's life on the basis of one's background.[109]

The ambiguity in Heidegger's notion of the One or Everyman affects his concept of authenticity, because the latter concept is defined as the opposite to being lost in the One. We become authentic, Heidegger says, as soon as we take hold of our Self in our own way (*"das Selbst eigens ergreifen"*).[110] How are we able to take hold of our Self if, as Heidegger claims, in our daily existence we flee from our Self into Everyman and into worldly occupations? Heidegger argues in the dazzling section 40 of division 1 that the very phenomenon of flight from our Selves is a clue here. We would not flee from ourselves unless seeing ourselves as we really are is frightening. And indeed, such an insight immediately provokes *Angst*. If so, the experience of *Angst*, from which we attempt to flee in daily life, will reveal the entire existential structure of Dasein as it really is.[111]

What we experience in *Angst* is that the world as a meaningful structure collapses. Everything becomes insignificant. If we ask someone who experiences *Angst* what he is afraid of, he will answer: nothing. And indeed, *Angst* is not an apprehension for particular things or events. Rather, it is a comprehension of the essential reliance of finite and vulnerable Dasein on a meaningful world, which is revealed by the very collapse of this world. In short, *Angst* reveals the world *as* world, and it discloses Dasein *as* a finite being-in-the-world. It is at this point that Heidegger's concept of authenticity emerges, and, as I said, it is contaminated by the ambiguity within his notion of the One. For Heidegger claims that in confronting one's Self in *Angst*, we do not reveal ourselves in our reliance on our cultural world, but, on the contrary, in a radical individuality (*Vereinzelung*). Because of the very fact that in *Angst* the meaningful world collapses, we cannot flee from ourselves into this world and into the They anymore, and our Dasein stands naked, as it were.[112] We realize that we are "thrown" into existence, and that we have freely to construct our existence by ourselves and to choose our course in life. Because Heidegger does not clearly distinguish between the phenomenon of a shared cultural background and the dictatorship of public opinion, he suggests that liberating oneself from the latter amounts to freeing oneself from the former as well. Authenticity, then, consists in a radical affirmation of our existential solitude. As Heidegger says, "anxiety individualizes Dasein and thus discloses it as '*solus ipse*.' "[113] Although, as Heidegger admits, this cannot imply that in existential solipsism the structure of being-in-the-world is dissolved, authenticity at first sight seems to consist in a complete autonomy of the Self, in which the individual does not rely on his cultural background except in the sense that he freely chooses the possibilities he wants to realize, or, as Heidegger says, his "heroes."[114]

Division 1 of *Sein und Zeit* culminates in an articulation of the existential structure of Dasein revealed in *Angst* (§§ 41–42) and in a critical discussion of the traditional notions of reality and truth (§§ 43–44). The totality of Dasein's existential structure is called *Sorge* (concern or care), which means that Dasein is a being that makes an issue of its being, and it consists of three aspects that are all disclosed in *Angst*. That in the face of which we have *Angst* is the fact that we are thrown into existence, so that in a sense we are radically contingent (*Geworfenheit, Faktizität*). That which we have *Angst* about is our freedom or potentiality to realize our being-in-the-world (*Ex-sistenz, Entwurf*). Finally, that into which we flee from our *Angst* is being absorbed in worldly affairs, handing over the responsibility for our existence to the They, and trying to understand Dasein in terms of worldly things. This flight is the falling of Dasein (*Verfallen*).

Heidegger stresses that the ontological analysis of Dasein in division 1 is merely preparatory, because, first, it concentrates on Dasein in its daily inauthentic mode of existence; second, it does not grasp Dasein in its totality (*Ganzsein*); and, finally, it does not explain the fundamental unity of the existential structure of concern (§ 45). In division 2 of *Sein und Zeit* Heidegger attempts to ground this preparatory analysis by what he calls a primordial existential interpretation of Dasein. It seems that in order to conceive of Dasein in its totality, we have to survey its existence from birth to death. But this is impossible in our own case, because as long as we are able to survey anything, our death has not yet arrived. Heidegger argues that we may nevertheless grasp our Dasein in its totality and that we may *be* wholly ourselves if we adopt an authentic relation to our death, and, indeed, that authenticity is nothing but being myself "in an impassioned *freedom toward death*—a freedom that has been released from the illusions of the One, and which is factical, certain of itself, and anxious" (§§ 46–53).[115] The possibility of being authentic in this sense is disclosed to us in the call of conscience, which incites us to being ready for *Angst* and to being resolute in realizing what we have decided to do (§§ 54–60). Authenticity is defined as a resolute anticipation of our own death, which enables us to be our Self as a whole. Only by being resolute can we integrate the phases of our life into a meaningful whole, whereas without resoluteness human life is *zerstreut* (dispersed).

Authenticity in this sense is the clue to understanding the unity of the structure of concern, because by resolutely anticipating our death, the finite temporal structure of existence is revealed, whereas the unity of the three aspects of concern (*Existenz, Geworfenheit, Verfallen*) is founded on the three dimensions of existential temporality (future, past, present). This is why Heidegger repeats his preparatory existential analysis of Dasein by elaborating in division 2 the temporal sense of the existentialia of division 1 (§§ 61–71). Finally, Heidegger claims that the temporal structure of Dasein explains why it is a historical being, so that historicity is another existential of Dasein (§§ 72–77). In the final chapter of division 2, Heidegger attempts to account for the origin of the ordinary concept of time as an endless continuum of equivalent moments, a concept that is very different from that of the existential time in which we live into a finite future. The ordinary conception of time, with which we calculate in daily existence and by which we often measure out our life, allegedly is derived from existential time, and Heidegger claims that it is due to the falling of Dasein (§§ 78–83).[116]

As I stressed before, I do not pretend to give a comprehensive summary of the published divisions of *Sein und Zeit*. My succinct hints as to the contents of this complex book merely aim at arousing the interest of the reader in Heidegger's question of being. It has been argued that Heidegger's ontology of Dasein is akin to American pragmatism as developed by John Dewey, so that analytical philosophers would be already familiar with some elements of Heideggerian thought. The main reason for this purported rapprochement is that in discussing the notion of world Heidegger focuses on our manipulation of tools. He argues that the world is primarily disclosed to us as a meaningful background in which we work and use tools and instruments. Accordingly, the primordial way in which things manifest themselves to us is as being *Zuhanden* (ready-to-hand), and not at all as things that are *Vorhanden* (simply exist and occur, are extant). In section 69b of *Sein und Zeit*, Heidegger tries to explain the genesis of the scientific view of the world as a collection of meaningless things on the basis of a breakdown of the primordial meaningful world of work. He argues that the scientific image of the world and the theoretical attitude in general are derivative, and that pseudoproblems arise if we try to regard the scientific worldview as the fundamental one. This analysis resembles Dewey's well-known critique of the "spectator theory of knowledge," which allegedly dominated Western thought from Plato on. The spectator theory of knowledge assumed that the theoretical attitude is the basis of the practical one, instead of the other way around.[117]

Notwithstanding these resemblances between Heidegger and Dewey, I think that manifest and important differences prevail. Whereas Dewey stressed the continuity between practical life and scientific inquiry, and reinterpreted science within the context of pragmatism as a process of inquiry that aims at resolving vital problems, Heidegger in *Sein und Zeit* squarely opposes the existential account of Dasein and world to the scientific view of the world. One might say that Heidegger wants to cancel the ontological aspect of the scientific revolution, according to which the corpuscular image of the world would have refuted the manifest image of common sense. Heidegger not only restores the primacy of the manifest image; he also argues that Dasein still misinterprets itself even in its commonsense interpretation, because it understands itself in terms of entities in the world.

This first difference is related to a second one. Dewey also stresses another continuity, the continuity between higher animals and man. His account of science as inquiry fits in well with evolution theory, and he often uses biological categories in the interpretation of human life.[118] Dewey is a naturalist, whereas according to Heidegger any naturalist interpretation of Dasein will necessarily fail to do justice to the fundamental structures of existence. Assimilating Heidegger's analysis of human existence to Dewey's pragmatism will easily lead to a superficial interpretation of Heidegger's works, which overlooks the radical and antinaturalist character of his philosophical enterprise.[119]

Sein und Zeit raises many questions of interpretation. Some of them are concerned with Heidegger's notion of authenticity. Apart from the tension within this concept due to the ambiguous notion of the One, there is a second difficulty. The ideal of authenticity, as developed in sections 40, 53, 60, and 62, is extremely individualistic and even "solipsistic," as Heidegger says. He argues that *Angst* and being free for death individuate (*vereinzeln*) us, and call our Self back from being lost in Everyman. The ideal of authentic resoluteness seems to require a radical independence from all others. But in section 74, which deals with the existential of historicity (*Geschichtlichkeit*), Heidegger proposes a very different ideal of authenticity. He claims that "Dasein's fateful destiny in and with its 'generation' goes to make up the full authentic performance of Dasein," where "destiny" is defined as the performance of a *Volk* (people).[120] What is the relation between Heidegger's individualistic notion of authenticity and this gregarious or *völkisch* notion, and how can the former suddenly turn into the latter, as it seems to do in section 74?

Among the many problems of interpretation concerning *Sein und Zeit* there is one problem that must be singled out as most fundamental. *Sein und Zeit* aims at raising the question of being. This question is the single and only question that Heidegger asked during his entire *Denkweg*. The question of being is also the theme of the present study. But what does this question amount to? And what is its relation to the fundamental ontology of Dasein in divisions 1 and 2 of *Sein und Zeit*? These problems will turn out to be difficult and complex. In order to reveal at least some of the difficulties involved, I now partly discuss the introduction to *Sein und Zeit*.

§ 4. THE QUESTION OF BEING: SIX PROBLEMS

Heidegger's question of being aims at revealing "the sense [*Sinn*] of being." To the extent that being (*das Sein*) is always the ontological constitution of a specific being (*ein Seiendes*), and for the reason that Heidegger in *Sein und Zeit* attempts to disclose the temporal sense of Dasein, one might suppose that Heidegger's question of being aims at revealing the ontological sense of human existence. According to this interpretation, what Heidegger means by *das Sein* is the temporal sense of our constitution of being, as Walter Schulz argued in the 1950s, or at least that which enables us to make sense of our existence and of the world.[121] Hubert Dreyfus endorses the latter view when he characterizes Heidegger's question of being as the attempt "to make sense of our ability to make sense of things."[122] It seems, then, that the relation between the question of being and the existential analysis of Dasein is unproblematic. They amount to the very same thing. This implies that there is no separate problem of interpretation with regard to the question of being. To the extent that we understand what Heidegger's existential analysis of human existence amounts to, we also understand the meaning of his question of being.

Unfortunately, things are not simple as that. According to the original plan of *Sein und Zeit*, its six divisions are preceded by an introduction, which is entitled "Exposition of the Question of the Sense of Being." This introduction was published along with divisions 1 and 2 of the book. In order to find out what Heidegger's question of being means, and how it relates to the fundamental ontology of Dasein in *Sein und Zeit*, we have to study the introduction. But no one who penetrates into this condensed and complex text will be able to subscribe to the elegant and simple interpretation of the question of being and its relation to the analysis of Dasein that I just outlined. In fact, the introduction raises more problems than it answers, problems that an interpretation of Heidegger's question of being has to solve. In the present section, I state six of these problems. A reader who is not interested in minute textual exegesis may skim through this section. One should remember, however, that we are preparing the grounds for an interpretation of Heidegger's thought, and that the only adequate basis for such an interpretation is a scrupulous analysis of the texts and of the problems they contain.

Heidegger's introduction consists of eight sections, divided into two chapters of four sections each. In the second chapter, Heidegger argues on the basis of a preliminary description of Dasein that there is a twofold task—a constructive and a destructive task (§§ 5 and 6)—in working out the question of being, maintains that the method of investigation has to be phenomenological or hermeneutical (§ 7), and sketches the structure of the book (§ 8). I have touched upon sections 5, 6, and 8 already, and I discuss section 7 below (in §§ 5, 8C, and 17B). This is why I concentrate now on the first chapter (§§ 1–4) of Heidegger's introduction. However, my first problem concerns page 1 of *Sein und Zeit*, a page that precedes the introduction and that is not referred to in the table of contents.

1. Page 1 of *Sein und Zeit* may be considered an introduction to the introduction. With reference to a quote from Plato's *Sophistes*, Heidegger introduces the question of being. He claims that we do not know an answer to the question, so that we have to raise the question once again. Moreover, because we are not perplexed by the question of being, Heidegger first has to reawaken an understanding of the meaning of the question. Having stated the objective (*Absicht*) and the provisional aim (*Ziel*) of the book, he says that its objective, its investigations, and its aim call for some introductory remarks. Most readers will turn over this first page without much reflection. Yet it contains one of the most vexing problems regarding the interpretation of Heidegger's question of being.

The reason is that the way in which Heidegger introduces the question of being is blatantly ambiguous. Page 1 of *Sein und Zeit* contains five formulations of the question of being, which fall into two kinds. According to one kind, the question of being is concerned with "what you mean when you use the expression 'being,' " or with "what we really mean by the word 'being.' " It aims at grasping the meaning (*Sinn*) of the word or expression "to be." The second kind of formulation suggests that the question of being rather seeks to make sense of a phenomenon. This time the word "being" is not put within quotation marks, and the question of being is characterized as "the question of the sense [*Sinn*] of being." Our first problem, then, is this: Does Heidegger's question of being aim at analyzing the meaning of a word, or does it seek to determine the "significance" or "sense" of a phenomenon, such as human existence? Depending on which interpretation we prefer, we must translate the German term *Sinn* either by "meaning" (What are the meanings of the verb "to be"?) or by significance (What is the significance of the phenomenon of human existence?).[123]

One might object that seeing a problem here is splitting hairs, because by determining the significance of the phenomenon of human existence, for instance, we may also fix the meaning of the expression "human being." But this objection does not annihilate the difficulty at all. Heidegger suggests in section 1 of *Sein und Zeit* that the question of being is concerned with ordinary uses of "to be" such as in "The sky *is* blue" and "I *am* merry."[124] Surely, in order to determine the meaning of the verb "to be" one has to analyze these ordinary uses, and this, it seems, is the task of linguists and logicians. Logicians usually distinguish among various functions of the verb "to be": it may express identity, as in "The morning star is the evening star," or predication, as in "The sky is blue," or existence (in the usual sense), as in "There is no greatest prime number." Most modern logicians will hold that the verb "to be" as used in these three ways is not a referring expression, so that there simply is no phenomenon called "being" in these senses. This does not exclude, the linguist will observe, that we may decide to use the expression "being" also in nonlogical ways, for instance, as a synonym for "the universe" or for "human life." But it seems that there is no reason at all to assume that an analysis of the significance or of the ontological constitution of human existence will have any bearing on the meanings of "to be" in its logical uses. Let me summarize the first problem as follows. Is Heidegger's question of being concerned with the meanings of expressions such as "being" and "to be," or is it concerned with a phenomenon, such as human existence? And if the answer turns out to be that it is concerned with both words and phenomena, what, according to Heidegger, is the relation between the two?

2. According to section 1 of *Sein und Zeit*, the question of being, which inspired the researches of Plato and Aristotle, has today been forgotten, and "what they wrestled . . . from the phenomena, fragmentary and incipient though it was, has long since become trivialized."[125] Moreover, on the basis of initial Greek contributions toward an interpretation of being, a number of prejudices have been developed that declare the question of being superfluous and sanction its neglect. Heidegger briefly discusses three of these prejudices, in order to show that it is necessary to raise the question of being once again. He concludes that the question of being lacks an answer and is itself obscure. It is interesting to see how Heidegger argues that an answer to the question of being is still lacking, for his argument contains some clues as to the precise meaning of the question of being as he understands it. His argument also raises problems, and I will state a problem concerning Heidegger's discussion of each of the three prejudices (problems 2, 3, and 4).

According to the first prejudice, the word "being" expresses the most universal concept.[126] Yet its generality cannot be the generality of a highest class or genus, as Heidegger observes, following Aristotle and the Scholastics. If we interpret Aristotle's categories (usually translated as substance, quantity, quality, relation, location, time, position, state, action, and passion) as the highest genera of everything there is, it would be misleading to say that "being" is an even higher genus that embraces everything. And if we interpret the ten categories as classes of different modes of saying something of an individual, we might say that the word "being" transcends the categories because it is used in each and every category.[127] In this sense, "being" is a *transcendens*, as the Schoolmen said. According to Aristotle, at least in the traditional interpretation, the unity of this transcendental universal ("being") is a unity of analogy in contrast to the multiplicity of the categories (see § 7, below, for discussion). Heidegger claims that Aristotle put the problem of being on a new basis with this discovery, although even Aristotle "failed to clear away the darkness of these categorial interconnections." Heidegger further claims that at the end of the metaphysical tradition, Hegel no longer paid heed to Aristotle's problem of the unity of being as over against the multiplicity of categories. Accordingly, from the fact that "being" expresses the most universal concept it does not follow that the notion of being is clear. It is rather the darkest notion of all, and this is why the question of being has to be raised once again.

Heidegger's discussion of the first prejudice raises the problem as to how much of the ontological tradition he endorses in *Sein und Zeit*. Does *Sein und Zeit* aim at solving Aristotle's problem of the unity of being, to which Hegel allegedly no longer paid heed? This is suggested by texts such as "Mein Weg in die Phänomenologie." More particularly, does Heidegger accept the idea that "being" is a *transcendens*? We have to answer this question in the affirmative, for he writes in section 7 of *Sein und Zeit*:

> Being, as the basic theme of philosophy, is no genus of an entity; yet it pertains to every entity. Its "universality" is to be sought higher up. Being and the structure of being lie beyond every entity and every possible character that an entity may possess. *Being is the transcendens pure and simple.* . . . Every disclosure of Being as the transcendens is *transcendental* knowledge.[128]

If Heideggerian being is the *transcendens* pure and simple, what does Heidegger mean by transcendens and "transcendental"? Does he want to say that the verb "to be" is used in all categories, and that "being" therefore is transcendent(al) in the Aristotelian and Scholastic sense? Or is being transcendent in the sense of the Neo-Platonic and Christian tradition, which used *esse* as another word for "God" and argued that Being is transcendent to the created temporal world? Or, finally, does Heidegger use the word "transcendental" in the Kantian sense, so that being is transcendent(al) because allegedly understanding being is a transcendental condition of the possibility of perceiving particular entities? The problem is that the text of *Sein und Zeit* does not enable us to answer these questions unambiguously.[129]

There is some discussion of the notion of transcendence in section 69, where Heidegger argues that the characteristic of Dasein, that it discloses itself and the world, is rooted in its temporality.[130] This characteristic is called the transcendence of Dasein. Furthermore, the world itself is called transcendent because the world, in Heidegger's sense of a meaningful background, allegedly is a condition of the possibility of our using tools or encountering entities. Heidegger draws attention to the fact that it is not possible to understand something as a piece of equipment (a hammer, for instance) without the pragmatic background of standardized procedures, other pieces of equipment, and institutionalized human practices and objectives. But it would be rash to conclude that the transcendence of the world or of Dasein is the same as the transcendence of being, and Heidegger nowhere in *Sein und Zeit* clearly explains what he means when he calls being transcendent. The present problem of interpretation, then, is concerned primarily with the notion of a transcendence of being. As we will see, Heidegger's discussion of the second prejudice raises a related problem.

3. The second prejudice says that the concept of being is indefinable. We can neither derive the concept of being from higher concepts by definition, nor can we present it through lower ones. However, the indefinability of "being" does not eliminate the question of its meaning; it rather demands that we look that question in the face.[131]

Heidegger's discussion of this second prejudice seems to be altogether trivial. Surely the verb "to be" and the noun "being" cannot be defined in the traditional way of a *definitio per genus proximum et differentiam specificam*, and surely this does not exempt us from analyzing their meanings.[132] Heidegger infers from the indefinability of "being" and "to be" (*Sein*) that these expressions cannot denote an entity.[133] This seems to be a trivial result as well. Did Kant not already argue that "being" in the sense of "existence" cannot be a real predicate? Yet, Heidegger's brief discussion of the second prejudice raises a number of crucial questions. How can we determine the meaning of "being" if "being" cannot be defined? Why does Heidegger not turn to logic and to linguistic analysis in order to clarify the meaning of "to be"? Finally, how does Heidegger distinguish being (*das Sein*) from beings (*Seiendes*)? In his later works, he stresses this distinction again and again, and calls it the "ontological difference."[134] He claims that the distinction has been forgotten in the tradition of metaphysics. But what does the distinction amount to? How does *being* relate to *beings*, and what does Heidegger mean by *being* (without quotation marks)? Should we conclude that the ontological difference and the idea that being is the *transcendens* pure and simple are two sides of the same coin? Is *being* transcendent to *beings* simply because it is not *a* being itself? If so, how can Heidegger attach such importance to the trivial fact that the verb "to be," at least in its logical uses, does not denote an entity?

These questions are not easily answered, and Heidegger seems to contradict himself concerning the relation between being and beings. There is a marked tendency in *Sein und Zeit* to interpret *being* as the ontological constitution of specific beings, such as ourselves.[135] We *are* in a way different from that of tools and from that of a stone or a mountain. When I say, "Charles is worried," this statement presupposes a constitution of being of Charles that is very different from the constitution of being expressed by "This stone is heavy." The statement that Charles is worried would not make sense unless Charles lived into his future and unless the deep structure of his existence were characterized by what Heidegger calls concern. If Heidegger uses the word "being" (*Sein*) as a technical term for the ontological constitution of specific beings, it follows that to specify the sense of being is nothing but to analyze different constitutions of being. Moreover, it follows that being is never without beings, and this is precisely what Heidegger affirms in *Sein und Zeit*.[136] However, in the postscript to the fourth edition (1943) of *Was ist Metaphysik?* Heidegger wrote that being *does* act (*west*) without beings, even though beings are never without being. This seems to contradict the idea that being is nothing but the ontological constitution of specific beings. Six years later, in the fifth edition (1949), Heidegger changed the text and wrote that being *never* acts without beings, so that the fifth edition of *Was ist Metaphysik?* contradicts the fourth edition, which, in turn, contradicted *Sein und Zeit*. What are we to make of these contradictions?[137] How are we to explain the fact that Heidegger specified the relation between being and beings in contradictory ways? Let me call this the problem of the ontological difference.

4. According to the third prejudice, the notion of being is self-evident. The various uses of "to be," as in "The sky is blue" and "I am merry," are intelligible without further ado. Heidegger's reaction to this prejudice is surprising:

> But here we have an average kind of intelligibility, which merely demonstrates that it is unintelligible. It makes manifest that in any way of comporting oneself toward entities as entities and in any being toward entities as entities there lies a priori an enigma. The very fact that we already live in an understanding of being and that the meaning of being is still veiled in darkness proves that it is necessary in principle to raise this question again.[138]

Many analytic philosophers will admit that our ability to use the verb "to be" without problems does not automatically imply that we are able to state and clearly distinguish its diverse meanings. Our knowing how to use a certain expression does not necessarily involve our knowing that such and such is true of this expression, and this explains why one easily commits fallacies of ambiguity when the verb "to be" is involved. However, analytical philosophers would not speak of an enigma in this context. Having the competence of applying linguistic rules enables us in principle to make them explicit and also to make them more precise. This is what we try to do in the study of grammar and in philosophical logic. I think that the first sentence of the quotation is the most interesting one. How can Heidegger claim that the fact that we understand the ordinary uses of "to be" demonstrates their *un*intelligibility? Does he perhaps presuppose a conception of meaning and language that linguists and analytical philosophers would not endorse? If so, what is this conception of meaning and language? Furthermore, what is, according to Heidegger, the connection between our understanding of the verb "to be" and an "enigma" that "lies in any way of comporting oneself toward entities as entities," an enigma that allegedly is revealed by the fact that we are able to use the verb "to be"?

5. In section 2 of *Sein und Zeit*, Heidegger discusses the "formal structure" of the question of being. He first tells us that each and every questioning is characterized by four different aspects: (1) it is based on a preliminary grasp of what it is aiming at; (2) there is a content (*das Gefragte*) that has to be specified; (3) there is something that is interrogated or investigated (*das Befragte*); and (4) the inquiry reaches its goal with that which is to be found out by questioning (*das Erfragte*).

Heidegger then specifies the first three aspects for the case of the question of being. Significantly, he omits a discussion of the fourth aspect. Perhaps this is only to be expected because, as we know from section 5, the answer to the question of being tells us merely how to conduct our concrete ontological research.[139]

According to Heidegger, the preliminary grasp of what the question of being is aiming at is what he calls our average understanding of being (*durchschnittliches Seinsverständnis*). We have seen that Dasein is characterized by an understanding of being. However, Heidegger's notion of an understanding of being is a difficult one, and it seems to contain many ambiguities. When Heidegger introduces the notion in section 4, he derives it from the fact that Dasein has a relation to its own being, because it has to live out its own existence. This relation is called "understanding of being" (*Seinsverständnis*). What it means is first of all that we more or less know how to live, and "understanding" in this context is a capacity word. This existentiell know-how would be impossible if we were not able to find our way in our environment, and this is why our understanding of being concerns both Dasein and the world. However, when Heidegger introduces the notion of understanding of being in section 2, he suggests that we possess understanding of being because we know how to use the verb "to be," even though we cannot state its meanings. In short, Heidegger's notion of an understanding of being is affected by the same ambiguity as the question of being itself: Is it concerned with a word or with a phenomenon, or with both? (see problem 1).

The content (*das Gefragte*) of the question of being, Heidegger continues, is being itself, whereas its aim (*das Erfragte*) is the sense of being. He specifies *being* as "that which determines a being as *a being*, that with regard to which entities are already understood, however we may discuss them in detail."[140] This is an obscure and ambiguous formula. Its first half, "that which determines a being as a being," reminds us of Plato and of medieval philosophical theology, whereas its second half, "that with regard to which entities are already understood," has a Kantian flavor. Heidegger stresses that *being* is not *a being* and that, therefore, we need both a special method and a special kind of concept in order to reveal the sense of being. My fifth problem is concerned with being as the content of the question of being. In order to introduce this problem, I have to turn to section 3 of *Sein und Zeit*, in which Heidegger argues for the "ontological priority" of the question of being on the basis of a rudimentary philosophy of science. In the remainder of section 2 and the entire section 4 of *Sein und Zeit*, Heidegger discusses that which has to be interrogated or investigated if we want to raise the question of being (*das Befragte*). He argues that this is Dasein, so that the question of being has to be developed by analyzing Dasein. The sixth problem I want to raise concerns this argument and its validity.

Let me first turn to section 3 of *Sein und Zeit*, in order to introduce my fifth problem. As the title indicates, Heidegger in this section wants to demonstrate the ontological priority of the question of being, or, as he calls it in the final sentence of the section, its objectively scientific priority.[141] In the two introductory paragraphs of section 3, he makes clear that by showing its ontological priority, he will have specified the function of the question of being, namely, that it is the most fundamental and the most concrete question.[142] However, in section 3 Heidegger merely explains why the question of being is the most fundamental question, omitting an explanation of its concreteness, and, as I said before, he does so on the basis of a rudimentary philosophy of science.[143]

Somewhat anachronistically, we might characterize this philosophy of science as a blend of Husserl's philosophy of science and Thomas Kuhn's notion of scientific progress by means of revolutions. The third and sixth paragraphs of section 3 are Husserlian, whereas the fourth and fifth are Kuhnian. According to Husserl's philosophy of science, each special science investigates a specific region or domain of being. Heidegger mentions history, nature, space, life, Dasein, and language as examples of these domains. Implicitly or explicitly, the special sciences are founded on what Husserl calls regional ontologies, which articulate the "essence" (Husserl) or the "fundamental constitution of being" (Heidegger: *Grundverfassung seines Seins*) of the entities in their domain. According to both Husserl and Heidegger, these founding ontologies are a priori, and the general insights they contain are essential and not contingent.[144] They both hold that the fundamental concepts which constitute a regional ontology may be "demonstrated" or "grounded" by a descriptive analysis of the essence or of the ontological constitution of entities in the domain under investigation.[145] Such a descriptive grounding of regional-ontological concepts is the proper task of the philosophy of the special sciences. With a sneer to the Neo-Kantians and logical positivists of his time, Heidegger says that a regional ontology is very different from the epistemology or methodology of the special sciences, a logic of science that would be sterile because it limps along with scientific progress. In contrast, regional ontologies are *productive* logics that precede scientific progress because they disclose regions of beings in the structure of their being, and make these structures available to the positive sciences as transparent assignments for their inquiry.[146]

According to the Kuhnian aspect of Heidegger's rudimentary philosophy of science, "the real 'movement' of the sciences takes place when their basic concepts undergo a more or less radical revision." Heidegger adds that "the level which a science has reached is determined by how far it is *capable* of a crisis in its basic concepts," and he briefly discusses such crises in mathematics, physics, biology, history, and theology.[147] Unfortunately, Heidegger does not explain how he intends to resolve the tension or even contradiction between the Husserlian and the Kuhnian aspects of his philosophy of science. Husserl's notion of science is fundamentally static. As soon as the philosophical foundation of a special science has been made explicit by means of a regional ontology, it has been laid once and for all, because it is a priori, and scientific progress can only consist in accumulating empirical results obtained within the conceptual framework of the relevant regional ontology. How is Heidegger able to endorse Husserl's conception on the one hand, accepting the idea that regional-ontological concepts can be justified a priori by a descriptive analysis of ontological structures, and on the other hand to acknowledge the fact, which had become obvious by 1927, that the basic concepts of the sciences may undergo fundamental revisions?[148] The tension between a Husserlian aspect and a Kuhnian aspect of Heidegger's philosophy of science is connected to other tensions in *Sein und Zeit*, such as the tension between the phenomenological and the hermeneutical aspects of Heidegger's own method. (I come back to the latter tension in §§ 8C and 9B, below, whereas the former tension will be resolved in § 9A.)

How does Heidegger argue for the ontological priority of the question of being on the basis of his apparently ambivalent philosophy of science? His argument is contained in the seventh and eighth paragraphs of section 3:

> Ontological inquiry is indeed more primordial, as over against the ontical inquiry of the positive sciences. But it remains itself naïve and opaque if in its researches into the being of beings it fails to discuss the meaning of being in general. . . . The question of being aims therefore at ascertaining the a priori conditions not only for the possibility of the sciences that examine entities as entities of such and such a type, and, in so doing, already operate with an understanding of being, but also for the possibility of those ontologies themselves which are prior to the ontical sciences and which provide their foundations.[149]

This passage could have been endorsed by Husserl as it stands, and indeed Heidegger derived his idea of a three-story edifice of knowledge from Husserl's mature philosophy. According to both Husserl and Heidegger in *Sein und Zeit*, the special sciences are founded on regional ontologies, which, in their turn, are founded on transcendental first philosophy. However, within this formal tripartite framework, Heidegger is highly critical of Husserl's conception. Husserl argued in the Fundamental Meditation (*Fundamentalbetrachtung*) of *Ideas* I that the *being* of regional entities consists in their being constituted by the transcendental ego. He explained this process of constitution as a multilayer interpretation by the transcendental ego of its hyletic data, its sensations. As a consequence, the constituted world allegedly is ontologically dependent on the transcendental ego, which itself exists as an independent and temporally infinite substance. As Husserl explained in the terminology of his third Logical Investigation, *being* falls apart into two types: ontologically independent being (the being of the transcendental ego or egos), and ontologically dependent being (the being of entities in the world). He later called this ontology "transcendental idealism."[150]

One might say, then, that Husserl already answered Heidegger's question of being. But it is also clear why Heidegger rejected Husserl's idealist answer.[151] I have argued elsewhere that Husserl's transcendental idealism is a solution to the traditional problem of the external world.[152] We have seen in section 3, above, that Heidegger rejects this problem as a pseudoproblem, and that he attributed the fact that the problem arose to a mistaken (scientistic) conception of the *being* of Dasein and world. This is a sufficient reason for asking the question of being anew, and for investigating the *being* of world and Dasein. In short, section 3 of *Sein und Zeit* shows that Heidegger derived his argument for the ontological priority of the question of being from the philosophical tradition, a tradition that started with Plato and Aristotle and led to Husserl. One of the reasons for raising the question anew was the rejection of Husserl's transcendental idealism.[153]

There was yet another reason related to Husserl, and this second reason brings me to the fifth problem I want to raise. As Heidegger says at the end of section 1.1 of *Sein und Zeit*, the philosophical tradition was not able to solve the problem of the unity of being as over against the multiplicity of categories. Heidegger objected to Husserl that transcendental idealism did not solve this problem of the unity of being either, because it divided beings into two classes, independent transcendental egos or monads and dependent mundane beings. What was the unitary meaning of the verb "to be" that allowed Husserl to say that both monads and mundane entities *are*?

Interestingly, Husserl gave an answer to this question, and the problem I want to raise is why Heidegger did not accept this answer. The answer is implied by Husserl's notion of a formal ontology. In section 13 of *Ideas* I, Husserl clarifies his distinction between regional or material ontologies on the one hand and formal ontology on the other hand by means of a distinction between generalizing and formalizing. By "generalizing" he means the activity of finding ever more general concepts under which something falls. If we start with *dog*, for instance, we might end up with the concept *living being*. Husserl calls such a most general concept a "highest material genus." A highest material genus defines a region of being, and regional ontologies have the task of articulating the *material categories* that determine the ontological structure of the various regions. Husserl seems to assume that the whole of being is unambiguously carved up into ontological regions.

Formalizing, on the other hand, is what we do in mathematics and formal logic, when we substitute variables for material expressions. The range of these variables is defined by what Husserl calls *formal categories*, such as property, relation, entity, predicate, proposition, class, part, whole, and the like. Formal disciplines whose variables range over propositions or parts of propositions are called apophantic logic, whereas formal disciplines whose variables range over entities and their parts, properties, relations, and classes of these are called formal ontology.[154] Now Husserl says, echoing and also clarifying Aristotle's notion of the transcendence of being, that it would be a fatal mistake to conceive of the notion of an entity in general (*Gegenstand überhaupt*) as a highest material category, for this would amount to mistaking the operation of formalization for a kind of generalization. The notions of *being* and *to be*, then, are *formal* notions and not material ones, and Aristotle's doctrine that being is not a *genus* and transcends the categories is a confused way of expressing the difference between formalizing and generalizing. It follows that the question of being, to the extent that it aims at clarifying the nonregional meanings of "being" and "to be," belongs to formal ontology or to philosophical logic. Material ontologies conceptualize the ontological structure of various regions of being. But the unity of the notions of "being" and "to be" is purely formal. This is an attractive view. It explains the universal scope of logic and arithmetic, that is, the validity of these disciplines for all material regions of being. Why did Heidegger reject this view? How are we to understand Heidegger's conviction that we even have to destroy formal logic in order to raise the question of being properly?

6. Let me now come back to section 2 of *Sein und Zeit*, in order to state the final problem concerning the interpretation of the question of being that I want to raise. We have seen that Heidegger stresses the ontological difference in section 1.2 of *Sein und Zeit*, and that he says that being (*das Sein*) is the *transcendens* tout court.[155] Being is not *a* being, nor a property or characteristic of beings. If so, it will come as a surprise that according to section 2 we need a *Befragtes*, something to be investigated, in order to be able to answer the question of being. Why should we investigate *a* being (*ein Seiendes*) in order to answer the question of being, if being (*das Sein*) is neither a property nor some other kind of characteristic of beings?

Even though being is the *transcendens* tout court, Heidegger affirms in sections 2 and 3 that being is always the being of a being.[156] In section 2 he speaks of "the characteristics of the being" of beings, and in section 3 of the basic constitution of being (*Grundverfassung seines Seins*) of a being. We may conclude that the question of being requires that we investigate particular beings to the extent that it aims at making explicit the various ontological constitutions of the beings of different regions. Only if "being" means the ontological constitution of regional entities, such as animals, Dasein, material objects, tools, linguistic units, and so on, will we need a *Befragtes* in order to answer the question. This is precisely what Heidegger stipulates at the beginning of the eighth paragraph of section 2.[157]

In this and the next paragraph of section 2, Heidegger argues that there is one regional being that is privileged, namely, Dasein. If we want to disclose the sense of being, we should start by investigating *its* ontological structure.[158] We may wonder why Heidegger thinks that there is such a privileged region of being at all. Admittedly, most philosophers of the tradition took a specific type of being as a paradigm in developing their general notion of being. As Heidegger says in section 6, the ancient notion of being, as instantiation of an *eidos* or as a concretum of matter and form, was based on the model of artifacts and then generalized to all beings.[159] But we have also seen, in section 3, above, that Heidegger objects to this kind of conceptual generalization in ontology. It is inherent in the very notions of a regional ontology and of a destruction of the history of ontology that "being" has a different sense relative to the various regions of being. As Heidegger himself says, "there are many beings that we designate as 'being,' and we do so in various senses."[160] If this is the case, why should there be one privileged region of being? Why did Heidegger not simply develop a series of regional ontologies, adding, as an answer to the general question of being, that he means by "being" the particular ontological constitution of each different region? What justifies Heidegger's favoritism with respect to Dasein? Why did he reject pluralism in ontology, which consists in the view that entities of different regions have different ontological constitutions, and that no region is more fundamental or more privileged than any other one? Or, finally, if ontological favoritism is permitted, why did Heidegger not choose the region of physical being as the fundamental one, an option more in harmony with the evolution of the universe?

This problem of the priority of Dasein for elaborating the question of being *tout court* is perhaps the most crucial problem we have to solve if we want to understand Heidegger's *Denkweg*. One hypothetical solution consists in the thesis that the primacy of Dasein in *Sein und Zeit* should be regarded as a parallel to and an implicit critique of Husserl's notion that the transcendental ego is the privileged and fundamental region of being. We saw in section 3 and under point 5, above, that Heidegger rejected the problem of the external world, which Husserl's transcendental idealism purported to solve. He considered the problem as a pseudoproblem due to a scientistic misinterpretation of Dasein and world. This may have been a reason to analyze Dasein and its relation to the world first, before turning to the other regional ontologies. Even so, the primacy Heidegger claims for the ontology of Dasein is stronger than a mere priority of order, and there are other solutions to the problem of the primacy of Dasein. I discuss several of them in sections 9, 11, 12C, and 13 of the present book.

It would have been helpful if Heidegger had given a clear and convincing argument for the primacy of Dasein in the introduction to *Sein und Zeit*. Heidegger in fact argues for the primacy of Dasein both in section 4 and in paragraphs 8 and 9 of section 2. However, his arguments are neither clear nor convincing. According to section 2, we have to analyze the ontological constitution of Dasein in order to raise the question of being in a fully transparent way, because the various aspects of this question, such as a preliminary understanding of being, belong to the activity of questioning, whereas that activity is an activity of Dasein. This argument is invalid, as a logical analogy shows. For we may just as well argue along the same lines that in order to raise the question as to the nature and causes of photosynthesis in a fully transparent way, we have to analyze Dasein's mode of being, which is patently absurd.

Perhaps Heidegger himself did not regard the argument of section 2 as a conclusive one, for at the end of the section he declares that "so far, our discussion has not demonstrated Dasein's priority," although "something like a priority of Dasein has announced itself."[161] This contrasts with the penultimate paragraph of section 4, where Heidegger assures us that this time he has shown the priority of Dasein, so that the ontological analytic of Dasein is what makes up *fundamental* ontology.[162] Accordingly, we have to look at section 4 in order to discover the argument for the primacy of Dasein that Heidegger regarded as conclusive. What is this argument?

In section 3 of his introduction, Heidegger argued for the ontological primacy of the question of being on the basis of an objective conception of science (*Wissenschaft*)—objective in the sense that the sciences are regarded as systems of propositions. He opens section 4 by declaring that this conception of science is not complete, and that it does not reach the sense (*Sinn*) of science.[163] Heidegger suggests that we will grasp the true sense of science only by considering science as an activity of Dasein, because, "as ways in which man behaves, sciences have the manner of being which this being—man himself—possesses."[164] Moreover, because Dasein has a special *ontical* primacy as compared to other entities, the *ontology* of Dasein is the fundamental ontology in relation to the other regional ontologies. In order to spell out this argument for the primacy of Dasein, Heidegger first specifies the "special ontical primacy" of Dasein (paragraphs 2–6). He then draws the conclusion that the ontology of Dasein is fundamental ontology (paragraphs 7–10), points out that the philosophical tradition has been dimly aware of the ontical-ontological primacy of Dasein (paragraph 11), and summarizes his conclusion (paragraphs 12–13). Let me now highlight the main points of Heidegger's argument. What is the special ontical primacy of Dasein, and why does this primacy imply that the ontology of Dasein is more fundamental than the other regional ontologies?

According to Heidegger, Dasein is ontically privileged because (a) it does not just occur among other entities but, in its very being, this being is an issue for it: Dasein has to effectuate its existence. In other words, Dasein has an understanding of being, which concerns its own being, the world, and worldly entities at the same time (paragraphs 2 and 7). Furthermore, (b) because the mode of being of Dasein is what Heidegger calls "existence" (paragraph 4), Dasein always has (c) the choice to be itself or not to be itself (paragraph 5). Surely one cannot say of a tree, a stone, or a hammer that it has such a choice. One will admit to Heidegger, then, that Dasein has many ontical privileges. But why does it follow that the ontology of Dasein is fundamental to other ontologies, and that developing such an ontology is the primary task if we want to elaborate the question of being? The crucial step of Heidegger's argument is contained in paragraphs 7 and 8 of section 4:

> Sciences are modes of being in which Dasein comports itself toward entities which it need not be itself. But to Dasein, being in a world is something that belongs essentially. Thus Dasein's understanding of being pertains with equal primordiality to an understanding of something like a "world," and to the understanding of the being of those entities that become accessible within the world. So whenever an ontology takes for its theme entities whose character of being is other than that of Dasein, it has its own foundation and motivation in Dasein's own ontical structure, in which a preontological understanding of being is comprised as a definite characteristic.
>
> Therefore *fundamental ontology*, from which alone all other ontologies can take their rise, must be sought in the *existential analytic of Dasein*.[165]

As I have said already, one might endorse Heidegger's premise that Dasein is an ontically privileged being because it understands its own being and that of other entities. This is why Dasein is able to develop the sciences. But does it follow from this *ontical* priority of Dasein that the *ontology* of Dasein is more fundamental than the other regional ontologies, as Heidegger claims in the conclusion of his argument? The problem with section 4 is that Heidegger's argument for the ontological primacy of Dasein seems to be identical to the patently invalid argument of section 2, of which even Heidegger himself admits that it does not amount to a demonstration.[166] For in section 4, as in section 2, Heidegger infers from the fact that Dasein is the entity which asks questions and develops sciences and ontologies, that the answer to the question of being must be based on the fundamental ontology of Dasein. However, from the fact that astronomy is a human activity it does not follow that the sciences of man are somehow more fundamental than astronomy. Similarly, from the fact that Dasein is able to develop ontologies of worldly things, it does not follow without more ado that the ontology of Dasein is the fundamental ontology, "from which alone all other ontologies can take their rise." In short, the ontic privileges of Dasein do not imply its ontological primacy, and from the fact that Dasein is the author of ontology and science it does not follow that Dasein should be its privileged topic.

We may conclude that the problem of the primacy of Dasein in relation to the question of being remains a *crux interpretum* of *Sein und Zeit*. In the introduction to that book, Heidegger neither explains clearly why the ontology of Dasein is fundamental ontology, nor does he clarify the sense in which this ontology is "fundamental" in relation to regional ontologies or in relation to the question of being as such. The problem is all the more crucial because, according to the received interpretation of Heidegger's *Kehre* (turn), Heidegger gave up the ontological primacy of Dasein in his later works. Whereas in *Sein und Zeit* Heidegger tried to grasp "being itself" on the basis of an interpretation of Dasein's understanding of being (*Seinsverständnis*), he reversed this priority in later works such as the *Brief über den "Humanismus"* (1947, *Letter on "Humanism"*), and defined Dasein on the basis of the relation (*Bezug*) that Being itself has to the essence of man. He said of being that it "*is* above all," and that the task of thinking is to accomplish what already *is*, namely, being and its relation to man.[167] However, six years after the first publication of the *Brief über den "Humanismus,"* Heidegger wrote in the preface to the seventh edition (1953) of *Sein und Zeit* that "the road this book has taken remains even today a necessary one, if our Dasein is to be stirred by the question of being." We may wonder, then, what justified the primacy of Dasein as against being in *Sein und Zeit*, why Heidegger reversed this primacy later, and, finally, why even after this reversal the road of *Sein und Zeit* remains a necessary one. Moreover, we may also wonder what the relation is between the ontological primacy of the question of being argued for in section 3 of *Sein und Zeit* and the primacy of Dasein of section 4. I call this complex of questions the problem of the primacy of Dasein.

§ 5. WAYS OF INTERPRETATION

It would be tedious to spell out all problems of interpretation concerning the question of being that are concealed in Heidegger's introduction to *Sein und Zeit*, let alone the problems added by the body of the book and by the later works. My aim in the previous section was merely to show that there are a number of problems that call for an interpretative solution. For this purpose, it was sufficient to focus on the first chapter of Heidegger's introduction and to develop a small sample of difficulties. But what type of interpretation will be suitable for resolving these and similar problems? This is the question I discuss in the present section.

I do not intend to delineate a comprehensive theory of interpretation. My purpose is to point out what assumptions regarding interpretation I am making in interpreting Heidegger's question of being. One reason for laying my cards on the table is that it is often objected to critical interpretations of Heidegger's work that they are naïve in that their authors have not understood the very nature of interpretation. The objector usually assumes that the account of interpretation given by Heidegger in *Sein und Zeit*, or by Gadamer in *Wahrheit und Methode* (*Truth and Method*), is the correct account. I will argue, however, that in order to do justice to Heidegger's works, we should not apply Heidegger's own doctrine of interpretation in interpreting his thought.

Everyone who has even a limited understanding of disciplines such as law, theology, history, classical philology, or literary criticism will know that there are many methods, techniques, and types of interpretation. *Interpretatio* and its Greek equivalent *hermeneia* were originally used for reading signs of the divine, like smoke, flights of birds, or configurations of the intestines of sacrificial animals, and the term *hermeneia* was seen as akin to "Hermes," the name of the Greek messenger of the gods.[168] Poets were often thought to be privileged interpreters or harbingers of deities.[169] Later, the notion of interpretation became restricted to attempts to make sense of unclear passages in written texts. However, both Dilthey and Heidegger in *Sein und Zeit* argued that this notion of textual interpretation is too narrow. First, all manifestations of human life, to the extent that they might be meaningful, may stand in need of an interpretation, whether they be linguistic or not. As a consequence, interpretation is the fundamental method of the moral sciences or *Geisteswissenschaften*. Second, they argued that in order to lay the foundations of the *Geisteswissenschaften*, and to explain why interpretation is the fundamental *modus operandi* of these disciplines, it must be shown that human life or Dasein itself is fundamentally "interpretative" and historical. As Heidegger says in section 32 of *Sein und Zeit*, interpretation (*Auslegung*) is rooted in Dasein's ontological structure. Whereas the term "hermeneutics" is often used for the methodology of interpretation, in the context of Heidegger's philosophy it primarily refers to the ontology of Dasein.[170] Because the ontology of Dasein allegedly is the foundation of all regional ontologies, Heidegger argues in section 7 of *Sein und Zeit* that hermeneutics works out the conditions for the possibility of any other regional ontology.[171] Furthermore, since special sciences are founded on regional ontologies, hermeneutics is supposed to be transcendental philosophy, the ultimate foundation of the scientific enterprise.

We saw that Dasein is conceived of by Heidegger as an essentially self-interpretative being. As a consequence, divisions 1 and 2 of *Sein and Zeit* should be viewed as an ontological autointerpretation of Dasein by Heidegger. This autointerpretation is itself a philosophical text. In fact, it is an extremely difficult philosophical text, mainly because Heidegger develops a new and idiosyncratic terminological network (the existentialia) in order to chart the ontological constitution of Dasein. This network and each of its key terms call for an interpretation in their turn, if only because there seem to be many ambiguities and difficulties in Heidegger's existentialia. By which type of interpretation should we try to make sense of Heidegger's ontological autointerpretation of Dasein and of his question of being?

It is often assumed, implicitly or explicitly, that in interpreting the existentialia of *Sein und Zeit* and Heidegger's oeuvre in general, one is not allowed to use a terminology or conceptual structure other than the one invented by Heidegger himself. The reason for this drastic restriction on our means of interpretation is not difficult to find. As we saw in section 3, above, Heidegger claims in *Sein und Zeit* that traditional understanding of Dasein and of being (*Sein*) is inadequate, because it is due to our falling. Traditionally, philosophers tried to understand Dasein's ontological constitution on the model of entities in the world, such as artifacts and tools (*Zeug*), or of things that are merely present (*Vorhanden*), and they interpreted being in general as being present in this sense. Because according to Heidegger Dasein is not such an entity, and because Dasein's ontological constitution is different from that of these entities, the traditional conceptual structures are inadequate, and Heidegger has to construct a new network of concepts, the existentialia. In particular, Heidegger rejects the traditional conception of a human being as a material substance to which some extras are added, such as consciousness or an immortal soul. He would have rejected, for instance, John Searle's notion of consciousness as an aspect of humans that causally supervenes upon their brains and yet is ontologically irreducible. Although Searle claims to have shown that the traditional vocabulary of the philosophy of mind is obsolete, Heidegger would have thought that Searle's own vocabulary still belongs to the tradition and that it is not less obsolete than the conceptual dichotomies that Searle allegedly repudiates.[172] Heidegger's rejection of traditional terminology and of traditional philosophical problems purports to be a radical one. It is much more radical than Searle's similar move, and indeed, Heidegger's strategy of philosophical radicalism aims at radically surpassing all other philosophical radicals.

If Heidegger's conceptual structure is radically novel, all attempts to clarify what he wants to say by means of traditional terms such as "consciousness" or "intentionality" are misguided, because they translate Heidegger back into the traditional conceptual structures that he tried to supersede. Accordingly, Heidegger's orthodox followers would dismiss from the outset attempts such as Mark Okrent's, in his book *Heidegger's Pragmatism*, to explain Heidegger's thought in terms of the problems of analytic philosophy. Only interpretations such as those by Pöggeler, Richardson, Schulz, and Kockelmans, which are *strictly internal* in the sense that they try to clarify Heidegger's texts in Heideggerian terms, would be acceptable from the orthodox point of view.[173]

I do not want to deny that strictly internal interpretations have a use. They might make Heidegger's *Denkweg* surveyable by summarizing it, and clarify many passages by collating them with other more intelligible passages. Strictly internal interpretations may be compared to induction in scientific procedure: they do not provide us with essentially more than the textual basis, because they merely offer a survey of this basis. However, there are at least three reasons for rejecting the strictly internalist doctrine if one wants to interpret the Heideggerian corpus.

First of all, Heidegger's conceptual network is not as new as he seems to claim at first sight. He borrows many technical terms from traditional philosophy, such as "being" and "transcendence," and he himself discusses terminological parallels with the tradition, such as the parallel between his notion of *Sorge* (concern) and the Latin *cura* (SZ, § 42). In fact, the great majority of Heidegger's key terms are traditional, and even when he transforms the meanings of these traditional terms, such as *Angst*, "concern," "conscience," and "guilt," there is a motivated path from the traditional meanings to Heidegger's new notions. Moreover, a novel conceptual structure would be unintelligible if it were not accessible from our existing language, and indeed Heidegger uses ordinary language in explaining the meaning of his neologisms. We must conclude that the strictly internalist requirement is both due to an exaggeration and based on misunderstandings concerning the nature of conceptual innovation.

Second, and more important, it is not possible to resolve crucial problems of interpretation if one uses Heideggerian terminology only. This is the case, for instance, where Heidegger's technical terms are ambiguous, as I argued with respect to his notion of *das Man* (the One), or if what he says remains mysterious even to someone who has studied his works thoroughly in the internalist or inductive manner. I would claim that this is our situation with regard to many themes of the later Heidegger, such as *Ereignis* (event of becoming ourselves), *Ankunft* (arrival), *Nähe* (nearness), and *die Stimme des Seins* (the voice of being).

Finally, there is an internal reason for rejecting the internalist dogma in general. Strict internalism in the sense defined above is not Heidegger's own method of interpretation when he elucidates texts of other philosophers and of poets. As a consequence, there is a contradiction between two different internalist requirements for interpreting Heidegger, both of which are rooted in the Heideggerian corpus. The *strictly* internalist requirement conflicts with another requirement, which might be called the *reflectively* internalist requirement: that we apply Heidegger's conception and method of interpretation when we interpret Heidegger's texts. If strict internalism is incompatible with reflective internalism, no interpretation of Heidegger's philosophy can be internal in all senses. I have given two reasons why strict internalism is undesirable if we really want to discover the meaning of Heidegger's writings. Let me now go into the questions whether and to what extent we must be reflective internalists. What is Heidegger's view of interpretation? Should we apply this view in interpreting his texts?

During his long career, Heidegger interpreted the works of many religious thinkers, philosophers, and poets.[174] In his *Habilitationsschrift* on *Die Kategorien- und Bedeutungslehre des Duns Scotus* (1916, *Scotus's Doctrine of Categories and Meaning*), he elucidated the tract *De Modis Significandi*, attributed to Scotus at the time, but which was in fact written by Thomas of Erfurt, and he planned a philosophical interpretation of Eckhart's mystical writings. Between 1909 and 1914 Heidegger had already discovered Hölderlin, Nietzsche, Kierkegaard, and Dostoiewski, and had begun to study Husserl, Hegel, Schelling, Rilke, Trakl, and Dilthey. In his early lectures at Freiburg University directly after the First World War, he discussed Aristotle, Dilthey, St. Paul, St. Augustine, Luther, and Kierkegaard, and tried to reconstruct the manner in which early Christianity experienced human life before it was "contaminated" by Greek philosophy. He argued that, according to this experience, the arrival of the saving supreme moment of Christ's second coming (*kairos, Augenblick, Ereignis*) is essentially unpredictable and beyond description. Human life allegedly is doomed as soon as we try to predict, calculate, characterize, or otherwise attempt to make available to ourselves this future moment. According to Pöggeler, Heidegger's thought was to be inspired forever by the conjecture that we are ill-fated as soon as we try to fix and calculate the moment yet to come.[175] As we will see in section 11, this is one of the most significant hints concerning the interpretation of Heidegger's later thought, the germs of which were already present in his early courses.

Heidegger's lectures in Marburg between 1923 and 1928 were devoted to an interpretation of the metaphysical tradition from the pre-Socratics to Thomas Aquinas and Kant. In these lectures, Heidegger gradually developed the insight, incisively expressed in *Sein und Zeit*, that the philosophical interpretation of our factual, historical life requires a destruction of traditional philosophy, because the traditional conceptual structures betray and conceal the way we perform the task of living. This is why an ontological interpretation of Dasein is inseparable from a destructive interpretation of the history of metaphysics, and why our Dasein, although it is ontically nearest and even identical to us, is ontologically furthest.[176] In Heidegger's later philosophy, the interpretation of the great metaphysicians of the past, such as Plato, Descartes, Kant, Schelling, Fichte, Hegel, and Nietzsche, acquired an even more central role. Metaphysics was now seen as the way in which Being revealed itself in the very act of its concealment, so that the metaphysical tradition supposedly is a veil or mask of Being. The thinker had the task of commemorating and elucidating traditional metaphysics, in order to enable us to cope with Being's concealment (*Verwindung der Metaphysik*) and to prepare a future advent of Being (see § 11, below). Interpretation, then, is the very medium of Heidegger's thought.

It would be misleading to say that Heidegger in all these interpretations applied one and the same method or doctrine of interpretation. However, in Heidegger's later writings there are a number of significant and startling pronouncements on the nature of interpretation or elucidation (*Erläuterung, Erörterung*). I will begin my discussion of Heidegger's notion of interpretation with one of these pronouncements, which Heidegger apparently regarded as important because he stressed its point repeatedly:

> Of course an elucidation [*Erläuterung*] does not have to derive the matter [*die Sache*] from the text only. It must also add to it something of its own, out of its matter [*aus ihrer Sache*], and it has to do so covertly [*unvermerkt*], without boasting about it. It is this extra [*Beigabe*] which, if compared to what he considers to be the content of the text, the layman experiences as something read into it [*ein Hineindeuten*], and which he censures as whimsical with the right which he claims for himself. However, a real elucidation never understands a text better than its author understood it, although it understands the text differently. And this different manner must be such, that it touches the same matter [*das Selbe*] about which the elucidated text is reflecting.[177]

Having rejected the requirement of a strictly internal interpretation, at least for interpreting Heidegger's texts, we will agree with Heidegger that an interpretation should add an *extra* to the text, an interpretative hypothesis, which sheds light on passages that would otherwise remain obscure. However, Heidegger claims two quite astonishing things about this procedure of adding an extra, a procedure that clearly is incompatible with the requirement of strict internalism, as I claimed above. He asserts in the first place that we should add the extra without marking it as such, that is, covertly or unobtrusively (*unvermerkt*), and in the second place that it should be derived from the matter or from the concerns of the interpreter or the interpretation (*aus ihrer Sache*), even though he also says that the extra should touch the subject matter of the text.[178] Heidegger's requirement of covertness is perhaps most shocking to those who are professionally engaged in the activity of interpreting texts. They will argue, as I will do at the end of this section, that the scrupulous interpreter should carefully and clearly distinguish between his interpretative hypotheses and the texts he is studying. This is why I will concentrate on the *requirement of covertness* in discussing Heidegger's hermeneutical doctrine.

To begin, Heidegger's hermeneutical practice usually conforms to the hermeneutical doctrine of covertness. His critics complain again and again that Heidegger does not sufficiently distinguish between what he himself is up to and what the author whose works he interprets wanted to say. As Zimmerman rightly observes, "the reader is never sure whether Heidegger was speaking for the other thinker or for himself."[179] It has often been argued, in relation to Heidegger's interpretations of Nietzsche, for example, that "Heidegger projected his own concepts onto Nietzsche's texts and forced them to speak an alien Heideggerian language."[180] If this practice is based on an official doctrine, it cannot be due to negligence on Heidegger's part. What, then, explains Heidegger's doctrine of interpretation? How are we to interpret his requirement of covertness?

Our first reaction will be that the Heideggerian requirement of covertness can never be justified, and that we should reject it without further ado. However, in doing so we risk overlooking important clues as to the overall meaning of Heidegger's philosophy. If this philosophy consists of interpretations through and through, it is crucial to discover the rationale for Heidegger's view of interpretation, because this view must somehow be central to his thought. Moreover, there are cultural and institutional situations of interpretation in which the requirement of covertness *is* justified, even though perhaps we will be prone to think that these situations themselves are not desirable. I will now briefly discuss two of these situations, in order to derive from them an interpretative hypothesis concerning Heidegger's requirement of covertness. After having tested this hypothesis, in part by analyzing what Heidegger says on interpretation in *Sein und Zeit*, and in part by anticipating my interpretation of his later works, I will conclude by specifying the kind of interpretation of Heidegger's philosophy I want to develop.

The requirement of covertness is justified in situations where on the one hand interpretation cannot be avoided and on the other hand interpretation cannot be allowed. In these situations, interpretation has to go underground, as it were, and it has to conceal the fact that something is added to the text. Interpretation cannot be avoided if texts that were written in the past and that cannot be changed have to be applied to present situations in order to enable us to live or to do certain things. One may be convinced that the application of religious texts is needed for living a moral life or for illuminating our present existence. It is necessary to apply legal texts (laws, precedents) for resolving many practical difficulties and for doing things that have some kind of official status. In such situations interpretation is inevitable for many reasons. Usually the texts are fairly general and not written with the details of the present situation in mind, so that we need to make them more specific, or even change their original sense, in order to be able to do what we have to do on their basis. Let me call the kind of interpretation needed to apply texts to practical situations or to our present life *applicative* interpretation.

In modern law and Western religions, it is generally acknowledged that applicative interpretations cannot be avoided, and there is no need to be covert about them. However, the maxim of covertness is called for in situations in which the authority of the text is assumed to be absolute, so that each and every interpretation is seen as a derogation from this authority. If, for instance, a holy book is accepted as a revelation by a deity, authoritarian religions might claim that the book should speak directly to us, without human interpretations. Because an applicative interpretation of passages of the book cannot be avoided if we want to apply holy texts to actual situations, the interpreter, usually a priest, should either dissimulate the fact that he is giving an interpretation (the maxim of covertness), or he should claim that his interpretation is directly inspired by the deity. Apart from authoritarian religions, there are legal situations in which the maxim of covertness is justified. During the French Revolution, for instance, the revolutionaries feared that conservative judges would pervert the intentions of revolutionary laws by interpreting them in a reactionary spirit. In order to prevent this, they professed the doctrine that the judge is nothing but the mouthpiece of the law (*la bouche de la loi*), a doctrine that simply prohibited interpretation. Yet the judges realized that in most cases the application of laws is impossible without an interpretation, so that they had to use the maxim of covertness in order to be able to do their job. We may conclude that the maxim of covertness is justified in cases of applicative interpretations of authoritative texts, where interpretation is thought to derogate from textual authority.

Later in this section, I develop a distinction between applicative and theoretical (objective, historical, critical) interpretations. In the case of applicative interpretations, we have particular situations in mind to which the text has to be applied in order to obtain specific results. However, when an archaeologist tries to decipher and interpret texts on Roman tombstones, he will not have in mind a present situation on which he wants to bring to bear the text, even though in Antiquity the text was used at the occasion of a funeral. The aim of his interpretation is a purely theoretical, historical, or epistemic one: to understand a culture of the past.

I do not think that within the context of such a theoretical interpretation the maxim of covertness can ever be justified. Consequently, the distinction between applicative and theoretical interpretations suggests an interpretative hypothesis to explain the fact that Heidegger endorses the maxim of covertness as an element of his doctrine of interpretation. If we will be able to discover in Heidegger's views on interpretation a bias toward applicative interpretation and an authoritarian conception of philosophical texts, we will have explained Heidegger's maxim of covertness. I will now argue, first, that the theory of interpretation of *Sein und Zeit* already shows such an applicative bias, and second, that Heidegger's later philosophy implies an authoritarian and applicative reading of metaphysical texts.

As I said, Heidegger claims in *Sein und Zeit* that hermeneutics as a methodology of interpretation must be based on hermeneutics in the sense of the fundamental ontology of Dasein, because the activity of interpretation is rooted in Dasein's ontological structure. Consequently, we will not understand what interpretation is and can be, unless we understand ontologically our own mode of being. Moreover, this implies that Heidegger's own hermeneutical method in *Sein und Zeit* is rooted in the results of *Sein und Zeit*, so that the book unwinds in a spiraling way. Having made some preliminary remarks on hermeneutics in section 7C, Heidegger in division 1 interprets the basic ontological structure of Dasein as being-in-the-world. This "preparatory" analysis enables him to see how interpretation (*Auslegung*) is founded on the fundamental ontological structure of Dasein, and to develop the structural aspects of interpretation (§§ 31–33). The elucidation of the nature of interpretation, in its turn, enables Heidegger to repeat the existential analysis of Dasein in a methodologically more self-conscious manner in division 2. In particular, Heidegger is now able to acknowledge that the ontological interpretation of Dasein inevitably is based on the projection (*Entwurf*) of a specific ideal of authentic life (§§ 62–63). Again and again, new insights into the ontological structure of Dasein lead to a deeper methodological consciousness, which, in its turn, yields deeper insights concerning Dasein's mode of being. In principle, this spiraling movement could be repeated until the point is reached at which no new results emerge. For our purposes, however, it is sufficient to analyze two turns of the spiral, which Heidegger develops respectively in sections 31–33 and 62–63.

After an introductory first chapter, which explains the very idea of a preparatory analysis of Dasein, Heidegger in division 1 discusses Dasein's fundamental ontological structure. In chapter 2, this structure is defined as being-in-the-world. Heidegger stresses that the fundamental ontological structure of Dasein is a complex whole, which has to be understood *as* a whole. Such a holistic understanding will not be possible unless the various aspects of the structure are analyzed in detail, even though each aspect cannot be understood properly without a grasp of the other aspects and of the whole to which it belongs. As a consequence, the spiraling movement I mentioned above is merely a special case of the inevitable method for the autointerpretation of Dasein in general: each analysis of particular aspects of Dasein's ontological structure sheds new light on the other aspects and on the whole of this structure, and each global analysis of the whole enables us to understand better the particular aspects. This is why the analysis of division 1 starts with a grasp of the whole (second chapter), then proceeds to discuss three aspects of being-in-the-world—(1) the worldlihood of the world (third chapter), (2) the "who" of our everyday being-in-the-world (fourth chapter: *das Man*), and (3) being-in as such (fifth chapter)—and ends up with rediscovering the whole on a deeper level, namely, as concern (sixth chapter). Sections 31–33 belong to the fifth chapter, in which Heidegger discusses being-in as such.

Heidegger's main purpose in chapter 5, as indeed in division 1 in general, is to show how Dasein's being differs from the ontological constitution of things we find in the world (*Vorhandenes*) and of other types of beings, such as tools (*Zuhandenes*). Heidegger wants to demonstrate this difference, we remember, because the metaphysical tradition applied the categories developed for things and artifacts also to Dasein's being, and thereby concealed the real ontological structure of Dasein (cf. § 3, above). Consequently, Dasein, although it is ontically nearest, is ontologically furthest from itself. The way Dasein is in the world, for instance, is radically different from the way in which things are in a container, or at a place, although we usually overlook this difference. Heidegger argues in chapter 5 that our being-in is constituted by three more specific aspects of being-in-the-world: *Befindlichkeit* (finding oneself in a situation, §§ 29–30), *Verstehen* (understanding, §§ 31–33), and *Rede* (discourse, § 34). He stresses that these aspects are equiprimordial (*gleichursprünglich*), so that they cannot be derived from each other. Moreover, because they pervade each other, one cannot understand one without understanding the others. Even so, I will only briefly comment on *Befindlichkeit* in order to focus on *Verstehen*. According to Heidegger, the structure of *Verstehen* is the ontological basis of the activity of interpretation.

It is seriously misleading to translate *Befindlichkeit* by "state of mind," because the category of a state typically applies to material substances, or to artifacts such as machines, while the notion of a mind is infected by traditional metaphysics.[181] Heidegger coined the neologism *Befindlichkeit* from a series of German idiomatic expressions, such as "Wie befinden Sie sich?" (How are you?), "Ich befinde mich wohl heute" (I feel well today), and "Wo befinde ich mich?" (Where am I?). The existential of *Befindlichkeit* expresses the structural characteristic of our ontological constitution that we always already find ourselves in a meaningful situation, and that, finding ourselves in a situation, we are disclosed to ourselves as having to live in it. In *Befindlichkeit*, the situation, our fellow humans, and our facticity (*Faktizität*) are disclosed to us simultaneously. Because we are not the architects of the situations in which we find ourselves, Heidegger says that *Befindlichkeit* reveals our *Geworfenheit*: that we are "thrown into" existence. As we have to live and act in the situations in which we find ourselves, *Befindlichkeit* also reveals our existence as a burden (*Last*), which we either assume or try to shake off. We might translate Dasein as "being there," and Heidegger plays with the word, splitting it up into *Da* and *sein*. He says that we *are* our *there*, because we are thrown into situations, and that we *find* ourselves in our *there*. He identifies the There (*das Da*) with the disclosure to ourselves of situations, of ourselves, and of others. It follows that the There (*das Da*) is the fundamental openness (*Erschlossenheit*) or clearing (*Lichtung*) we have for ourselves, the world, and the others.

The philosophical tradition identified this fundamental openness with the outer or inner perception of an object by a subject. It is Heidegger's revolutionary thesis in the fifth chapter of division 1 that what Husserl called "objectivating acts," such as perceptions of objects and the detached theoretical attitude, are not fundamental but derived, and that the most fundamental openness for ourselves and the world consists in *Stimmungen* (moods) such as boredom and in what he calls *Verstehen* (understanding). Reversing the famous *dictum* of Brentano and Husserl that an affection such as fear must be based on a representation (*Vorstellung*), Heidegger claims that "the mood has already disclosed, in every case, being-in-the-world as a whole, and makes it possible first of all to direct oneself toward something."[182] In other words, intentionality is not a fundamental characteristic of our openness, as Husserl and Brentano claimed, but a derived one. Fundamental are moods and understanding. Moods are the modes of finding ourselves in situations (*Befindlichkeit*), but what is, according to Heidegger, the existential of understanding (*Verstehen*), and how does this existential determine the structure of interpretation?

Our being-in situations has two opposite aspects, which traditional philosophers would have called a passive and an active one. On the one hand we find ourselves in a meaningful situation and on the other hand we have to construct our life in this situation. As we saw, Heidegger calls our disclosure of finding ourselves in situations *Befindlichkeit*, whereas he identifies the existential of understanding (*Verstehen*) with our opening up possibilities of effectuating ourselves (§§ 31–32). Finding oneself reveals one's thrownness (*Geworfenheit*), but understanding one's possibilities always reveals the *projects* (*Entwürfe*) one has wittingly or unwittingly projected: it is the capacity to live into the future. Because we live into the future, we *are* in a sense the possibilities we project. And only because we already are the possibilities we have projected, we may say to ourselves: "become who you are." Combining the two modes of disclosure of our There, *Befindlichkeit* and *Verstehen*, Heidegger says that Dasein is a *geworfener Entwurf* (a thrown project). The best translation of the existential *Verstehen*, then, is "know-how to live in a situation," and understanding in Heidegger's sense of *Verstehen* is primarily a capacity word.[183]

Heidegger's notion of understanding (*Verstehen*) as projection of existentiell possibilities is an idiosyncratic one, and it both stretches and narrows down the usual notion of understanding.[184] However, Heidegger's redefinition of the concept of understanding has a philosophical point. Heidegger claims that all other kinds of understanding, such as understanding texts and even understanding natural phenomena in science, are rooted in the existentiale of understanding, so that they share its structure. What, then, is the structure of the existentiale of understanding? And what are the implications of Heidegger's claim for his theory of interpretation and for his theory of science?

According to Heidegger, Dasein exists for the sake of itself. This implies that the ultimate "for-the-sake-of-which" (*Worumwillen*) of all Dasein's projects is Dasein's own existence: it is the kind of human being an individual Dasein wants to be. Projecting our being as possibility, we not only open up possibilities for self-realization. Our project (*Entwurf*) also involves an open space or framework of possibilities (*Spielraum*), and a referential structure (*Bewandtnisganzheit, Welt*) that gives significance to tools and entities that we encounter. For instance, my global project of becoming a just man involves a certain world, the world of the just, and my particular project of climbing the Matterhorn implies that each feature of the crest before me will take on the significance of a possible grip or of a dangerous trap to be avoided.

Because our projects and the referential structures they involve give meaning to our actions, and also to instruments and natural phenomena we need in order to effectuate these projects, Heidegger defines the notion of meaning or sense (*Sinn*) as the *Woraufhin des Entwurfs*: that toward which we project our projects (p. 151). We might say that the sense of our life is our ultimate direction, as structured by a space of possibilities and by a referential structure, and that, in Heidegger's view, it is only in the light of this ultimate direction and its referential structure (*Woraufhin*) that all other meaningful entities, occurrences, relations, things, and instruments get their significance. A hammer, for instance, is interpreted *as* a hammer in the light of a project of making a cupboard or of building a house, and such projects ultimately derive their meaning from the fact that each Dasein exists for the sake of itself with other Daseins in a world. All understanding of something *as* something is rooted in Dasein's ultimate project. Of course, the term "project" in this context should not be understood as a deliberate plan.[185]

Heidegger rejects the traditional thesis that we have to be able to perceive something in order to be able to understand it *as* something. He claims, on the contrary, that understanding something *as* something, as a hammer for instance, is more fundamental than "objective" perception. The latter allegedly is an impoverished derivative of the former (p. 149). In short, all objective ways of perceiving and understanding are based on understanding in the sense of projecting possibilities. As a consequence, they share its basic structure (§ 32).

Because understanding in the basic sense of knowing-how-to-live consists in projecting possibilities, understanding (*Verstehen*) and its explicit mode (*Auslegung*) are characterized by what Heidegger calls a *Vor-struktur* (fore-structure; § 32). In understanding something, we always interpret it in the light of a projected and future "toward which" (*Sinn*). In the case of understanding explicitly (*Auslegung*), this fore-structure has three aspects, which Heidegger calls *Vorhabe, Vorsicht,* and *Vorgriff* (p. 150). The first of these terms is a Heideggerian neologism, whereas the second and third are used in an idiosyncratic way. The word *Vorhabe* is derived from the German verb *vorhaben*, which means to intend, to have planned. The term *Vorhabe* calls attention to the fact that in pro-jecting our Dasein, we "have in advance" (*vor-haben*) a referential structure of instruments, institutions, and possibilities (*Bewandtnisganzheit*) that derives its point from Dasein as the ultimate "for the sake of which," and that functions as a background for interpreting entities or texts. The German word *Vorsicht* means circumspection or prudence. Heidegger uses it, however, as connected to *Hinsicht*: it refers to the point of view (*Sicht*) from which we want to understand something, a point of view we always have already adopted in advance (*vor-*) by projecting a project. *Vorgriff*, finally, literally means anticipation, and it is related to both *vorgreifen* (to anticipate) and *begreifen* (to understand). It denotes the conceptual structure that we beforehand have decided (*entschieden*) to use in order to understand something. Heidegger's explanation of this threefold fore-structure of understanding is not very clear. What is clear, though, is the fact that according to Heidegger all understanding has a fore-structure because it is rooted in Dasein's projective manner of being. I will now briefly discuss the consequences of this theory of understanding for Heidegger's theories of interpretation and of science.

The crucial question here is whether Heidegger's projective theory of understanding, if applied to interpretation and scientific method, leaves room for more or less objective tests of interpretative or explanatory hypotheses and conceptual structures. There are ample grounds for thinking that the theory excludes in principle the possibility of such tests. First, if everything that has meaning ultimately derives its meaning from "that toward which" (*Woraufhin*) we project our projects, all meaning is determined beforehand by *our* existentiell project. It seems that in order to assign meaning to something at all, we have to envisage it in the light of an endeavor to construct our life, and of the referential structure involved. Moreover, since interpretations primarily reveal possibilities of self-realization, they will simply not be evaluated in terms of "true," "false," "correct," or "incorrect," but rather in terms of success or authenticity. Second, Heidegger's notion of an inevitable *Vorgriff* in all interpretation and explanation expresses the idea that we always have decided beforehand in terms of which conceptual structure we are going to understand something, because our projecting implies such a structure. It seems to follow from these two points that one and the same text or one and the same natural phenomenon will be capable of being interpreted quite differently by interpreters who assume different projects of their life, and that the interpretations or explanations will be incommensurable. As a consequence, Heidegger's theory of understanding destroys the crucial distinction between correct and incorrect interpretations and explanations.

In the third place, this conclusion is further substantiated by what Heidegger says on the ontological interpretation of Dasein itself in sections 62 and 63 of *Sein und Zeit*. If interpretation is only possible in the light of an existentiell or ontic project, the existential or ontological interpretation of our constitution of being must presuppose a particular ideal of life, an ideal of authentic existence. This is the very conclusion Heidegger stresses at the end of section 62. But this conclusion raises a powerful objection, which Heidegger discusses in section 63. Assuming that the ontological interpretation of Dasein is based on a presupposed ontic ideal, will its results not be arbitrary, because the presupposed ideal is a matter of free choice? Will we not interpret the ontological structure of Dasein differently if we choose another ontic ideal of authentic existence? If this is the case, as it seems to be in view of the many different interpretations of human existence by Sartre, Merleau-Ponty, Levinas, and others, should we not abandon the claim that the ontological analysis of Dasein yields knowledge?

In section 63, Heidegger denies that this skeptical conclusion is justified. But his argument confronts him with a dilemma. He stresses that there are formal aspects of the ontological structure of Dasein as interpreted by him, such as the self-interpretative nature of Dasein in general, which do not depend on a particular ontical project.[186] The problem is that this thesis conflicts with Heidegger's theory of interpretation, according to which all features of Dasein's ontological structure can be discerned *only* in the light of a *specific* existentiell project and its fore-structure. As a consequence, Heidegger should either admit that he contradicts his theory of interpretation, or he should restrict the scope of this theory to applicative interpretations and leave room for other types of interpretation, such as objective or theoretical interpretations. In the latter case, he could draw a distinction within the analysis of Dasein in *Sein und Zeit* between purely ontological analyses, which are independent of any specific ontic ideal, except of course the ideal of seeing the ontological constitution of human life as it is, and ontically contaminated analyses, which presuppose a specific ontical ideal. I argue below that amending *Sein und Zeit* in the latter sense is mandatory.

Heidegger does not resolve this dilemma. On the one hand he defends his projective theory of interpretation as a completely general theory on the basis of the allegedly projective structure of understanding, and on the other hand he says things which suggest that there must be a more "objective" kind of interpretation, which is independent from specific existentiell projects. What does he mean, for instance, when he writes that either "the way in which the entity we are interpreting is to be conceived can be drawn from the entity itself, or the interpretation can force the entity into concepts to which it is opposed in its manner of being" (p. 150)? How are we to interpret his claim that genuine knowledge can be achieved only if we "make the scientific theme secure by working out these fore-structures in terms of the things themselves" (p. 153)?[187] Does Heidegger mean by "the entity itself" and "the things themselves" beings as they manifest themselves independently of any specific existentiell project and fore-structure? Or does he imply that things themselves are *constituted* by such projects, so that a river, for instance, is in itself a different phenomenon within the projects of, say, early Greek civilization and modern technological society? The latter interpretation (internal realism) coheres with Heidegger's projective theory of understanding, whereas the former contradicts it. Heidegger might object that there is no contradiction in the former case, because it might be in the very nature of our existentiell project to reveal things as they are. However, this attempt to avoid a contradiction with the projective theory of understanding will not do. If it is possible that our conceptual structure is adapted to the things as they are in themselves, and not determined in its content by an existentiell project, understanding in such a case is *receptive* and not projective in Heidegger's sense.[188] Yet Heidegger's projective theory of understanding means that there can never be a mere receptive understanding. The real problem is not only that Heidegger fails to elaborate his projective theory of understanding in a coherent way; it is also that the very conceptual apparatus he uses in attempting to do so is based on dubious assumptions. He seems to think that a conceptual structure that we use in understanding something is either "drawn from the entity itself" or "forces the entity into concepts to which it is opposed in its manner of being" (p. 150). The assumption is that concepts simply originate in experiences of entities, as Hume and Husserl thought, and that concepts are either adequate or not adequate in relation to the ontological constitution of these entities. (I criticize this assumption in § 17B, below.)

Finally, when Heidegger argues in section 63 that interpretations must be *gewaltsam* (violent), does he not presuppose an objective standard without which interpretations cannot be judged to be violent? Heidegger suggests that we have such an objective standard at our disposal in the case of the ontological interpretation of Dasein. He says that this interpretation is violent because it has to destroy the concealing self-interpretations due to *Verfallen* (falling) in order to reveal the ontological structure of Dasein as it really is. Violence is done, then, to the alienating self-interpretations of the philosophical tradition, and ultimately to Dasein's own tendency to cover things up, but *not* to the ontological structure of Dasein as it is, or to Heidegger's own interpretation of this structure, which is assumed to be the objectively adequate one. But if it is possible to violently destroy Dasein's misinterpretations of itself on the basis of an adequate interpretation, how can Heidegger go on to claim that, even though this violent nature of interpretation "is specially distinctive of the ontology of Dasein, it belongs properly to *any* interpretation, because the understanding that develops in interpretation has the structure of a projection"?[189] Either some interpretations may be called violent, if measured by the standard of more objective and historically adequate interpretations, or, if all interpretations are "projective," it simply does not make sense to speak of violent interpretations.

Heidegger does not succeed, then, in formulating his projective theory of interpretation unambiguously and consistently. This should not surprise us, because the theory confronts him with something like the paradox of the liar. Heidegger's view of interpretation, as indeed his view of truth, which I have not yet discussed, resembles Nietzsche's claim that truth is a product of a will to power, or Marx's claim that truth is a product of class interests, in that it is reflectively incoherent. Because these theories purport to be general theories about the nature of theory or interpretation, they immediately invite us to ask: Is the theory itself also a projection, or a product of a will to power, or an outcome of class interests? If so, why should we accept it? If not, it cannot be a completely general theory. In the *Prolegomena* to his *Logical Investigations*, Husserl analyzed theories of this type (§§ 32–40). According to his diagnosis, which we should endorse, Heidegger's theory of interpretation is skeptical in the strict sense that its content contradicts necessary (constitutive) conditions for the possibility of theories of interpretation in general.

I conclude that even though some interpretations may conform to Heidegger's projective theory of interpretation and understanding, it cannot be the case that all interpretations conform to it. There must be another, objective or theoretical, type of interpretation. Only if we measure interpretations of the former type by the standard of the latter type, may we say that they are "violent." In formulating his projective theory of interpretation, Heidegger implicitly presupposes the possibility of a more objective kind of interpretation, even though he explicitly denies this possibility. The reader will easily see that the interpretations that conform to Heidegger's projective theory are what I have called "applicative" interpretations. The very point of these interpretations is to make sense of phenomena, instruments, or texts in the light of a preconceived project and of our present situation. Clearly, applicative interpretations have to add an extra to the text, an extra that derives from the matter or the interests (*Sache*) that is or are vital to the application.

When one keeps applicative and theoretical interpretations clearly apart, there is no point in calling the former violent as compared to the latter. There is no point, for instance, in telling a judge who interprets the legal term "material object" as encompassing electricity that he misinterprets the law because the law was written before electricity was discovered. The judge wants to apply the interdiction of theft in penal law to tapping electricity, even though "theft" is defined as illegally taking a material object that belongs to someone else. Such an application may be juridically justified, even though the interpretation is incorrect from a purely historical point of view.[190] While theoretical, historical interpretations aim at discovering what a text meant in the historical circumstances in which it was written, applicative interpretations purport to apply texts in order to do specific things in present situations, that is, to carry out "projects," or in order to illuminate our present existence. In order to do so, applicative interpretations often have to read into the text meanings that its author did not intend.

Heidegger's projective theory of interpretation, then, shows an *applicative bias* because he generalizes to all interpretations a theory of interpretation that is correct for applicative interpretations only.[191] As we have seen, this cannot be done without inconsistency. Moreover, such a generalization yields a destructive ideology, which explodes the ideal of objectivity inherent in historical or theoretical interpretations, the ideal that they should try to reconstruct what the text meant in the historical circumstances in which it was written. For if each and every interpretation presupposes an existentiell project, which derives its ultimate point from the fact that the interpreter's Dasein exists for the sake of itself, and which fixes in advance the conceptual framework in terms of which a text is read (*Vorgriff*), we will get as many different interpretations of a text as there are different existentiell projects, and interpretation will become an arbitrary game of "dissemination," as indeed it has become in the hands of Heidegger and his pupils. Moreover, we will never really learn from the author whose works we are trying to interpret. Having decided in advance in terms of which conceptual structure we are going to interpret these works, we are always forcing them into our own mold, projecting our preconceptions into them. There is also a moral matter involved. By interpreting someone else's words projectively, we will violate his or her and our integrity because we disregard what he or she wants to say.[192]

It is no coincidence, of course, that this is the very objection that is raised against Heidegger's interpretations of other philosophers. Heidegger's practice of interpretation was based on his doctrine of interpretation and on the maxim of covertness in particular, and this maxim is explained, in part, by the applicative bias of Heidegger's projective theory of interpretation in *Sein und Zeit*. In order to explain the maxim of covertness more fully on the basis of my interpretative hypothesis as developed above, I have to show as well that Heidegger endorses an authoritative view of the metaphysical texts he interprets in his later works. As we will see (§ 11, below), in the later works Heidegger interpreted the canonical corpus of metaphysical texts as some sort of revelation by Being, in which

Being revealed itself in the very act of dissimulating itself. Because Being dissimulates itself in these texts, we should add something (*Beigabe*) in order to discover their meaning. On the other hand, because Being also reveals itself in these texts, the texts have an authority similar to that of religious revelations, so that explicitly adding an extra would derogate from their authority. Moreover, because Heidegger conceived of his later interpretations of metaphysics as preparing a future advent of Being, they also have an applicative function.

The maxim of covertness is explained, then, by the applicative bias of Heidegger's theory of interpretation in *Sein und Zeit*, and by the authoritative and applicative conception of metaphysical texts in the later works. At the present stage of my argument, this interpretation of the maxim of covertness remains speculative as far as Heidegger's later work is concerned, and it has yet to be substantiated (see § 11).

We are now fully prepared to answer the question as to what extent we should apply Heidegger's own doctrine of interpretation in interpreting his oeuvre, that is, to what extent we should apply the maxim of reflective immanence. What would it mean to use Heidegger's projective theory of interpretation in the interpretation of his philosophy? It would mean that we would read Heidegger in the light of a project of our own, and that the "toward which" (*Woraufhin*) of this project constitutes the meaning (*Sinn*) that Heidegger's oeuvre will have. Now I do not deny that the ultimate aim of my book is to decide what significance Heidegger's philosophy can have for us. Yet we should distinguish between the significance of a philosophy for us and the meaning of the relevant texts. Perhaps the fact that the German term *Sinn* is used both for significance and for textual meaning was instrumental to Heidegger's neglect to make this crucial distinction. To my mind, it would be begging the question if we wanted to decide about the significance of Heidegger's philosophy on the basis of a projective interpretation of his works. A critical decision about the significance of Heidegger's philosophy will be premature and corrupt unless it is based on a scrupulous historical and nonapplicative interpretation of what Heidegger himself wanted to say. In other words, critical decisions must be based on an optimally objective and historical interpretation. Significance is the proper object of criticism, not of interpretation, whose exclusive object is verbal meaning.[193] Only by attempting to interpret Heidegger in a nonprojective way, and to determine what he himself wanted to say, will we be able to learn from him and to do justice to his texts.

It is this very aspiration to objectivity that is usually rejected by followers of Heidegger. It would be a naïve illusion that objectivity is possible, even to a limited extent. Objectivity would be excluded by the hermeneutical circle and by the nature of understanding. At the risk of being repetitive, I will round off this section by analyzing Heidegger's discussion of the hermeneutical circle in *Sein und Zeit*. The problem with this discussion is that some elements of what Heidegger calls the hermeneutical circle pertain to all interpretations, whether applicative or theoretical, whereas other elements are typical of applicative interpretations.

Because Heidegger in his analysis of interpretation does not bother to distinguish between these and other types of interpretation, what he says about the hermeneutical circle is confusing.

When we speak or write, we use an existing language, and this is also true when we use this language partly in an idiosyncratic and innovative manner. As was clearly realized by most philosophers of the German romantic movement, such as Herder, whose insights strikingly resemble typical Heideggerian themes, it is impossible to understand a language fully unless one shares the historical form of life (*Lebensform*) of which the language is part and parcel.[194] Even contemporaries who share a language may have difficulties in understanding each other, because there may be differences between local forms of life and because there is a linguistic division of labor. No individual masters a language completely. In fact we do not know what "completeness" would mean here. Languages are ever-evolving structures, and each speaker may try to add new uses and expressions to existing ones, although this does not happen very often.

As linguistic structures are relatively stable over time, we are able to understand texts that were written long ago in a language we know. However, because quite often the point of textual passages, if it was clear at all, was clear only within the contingent historical circumstances, which change more rapidly than linguistic structures, texts written in the past will contain passages that are obscure to us. We will misinterpret such passages if we naïvely read them in the light of the form of life of which we are part ourselves. One of Heidegger's crucial insights was that in interpreting texts, we cannot but begin to read them within the situation of our form of life. As Heidegger says in section 32 of *Sein und Zeit*, "an interpretation is never a presuppositionless apprehending of something presented to us. If, when one is engaged in . . . exact textual interpretation, one likes to appeal to what 'stands there,' then one finds that what 'stands there' in the first instance [*zunächst*] is nothing other than the obvious undiscussed assumption of the person who does the interpreting."[195] In interpretation, then, one cannot but begin with implicit or partly explicit presuppositions and an implicit background, just as in scientific investigations one cannot but begin with implicit or partly explicit hypotheses and a background of accepted theory and customary practices of research. This is true even in the case of conversations with friends, though in this case the presupposed forms of life will be nearly the same, so that "interpretation" is usually superfluous.[196] We may conclude that understanding and interpretation have a presuppositional nature, which is one aspect of what Heidegger calls the hermeneutical circle. As he says, we cannot avoid this circle: "What is decisive is not to get out of the circle but to come into it in the right way."[197] Even this warning is an understatement. For being raised into a form of life, we always already are in the hermeneutical circle.[198]

The crucial question is, as I said, whether it is possible in principle to test our interpretative presuppositions in a more or less objective manner. Is it not obvious that by exploring the historical background of a text, we might discover that our initial reading is mistaken, and that the mistake was due to our underestimating the differences between our *Lebensform* and that within which the text was written, or to the fact that we overlooked crucial connections with other texts or with historical events? Admittedly, in many cases it is difficult to discover much of a past form of life, because it is lost forever and not many traces may remain. But this is a factual and incidental matter. In other cases the background of a text is an existing form of life, or a past one about which we have a great deal of information. The question is not whether in fact we have the means to reconstruct the historical situation of a particular text, or even to reconstruct texts themselves, but whether the *ideal* of objectively testing our presuppositions is legitimate in principle, so that it makes sense to try to attain it, even though we will often fall short of realizing it fully. Heidegger's analysis of the hermeneutical circle is so alarmingly ambiguous because on the one hand he denies that the ideal of objectivity makes sense, whereas on the other hand he uses expressions that presuppose it.

Heidegger discusses the hermeneutical circle in three sections (2, 32, 63) of *Sein und Zeit*. As he says in passing in section 32, there are two mutually connected aspects of the circle, which I will call the holistic aspect and the presuppositional aspect. Understanding Dasein and its historical or cultural worlds is *holistic* because the various aspects and elements refer to each other, so that they form some kind of organized whole. Furthermore, interpreting texts and other manifestations of human life is *presuppositional* because we cannot but begin the interpretation within the situation of our own form of life.[199] In sections 2 and 63, the discussion of the hermeneutical circle focuses on its holistic aspect, in particular, on the holistic structure made up by Dasein and being (*Sein*). Heidegger argued in sections 2 and 4 of *Sein und Zeit* that we have to analyze Dasein in order to grasp *Sein*. But if Dasein is said to *be* itself, must we not clarify the notion of being in order to be able to analyze Dasein? Heidegger resolves this circle by means of what I have called the spiraling movement of interpretation. In order to analyze Dasein, we must indeed presuppose some vague notion of being, but not a developed concept of being. This vague notion belongs to our average understanding of being. Having developed an ontological interpretation of Dasein, we will then be able to articulate the notion of being more fully, and so on.[200] Only if we overstate the holistic thesis and claim that it is impossible to have even a partial understanding of parts unless we have an entire understanding of the whole first, would it lead to a vicious circle and to skepticism. This is not what Heidegger claims.

In section 32, on the other hand, Heidegger concentrates on the presuppositional aspect of the circle. Because this aspect is due to the fact that we always already find ourselves in a form of life and in a language that belongs to that form of life, it is surprising that Heidegger connects the presuppositional aspect to *Verstehen* and the projective nature of Dasein and not to *Befindlichkeit* and "thrownness." However this may be, nobody will object to Heidegger's notion of the hermeneutical circle to the extent that it draws attention to the presuppositional nature of interpretation. It is a platitude in the philosophy of science that no research is possible without some kind of hypothesis and without a background of existing knowledge and skills. Why should this be different in the case of interpreting texts? To repeat, the crucial question is whether Heidegger allows for a more or less objective testing of interpretative presuppositions or hypotheses. In order to answer this question, we must carefully follow the argument concerning the hermeneutical circle of section 32 of *Sein und Zeit* (pp. 152–153).

Heidegger starts the argument by comparing the presuppositional circle in interpretation with an ideal of scientific knowledge, according to which science should prove its results without presupposing them. Does the presuppositional nature of interpretation not exclude that we ever realize this ideal in the case of historical interpretation? Should we not exclude interpretation and history from the province of scientific knowledge (in the broad sense of the German *Wissenschaft*)?[201] Heidegger stresses that the historian himself endorses the ideal of objectivity: "even in the opinion of the historian himself it would admittedly be more ideal if the circle could be avoided and if there remained the hope of creating some time a historiography that would be as independent of the standpoint of the observer as our knowledge of Nature is supposed to be."[202]

Heidegger could have continued by pointing out that making presuppositions is not at all incompatible with the ideal of scientific objectivity, as long as some form of objective testing of the presuppositions remains possible. He could have argued that even in science research is impossible without hypotheses and a background of knowledge and skills, and that, therefore, science and interpretation possess the very same hypothetical-deductive structure. In other words, he could have argued that the ideal of presuppositionlessness as defended by Husserl, for example, is not the only possible conception of objectivity in science, and that in fact the idea of objectivity as presuppositionlessness is hopelessly inadequate as a philosophy of science. But this is not at all how Heidegger continues. On the contrary, he endorses the idea that the presuppositional nature of understanding excludes the ideal of objectivity, and goes on to argue that this ideal is an illusion because it stems from misunderstanding the circular nature of *Verstehen* and, indeed, the circular nature of projective Dasein: "this circle of understanding is not an orbit in which any random kind of knowledge may move; it is the expression of the existential *fore-structure* of Dasein itself." And: "an entity for which, as Being-in-the-World, its being is itself an issue, has, ontologically, a circular structure."[203]

Clearly, then, Heidegger rejects the ideal of objectivity in historical research as an illusion, based on a misunderstanding of the nature of Dasein, even though he uses again the confusing expression "things themselves" on which I have already commented.[204] Perhaps his argument was inspired by Nietzsche's famous 1874 essay "On the Use and Abuse of Historiography for Life," to which Heidegger refers in section 76 of *Sein und Zeit*. Nietzsche also argued that the three functions of historiography that are useful for life were incompatible with scientific objectivity. And like Nietzsche, Heidegger claims in section 32 that the ideal of objectivity in the natural sciences is itself an illusion, because these sciences are mere subspecies of *Verstehen* or interpretation (p. 153).[205] We may conclude that Heidegger's analysis of the hermeneutical circle confirms my diagnosis of his theory of interpretation, that it shows an applicative bias. According to Heidegger, the circular structure of interpretation is an expression of the circular structure of Dasein, which projects its existence, a space of possibilities, and a referential structure, for the sake of itself.

We saw that Heidegger did not succeed in formulating his projective theory of interpretation consistently. He could not succeed in doing so, because the projective theory is confronted with the paradox of the liar. In Husserl's terms, it is a skeptical theory in the strict sense. We concluded that Heidegger's theory holds at best for applicative interpretations, and that we should aim at a maximally objective and historical interpretation of Heidegger's works in order to do justice to his thought and to be able to assess it. But what should one say when someone objects, like Heidegger in section 32 of *Sein und Zeit*, that the ideal of objectivity is an illusion because it is founded on misunderstanding the projective nature of Dasein?

I suggest that we do not sever the link between the ontological analysis of Dasein and the nature of interpretation. If, therefore, Heidegger's analysis of Dasein implies the projective theory of interpretation, and if the projective theory is reflectively inconsistent, we should conclude by *modus tollens* that there is something wrong with Heidegger's analysis of Dasein. Indeed, it is patently absurd to conceive of all interpretation and knowledge as based on *Verstehen* in the sense of projecting projects for realizing Dasein. Heidegger's analysis should be corrected on two points. First, the presuppositional nature of interpretation is related to *Befindlichkeit* rather than to *Verstehen*, because it derives from the fact that we always already find ourselves in a common form of life that we did not invent. Only in the case of applicative interpretations is the content of our interpretative hypothesis determined in part by the project we want to realize by means of the interpretation. Second, I think that Heidegger in his revolutionary ardor overstated his case when he reversed the traditional thesis of Brentano and Husserl. According to this thesis, emotive experiences such as fear are founded on (re)presentational acts such as perception, imagination, or thought, in the sense that the former are not possible without the latter. Similarly, interpreting something *as* something would be founded on a simple representation or perception. In sections 29 and 32 of *Sein und Zeit*, Heidegger argues that, on the contrary, moods and projects are the fundamental ways in which the world is revealed to us, and that "objectivating" perception and thought are privative derivations of moods and projects. This is why, correlatively, the world is primarily the world of equipment and work (*Zuhandenheit*), whereas the world of objective perception and science (*Vorhandenheit*) allegedly is an alienating abstraction. Is it not more plausible to assume that the ways in which objective perception and science reveal the world are at least equiprimordial (*gleichursprünglich*) with other ways, such as moods and projects? Why does Heidegger not apply the notion of equiprimordiality here, whereas he stresses this notion again and again elsewhere? Such a move would have saved the ideal of objectivity, an ideal that we cannot reject consistently.

Let us then admit to Heidegger that all science and all interpretation begin with presuppositions or hypotheses within the framework of a shared form of life, and that, in this sense, interpretation is presuppositional. However, this hermeneutical a priori is not at all incompatible with the ideal of objectivity, because in itself it is a defeasible a priori and does not exclude a more or less objective testing of hypotheses. Depending on the type of interpretation we want to develop, there are different sets of constraints on permissible hypotheses, and different rules and criteria for testing them. Let me briefly comment both on these constraints and on these rules or criteria.

All interpretation inevitably starts within the language and form of life of the interpreter. Against the background of this implicit "presupposition," explicit hypotheses of interpretation may be formulated. In the case of applicative interpretation, these interpretative hypotheses will derive their point from a project (*Entwurf*). In law, for instance, we want to resolve practical problems in a way that is acceptable to present-day society. The ultimate criteria for evaluating the quality of the interpretation are both pragmatic and normative: Does the interpretation yield a "just" solution that "works" in the present-day situation? However, depending on the province of law and on the structure of the legal system, there will also be a set of purely legal or juridical criteria for evaluating or testing an interpretation. In penal law, for instance, interpretation should not be ampliative, so that purely historical interpretations to a large extent function as boundary conditions for admissible applicative interpretations. Interpretation in civil law may be much less restrictive. Libraries of books have been written on interpretation in law. My aim here is merely to distinguish clearly applicative interpretation from another type of interpretation, which I have called objective, critical, or historical interpretation.

In this latter type of interpretation, our only aim is to discover what the author wanted to say, or, in other words, what the historical meaning of an unclear text is. This objective is not at all "pragmatic." Our objective is truth or historical correctness. In order to realize the purpose of critical interpretations, we must try to locate the text within the historical circumstances in which it was written, and we must understand its language as it was understood at the time and within the form of life of the author. Sometimes we also have to reconstruct the individual situation of the author: we must study her or his life and its major events, and we must read what the author read, in order to discover clues to obscure passages in her or his works. In the case of critical interpretations, interpretative hypotheses are admissible only if they aim at historical adequacy. We may suppose, for instance, that an unclear passage should be understood against the background of works of another author only if our text is written by someone who, directly or indirectly, was acquainted with these works. In testing such hypotheses, we investigate whether they are in fact historically adequate, and we also verify to what extent they make sense of the passages we want to interpret.

It would be trivial to object that even objective or historical interpretations will be part of an existentiell project of the interpreter, because it is an existentiell project to search for a historically correct interpretation. Maybe our ultimate aim (*Woraufhin*) of such an epistemic project is to become happy, to lead a noble life, or to have a successful academic career. The crucial point is, however, that this *Woraufhin*, which Heidegger calls *Sinn*, should in no way determine the meaning that we will attribute to the text we are interpreting. If it does, our interpretation should be rejected as subjectively biased, and our existentiell project of discovering the correct interpretation would be frustrated. The name of the game of historical interpretation is truth or correctness, even if we play this game for ultimate reasons of our own.

In this book, I am aiming at such an objective historical interpretation. In some cases, such as those of the pre-Socratics, the aim of objective interpretation is difficult to attain because only textual fragments survive. In Heidegger's case, the task of objective interpretation is difficult to carry out because we suffer from the opposite problem: there is an abundance of information and textual material, and it would take many scholarly careers to explore all the contexts and historical situations that might be relevant to the interpretation of Heidegger's oeuvre.[206] As a consequence, interpretations of Heidegger's philosophy will be partial. However, being partial, they nevertheless may be historically adequate. It must be possible to understand aspects of Heidegger's thought correctly without fully understanding the whole. If not, Heidegger himself could not have understood what he wrote until he had written his very last word. Focusing on Heidegger's main and unique question, the question of being, I will try to elucidate the fundamental structures of his thought. As far as the textual basis of my interpretation is concerned, I have decided to take the texts published by Heidegger himself as the main *interpretandum*, and to use lecture notes and other materials published in the *Gesamtausgabe* as secondary sources.[207] The most important exception to this rule is *Beiträge zur Philosophie*, a book that I consider as a primary source, indeed, as the hidden fountain from which Heidegger's later publications flowed forth. In the next two chapters, my interpretative hypothesis is developed and partly tested.

Analysis

IN THE PREVIOUS, introductory chapter I tried to show why it may seem impossible to make sense of Heidegger's question of being and why we should nevertheless try to do so (§§ 1–3). Moreover, I stated six problems of interpretation, by way of examples, because interpretations easily degenerate into mere summaries unless they purport to answer carefully formulated questions regarding textual unclarities (§ 4). Finally, I argued that we should neither aim at a strictly immanent nor at a reflectively immanent interpretation of the question of being if we want to grasp the textual meaning of Heidegger's works, and to use our interpretation as a basis for critically evaluating his philosophy (§ 5). Instead, we should attempt to formulate an interpretative hypothesis, to test its historical adequacy, and to explore its clarifying power.

It is the aim of the present chapter and the next chapter to develop and partly assess such an interpretative hypothesis. In section 6, I sketch its contours. Heidegger's question of being, I hold, is not really one question, nor is it a patchwork of loosely related themes. There are five fundamental strands or leitmotifs in the question of being, which are multiply connected and interwoven. In order to develop this hypothesis, I first analyze the leitmotifs separately (*Analysis*: §§ 7–11 of this chapter) and then study their interconnections (*Synthesis*: next chapter). In the course of these two central chapters, the interpretative problems stated in section 4 will be resolved in several ways. Furthermore, many new problems will emerge. As is the case in science, in the field of textual interpretation the problem-generating capacity of a hypothesis should be considered as a virtue.

Because only very precise interpretative hypotheses will be able to generate new problems of interpretation, and thereby enable us to discover what Heidegger meant by his question of being, I object to a tendency among American Heidegger scholars to move away from the texts in favor of an attempt to "examine and extend the range of phenomena he [Heidegger] introduced into philosophy, and to continue his attempt to relate his thinking to current practices." If indeed it is the case that "the secondary literature on Heidegger that tries to capture Heidegger's powerful new insights by looking solely within his texts has been largely a huge and growing wasteland"—and this is to some extent the case—the solution is not to look for the Heideggerian "meaning of being" in our "everyday practices."[1] In order to find a way out of this wasteland, one should rather develop an accurate and strictly historical interpretation of Heidegger's works, instead of yet another applicative interpretation. Without such a historical interpretation of the texts, one simply does not know what Heidegger meant by the question of being. If one then analyzes everyday practices or other phenomena in Heidegger's name, one's analyses may very well turn out to be Wittgensteinian or pragmatist rather than Heideggerian. As I argued in section 5, an evaluation of Heidegger's significance for our own philosophical stance must be based on a strictly historical interpretation of his works. This is why the interpretative chapters 2 and 3 precede the critical analyses of chapter 4.

§ 6. AN INTERPRETATIVE HYPOTHESIS

In the existing secondary literature there are a large number of interpretative hypotheses regarding Heidegger's question of being. Although I do not want to commit the error of discussing them all, it is useful to present the two most extreme types of interpretation, and to explain why one should avoid them. Avoiding these two extremes implies that one will have to accept an interpretation of the type to which the one I am proposing belongs, even if one does not agree with the details of my proposal.

As Heidegger suggests that during his entire *Denkweg* he was stirred by one unique question, the question of being, the first interpretative hypothesis we should try out is what I will call the *unitarian* interpretation. According to this interpretation, there is *one* more or less precise meaning of Heidegger's question of being that remains the same throughout his philosophical career. Interpretations of the unitary type incur the risk of being vacuous if they are coupled with the admission that there are a number of quite drastic shifts or turns in Heidegger's philosophical development. Unitary interpretations that tell us, for instance, that Heidegger's question of being aims at discovering "what the being of beings consists in," or at disclosing "the source of the intelligibility of beings as beings," do not clarify very much. Obviously, we should aim at a more substantial interpretation. Let me briefly discuss one arbitrarily chosen example of such a substantial unitarian exegesis.

Without any doubt, Hubert Dreyfus's discerning view of the question of being should be regarded as a unitarian interpretation. According to his commentary on division 1 of *Sein und Zeit*, Heidegger means by "being" the "intelligibility correlative with our everyday background practices."[2] By asking the question of being, Heidegger wanted to explore the various ways in which we understand beings as beings of a specific type, for example, as tools, as occurrent things, as works of art, or as fellow men. Heidegger's assumption would have been that this "intelligibility" of beings, that is, the framework within which we understand them as meaningful, "is in our background practices."[3] Dreyfus's interpretation may be called Wittgensteinian or pragmatist. Wittgenstein argued in his later work that it is impossible to understand language games if one abstracts from the forms of life or from the background practices with which they are connected. Because according to Heidegger the phenomenon of meaning is not restricted to language—all beings we encounter have some meaning for us— it seems plausible to extend Wittgenstein's insights and to interpret Heidegger as saying that all "meaning" or intelligibility is rooted in, or connected to, background practices.[4] If this is correct, Heidegger's central insight resembles that of American pragmatism.[5]

Dreyfus defends this interpretation of Heidegger's question of being also with regard to the later writings. As he writes in a footnote to his commentary, Heidegger's claim that "being needs man," put forward in works such as *Unterwegs zur Sprache* (*On the Way to Language*), just means "that intelligibility is correlative with those skills that make up human background practices or customs and thus needs human beings."[6] However, this interpretation of the later works is altogether implausible. Heidegger elaborates the idea that being needs man by saying that man should be attentive to the "voice of being" (*"Achtsamkeit auf die Stimme des Seins"*), that being claims man in his essence (*"den Menschen in seinem Wesen in den Anspruch nimmt"*), and that man should be prepared for *Angst* in order to experience being in nothingness.[7] How will one manage to fit such pronouncements into the idea that Heideggerian *being* is nothing but the intelligibility of beings that is rooted in our background practices? Dreyfus's Heidegger is a domesticated Heidegger, made *salonfähig* for American academic circles by reducing him to a pragmatist or to a Wittgensteinian philosopher.

In order to domesticate Heidegger, Dreyfus has to exorcise those aspects of Heidegger's later thought which suggest that the "ungrounded ground" of all intelligibility does not reside in social practices at all, but in Being as some kind of absent god. This latter, "theological" interpretation, which would explain the phrases in Heidegger's later works I just quoted, squarely contradicts Dreyfus's conviction that according to Heidegger the source of all intelligibility is not hidden but lies open to view in our background practices.

It is interesting to see how this exorcising is done. In the introduction to a collection of essays on Heidegger published a year after Dreyfus's commentary appeared, Dreyfus and Hall discuss the theological interpretation I am referring to.[8] They admit that "the professional interpreters of Heidegger" have been attracted to the idea that Heideggerian Being, the alleged ground for understanding the meaning or significance of everything, lies "in an intelligibility that was concealed from the common run of people." Instead of showing on the basis of textual evidence that such an interpretation is mistaken, Dreyfus and Hall argue that a theological interpretation of Heidegger's philosophy leads to "disappointment with the master." For if the meaning of being cannot be found in our social practices, "where was a scholar to search for Heidegger's elusive meaning of being? Once everyday practices are eliminated, there simply is no other place, no point of reference for seeing what Heidegger is talking about, except the Heideggerian texts themselves." Unfortunately, "the secondary literature on Heidegger that tries to capture Heidegger's powerful new insights by looking solely within his texts has been largely a huge and growing wasteland." For this reason, we should try to put Heidegger's "jargon into clear terms," "to examine and extend the range of phenomena he introduced into philosophy, and to continue his attempt to relate his thinking to current practices."

I want to make two points in relation to Dreyfus and Hall's discussion. The first is that exorcising recalcitrant texts is an inevitable subterfuge for all unitarian interpretations, for the simple reason that there is no unique substantial sense of Heidegger's question of being, as I argue below. Second, the exorcising practice endangers our intellectual integrity, because it confuses two questions that we should keep separated: the interpretative question as to what Heidegger meant and the evaluative question as to what we are to think of what he meant. There is no point in trying to answer the evaluative question before we have answered the interpretative question as scrupulously as we can, because, in doing so, we risk projecting our own preferred doctrines onto Heidegger and overlooking passages that refute our preconceptions. I admit that such a projective interpretation is a way to prevent "disappointment with the master," because we will agree with the projection of our own views. In trying to answer the interpretative question, however, the argument that a certain type of interpretation will lead to disappointment with the master is irrelevant. We cannot rule out in advance the possibility that what Heidegger really meant *is* disappointing to us.

Furthermore, the interpretative question is concerned with the texts only: it aims at establishing the textual meaning of unclear passages. Even though it may be necessary to investigate the subject matter of a text in order to be able to understand the text, we should always distinguish between what the author writes about the subject matter and what we ourselves think of it. We may understand the subject matter better than the author appears to do. It does not follow that in this case we understand the text better than the author did, as is often claimed. Admittedly, if a text deals with a subject matter that is hidden or concealed, such as an absent god, we will not be able to investigate its subject matter, and it will be difficult to understand the text. However, is it really plausible to suggest that we would be able to understand the text better if only we assumed that it speaks of something else than it appears to do, something that we *can* investigate?

Let me come back to my first point. Unitarian interpretations will provide a uniform explanation of the wide influence of Heidegger's thought. We are not surprised to read that according to Dreyfus and Hall this influence is due to the fact that Heidegger grounds his thinking "in average, everyday *practice*," and not, for instance, in some hidden source of intelligibility such as an absent deity. But there are other unitary interpretations that squarely contradict the interpretation by Dreyfus and Hall. Karl Löwith, one of the most sensitive and well-informed readers of Heidegger's works, who was intimately acquainted with Heidegger before the Second World War, attributes Heidegger's immense influence to the fact that at the basis of everything Heidegger said lies something he never clearly expressed but which he strongly suggested: the religious theme, which is the more effective because it has been detached from Christianity, and appeals to those who want to remain religious even though they have grown dissatisfied with the traditional churches.[9] Clearly, there are contradictory unitarian interpretations of Heidegger's question of being, which imply contradicting unitarian explanations of Heidegger's influence. Since each of these unitarian interpretations is based on a large sample of Heidegger's texts, we must conclude that the very project of a unitarian interpretation is doomed to fail. If the best unitarian interpretations that can be developed on the basis of Heidegger's texts are mutually exclusive and each neglect important texts that are taken into account by rival unitarian interpretations, there probably cannot be a unique substantial unitarian interpretation of the question of being that accounts for the entirety of his works.

Thus disillusioned, we will perhaps be tempted to resort to the other extreme of the scale and endorse a patchwork interpretation of Heidegger's writings. Hans Vaihinger and Norman Kemp Smith once proposed a patchwork theory in order to explain the unclarities and contradictions in Kant's first Critique. The *Kritik der reinen Vernunft* was written very quickly after ten years of research. According to the patchwork theory, it is a collage made up of jottings written down over the years. Similarly, one might propose a patchwork interpretation of Heidegger's *Sein und Zeit*, and indeed of his entire oeuvre. Even though I have not found a proponent of the patchwork interpretation in the secondary literature on Heidegger, I will briefly sketch such an interpretation, because in the past I have been attracted to the idea myself.[10]

According to the patchwork interpretation, there is no substantial meaning of Heidegger's question of being. The formula of the question of being is an empty one, or at best a chameleon that changes its meaning from passage to passage, and it suggests a unity of Heidegger's work that in fact does not exist. Heidegger's philosophy is a patchwork made out of many different materials that Heidegger borrowed from others and transformed to suit his purposes, materials that do not fit together very well. The biographical argument in favor of the patchwork theory in the case of *Sein und Zeit* is the same as in Kant's case. Heidegger composed *Sein und Zeit* in a relatively short time on the basis of materials collected over ten years.[11] This holds especially for the second division, which Heidegger had to complete in a hurry in order to get Hartmann's chair in Marburg. The patchwork interpretation may seem to be a lazy exegesis, because it excuses us from the task of inventing a coherent interpretation of Heidegger's philosophy. Still, it is less lazy than most interpretations because its rationale is derived from the fact that there are many tensions and contradictions in the text. In order to justify the patchwork interpretation, its proponent has to present clearly these tensions and contradictions on the basis of minute textual analysis, and he has to argue that the patchwork interpretation is the best explanation for them. Justifying the patchwork interpretation requires more textual analysis than we find in most books on Heidegger.

I should add that the patchwork interpretation, if correct, rules out some of the central questions of my book. For example, in the preface I wondered whether

Heidegger's National Socialist pronouncements, such as the passage where he says that "the *Führer* himself and alone *is* the present and future German reality and its law," move at the periphery of his thought or occupy its very center. According to the patchwork interpretation, however, we cannot distinguish a center from a periphery of Heidegger's thought. What, then, pleads in favor of the patchwork theory? It is not easy to establish its correctness, because the patchwork theorist has to argue that each and every more or less unified interpretation is refuted by obstinate passages, so that he needs an enumeration of all possible interpretations in order to substantiate his case. Let me give some examples of the tensions and contradictions that the patchwork theorist wants to explain by his hypothesis.

Sein und Zeit seems to contain a large number of such tensions and contradictions. If one makes a list of everything Heidegger says about being (*Sein*) in this book, one ends up with a plethora of heterogeneous passages. As we saw, Heidegger takes being both as the word "being" and as a phenomenon. On the one hand he says that being is the *transcendens schlechthin* (p. 38), and on the other hand he stresses that being is always a particular ontological constitution of a particular type of being (pp. 6–7). Furthermore, he identifies being both with "that which determines beings as beings" and with "that in the light of which [*woraufhin*] beings are already understood" (p. 6). Finally, "being" (*Sein*) is quite often used as a term for human existence.[12] If one despairs of giving a coherent interpretation that unites these different claims, one will resort to a patchwork interpretation and explain them as a miscarried attempt to combine what, say, Plato, Aristotle, Duns Scotus, Eckhart, Kant, Kierkegaard, and Husserl said about being.[13]

Another example of a tension where the patchwork interpretation has a foothold is the notion of authenticity (*Eigentlichkeit*) in *Sein und Zeit*. As we saw in section 3, Heidegger seems to defend two quite different conceptions of authenticity, a solipsistic or individualistic one and a communal one. In sections 40 and 53 of *Sein und Zeit*, Heidegger stresses that *Angst* and the anticipation of death individualize us (*vereinzeln*) and disclose our Dasein as *solus ipse* in the sense that they bring it face to face with itself as Being-in-the-world. This is why authenticity would consist in a passionate and anguished "freedom toward our own death," which is essentially individual. According to section 74, however, full authenticity consists in resolutely assuming the possibilities provided by our heritage (*Erbe*) and thereby endorsing our fateful destiny (*Geschick*) "in and with our generation."

Instead of trying to smooth over the apparent contradiction between these two notions, the patchwork theorist might explain it as the result of an attempt to combine two incompatible ideals of authenticity, that of Kierkegaard on the one hand and that of Hegel, Herder, or Dilthey on the other hand. According to Kierkegaard, authenticity consists in facing the fact of our solitary, sinful, and paradoxical existence. Facing it in *Angst* finally motivates the jump to religion and will bring the isolated individual before God. In order to become authentic in this sense, we have to disrupt our social relations and concentrate on our individual spiritual and eternal self, which constitutes our real identity. Hegel, Herder, and Dilthey stressed, on the contrary, that our personal identity is thoroughly determined by the historical culture in which we grow up, so that authenticity would consist in consciously endorsing a contingent cultural heritage. Heidegger mutilated Kierkegaard's individualistic conception of authenticity beyond recognition by secularizing it, and ran into contradictions because he wanted to blend it with the historicist and communal conception of Hegel, Herder, and Dilthey, so the patchwork theorist might argue.[14]

Compared to the later works, *Sein und Zeit* is a relatively unified whole. Indeed, the later oeuvre provides the real playground for the patchwork theorist. He will argue that the main themes of Heidegger's later philosophy were borrowed from others and that, even though Heidegger transformed what he borrowed, they do not fit together at all. Let me draw attention to some of the most striking examples. Heidegger's preoccupation with authentic producing and his critique of modern technology were consonant with the first stage in the official Nazi propaganda, which around 1933 "almost demonized technology and . . . affirmed the importance of human-scale workshops that promoted the well-being of the *Volk*."[15] Like many Germans from a rural background, Heidegger experienced Germany's rapid industrialization as a threat to authentic life and to traditional spirituality, and National Socialist propaganda cleverly took advantage of this widespread feeling. Heidegger's notion of art as a world-disclosing event, which might renew the German nation, was also in the air and it was equally exploited by the National Socialists. "It was no accident," Zimmerman writes, "that Heidegger read the first version of his essay 'The Origin of the Work of Art' in 1935, not long after Hitler's Nuremberg speech about art and architecture."[16] While Hitler claimed that National Socialism "would provide the German people with the new work of art, the new myth, necessary to lead them out of the wasteland of modernity and industrial technology," Heidegger's interpretation of art "was at least in part an attempt to provide National Socialism with a proper understanding of the role of art in the 'new' Germany."[17] Furthermore, the idea that Germany has a preferential relation to ancient Greece had been a theme in German philosophy and literature since romanticism; one should not be astonished that Heidegger and the National Socialists took it up. The same holds for the notion that Germany, as the Middle Realm, has a world-historical vocation, and that it has to realize this vocation by finding a third way between Russian Bolshevism and American capitalist democracy.[18]

Heidegger's surprising interpretation of Nietzsche, according to which Nietzsche's metaphysics of the will to power expresses the advance of modern technology, was inspired by Ernst Jünger, who argued in *Der Arbeiter* (*The Worker*, 1932) that the eternal will to power expressed itself around 1930 in the *Gestalt* of the worker, and that humanity should adapt itself to this *Gestalt* by a "total mobilization."[19] Jünger defined *Gestalt* as a transcendental ordering principle that shapes a new age, and it has been shown that Jünger's *Gestalt* of the worker prefigures Heidegger's later notion of *Gestell* (frame, violent setting-upon).[20] After 1934, Heidegger grew more and more dissatisfied with the official line of the National Socialist Party. Farias has argued, not quite convincingly, that Heidegger belonged to the Röhm faction, and that the purge of 30 June 1934 eliminated him as a candidate for being the official Party philosopher.[21] Another reason for Heidegger's disillusionment with the dominating Nazi factions may have been that from 1936 on, the "earlier veneration of pre-industrial ways of life was suppressed in favour of the exaltation of . . . industrial technology" in the Party propaganda, obviously because Hitler wanted to prepare a next war.[22] Perhaps Heidegger could not join in this *volte-face*, and began to use Jünger's interpretation of the *Gestalt* of the worker as an expression of the will to power against Jünger himself. The will to power was not an eternal force, as Jünger thought, following Nietzsche, but merely a historical metaphysical stance, expressing itself in the domination of technology, a stance that should be overcome.[23] When Heidegger finally delivered his lecture on the essence of technology at the polytechnic in Munich on 18 November 1953, he could join in a debate on technology and its autonomous power that had been started before by the evangelical church, politicians, and authors such as Alfred Weber and Friedrich Georg Jünger, Ernst Jünger's brother.[24] Many reactionary Germans embraced a pessimistic interpretation of technology after the end of the Second World War, implicitly blaming the powers of technology for Germany's defeat.

Both in *Sein und Zeit* and in the later works, Heidegger developed his notion of the world in opposition to the scientific worldview. Whereas in *Sein und Zeit*, the worldliness of the world consists in a meaningful referential framework within which tools and human institutions manifest themselves as such, he later came to embrace a mythical notion of the world as the fourfold (*Geviert*) of earth and sky, gods and mortals.[25] As Zimmerman argues, Heidegger's account of the world as fourfold is borrowed from Hölderlin.[26] And Rilke's reflections on Cézanne's portrait of Madame Cézanne may have influenced Heidegger's ruminations over The Thing (in "Das Ding"), for both according to Heidegger and to Rilke, a thing such as a work of art or a jug provides a focal point around which the world "worlds."[27]

Exploiting the many tensions in Heidegger's oeuvre and drawing on a contextual investigation of Heidegger's sources, the patchwork theorist will propose his own explanation of Heidegger's immense influence. Heidegger was not an untimely philosopher, as Nietzsche wanted to be, far ahead of his age.[28] On the contrary, Heidegger should be seen as a master patchworker, who ably cashed in on the popular themes of the period and country he lived in, condensing these themes into his abstract and abstruse jargon and lending them the appearance of deeper truths by carefully disguising their time-bound origins.[29] Because there is such a large number of these themes, and because their plurality is concealed by the uniform but empty formula of the question of being, numerous readers are able to find in his texts what they fancy to be there, and many incompatible interpretations coexist.

However attractive it may seem at first sight, I suggest that we reject the patch-work interpretation, as we had to reject interpretations of the unitarian genre, but for different reasons. In my view, substantial unitarian interpretations always will be shipwrecked because Heidegger's textual corpus admits of different incompatible unitarian interpretations, as I showed using the examples of Dreyfus and Löwith. It follows that there is no unique substantial meaning of the question of being, and I predict that all unitarian interpretations will be confronted with textual passages that refute them. However, it would be premature to rush to the other extreme, and to suggest that there is no substantial meaning of Heidegger's question of being at all. In interpreting Heidegger's question, we should apply the principle of charity as extensively as we can. If unitarian interpretations are ruled out, so that we have to admit plurality in the question of being, we should try to restrict plurality and to show that plurality does not altogether exclude unity. The patchwork interpretation, which would destroy many of the claims Heidegger made in behalf of his philosophy, cannot be established unless we possess a complete enumeration of other possible interpretations, for we should not resort to the most uncharitable interpretation before having tried out more charitable views. This methodological maxim implies that we should attempt first to develop an interpretation of Heidegger's question of being that, although it admits of multiple substantial meanings, also shows that these meanings are interconnected, so that unity is restored to some extent. The interpretation I am proposing is of this type.

In a pilot study of my interpretation, I compared Heidegger's texts with the overtures of Richard Wagner.[30] In his overtures Wagner sketches the content of the opera in question by means of so-called leitmotifs, musical phrases that each suggest a personage, an idea, or a theme of the plot, and that will be repeated and interwoven, so that the plot is not only told by the text of the libretto but also by the music itself. The overtures are enchanting pieces of music, and one may be enthralled by their spell without having analyzed the interplay of leitmotifs. In this case, however, one does not really understand what is going on in the music. Similarly, I propose that in Heidegger's texts on the question of being there are a number of leitmotifs that are skillfully interwoven to produce the desired effect. One may be deeply impressed by these texts and feel that something important is going on, but will not clearly understand what it is unless one analyzes the leitmotifs and studies their interweavings.[31]

In sections 7–11 of this chapter, I analyze the five leitmotifs or themes which, according to my interpretative hypothesis, constitute the meaning of Heidegger's question of being. They may be regarded as the fundamental structures of Heidegger's philosophy. If there are fundamental structures, it will make sense to ask questions such as whether Heidegger's National Socialist pronouncements belong to a fundamental structure of his philosophy or whether they are contingent details which, even though they are connected to the relevant structure, are not necessitated by it. I argue that the latter alternative is the correct one. For ease of exposition, I have labeled the five leitmotifs as follows: (A) the meta-Aristotelian theme,

(B) the phenomenologico-hermeneutical theme, (C) the transcendental theme, (D) the Neo-Hegelian theme, and (E) the postmonotheist theme.

These labels will sound familiar to those who are acquainted with Heidegger's works. One might object that the proposed interpretation means no news in the trench war of Heidegger scholarship, but this is not true at all. First, although the main substantial interpretations in the field all acknowledge that Heidegger was deeply influenced by, say, Aristotle, Husserl, Dilthey, Kant, Hegel, and the religious tradition, they aim at a unitarian interpretation of the question of being. I am arguing that such a unitarian interpretation is impossible, and that there is a fundamental plurality of meanings in Heidegger's question of being. Second, only by developing the five themes separately will we get a clear view of their interconnections and of the tensions between them, and be able to suggest a host of new "relational problems." It will become clear in detail why unitarian interpretations must fail. Finally, the pluralistic interpretation that I propose will enable us to assess the five fundamental structures of Heidegger's question of being separately (ch. 4), whereas, taken as an unanalyzed whole, Heidegger's philosophy is as difficult to assess as it is difficult to swallow a whale. If we try to do so without dissection, we will risk being swallowed by it.

As far as the unity of Heidegger's question of being is concerned, I distinguish various types of unity (ch. 3). Let me mention two of them here. First, there is material unity, effected by motivational links between the different fundamental structures or leitmotifs. I will explore a number of these links, especially in the next chapter. Second, there is a formal framework of the question of being, which is the same in each of the five leitmotifs. We might say that the five fundamental structures of Heidegger's question of being are interconnected by means of a formal analogy, or by a common "grammar," which consists of nine formal features. In each of the five leitmotifs, these formal features are provided with a somewhat different semantic content.

This formal structure is as follows. According to Heidegger, there is (1) one unique and fundamental question of philosophy or thought: the question of being (*Seinsfrage*). Man has (2) an understanding of (this question of) being, and this understanding characterizes man in his essence (*Seinsverständnis*). Nevertheless, (3) we live in forgetfulness of the question of being, and, indeed, of being itself (*Seinsvergessenheit*), because (4) we do not distinguish between being and beings, that is, we fail to observe the ontological difference (*ontologische Differenz*). Implicitly or explicitly we endorse (5) the ontology of presence (*Ontologie der Vorhandenheit*). The task of the thinker is (6) to wrest us from the oblivion of being by (7) raising the question of being anew and by (8) retrieving the tradition of metaphysics, which embodies the ontology of presence (*Destruktion, Verwindung*). Only in this manner (9) will man turn in upon his essence and origin again.

In the following five sections, I will develop each of the leitmotifs of Heidegger's question of being, and show what semantic content the nine formal features of their common grammar take within each leitmotif. I will partly substantiate the interpretative adequacy of the five hypothetical leitmotifs by presenting the relevant texts in the notes. Readers will be able to assess my hypothesis further by examining its clarifying power for other Heideggerian texts of their own choice. In doing so, one should be on one's guard against Heidegger's interpretations of his earlier texts. As is now generally acknowledged, these autointerpretations mostly are reinterpretations, and they should not have a special authority if one aims at a strictly historical interpretation of Heidegger's oeuvre. Instead of being a privileged and authoritative ingredient of our interpretation, they belong to the material to be interpreted (see §§ 12B and C).

§ 7. THE META-ARISTOTELIAN THEME

Heidegger claims that the question of being is the fundamental question of philosophy, and according to his autobiographical sketch "Mein Weg in die Phänomenologie," he derived this question from Brentano's dissertation on the Aristotelian doctrine of being.[32] This is why I propose the Aristotelian theme as the first leitmotif in Heidegger's question of being. From a methodological point of view, it is mandatory to investigate in the first place to what extent Heidegger's question of being may be elucidated by taking the Aristotelian theme as a guiding principle. Heidegger not only insists that he derived the question of being from Aristotle. He also holds that Aristotle did not really manage to develop the problem of being, let alone solve it, and that the problem of being fell into oblivion, even though the conceptual structures of Aristotelian ontology allegedly determine our ways of thinking up until the present day.[33] Although Heidegger claims to have inherited the question of being from Aristotle, he aims at stating and solving the problem of being in a more adequate manner. Consequently, the Aristotelian theme in Heidegger's question of being is in fact a meta-Aristotelian theme: Heidegger uses, or seems to use, Aristotle with the objective of going beyond Aristotle.

In order to develop the meta-Aristotelian theme, we have to address three questions. First, (A) why do Aristotle and Heidegger assume that there is one and only one fundamental question, the question of being, and why do they hold that it is the task of philosophy to raise and answer this question? We will never understand the content of the question of being unless we will have resolved what I will call the problem of the primacy of the question of being.[34]

Whereas Heidegger fully endorsed the primacy of the question of being, he criticized Aristotle for not having adequately developed the problem of being. Heidegger's relation to the Aristotelian doctrine of being is characterized by a similar ambiguity. On the one hand, his philosophical terminology is quite often inspired by Aristotle's, and many Heideggerian neologisms, such as *Woraufhin* (the upon-which), *Lichtung* (clearing), and *Umsicht* (circumspection), can be traced back to Aristotle's Greek. Heidegger justifies his strained usage of the

German language in *Sein und Zeit* partly by reference to "the altogether unprecedented character of those formulations that were imposed on the Greeks by their philosophers."[35] And indeed, comparing Aristotle's usage of Greek and Heidegger's usage of German, one will conclude that Heidegger would never have invented his highly original philosophical jargon had he not been inspired by Aristotle and, to a lesser extent, by Plato. On the other hand, Heidegger rejects Aristotle's doctrine of being for the reason that Aristotle's ontological concepts originated from experiences that do not touch the heart of the ontological matter.

In order to see clearly, then, to what extent Heidegger accepted Aristotle's doctrine of being, and to what extent and for which reasons he rejected this doctrine, we have to answer two further questions: (B) What is Aristotle's doctrine of being? (C) Why and to what measure did Heidegger reject this doctrine? In developing the meta-Aristotelian theme, I will discuss these three questions in this order, and I will be brief and somewhat dogmatic, skipping many exegetical subtleties regarding Aristotle's texts to prevent this section from growing into a book on Heidegger's relation to Aristotle.

A. The Primacy of the Question of Being

The problem of the primacy of the question of being is related to that of grasping Aristotle's notion of first philosophy, because according to Aristotle it is the task of first philosophy to deal with the question of being. There is yet another complexity: we are interested in Heidegger's interpretation and reception of Aristotle's question of being. Heidegger conceived of his relation to philosophers of the past as "retrieval" (*Wiederholung*). By tracing their concepts and problems back to the experiences from which they originated, he wanted to renew and reanimate these problems and concepts, and to show their positive possibilities and their limits (cf. *Destruktion*, § 3, above).[36] Hence, two separate issues are involved in the problem of the primacy of the question of being: How did Heidegger retrieve Aristotle's question of being and his notion of first philosophy? How did Aristotle himself justify the primacy of the question of being and his notion of first philosophy?

I will argue that Heidegger's retrieval was a partial one, and that he failed to discuss and assess Aristotle's main justification for the notion of first philosophy, which was based on the Aristotelian philosophy of science, that is, on his view of true knowledge (*epistēmē*). Heidegger's idea of retrieval derives its point from an insight common to German historians of the nineteenth century: that we will be influenced unwittingly by traditional conceptions unless we explicitly digest and assess them. If so, the fact that Heidegger's retrieval of Aristotle was only a partial one is a serious defect, for it implies that in assuming the primacy of the question of being, Heidegger's thought may have been determined inadvertently by Aristotle's philosophy of science. As we will see, this is indeed the case.

Let me first discuss Heidegger's retrieval of Aristotle's notion of philosophy and inquire whether this retrieval explains why Heidegger considered the question of being the most fundamental question that a human being can ask. Between 1921 and 1927, the year in which *Sein und Zeit* was published, Heidegger lectured on Aristotle a great number of times: in the winter semester of 1921–22 and the summer of 1922 at Freiburg University, and at Marburg University during the winter semester of 1923–24, the summer semester of 1924, in his important course on Plato's *Sophistes* of the winter semester 1924–25, during his course on philosophical logic in the winter semester of 1925–26, his course on the fundamental notions of ancient philosophy in the summer of 1926, and in the course on the fundamental problems of phenomenology of 1927.[37] He held seminars on Aristotle a great many times as well.[38] Moreover, between 1919 and 1923, Heidegger was working on a book on Aristotle, due to appear as volume 7 (and perhaps 8) of Husserl's *Jahrbuch*, but which was never published. Doubtless, the most interesting text on Aristotle from this period is a fifty-page manuscript that Heidegger wrote between 22 September and 30 October 1922, and which Husserl sent to Natorp in order to get Heidegger a position as *extraordinarius* in Marburg.[39] This manuscript, usually called the "Natorp essay," is a densely written, more or less programmatic summary of Heidegger's studies on Aristotle. Although it was thought to be lost because Natorp's copy perished in the bombings of Leipzig,[40] Heidegger's own copy has been found in Josef König's papers. The essay was published in the *Dilthey-Jahrbuch* of 1989. How did Heidegger retrieve Aristotle's notion of first philosophy in this summary of his *Phenomenological Interpretations concerning Aristotle*, as the book was to be called?

The Natorp essay is of crucial importance for understanding the genesis of *Sein und Zeit*, for Heidegger said that he took the first steps toward *Sein und Zeit* around 1922–23.[41] What strikes us primarily when we read the essay is that its composition resembles the bipartite scheme of the original plan of *Sein und Zeit*, according to which a constructive part about Dasein is followed by a destruction of the ontological tradition.[42] Heidegger's summary of his interpretations of Aristotle is preceded by an elaborate "indication of the hermeneutical situation," which takes up the first twenty-eight pages of the manuscript. In this "indication" Heidegger analyzes the ontological structure of Dasein, and he anticipates many of the themes of *Sein und Zeit*. It is easy to imagine that in the subsequent years, the focus of Heidegger's investigations shifted from the destructive to the constructive enterprise, and that the published divisions of *Sein und Zeit* grew out of the "indication of the hermeneutical situation" written in 1922.

Heidegger starts his "indication" by arguing that as our present situation inevitably is the starting point for interpretations of earlier philosophers, the better we understand this situation, the better we will be able to reveal the meaning of their works. In particular, our present conception of philosophy will determine the attitude we have toward its history. This implies that Heidegger has to state his own conception of philosophy in order to elucidate the hermeneutical situation from which he is going to interpret Aristotle. In 1922, Heidegger does not define philosophy as the search for being as such. Rather, the object of philosophy is to investigate human Dasein in its manner of being (*Seinscharakter*).[43] Philosophy has to interpret factical human life out of itself, so that philosophical research is part and parcel of our Dasein. It is the attempt to grasp the fundamental movement (*Grundbewegtheit*) of human life, and in this manner to intensify its questionable nature. Philosophy is the act of explicitly performing (*expliziter Vollzug*) the movement of factical existence.[44] It is easy to see why historical investigations of a specific kind are relevant to philosophy in this sense. They should reveal the way in which philosophers of the past interpreted human existence. A confrontation between our and their view of Dasein will lead to a fruitful antagonism (*fruchtbare Gegnerschaft*), which enables us to criticize both past and present human self-understanding and to grasp decisive possibilities of existence.[45]

   This conception of philosophy, which Heidegger derived from Luther, Kierkegaard, and Dilthey rather than from Aristotle or Husserl, is the basis both of the structure of the Natorp essay and of Heidegger's interpretations of Aristotle. Heidegger first develops a hermeneutic of human Dasein as it experiences itself in Heidegger's own generation, for it "follows from the notion of facticity that in each time only the *authentic* [*eigentliche*], in the literal sense of *one's own*, life, that is, the perspective of one's own time and generation, is the real object of investigation."[46] However, because he claims, as in *Sein und Zeit*, that Western self-understanding is unwittingly determined by the concepts of Greek philosophy in general and by Aristotle's philosophy in particular, we have to retrace or "destroy" the Aristotelian tradition in order to liberate ourselves and to reach a proper understanding of the movement and possibilities of our Dasein.[47] Clearly, the Natorp essay has the same constructive-destructive composition as *Sein und Zeit*.[48]

   Let me now focus on Heidegger's retrieval of Aristotle's notion of first philosophy. Does Heidegger reveal Aristotle's reasons for regarding the question of being as the fundamental question of first philosophy? In the Natorp essay, Heidegger studies the genesis of Aristotle's notion of (first) philosophy or wisdom (*sophia*) on the basis of the first two chapters of *Metaphysics* (Met. A, 1–2). The fundamental sense (*Grundsinn*) of "philosophy," Heidegger argues, is determined both by the way in which Aristotle gains access to the phenomenon of *sophia*, a phenomenon that Heidegger calls "pure understanding" (*reines Verstehen*), and by the manner in which Aristotle interprets *sophia*.[49] Heidegger stresses that in *Metaphysics* A, 1–2, Aristotle develops the notion of *sophia* as the last stage of a series of degrees of knowledge. The first stages of the series, such as sensation (*aisthēsis*), memory (*mnēmē*), and art (*technē*), clearly derive their point from the concerns of practical life.[50] In other words, Aristotle gains access to his notion of *sophia* via the point of view of practical human concerns. From this observation on the genesis of the notion of *sophia* Heidegger draws a conclusion that also stands out prominently in *Sein und Zeit*: that purely theoretical knowledge—that is, both *epistēmē* and *sophia* in Aristotle—somehow originates from the fact that we are concerned with our own life. Apparently, in its tendency to gain more and more insight, factical life comes to the point of giving up its concerns with acting and making, for factical life does not figure in Aristotle's interpretation of *sophia* itself.[51] This exegesis leads Heidegger to a radical critique of Aristotle's notion of (first) philosophy. If Aristotle derives his notion of philosophy from an interpretation of a factical tendency of human concern, it is paradoxical that in *sophia*, the last stage of this tendency in human life, human life disappears as an object of our concern: according to Aristotle, philosophy is not concerned with human life, but with first principles and with the Deity.[52] Furthermore, Heidegger rejects also Aristotle's notion of the Deity, according to which the Deity is not concerned with humans but merely reflects on itself. As Heidegger says, "for Aristotle . . . the idea of the divine did not derive from an explication of something that became accessible in a religious fundamental experience." On the contrary, Aristotle's conception of the Deity is the result of his analysis of movement, which requires an unmoved mover as a highest being.[53] In other words, both Aristotle's notion of (first) philosophy and his notion of the Deity, which have decisively influenced the Christian conception of God's relation to man and of man's relation to himself, disguise the fact that they originated from human concerns. These notions are articulated in categories that were derived from the analysis of movement (*kinēsis*) in Aristotle's physics, not from the phenomenon of human existence. As a result of Aristotle's influence on Christianity, human life and man's relation to God have been understood in the Christian tradition in terms of categories that have been borrowed from another ontological region; hence the Christian tradition has been alienated from itself.[54]

Although the critical tendency of Heidegger's retrieval is not as clear in the Natorp essay as it would become later, we may conclude that Heidegger wanted to destroy the Aristotelian notions of philosophy and of God, because they allegedly express an alienation. Whereas their origin lies in human concerns, Aristotle derived their content from the physical analysis of movement. This tension between origin (human) and content (nonhuman) supposedly explodes the Aristotelian conceptions. One might say that Heidegger used Aristotle in order to criticize Aristotle. Accepting the Aristotelian genesis of the idea of philosophy, he felt himself justified in rejecting its content, because the content allegedly contradicts the genesis. Heidegger's retrieval of the Aristotelian notion of philosophy seems to be a prime example of internal criticism or deconstruction.

However, there is another view of the Natorp essay that comes nearer to the truth. According to this alternative view, which I endorse, the essay is not an internal criticism of Aristotle at all. Heidegger interpreted Aristotle's notion of philosophy from the point of view of his own notion, which he derived from Luther, Kierkegaard, and Dilthey. Only because he had decided in advance that philosophy has to be an autointerpretation of human existence, he felt justified in rejecting the content of Aristotle's notion of philosophy, according to which philosophy is concerned with the first principles and with the Deity. Heidegger's destruction of Aristotle is motivated not by internal tensions in Aristotle but by his own preconceptions, and in the Natorp essay he already practices the applicative method of interpretation he advocates in *Sein und Zeit*. There is no attempt at all in Heidegger's retrieval of Aristotle to list everything Aristotle says about first philosophy and to explain the latter's notion of philosophy in a purely historical manner. Heidegger's retrieval is a partial one, and it explains neither the notion of first principles nor, interestingly, the fact that first philosophy should raise the question of being, even though in Aristotle these two topics are narrowly related. To the extent that the question of being emerges at all in the Natorp essay, it is primarily concerned with our own human mode of being, and Heidegger claims, as he does in *Sein und Zeit*, that the point and sense of regional ontologies is derived from the ontology of our factical life.[55] In short, Heidegger's retrieval of Aristotle in 1922 neither explains nor justifies the primacy of the question of being at all.

Having analyzed Heidegger's retrieval of the Aristotelian notion of (first) philosophy, we should now compare his retrieval with a purely historical attempt to interpret this Aristotelian notion. What was Aristotle's conception of first philosophy and why did Aristotle hold that first philosophy is concerned with the question of being? What is the meaning of this question in Aristotle? Only by using such a historical reconstruction as a standard of comparison will we be able to see clearly to what extent Heidegger's retrieval is contaminated by his own preoccupations. I will also discuss the important question as to whether Heidegger's thought was determined inadvertently by the aspects of Aristotle's notion of philosophy that Heidegger failed to retrieve, and, for that reason, was unable to assess critically.

In his *Metaphysics*, Aristotle characterizes first philosophy or *sophia* in a great number of ways. The most important characterizations are as follows. (1) *Sophia* is concerned with the first principles and causes (Met. I.1), so that the search for *sophia* is first philosophy in contradistinction to second philosophies such as physics. Furthermore, knowledge of the first principles and causes is the most true knowledge, about which one cannot be mistaken because it is necessary, and it is purely theoretical.[56] Because what is first in virtue of itself is the most difficult thing to discover, first philosophy, which in itself precedes physics, can be acquired only after physics, so that in the pedagogical order first philosophy is "meta-physics," a term introduced by early followers of Aristotle.[57]

(2) According to a second series of characterizations, first philosophy is the science that embraces everything, because the first principles are the most universal.[58] It is the theoretical science about each being in so far as it is (*to on hēi on*) and, accordingly, about beings as such. Much later, the term "ontology" was introduced for first philosophy in this sense.[59] According to Aristotle, the main

topic of the science of beings as such is what the Greeks called *ousia* (substance), that which *is* in the fullest sense of the word.[60]

(3) Finally, Aristotle characterizes first philosophy as theology, both in the sense that it is the most divine knowledge, which the Deity possesses, and in the sense that it is concerned with the Deity. In *Metaphysics* I.2, Aristotle suggests that first philosophy is *also* theology, because the Deity is the ultimate or first final cause of all movement in the cosmos, so that a science of the first causes should be concerned with the Deity. But there are two other texts in which Aristotle seems to claim that first philosophy is theology *only*. For the most noble science should be concerned with the most noble entity, that is, an entity that exists in itself and eternally. Although the objects of physics exist in themselves, they are not eternal. The objects of mathematics, on the contrary, may be eternal but they do not exist in themselves. For this reason, there must be a third theoretical science, first philosophy, which investigates an eternal entity that exists in itself, the Deity.[61]

There are many interpretative problems regarding Aristotle's notion of first philosophy. Why, according to Aristotle, should there be something like first philosophy at all? Why is it concerned with being as such? How is a science or doctrine of being possible if, as Aristotle says, being is not a highest genus, whereas all scientific disciplines are defined by the highest genus of objects they are concerned with? Finally, how can first philosophy be both ontology and theology? The latter problem, concerning the ontotheological unity of metaphysics, was elegantly solved by the Neo-Platonic reception of Aristotle within the Christian tradition. Ontology is concerned with Platonic forms for it studies of each being what-it-is-in-itself-in-virtue-of-itself; these forms are ideas in God's mind, and because in the act of creation God modeled the world on these ideas, the all-embracing science of the world (ontology) coincides with theology. It is not surprising that when secularization set in, this solution lost its hold. In Aristotle-scholarship, Paul Natorp raised the problem of the ontotheological unity of Aristotle's thought in 1888. According to Natorp, whom Heidegger got to know well during his years in Marburg (1923–28), the ontological and theological characterizations of first philosophy contradict each other, and he tried to eliminate the latter, interpreting them as later interpolations.[62] Werner Jaeger agreed with Natorp about the contradiction, but he argued in 1923 that the theological definition of first philosophy reflects an early stage in Aristotle's development that was overcome later.[63]

Heidegger was right, I think, to apply the principle of charity and to reject the hypothesis that there is a contradiction in Aristotle on this point. However, Heidegger did not go far enough in applying the principle of charity. According to the lectures of 1926 on the fundamental concepts of ancient philosophy, the ontological and theological determinations of first philosophy "with objective necessity belong to a problem that Aristotle did not manage to solve and did not even formulate as such," to wit: the problem of being, or more precisely, the problem of the ontological difference between being and beings.[64] It would be more charitable to assume that the determinations fit into Aristotle's doctrine of being, and that an interpretation of this doctrine should attempt to show why this is the case.

Although Heidegger rejects Aristotle's doctrine of being (see under B and C, below), he fully accepts the primacy of the question of being and the formal idea of a fundamental science. This means that apart from merely giving an interpretation of Aristotle, Heidegger must also have thought that Aristotle's arguments for the primacy of the question of being and for the existence of first philosophy as a fundamental science are convincing. Here we come to the most astonishing fact about Heidegger's retrieval of Aristotle, not only in 1922 but also in 1926: Heidegger does not even attempt to trace Aristotle's argument in favor of the primacy of the question of being, and consequently he was not able to assess it. This argument heavily relies on the philosophy of science (*epistēmē*) that Aristotle developed in his *Posterior Analytics*. Heidegger nowhere discusses this tract and its relation to the Aristotelian conception of first philosophy. In the lectures of 1926, for instance, he starts by stipulatively defining philosophy as a critical discipline, which distinguishes (*krinein*) between beings and being. In other words, philosophy should acknowledge the ontological difference and raise the question of being. Although Heidegger pretends to show in the body of the lectures that Greek philosophers aimed at raising this question, he in fact demonstrates that they did not succeed in doing so. He concludes that the question of being has to be raised anew, and that the difference between being and beings is as yet to be made. According to Heidegger, then, there is merely an implicit tendency in Greek philosophy toward raising the question of being in the sense in which he wants to raise it himself, a tendency that culminated in Aristotle. As a consequence, Heidegger is able to disregard the arguments for raising the question of being in Aristotle's sense, arguments that Aristotle explicitly formulated. This implies that Heidegger's retrieval of Aristotle neither provides us with a justification of his idea that there must be a fundamental discipline, philosophy, which raises the question of being, nor enables us to elucidate the content of this question. It follows that the meta-Aristotelian theme cannot be the only, or even the most fundamental, leitmotif in Heidegger's question of being, because it does not provide us with explicit reasons for raising this question at all.

There were such reasons in Aristotle's case, and, as I said, these reasons are based on Aristotle's philosophy of science or true knowledge (*epistēmē*). In his *Posterior Analytics*, Aristotle defines scientific knowledge as knowledge of truths by demonstration. We cannot be said to know that p unless we have validly deduced p from premises that we know to be true. However, this definition of scientific knowledge leads to a trilemma. Either (1) the chain of proofs of p and its premises goes back in(de)finitely. In this case we will never be able to possess knowledge, because the capacities of the human mind are finite. Or (2) the chain of proofs is circular. If so, we do not possess knowledge either, for although circular deductions are logically valid, they do not amount to proofs of the truth of the conclusion. This implies that Aristotle's definition of knowledge leads to skepticism, unless (3) the chains of proofs are based on first principles, which we are able to know without proof, because they are necessary and self-evident.

In this manner, Aristotle's conception of scientific knowledge as knowledge by proof leads to the conclusion that there must be a more fundamental kind of knowledge, knowledge of the first principles. It is interesting to compare Aristotle's philosophy of science with *The Elements* of Euclid, who practiced Aristotle's ideal. Euclid must have flourished around 300 B.C., and he was somewhat younger than Aristotle (384–322 B.C.). However, his mathematical works stand in the Platonic tradition, and probably he received his training from pupils of Plato. It is not far-fetched to assume that Aristotle's philosophy of science was inspired by a tradition in mathematics that culminated in Euclid. Both according to Aristotle's theory and to Euclid's practice, sciences should be construed as axiomatic-deductive systems. Aristotle stresses more than Euclid, however, that the first principles must be evidently and necessarily true if we are to be able to derive truly scientific knowledge from them.

Both Euclid and Aristotle distinguish between two kinds of first principles: postulates and axioms proper. The difference is that postulates belong to a particular scientific discipline and specify "essential attributes" of the objects of its domain, whereas the axioms are "common notions": they hold for all disciplines.[65] One might express this distinction differently, in order to show the relation between Aristotle's philosophy of science and his conception of first philosophy. The postulates are concerned with beings *in so far as* they have some specific, regional essence. Geometry studies beings to the extent that they have shapes; psychology studies beings *qua* human, to the extent that they are gifted with perception and thought. In contrast, the axioms are concerned with beings in general, or with beings *in so far as* they are or exist at all, beings *qua* beings. And this is precisely Aristotle's formula for the subject matter of first philosophy: *to on hēi on*. First philosophy, then, is ontology because it is concerned with *to on hēi on*, beings *qua* beings, and it is the general foundation of all scientific disciplines or "second" philosophies because it contains the universal principles underlying these disciplines.

One must conclude that Aristotle's conception of first philosophy as ontology, and indeed his question of being as a primary question, are derived from his philosophy of science. Only if one conceives of scientific knowledge as knowledge of truths by proof will one have to assume that there is another kind of knowledge (*sophia*), which is more fundamental than the sciences: unprovable knowledge of the general first principles and of fundamental concepts that hold for beings as such.[66] Aristotle's philosophy of science implies the notion of first philosophy, which raises the question of being in the sense of the question of what characterizes all beings as beings. Conversely, the idea that the question of being(s) is the most fundamental question we might raise, and that first philosophy has the task of raising it, will lose its justification as soon as one rejects Aristotle's philosophy of science.

Aristotle's view of science, and his concomitant conception of ontology as first philosophy, have been extremely influential in the history of philosophy. During the scientific revolution the Aristotelian sciences and ontology were rejected. They were rejected, however, for the very reason that they failed to realize the ideal of science that was formulated in Aristotle's philosophy of science, an ideal that was endorsed by philosophers such as Descartes and Newton. Descartes argued in the *lettre-préface* to the French translation of the *Principia Philosophiae* (*Principles of Philosophy*) that Plato and Aristotle were not able to know with certainty the first principles, because they did not possess the correct method, methodical doubt and intellectual intuition. Similarly, Kant accused his predecessors of not having been able to justify the synthetic a priori principles of science, and he argued that we need a transcendental philosophy for doing so.

It is not difficult to see that Heidegger was influenced by this Aristotelian tradition in the philosophy of science. Like Kant and Husserl, Heidegger assumes in *Sein und Zeit* that philosophy is more fundamental than the sciences. Moreover, philosophy consists of two levels. Regional ontologies have the task of elaborating a priori the fundamental concepts of specific regions of being.[67] First philosophy, however, is concerned with the nature of being as such, and with the way being is related to the knowing subject (see § 9, below, for details). As Heidegger says in sections 3, 4, and 7 of *Sein und Zeit*, (first) philosophy is fundamental ontology, concerned with being as such and with human understanding of being.

Heidegger never really abandoned this Aristotelian, foundationalist conception of philosophy, even though he gave up the notion of a fundamental ontology. In his rectoral address of 1933, Heidegger defines science (*Wissenschaft*) as "maintaining one's questioning attitude amidst the totality of being, which hides itself permanently,"[68] and he stresses that there is an intimate connection between science and the German *Volk* (people). The "full essence of science" would be constituted by three "services" for the nation or the *Volk*: labor service, military service, and service of knowledge.[69] Apart from this *völkisch* and perhaps even National Socialist notion of scientific knowledge, the rectoral address also shows the influence of the Aristotelian conception of science: Heidegger claims that all science is philosophy, and that it remains attached to its origins: the emergence of Greek philosophy.[70] Five years later, in a text from 1938 on "Die Zeit des Weltbildes" ("The Age of the World View"), Heidegger raises the question as to which conception of being and truth grounds the essence of modern science. He assumes, without further argument, that science is founded on a "metaphysical basis," an assumption inherent in the Aristotelian conception of science.[71] In his celebrated lecture on the origin of the work of art, which dates back to 1935, Heidegger derives from his Aristotelian conception of science and philosophy the conclusion that science is not an "original happening of truth."[72] We discern traces of the Aristotelian foundationalist conception of science and philosophy even in Heidegger's last writings, such as the essay entitled "Das Ende der Philosophie und die Aufgabe des Denkens" ("The End of Philosophy and the Task of Thinking"), published in 1969, where Heidegger claims that the sciences implicitly speak about the being of beings when they posit their regional categories, and that they cannot get rid of their origin in philosophy.[73]

We are justified in concluding that Heidegger maintained the Aristotelian thesis of the primacy of philosophy and of the question of being in relation to the sciences during his entire philosophical career, even though he did not retrieve and critically assess the Aristotelian argument for this thesis. Because Heidegger never reflected on the connection between the primacy thesis and Aristotle's philosophy of science, he did not bother to rethink his own rudimentary philosophy of science, although he was acutely aware of the scientific revolutions of the first half of this century, revolutions that in fact necessitated a revolution in the philosophy of science as well.[74] This revolution in the philosophy of science, which in fact took place in the works of many philosophers of science in this century, dethroned metaphysics and the Aristotelian question of being from the position of first philosophy. As a consequence, Heidegger is faced with a dilemma. Either the justification for the primacy of the question of being is derived from Aristotle. If so, the primacy thesis is refuted by later developments in the philosophy of science. Or the primacy of Heidegger's question of being, and perhaps this question itself, was not derived directly from Aristotle, but from, say, Neo-Scholastic philosophical ontotheology such as that of Heidegger's master Carl Braig.[75] But this contradicts what Heidegger says on the matter in "Mein Weg in die Phänomenologie."

B. Aristotle's Doctrine of Being

My reconstruction of Aristotle's notion of first philosophy, and of the primacy of the question of being in Aristotle's sense, leaves unexplained a number of characteristics that he attributes to first philosophy. We have seen why according to Aristotle there must be a first philosophy about being(s) in general. But we do not yet understand why first philosophy studies the first causes, and how it can be concerned both with *ousia* and with the Deity. To put it differently, I have only retrieved Aristotle's formal conception of first philosophy, and his rationale for the primacy of the question of being, but not the way in which Aristotle tried to realize this conception, that is, his doctrine of being. However, in order to understand Aristotle's doctrine, we must first reconstruct his problem of being.

The problem of being, as Aristotle saw it, may be put as follows: How is first philosophy, the study of being(s) as such, possible as a rigorous science? According to *Posterior Analytics* I.7, a scientific discipline is always concerned with objects of one highest genus. However, being as such is not a genus. The general axioms of the sciences, which hold for beings in general, such as the axiom that if equals be subtracted from equals, the remainders are equal, apply only analogically in different sciences: the axiom means something different in geometry and in arithmetic.[76] But analogy destroys the unity of a genus. Moreover, "being" is said in many ways (*pollachōs*), as Aristotle repeatedly affirms. For these reasons, it seems, first philosophy as a science of being(s) as such is impossible. Whereas Aristotle's philosophy of science on the one hand implies that there must be such a science, it on the other hand excludes there being one. I will argue that Aristotle's doctrine of being should be understood as an attempt to solve this problem of the possibility of a science of being(s).

Aristotle's problem of being is very different from the problem of being that Heidegger wanted to elaborate, the problem of the ontological difference, and it should not astonish us that from the point of view of his own problem, Heidegger said that Aristotle never formulated the problem of being. As in the case of the primacy of the question of being, Heidegger only partially retrieved Aristotle's problem of being. Because he did not bother to reconstruct Aristotle's problem in a purely historical manner, he never discovered how according to Aristotle the different characterizations of first philosophy hang together. Nevertheless, there is a formal or structural resemblance between Aristotle's and Heidegger's problems of being. Both problems consist of a tension between two poles, which I will call the pole of differentiation and the pole of unity.

In Aristotle's case, there is a pole of differentiation because he affirms that "being" is said in many different ways (*pollachōs*).[77] As I noted in section 1, above, the most important distinction between ways in which "being" is said is that of *Metaphysics* V.7, where Aristotle distinguishes between (1) being in the sense of things that are named according to a coincidental mode of being (*kata sumbebēkos*), (2) being in a substantial sense (*kath' hauto*), as specified in the ten categories, (3) being in the sense of being true, and (4) being in the sense of being something potentially or actually. If this plurality of senses of "being" were irreducible, a science of being as such would be impossible, because each science must be concerned with one homogeneous domain or genus. In order to solve the problem of the possibility of first philosophy, then, Aristotle has to show that the plurality of senses of "being" somehow reduces to one, and that there is one genus with which first philosophy is primarily concerned. In other words, apart from a pole of differentiation, there is also a pole of unity.

Aristotle's doctrine of being is an attempt to effectuate this reduction. I now try to reconstruct this doctrine, which has to be reassembled from Aristotle's *Metaphysics*. Then I state Heidegger's criticisms of the Aristotelian doctrine as he saw it in subsection C. We will see that Heidegger's problem of being also has a pole of differentiation and a pole of unity, but that his problem is different from Aristotle's, among other reasons because Heidegger did not conceive of the unity of being as reducibility to one genus.

We may distinguish three stages in Aristotle's reduction of the plurality of being to a generic unity. First, he eliminates two senses of the term "being" as irrelevant to first philosophy. "Being" in the sense of (1) being something coincidentally is irrelevant because what something is coincidentally must escape seri-ous scientific examination.[78] And "being" in the sense (3) of being true does not belong to the province of ontology either, for being true and being false do not exist in the world: they pertain to thought.[79] As a consequence, the problem of being is primarily concerned with the second and the fourth ways of saying being, that is, with (2) being as it is divided into the categories, and with (4) being potentially and actually. Aristotle discusses categorial being in books VII and VIII of *Metaphysics*, while actuality and potentiality are dealt with in book IX. However, because act and potentiality are modes of being of the first category, substance (*ousia*), the problem of being is in fact reduced to a problem concerned with one way of saying being only: (2) being in the sense of the categories.

This first reduction of four ways of saying "being" to one, that of the categories, does not yet solve the problem of being. As soon as we focus in on the categories, we see that a new differentiation emerges, because there are ten categories. This is why Aristotle repeats the *pollachōs*-dictum in the first sentence of book VII of the *Metaphysics*. "Being" is used differently in the various categories, such as in "Socrates being a man" (category of substance), "Plato being taller than Socrates" (category of relation), or "Socrates being well trained" (category of *hexis*).[80] How, then, is a homogeneous science of being possible if being is not said homoge-neously in the categories? Clearly, a second reduction is needed. Because there is much confusion about this second reduction in the secondary literature, we must briefly pause and wonder what Aristotle means by his *pollachōs*-dictum.

In the first chapter of the *Categories*, Aristotle discusses homonymy and par-onymy as two ways in which something may be said *pollachōs*. It is important to remember that quite often Aristotle does not distinguish between talking about words, as when we say that the noun or gerund "being" is used in many ways, and talking about beings, for he in fact claims that things and not words are homonymous or paronymous.[81] Many commentators have observed that Aristotle assumes a harmony between language and reality, and that the *Categories* are about things *as* they are addressed in language. This is not as strange as it may seem. If we say that the Morning Star is identical with the Evening Star, we neither assert something about the thing as it is in itself (this would be uninforma-tive: each thing is identical with itself), nor about the names only (if so, the identity would merely express a convention about names, and not an empirical discovery): we assert something about the things *as* they are addressed by us in language.[82]

According to the *Categories*, things are homonyms if they have the same name but not the same definition. They are synonyms if they share both name and definition. Homonymous things are said *pollachōs*, synonymous things are not. Apart from homonymy, Aristotle mentions a second kind of being said *pollachōs*: paronymy. Paronymous things are addressed by the same (or nearly the same) name, and they almost share the definition, because name and definition are re-lated to one paradigmatic thing or focal entity. The best example of paronymy is health. We call food, or sports, or a way of living "healthy" because they are positively related to the health of a human being.[83]

If "being" were said synonymously, Aristotle's problem of being would not arise, for being would be a homogeneous genus. If, on the other hand, "being" were said homonymously, the problem of being would be insoluble, because the different ways of using "to be" would have nothing in common. Since it is quite clear that Aristotle considered the problem of the possibility of first philosophy as a soluble problem, he must have assumed a relation between the ways in which "being" is said in the ten categories that is both stronger than mere homonymy and weaker than synonymy. There are two interpretative hypotheses in the literature about the nature of this relation, which both seem to find support in the text of *Metaphysics*. According to some, the relation is one of analogy. Others suppose it to be a relation of paronymy. I will defend the latter alternative.[84]

It is important to distinguish clearly between analogy and paronymy, because they are often confused with each other.[85] In his retrieval of Aristotle's metaphysics, Heidegger does not even differentiate between these two relations.[86] Analogy in the usual sense of the term should also be distinguished from metaphor. In speaking metaphorically, we make use of a similarity between states or properties. We say, for instance, that someone has a *green thumb* if he is good at gardening (in producing green things). Analogy is based on a similarity between relations. We say that old age is the *autumn of life* because A (the autumn) relates to B (the year) as C (old age) to D (life). Aristotle uses analogy quite often in defining the basic concepts of his metaphysics. A piece of marble *is* a statue in the same way as a sleeping student *is* studying, namely, potentially. Similarly, a waking man relates to a sleeping man in the same way as someone who is looking relates to someone who has his eyes closed, to wit, as actuality to potentiality. Aristotle claims that it is not necessary to define explicitly the notions of actuality and potentiality. It is sufficient to grasp the stated analogies in order to grasp these notions. One might say that Aristotle defines them by analogical abstraction.[87] Analogy is a relation very different from paronymy. In the case of analogy, there are similar relations between heterogeneous terms. In the case of paronymy, however, things are called F (healthy, for instance) because they have different relations to one thing (*pros hen*) which is called F in a primary or fundamental way. Unfortunately, Aristotle uses the term "analogy" at least once for the *pros hen* relation of paronymy as well.[88]

There is no doubt that according to Aristotle there is an analogy between the ways we use "being" in the ten different categories. He says, for instance, that *being even* relates to *being a number* as *being white* relates to *being colored*.[89] Moreover, the formal axioms of the sciences apply analogically in each science.[90] It does not follow, however, that Aristotle tried to solve his problem of being by means of this type of *analogia entis*: such an attempt would have been doomed to fail from the start. In order to solve Aristotle's problem, we have to find a homogeneous genus "being" as the subject matter of first philosophy or ontology.

But the relation of analogy is a formal one only, and it cuts through genera. According to the doctrine of the analogy, we use "being" analogously in the different categories. There is an analogy of being, for instance, between *Socrates being a man* and *courage being a virtue*, because in both cases we subsume an individual under a general name. This formal analogy holds in spite of the difference between the categories substance and quality. Now we might conceive of the ten categories as highest genera: the category substance is the highest genus of all substances; the category quality the highest genus of all quality; and so on.[91] It follows that the *analogia entis* in this strict sense of "analogy" will never specify a homogeneous genus as the subject matter of first philosophy.

The situation is different in the case of paronymy, the *pros hen* relation. We may conceive of Aristotle's *Categories* in a second way: as a classification of different kinds of things we say of a concrete individual. One might speak of Socrates, for example, calling him a man (substance), saying that he is in Athens (place), or that he was living a long time ago (time). According to this latter conception of the categories, using the notion of being in all categories is related to the first category of concrete individuals. Because a concrete individual or substance such as Socrates is neither *in* something else nor said *of* something else, it *is* in the most fundamental way, and all other ways of saying "is" and talking about something are related to it as to the one, primary being. Combining this latter conception of the categories with the former conception of the categories as highest genera, we may say that the use of "being" in the categories 2–10 is paronymically related to saying "being" in one highest genus, namely, the first category of substance (*tode ti*). Aristotle endorses this solution to his problem of being explicitly in *Metaphysics* IV.2 and VII.1. Because all ways of saying "being" are related *pros hen* to one fundamental way, that of the first category, substance or *ousia* has to be the primary subject matter of first philosophy. Aristotle refers to this solution at the beginning of *Metaphysics* VIII and IX as something which by now should be clear. And he repeats it in *Metaphysics* XI.3 and XII.1.[92] We must conclude that the second reduction that Aristotle needs in order to explain how first philosophy is possible is a paronymous reduction of using "to be" in all categories to using it in the first category, that of *ousia* or substance. According to the conception of the categories as highest genera, *ousia* is a highest genus, so that ontology is possible as a science of one homogeneous genus, the genus of substance. Indeed, Aristotle's doctrine of substance is the heart of his metaphysics.

In order to complete my brief summary of Aristotle's doctrine of being, I will now discuss the problem of the so-called ontotheological unity of his metaphysics. Why does Aristotle say that first philosophy is both concerned with *ousia* and with the Deity? And what is the relation between this ontological or ousiological definition of first philosophy and its theological definition? Heidegger mistakenly claims that Aristotle never formulated this problem as such.[93] But even if he were right, this would not exempt us from the obligation of trying to reconstruct Aristotle's problem and his solution. In doing so, I will heavily rely on Routila's book.[94] According to Routila, first philosophy as ontology or ousiology reduces paronymically to theology. This is the third stage in the reduction of the differentiation of being to unity, and, like the second, it is a *pros hen* reduction. Why is this third reduction necessary? Did we not already find a homogeneous domain for first philosophy, the domain of *ousia*? Again, we must try to reconstruct Aristotle's problem before we can understand his solution. And again, the problem concerns the possibility of a science of being as such.

This time, the requirement that causes the problem is not that of generic unity. Rather, it is the requirement that scientific knowledge (*epistēmē*) should be concerned with eternal objects, a requirement that applies to metaphysics as well, because metaphysics is the highest and most fundamental kind of true knowledge. All scientists aim at universal knowledge, because universal knowledge, if true, does not become obsolete: it is applicable in all situations of the relevant kind. Plato and Aristotle erroneously assumed that universal knowledge, because it is in itself immutable, must be concerned with immutable objects, such as ideal geometric forms. Consequently, scientific knowledge is impossible unless there are immutable entities. In Plato's case, these entities are the immutable Forms, which are supposed to exist apart from temporal reality, and Plato identifies *ousia* with Form. However, the immutability requirement causes a problem for Aristotle, because Aristotle denies that the Forms exist separately, apart from spatio-temporal reality. According to Aristotle's view of *ousia* or substance, the *ousia* is typically a concrete individual entity consisting of Form and Matter, such as an individual animal, plant, or human being. But if the *ousia* is a concrete individual, which changes over time and perishes in the end, how is a science of *ousia* possible? Aristotle's conception of *ousia* seems to exclude that first philosophy as a science of *ousia* is possible, because science requires immutable objects, whereas the individual *ousia* is perishable. This, Routila suggests, was the problem that forced Aristotle to connect ousiology and theology. Why and how did he do so?

The clue to this problem is to be found in the composition of book XII of Aristotle's *Metaphysics*, the book on theology. In chapter 1, Aristotle distinguishes three kinds of substance (*ousia*): (1) sensible and perishable, (2) sensible and eternal, and (3) not sensible and eternal. Substances of the first kind, such as plants and animals, are the object of Aristotelian physics; substances of the second kind are the object of astronomy; and substance of the third kind is the object of theology. In chapters 2–5 of book XII, Aristotle discusses change and perishable objects, whereas he starts his discussion of theology in chapter 6 and discusses astronomy in chapter 8. Now Routila suggests —correctly— that the composition of book XII is explained by the hypothesis that according to Aristotle perishable substances are *pros hen* connected to the Deity in the same sense in which heavenly bodies are connected to the Deity.

In chapter 6, Aristotle proves the existence of the Deity by arguing that time is eternal (it cannot begin or stop, for in that case there would be something before or after time, and "before" and "after" presuppose time), and that according to the *Categories* time cannot exist without substance, so that there has to be an eternal substance.[95] Moreover, time is impossible without movement; hence the eternity of time requires an eternal movement, which has to be circular because space is finite. This eternal movement is the rotation of the outer heavenly sphere, the sphere of the fixed stars, and Aristotle thinks that its rotation is caused teleologically by the Deity, which he calls the unmoved mover. According to Aristotle, the cosmos is a finite spherical entity, consisting of an inner sublunary realm and fifty-six concentric rotating spherical shells, in which the heavenly bodies are fixed. The Deity causes the rotation of the outer shell directly and the other rotations indirectly. Consequently, Aristotle's astronomy and his theology are closely connected: both the rotations of the heavenly bodies and time presuppose the Deity, which provides time by inspiring movement.

Although local movements in the sublunary sphere are never infinite or circular, Aristotle nevertheless assumes some kind of eternal recurrence in the domain of perishable living beings as well. He thinks that the specific Forms of plants, animals, and man are in some sense eternal, because they are transferred eternally by procreation from one individual to another. Routila's hypothesis is that this eternal recurrence of Forms solves Aristotle's problem of the possibility of a science of the *ousia*: although individual substances are perishable, they can be known scientifically as far as the recurrent Form is concerned. Within the framework of Aristotle's philosophy, this solution would not work if the movement of eternal recurrence of Forms were not inspired by the Deity in the same way as the heavenly rotations are. Moreover, Form as an eternal substance without matter can only exist if it is perceived by the Deity, as Aristotle suggests in chapter 9 of book XII.[96] For these reasons, ontology as ousiology is related to theology: the eternal recurrence of Forms is not possible without the unmoved mover as its *telos*, and the Form as an eternal structure exists only in the mind of the Deity.

This Aristotelian doctrine of a *pros hen* relation between Deity and individual substances was modified by the Scholastics during the thirteenth century in order to fit Christian creationism. The creatures are *pros hen* related to God, because God *is* primarily and transfers *being* to the creatures in the act of creation. According to Eckhart, for instance, God has being (*esse*) in the primary sense, whereas the creatures have being only from God and in God. Eckhart concludes that to the extent that we *are* at all, our being is fundamentally God's being. Misleadingly, this idea of a paronymic relation between God and creatures has been called the doctrine of the *analogia entis*.

C. Heidegger and Aristotle on Being

Having reconstructed Aristotle's doctrine of being, I now come to my third question: Why, and to what extent, did Heidegger reject this doctrine? It is crucial to see that Heidegger could not accept Aristotle's doctrine of being because his conception of philosophy, and indeed of the question of being, were already different from Aristotle's. Admittedly, both Aristotle and Heidegger believed that (first) philosophy is the most fundamental discipline, and that it raises the question of being. They also believed that philosophy is essential to human life, because by doing philosophy we become really ourselves, either by actualizing our specific Form (Aristotle) or by grasping the possibility of authentic existence (Heidegger).

However, this formal similarity masks a fundamental difference between Aristotle's and Heidegger's conceptions of philosophy. Whereas according to Aristotle, philosophy is the science of the first principles and causes, which studies being(s) in general and provides man with a comprehensive view of the cosmos, Heidegger defines philosophy in the Natorp essay as the attempt to grasp explicitly the fundamental movement of human life. In 1922, Heidegger's question of being is primarily concerned with our own mode of being, and this is still the case in *Sein und Zeit*, even though Heidegger's formal definition of philosophy in 1927 is nearer to Aristotle's than in 1922. Moreover, whereas according to Aristotle philosophy makes man divine, because philosophy consists in the pure activity of contemplation that characterizes the Deity, Heidegger stresses in Paulinian manner that philosophy should make life more human by making it more difficult, because the human condition *is* difficult. By explicitly grasping the fundamental movement of human life, philosophy annuls the alienation that consists in our attempt to make ourselves comfortable and to flee into worldly occupations.[97]

In the Natorp essay, Heidegger stresses that philosophy should be atheistic, and I will argue in chapter 3 that *Sein und Zeit* is also atheistic in this sense. But Heidegger's atheism does not consist in the conviction that God does not exist. It rather springs from the notion that philosophy, which seeks to grasp the most authentic possibilities of human existence, should restrict itself to possibilities that are within its own power, and that theorizing about God *à la* Aristotle is a temptation that leads us astray. Heidegger says that only in this manner can philosophy stand honestly before God.[98] If Heidegger read Aristotle from the vantage point of his own notion of philosophy, we must conclude that Heidegger's question of being cannot be derived primarily from Aristotle. On the contrary, Heidegger approached Aristotle from an external, Christian point of view, and Heidegger's "destruction" of Aristotle resembles Luther's attempt to liberate the Christian experience of life from the Scholastic, Aristotelian tradition, as I will argue in section 11.

There is a similar tension between formal similarity and material divergence with regard to Aristotle's problem and doctrine of being. Both Aristotle's and Heidegger's questions of being possess two opposite poles: a pole of differentiation and a pole of unity. The task of the pole of differentiation is to explore the many different ways in which "being" is said. The pole of unity, on the other hand, consists in the attempt to relate or even to reduce these different ways to one fundamental sense of "being." The Aristotelian leitmotif in Heidegger's question of being is a meta-Aristotelian theme, because Heidegger both radicalizes the pole of differentiation and transforms the pole of unity of Aristotle's question of being. As Heidegger rejected Aristotle's doctrines concerning the differentiation and unity of being, he wanted to raise the question of being anew. I will now briefly specify what Heidegger rejected, and thereby show why, according to Heidegger, the question of being had to be raised again.

Aristotle's differentiation of the ways in which we say "being" is twofold: he first differentiates among the four ways of *Metaphysics* V.7 and then among the ten categories. Unity is restored by eliminating "being" in coincidental designations and "being" as being true, and by two *pros hen* reductions: one of the categories to the first category, *ousia*, and a second of the *ousia* to the Deity.

Heidegger's retrieval of the Aristotelian doctrine of being in the Natorp essay is based on one guiding question: How does Aristotle interpret human existence? Is Aristotle's interpretation of human life derived from a fundamental experience of life itself, or does he simply conceive of human Dasein as being an entity that belongs to a more comprehensive domain of entities? How does Aristotle conceptualize our human mode of being, and being in general?[99] This guiding question is implied by Heidegger's conception of philosophy in 1922. Moreover, it presupposes the antinaturalist assumption that if one wants to interpret human life on the basis of a fundamental experience of Dasein itself, one should not conceive of Dasein primarily as an entity belonging to a more extensive domain, for instance, the domain of all living beings.

Heidegger argues in 1922 that Aristotle's ontological concepts, such as *ousia*, *form*, *matter*, *dunamis*, *energeia*, and *entelecheia*, are drawn from the sphere of artifacts or manufactured goods. Although these notions originate in Aristotle's analysis of change (*kinēsis*) and growth in his *Physics*, their real empirical source is the structure of artifacts, which are Aristotle's typical examples where he develops his ontological concepts. When an artifact is completed, a *matter* is *formed* and an *entelecheia* has passed from *dunamis* to *energeia*. Being is being at rest, being completed, being manufactured, and being available.[100] Aristotle generalizes these concepts and applies them in his analysis of human existence in the *Nicomachean Ethics* and in *De Anima*. According to Heidegger this implies, however, that Aristotle analyzes human existence in terms that are alien to Dasein, so that Aristotelian ontology is an alienation that has to be destroyed if we want to be able to grasp the movement of our life as it really is.[101] We have seen in section 3, above, that this very same thesis informs *Sein und Zeit*.

According to section 3 of *Sein und Zeit*, there is a plurality of ontological domains or "regions." Each of these regions has its own structure of fundamental concepts. The destruction of the traditional, Aristotelian ontology purports to trace back traditional ontological concepts to their regional origin, so that both their positive meaning and their limited validity are revealed. This thesis of the regionality of being, which Heidegger inherited from Husserl and, indirectly, from Aristotle, is a radicalization of the pole of differentiation in the question of being. Instead of one system of categories for being, we now have a plurality of systems.[102] According to Heidegger, Aristotle's system of categories is rooted in the ontological domain of artifacts.[103] Instead of generalizing this system into a universal ontology, we should recognize its limits and develop other systems as well, primarily a system of existentialia that characterize our own mode of being.

Heidegger not only radicalizes the pole of differentiation in the question of being; he also transforms the pole of unity, and he does so in two ways. First, the notion of the regionality of being does not exclude, either in the Natorp essay or in *Sein und Zeit*, that there is a privileged or fundamental region, to which the other domains are *pros hen* related. In this respect, Heidegger's analysis formally resembles Aristotle's first *pros hen* reduction to the region of the *ousia*. But whereas Aristotle mistook the *ousia* for a general region, even though his analysis was inspired by the domain of artifacts, Heidegger singles out the domain of human Dasein as the fundamental ontological region to which the others are related. As he says in the Natorp essay, the analysis of factical life is *prinzipielle Ontologie*, because the specific mundane regional ontologies receive the ratio and the sense of their problems from the ontology of factical existence.[104] Clearly, Heidegger already in 1922 endorsed the thesis of the primacy of Dasein and the notion of a fundamental ontology, which stand out so prominently in *Sein und Zeit*.

This primacy of Dasein is also why Heidegger rejects Aristotle's second *pros hen* reduction, the reduction of the *ousia* to the Deity. As we saw, Heidegger repudiates Aristotle's conception of the Deity as an unmoved mover precisely because this conception was derived from the analysis of movement and was not inspired by something that is accessible in religious fundamental experience.[105] In other words, according to Heidegger the experience of human life has to be the origin of the notion of, and of our quest for, God, and not the experience of animal life and cosmic movement. The same holds for the notion of time. As in *Sein und Zeit*, Heidegger argues in the Natorp essay that only by resolutely anticipating our death can we get a clear view of human life, and that *Sein-zum-Tode* (being-toward-death) is the phenomenon that reveals the fundamental sense of time.[106] The notion of time, then, should not be derived from cosmic movement but from human existence as being-toward-death. Finally, Heidegger draws similar conclusions with regard to logic. Traditional logic mirrors traditional, Aristotelian ontology, for the subject-predicate structure is akin to the substance-property structure. Logic too has to be derived from the analysis of human existence, not from the ontology of the *ousia*.[107] The ultimate point of this Heideggerian critique of Aristotle will become clear in the course of the present book. What can be established now is merely that its source of inspiration must be external to Aristotle.

A second transformation of the pole of unity was probably developed after 1922. As we saw, Heidegger argues in the lectures on the fundamental concepts of ancient philosophy of 1926 that philosophy is the critical discipline that distinguishes between beings and being. Even though Aristotle's ontology aimed at raising the question of being, he did not succeed in doing so because he reduced the *being* of entities to yet another entity, the Deity. In other words, Aristotle did not fully acknowledge the ontological difference; he was unable to grasp the fundamental distinction between beings (entities) and being. Unfortunately, Heidegger does not explain this distinction clearly in the lectures of 1926 either, so that Heidegger's question of being remains nearly as obscure. We can only conclude that a study of Aristotle's writings does not allow us to elucidate the content of Heidegger's question of being, because this question turns out to be derived from a source external to Aristotle. There is merely a formal resemblance between Aristotle's question of being and Heidegger's question of being. Both questions are regarded as ultimate and fundamental, and both questions have a bipolar structure.

In elaborating the meta-Aristotelian leitmotif, we have discovered in passing the formal structure of the question of being as specified in section 6, above. Although Aristotle raised the question of being (1), Heidegger claims that he did not succeed in really doing so, because he reduced being to an entity, God, and because he applied alien categories to human existence. That is, Aristotle allegedly overlooked the ontological difference (4). As a consequence, he became the founding father of (3) forgetfulness of being and (5) the ontology of presence. This is why we have to destroy Aristotelian ontology (8) and raise the question of being anew (7), in order to wrest us from the oblivion of being, that is, of our own being (6). Heidegger rejects Aristotle's notion of philosophy because Aristotle betrays the fact that philosophy should be concerned with the mode of being of us humans, that is, with our understanding of our own manner of being (2). Finally, we saw that Heidegger's question of being, like Aristotle's, has two poles, a pole of differentiation and a pole of unity, and that Heidegger transforms both poles. Nevertheless, we are still groping after the content of Heidegger's question of being.

At first sight, the meta-Aristotelian theme may seem to have originated from a purely internal criticism of Aristotle, as Heidegger himself suggests in his lectures of 1926. But we have discovered that this is not true. Heidegger's conception of philosophy of 1922 as "explicitly grasping the movement of human life" is not Aristotelian, and Heidegger only in part retrieves Aristotle's own conception of philosophy, which, for that reason, he was unable to assess critically. A similar point can be made with regard to Heidegger's rejection of the Aristotelian notion of God as a prime mover. How is Heidegger able to say that this notion did not derive from a religious fundamental experience? Could it not have been the case that the Greek religious experience was partly cosmological, so that, if the Greek conception of heavenly rotations gave rise to Aristotle's notion of the Deity, one cannot conclude that this notion is areligious? Is it rash to assume that Heidegger read Aristotle's texts with a notion of religious experience in mind which was alien to Aristotle, and which he acquired during his Catholic upbringing and his studies of St. Paul, the Scholastics, Luther, and Kierkegaard? Such a hypothesis is the more probable because Heidegger argued in his lectures of the winter semester 1920–21 that the problem of characterizing the movement of factual human life was discovered by early Christianity.[108] Finally, what justifies Heidegger's critical view, developed in the lectures of 1926, that Greek philosophy did not succeed in acknowledging the ontological difference between being and beings, although acknowledging this difference would have been its internal *telos*? Should we not rather conclude that Heidegger projected the notion of an ontological difference onto the Greeks? If this was the case, what does this notion mean and where does it come from?

These questions are of crucial importance. If Heidegger read Aristotle from the point of view of a notion of philosophy and of being external to Aristotle, there must be other leitmotifs in Heidegger's question of being, apart from the meta-Aristotelian theme.[109] One of these other leitmotifs is the phenomenologico-hermeneutical theme.

§ 8. THE PHENOMENOLOGICO-HERMENEUTICAL THEME

Heidegger claimed in "Mein Weg in die Phänomenologie" that he derived his question of being from Brentano's dissertation on the manifold sense of being in Aristotle.[110] For this reason, I introduced the meta-Aristotelian theme as the first leitmotif in Heidegger's question of being. By exploring the meta-Aristotelian theme, we hoped to discover why Heidegger holds that the question of being is the most fundamental question man can raise (primacy of the question), what this question amounts to (content and structure of the question), and, finally, how it might be answered (doctrine of being).

Concerning the primacy of the question of being we were disappointed by the meta-Aristotelian leitmotif. Admittedly, Aristotle himself justifies the primacy of the question of being on the basis of his philosophy of science. The difficulty was, however, that Heidegger neither retrieved nor critically assessed Aristotle's justification for the primacy of the question of being. Although Heidegger's thought turned out to be influenced by the Aristotelian conception of scientific knowledge, Heidegger never argued explicitly for the primacy of the question of being on its basis. As a consequence, we still do not know why, according to Heidegger, the question of being is the most fundamental question man can raise.

To the extent that Heidegger develops a doctrine of being in *Sein und Zeit*, this doctrine turned out to be very different from Aristotle's doctrine. Yet we discovered a structural similarity between the two doctrines, due to the fact that both in Heidegger's and in Aristotle's question of being there are two poles: a pole of differentiation and a pole of unity. Heidegger transforms both the pole of differentiation and the pole of unity of the question of being. According to Aristotle, the notion of being is used in various ways within the system of the categories, whereas this system and its basic category of a substance would hold universally. Heidegger claims, on the contrary, that the traditional notion of a substance at best fits artifacts and occurrent things; it does not fit Dasein. In other words, according to Heidegger, "being" is not only differentiated within a system of categories. We must acknowledge different systems of categories. In particular, we must develop a proper system of categories (existentialia) in order to grasp the mode of being of Dasein.

As we will see, Heidegger's point in *Sein und Zeit* is not simply that Dasein is capable of having another range of properties, states, dispositions, or modifications than, say, artifacts such as tables or occurrent things such as stones. We will easily admit that a human being may be courageous, for instance, and that it is nonsensical to say of a stone that it is, or is not, courageous. Heidegger's point purports to be a deeper one: that what it *is* for a human being to have such a property is different from the way a stone has a property. Being courageous is a manner in which we pro-ject our Dasein into the future. Dasein can only *be* courageous because it is already concerned with itself, because its own being is an issue for it, and because it has to live out its being. The possibility of Dasein's being courageous or not courageous presupposes the entire existential and temporal structure of concern and being-with-others-in-the-world as the "condition of its possibility." Being courageous is a way of "performing" (*vollziehen*) our existence. Logically speaking, Heidegger claims that our uses of the copula "is" are not topic-neutral. When we say that Alexander is brave, the verb "is" expresses an existential project, not a state or property of a substance. In expressing an existential project, the verbal form "is" indicates the specific ontological constitution of humans, Dasein.

In view of this radical differentiation of being, we may wonder why Heidegger in his question of being assumes a pole of unity at all. Why does Heidegger postulate that there is one fundamental sense of being? Why does he not simply acknowledge multiple senses of the expressions "being" and "to be"? It is not difficult to understand why Heidegger in *Sein und Zeit* rejects the way Aristotle unified the senses of being. Aristotle reduced all senses of "being" to being as a substance, and ultimately to being as the Deity. He did so because he assumed, like Plato, that only what is immutable and eternal really *is.* In other words, Aristotle implicitly presupposed that the verb "to be" has the fundamental meaning of *always being present.* As a consequence, beings that are neither eternal nor immutable have a derived and secondary kind of being. In *Sein und Zeit*, Heidegger rejects Aristotle's doctrine of the unity of being for two reasons: (1) Aristotle did not explicitly distinguish between beings, such as the Deity, and the sense of "to be"; he did not reflect on his fundamental assumption that "being" ultimately means "being eternally present"; (2) this implicit sense of "to be" does not suit at all the way Dasein is, for Dasein is in the manner of finite temporality.[111] Projecting its finite possibilities, Dasein is always ahead of itself, anticipating its death. Accordingly, in order to understand the sense of being-there (Da-sein), we must explicitly reflect on the temporal structure of our existence. Finite temporality is the horizon of understanding our own being, and, indeed, the horizon of our being itself. But again, why does Heidegger not infer from his rejection of Aristotle's unification of being that there simply is no pole of unity in the question of being? How does he justify the first main thesis of *Sein und Zeit*, that finite temporality is not only the horizon of understanding being as Dasein, but also of understanding being *tout court* (cf. § 3, above)? Why should there "be" something like a unitary being *(Sein)*? The meta-Aristotelian theme does not provide an answer to this question.

Unfortunately, it does not provide a clear solution to the problems of interpretation I stated in section 4 either. Why does Heidegger assume, for instance, that the question of being is concerned both with the meanings of the verb "to be" and with the sense *(Sinn)* of certain phenomena (§ 4.1)?[112] What does he mean by the transcendence of being (§ 4.2)? How does Heidegger conceive of the relation between being and beings, and why do we find contradictory statements on this relation in his works (§ 4.3)? What conception of language enables Heidegger to claim that we do not really understand the meaning of the verb "to be," even though we are able to use this verb correctly and explain its uses to others (§ 4.4)? Why does Heidegger not endorse Husserl's distinction between formal-ontological categories and material categories (§ 4.5)? And finally, how should we understand the problem of the primacy of Dasein in *Sein und Zeit* (§ 4.6)?

In the present section, I argue that the problems of sections 4.1–4.5 may be solved at least in part by introducing a second leitmotif, the phenomenologico-hermeneutical theme. This theme will be developed in three stages. As Heidegger says in his autobiographical essay "Mein Weg in die Phänomenologie" (1963), Husserl's *Logische Untersuchungen* played a decisive role in elaborating the question of being. By investigating (A) what exactly this role may have been, we will be able to solve the problems of sections 4.1 and 4.4. The solution to these problems will raise (B) the question I elucidated in section 4.5: Why did Heidegger not endorse Husserl's distinction between formal and material categories? Since Heidegger nowhere argues against this distinction in a clear manner, I will offer a somewhat speculative answer to this question, an answer that also explains in part why Heidegger could not accept the "authority" of formal logic (see § 2, above). Finally, (C) we have to understand why Heidegger transformed Husserl's notion of phenomenology in section 7 of *Sein und Zeit*, and why, according to Heidegger, phenomenology has to be "hermeneutical." This will solve the problems of sections 4.2 and 4.3. We will see that there is a tension in *Sein und Zeit* between the phenomenological and the hermeneutical aspect of the phenomenologico-hermeneutical leitmotif.

A. *The Principle of Referentiality*

As I argued in section 4.1, Heidegger introduces the question of being in *Sein und Zeit* both as a question concerned with the meaning(s) of the verb "to be" and as a question concerned with a phenomenon called being *(das Sein)*. According to section 7 of *Sein und Zeit*, being is indeed the *phenomenon par excellence*.[113] This duality in Heidegger's formulations cannot be due to careless writing. A charitable interpreter of *Sein und Zeit* should assume that the duality is intentional. Only by taking seriously Heidegger's text in this manner will we be able to raise a productive problem of interpretation: how to explain the fact that for Heidegger the question as to the meaning(s) of the verb "to be" coincides with a question concerning the sense (*Sinn*) of a phenomenon, the phenomenon of being. I will argue that this coincidence is not accidental. On the contrary, it is due to a specific theory of language, which Heidegger never states, a theory of language he inherited from Husserl.[114] This theory explains why Heidegger thought that the question concerning the meaning(s) of "to be" may be answered by the phenomenological method. In order to substantiate my interpretation, I first summarize what Heidegger says about the question of being taken as a question regarding the meaning(s) of the verb "to be," and I stress that at first sight what he says is not at all plausible. Next, Heidegger's pronouncements about Husserl's influence on his thought will be considered, and we will see that they point the way to the view on the workings of language that Heidegger presupposes in his question of being.

In *Sein und Zeit*, Heidegger suggests that the question of being is concerned with all uses of the verb "to be" and its gerund "being." He quotes uses as a connecting verb, such as in "The sky *is* blue" and "I *am* merry" (p. 4), and he lists some uses of "to be" that traditional philosophy distinguished, such as existence, predication, being in the sense of reality, being present, continued existence, being valid, being there (*Dasein*), and the expression "there is . . . " (*es gibt*). He stresses that we might call "being" everything we talk about, everything we have in view, and everything toward which we comport ourselves in any way.[115] Heidegger explicitly acknowledges the pole of differentiation in the question about the meanings of "to be." As he says, we use "being" in many different senses.

If the question of being is really concerned with the meanings of the verb "to be" and its inflections, we may wonder why Heidegger did not resort to the works of linguists and logicians in order to answer his question. Linguists will distinguish various uses of "to be," like the uses as an auxiliary verb or as a connecting verb, which show in the structure of sentences. They will note that the German verb *sein* lacks some of the uses of "to be," such as in forming the continuous tenses of verbs ("I am writing"—"Ich schreibe") or in expressing what must or must not happen ("You are not to smoke in this room"—"Sie müssen nicht rauchen in diesem Zimmer"). Logicians, on the contrary, are neither concerned with the grammatical structure of sentences nor with the particular features of specific languages. They will take the logical powers of propositions as a criterion for distinguishing senses of "to be." First, they will differentiate between uses of "to be" as a logical word, on the one hand, and nonlogical uses on the other hand, as in "a human being." Next, various logical uses, such as existence ("There is a queen of The Netherlands"), class membership ("Louis is bald"), class inclusion ("The dog is a mammal"), and identity ("The Morning Star is the Evening Star"), are distinguished, and their interrelations are analyzed.

In Heidegger's oeuvre, we find neither extensive linguistic analyses of the uses of "to be," nor interesting logical discoveries, although Heidegger did study what traditional logicians had to say on the matter.[116] He thought, apparently, that neither linguistics nor logic is qualified to answer the question of being, and that the correct approach is *phenomenological*. Why did he think so? Heidegger made at least three important assumptions concerning the question of "being," that is, the question of being taken as a question regarding the meanings of "to be," and these assumptions will point the way to understanding the rationale of Heidegger's phenomenological approach.

First, Heidegger assumes that if "being" is used in many ways, there must be a "leading fundamental meaning" of "to be." He even tends to identify his question of being with what I called the pole of unity. Recall, for instance, the way Heidegger expresses the question of being in "Mein Weg in die Phänomenologie" (1963): "if being [*das Seiende*] is said in multiple meanings, what, then, is the leading fundamental meaning? What does to be mean?"[117] Linguists and analytical philosophers will retort that there need not be one fundamental meaning of "to be," from which the other meanings are derived. Words may be simply ambiguous, or there might be a family of interrelated meanings, no one of which is more "fundamental" than the others. One of Heidegger's pupils, Karl-Otto Apel, once argued that the logical uses of "to be," existence, predication, and identity, have one common root of meaning, but his arguments are fallacious.[118] Instead of postulating an underlying unity that would explain the diverse uses of "to be," we should rather make a survey of the ways in which the verb is actually used. This is not at all the manner in which Heidegger proceeds. What, we may wonder again, justifies Heidegger's assumption that there must be one fundamental meaning of "to be"? Why does his question of being have a pole of unity?

Second, Heidegger assumes that in order to elucidate the meanings of "to be," we must not only analyze these meanings: we should also and primarily analyze the "things themselves." As he says in section 20 of *Sein und Zeit*, where he discusses the traditional notion of being as a substance: "Behind this slight difference of meaning . . . there lies hidden a failure to master the basic problem of being. To treat this adequately, we must 'track down' the equivocations *in the right way*. He who attempts this sort of thing does not just 'busy himself' with 'merely verbal meanings'; he must venture forward into the most primordial problematic of the 'things themselves' to get 'nuances' straightened out."[119] Why should we study "things themselves" in order to analyze the equivocations of words such as "to be"? The expression "things themselves" is an implicit reference to Husserl, for Husserl used the slogan "back to the things themselves" as the slogan of phenomenology, meaning that we should carefully describe the way in which things appear to us in mental acts instead of formulating speculative theories about the relation between consciousness and world. Why, then, does an analysis of the meanings of "to be" require a phenomenology of things themselves, and what are these "things"?

Finally, in section 4.4, above, I have already commented on Heidegger's surprising statement in section 1.3 of *Sein und Zeit* concerning the fact that in ordinary language our uses of "to be" are mostly unproblematic. As Heidegger says, the expression is intelligible "without further ado." We are able to use the verb "to be," and, if we have some training in logic and grammar, we are able to explain its diverse uses to others. Surely this is what knowing the meaning of a word consists in. Why, then, raise the question concerning the meanings of the verb "to be" at all? Heidegger apodictically replies: "But this average kind of intelligibility only demonstrates that it is unintelligible."[120] Apparently, he assumes that there must be a level of understanding the meaning of "to be" which is deeper than ordinary linguistic competence, so that we may be fully competent in our uses and elucidations of the verb "to be" without really understanding its meaning.

According to my interpretative hypothesis, these three surprising assumptions concerning the question about the meanings of "to be" are due largely to Husserl's influence on Heidegger. What was this influence, and how does it explain Heidegger's three assumptions?

Let me begin by reviewing Heidegger's own statements on the manner in which Husserl's philosophy helped him develop the question of being. In "Mein Weg in die Phänomenologie," Heidegger is relatively clear about Husserl's importance.[121] He describes the birth of the question of being as the fruit of a combined reading of Aristotle, triggered by Brentano's dissertation, and of Husserl. Because Heidegger knew that Husserl's way of thinking had been decisively influenced by Brentano, Husserl's *Logische Untersuchungen* (*Logical Investigations*) was lying on his desk from his first semester in theology in 1909–10 on. Heidegger hoped to receive from *Logische Untersuchungen* an important stimulus for resolving the question suggested by Brentano's dissertation: "If being is used in diverse senses, what is the leading and fundamental meaning?"

Heidegger seems to have been so deeply fascinated by Husserl's book that he read and re-read it without coming to understand the source of his fascination. "The spell emanating from this work spread out over its external aspect, its typography and its title page," he remembers in 1963.[122] Indeed, Heidegger's way to phenomenology seems to have been paved with the *Logische Untersuchungen*. According to "Mein Weg in die Phänomenologie," Heidegger plunged into the recesses of the *Investigations* at least four times, in 1909, in 1911–12, after 1913, and again in 1919. Which aspect of Husserl's book turned out to be crucial for developing Heidegger's question of being? Heidegger is clear on this point:

When, from 1919 on, I began to practice the phenomenological manner of seeing, teaching, and learning in proximity to Husserl, and at the same time tried out in the seminar a modified approach to Aristotle, my interest was once again drawn toward *Logische Untersuchungen*, especially the first edition of the sixth investigation. The distinction worked out there between sensible and categorial intuition revealed itself to me in all its importance for the determination of the "manifold meaning of being."[123]

What Heidegger says here is corroborated by many other texts. For instance, during the seminar at Zähringen, held in 1973, Heidegger said that "in order to be able to unfold the question concerning the meaning of being, being had to be given, so that one could inquire its meaning from it." Husserl's achievement allegedly consisted in showing that being, as a category, is phenomenally present. Because of this discovery, Heidegger "finally gained ground": being turned out to be "not a mere concept, not a pure abstraction."[124] In his important lectures of 1925 on the history of the concept of time, which contain an early version of *Sein und Zeit* preceded by an extensive critical survey of Husserl's phenomenology, Heidegger also stressed the "decisive importance" of the discovery of categorial intuition in Husserl's sixth investigation: "by means of the discovery of the categorial intuition one has gained for the first time the concrete method of a disclosing and real investigation of the categories."[125] We may conclude that it was Husserl's doctrine of categorial intuition as developed in his sixth logical investigation, which meant a breakthrough in the development of Heidegger's question of being. As Heidegger says, this doctrine provides the "concrete method" for an investigation of the categories. We know that Heidegger's method for resolving the question of being was phenomenological. What, then, is Husserl's doctrine of categorial intuition? Why does it imply that the problem of being has to be resolved by the phenomenological method?

Husserl's doctrine of categorial intuition is a corollary of the theory of meaning stated in the first of his *Logical Investigations*. Husserl would never have developed the doctrine of categorial intuition, had he not endorsed a fairly traditional principle in the theory of meaning, which I will call the principle of referentiality.[126] According to Husserl's first investigation, linguistic signs have two aspects: their physical aspect (sounds, marks in ink) and their meaning. The main task of a philosophical theory of meaning is to make clear what the meaning of expressions consists in. Assuming the dualistic framework of the Cartesian tradition, Husserl argues from the fact that the meaning of a sign is not a physical property to the conclusion that meaning must be mental. The meaning of an expression in its concrete use allegedly consists in (an ingredient of) a special mental act, a "meaning-intention" (*Bedeutungsintention*), and the expression expresses this very intention. However, Husserl develops this traditional view in two ways. First, he carefully distinguishes between meaning as a token and meaning as a type. Whereas the former consists in an ingredient or aspect of a mental act, which exists in time, the latter is an "ideal species" or Platonic form of such an ingredient or aspect, which exists separately in a timeless realm. Husserl holds that formal logic is about meanings and propositions in a timeless sense, and this doctrine enables him to avoid psychologism in logic.[127] Second, Husserl is much more sophisticated than, say, the British empiricists, in determining precisely in what kind of mental acts meaning consists. He distinguishes between "signitive" and "intuitive" mental acts, and holds that acts of meaning are not intuitive (such as mental images, for instance), but signitive: these acts are essentially mental acts of interpreting signs and cannot exist without a "signitive content." John Searle's theories of meaning and intentionality may be regarded as grandchildren of Husserl's views.

Two aspects of Husserl's theory of meaning are especially relevant for the theory of categorial intuition. Because Husserl defines the notion of a mental act by means of the notion of intentionality or object-directedness, he assumes that signitive acts not only provide signs with meanings but also with references. As he says in section 15.2 of the first investigation, "In the meaning the relation to the object is constituted. Therefore, to use an expression meaningfully and to refer to the object by means of the expression (to represent the object) are one and the same thing, irrespectively of whether the object exists."[128] As Husserl says that each meaningful part of speech (morpheme) counts as an expression, it follows that all morphemes are referential: we cannot use them meaningfully without referring to something.[129] This principle, according to which there is no meaning without reference, is what I call the principle of referentiality.[130]

The principle of referentiality is narrowly related to the second aspect of Husserl's theory of meaning, which I want to stress. If all meaning is referential, it seems natural to assume that perceptual acquaintance with the referent of an expression will show us what the meaning of the expression is. Husserl indeed endorses such a principle of acquaintance. He holds that meaning-intentions may be satisfied ("fulfilled") by intuitive mental acts, such as perceptions, reflections, or acts of the imagination, and that the process of fulfillment will clarify the relevant meanings. Somewhat misleadingly, he calls this process the analysis of the origins (*Ursprünge*) of meaning.[131] We will see presently why Husserl's principles of referentiality and of acquaintance compelled him to invent the doctrine of categorial intuition.

In *Logische Untersuchungen*, Husserl not only wanted to develop a coherent nonpsychologistic philosophy of logic; he also wanted to elucidate the basic concepts of logic. He conceived of logic as an axiomatic-deductive system, consisting of logical truths.[132] Whereas the truths of the theorems could be proved by deducing them from the axioms, a task that Husserl delegated to the mathematician, the truth of the axioms, being analytical, should be established by elucidating the relevant concepts, and Husserl held that this was a job for the philosopher of logic.[133] In the introduction to volume 2 of *Logische Untersuchungen*, Husserl calls it the "great task of restoring the logical ideas, that is, the concepts and laws, to their epistemological clarity and distinctness."[134] Logical concepts may be divided into two classes: concepts of the second order (concepts of concepts) such as "proposition," "concept," "meaning," "knowledge," and "truth" on the one hand, and concepts of logical constants or logical forms such as conjunction, disjunction, and implication on the other hand.[135]

Husserl's sixth investigation is especially concerned with the notions of knowledge and truth, and with the logical constants. In its first division, Husserl analyzes knowledge as the fulfillment of signitive acts (meaning-intentions) by intuitive acts. When we perceive what we at first only thought to be the case, our thought is verified by perception. Self-evidence consists in the awareness of such a verification, that is, in the fact that we explicitly identify what we perceive *as* the very thing which we merely meant before. Husserl rejects the empiricist notion that self-evidence is a feeling of being convinced, because this notion leads to skepticism. The concept of truth is defined primarily as the identity between what we meant and what is really given in perception, and truth is experienced in the act of verification. In a derived sense, the perceived object may be called "true" to the extent that it satisfies a judgment, and the judgment may be called "true" if it can be verified.[136] Perceptions may be more or less adequate, and Husserl distinguishes many degrees of evidence, degrees that point to the ideal of absolute adequacy, where the perceptual act as it were wholly includes the perceived object.

Because Husserl takes "being" and "to be" as logical constants or meaning-forms (*Bedeutungsformen*), we now have to turn to the second division of the sixth investigation, which is concerned with logical form, to see how according to Husserl these forms may be elucidated and "fulfilled." Husserl's principle of referentiality implies what I have called elsewhere an atomized correspondence theory of truth.[137] As each meaningful part of language allegedly owes its meaning to an intentional mental act that refers to something, the complex referent of a true statement must contain a specific partial referent or objective counterpart for each meaningful expression, and the latter may be said to be true of the former. Moreover, Husserl endorses the traditional distinction between complex expressions, which can be defined verbally, and simple expressions, which cannot. Like the British empiricists, he assumes that all simple meaningful expressions must be elucidated on the basis of perception, reflection, or some other kind of intuition. This is precisely what the principle of acquaintance says. Combining the principles of referentiality and of acquaintance, we come to the conclusion that according to Husserl, each simple meaningful expression must have a possible referent of which it is true, and that we have to perceive or otherwise intuit the referent in order to elucidate the meaning of the expression.

These assumptions explain the way in which Husserl stages the problem of logical form in chapter 6 of the sixth investigation. We agree, he says, that we are able to verify the statement "this paper is white" by looking at this paper. But what do we have to perceive in order to verify the statement? Surely, we perceive visually the paper and its white surface. However, Husserl's atomized theory of truth requires that there must also be objective counterparts to the expressions "this" and "is." His problem is, of course, that there are no such counterparts that are possible objects of sense perception or reflection on mental phenomena.

Husserl does not conclude, as Wittgenstein did in the *Tractatus*, that the principle of referentiality must be rejected for logical form.[138] On the contrary, he claims that the simple model of a name and its bearer holds for language in general, and that this model must be the "guiding thought" for resolving the problem of logical form.[139] If, as Husserl stresses, there is neither a material nor a mental referent for the expression "is," there must be a nonmaterial and a nonmental referent. And if we cannot perceive this referent by sense perception or reflection, there must be a third kind of perception that enables us to perceive the *is* itself. Husserl calls this third kind of perception *categorial perception*, and the perceived forms *categorial objects*. The categorial, then, is the formal, and it does not belong to reality defined as what is a possible object of sensation or reflection. Apart from real elements, such as paper and its whiteness, the state of affairs that this paper is white also contains irreal, formal, or categorial elements, such as the *is*, which may be perceived by categorial perception. If we are acquainted with the *is* by means of categorial perception, we will be able to elucidate the meaning of the word "is." This is part of what the philosophy of logic should do.

Without going deeper into the subtleties of Husserl's theory of categorial intuition, we are now able to see why Heidegger could think that this theory was of crucial importance for his question of being. Indeed, Husserl's theory of categorial intuition explains to a large extent the three assumptions of Heidegger's question of "being" that I discussed above. It entirely explains Heidegger's second assumption, the assumption that in order to elucidate the meanings of "to be," we have to analyze not only the uses of words but also a phenomenon, the phenomenon of being. This solves the problem of interpretation I raised in section 4.1, above. The theory of categorial intuition partly explains Heidegger's third assumption, the assumption that we may not really know the meanings of "to be" even though we are able to use this verb correctly. For if it is supposed that really knowing the meaning of a word involves acquaintance with its referent and identifying it as such, we might perhaps use a word correctly without really knowing its meaning, that is, without being acquainted with its referent. In most cases, Husserl would deem this improbable, as improbable as it is that we always correctly use the word "red" without being able to identify some red object *as* red. But Heidegger added to Husserl's principle of acquaintance a theory of tradition which, I suggest, he derived from the theology of revelation (see § 11). As is clear from section 6 of *Sein und Zeit*, Heidegger thought that the acquaintance with the referents of crucial philosophical terms such as "being" may have been an event in the distant past, an event that has long since been forgotten. Because we go on using these terms without renewing the acquaintance with their referents, our "average intelligibility" of these terms merely demonstrates "that they are unintelligible." In our ordinary uses of "to be" we supposedly do not really know what we are talking about because we are not acquainted with the phenomenon of being. Finally, Husserl's theory of categorial intuition is also a possible, though not at all sufficient, condition for understanding Heidegger's postulate that there must be one fundamental meaning of "being." For it could be that the verb "to be," in all its diverse uses, finally refers us back to one unique phenomenon of being. However, there is nothing in Husserl that would justify this assumption of unity, so that we are still far removed from understanding the pole of unity in Heidegger's question of being.

I conclude that Husserl's theory of categorial intuition fully explains why Heidegger thought that the question of being, interpreted as a question concerning the meanings of the verb "to be," should be answered by the phenomenological method and not by mere linguistic or logical analysis. Meanings of "to be" have to be elucidated by analyzing the phenomenon or the phenomena of being. Yet the Husserlian background leaves many aspects of Heidegger's question of being unexplained, in particular, its pole of unification. It equally leaves unexplained Heidegger's obsession with the verb "to be." For according to Husserl, "being" is only one of many logical forms. From a logical point of view, there is no reason why we should concentrate on "being" only, and not also raise the question as to the meanings of "or," "and," "all," "some," "not," "if . . . then," and so on. Although Heidegger developed a view on negation, as we saw in section 2, he wholly neglected the other logical constants such as "or," "if . . . then,", and "and."

Moreover, my interpretation raises a number of new questions. First, we might ask the critical question as to whether Husserl's theory of categorial perception is not a philosophical delusion, produced by his mistaken principle of referentiality, as I will indeed argue in chapter 4 (§ 17B). Such a criticism, if valid, has devastating consequences for Heidegger's idea that the question of being can be concerned both with the verb "to be" as we use it in ordinary language and with specific phenomena, at least to the extent that this idea is based on Husserlian assumptions. Second, my exegesis raises at least two problems of interpretation. (1) Husserl thought that the categorial phenomenon of copulative being is an aspect or dependent part of a state of affairs, the state of affairs that *a is F*. But Heidegger seems to think that we may discern the phenomenon of being in all beings, not only in states of affairs but also in Dasein, for instance. What explains this extraordinary generalization of Husserl's notion of the categorial? Furthermore, (2) Husserl in the sixth investigation sharply distinguishes between the formal or the categorial on the one hand, and the material on the other hand. One and the same matter, belonging to mental or physical reality, may be categorially formed in many ways. For instance, "This paper is white" and "this white paper" are two different categorial formings of one and the same matter.[140] Even though Husserl changes his terminology in the first book of the *Ideen* of 1913, where he uses the term "category" also for the highest concepts of material regions, he maintains his sharp distinction between the formal and the material. Material categories such as "spatial shape" or "sensuous quality" belong to material or regional ontologies, whereas formal categories such as "something" or "being" belong to formal ontology.[141] We do not find this crucial distinction between the formal and the material in *Sein und Zeit*. Instead, we come across another distinction, the distinction between phenomena in the "vulgar" sense, by which Heidegger means empirical phenomena, and the "phenomenological" phenomenon of being.[142] The latter cannot be Husserl's formal category of being, because this category is the same in all ontological regions, whereas Heidegger claims that "being" has different senses in the different ontological regions. Obviously, Heidegger rejects Husserl's distinction between the formal and the material, between formal ontology and regional ontologies, as I already noted in section 4.5, above. Why does he do so? In the next subsection I will try to answer these two interpretative questions.

B. Formal Ontology and Formal Indication

Let me begin with problem (1)—why Heidegger thought that the phenomenon of being is inherent in all entities. At first sight, this is a drastic departure from Husserl's view on the categorial. I stressed that Husserl in sections 60–62 of his sixth logical investigation sharply distinguishes between the categorial or the formal, and the material or the sensuous. Sensuous concepts such as "color," "house," "judgment," or "wish" are derived from the data of sensation or reflection, whereas categorial concepts such as "unity," "plurality," "relation," and "conjunction" are derived from categorial intuition. Husserl's empiricist principle of acquaintance implies that differences in origin must correspond to differences in concepts or meanings. He also acknowledges mixed concepts, which have both a sensuous and a categorial origin, such as "being-colored," but he denies that all concepts are mixed. He stresses, for instance, that copulative being is an aspect of states of affairs only.[143] Clearly, then, Heidegger's thesis that being as a categorial phenomenon is present in *all* entities contradicts Husserl's theory, and we may wonder what justifies Heidegger's departure from Husserl's views.[144]

However, if we analyze the text of Husserl's *Logische Untersuchungen* more closely, we will see that Heidegger's thesis about the omnipresence of being is implied by what Husserl says in one, somewhat isolated, passage in section 40 of the sixth investigation. As we have seen, Husserl defines the categorial as the formal, and opposes it to matter in the sense of each possible object of sensation or reflection. Accordingly, in order to circumscribe the domain of the categorial, Husserl delimits those elements of language that do not refer to possible objects of sensation or reflection. In "This paper is white," for instance, "this" and "is" do not refer to such objects. Husserl goes on to claim that even an expression such as "white paper" implies a reference to a categorial form, because it means "paper *being* white." Then follows a revealing passage, which contradicts what Husserl says in sections 60–62:

> And does not the same form repeat itself also in the noun "paper," although in an even more concealed manner? Only the meanings of words for properties, which are united in the concept of paper, are fulfilled in sensation. Yet the whole object is recognized as

paper. Here also we have a completing form, which contains being, although being is not the only form.[145]

According to this text, nouns such as "paper" express categorially mixed concepts, whereas in section 60 Husserl says that the noun "house" expresses a purely sensuous concept. There clearly is a contradiction between section 40 and section 60.[146] However, the passage of section 40 is the more sophisticated one, and it is not difficult to see what Husserl means when we take into account his empiricist background. Husserl seems to assume that paper is a substance with a number of perceptible characteristics. The experiential origin of the concepts of these characteristics lies in sense perception or sensation. But how can sensation be the origin of the notion of a *substance* or a *thing that has* these characteristics? In other words, each noun that refers to a concrete particular implicitly contains the categorial notion of "being" (of an x *being* F, G, H . . .), so that each concrete entity also contains being itself, in the double sense of a *being* or entity *being* F, G, H . . . This, I suppose, is also Heidegger's view, and in his lectures of 1925 on the history of the concept of time he repeatedly stresses that a categorial intuition is implied in each and every experience.[147] As Husserl says, being is "concealed" in all particulars, and this is one possible explanation of why Heidegger claims, in section 7C of *Sein und Zeit*, that the being of beings, which is the phenomenon that his phenomenology purports to investigate, "lies *hidden*" and "shows itself only *in disguise*."[148] Moreover, because the phenomenon of being is not present in sensation, it must have been added by the intentional mental act. Hence an "understanding of being" must be implicit in each and every *intentio*. We may conclude that Heidegger was justified in considering his thesis of the onmipresence of being as an interpretation of Husserl's doctrine of the categorial, and our first problem of interpretation arose because Husserl contradicts himself. Incidentally, Heidegger never realized that in proclaiming the ubiquity of being in this manner, he was implicitly endorsing Husserl's empiricist, Lockean assumptions.

I now turn to problem (2), which I raised in section 4.5. One might say that Husserl had already answered the question of being by his conception of formal ontology. Categorial or formal concepts such as "being" or "entity" should be strictly distinguished from material concepts such as Dasein in the sense of human existence, or "spatial form." Whereas the latter are the products of a generalizing abstraction, the former arise by formalization, and we may use them in the same sense for entities of all material regions of being. This is why formal ontology and formal logic apply universally, and why universal logical laws are very different from universal material statements. Because "being" is a formal category, Heidegger should have turned to formal logic and to formal ontology in order to answer his question of being, so Husserl might have thought. As Husserl conceived of formal logic and ontology as being topic-neutral, he would have deemed it a serious mistake that Heidegger wanted to solve the problem of being primarily by means of an analysis of human existence, that is, by elaborating a specific regional ontology. Why, then, did Heidegger not endorse Husserl's distinction between formal ontology and material ontologies as a basis for elaborating his question of being?

My solution to this problem is somewhat hypothetical, because, as far as I know, there is no explicit attempt in Heidegger's own published writings to criticize Husserl's distinction.[149] The only elaborate critical discussion of Husserl's notion of formal ontology is to be found in Heidegger's lectures of November 1920. The original manuscript of these lectures seems to be lost. Although we know about their contents from the edition in *Gesamtausgabe* volume 60, which has been established on the basis of lecture notes made by Oskar Becker and others, we do not know enough to resolve this problem with certainty. According to Kisiel, Heidegger's methodological considerations in these lectures are "abstruse," and the notion of a *formale Anzeige* (formal indication), which Heidegger develops as an alternative to Husserl's notion of formal ontology, is "ever more esoteric."[150] Finally, the lectures were broken off at a crucial point on 30 November 1920, probably as a result of student complaints to the dean of the philosophical faculty about the lack of religious content in a course on the philosophy of religion.[151] As a result, we will have to resolve our problem of interpretation by a hypothesis developed on the basis of the Husserlian background, the lecture courses of 1920 and 1925, and of *Sein und Zeit*.

I suggest that Heidegger rejected Husserl's notion of a formal ontology as an answer to the question of being for two reasons. First, while he derived from Husserl's sixth investigation the thesis that being as a categorial aspect is present in all particulars, he rejected the notion that "being" as a category is topic-neutral. As I argued in the introduction to this section, Heidegger held that what it is for an x to *be* F is different in the different material regions. The way in which a particular Dasein *is* courageous is different from the way in which a stone *is* heavy, and this difference is due to a difference between the respective "modes of being" or ontological constitutions of Dasein and a stone.[152] Only because Dasein has the ontological constitution of future-directed concern can it be brave or cowardly. Now Husserl uses in *Ideen* I the expression "mode of being" (*Seinsweise*) in order to characterize the differences between material regions. He says, for instance, that consciousness has a different mode of being from material objects. But he distinguishes sharply between these regional modes of being on the one hand, and being in the formal sense on the other hand. If, however, being in the formal-categorial sense is not topic-neutral, this distinction is illegitimate. The formal category of being would in fact be determined by material, regional categories, that is, by specific modes of being in the material sense. Indeed, Heidegger argued already in the Natorp essay of 1922 that the traditional category of substance had been derived from a particular ontological region, the region of artifacts.

Heidegger's rejection of the formal-material distinction has drastic consequences for the status of formal logic. If formal categories are materially condi-
tioned, one might either conclude that although logic applies to (statements about)
all regions of being, it only applies analogously. There would be differences of
sense between the logical operators from region to region. It has been argued by
the later Wittgenstein, for instance, that the universal quantifier is not topic-neutral. We may analyze "all countries of the world" as a logical product, but not
"all real numbers." However, Heidegger's thesis would be more specific and more
problematic: he supposedly holds that the formal categories have different meanings relative to the respective material regions in which they are applied. For
example, the copula "is" would have a different meaning if used in the domain
of history from the meaning in which it is used in biology. This is not a very
plausible thesis.[153] Or, alternatively, one might conclude that formal logic does
not apply to all regions. There is a tendency in Heidegger's writings to suggest
that formal logic is related to traditional ontology. Indeed, traditional Aristotelian
logic, which conceives of propositions as having a subject-predicate structure,
mirrors the ontology of substances and attributes.[154] If the traditional ontology of
presence is due to the falling of Dasein and does not apply to it, as Heidegger
argues in *Sein und Zeit*, this would hold for logic as well.[155] (In § 17B of chapter
4, I will critically assess these claims, which constitute one of the possible explanations for Heidegger's rejection of logic in *Was ist Metaphysik?* of 1929.)

The second reason why Heidegger rejected Husserlian formal ontology stems
from a very different source. Thus far, I have traced the influence of Husserl's
theory of categorial intuition on Heidegger's question of being, taking Heidegger's own statements about this influence as a lead. To this end, I began by con-
struing the question of being as a question concerned with the meaning of the
verb "to be." We have seen why Heidegger assumes that we have to analyze a
phenomenon of being in order to elucidate the meaning of "to be," and also why
Heidegger drops Husserl's distinction between the formal and the material. In this
manner, we may try to understand that Heidegger's question of being seems to
be concerned both with a material region such as Dasein and with formal categories. In his lectures of 1920, however, Heidegger entirely rejects Husserl's program of a formal ontology. He does so on the basis of a definition of philosophy
that has no relation whatsoever to Husserl's theory of categorial intuition.

In 1920, Heidegger defines philosophy as the attempt to come to terms with
factical life experience. Philosophy springs from life experience and then jumps
right back into life experience again.[156] This definition prefigures the one of the
Natorp essay of 1922, that philosophy is the attempt to grasp explicitly the way
we "perform" (*vollziehen*) life, in order to intensify life itself. It is still echoed in
section 7C of *Sein und Zeit*, where Heidegger says that philosophy "takes its
departure from the hermeneutic of Dasein, which . . . has made fast the guiding-
line for all philosophical inquiry at the point where it *arises* and to which it
returns."[157] Because the aim of philosophy in this sense is to intensify life, and

especially to deepen our sense of "falling," the philosophical attitude is very different from the theoretical attitude. Instead of aiming at a rigorous science, as Husserl did, philosophy in Heidegger's sense (1920) should reject all theoretical and scientific enterprises as dangerous temptations: it should try to be pretheoretical, and it should destroy all theoretical objectivations.[158]

Traditional philosophy, when it wanted to conceptualize how we experience ourselves in factical life, tended to assume some theoretical concept of the mental, such as soul, stream of mental acts, or transcendental consciousness. According to Heidegger these concepts alienate us from our life experience. They are an expression of a tendency of factical life to lapse (*abfallen*) toward objective determinations, a tendency that philosophy indulged in from Plato on.[159] Heidegger wanted to revolutionize philosophy in order to liberate it from the danger of secularization into science or into a doctrine of worldviews.[160] Because he claims that the categories of formal ontology entirely belong to the domain of the theoretical, Heidegger in 1920 squarely rejects Husserl's project of a formal ontology.[161]

If we compare this second reason for rejecting the project of a formal ontology with the first, we may be tempted to conclude that we have exhausted the possibilities of a rational reconstruction of Heidegger's philosophy on this point. It seems that there is an unbridgeable gap between Heidegger's question of being as influenced by the doctrine of categorial intuition, and Heidegger's question of being as the attempt to grasp explicitly, and to intensify, the movement of our life. Whereas the first aims at a theoretical elucidation of meanings, the second is fiercely antitheoretical. And whereas the first is primarily concerned with the meanings of logical words, the second is concerned with the significance of human existence. Because these two entirely different "questions of being" both enter into "the" question of being in *Sein und Zeit*, it seems to follow that this book is a patchwork of incompatible elements, and that Heidegger's question of being is a hollow formula that covers a number of disparate philosophical problems and programs.

Yet it is rash to take recourse to the patchwork interpretation even at this point. One of the reasons why Heidegger may be considered as a "great" philosopher is that he was able to meld many disparate elements into a unified whole. There is indeed a unifying link between the theoretical program of elucidating logical categories and the antitheoretical attempt to grasp the movement of human life, an attempt that derives from Kierkegaard, Dilthey, and the Christian tradition rather than from Husserl's philosophy as a rigorous science. This link is forged from Husserl's idea, already present in section 65 of his *Prolegomena*, that in order to understand the conditions of possibility of the sciences, we should distinguish between subjective conditions, pertaining to the knowing subject, and objective conditions, pertaining to logical form.[162] Whereas Husserl stressed the objective conditions in *Prolegomena*, his attention shifted to the subjective conditions already in the second volume of *Logische Untersuchungen*. In his later phenomenology, Husserl held that in order to understand science philosophically, we should not primarily consider it as a system of propositions, but rather study the way in which its objects and propositions are "constituted" in our subjective conscious activities.

Heidegger echoes this Husserlian conception when he says in his lectures of November 1920 that the sciences can no longer be regarded as objective formations of sense or ordered constellations of true propositions. They too must now be grasped concretely "in act," realizing themselves practically, developing historically, and actively assuming the "finished" shapes out of factical life experience.[163] Likewise, Heidegger argues in *Sein und Zeit* that in order to establish the meaning (*Sinn*) of science (*Wissenschaft*), we have to conceive of science as an activity of Dasein and not as a system of propositions. Science, he claims, has the mode of being of Dasein, and further on in *Sein und Zeit* science turns out to belong to a special modification of Dasein called its falling (*Verfallen*).[164] Elucidating logical categories and grasping pretheoretical life, then, are linked together because constituting logical forms is an activity in life, and because we should understand this activity in order to elucidate the categories, at least according to Husserl's later conception of phenomenology. But in Heidegger's view, the link between life and logic is degrading rather than fruitful. Heidegger argued in 1920 that logical categories are correlates of a specific attitude (*Einstellung*), the theoretical attitude, and that this attitude precludes an understanding of life as it really is. For this reason, a phenomenology of human life should eliminate the theoretical attitude by what Heidegger calls a *formale Anzeige* (formal indication).[165]

This notion of a formal indication replaces in Heidegger's early works the Husserlian notion of a formal ontology. However, its sense is a totally different one. In his lectures of November 1920, Heidegger tried to pull off the difficult feat of developing his notion of a formal indication on the basis of Husserl's conception of formal ontology.[166] Whereas he pretends to "develop" (*weiterbilden*) Husserl's notions of formalization and of a formal ontology, in fact he repudiates them radically. To the extent that Heidegger's argument on this point is clear at all, it may be reconstructed as follows. According to Husserl, material categories that belong to a regional ontology refer to specific "material" features of entities. Formal categories such as "object," "relation," or "property," however, cannot refer to specific material features of entities, because they apply to all entities whatsoever. Heidegger concludes that formal categories must express a way in which human beings *relate* to entities, and that they spring from the *sense* of the attitude that we adopt vis-à-vis entities.[167] But what is the "sense" of the attitude in which we predicate formal categories of entities? Heidegger claims that this attitude is the "theoretical" attitude and that the theoretical attitude conceals the way in which human beings relate to the world in the most fundamental manner.[168] It follows that phenomenology, which wants to study the way in which human beings relate to the world, must reject Husserlian formal ontology. Phenomenology, especially the phenomenology of religion, should not adopt the theoretical attitude at all. On the contrary, it should *preclude* that phenomena are envisaged in the theoretical attitude. To prevent this attitude is the very function of what Heidegger calls "formal indication."[169] Clearly, in this expression Heidegger uses the word "formal" in a sense that is radically different from Husserl's.[170] He has only a weak justification for using it. Because formal categories express the theoretical *manner of relating* to entities instead of capturing features of entities, we might "formalize" on a deeper level by leaving even our manner of relating to entities *undetermined*. This is what we do when we envisage phenomena by means of "formal indications."[171] Heidegger's "development" of Husserl's notion of a formal ontology leads him to a position that is diametrically opposed to Husserl's. Instead of Husserl's program of phenomenology as a rigorous science, Heidegger now calls for a phenomenology that essentially adopts an antiscientific attitude. (We will discover the ultimate rationale for this Heideggerian revolution in phenomenology later on, in §§ 12C and 13C, below.)

C. Phenomenology and Hermeneutics

It seems, then, that there are two different reasons why Heidegger claims that his question of being is to be answered by phenomenology. First, in order to elucidate the meanings of "to be," we must study the phenomenon or phenomena of being. This claim is rooted in Husserl's theory of categorial intuition. Second, to the extent that the question of being is concerned with human being, that is, with the ontological constitution of our own factical life, we have to use the phenomenological method as specified by Heidegger's notion of a formal indication (*formale Anzeige*). Interpreting the concepts that we use in reflecting on our factical life as "formal indications," we will ward off scientific conceptions of life, which conceal life as it really is and which belong to the falling of Dasein.[172] But even though we understand why, according to Heidegger, the question of being has to be answered by phenomenology, we do not yet know what phenomenology is. As Heidegger took his conception of phenomenology primarily from Husserl, I will now turn to Husserl's notion of phenomenology as it developed from *Logische Untersuchungen* (1901) to *Ideen I* (1913), and try to explain briefly how and why Heidegger transformed this notion in section 7 of *Sein und Zeit*.

In 1901, when he published the first edition of the second volume of *Logische Untersuchungen*, Husserl identified phenomenology with descriptive psychology.[173] This definition has a history, which goes back to Locke's and Hume's attempt to establish psychology as a complementary science to Newton's mechanics; the notion of descriptive psychology came from Franz Brentano, who had been deeply influenced by the British empiricists. Brentano distinguished between descriptive psychology, which should scrupulously describe and conceptualize mental phenomena, and genetic or explanatory psychology, which should causally explain these phenomena. Because Brentano thought that the origin of mathematical and logical concepts lies in mental operations, he conceived of descriptive psychology as the philosophical basis of the a priori sciences, a conception Husserl still adhered to in *Philosophie der Arithmetik* (*Philosophy of Arithmetic*, 1891). According to this early version of Husserl's principle of acquaintance, describing the relevant mental operations elucidates the fundamental concepts of logic and arithmetic, and thereby establishes the fundamental analytical laws of these sciences.

Although this conception of phenomenology both as descriptive psychology and as the philosophical basis of the a priori sciences is still present in the introduction to volume 2 of the 1900–1901 edition of *Logische Untersuchungen*,[174] Husserl in fact undermines it in the second part of the sixth investigation. In sections 44–51 of the sixth investigation he forcefully argues, as we have seen, that the experiential "origin" of the fundamental concepts of logic does not lie in reflection on mental operations, but in categorial intuition of objective categorial aspects of states of affairs. The concept of number, for instance, cannot have the same origin as the concept of counting. The origin of the first is categorial, whereas the origin of the second is mental. The conception of categorial intuition, then, landed Husserl in a dilemma: either phenomenology grounds logic and mathematics, but then it cannot be identical with descriptive psychology, or phenomenology is descriptive psychology, but then it cannot ground logic and mathematics. Husserl chose the first horn of this dilemma, and launched a series of transformations of his conception of phenomenology, which resulted in the doctrine expressed in *Ideen* I of 1913.

Apart from the notion of categorial intuition, there was a second motive for transforming the concept of phenomenology, which I will call the Cartesian or epistemological motive. Husserl held, as Brentano did, that our own mental life is present with absolute certainty in reflection, or inner perception as he called it, whereas physical reality can never be given in perception with this degree of certainty. Furthermore, he conceived of epistemology as the fundamental philosophical discipline that has to solve the problem of the external world. In doing so, epistemology should draw its concepts from the sphere of the apodictically given only, that is, from the sphere of consciousness. This is why in the introduction to volume 2 of *Logische Untersuchungen* (1901), Husserl accepts the following equations: epistemology = (part of) descriptive psychology = phenomenology.

As I have explained elsewhere at great length, Husserl came to reject the equation phenomenology = descriptive psychology, while maintaining the equation epistemology = phenomenology.[175] In 1903, he acknowledged that the notion of psychology involves claims that transcend the sphere of apodictically given consciousness, because psychology purports to investigate conscious phenomena that belong to human beings and causally depend on human organisms. Furthermore, in 1907 he claimed that the objective correlates of mental acts as such, which he later called *noemata*, belong to the sphere of the apodictically given, hence phenomenology should study the *correlation* between conscious mental acts and their intentional correlates as such. And in 1913 he finally argued that studying the way in which these intentional correlates are "constituted" in mental acts is equivalent to an elucidation of the ontological status of whatever exists, because the world is nothing but an intentional correlate of consciousness, whereas the latter exists in itself as a transcendental substance. Such is Husserl's doctrine of transcendental idealism. In *Ideen* I, phenomenology is defined as a transcendental science of consciousness and its intentional correlates.

Husserl's mature conception of phenomenology is characterized by four elements: (1) phenomenology is a purely descriptive discipline, which avoids all theorizing; (2) phenomenological description of the way in which entities are "given to" or "constituted in" transcendental consciousness is equivalent to an ontological elucidation of their mode of being (*Seinsweise, Seinssinn*), because (3) the "being" of entities is identical with their being constituted in transcendental consciousness. Finally, (4) transcendental phenomenology is possible as an "eidetic" discipline, which consists of synthetic a priori propositions about essential structures. Clearly, each of these four tenets is problematic. The principle of description (1) presupposes that theory-free description is possible. The idea of a phenomenological ontology (2) assumes that the manner of being of entities or their ontological constitution is identical to the manner in which they appear to us, and this, in its turn, presupposes Husserl's transcendental idealism (3), that is, the view that the world, and all entities other than transcendental consciousness, are ontologically dependent on transcendental consciousness because they are constituted by it.[176] Element (4), finally, will be rejected by the great majority of modern philosophers, for they repudiate the notion of a synthetic a priori discipline.

In section 7 of *Sein und Zeit*, where he elucidates his notion of phenomenology, Heidegger at first endorses (1), (2), and (4), whereas he rejects Husserl's transcendental idealism (3). Heidegger thought, correctly, that transcendental idealism was nothing but yet another solution to the problem of the external world. Husserl's solution, although different from Berkeley's and Kant's, strikingly resembles these traditional idealisms. According to Husserl, worldly entities are correlates of transcendental consciousness, and they are ontologically dependent on it. Transcendental consciousness, on the other hand, is a substance in the traditional sense that it does not need anything else in order to exist.[177] As we have seen in section 3, above, Heidegger officially rejected the Cartesian epistemological tradition of which Husserl's transcendental idealism was a final offspring. Heidegger objects to Husserl's argument for transcendental idealism that it does not at all start with a reflection on the way we experience ourselves in ordinary life, as Husserl claims.[178] By using the traditional notions of consciousness, material object, and substance, Husserl infected his analysis with concepts that do not derive from pretheoretical human experience, but from a scientific conception of the world that goes back to Descartes and, ultimately, to Aristotle.[179] This criticism by Heidegger resembles what Gilbert Ryle argues in *The Concept of Mind*, and perhaps it is not far-fetched to assume that Ryle borrowed his criticisms of Cartesian dualism in part from *Sein und Zeit*, a book that he reviewed in 1929, and transposed them from a phenomenological to a linguistic level. Our life, as we experience it in the very movement of living, is Dasein or the whole person, and not a substance called consciousness mysteriously linked to a body.

Heidegger's diagnosis and rejection of transcendental idealism, according to which the very start of Husserl's argument for idealism was already misconceived because Husserl misunderstood the manner of being of us, humans, can be seen as a radicalization of Husserl's principle of theory-free description (1). It also explains to some extent that the phenomenological ontology of Dasein assumes such a central role in *Sein und Zeit*. Finally, although Heidegger does not explicitly criticize transcendental idealism in section 7 of *Sein und Zeit*, it explains the first of two fundamental changes that Heidegger made in Husserl's conception of phenomenology.

Whereas phenomenology in Husserl's sense had to study the correlation between beings in their constitution of being and transcendental consciousness, Heidegger drops the idea of transcendental consciousness. Having distinguished several notions of a phenomenon in section 7A, such as appearance and symptom, he argues that the most fundamental notion of a phenomenon is "that which shows itself in itself" (*das sich-an-ihm-selbst-zeigende*). He goes on to argue in section 7B that the most fundamental meaning of *logos* or *legein* in Greek is "to show something as it is." Hence phenomenology means "to let that which shows itself be seen from itself in the very way in which it shows itself from itself" (§ 7C).[180] This, however, is only a "formal" notion of phenomenology, which characterizes its method but says nothing about its subject matter. The latter is specified by Heidegger's distinction between "vulgar" or empirical phenomena, which are studied and explained by the empirical sciences, and the phenomenological phenomenon of being (*das Sein*). Phenomenology studies being (*das Sein*), not beings (*das Seiende*).[181]

In a great number of passages of *Sein und Zeit*, being is conceived of as the manner of being or ontological constitution (*Seinsweise*) of specific kinds of beings, such as Dasein, artifacts, natural phenomena, mathematical objects, and so on.[182] According to this conception, which I will call Heidegger's phenomenological notion of being, phenomenology has to elucidate and conceptualize the ontological constitution (*Seinsweise*) of the various types of being ("regions") by pretheoretically describing these modes of being (1). Phenomenology in this sense is ontology, as Husserl already held (2), and it analyzes essential structures, not bare facts (4).[183] Because Heidegger holds that each region or kind of being has a specific ontological constitution, the phenomenological notion of being implies that there must be a number of different regional ontologies, as Heidegger stresses in section 3 of *Sein und Zeit*. He also argues, as we saw, that one of these regional ontologies, that of Dasein, is more fundamental than the others (§ 4 of *Sein und Zeit*). This thesis of the primacy of Dasein implies a second fundamental change with respect to Husserl's conception of phenomenology, which occurs quite suddenly, at the end of section 7C of *Sein und Zeit*.

There Heidegger claims that Dasein is disclosed to itself primarily because it *understands* its own being (*Seinsverständnis*). In section 3, above, I explained that for Heidegger the most fundamental mode of understanding ourselves is a pretheoretical know-how-to-live, and this consists in projecting concrete possibilities of existence. Making explicit such a self-understanding, and ontologically elucidating its structures, is not description in Husserl's sense, but interpretation (*Auslegung*). As we saw in section 5, above, Heidegger claims that interpretation has the same projective structure as understanding (*Verstehen*), so that the ultimate sense which an interpretation reveals is a "that-toward-which" (*Woraufhin*) of a project. Consequently, Heidegger's ontology of Dasein turned out to depend on a specific ontic ideal, an ideal of authentic existence. The second fundamental change in Husserl's conception of phenomenology is, then, that according to Heidegger phenomenology must be interpretative or hermeneutical. As Heidegger says, the phenomenology of Dasein is hermeneutics.[184]

The phenomenologico-hermeneutical leitmotif implies a particular way of understanding the formal structure of Heidegger's question of being, as specified at the end of section 6, above. This structure has nine elements, which take the following semantic contents within the framework of the phenomenologico-hermeneutical theme. (1) The question of being is concerned with the ontological constitution of regional beings, such as nature, space, life, Dasein, language, and the like. Heidegger presupposes, like Husserl, that the totality of what there is may be carved up neatly into ontological regions. He also believes, in contradistinction to Husserl, that formal categories are bound to regions. An analysis of a mode of being pertaining to such a region yields a regional ontology. In order to distinguish them from formal logic and from philosophy of science, Heidegger calls such regional ontologies "productive logics."[185] (2) We have an implicit understanding of our own regional being (*Seinsverständnis*), and, indeed, of the being of other regions. (3) If, however, we live in forgetfulness of being, this is because we conceive of our own mode of being on the traditional model of things or artifacts (the ontology of presence [5]), and because, in general, we conceive of the being of all beings in terms of this particular ontological model. Forgetfulness of being (*Seinsvergessenheit*) means, then, that we overlook the categorial differences among the various ontological regions, and that we misconceive our own mode of being. (4) This is because we do not observe the ontological difference (*ontologische Differenz*), that is, the difference between beings and their respective modes of being. Forgetfulness of being may be abolished, however, by (7) explicitly raising the question as to the different modes of being and by (8) showing that the fundamental concepts of traditional ontology were derived from one ontological region only and illegitimately applied to the other regions. In this manner, (9) Dasein will be able to construct an adequate ontology of itself, and to distinguish the ontology of Dasein clearly from other regional ontologies. By doing so, Dasein will finally understand itself as it really is and become authentic.

In elaborating the phenomenologico-hermeneutical theme, most of the problems of section 4 were solved. Since Heidegger implicitly endorsed Husserl's principle of referentiality, he thought that the meanings of the verb "to be" should be analyzed by studying phenomena of being, using the phenomenological method (§ 4.1). If Heidegger calls being "transcendent," he might mean that the mode of being of an entity is not one of its properties and that being in the sense of an ontological constitution is different from beings (§ 4.2). As a consequence, the relation between being and beings is such that there is no being without beings: being is the mode of being, or ontological constitution, of a being (§ 4.3). Furthermore, Heidegger's principle of acquaintance implies that we might be able to use the words "being" and "to be" even though we do not know their real meaning, because we do not pay heed to the phenomena of being (§ 4.4). Finally, I suggested that Heidegger rejects Husserl's distinction between the material and the formal, and between regional ontologies and formal ontology, because he believed that logical form is not topic-neutral (§ 4.5).

Not all problems of interpretation are solved by the phenomenological leitmotif, however, and new problems emerged. Apart from problems of interpretation, we should consider an intrinsic problem in the method of *Sein und Zeit*, which is due to a tension within the phenomenologico-hermeneutical theme. This tension may be brought out in two ways. First, Husserl claimed that phenomenology is a theory-free description of phenomena, and that the concepts which phenomenology uses are derived from the phenomena themselves. According to Heidegger's notion of hermeneutics, however, interpretation has a projective nature, and the concepts it uses derive their meaning from the ultimate sense or direction of a project. How, then, can a philosophical investigation be both phenomenological and hermeneutical? The very coinage "phenomenologico-hermeneutical" seems to imply a contradiction. Husserl's method of theory-free description rests on the so-called principle of presuppositionlessness, according to which only the phenomena themselves should justify our descriptions. Heidegger's notion of a hermeneutical circle is incompatible with Husserl's principle, as I argued in section 5. The difficulty is that Heidegger often uses Husserl's rhetoric of objectivity, of things themselves, of phenomena that show themselves, and of phenomenology as the method of letting us see beings as they are, but that his conception of hermeneutics and of the hermeneutical circle undermines the justification for using this rhetoric.

Second, Husserl conceived of phenomenology as an eidetic science, which is able to yield synthetic a priori descriptions of essential structures. These essential structures were assumed to be ahistorical. On the other hand, interpretation, as Heidegger conceives it, is radically historical. We start our interpretations always in a historically determined situation, and as we saw in section 5, above, Heidegger tends to deny that we are able to transcend the limitations of this situation in interpreting expressions of life of another epoch. Again, we see in *Sein und Zeit* that Heidegger goes on using the rhetoric of essential structures. He claims in

section 5, for instance, that the ontology of Dasein analyzes "not just any accidental structures, but essential ones which, in every mode of being that factical Dasein
may possess, persist as determinative for the character of its being."[186] How is
Heidegger able to justify this essentialist claim, if he holds that phenomenology
is hermeneutical and that hermeneutics is historical?[187] Although Heidegger nowhere in *Sein und Zeit* specifies the extension of the notion of Dasein, it seems
that the book purports to provide an ontology of adult human existence that holds
for all times and all places. Such an essentialist claim is undermined by what
Heidegger says about the historical nature of interpretation. In short, *Sein und
Zeit* seems to be caught in a contradiction between Husserlian essentialism and
historical relativism *à la* Dilthey. It has been argued that Heidegger solved this
problem by considering historicity itself as an essential structure of Dasein. We
will see in section 10, below, that this solution was adopted in *Sein und Zeit* but
rejected later.

§ 9. The Transcendental Theme

Do we get an adequate interpretation of the question of being as it unfolds in
Sein und Zeit if we add the phenomenologico-hermeneutical theme to the meta-
Aristotelian leitmotif? The answer must be negative. Although many points of
interpretation have been clarified, other issues remain obscure. Let me mention
three unresolved problems in particular.

A first problem concerns the primacy of the question of being. Admittedly, the
phenomenological interpretation of being as the mode of being or ontological
constitution of specific regional entities sheds some light on the primacy of Heidegger's question. The question of being in this sense is fundamental because
Heidegger conceives of regional ontologies as "productive logics," which "run
ahead of the positive sciences," disclosing the ontological structure of regional
entities in an a priori manner.[188] However, as there are many regional ontologies,
the phenomenological notion of being merely explains the primacy of the question
of being in the sense of its pole of differentiation. Heidegger claims in section 3
of *Sein und Zeit* that differentiation of being presupposes unity. Accordingly, the
question as to the unity of being would be even more fundamental. Why is this
the case?

Second, it is problematical why there must be a pole of unity in the question
of being at all. If Heidegger rejects Husserl's notion of a formal ontology, should
he not conclude that the plurality of regional ontologies is irreducible? For what
reasons does Heidegger hold that there is one fundamental meaning of "to be"
from which the other meanings are derived? In other words, why does he presuppose that the phenomenological analysis of the various regions of being needs a
fundamental sense of being and a fundamental ontology in which this sense is
investigated? Could we not say that "being" in *Sein und Zeit* just means regional

constitution of being (*Seinsweise*), and then add that there are as many ontological constitutions as there are ontological regions? Heidegger seems to claim that the regions are unified in a more substantial way, because they are founded upon a fundamental ontology, but it is neither very clear why this ontology is needed nor what it embraces.

Third, the issue of the primacy of Dasein (see § 4.6, above) has not been settled. We saw that Heidegger in 1920 and in 1922 defines philosophy as an attempt to grasp the dynamics of human existence, so that in philosophy Dasein would be primary by definition. But in his lectures of the summer terms of 1926 and of 1927 he defines philosophy as the "critical" discipline that distinguishes between beings (*Seiendes*) and being (*Sein*). According to this latter definition, which is also that of *Sein und Zeit*, being (*Sein*) is the theme of philosophy.[189] It is from the point of view of the second definition that the problem of the primacy of Dasein has to be raised: If *being* is the theme of philosophy, why should the disclosure of being take its departure from one regional ontology, the ontology of Dasein, as Heidegger unconvincingly argues in sections 2 and 4 of *Sein und Zeit*? Correlatively, why should Dasein's finite temporality be the horizon not only of understanding Dasein's mode of being, but also of understanding other regions of being, and, indeed, of understanding being *tout court*? Furthermore, why does the hermeneutical nature of the phenomenology of Dasein imply that *all* phenomenology is hermeneutical? In other words, why does Heidegger say that the ontology of Dasein is *fundamental* ontology?[190]

These problems may be solved by introducing a third fundamental structure or leitmotif into Heidegger's question of being, which I will call the transcendental theme. Heidegger amply uses the jargon of transcendental philosophy, and there can be no doubt that there are transcendental arguments in *Sein und Zeit*.[191] Heidegger explicitly draws parallelisms between his question of being and the Kantian question concerning the conditions of the possibility of experience. In section 7A of *Sein und Zeit* he says that Kantian space and time as forms of intuition are instances of the phenomenon of being. Empirical phenomena allegedly presuppose the phenomenon of being, because the latter shows itself unthematically prior to the former.[192] And according to section 31, it is not accidental that the question about X's *being* aims at "conditions of its possibility."[193] We might conclude that *being* in one of Heidegger's senses is the totality of transcendental structures that condition the possibility that specific beings become manifest to us.

Transcendental arguments proceed in two stages. First, it is argued that some set of "subjective" conditions is necessary for *experiencing* entities, or for some other kind of intentional behavior vis-à-vis entities. Second, one argues that these very same conditions specify the necessary conditions that these entities must satisfy in order to *be*, in the sense of being accessible to us.[194] If we identify Heideggerian understanding of being (*Seinsverständnis*) with the set of conditions for experiencing entities, and Heideggerian being (*Sein*) with the set of conditions for entities being accessible to us, we get the following interpretation of the question of being in *Sein und Zeit*. In order to answer the question of being, we first have to interpret our implicit understanding of being, for doing this is the first stage of the transcendental argument of *Sein und Zeit*. Analyzing our understanding of being means analyzing the temporal existential structure of Dasein, because Dasein is characterized by understanding (*Verstehen*). The first stage in Heidegger's transcendental argument explains, then, why an analysis of Dasein is primary in developing the question of being.

Within this first stage, there are a number of more specific transcendental arguments. Heidegger contends, for instance, that a "scientific" encounter of entities as meaningless multiplicities of objects presupposes a more fundamental "practical" involvement with the world as a meaningful structure, within which we meet our fellow humans, manipulate tools and equipment, and construct our lives. This practical involvement, in its turn, presupposes the existential structure of understanding as pro-jecting, which is one aspect of the complex existential structure of concern or care (*Sorge*). The reason is that understanding something as a tool presupposes a framework of means-end relations, future-directed human projects, and a horizon of human institutions and standardized social roles. At a still deeper level, the future-directed and finite time structure of Dasein is the condition of the possibility of understanding as projecting. This time structure allegedly is "the" ultimate condition of the possibility of understanding being (*Seinsverständnis*), not only of understanding our own being, but of understanding the mode of being of other entities as well.

According to the second stage of Heidegger's transcendental argument, *Seinsverständnis*, which is the condition that enables us to experience entities, is identical to, or at least equivalent to, *Sein*, which enables entities to *be*. Being is simply *what* we understand in understanding being, and it is *as* we understand it. This implies that the time-structure of Dasein is also the ultimate condition of the possibility of being. Heidegger expresses the second stage of his argument in sections 43c and 44c of *Sein und Zeit*, where he says that "only as long as Dasein, the ontical possibility of understanding of being, is, 'there is' being"; that "Being—not entities—is something which 'there is' only in so far as truth is," and that "truth *is* only in so far and as long as Dasein is."[195] Heidegger interprets truth in its most fundamental sense as being-uncovering or being-disclosing, as the fundamental disclosure (*Lichtung*) that Dasein is in relation to itself, to others, and to worldly entities. Clearly, the thesis that "there is" being only in so far as, and as long as, there is Dasein's fundamental disclosure is nothing but the second stage of a transcendental argument.

The transcendental interpretation of the question of being in *Sein und Zeit* not only explains the primacy of Dasein. It also explains why the ontology of Dasein is a fundamental ontology rather than a regional ontology of human life. *Da-sein* is the fundamental disclosure of beings, the condition of the possibility that beings manifest themselves. Although Heidegger claims that only humans have or are

Dasein in this sense, it is misleading, at least from the transcendental point of view, that he sometimes identifies the ontology of Dasein with the ontology of human life.[196] The ontology of Dasein is transcendental philosophy, an ontological analysis of the transcendental structure *in* human beings. As Heidegger explains in *Kant und das Problem der Metaphysik*, fundamental ontology should not be confused with philosophical anthropology, and in this book of 1929 he consistently speaks of Dasein *in* man.[197] Furthermore, the transcendental interpretation shows why and how there can be a pole of unity in Heidegger's question of being, because regional ontologies are rooted in Dasein's understanding of the mode of being of regional entities, so that the fundamental ontology of Dasein is the pole of unity. Both the question regarding time and the question concerning hermeneutics are answered by the transcendental interpretation. As in Kant and Husserl, transcendental time is the horizon of understanding being in general. And since the conditions of understanding being (*Seinsverständnis*) are the conditions of being (*Sein*), the hermeneutical phenomenology of Dasein "becomes a 'hermeneutic' in the sense of working out the conditions on which the possibility of any ontological investigation depends."[198] Finally, the transcendental interpretation explains the primacy of the question of being itself: this question is even more fundamental than regional ontologies, because it is concerned with the conditions of the possibility of these ontologies. It is the most fundamental philosophical question man can ask.

One cannot doubt, then, that the transcendental interpretation is a correct exegesis of Heidegger's question of being in *Sein und Zeit*, or, more precisely, of one strand in this question. The interpretation is corroborated by *Kant und das Problem der Metaphysik* of 1929, which covers the same grounds as the unpublished first division of the "destructive" second part of *Sein und Zeit*.[199] In this book, Heidegger interprets Kant's first *Critique* from the point of view of human finiteness. *Sein und Zeit* is staged as a "retrieval" (*Wiederholung*) of Kant's transcendental problem. Kant was the first who conceived of the question of being, raised in Antiquity, as a question about "the inner possibility of understanding being."[200] Heidegger tries to show that in exploring this inner possibility, Kant shrinks back or withdraws (*zurückweichen*) when confronted with its deepest root or source, transcendental imagination and its time structure.[201] As Heidegger says in *Sein und Zeit*, Kant failed to provide a proper ontology of Dasein, because he took over Descartes' ontological position, according to which the subject is an eternal substance.[202] The retrieval of Kant's transcendental problem has the task of showing that Kant's analysis, which starts with human finiteness, points to the transcendental phenomenon of finite time or temporality. In Heidegger's hands, Kant's transcendental imagination becomes Dasein's projective understanding, which is rooted in future-directed finite time as being-toward-death.

In spite of its overwhelming plausibility, the transcendental interpretation of *Sein und Zeit* as a retrieval of Kant's problem is also problematical. According to Heidegger, a "retrieval" of a traditional philosophical problem is not merely an attempt to obtain historical knowledge. Rather, it is an endeavor to grasp the inner dynamics of the problem, to open up its future possibilities, and to transform the problem in a fruitful way.[203] We saw that in the case of Aristotle, Heidegger interpreted Aristotle's question of being within the *fore-structure* of a notion of philosophy that is alien to Aristotle, and that he did not succeed either in elucidating Aristotle's own problem of being or in retrieving Aristotle's reasons for the primacy of the question of being. By analogy, we expect that there may be many different reconstructions of the inner dynamics of Kant's transcendental problem, and that Heidegger's reconstruction is perhaps not the most adequate one from a historical point of view. In the preface to the fourth edition of his book on Kant (1973), Heidegger with rare candor admits the biased nature of his interpretation. He says that the question of being as raised in *Sein und Zeit* functioned as a *Vorgriff* (fore-conception) for the attempted interpretation of Kant.[204] He concludes that "Kant's text became a refuge for seeking in Kant an advocate of the question of being as raised by me."[205] Not very much is gained, then, in stating that *Sein und Zeit* is a treatise in transcendental philosophy.[206] It is crucial to develop the transcendental leitmotif, and to discern how Heidegger's retrieval of Kant's transcendental problem is related to a purely historical reconstruction of the problem. Only in this manner might one succeed in specifying the precise sense in which the question of being in *Sein und Zeit* is "transcendental."

I develop the transcendental theme in three stages. First (A), we may wonder what makes Heidegger's transcendental turn necessary. In Kant's case, the transcendental turn or Copernican revolution was necessitated by the problem of the possibility of synthetic a priori propositions. Heidegger in his book on Kant plays down the importance of this problem. What justifies the Copernican revolution in Heidegger's case?

Second (B), we may be puzzled about the possibility of Heidegger's transcendental turn. In the philosophy of Kant, the transcendental turn was possible only because Kant assumed, in line with the theories of perception of Descartes and the empiricists, that in perception a manifold of sensations is given, which is then synthesized by operations of the mind, especially of the *sensus communis* and the imagination. Moreover, Kant's transcendental turn was inextricably bound up with transcendental idealism. This holds for Husserl's transcendental turn as well, albeit in a somewhat different manner.[207] In *Sein und Zeit*, Heidegger rejects both the traditional sense-datum theories of perception and transcendental idealism. How is his transcendental turn possible, if he repudiates the notion of perception, which was a necessary condition for its possibility in Kant's and Husserl's case? What does Heidegger's transcendentalism mean, if he rejects transcendental idealism?

According to Kant's celebrated definition of transcendental philosophy, transcendental knowledge is not concerned with objects, but with the manner in which we are able to obtain a priori knowledge of objects.[208] This definition fits in well with the transcendental interpretation of *Sein und Zeit*: being (*Sein*) in Heidegger's sense is a priori because in understanding being (*Seinsverständnis*) a specific sense of being, such as being-available as equipment or being-occurrent, is projected by Dasein as a global framework, without which entities cannot manifest themselves to us. Heidegger calls the projective understanding of a sense of being by Dasein the *transcendence* of Dasein, both because Dasein transcends itself by projecting a sense of being and because such a global framework transcends individual entities.[209] In the latter sense, the world as a meaningful global framework in which we live and act is also called transcendent.[210]

We should carefully distinguish this Heideggerian notion of transcendence both from Kant's notion of the transcendental and from the official sense in which Kant understood the term "transcendent" in opposition to "immanent." According to Kant's definitions, something is transcendent if it is beyond any possible experience, whereas things within the domain of possible experience, including the a priori structure of this domain, are called immanent.[211] Accordingly, Kant distinguishes between immanent metaphysics, which is the synthetic a priori ontology of the phenomenal world, and transcendent metaphysics, which is concerned with God, the immortal soul, and the cosmos as creation. His transcendental turn implies that immanent metaphysics is possible as a science, whereas transcendent metaphysics is not. Kant's definitions do not entirely cohere with Heidegger's. Heidegger calls the world as a global meaningful structure "transcendent"; Kant would have called it "immanent," although it transcends the experience of individual entities.[212] In spite of these terminological differences, Heidegger's views may be called transcendental in a Kantian sense.

My third problem (C) is concerned with the possible senses of Heidegger's expression "the transcendence of being." I raised this problem in section 4.2 of the first chapter. According to the transcendental interpretation as developed up to this point, being is "transcendent" because it is a global meaningful framework or horizon whose a priori projection by Dasein's understanding of being is a condition for the possibility of entities showing up for us. Is this the only sense in which Heidegger calls being "transcendent"? In section 7C of *Sein und Zeit*, Heidegger says that being is the *transcendens pure and simple*."[213] What does he mean by "pure and simple" (*schlechthin*)? Moreover, in the last section of *Sein und Zeit*, Heidegger claims that the fundamental-ontological analysis of Dasein and its temporal structure is merely *a way*, and that the ultimate destination or objective of this way is to work out the question of being as such.[214] This seems to be surprising from the point of view of the transcendental interpretation: If the sense of being is identical to what is projectively understood by Dasein as the sense of being, why does something remain to be "worked out" in the question of being once the transcendental analysis of Dasein and its understanding of being has been completed? Should one conclude that the expression "transcendence of being" has yet another sense than the transcendental one? Does section 83 of *Sein und Zeit* transcend the limitations of the transcendental interpretation?

A. Why Is Heidegger's Transcendental Turn Necessary?

Concerning the necessity of the transcendental turn, there is not much room for interpretation in Kant's case. In the first *Critique*, Kant explains clearly why he claims that the transcendental or Copernican revolution is justified. In the introduction to the *Critique* Kant raises a problem, and in the body of the book he argues that the Copernican revolution is the only possible solution to this problem. I will summarize Kant's justification for his transcendental turn, then discuss the question as to whether Heidegger in his interpretation of Kant "retrieved" Kant's justification, and finally make a guess about Heidegger's own reasons for his transcendental turn in *Sein und Zeit*.

Kant's problem has three parts. It is primarily concerned with the possibility of metaphysics as a science (*Wissenschaft*). Although we are naturally inclined to raise metaphysical questions, it had become doubtful in Kant's time whether a scientific answer to these questions was possible. Because metaphysics was conceived of as a nonempirical informative science, it would consist mainly of so-called synthetic a priori propositions, that is, propositions that are both necessarily true or independent of experience (a priori), and which cannot be discovered to be true by mere conceptual and logical analysis (synthetic). This is why the problem of whether metaphysics is possible reduces to the question as to whether metaphysical synthetic a priori propositions can be known to be true. Kant's strategy for investigating this question depended on his philosophy of science. For he assumed that we in fact know that specific synthetic a priori propositions are true both in mathematics and in Newtonian physics. On the basis of this assumption, he could raise two other questions that were also part of his problem: How are synthetic a priori propositions possible in mathematics? And how are they possible in physics? Kant answered the question of whether metaphysics is possible by first investigating how synthetic a priori propositions in mathematics and physics are possible.

In the body of the first *Critique*, he argues that mathematics is possible in an a priori manner, that is, without having recourse to experience, because the structures that mathematics explores are inherent in the knowing subject. Kant takes for granted that these structures are absolute space and absolute time in Newton's sense, and he concludes that space and time are subjective "forms of intuition," which may not belong to the world as it is in itself. Similarly, the fundamental principles of Newtonian physics, such as the deterministic law of causality, are argued to be known a priori because categories such as causality are part of the workings of the knowing subject. The categories and forms of intuition are subjectively necessary in that we cannot think and form representations unless we do so in terms of the categories and in the forms of space and time. Here we recognize the first stage in Kant's transcendental argument. But if space, time, and causality are subjective in this sense, how can the a priori propositions of mathematics and of physics be (known to be) true of the real world? How can they be synthetic?

It is at this point that Kant's Copernican revolution becomes relevant. According to Kant's preface to the second edition of the first *Critique*, all disciplines that have become scientific (*wissenschaftlich*), such as logic, mathematics, and physics, have become so because of a revolution in their manner of thinking. Kant claims that his Copernican revolution is such a revolution, which will make metaphysics into a science. It consists in assuming that the objects of our knowledge are constituted in part by the epistemic mechanisms of the knowing subject, instead of assuming, as traditional philosophy did, that knowledge must be derived from its objects. This revolution explains how a priori propositions can be synthetic, because the objects of which these propositions are true have been constituted by the very same epistemic mechanisms which, because they inhere in the knowing subject, explain that such propositions can be known in an a priori manner. For example, Euclidean geometry is true of actual spatial objects (synthetic), because these objects are constituted by the spatial form of intuition that enables us to develop Euclidean geometry in an a priori way. This is the second stage of Kant's transcendental argument.

Kant's transcendental turn implies a distinction between on the one hand the objects as we may experience them (*phenomena*), which are partly constituted by the knowing subject, and on the other hand entities as they are in themselves (*noumena*). Because Kant's transcendental turn explains the possibility of synthetic a priori judgments for the phenomenal world only, he claims that mathematics, physics, and metaphysics, to the extent that they are scientific, are concerned with the phenomenal world and not with the world in itself. In other words, scientific metaphysics must be "immanent." Since Kant thought that Newtonian physics was the most fundamental science of material nature, he identified scientific metaphysics of material nature—the *metaphysica generalis* of the phenomenal material world—with the synthetic a priori principles of Newtonian physics.[215] However, to the extent that metaphysics transcends the boundaries of the phenomenal world, because it aims at knowledge of God, the immortal soul, or the cosmos as creation (*metaphysica specialis*), it is not possible as a science. Kant tried to show in his transcendental dialectics that transcendent metaphysics inevitably runs into contradictions.

Most modern cognitive scientists would agree with Kant that there is a distinction between the phenomenal and the noumenal worlds, a distinction that is relative to specific organisms. If we conceive of knowing organisms as information-processing machines, we might say that the input of these machines is provided by the world as it is in itself, whereas the output is the world as it is experienced by the organism. A fly will see the world differently from us, even if its visual input is the same, because its eyes and nervous system are different from ours. As the output is constituted by two factors, the input and the information-processing mechanisms in the organism, it follows that, given the output, the input must be poor if the information added by the processing mechanisms is rich and *vice versa*. In the limiting case that there is no information added during the processing, the organism will perceive the world as it is in itself, and this is what Gibsonians argue. In the opposite limiting case, there is no input and the information-processing machine creates its own world. This is God's case.[216] What makes Kant's theory special, then, is not that Kant distinguished between a noumenal and a phenomenal world. It is, rather, that he attributed fundamental features such as time, space, and causality to the information-processing mechanism in the knowing subject instead of to the input, so that he conceived of information processing as *adding* very substantial information (spatial structure, linear temporal ordering, causal relations) to the input instead of merely decoding it. Consequently, the input of perception had to be thought of as a pure manifold, of which we cannot even say that it is in time and space. This implies that if Kant's theory is true, the noumenal world must be unknowable. This peculiar theory could be justified, Kant thought, as being the only solution to the problem of how mathematics and the principles of physics are possible.

Kant's justification of his transcendental turn may be criticized in two ways. One might either claim that there are other possible solutions to Kant's problem, such as the solution of Descartes, who thought that God guarantees that there is a harmony between clear and distinct a priori principles and nature, and a Darwinian solution, according to which the truth of innate knowledge might be accounted for by the notion of natural selection. Kant argued, however, that we cannot know God, and he might have argued that a Darwinian solution leaves unexplained the necessary nature of synthetic a priori knowledge. Or, alternatively, one might reject Kant's problem, and this is what most critics have done in the twentieth century. Kant's assumption that mathematics and the principles of physics are synthetic a priori is essential to his problem. Without this alleged "fact," an explanation of its possibility is superfluous. Subsequent developments in mathematics and physics have shown that there is no such fact. The invention of non-Euclidean geometries compelled philosophers of science to distinguish between pure and applied mathematics. Because the application of geometry to space requires a physical interpretation of mathematical concepts such as "straight line," the question as to whether space is Euclidean becomes a complex and partly empirical question, which was answered in the negative by Eddington's confirmation of Einstein's theory of relativity. Furthermore, the idea that a deterministic principle of causality is a priori true of nature has been undermined by quantum mechanics. Both the development of physics and the subsequent philosophy of science have refuted the assumption of Kant's problem that there is in fact true synthetic a priori knowledge. Consequently, Kant's justification for his transcendental turn collapsed at the beginning of the twentieth century.

Before I pass on to Heidegger's retrieval of Kant's transcendental problem, I should stress that although Kant claims to have discovered the notion of synthetic a priori propositions, this notion fits in well with the traditional philosophy of science of Aristotle and Descartes. Aristotle, Descartes, and Kant conceived of science as a system of true propositions that must be based ultimately on first principles that are necessary and apodictically true.[217] Because Descartes' a priori foundation of physics was refuted by empirical findings such as Rømer's discovery of the finite speed of light, many philosophers became empiricists at the end of the seventeenth century. However, the empiricist philosophy of science led to skepticism, because on the one hand it did not radically abandon the notion of science as true knowledge by proof, whereas on the other hand the problem of induction showed that empirical proofs of scientific laws are impossible. Kant saw a contradiction between the skeptical philosophy of science of the empiricists, according to which science is impossible, and the brute fact of Newtonian mechanics, which in the eighteenth century was widely acclaimed as a paradigmatic science. Instead of concluding, as Popper, Reichenbach, and many others did in our century, that the empiricist revolution in the philosophy of science had not been sufficiently radical, because it did not reject the Aristotelian notion of science as knowledge by proof, Kant took refuge in the old rationalist conception of a priori principles of physics. This historical background explains why Kant felt safe in assuming the existence of synthetic a priori propositions in mathematics and physics, in spite of the poor arguments by which he tried to substantiate this assumption in the introduction to the first *Critique*.[218]

What strikes us most when we read Heidegger's interpretation of the first *Critique* in *Kant und das Problem der Metaphysik* is the fact that Heidegger altogether disregards this historical background. Newton is not even mentioned, and Heidegger attempts to reconstruct Kant's transcendental problem by a purely internal reading of Kant's texts.[219] Moreover, the relevance of Kant's assumption that there are synthetic a priori propositions in mathematics and in physics to his strategy for solving the problem of the possibility of metaphysics is left unnoticed in Heidegger's discussion of the introduction to the first *Critique*.[220] In his zeal to combat the epistemological interpretations of the Neo-Kantians, Heidegger even claims that the *Critique of Pure Reason* has nothing to do with epistemology or philosophy of science.[221] In fact, Kant could not justify his Copernican foundation of metaphysics without a theory of mathematics and of physics, as he himself makes abundantly clear. We should conclude that Heidegger only partially retrieves Kant's transcendental problem, and that he eliminates the essential role that Kant's conception of science as knowledge by proof played in the construction of the problem. In this respect, Heidegger's partial retrieval of Kant resembles his partial retrieval of Aristotle.

As a result, Heidegger is not able to explain the necessity of Kant's Copernican revolution. According to Heidegger's reconstruction in *Kant und das Problem der Metaphysik*, Kant wanted to show the inner possibility of ontology or metaphysics. He did so by reflecting on the essential finiteness of human knowledge. As Heidegger correctly observes, Kant contrasted finite human knowledge with infinite divine knowledge. God's knowledge is creative intuition, *intuitus originarius*, because when God intuits individual beings, he *eo ipso* creates them. Human knowledge consists of thought and intuition. In contrast to God's intuition, however, human intuition is receptive and not creative. Because human intuition is finite, it needs an external stimulus, and according to Heidegger this explains the necessity of the senses for human intuition. Human intuition also needs the detour of the understanding (*Verstand*), because without understanding, human knowledge would be limited to particular cases. Starting from the mere topic of the finiteness of human knowledge, Heidegger reconstructs Kant's notions of receptivity, the senses (*Sinnlichkeit*), and understanding. As the interaction between sensibility and understanding is mediated by transcendental imagination, imagination becomes the pivotal concept of Heidegger's interpretation.[222]

How does this meditation on the finite nature of human knowledge solve Kant's problem of the possibility of ontology or metaphysics? Ontology is a priori knowledge of objects. From the finite nature of human knowledge it does not follow that ontology must be possible. Rather, it seems to follow that all human knowledge is empirical, since finite knowledge needs external stimuli. How does Heidegger solve this crucial problem in his interpretation? He claims, without further argument, that objects can only manifest themselves to us in perception if we first give them the possibility of doing so by turning ourselves to them (*zuwenden*). This preliminary turn toward objects is then identified both with Kant's a priori epistemic mechanisms and with the preliminary understanding of being (*vorgängiges Seinsverständnis*) of *Sein und Zeit*.[223] Now it may be admitted that in some cases we must turn to an object in order to be able to perceive it, for instance, if we want to see something that is behind our backs. But this is not true for all cases (hearing, for example), and it is arbitrary to identify this "turn toward objects" with an a priori structure in the knowing subject that incorporates time, space, and the categories. We must conclude that Heidegger is not able to elucidate the main problem of the *Critique of Pure Reason*, the problem of how metaphysics is possible as a science, because he tries to reconstruct Kant's theory merely from the point of view of human finiteness, and omits the epistemological problem of how synthetic a priori propositions are possible in physics and mathematics. Heidegger's attempt to eliminate the philosophy of science from Kant's transcendental philosophy is a blatant failure.

Perhaps the reader will wonder why this analysis of Heidegger's retrieval of Kant in contrast with a historical reading of the first *Critique* is relevant to the interpretation of the question of being in *Sein und Zeit*. Yet its relevance is quite direct. The transcendental interpretation of *Sein und Zeit* explains both the primacy of the question of being and the primacy of Dasein. According to Heidegger's transcendental turn, understanding of being (*Seinsverständnis*) is somehow a priori. Moreover, if understanding of being is a preliminary condition for the possibility of experience and intentional behavior, being-as-understood is a condition for the possibility of entities, to the extent that they are accessible for us.

Here we recognize the two stages of a transcendental argument. But what, we may wonder, justifies Heidegger's transcendental turn? If Heidegger did not retrieve the justification of Kant's transcendental turn, did he perhaps take over the transcendental theme from the philosophical tradition without critically assessing it? In this case, Heidegger was unwittingly influenced by the superseded philosophy of science which Kant still presupposed, and this conclusion confirms what I said in section 7, above.

Even so, Heidegger must have had his own reasons for going transcendental. What justifies his view that the meaning of being that we "pro-ject" in projective understanding is a priori, in the sense that it constitutes a global meaningful horizon without which entities cannot become manifest to us? This connotation of the term "project" (*Entwurf*) is certainly not included in the "existentialist" notion of Dasein as a project, according to which human life is a project because we have to construct our life by projecting it into the future. In other words, which philosophical problems did Heidegger want to solve by this theory? Heidegger, like Husserl, did not state explicitly the problems that explain his views. They both held that philosophy is purely descriptive, and this descriptivist ideology prevented them from developing their problems thematically. For this reason, an interpretation has to reconstruct Heidegger's problematic, and a hypothetical reconstruction is adequate if it is the best explanation of the texts. My hypothesis is that Heidegger took the transcendental turn because he wanted to solve the problem of the manifest image and the scientific image, to use Wilfrid Sellars' terminology, and that he solved it in an antinaturalist way.

The problem of the manifest and the scientific image is one of the most fundamental problems of modern philosophy.[224] If *Sein und Zeit* can be read as an attempt to solve it, Heidegger ceases to be what he is according to most analytic philosophers, an obscure German sage from the Black Forest. His work becomes relevant to mainstream analytical philosophy. Let me first elucidate the problem of the manifest and the scientific image, and then attempt to show that Heidegger in *Sein und Zeit* proposed a solution by means of a transcendental turn.

The problem of the manifest and the scientific image originated during the scientific revolution in the seventeenth century. According to Aristotle and common sense, human beings live in a world which is meaningful to them, and which appeals to them because it contains a wealth of qualities that we perceive by the senses, such as colors, thermal properties, odors, and sounds. The philosopher-physicists of the scientific revolution rejected this manifest image of the world. They argued that the material world, as it really is in itself, lacks both significance and the "secondary" qualities as we perceive them by the senses. Material objects merely possess the "primary" and measurable properties and powers that theoretical physics attributes to them, because such objects consist of imperceptible particles (corpuscles) that cannot have sensible qualities. Material reality is a meaningless multiplicity of corpuscles, and both meaning and sensuous qualities are projections of the knowing subject. In other words, the scientific image of the world is incompatible with the manifest image. Let me call this result the incompatibility thesis.

The incompatibility thesis yields the problem I am referring to: Which image of the world is the true or the most fundamental one, assuming that they are mutually incompatible? Is the manifest image merely a useful subjective illusion, as Descartes argued, or should we conclude that the scientific image is somehow misconceived? It is not difficult to map all possible solutions to this problem on an intellectual chart. The philosopher-scientists of the seventeenth century opted for the primacy of the scientific image. Physics would characterize the material world as it really is. If physics contradicts common sense, common sense must be mistaken. I call this position classical naturalism. As I explained in section 3, above, classical naturalism leads to a number of tricky ontological and epistemological problems. At the end of the nineteenth century, all possible solutions to these problems had been developed, and none of them was satisfactory. My hypothesis is that Heidegger in *Sein und Zeit* concluded that we must reject classical naturalism, or *die Ontologie der Vorhandenheit* (the ontology of occurrentness), as he calls it. Because he endorsed the incompatibility thesis, he had to argue that the meaningful world of everyday life (*Alltäglichkeit*) is more fundamental than the scientific image. What, then, were the problems raised by classical naturalism, and why are they insoluble?

Let me start with the ontological problem of secondary qualities such as color. According to common sense, the color of a material object is a real property of this object, which humans are able to perceive if they are not color-blind. Classical naturalism claims, however, that material objects cannot possess secondary qualities or "qualia" such as colors as we perceive them. What, then, is the ontological status of colors? Galileo argued that colors are subjective impressions in the perceiving organism, which are caused by colorless physical processes. However, if the perceiving organism is a material object among others, as Descartes held, and if colors as we perceive them cannot exist in matter, this solution will not do. Descartes concluded that at least in our own case the perceiving subject must be an immaterial soul or mind, which contains colors as immanent sensations, and that mind is essentially different from matter. If one accepts the incompatibility thesis, Cartesian dualism follows from classical naturalism. Naturalism leads to the paradoxical conclusion that the knowing subject cannot belong to the natural material world, because it is a mind that is essentially different from matter. Descartes welcomed this conclusion on religious grounds. It must be unacceptable to the scientist, however, who wants to include the knowing subject among the objects to be studied by science. Accordingly, contemporary materialists have tried to eliminate qualia and consciousness altogether, in order to vindicate naturalism as an unrestricted image of the world. This solution will not do, because it conflicts with the obvious fact that we do perceive colors.[225]

The thesis that secondary qualities such as colors are sensations in the mind instead of objective properties of material objects, whereas these objects merely possess the powers to cause sensations in us, may be called the principle of immanence. The principle of immanence not only implies ontological dualism. It also raises epistemological problems concerning perception. If colors as we perceive them are sensations in the mind, perception must consist of a projective mechanism, because we do not perceive colors *as* sensations in the mind, but as objective properties of material objects. According to the theories of perception necessitated by the principle of immanence, the psychological aspect of perception consists in our having immanent sensations, which are projectively interpreted as objective properties. However, if perception is projection, how can we know that the world that we perceive exists independently of the perceiving mind? According to the classical naturalist, our subjective impressions are caused by objective physical processes, but we do not perceive these processes; we perceive our own projected sensations that allegedly are caused by them. Classical naturalism, then, implies the problem of the external world, and it is not accidental that this problem emerges for the first time in Descartes' *Meditations*. As Russell says, "the observer, when he seems to himself to be observing a stone, is really, if physics is to be believed, observing the effects of the stone upon himself. Thus science seems to be at war with itself: when it most means to be objective, it finds itself plunged into subjectivity against its will."[226]

The paradox of classical naturalism, if coupled to empiricism, is that it starts with a theory of matter and ends up doubting the existence of matter. If we do not perceive material objects as they are, but our own projected sensations instead, we should prove the reality of the material world by arguing that it causes our sensations. Both Berkeley and Husserl denied that we can have a conception of matter as distinct from sensuous qualities. They inferred that God causes our sensations, and became idealists. Hume argued that a causal proof of the external world on the basis of our sensations is impossible, because we have to be able to observe both cause and effect in order to establish causal laws. He held, however, that this impossibility demonstrates the impotence of the human intellect, and that we should trust our instinctive belief in the reality of the external world. Kant tried to refute idealism by proving the existence of the external world. What he proved was merely the existence of the mind-dependent phenomenal world, which no one ever doubted, not the existence of a world *an sich*. The assumption of the latter as a cause of our cognitive input contradicts Kant's transcendental theory, which says that the category of causality cannot be applied outside the domain of possible phenomena. The hypothetical realists, finally, argued that the hypothesis of a mind-independent material world is the best explanation of our having the sensations we happen to have, even though we will never be able to prove this hypothesis. But it is peculiar to say that the existence of a mind-independent world is a hypothesis only. Why should this hypothesis be better than the theological one, which has the virtue of simplicity? Neither the idealist nor the realist solutions to the problem of the external world seem to be acceptable. Contemporary ontology and philosophy of mind, as practiced by Quine, Rorty, Searle, or Churchland, have not been able to free themselves from the assumptions of classical naturalism.[227] As a consequence, these philosophers still wrestle with the problem of realism, and old solutions, made sophisticated by means of theories of language, are presented under new labels, such as internal realism. Should we not rather admit that the problem is insoluble, and reject the assumptions that implied it in the first place? This is what Heidegger attempted to do in *Sein und Zeit*.

According to the interpretation put forward here, Heidegger endorsed the incompatibility thesis. As a consequence, he could only reject ontological dualism and the problem of the external world by repudiating classical naturalism. In *Sein und Zeit*, Heidegger claimed that the manifest image is fundamental, and that the scientific image is derived, impoverished, and even false in a sense. I will now try to substantiate this interpretation by briefly summarizing the relevant parts of *Sein und Zeit*. Heidegger's argument consists of two steps: he argues that the scientific image is possible only on the basis of the manifest image, and he argues that the scientific image is the product of a project (*Entwurf*). Because Heidegger's argument is a transcendental one, he concludes that the very *being* of the objects that science claims to discover depends on the framework of the projected scientific image of the world.

Heidegger argues in sections 12 and 13 of *Sein und Zeit* that Dasein is primarily being-in-the-world. The world in which Dasein exists is a meaningful structure or horizon, within which we lead our daily life (*Alltäglichkeit*). As I said in section 3, above, world is a constitutive existential of Dasein. Accordingly, Dasein, if well understood ontologically, cannot be thought of as without its world. From this point of view, the problem of the external world is a nonsensical problem (§ 43a). In sections 15–18, Heidegger develops his notion of world by analyzing the way in which we manipulate equipment (*Zeug*). The mode of being of equipment (*Zuhandenheit*: usually translated as "readiness-to-hand"), Heidegger argues, is fundamental for our daily existence in the world. In daily life, we manipulate equipment and other meaningful entities, and manipulating equipment presupposes the world as a global meaningful structure (*Bewandtnisganzheit*).[228]

The scientific view of the world as a multiplicity of meaningless entities must be due to a *deficiency* in our daily commerce with equipment and fellow humans, if the world in reality is a meaningful structure.[229] It is the product of a new ontological attitude (*Seinsstand*) vis-à-vis the world which always is already revealed as meaningful in daily life.[230] This new ontological attitude, which opens up the world as a totality of purely present things (*Vorhandenheit*), is secondary in relation to, and based on (*fundiert in*) our primary dwelling in the world. It passes over (*überspringen*) the phenomenon of the world in the primary sense (§§ 14, 21). For instance, a knife loses its instrumental meaning of a tool that is useful for realizing specific practical aims as soon as it is studied by physics and reduced to a piece of matter.

If Heidegger says that the scientific view of the world *passes over* the phenomenon of the world, should we not conclude that according to him the scientific image of the world is in some sense false, because it leaves out the phenomenon of the world as it really is? By arguing that the scientific view of the world is due to a *deficiency*, that it is *secondary* in relation to the manifest image of daily life, and that it *skips* (*überspringt*) the phenomenon of world, Heidegger in fact chooses the antinaturalist horn of the dilemma of the manifest versus the scientific image. He further argues in section 21 of *Sein und Zeit* that it is impossible to understand the meaningful world of daily life on the basis of the scientific image. We cannot reconstruct this meaningful world as a higher stratum, built on the basic stratum of physical objects, as philosophers such as Nicolai Hartmann, who was Heidegger's colleague in Marburg, tried to do.

We will be interested to know how, according to Heidegger, the attitude of theoretical discovery arises out of the more original practical involvement with the world. Heidegger sets out to deal with this topic in section 69b of *Sein und Zeit*. The way in which he words his question has a Kantian flavor: "Which of those conditions implied in Dasein's ontological constitution are existentially necessary for the possibility of Dasein's existing in the way of scientific research?"[231] How is this revolution (*Umschlag*) to be accounted for? We expect that in this section Heidegger will explain what in our daily manipulation of equipment *motivates* the revolution in ontological attitude from practical involvement in the world to theoretical investigation. Indeed, he starts with an (abortive) attempt to do so. Is it perhaps the case that the theoretical attitude emerges when we simply hold back from any kind of manipulation of equipment?[232] This cannot be so, because "theoretical research is not without a praxis of its own": we have to set up experiments, make measurements, excavate archaeological data, and so on.[233] Or is it rather the case that the theoretical attitude, which takes entities as purely present objects (*vorhanden*) without instrumental significance, emerges when tools turn out to be unusable or damaged, not properly adapted for the use we had decided on?[234] On the contrary: we discover the unusability of tools not by detached theoretical research, but by the very kind of practical circumspection that is typical of our primary involvement with the world.[235]

When in section 69b Heidegger finally characterizes the way in which "circumspective concern" changes over into "theoretical discovering," we must conclude to our disappointment that he does not offer a substantial explanation of this change. Heidegger is not able to identify a motive in our practical involvement with the world for changing over into the theoretical attitude. What he comes up with seems to be a mere tautology. Why is it that we first manipulate a hammer as a hammer, and then suddenly perceive it as a physical object with measurable properties? "*The understanding of being* by which our concernful dealings with entities within-the-world have been guided *has changed over*."[236] To what else does this amount than to saying that we understand the hammer differently because we understand it differently?

Yet there is a nontautologous explanation here. Heidegger assumes that our understanding of being (*Seinsverständnis*) implies a global framework of implicit categories and relations, which we project onto beings. Only because we project such a global framework will individual entities become manifest to us *as* tools or *as* physical objects. For instance, we cannot understand something as a hammer in isolation. A hammer only shows up for us as such within a framework of other tools and materials, such as planks and nails, which is structured by a social world of practices and standardized procedures, and by our purposeful actions. Heidegger holds that this framework is pro-jected by Dasein and that this projection is made possible, ultimately, by the transcendental time-structure of concern and being-toward-death. I discussed Heidegger's projective theory of understanding in section 5, above. He applies this theory in section 69b, when he characterizes the worldview of mathematical physics as a "projection" (*Entwurf*). This substantiates the Kantian interpretation of *Sein und Zeit* as follows.

In order to be able to *perceive* entities as physical objects, Dasein must project the ontological framework of mathematical physics onto entities. This is the subjective aspect of Heidegger's transcendental deduction, or the first step in his transcendental argument. Heidegger also subscribes to the objective aspect of the transcendental deduction. The second step in his argument consists in claiming that the *being*, or the sense of being (*Seinssinn*), of entities is determined by such a projection. "What is decisive for the development of mathematical physics," Heidegger says in section 69b, "does not lie in its higher esteem for the observation of 'facts,' nor in its 'application' of mathematics in determining the character of natural processes; it lies rather in the *way in which Nature herself is mathematically projected. . . .* Only 'in the light' of a Nature which has been projected in this fashion can anything like a 'fact' be found."[237] The facts of natural science only show up for us on the basis of a global conception of natural being, which is a priori in the sense that it is a projection without which we cannot discover scientific facts at all. What is more, there simply *are* no scientific facts apart from such a projection. That Heidegger's notion of understanding of being (*Seinsverständnis*) may be interpreted in this Kantian sense is also confirmed by *Kant und das Problem der Metaphysik*. In that book, Heidegger often uses the term *Seinsverständnis* for the Kantian a priori structures of experience.[238]

Heidegger's Copernican turn, according to which a holistic projective understanding of being determines the mode of being in which entities show up for us, is an antinaturalist solution to the problem of the manifest and the scientific image. This interpretation is supported by the following grounds:

1. According to Heidegger, the scientific view of the world is not established as true, probable, or plausible, or warranted on the basis of more or less neutral facts. On the contrary, we can only discern scientific facts on the basis of an a priori projection of nature-as-scientific. In terms of contemporary philosophy of

science, this implies that facts and perception are radically theory-laden, and that there is an incommensurability between the scientific and the manifest image. If this radical view were correct, we would not be able to substantiate the claim that scientific knowledge is superior to religious, mythical, or other prescientific systems of knowledge.

2. In projecting the scientific view of the world, we skip (*überspringen*) the world as it is in daily existence: a meaningful world in which we live and work.[239] Heidegger claims that the meaningful world of daily existence is the world *as it is "in itself."*[240] This implies that the world as science sees it is *not* the world as it is in itself. Moreover, Heidegger claims (but fails to argue effectively in § 69b of *Sein und Zeit*) that the scientific view and scientific practice are parasitic on the primary practice of daily life. As a consequence, the scientific image is deficient in relation to the manifest image (*Alltäglichkeit*), and the manifest image is primary.

3. Whereas Kant thought that the transcendental structures of experience are operative necessarily, so that we cannot help viewing the phenomenal world in a scientific, Euclidean, and deterministic manner, Heidegger claims that the scientific view of the world is due to an antecedent projection (*Entwurf*) of nature as a meaningless, "mathematical" multiplicity.[241] Admittedly, Heidegger warns against interpreting the notion of *Entwurf* as a deliberate plan or project.[242] This warning is essential for understanding the sense in which Dasein may be said to project its possibilities of self-realization. Yet, in relation to natural science, the term *Entwurf* suggests that the scientific view of the world is somehow optional, and that we may decide to reject the scientific view of the world without going against any independent evidence.

4. I now want to suggest that such an antinaturalist decision is one of the most important objectives of Heidegger's quest. Even though he often seems to give science its due, Heidegger's deepest intentions were to undermine the hold of the scientific view of the world, because this view allegedly deprives the world of its "meaningfulness." As Heidegger says in his second book on Kant, *Die Frage nach dem Ding*, philosophical questioning has the objective of preparing us for a decision. We must decide whether science (*Wissenschaft*) provides the sole criterion of knowledge. Heidegger suggests that there is a deeper kind of knowledge, which fixes the grounds and limitations of the sciences.[243]

Let me conclude. Although Heidegger did not retrieve Kant's justification for the transcendental turn, he had reasons of his own for going transcendental. In *Sein und Zeit*, he wanted to resolve the conflict between the scientific image and the manifest image. His transcendental turn enabled him to argue in favor of an antinaturalist stance, which restores our life and the world to their "meaningfulness." Although Heidegger rejects transcendental idealism and overlooks Kant's justification for going transcendental in his book on Kant of 1929, his transcendental turn brings him close to Kant's own solution to the conflict between the Newtonian picture of the world on the one hand and religion and morality on the other hand. Like Kant, Heidegger argues that the "meaningfulness" of life resides in the world as it is *an sich*, whereas the world of physics is merely phenomenal. (The antinaturalist interpretation of Heidegger's question of being will be corroborated more amply by §§ 11–13, below.)

B. How Is Heidegger's Transcendental Turn Possible?

Having put forward a hypothesis that explains why Heidegger's transcendental turn was necessary, I now come to the topic of its possibility. Here, too, it is instructive to compare Heidegger with Kant, and I will do so at the risk of being somewhat repetitive. Kant's transcendental turn would not have been possible if Kant had not inherited the theory of perception developed by Descartes. According to this theory, processes in the physical world impinge upon our sense organs. Stimulations of the senses are transmitted to the brain by physical mechanisms, and the physical effects in the brain cause mental impressions in our minds. These impressions or sensations do not resemble their physical causes, because they are representations of secondary qualities (such as warm and red), which Descartes denied to the physical world. Impressions are then interpreted, processed, and projected by a mental mechanism. As a result we perceive a (phenomenal) world that contains secondary qualities.

Kant radicalized this traditional theory of perception. In order to solve his problem of synthetic a priori propositions, he had to argue that structures such as time, space, and causality are part of the information-processing mechanisms in the mind, instead of being properties of the world as it is in itself. He could not explain that a priori knowledge can be synthetic except by assuming that the objects of a priori knowledge are constituted by the same epistemic mechanisms that enable us to acquire such knowledge in an a priori manner. This Copernican turn, which exploits the Cartesian distinction between a physical world in itself and a subjectively constituted phenomenal world, implies that physics must be concerned with the phenomenal world and not, as Descartes thought, with the world as it is in itself. It also implies transcendental idealism in the sense that the phenomenal world is subject-dependent. Kant's theory led to the paradoxical result that the theory of perception, which had to be assumed in order to develop transcendental philosophy in the first place, had to be rejected once this philosophy had been accepted. According to Kant's transcendental theory, the category of causality cannot be validly applied outside of the phenomenal world. As a consequence, it would be incompatible with this theory to say that the sensations of which the phenomenal world is constituted are caused by processes in a world *an sich*. Jacobi was one of the first philosophers to discern this paradox, which became known in subsequent German philosophy as the problem of the *Ding an sich*.

In *Sein und Zeit*, Heidegger rejects both the traditional (Cartesian) theories of perception and transcendental idealism.[244] This raises the question as to how a transcendental theory is possible without them. What can be the content of such a theory? In what sense can we say that the object of knowledge is constituted by subjective conditions if we reject transcendental idealism? I will answer these questions by briefly stating the differences and parallelisms between the transcendental theories of Kant, the later Husserl (*Ideen* I), and Heidegger, respectively. Let me choose three points of comparison: (1) their conceptions of the phenomenal world, (2) their conceptions of the world *an sich*, and (3) their views on the ontological status of the transcendental subject.

1. *The Phenomenal World*. According to Kant and Husserl, the phenomenal world is constituted by transcendental subjectivity on the basis of a "matter" of sensations that the transcendental subject finds in itself. As a consequence, this world is ontologically dependent on the transcendental subject (transcendental idealism). As far as its structure is concerned, Kant's phenomenal world consists of material and mental phenomena. His conception of material phenomena is modeled on Newton's physics, and the phenomenal material world is identical with the physical world. In the second half of the nineteenth century, many Neo-Kantians rejected this dualistic conception of the phenomenal world. After the pace of history had been quickened by the French Revolution and the Napoleonic wars, history had established itself as a major intellectual discipline. Consequently, Neo-Kantians wondered whether the phenomenal world should not make room for objective spirit and history. As a result of this development, Husserl distinguished various ontological domains or regions in the world, such as material object, animal nature, person, and objective spirit in Hegel's sense. Whereas causality is a category basic to the region of matter, motivation would be a defining category of the regions of persons and objective spirit. Heidegger borrowed from Husserl and the Neo-Kantians this regionalization of being, which he also found in Aristotle. There is another innovation of Husserl's that Heidegger endorsed: the distinction between life-world and the world of physics. Husserl argues in *Ideen* I (§ 52) and in *Krisis* that the life-world is ontologically fundamental, and that the world of physics should not be conceived of as a transcendent cause, but rather as constituted on the basis of the life-world. As we saw under (A), this is also Heidegger's opinion. Husserl's notion of a life-world is not incompatible with his transcendental idealism, as is often thought. On the contrary, Husserl claims that the life-world is ontologically dependent on transcendental subjectivity.[245]

The main difference between Husserl's and Heidegger's transcendental doctrines is that Heidegger rejects transcendental idealism. According to Heidegger, the transcendental subject (Dasein) and world are equiprimordial, because Dasein is being-in-the-world. As I argued in section 3, this new conception is a drastic departure from the philosophical tradition of the West, because Heidegger claims that being-in-the-world cannot be understood within the matrix of traditional philosophical categories such as subject, object, substance, property, consciousness, and matter. The question is, however, in what sense Heidegger's conception of Dasein as being-in-the-world may be called transcendental. If the world is as fundamental as Dasein, how can Heidegger endorse the second stage of a transcendental argument, according to which phenomenal objects are constituted by subjective conditions?

2. *The World in Itself.* Because Kant included space, time, and categories such as substance and causality in the epistemic mechanism of the transcendental subject, he had to conclude that the input of this mechanism is nothing but a pure manifold of sensations. The knowing subject cannot create sensations, because a finite knower is receptive. This is why Kant had to assume a *Ding an sich*, which causes our sensations. However, such an assumption is puzzling for two reasons. First, if even time and space are subjective, we cannot know anything of this world in itself. Second, the assumption contradicts the very idea of the Copernican turn, which implies that the category of causality can only be applied to phenomena. Both Fichte and Husserl felt that the Kantian notion of a *Ding an sich* had to be eliminated. In *Logische Untersuchungen* and in *Ideen* I, Husserl argued that the concept of an essentially unknowable object is nonsensical. He redefined the notion of a *Ding an sich* as an ideal limit, inherent in the process of sense perception. When we perceive ever more aspects of an object, we will form the conception of the object-as-completely-perceived, that is, of the object as it is *an sich*. This conception is an "idea in the Kantian sense," because it can never be actualized.[246]

Husserl's new definition of the notion of a *Ding an sich* had drastic implications for his notion of the world. If an object as it is in itself is a mere ideal limit, implied by a series of perceptions as the ultimate objective correlate of this series, the phenomenal world is the only world there is, and the world is ontologically dependent on the transcendental subject. Also, we should now say that the object in itself is not an object different from the object that we perceive: the former is an ideal limit of the latter. Heidegger in *Sein und Zeit* follows Husserl in abolishing the distinction between a phenomenal and a noumenal world. According to Heidegger, things *manifest* themselves to us primarily as tools. He concludes that "readiness-to-hand (*Zuhandenheit*) is the way in which entities as they are *in themselves* are defined ontologico-categorially."[247] In *Kant und das Problem der Metaphysik*, Heidegger projects back into Kant's texts his Neo-Kantian understanding of the *Ding an sich*. Phenomena and noumena are not different kinds of objects. Rather, there is only one object, which functions as a phenomenon when it manifests itself to finite knowers, whereas God sees it as it is in the act of creating it (noumenon).[248] Again, we should ask how Heidegger is able to set up a transcendental argument in *Sein und Zeit* if noumenon and phenomenon are identical.

3. *The Ontological Status of the Transcendental Subject.* According to Husserl, Kant never succeeded in defining unambiguously the ontological status of the transcendental subject. On the one hand, Kant distinguished between transcendental and empirical egos. On the other hand, he assumed that even the transcendental ego is affected by a world *an sich*. Kant held both that the transcendental ego

constitutes the (phenomenal) world, and that the transcendental ego is somehow *in* the world. From Husserl's point of view, this amounts to a contradiction, because the phenomenal world and the noumenal world are in fact the same. If so, Husserl ended up in a dilemma: either the transcendental subject constitutes the world by making sense of its stream of immanent sensations. In that case the transcendental subject cannot be *in* the world, because it is the constitutive source of the world. Or, alternatively, we assume that the transcendental subject is in the world. In that case we have to give up the idea that the world is constituted by it. This latter alternative seems to imply that one gives up transcendental philosophy.

Husserl chose the first horn of this dilemma. His theory of perception implied constitutionalism. He resolved the "paradox of human subjectivity," which consists in the antinomy that the subject is both in the world and constitutes the world, by making a radical distinction between empirical or "mundane" human subjects in the constituted world and transcendental subjects (monads) that constitute the world, and which therefore cannot be *in* it. Transcendental subjects are substances in the Cartesian sense that they do not need anything else in order to exist, whereas the constituted world is ontologically dependent on transcendental subjects. Husserl's transcendental idealism is different from Berkeley's subjective idealism because of this distinction between mundane and transcendental subjects.[249] It also resembles Berkeley's view. Like Berkeley, Husserl claims that substantial reality is purely spiritual and he ventures the hypothesis of a radically transcendent God in order to account for the fact that the transcendental subject finds in itself ordered series of sensations, which enable it to constitute a world.[250]

Heidegger opts for the other horn of Husserl's dilemma. Dasein as a transcendental subject is said to be *in* the world. This fits into the manifest image, which Heidegger endorses. As a consequence, Heidegger rejects Husserl's constitution-theory of perception. It seems, however, that Heidegger's solution raises a second dilemma. We should remember that transcendental arguments consist of two steps. It is first argued that specific conditions in the knower are necessary for being able to *experience* objects. Second, it is argued that these very same conditions are necessary for objects in order *to be*. The dilemma I am referring to can now be stated as a dilemma between weak and strong transcendentalism. If one identifies by a stipulative definition an object's "being" with our experiencing it, the two stages of the transcendental argument collapse into one, and transcendentalism becomes a tautology. I call this trivial position weak transcendentalism. In strong transcendentalism, the two stages must be clearly distinguished, as is the case in Husserl and Kant. Husserl's view of the world as nothing but an ontologically dependent correlate of the transcendental subject is a clear example of strong transcendentalism. Heidegger's problem is as follows: how to avoid weak transcendentalism if one rejects transcendental idealism and a constitution theory of the world. It seems that Heidegger has a choice between strong transcendentalism, which implies transcendental idealism, and weak transcendentalism, which is trivial. How does he resolve this dilemma?

Heidegger argues in section 43 of *Sein und Zeit* that real *entities* do not depend on Dasein's understanding of being (*Seinsverständnis*). This amounts to a rejection of transcendental idealism.[251] He claims that only *being itself* depends on understanding of being.[252] These two statements imply, however, that entities cannot depend on being itself, because the relation of "depending on" is transitive. If this is the case, how can *being* be defined as that which determines entities as entities, as Heidegger says in section 2?[253] Weak transcendentalism seems to be the only plausible solution to this contradiction. The second stage of Heidegger's transcendental argument (understanding of being determines being) must be identical to the first stage (understanding of being is a condition of experiencing entities). What Heidegger must mean by "being" is nothing but the sense in which we understand entities ontologically, that is, as tools, or as purely present objects. The expressions "the sense of being" and "being" must be equivalent. Does this identification of being with ontological sense reduce Heidegger's position to a trivial one? It seems that his ambiguous terminology ("being" instead of "ontological sense" or "significance") only masks the fact that his view comes dangerously close to the position that the entities which we manipulate and know *exist* independently of Dasein, even though Dasein determines the *significance* which these entities have for it. This commonsensical view should not be called transcendentalism. It merely sounds like a transcendental view because Heidegger uses the term "being" in a new and idiosyncratic sense, as synonymous with "significance." Apart from "being" in this peculiar sense, Heidegger still needs the usual notion of being as existence in order to state his position: entities *exist* independently of Dasein, even though they *are* not independent of Dasein. Clearly, Heidegger's antinaturalism threatens to collapse if this were his position, because a scientist might claim that science merely abstracts from the ontological sense that Dasein projects upon preexisting entities, and investigates them as they are in themselves. This was Descartes' position, which is not at all "transcendental." In what sense, then, is *Sein und Zeit* a treatise in transcendental philosophy?

In the first stage of his transcendental argument, Heidegger claims that we can only encounter entities on the basis of a global understanding of being, which projects on entities a holistic framework of significance.[254] In the second stage, he argues that entities derive their ontological sense from this global framework.[255] Because Heidegger rejects transcendental idealism, he has to deny that the existence of entities depends on this framework.[256] As a consequence, the two stages of his transcendental argument collapse into one. Nevertheless, there is a real Kantian flavor to Heidegger's position, because it is claimed that the sense or significance of entities depends on a *holistic* framework, projected by understanding of being. In the case of tools, this framework is inherent in our human practices.[257]

As we saw under (A), the assumption of a holistic projected framework is essential to Heidegger's solution of the problem of the manifest and the scientific image. Because scientific facts allegedly do not show up for us except within a projected framework of a holistic mathematical understanding of nature, there *are* no neutral and independent facts that might compel us to accept the scientific view of the world. Consequently, accepting this view must be a matter of free choice or projection, not of facts. Heidegger's philosophy aims at preparing us for such a choice. If, however, the assumption of holistic frameworks is false or nonsensical, as I will argue in chapter 4, there is no room for choice here, and Heidegger's antinaturalism is shipwrecked.

We must conclude that Heidegger's transcendental theory in *Sein und Zeit* is a variety of weak transcendentalism.[258] "Being" in Heidegger's idiosyncratic usage is identical to the ontological sense projected by Dasein. Yet the theory is non-trivially transcendental because Heidegger claims that entities can manifest themselves to us *as* equipment or *as* merely extant only on the basis of a global a priori framework, which Dasein projects onto them. In the terminology of *Kant und das Problem der Metaphysik*, he claims that we have to "turn ourselves toward" entities (*Zuwendung*), in order that they may manifest themselves. It is merely this assumption that an a priori and holistic framework of significance must be projected on preexisting entities in order that they may show up for us, which distinguishes Heidegger's weak transcendentalism from the trivial view that humans give significance to preexisting things. Unfortunately, Heidegger provides no arguments for his weak transcendentalism and it does not follow from his phenomenological description of equipment. From the fact that a hammer refers to nails and planks one cannot infer that something would not show up for us as a hammer unless a *global* and *a priori* framework of significant relations has been projected.

C. The Transcendence of Being

Up until now, I have specified two different senses in which Heidegger uses the term "being" (*Sein*) in *Sein und Zeit*. According to the phenomenological leitmotif, "being" means the fundamental mode of being or ontological constitution (*Seinsweise, Grundverfassung des Seins*) of ontological regions such as history, nature, space, life, Dasein, and language. It is the task of regional ontologies to develop basic concepts that capture these different modes of being. According to Heidegger, regional ontologies are a priori in that they disclose areas of being and make the relevant conceptual structures available to the positive sciences. Regional ontologies are the foundations of the specific sciences.[259] In a second, Kantian sense, "being" is a global meaningful structure, projected by Dasein, which enables entities to manifest themselves with a specific ontological significance, and "being" is also used as a synonym for "ontological significance" (weak transcendentalism). For instance, Heidegger claims that we can encounter entities such as tools only within the framework of what he calls a *Bewandtnisganzheit*, a global meaningful structure of instrumental relations. This framework is also a priori, because according to Heidegger entities cannot show up for us without a prior projection of such a framework. A *Bewandtnisganzheit* is a condition of the possibility that entities appear to us *as* tools.[260]

Heidegger nowhere in *Sein und Zeit* discusses the interrelations between these two concepts of being, and, indeed, he does not distinguish them explicitly. It is clear, however, that they are not equivalent. The notion of a regional ontology is logically independent from the Neo-Kantian notion of a holistic framework, projected on entities, and *vice versa*. If the notion of a regional ontology seems to presuppose that the furniture of the world is neatly divided into different domains, a global projected framework does not need to respect these domains; it may cut across them. Entities from different regions, such as animals, stones, and pieces of wood, will be integrated into the primary framework of readiness-to-hand (*Zuhandenheit*). Moreover, according to the phenomenological conception, Dasein is a mere region of being, whereas in the Kantian conception it is fundamental or transcendental because it projects ontological frameworks. In section 2 of *Sein und Zeit*, Heidegger uses two different formulas to specify what he understands by "being": "that which determines entities as entities," and "that with regard to which entities are already understood."[261] One might say that the first formula fits the phenomenological interpretation of "being" and that the second expresses the Neo-Kantian conception.[262]

Are these two notions of being the only ones in *Sein und Zeit*? There is a passage at the end of section 7C that suggests that Heidegger uses "being" in yet a third sense:

> Being, as the basic theme of philosophy, is no class or genus of entities; yet it pertains to every entity. Its "universality" is to be sought higher up. Being and structure of being lie beyond every entity and every possible character which an entity may possess. *Being is the transcendens pure and simple.*[263]

For two reasons it is difficult to read this passage either in the phenomenological or in the Kantian sense. First, there is a suggestion that being is one and unique. This is not the case according to the phenomenological and the transcendental interpretations. There are many ontological regions and there are various possible transcendental frameworks. Second, there is a suggestion that being is *higher* than beings. The phenomenological and transcendental interpretations do not enable us to make sense of such a suggestion either.

Those who are familiar with the philosophy of the Schools, as Heidegger was, will recognize the idiom of the quoted passage. In fact, there are two pre-Kantian notions of transcendence of being that might be involved here, one derived ultimately from Plato and another from Aristotle. According to Plato, real beings are eternal Forms, which are transcendent in relation to the perishable world that we perceive by the senses. The form of the Good even transcends the realm of Forms. In the Platonic sense, the Good is a transcendens pure and simple, and it is "higher" than ordinary beings. The Aristotelian notion of the transcendence of being is less lofty. Aristotle observed that we may use "being" in all categories.

We say, for instance, that Socrates *is* a man (substance), that it *is* five o'clock (time), and that he *is* five feet tall (quality). In this sense, the verb "to be" transcends the categories: its usage is not limited to one of them. However, it does not transcend the categories because it is a higher genus than the categories are. The categories may be seen as highest genera of ontological kinds, whereas the verb "to be" does not denote entities that belong to a genus; it functions in speaking about beings in all categories. What holds for "to be," that it transcends the categories, also holds for "true" and "good," which may be used in all categories as well.

The Scholastics, especially Thomas, tended to identify Plato's Good with the Christian God, and to conflate the sense in which the Good is transcendent with that in which "to be" or "good" are transcendent. "Being" (*ens, esse*) was also used as another word for God, who was supposed to *be* par excellence, and it was thought that the plenitude of being in God filters though the Forms into created entities. Clearly, Being in this sense is a *transcendens pure and simple*; it is one of the celebrated *transcendentalia*. It is both transcendent to experience and transcendental in the sense that it is a condition for the possibility of all entities. According to Thomas and to Eckhart's mysticism, the actuality of Being is shared in some degree by all created beings, so that Being is a phenomenon hidden in all entities. Is this what Heidegger means in the quoted passage? A great many obscure sentences in *Sein und Zeit* seem to receive a sudden illumination from this interpretative hypothesis. For instance, what should we think of section 2, last paragraph, where Heidegger intimates that Being has an "essential pertinence" to Dasein, and that for this reason Dasein is perhaps related in a special way to the question of being?[264] Heidegger's thesis in section 7C of *Sein und Zeit*, that being is a phenomenon which is hidden in all entities, could also have this Eckhartian sense, apart from its phenomenological interpretation. Yet, the text of *Sein und Zeit* does not enable us to decide on the value of the hypothesis, and I will come back to it in section 11.[265] Let me now try to derive from the text of *Sein und Zeit* some hints as to the way in which we should interpret the notion of being as a transcendens pure and simple (*transcendens schlechthin*). These hints are implied in the hermeneutical structure of the book.

1. In section 5, above, I distinguished two mutually connected aspects of the hermeneutical circle: a holistic aspect and a presuppositional aspect. According to Heidegger, Dasein and being (*Sein*) make up a hermeneutical whole. We cannot understand being without understanding Dasein, as Heidegger argues in sections 2 and 4 of *Sein und Zeit*, whereas the notion of being (*Sein*) is also implied in that of Da*sein*, so that we cannot understand Dasein without understanding being. The solution to this hermeneutical circle is what I have called the spiraling movement of interpretation: Heidegger starts with a vague and implicit notion of being. Using this notion, he develops an explicit ontological interpretation of human understanding of being (*Seinsverständnis*), that is, of Dasein.[266] Unfortunately, the published part of *Sein und Zeit* breaks off at the climax of this ontological

interpretation, the analysis of the temporality of Dasein. We will see later on that this rupture is not at all accidental (§§ 12C and 13C).

2. As we know from section 8 of *Sein und Zeit*, Heidegger had planned a third division of the first, constructive, part of the book. The title of this division, "Zeit und Sein," is a reversal of the title of the book itself, *Sein und Zeit*. What does this reversal of title mean? According to section 8, the first part of *Sein und Zeit* should develop two topics: the interpretation of Dasein in terms of temporality, and the explication of time as the transcendental horizon for the question of being.[267] It is plausible to assume that the first topic is dealt with in the two published divisions, so that the unpublished third division of part 1 is reserved for "the explication of time as the transcendental horizon for the question of being." From a purely formal point of view, we may say that the third division ("Zeit und Sein") is just the next turn in the spiraling movement of Heidegger's hermeneutics. Having analyzed Dasein, he must now turn to *Sein*, and develop an explicit notion of being *tout court*. After that, yet another turn might be necessary, from *Sein* back to Dasein, for the explicit notion of *Sein* might shed new light on the ontology of Dasein.[268] This second turn was not planned in the setup of *Sein und Zeit*.

3. What is the hermeneutical turn from Dasein to *Sein* in the third division of *Sein und Zeit* supposed to teach us? We do not possess a manuscript of this third division. As Heidegger later said in the Letter on "Humanism," he held back the third division of part 1 because "thinking failed in the adequate saying of this turning [*Kehre*] and did not succeed with the help of the language of metaphysics."[269] He also says that in this division, "the whole is reversed."[270] We must conclude, perhaps, that Heidegger's attempt to develop the third division in his lectures of the summer semester of 1927 was also a failure.[271] Should we even conclude that the interpreter of Heidegger cannot answer the question as to what Heidegger meant by the expression "being" as a "transcendens pure and simple" in *Sein und Zeit*? Heidegger intended to give an explication of this expression in the third division of part 1. We do not possess this division. How can one interpret a nonexisting text?

This latter conclusion, however, is somewhat rash. For Heidegger's view of hermeneutics as a spiraling movement implies that what becomes explicit at the next turn must be implicit in the present one. We should be able to derive hints as to the content of Heidegger's notion of being as a transcendens pure and simple from the extant divisions of *Sein und Zeit* and from the lectures of 1927. Even if the relevant part of these lectures is a failure, this failure might reveal what Heidegger intended to do.

4. As far as *Sein und Zeit* is concerned, we may infer from the inversion of titles that in the third division the order between being and time was to be reversed. Whereas Heidegger in the first two divisions starts with interpreting a specific being, Dasein, and ends up with temporality, he seems to have anticipated for the third division a route from temporality to being as a *transcendens pure*

and simple. One possible interpretation of such a route is a traditional religious one: by reflecting on our finite temporality, that is, on our mortality, we might find a route to Being or God as an eternal and even atemporal being. It may seem that this cannot be Heidegger's objective in *Sein und Zeit*.[272] The reason is that his aim was a drastic reinterpretation of the notion of being itself, and that he stresses again and again the "ontological difference" between being and beings.[273]

There are many hints as to the nature of this reinterpretation in the published text of *Sein und Zeit*. Heidegger's revolution in the interpretation of being purported to overthrow two millennia of philosophical thought. From Parmenides and Plato on, eternal or atemporal being has been considered as more "real" than temporal being. According to this tradition, only what is eternal can be an object of real knowledge. Greek philosophy decisively influenced the interpretation of Christianity. The Christian God was conceived of as an eternal or atemporal substance, as was man's immortal soul. We find this Neo-Platonic view of God and soul in Descartes and in much of subsequent philosophy. According to Kant, the transcendental subject has to be immutable and timeless, because time itself is an ordering structure in this subject. In *Ideen* I, sections 81–82, Husserl tried to show that the stream of transcendental consciousness must be infinite. We might summarize the traditional notion of being in the maxim that if real being is timeless, our own real being must be timeless or eternal as well. As Heidegger says, the traditional notion of being is that of always being present (*ständige Vorhandenheit*).

It is in its application to human existence that the traditional notion of being shows its absurd consequences in the clearest way. As Heidegger argues in *Sein und Zeit*, we will never understand our own mode of being as care (*Sorge*) unless we accept and acknowledge our finite temporality as being-toward-death. How could we be really concerned about our life if we did not live into a finite future? This is why a destruction of the traditional notion of being should start with a hermeneutical analysis of human existence. As Heidegger says in the second half of section 5, temporality (*Zeitlichkeit*) is the horizon of understanding being, because temporality is the most fundamental ontological structure of Dasein, and because Dasein has understanding of being.[274] Most modern readers of *Sein und Zeit* will have no difficulties in accepting that human existence is inescapably finite, and that it should be understood on the basis of finite temporality. This does not explain, however, why Heidegger thinks that being *tout court* is temporal as well.[275] Heidegger's grandiose hermeneutical movement in *Sein und Zeit* seems to have been planned as follows. In the first and the second division, the grip of the traditional timeless notion of being is undermined by an analysis of the temporality (*Zeitlichkeit*) of Dasein. In the third division, Heidegger wanted to turn to being as such, and show that it is temporal as well (*Temporalität des Seins*).[276] How should one interpret this idea of the temporality of being itself?

5. At this point, two possible interpretations suggest themselves. First, we might stress the fundamental role of temporality in the transcendental philoso-

phies of Kant and Husserl.[277] According to Husserl, for instance, all regional entities, even the "timeless" spatial forms studied by Euclidean geometry, are constituted in transcendental time. Extrapolating this Husserlian doctrine to Heidegger,
we might suppose that according to Heidegger "being itself" is temporal in the
sense that the different regional notions of being are distinguished by temporal
characteristics, so that time functions as the "horizon" for interpreting being. This
could then be explained by the transcendental doctrine that all ontical regions are
somehow constituted (in the weak sense of projectively understood) by temporal
Dasein.[278] Such an interpretation fits in well with section 3 of *Sein und Zeit*, where
Heidegger says that we must have a preliminary understanding of the notion of
being as such in order to derive the different regional modes of being by means
of a "nondeductive genealogy."[279] As in the case of Kant and Husserl, Heidegger's
conception of transcendental philosophy implies a three-story edifice of knowledge. The sciences and humanities are based on a priori regional ontologies,
which, in turn, are based on an even more fundamental science of the transcendental realm. According to Heidegger, Husserl and Kant failed to dwell on the universal notion of being that we use when we say that regional entities and the transcendental subject "are." This universal notion should be arrived at by a reflection on
transcendental subjectivity. In Heidegger's case, it is the notion of being as finite
temporality, whereas Kant and Husserl assumed that the transcendental subject is
eternal.

This transcendental interpretation solves one of the two problems raised by the
quotation I started with, the problem of why there should be one unified notion
of being. However, as it fails to solve the other problem, concerned with the
suggestion that being as such is *higher* than beings, there remains room for a
second interpretative hypothesis. What can this second hypothesis amount to,
if the theological one, derived from Scholastic usage of "Being," is excluded?
Regarding the "highness" of being as such, there is a paradox in Heidegger's
writings, which becomes quite pressing in the later works. On the one hand, much
of what Heidegger says in relation to being becomes easy to understand if one
substitutes "God" for "Being." On the other hand, Heidegger stressed many times
that philosophical thought cannot be theology.[280]

By and large, Heidegger's lectures of the summer semester of 1927 on the
Fundamental Problems of Phenomenology seem to corroborate the transcendental
interpretation. In part 2 of these lectures, Heidegger develops his conception of
the finite temporality of Dasein in contrast with Aristotle's notion of time. He
distinguishes three conceptions of time: (a) the traditional "vulgar" notion of time
as an infinite linear continuum of meaningless moments, (b) the everyday notion
of time as time for doing or not doing something, and (c) the fundamental finite
temporality of *Dasein*. Heidegger argues that Dasein's fundamental temporality
is a condition of the possibility of intentionality and of all human behavior and
experience, because it enables Dasein to understand being. In a Kantian manner,
transcendental time is conceived of as a precondition for projecting a priori holis-

tic schemes, which, in their turn, are preconditions for experience and for manipulating tools. The transcendental interpretation explains why Heidegger says that all time essentially belongs to Dasein.[281] Both in the lectures (§ 19) and in *Sein und Zeit* (§ 81), Heidegger argues that the "vulgar" notion of time (a) is due to Dasein's falling, that is, to the tendency of Dasein to interpret itself and its temporality on the model of purely present things. Because time in the most fundamental sense is claimed to be transcendental, Heidegger has to explain the fact that most people erroneously believe that time is primarily a cosmic phenomenon. Heidegger also argues that time in the sense of the everyday-conception (b) is "given" beforehand by Dasein. Whenever we look at our watch, for instance, "we already gave in advance time to the watch."[282] Allegedly, Dasein is the transcendental time-giving agency.[283] In our Dasein, original time (c, *ursprüngliche Zeit, Zeitlichkeit*) brings about (*zeitigt*) time (*Zeit*), as Heidegger says with a pun on the verb *zeitigen* (to bring about).[284]

There is also another strand in the lectures of 1927. At crucial moments in this text, Heidegger refers to Plato's notion of the Good as radically transcendent, and to the Platonic image of the cave.[285] He claims that in our understanding of being, we have to project being with respect to something, and that this *woraufhin* is transcendent even to being.[286] The *woraufhin* of understanding being turns out to be transcendental temporality. What is the relation between transcendental temporality and Plato's idea of the Good? Should we assume that transcendental temporality, which is the fundamental structure of Dasein, is somehow also radically transcendent to Dasein and to *Sein*? What, precisely, is the status of transcendental temporality?

At this point in the lectures, Heidegger's formulations become exasperatingly ambiguous. He says both that temporality is Dasein's fundamental structure, which enables Dasein to project itself, and that "temporality is in itself the original auto-projection as such."[287] What does he mean by this latter, obscure formula, which seems to remind us of the notion of Divine creation? Why does Heidegger continue the relevant passage by abstrusely discussing the notions of Light and of Nothing? Again, the texts seem to acquire a theological flavor without being theological. Should we suppose that there is yet a third meaning of "being" after all, apart from the phenomenological and the transcendental ones? I will come back to this question in section 11, below.[288]

By way of a summary, we may now specify the formal structure of the question of being (see § 6 above, *in finem*) in terms of the transcendental leitmotif. Within the framework of the transcendental theme, the nine aspects of this formal structure acquire the following meanings. (1) The unique and fundamental question of philosophy is concerned with being in the transcendental sense. Because nothing can be manifest to us except on the basis of a holistic interpretative scheme, which is a priori in the sense that Dasein has to project it on entities in order to enable them to become manifest, the question as to the nature of such a scheme is more fundamental than questions of science or regional ontology. This question may be called the question of being, for transcendental schemes specify the onto-logical sense ("being") of entities. (2) Man has an implicit understanding of the question of being, because projective Dasein is man's existence. By interpreting our ontological constitution, we will make explicit the projective nature of our understanding of being, and the difference between entities and being.[289]

If (3) we do nevertheless live in forgetfulness of being, this means, on the transcendental interpretation, that in ordinary life the projecting activity of Dasein goes unnoticed. Similarly, Kant and Husserl claimed that usually we are not aware of our transcendental activity of constitution.[290] Forgetfulness of being may be annulled by some kind of transcendental reduction. In Heidegger's case, the tran-scendental reduction consists in changing over from the *existentiell* level of re-flection to the *existential* level, that is, from reflection on entities to reflection on their being, more precisely, to reflection on our projectively understanding their being.[291] Because in daily life we have an implicit ontological understanding of being, this changing over is motivated by daily life, especially by the fundamental experience of *Angst*, and it may be actualized by an explicit hermeneutics of Dasein. (4) Forgetfulness of being consists in overlooking the ontological differ-ence between entities and their ontological sense or "being." In the traditional sense of "existence," we may say that entities exist independently of Dasein. But according to the transcendental leitmotif, the ontological sense or "being" of entities is due to a holistic framework, projected by Dasein. Since we do not explicitly acknowledge the difference between beings and being, and because we tend to be absorbed in the world, we (5) tend to endorse the ontology of presence, according to which all entities, including humans, *are* in the sense of being purely present.[292] However, we may (6) wrest ourselves from the oblivion of being by (7) raising the transcendental question as to the nature of being as projecting ontological sense, and as to being in contradistinction to beings. In doing so we will (8) destroy the tradition of metaphysics by means of a temporal interpretation of the notion of being, which will enable us (9) to become authentic, and to acknowledge the fact that we are beings who are-to-death, and who project or understand being.

§ 10. The Neo-Hegelian Theme

According to the interpretative hypothesis I am proposing, the question of being in *Sein und Zeit* is an interplay among three different leitmotifs, the meta-Aristote-lian theme, the phenomenologico-hermeneutical theme, and the transcendental leitmotif. One might say that the meta-Aristotelian theme provides a formal framework, consisting of a pole of differentiation and a pole of unity, while the two other themes each materialize one of these poles. In *Sein und Zeit*, the pheno-menologico-hermeneutical leitmotif is the pole of differentiation, because there are many different ontological regions, whereas the transcendental leitmotif is the pole of unity, Dasein being the unique transcendental subject that unifies beings by projecting being. But how should we interpret the question of being in the works written after *Sein und Zeit*? Is Heidegger's question in the later works identical to the question of being in that seminal book? In order to provide an answer to these questions, we must have a firm grasp of the chronology of Heidegger's later oeuvre.

Heidegger's masterpiece *Sein und Zeit* appeared in 1927, and it was his first major philosophical publication since the doctoral dissertation and the *Habilitationsschrift*. Two years later, in 1929, Heidegger published *Kant und das Problem der Metaphysik*, which covers the grounds of the unpublished first division of part 2 of *Sein und Zeit*. In 1929 he also published the inaugural lecture *Was ist Metaphysik?*, delivered at Freiburg University on 24 July of that year, and a contribution to the festschrift for Husserl's seventieth birthday, entitled "Vom Wesen des Grundes." Three divisions of *Sein und Zeit*, the third division of part 1, entitled "Zeit und Sein," and the second and third divisions of part 2 would never appear. Heidegger once told F.-W. von Herrmann that the third division of part 1 had been drafted along with the published fragment of *Sein und Zeit*, but that he burned the draft because it did not satisfy him.[293]

Between 1929 and 1947, Heidegger did not publish much, even though he wrote voluminous manuscripts, such as *Beiträge zur Philosophie*, which counts 933 pages in autograph (1936–38), or *Besinnung*, a manuscript of 589 pages (1938–39), and an impressive series of lecture notes, most of which are now edited in the *Gesamtausgabe*.[294] In 1933 Heidegger's rectoral address appeared, in which he blended his philosophical idiom with terminology borrowed from Nazi propaganda. He argued that if one wants to realize the essence of German university, one should conceive of science (*Wissenschaft*) as the will to effectuate the historical spiritual mission of the German people in its state.[295] *Wissenschaft*, instead of being an international enterprise without essential links to specific nations or peoples, had to be redefined by means of three relations to the German nation-state. A first relation, to the German people (*Volksgemeinschaft*), would oblige students to take part in *Arbeitsdienst* (labor service); a second relation, to the German state, would oblige them to enroll in *Wehrdienst* (military service); and a third relation, to the spiritual task of the German people, would require a commitment to *Wissensdienst* (knowledge service), knowledge being defined heroically as "the most acute risking of Dasein in the midst of the predominance of being."[296] Summarizing his description of these three relations, Heidegger wrote that only together they constitute the original and full essence of science (*Wissenschaft*).[297] Whereas Karl Jaspers could still read the ambiguous text of the rectoral address as an attempt to revive Greek thought, interpreting the National Socialist overtones as external to Heidegger's real intentions, Heidegger's speech in Tübingen on 30 November 1933 clearly revealed what he was up to. He wanted to replace Wilhelm von Humboldt's conception of a university, according to which the state should not interfere with the universities funded by it, by a totalitarian conception.[298] Universities should become organic parts of the National Socialist state, hence their traditional identity as islands of academic freedom had to be destroyed.[299]

At the beginning of the same month, Heidegger's appeal to the German students appeared in the *Freiburger Studentenzeitung*. In this incriminating piece, Heidegger insists that all students must take part in the Nazi revolution, which transforms German Dasein, and that their life should not be guided by articles of faith or ideas, because "only the *Führer* himself *is* the present and future German reality and its law." According to Hugo Ott, the fact that Heidegger wrote the verb "is" in italics might betray a relation between his political engagement and the question of being.[300] On the eleventh of November, Heidegger had summoned his compatriots during a speech in Leipzig to vote for Hitler's decision to leave the League of Nations, using again a sinister mixture of his philosophical jargon and National Socialist slogans.[301] Heidegger remained rector of the Freiburg University until 23 April 1934, the day on which he abdicated.[302]

Heidegger's first philosophical publication after his fiasco as a rector was on Hölderlin, entitled "Hölderlin und das Wesen der Dichtung" (*Hölderlin and the Essence of Poetry*), and it appeared in 1936 in the ultraconservative periodical *Das Innere Reich*, in which only authors who more or less followed the line of the National Socialist Party could publish.[303] This text contains many of the themes that have become familiar from Heidegger's publications after the war, themes that I explore in section 11. According to Heidegger/Hölderlin, language is not a tool of humans, but the *Ereignis* (Event) that determines "man's highest possibility." Language *is* essentially only in *Gespräch* (conversation). The conversation that we humans *are* is nothing but *Nennen der Götter* (calling or naming gods) and *Wort-Werden der Welt* (the World becoming Word). Moreover, if we call or name gods, our word is an answer to an *Anspruch* (claim) that they address to us. The poet has the task of calling or naming the gods, and of founding being (*Stiftung des Seins*) by naming beings. In doing so, the poet "founds" or "establishes" (*gründen*) human Dasein: he gives its ground to it. Because the gods merely speak to us by giving *Winke* (hints), the poet has to pick up these hints and pass them on to his people. The act of founding being is bound by the hints of the gods. Our time is a wretched one (*dürftige Zeit*), because the gods have escaped (*entfliehen*), and the coming God has not yet arrived.[304]

Until 1947, when the "Brief über den 'Humanismus'" (*Letter on "Humanism"*) appeared, Heidegger published only six other philosophical pieces: one short piece called "Wege zur Aussprache" (1937),[305] one on Hölderlin's hymn "Wie wenn am Feiertage" (1941), one on Plato's doctrine of Truth (1942), the essay "Vom Wesen der Wahrheit" (1943), based on a lecture that Heidegger delivered for the first time in 1930 under the significant title "Philosophieren und Glauben,"[306] an elucidation of Hölderlin's poem "Andenken" (1943), and an elucidation of Hölderlin's poem "Heimkunft / An die Verwandten" (1944). After 1947,

Heidegger's publications became an ever growing stream, which finally discharged itself into the majestic river of the collected works (*Gesamtausgabe*). The first volume of the *Gesamtausgabe* appeared in 1975, one year before Heidegger's death on 26 May 1976. With the project of the collected works Heidegger secured himself a series of publications officially and misleadingly called final authorized editions (*Ausgabe letzter Hand*), which will continue to appear well into the third millennium.[307]

It is customary to designate all texts written by Heidegger after 1927 as his "later works," in contradistinction to *Sein und Zeit*, which may be considered the culmination point of the early Heidegger's development. With the exception of *Kant und das Problem der Metaphysik*, which clearly fits into the project of *Sein und Zeit*, the later works belong to literary genres different from that of Heidegger's masterpiece. Whereas *Sein und Zeit* is a philosophical treatise in the grand German style of Kant and Hegel, the later works are lectures, essays, letters, a few dialogues, occasional speeches, and elucidations of poetry. If Heidegger published books, they were either collections of essays, such as *Holzwege* (1950), *Vorträge und Aufsätze* (1954), *Unterwegs zur Sprache* (1959), *Wegmarken* (1967), and *Zur Sache des Denkens* (1969), or they were polished editions of often earlier lecture notes, such as *Einführung in die Metaphysik* (1953), *Was heißt Denken?* (1954), the two volumes of *Nietzsche* (1961), and *Die Frage nach dem Ding* (1962), or, finally, they were a mixture of these two genres, such as *Der Satz vom Grund* (1957). What explains this radical change in the literary form of Heidegger's writings?[308]

There is not only a shift in the form of Heidegger's publications after 1929; the content undergoes a drastic metamorphosis as well. The notion of a *Fundamentalontologie* (fundamental ontology) is abandoned and the claim of Heidegger's philosophy to be *wissenschaftlich* (scientific, academic) is dropped. The jargon of transcendental philosophy nearly disappears, as do the methodological claims of phenomenology and hermeneutics. Existentialia of Dasein, such as *Lichtung* (clearing), *Sorge* (Concern), and *Stimmung* (mood), to the extent that they occur in the later works, receive an interpretation very different from that of *Sein und Zeit*. Should we conclude that Heidegger's question of being, which remains the focus of his thought, is subjected to a metamorphosis as well?

However this may be, it seems clear that the metamorphosis both in form and in content of Heidegger's publications after 1929 must be related to the celebrated *Kehre* (turn). The German word *Kehre*, which Heidegger himself uses to mark the transition between the philosophy of *Sein und Zeit* and his later thought, has the literal meaning of a sharp turn or bend in a road, and it fits in well with Heidegger's characterization of his thinking as a road, a characterization we find already in *Sein und Zeit* (§ 83). However, because the stem *-kehr-* also occurs in German words such as *Bekehrung* (conversion) and *Umkehrung* (reversal, inversion, a change of one's ways, a turning back), many commentators have attributed a deeper meaning to this term, such as conversion. I will translate *Kehre* by "turn," in order to avoid prejudging the issue of interpretation (see § 13, below).

Dating the turn in Heidegger's philosophy is not irrelevant for the interpretation of the later works. Did the turn occur before Heidegger's involvement with the Nazis or after the fiasco of the rectorship in 1934? In the former case there is no doubt that Heidegger's political commitment, to the extent that it is philosophically relevant, has to be taken into account in an interpretation of his later thought. In the latter case his thought after the turn might be interpreted in part as a response to the events of 1933–34, and perhaps as an attempt to dissociate himself from National Socialism. After the war, Heidegger dates the turn in two crucial letters that he wrote to foreigners, the "Brief über den 'Humanismus,' " addressed to Jean Beaufret in the fall of 1946 and published in 1947, and the letter to William Richardson of April 1962, published as a preface to Richardson's book on Heidegger of 1963.

In the "Brief über den 'Humanismus' " Heidegger suggests that the turn had been anticipated already in *Sein und Zeit*, and that the lecture "Vom Wesen der Wahrheit" (On the Essence of Truth), delivered for the first time in 1930 and published in 1943, provides a certain insight into the thinking of the turn from "Being and Time" into "Time and Being." He adds that: "This turning [*Kehre*] is not a change of the standpoint of *Sein und Zeit*, but in it the thinking that was sought first arrives at the location of that dimension out of which *Sein und Zeit* is experienced."[309] One will conclude that the turn must have occurred as early as between 1927 and 1930. At first sight, the letter to Richardson seems to confirm what Heidegger says in the "Brief über den 'Humanismus.' " He stresses again that, although the turn *is* a change (*Wendung*) in his thought, it is not the consequence of altering the standpoint or of abandoning the fundamental question of *Sein und Zeit*. Rather, the thinking of the turn results from the fact that Heidegger stayed with the *zu denkenden Sache* (matter-for-thought) of *Sein und Zeit*. However, when it comes to dating the turn in the development of his thought, Heidegger surprisingly refers to a period very different from 1927–30. He says that what is designated as the turn was already at work in his thinking ten years prior to 1947, that is, around 1937, when he wrote *Beiträge zur Philosophie*.[310] As a consequence, it seems that Heidegger's own indications concerning the moment of the turn do not enable us to decide whether it occurred before Heidegger's involvement with Nazism or after the debacle of the rectorship.

This aporia concerning the dating of Heidegger's turn can be resolved only by means of a detour. First, we have to interpret the question of being in Heidegger's works written after 1934 and especially after 1937 (§§ 10–11). Having obtained in this manner a clear view of Heidegger's thought after the turn, we then may try to trace the incipience of the turn back to the period of 1927–30 (§§ 12–13). Only then we will be able to decide whether Heidegger's question of being in *Sein und Zeit* is the same question as the question of being in the later works, and whether Heidegger was faithful to the original intentions he had in writing *Sein und Zeit* when he said much later that his thinking after the turn was not a consequence of altering the standpoint of that book.[311] And only then will we be able to decide whether Heidegger's political commitment to Hitler, if it has a philosophical relevance, fits in with the philosophy of *Sein und Zeit*, as Heidegger told Karl Löwith during his visit to Rome in 1936, or with his thought after the turn, or perhaps with both.[312]

According to the letter to Richardson, there is one unique subject matter of philosophical thought (*Sache des Denkens*). Because this unique subject matter is intrinsically manifold (*in sich mehrfältig*) and abounds in plenitude (*Fülle bergend*), it requires manifold thought (*mehrfältiges Denken*).[313] In compliance with what Heidegger says here, I propose as an interpretative hypothesis that Heidegger in the later works incessantly tried to say the same thing, albeit in many different ways and from somewhat different perspectives.[314] Accordingly, the philosophical deep structure of Heidegger's later thought is relatively simple. It may be seen as an interplay of two fundamental themes or leitmotifs that complement each other. I call these leitmotifs respectively the Neo-Hegelian theme and the postmonotheist theme. Although the postmonotheist theme is more fundamental, I start with discussing the Neo-Hegelian leitmotif.

As the Neo-Hegelian and the postmonotheist themes are fundamental to all Heidegger's later works, they may be developed on the basis of an arbitrary selection of texts, and I refer to other texts in the notes. Yet some passages are clearer than others. The Neo-Hegelian theme is particularly conspicuous in works such as *Die Frage nach dem Ding* (*The Question Concerning the Thing*), based on lectures given in the winter semester of 1935–36 and published in 1962; "Die Zeit des Weltbildes" ("The Time of the World Picture"), a lecture of 1938 published in *Holzwege* (1950); "Die Frage nach der Technik" ("The Question Concerning Technology"), a lecture of 1953, and "Überwindung der Metaphysik" ("Overcoming Metaphysics"), which contains notes written between 1936 and 1946, both published in *Vorträge und Aufsätze* (1954); "Zur Seinsfrage" ("A Propos The Question of Being"), written for the sixtieth birthday of Ernst Jünger in 1955 and published in *Wegmarken* (1967); "Die Onto-Theo-Logische Verfassung der Metaphysik" ("The Ontotheological Constitution of Metaphysics"), which is the concluding lecture of a seminar given during the winter semester of 1956–57 on Hegel's *Wissenschaft der Logik*, published in *Identität und Differenz* (1957); and "Das Ende der Philosophie und die Aufgabe des Denkens" ("The End of Philosophy and the Task of Thinking"), read during the colloquium *Kierkegaard Vivant* in 1964 and published in *Zur Sache des Denkens* (1969). Further important passages are to be found in the second volume of *Nietzsche* (1961), especially in "Die Metaphysik als Geschichte des Seins" ("Metaphysics as History of Being") from 1941, in *Beiträge zur Philosophie* (*Contributions to Philosophy*) and in a great number of lecture notes edited in the collected works.

I develop the Neo-Hegelian leitmotif in three stages. First (A), I state and elucidate nine theses that in conjunction constitute the Neo-Hegelian theme in its most complete version. Second (B), I try to reconstruct the relation between the Neo-Hegelian leitmotif and the philosophy of *Sein und Zeit*: Why did the transcendental philosophy of *Sein und Zeit* turn into Neo-Hegelianism? Finally (C), I compare Hegel's grand strategy with Heidegger's, and point to the need of a fifth fundamental theme in Heidegger's question of being: the postmonotheist leitmotif.

A. *The Composition of the Neo-Hegelian Theme*

According to the celebrated definition of philosophy in the preface to Hegel's *Philosophy of Right*, philosophy is "its epoch comprehended by thought."[315] On this definition, it is the task of philosophy to conceptualize one's historical era and to give a diagnosis of the state of one's culture. Because the present epoch grew out of former epochs, philosophy must encompass diagnoses of the former stages of civilization as well. In the later works Heidegger endorses a variety of this Hegelian notion of philosophy. There is a Neo-Hegelian leitmotif in Heidegger's question of being.[316]

One may wonder how philosophy is supposed to be able to comprehend its epoch by thought. The present state of our culture is investigated by many disciplines, such as economics, history, sociology, ecology, political science, art history, geography, and demography. Moreover, these disciplines, and indeed all sciences, belong to the present state of culture, so that this state contains the most recent developments in physics, astronomy, mathematics, biology, technology, and chemistry. No human being is able to grasp even a billionth part of the amount of information available in our epoch. How, then, should the philosopher comprehend his epoch by thought, and what is the relation between philosophy in this sense and the empirical sciences of culture?

Clearly, the Neo-Hegelian notion of philosophy makes sense only if the amount of information is drastically reduced by a number of methodological decisions. Heidegger makes such decisions without explicitly discussing them. As a consequence, he conceals the serious epistemological problems involved in the Neo-Hegelian notion of philosophy. Depending on the methodological decisions that reduce the amount of information involved, different varieties of Neo-Hegelianism will arise. If one thinks, for instance, that economic structures are the essence of a historical era, as Marxism did, one will adhere to an "economic" variety of Neo-Hegelianism. According to the economic variety, studying economical phenomena is the main thing if one wants to grasp an epoch by thought.

The example of Marxism shows that Neo-Hegelianism will always be bound up with some kind of foundationalism. In Marx's case, it is assumed that human culture with the exception of economic structures is rooted in, and determined by, the means and relations of production. As we will see, Heidegger's variety of Neo-Hegelianism is also foundationalist: it claims that metaphysics is the foundation of a historical human culture as a whole. This conclusion is important because it contradicts a current interpretation of the later Heidegger, endorsed by Richard

Rorty and many others, according to which Heidegger in his later works broke free from foundationalism.[317] Let me now reconstruct Heidegger's variety of Neo-Hegelianism, which informs a great number of the later works. It may be expressed in the following nine theses:

1. Fundamental Stances. Fundamental to each historical epoch is what Heidegger calls a *Grundstellung* or *Grundzug der Haltung und des Daseins*, that is, a fundamental stance or attitude that each and every Dasein has toward itself, its fellow human beings, and indeed the totality of beings.[318] According to one text, such a fundamental stance consists of two aspects: the way in which humans treat, process, or manipulate beings on the one hand, and the way in which humans pro-ject a general and fundamental epistemic scheme on the other hand.[319] Mostly, however, these two aspects are taken together. A fundamental stance may then be characterized as the way in which everything there is shows up for us.[320] Such a way of manifesting is due to a projection (*Entwurf*) of a general scheme of disclosure. This first thesis may be seen as a historicist application of Heidegger's Kantian views in *Sein und Zeit*, according to which the way things are disclosed to us is determined by an a priori pro-jection of a holistic framework of significant relations. In the later works, Heidegger seems to assume that each historical epoch is determined by one specific scheme of disclosure.

2. Fundamental Stances All-embracing. Fundamental attitudes are totalitarian (my term) in that they determine the way in which everything manifests itself to us.[321] This second thesis, which is implied by the first, has far-reaching consequences. According to Heidegger, we are now living in the epoch of technology. What he means by this is not that technology in the usual sense plays a substantial role in contemporary Western culture, even though that is of course true, but that our fundamental stance is that of technology. This is to say that, according to Heidegger, everything shows up for us as raw material for production, processing, consumption, and exploitation. Even human beings tend to be viewed as a means of production only.[322] We might object that a great many phenomena in contemporary culture, such as the ecological movement and the notion of the fundamental rights of man, refute Heidegger's thesis of *das Wesen der Technik* (the reign of technology) as a monolithic fundamental stance. However, because Heidegger assumes that fundamental attitudes are totalitarian or holistic, he would stigmatize such objections as symptoms of false consciousness. A tourist may view the river Rhine poetically as a natural stream charged with symbolic significance. In reality, Heidegger argues in "Die Frage nach der Technik," the Rhine River in the present epoch *is nothing but* a water-power supplier, and if the tourist admires the river in the landscape, in fact river and landscape are objects calling for inspection by a tour group ordered there by the vacation industry.[323] Similarly, a forester who loves the woods and thinks that he walks through them as his grandfather did is in reality a function of the timber industry, "whether he knows it or not."[324] Heidegger's Neo-Hegelian foundationalism, like Marx's variety of Neo-Hegelianism, implies the thesis of a global false consciousness: anyone who thinks that there are exceptions to the present reign of technology must be mistaken, because the fundamental stance of technology determines the way in which *everything* manifests itself to us. Clearly, theses (1) and (2) are akin to structuralism, and it is not surprising that the later Heidegger deeply influenced structuralists such as Michel Foucault.

3. Metaphysics, The End of Philosophy, Fundamental Moods. We should wonder how the philosopher is able to grasp these totalitarian fundamental attitudes, which allegedly determine the way things manifest themselves in a specific historical era. This epistemological issue is the more delicate because Heidegger admits of the possibility that fundamental attitudes are at variance with the attitudes we consciously adopt vis-à-vis ourselves, our fellow humans, and natural phenomena. As we saw, Heidegger claims in "Die Frage nach der Technik" that our present era is characterized by the fundamental stance of technology, even though, consciously, we often do not regard ourselves, our fellow man, and natural phenomena as a matter for exploitation and production. Heidegger nowhere discusses the epistemology of grasping fundamental attitudes at length, and we have to reconstruct his views from hints and isolated observations.

The fundamental attitudes that were at the basis of past historical epochs in Western civilization are expressed by the philosophers of these epochs in their systems of metaphysics. At least this is what Heidegger claims.[325] The reason is that a fundamental stance determines how *all* beings manifest themselves to us, whereas metaphysics is traditionally defined as the science of beings as such, that is, of the fundamental characteristics all beings have in common. Metaphysics, then, is nothing but an explicit conceptual articulation of a fundamental stance.[326] As a consequence, we would be able to discern the fundamental stances of the past by studying the history of metaphysics. Of course this answer does not yet solve the problem of how the metaphysicians of the past managed to grasp fundamental stances. Sometimes Heidegger suggests that they provided historical epochs with a fundamental stance by interpreting "the totality of beings" in a certain way.

This Heideggerian notion of metaphysics differs from the traditional Aristotelian notion in two respects. First, Heidegger holds that metaphysics is fundamental to a cultural era as a whole, whereas Aristotle merely claims that metaphysics is fundamental to the sciences because it provides them with their first principles and causes. The Aristotelian notion of metaphysics, which informs the Western philosophical tradition from Plato and Aristotle via Descartes and Kant until Husserl and the early Heidegger, is an implication of Aristotle's philosophy of science, as we saw in section 7. Second, Heidegger takes it that each historical epoch has a different metaphysical foundation, whereas according to the notion of metaphysics we find in, say, Aristotle, Descartes, and Kant, metaphysical principles should be valid for all times, because they are necessarily true and a priori. In this respect, Heidegger is closer to Hegel and Fichte than to Aristotle and Kant.

There is a tradition in German philosophy, which starts with Hegel and continues with Marx and Nietzsche, according to which metaphysics has been completed. These thinkers endorse the slogan of "the end of philosophy (metaphysics)." Hegel claims that metaphysics has been completed because in his own
philosophy the Absolute overcomes its self-alienation in nature and becomes fully
conscious of itself. Marx and Nietzsche, who take metaphysics as a doctrine about
a suprasensible world, claim that metaphysics is an illusion, which either serves
the mighty in their oppression of the working classes (Marx), or, conversely,
assists the slaves and the weak in their power struggle against the masters and the
strong (Nietzsche). Heidegger also endorses the thesis of the end of metaphysics.
Philosophy in the sense of metaphysics has come to an end, he claims in "Das
Ende der Philosophie und die Aufgabe des Denkens" (1964), because with
Nietzsche it has exhausted its possibilities (see §15A, below). In this text, Heidegger argues for the thesis of the end of philosophy on the basis of a Neo-Platonist
notion of metaphysics (metaphysics as science of the suprasensible) and not on
the basis of his usual, Aristotelian notion (metaphysics as a general theory on the
totality of beings). Because Nietzsche and Marx "reversed" Platonism by saying
that the sensible world is the only real world there is, metaphysics allegedly exhausted its possibilities. According to Heidegger, the end of metaphysics does not
mean that we simply stop producing metaphysical systems. The end of philosophy
(metaphysics) is rather "that place [*Ort*] in which the totality of its history is
gathered in its most extreme possibilities."[327] As we will see, this ultimate station
is the reign of technology (*das Wesen der Technik*).

It follows from the thesis of the end of philosophy that Heidegger himself will
not attempt to express our alleged fundamental stance in a new metaphysical
system. Often he claims that Nietzsche already did so by his doctrine of the will
to power, for the reign of technology supposedly is the realization of Nietzsche's
philosophy. Heidegger was heavily indebted to Ernst Jünger for this somewhat
far-fetched interpretation of Nietzsche and of the modern era.[328] How, then, should
the philosopher articulate the fundamental stance of the present epoch, if not by
means of a metaphysical system? How is he supposed to know what this fundamental stance is?

In *Sein und Zeit*, Heidegger claimed that moods (*Stimmungen*) are the most
fundamental way of opening up the world (§ 29). Moods would be more fundamental than intentionality: "*The mood has already disclosed, in every case, Being-
in-the-world as a whole, and makes it possible first of all to direct oneself toward
something.*"[329] In his later works, Heidegger advances the similar claim that fundamental attitudes are revealed to us primarily in fundamental moods (*Grundstim-
mungen*).[330] The philosopher should try to arouse such a fundamental mood. He
should intensify a latent fundamental mood, such as *Langeweile* (boredom), in
order to make us aware of the fundamental stance that it expresses. Heidegger's
later writings are often meant to realize this objective. To the uninitiated reader,
they may seem to be attempts to rouse popular feeling, pieces of rabble-rousing,

but in fact their powerful rhetorical nature is inherent in Heidegger's Neo-Hegelian theme. The only thing to be deplored is that Heidegger never tells us how we are to distinguish fundamental moods from other moods, and how we might distinguish the allegedly unique fundamental stance that is basic to our epoch from other, more mundane, attitudes we happen to have. Perhaps he could not make the distinction himself, and this might explain why Heidegger took Hitler's rabble-rousing for a philosophical revelation of a fundamental stance.

4. Heidegger's Later Foundationalism. Metaphysics in the traditional, Aristotelian sense is thought to be a priori in relation to the sciences, because it provides the sciences with true first principles. While Heidegger generalizes the foundational import of metaphysics to an epoch of civilization as a whole, he obviously holds on to the notion that metaphysics, and indeed all knowledge of fundamental attitudes, is a priori in relation to the empirical sciences. This foundationalist thesis reduces the amount of information needed to "comprehend our epoch in thought" in a drastic way. No empirical research into the present state of civilization will be needed in order to grasp its fundamental stance, because this stance is more fundamental than empirical science.[331] By claiming that the unique fundamental stance of our epoch becomes accessible by arousing a fundamental mood, and that this epistemic access is more fundamental than empirical research, Heidegger radically dissociates philosophical insight from empirical studies of culture and society. He professes to discover the technological stance as fundamental to our time without ever discussing the empirical history of technology, and without investigating the factual extent to which technology dominates modern life. By claiming that a fundamental stance is totalitarian in the sense defined under (2), he also makes his diagnosis of the present state of Western civilization immune to criticisms raised by empirical studies of society. In Heidegger's hands, philosophical thought regains the position of queen of the sciences, a position that was threatened by Neo-Kantians and logical positivists, who reduced philosophy to epistemology and theory of science. As Bourdieu observed, Heidegger's philosophical radicalism serves the ultimate aim of a conservative revolution in philosophy, which purports to make philosophy fundamental again.[332]

5. Being Historicized. Being (*Sein*) within the framework of the Neo-Hegelian leitmotif becomes a word for the history-shaping ways in which entities reveal themselves in a specific epoch.[333] Traditional metaphysics allegedly suffers from an oblivion of being (*Seinsvergessenheit*) because, although it provides a conceptual articulation of the fundamental characteristics of the totality of beings, it refrains from reflecting on the fundamental sense of "being" (*Sein*) itself, which gives unity to each fundamental stance. Postmetaphysical thinking in Heidegger's sense has not only the objective of bringing to the fore the present fundamental stance by means of arousing a fundamental mood. It should also reflect on the history of metaphysics, in order to trace the various senses of "being" that inform the respective historical stances of Western civilization.

6. Real History. "History" in the habitual sense of the word designates both the sum of human actions, artifacts, and forms of life in the past, and the discipline that studies these actions and forms of life. Because Heidegger in section 7 of *Sein und Zeit* calls empirical phenomena "vulgar" phenomena, we might label empirical history "vulgar" history. To vulgar history, Heidegger opposes real or authentic history (*eigentliche Geschichte*), which is the sequence of fundamental stances underlying vulgar history. Real history is "necessarily hidden to the normal eye." It is the history of the "revealedness of being" (*Offenbarkeit des Seins*).[334] Heidegger's later "historical mode of questioning" (*geschichtliches Fragen*) aims at making explicit fundamental stances of Dasein amidst the totality of beings.[335] Since these stances allegedly can be studied independently of empirical history as an intellectual discipline, Heidegger's doctrine of real history implies that the philosopher is the real historian, and that by reconstructing the sequence of metaphysical structures, he does a more fundamental job than the historian in the usual sense is able to do. Heidegger often intimates that his historical questioning is also more fundamental than historical research done by historians of philosophy, and that it may brush aside the methodological canon of historical philology and interpretation. As Joseph Margolis observes, Heidegger's doctrine of real history "manages to ignore the concrete history of actual existence and actual inquiry."[336]

7. The Logic of Real History. Real history has its hidden logic, and it is one of the major objectives of the Neo-Hegelian leitmotif to trace this logic in the sequence of fundamental stances. According to Heidegger, the logic of real Western history is the logic of "productionist metaphysics."[337] As Heidegger says in the "Brief über den 'Humanismus,' " the reign of technology (*das Wesen der Technik*) is a fundamental stance or a *Gestalt* of truth that is rooted in the history of metaphysics. The history of metaphysics itself is only a phase in the history of being (*Geschichte des Seins*).[338] Why does Heidegger claim that the present fundamental stance of technology is rooted in the history of metaphysics? We find several versions of the logic of real history in Heidegger's later writings, but the underlying idea is always the same. The fundamental concepts of Greek metaphysics, such as matter (*hylē*) and form (*morfē*), are derived from the domain of artifacts, and these concepts inform all later metaphysics. This is a thesis Heidegger already advanced in the Natorp essay of 1922 and in *Sein und Zeit*.[339] It implies that from Plato and Aristotle on, "to be" has been understood as "being produced." According to the later Heidegger, the subsequent development of Western metaphysics is essentially nothing but a further elaboration of this notion of being. According to the Scholastics, "to be" means to be created by an all-powerful God. Descartes inherits this notion, but he also interprets human beings as creators, namely, creators of a representation of the world. In fact, the world becomes a man-made representation in the hands of Descartes and his followers, such as Kant, Schopenhauer, and Nietzsche.[340] Nietzsche is the metaphysical culmination point of the development of productionist metaphysics, because he claims that all entities are posits of a will to power. Nietzschean metaphysics allegedly is an articulation of the fundamental stance that is still extant in the present epoch, the reign of technology, because in our epoch everything manifests itself either as raw materials for production or as a product of technological power. In short, the metaphysical tradition that began with the productionist notions of matter and form in Plato and Aristotle has been completed in our modern technological epoch. This is why we live in the time of the end or completion of metaphysics.

In his later works, Heidegger describes the period of the end of metaphysics in apocalyptic terms, which may have been inspired by the destructions of the Second World War. The earth is destroyed, man errs (*Irre*), the world becomes monstrous (*Unwelt*), everything is consumed or wasted (*vernutzt*), including the raw material called "man" (*der Rohstoff "Mensch"*), and human action is meaningless.[341] This is the sinister epoch of the reign of technology. If Heidegger is right about the logic in the development of metaphysics and about fundamental stances in general, the present era of technology is nothing but the logical outcome of Plato's and Aristotle's decision to describe beings in terms derived from artifacts. For the history of metaphysics supposedly determines the actual history of the West.[342]

8. The Decision. As Heidegger says in *Die Frage nach dem Ding*, it is also the aim of historical questioning to prepare a decision. Of course, to engage in historical questioning at all is already the outcome of a decision, the decision to ask in a manner that "exceeds all other questioning in scope, depth, and certainty." We decided, Heidegger says, to engage in a questioning "which is long-winded and long-lasting, and which will remain a questioning during decennia." Only in this manner are we able to master that which will crush us if it remains natural to us: the fundamental stance of our epoch.[343] The ultimate objective of Heidegger's historical questioning is to prepare a second decision, a decision about the very stance that is fundamental to our epoch. Heidegger sometimes characterizes this stance as a projection (*Entwurf*), which belongs to the domain of our freedom. If we become conscious of the fundamental stance that determines our epoch, we might perhaps become free to change this stance. Only by changing the stance of technology and of the domination by science might we be "saved."[344] We should "let things be" (*seinlassen*) instead of dominating them by means of science and technology. No wonder that Heidegger's later thought has been annexed by the movement of deep ecology, which holds that only a fundamental change in our ways of thinking and acting will prevent an ecological catastrophe.

It is not clear how this notion of historical freedom should be reconciled with the notion of a logic of real history, which determines the sequence of fundamental attitudes. Have we become free to adopt a new stance only now, because the logic of productionist metaphysics has reached its completion? This is perhaps suggested by Heidegger, when he quotes Hölderlin's lines: "But where danger is, grows/ The saving power too."[345] Furthermore, Heidegger often seems to contradict the idea that we might decide on the issue of which fundamental stance to take. In "Die Frage nach der Technik," for instance, he says that "the essence of history . . . is neither the object of historical research, nor merely the process of human activity." He adds that the essence of freedom is *originally* not connected with the will or even with the causality of human willing.[346] What, then, does Heidegger mean when he tells us that historical questioning prepares us for a decision? The contradiction is not removed when he redefines freedom as "the realm of the destining that at any given time starts a revealing on its way."[347] As we will see, these questions can only be answered if we admit yet another leitmotif in Heidegger's question of being, the postmonotheist theme.

   9. Overcoming Metaphysics. The Neo-Hegelian leitmotif explains why the later Heidegger develops his thought mainly by interpreting the history of Western metaphysics. The theme of the destruction of metaphysics, which figured prominently in *Sein und Zeit*, now becomes the theme of *Überwindung der Metaphysik* (Overcoming of Metaphysics): by tracing the logic inherent in the sequence of fundamental stances, we will see that Western metaphysics has reached its consummation in the present era of technology, which, Heidegger says, will last a very long time. This insight will prepare us for a new beginning.[348] Incidentally, the theme of the destruction of metaphysics will undergo yet another metamorphosis in the context of the postmonotheist leitmotif, and emerge as "getting over metaphysics" or "coping with metaphysics" (*Verwindung der Metaphysik*).

   These nine theses and themes, which emerge again and again in Heidegger's later writings, constitute what I have called the Neo-Hegelian leitmotif in the question of being. The Neo-Hegelian leitmotif shows all formal characteristics of the question of being as specified in section 6, above. As is the case with the other leitmotifs, the Neo-Hegelian leitmotif provides each of these formal characteristics with a semantic content that is peculiar to this theme (the arabic numerals refer to those in § 6). (1) Being is the history-shaping way in which entities disclose themselves in historical epochs, and it is related to a fundamental stance. The *question of being* aims at revealing these ways of disclosure and the inner logic of their succession. (2) Dasein has an understanding of being (*Seinsverständnis*) because it implicitly grasps the sense of being in its epoch. Grasping (a sense of) being is the essence of Dasein, because it determines its historical identity. (3) Nevertheless, we live in forgetfulness of being (*Seinsvergessenheit*) because we do not reflect thematically on the present sense of being. Even traditional metaphysics is characterized by oblivion of being: although it reflected on the totality of beings as such, it did not articulate the sense of being that informed it: being as being produced. This is because (4) traditional metaphysics did not acknowledge the *ontological difference* between beings (*Seiendes*) and being (*Sein*). Since metaphysics did not reflect on the sense of being that informed it, it uncritically endorsed a productionist ontology (5) and it followed the logic implied by this ontology (cf. the ontology of presence in *Sein und Zeit*). The task of the thinker is (6) to wrest us from oblivion of being by (7) raising the question of being anew and by (8) retrieving the tradition of metaphysics. This will (9) liberate man for a new fundamental stance.

Heidegger's Neo-Hegelian theme may be seen as a reversal of this theme as developed by Marx. Whereas Marx claimed that economic structures determine the superstructure of civilization to which philosophy and metaphysics belong, Heidegger holds that metaphysics is a conceptual articulation of the foundations of civilization, because it comprehends in thought fundamental stances. Productionist metaphysics, as it developed from Plato and Aristotle on, allegedly explains the present technological era, so that the philosopher possesses the key to the temple of historical knowledge. From Heidegger's point of view, Marx's philosophy itself is a typical symptom of the reign of technology because it proclaims that manipulating and processing entities by means of labor is the essence of man.[349] The philosophies of both Marx and the later Heidegger, then, are opposing varieties of the same Neo-Hegelian theme. If Marx reversed Hegel by considering economic structures of production as the underlying basis of world history, instead of Hegel's autodevelopment of absolute spirit, does Heidegger's reversal of Marx bring us back to Hegel's view? As we will see, Heidegger's Neo-Hegelian theme in a sense is a reversal of Hegel as well. However, before discussing Heidegger's relation to Hegel, we should raise the question of how the philosophy of *Sein und Zeit* could turn into the Neo-Hegelian leitmotif.

B. From Neo-Kantianism to Neo-Hegelianism

How does the Neo-Hegelian leitmotif relate to the philosophy of *Sein und Zeit*? We remember that Heidegger's masterpiece was planned to consist of six divisions, of which only two divisions were published. Moreover, it was divided into a constructive, systematic part, and a destructive, historical part. The most simple and elegant hypothesis about the connection between *Sein und Zeit* and Heidegger's later Neo-Hegelian leitmotif would be that the Neo-Hegelian theme is a somewhat delayed and developed realization of part 2 of *Sein und Zeit*. It is the "destruction of the history of ontology" that Heidegger sketches in section 6 of that book. Indeed, there are authors, Safranski, for example, who assume that an essay such as "Die Zeit des Weltbildes" (1938), which squarely belongs to the Neo-Hegelian theme as reconstructed above, is part of Heidegger's destruction of the history of metaphysics as announced in *Sein und Zeit*.[350]

In order to substantiate this hypothesis, one might point to a great number of analogies between the destruction of the history of metaphysics and the Neo-Hegelian theme. What is meant by the program of a destruction of metaphysics? According to section 6 of *Sein und Zeit*, our understanding of ourselves as, say, mind-endowed bodies, is unwittingly determined by the metaphysical tradition. This tradition, in its turn, is shaped by the tendency of Dasein to interpret itself in terms of worldly objects. Because Dasein is inclined to get totally absorbed in its world (*Verfallen*), it understands itself in terms of that world by reflection.[351] Accordingly, in traditional metaphysics human existence is interpreted either in terms derived from the world of artifacts (*Hergestelltheit*), or in terms derived from natural objects in the broadest sense.[352] Because Heidegger in *Sein und Zeit* sharply distinguishes between on the one hand the ontological realms of nature in the sense of what is purely present or occurrent (*Vorhanden*) and of artifacts (*Zeug*, *Zuhandenheit*), and on the other hand the region of Dasein, he holds that Dasein cannot be adequately understood in categories derived from the world. The tradition of metaphysics, which determines human self-understanding, in fact prevents us from interpreting our Dasein as it is in its innermost being. In order to understand Dasein authentically, then, traditional metaphysics has to be "destroyed," that is, it has to be shown that its categories are not derived from Dasein but from worldly objects.

According to the Neo-Hegelian theme, it is also the case that present human self-understanding is determined by traditional metaphysics. The age of technology, in which everything is interpreted as raw material for production, is the completion of the productionist metaphysical tradition. As was the case in *Sein und Zeit*, we are urged to overcome the metaphysical tradition because it leads us astray. However, in spite of these parallelisms, there are also differences between the program of destroying traditional ontology and the Neo-Hegelian leitmotif. Clearly, the former program is rooted in the phenomenological theme in *Sein und Zeit*. According to the phenomenological theme, the totality of beings is carved up into ontological regions. Each of these regions should be explored by a proper regional ontology, and the mistake of traditional metaphysics was that it applied categories developed for the regions of artifacts or of nature in the sense of occurrentness (*Vorhandenheit*) to the region of Dasein. Traditional metaphysics may be destroyed by discovering the "original experiences" from which metaphysical concepts were derived.[353] It will then become clear that the traditional categories of metaphysics belong to one ontological region only, and that they cannot be generalized to all regions. According to the phenomenological theme, the question of being aims at developing a special set of categories for each ontological region in order to characterize the ontological constitution (*Seinsweise*) of entities belonging to that region.

This notion of the regionality of being is lacking in Heidegger's later Neo-Hegelian theme. As a consequence, the Neo-Hegelian "overcoming" of metaphysics cannot be identical to Heidegger's destruction of metaphysics in *Sein und Zeit*, for the latter notion is essentially informed by the idea of the regionality of being. Let me illustrate this difference by comparing the notion of *Zeug* (equipment, tools, paraphernalia) in *Sein und Zeit* with Heidegger's later notion of *das Wesen der Technik* (the reign of technology). From the point of view of *Sein und Zeit*, it would be mistaken to understand Dasein in terms derived from equipment or artifacts, as when one says that in reality man is like a machine or a computer. Dasein has an ontological constitution, called existence, which is different from the constitution of equipment. On the other hand, it is not erroneous to interpret things in the world as they manifest themselves to us primarily in terms of equipment or raw materials. On the contrary: it is one of the central theses of *Sein und Zeit* that things in the world primarily and in themselves *are* equipment (*Zeug*), and that the scientific image of things as meaningless presences (*Vorhandenes*) is an abstraction.[354] *Zeug* is a different ontological region from Dasein, and of course there is nothing wrong with understanding entities in the world as *Zeug*.

The situation is entirely different in "Die Frage nach der Technik" (1953). According to this lecture, the allegedly universal view of everything as raw material or products should not be "destroyed" by limiting it to its proper domain. On the contrary, it is suggested that this universal *Entbergung* (disclosure) of beings is a *Geschick* (fate), which is *uns geschickt* (sent to us). This fate is a danger that humans alone cannot avert.[355] It seems that according to the later Heidegger even the view of specific entities in the world, say trees, as raw material, is somehow fatal or dangerous. The reign of technology should not be overcome by limiting its scope, but by substituting a new fundamental attitude for it, although, of course, humans cannot refrain from using equipment and exploiting natural resources. This new fundamental attitude will be as holistic as the reign of technology.

Clearly, then, the Neo-Hegelian leitmotif is not a simple continuation of *Sein und Zeit*. The destruction of the history of ontology planned in Heidegger's chef d'oeuvre is not identical to the later Neo-Hegelian theme: it is structurally different. We should rather conceive of the Neo-Hegelian theme as resulting from *tensions* in *Sein und Zeit*. One of these tensions, the most important one in this respect, was sketched at the end of section 8, above. It is the tension between what might be called Husserlian essentialism and historical relativism.

According to Husserl, phenomenology should describe things as they are, and it should reveal essential structures, which are always and everywhere the same. Heidegger echoes this Husserlian desideratum where he says, in section 5 of *Sein und Zeit*, that the ontological structures which the analysis of Dasein brings out are "not just any accidental structures, but essential ones which, in every kind of being that factical Dasein may possess, persist as determinative for the character of its being."[356] Although Heidegger does not explicitly fix the extension of his notion of Dasein, he usually equates Dasein with human being. Consequently, it seems that the ontology of Dasein in *Sein und Zeit* is meant to be valid for human beings in general, irrespective of historical and local cultural circumstances.

This essentialist conception of the phenomenology of Dasein is not easy to square with Heidegger's historicist notion of hermeneutics, which was derived from Schleiermacher and Dilthey. A historicist would claim that there simply is no invariant essence of human existence to be found. Even our biological nature has no essence, because of the considerable amount of genetic variation among humans. The identity of human existence is determined by historical circumstances; it is a function of locally and historically determinate civilizations. This identity is nothing but the way in which human beings interpret the world and themselves, and this way will vary as a function of time and place. By means of historical interpretations of other cultures we should try to understand how humans interpret themselves and the world in these cultures. The very attempt to interpret other civilizations and to engage in historical hermeneutics is itself part of the historical culture of the West. As this attempt cannot but start within the horizon of its own culture, a self-conscious hermeneutical enterprise should first try to elucidate the present hermeneutical situation, that is, the way in which we understand ourselves in our time. This was the reason why, in the Natorp essay of 1922, Heidegger wanted to analyze contemporary Dasein before engaging in an interpretation of Aristotle. And this notion of historical hermeneutics also informs many passages in *Sein und Zeit*, such as the following text from section 6:

> On the other hand, if Dasein has seized upon its latent possibility not only of making its own existence transparent to itself but also of inquiring into the meaning of existentiality itself . . ., and if by such inquiry its eyes have been opened to its own essential historicality [*Geschichtlichkeit*], then one cannot fail to see that the inquiry into being . . . is itself characterized by historicality [*Geschichtlichkeit*]. . . . The question of the meaning of being . . . thus brings itself to the point where it understands itself as historiological [*historische*].[357]

How can one reconcile the historicist view of a hermeneutics of Dasein with the essentialist view of a phenomenology of Dasein? According to the former, the ontology of Dasein merely expresses human self-understanding in Germany in the 1920s. Taking this self-understanding as an inevitable point of departure, Heidegger could then try to trace its historical antecedents. Reviving Greek culture, for instance, might open up human possibilities for ourselves. We could "choose our heroes," as Heidegger likes to say, and by confronting Greek heroes with daily existence as it is now, we might become more authentic. This conception, which resembles Nietzsche's notion of monumental history, informs both the Natorp essay and sections 74 and 76 of *Sein und Zeit*.[358] But how can such a historicist notion of the hermeneutics of Dasein ever yield "essential structures, which persist as determinative for the character of Dasein's being," whenever and wheresoever it exists? How is one supposed to reconcile it with the latter, essentialist view?

In *Sein und Zeit*, this tension is resolved (*aufgehoben*) by what I have called the transcendental leitmotif. The transcendental leitmotif both radicalizes historical hermeneutics and reconciles it to essentialism. It radicalizes historical hermeneutics because, according to the transcendental theme, the way in which beings disclose themselves is determined by a holistic scheme, which is projected by Dasein. As we saw, Heidegger claims that the facts discovered by natural science are not disclosed to us except on the basis of such a holistic scheme: a good, old-fashioned Kantian claim. However, whereas Kant held that this holistic scheme is part of our makeup, so that we cannot change it, Heidegger holds it to be variable: it is a framework (*Entwurf*), projected by temporalizing

Dasein. From this point, it is but a small step to the Neo-Hegelian leitmotif, according to which a series of such frameworks is fundamental to the development of civilization.

The transcendental theme entails a radicalization of historicism because Heidegger suggests that criteria of truth and falsity, such as criteria for theory choice in physics, are internal to a projected framework or scheme. Consequently, we do not have the means of evaluating the frameworks themselves in terms of truth and falsity, nor can we evaluate theories or doctrines belonging to different frameworks in epistemic terms.[359] We cannot say anymore, for instance, that modern physics is epistemically superior to the worldview of the Hopi Indians. To be more precise: we will probably say it, because it characterizes our present framework to think that this is true, but we will not be able to justify such a statement in an objective and framework-neutral manner. Surely this position is full-blown historical relativism.[360] In *Sein und Zeit*, Heidegger reserves the term "truth" for the very act of opening up a world by projecting a scheme. Because he holds that the act of projecting is free, his notions of truth and of freedom are intimately related, as is still the case in "Vom Wesen des Grundes" (1929) and "Vom Wesen der Wahrheit" (1930, published in 1943).[361]

If the transcendental theme radicalizes historicism, how can it also reconcile Heidegger's historicist notion of hermeneutics to his Husserlian essentialism? It does so by locating the essence of Dasein on a transcendental level. Human understanding of itself and of the world is a product of projected frameworks. However, if this is the case, should we not wonder who does the projecting? It seems that there must be a projecting agency that escapes historical relativism, because it is at the basis of history itself. In other words, as soon as we ask what enables humans to project transcendental schemes, we will discover Dasein as a temporalizing transcendental structure *in* humans, which is ahistorical because it is the very condition of the possibility of history and time. This transcendental structure is what Heidegger calls historicality (*Geschichtlichkeit*). According to *Sein und Zeit*, it is the happening (*Geschehen*) of Dasein, the fact that Dasein produces (*zeitigt*) time (*Zeit*).[362] Only because Dasein is the transcendental source of time is history possible. And only because Dasein projects a world whenever it happens is there world-history. The fundamental ontology of *Sein und Zeit* is itself ahistorical, we may conclude, because it purports to discover the transcendental conditions for the possibility of history.[363]

Thus far, I have argued that the Neo-Hegelian theme is different from the destruction of ontology planned in *Sein und Zeit*, and that it is a solution for tensions within the philosophy of that book. But why did Heidegger need a Neo-Hegelian theme, if these tensions were already resolved by the transcendental leitmotif? The answer is that the transcendental solution for the tension between historicism and essentialism is an unstable one, which tends to degenerate into Neo-Hegelianism. If the projected frameworks that open up a world are really *all*-embracing, as the transcendental theme implies (thesis 2, above), should we not conclude that transcendental philosophy must be located *within* such a framework? Indeed, is transcendental philosophy not a philosophical possibility opened up within the tradition of subjectivism that started with Descartes? If frameworks really are all-embracing, no intellectual discipline, not even fundamental ontology, can claim to be more fundamental than all frameworks. Instead of giving up the notion of an all-embracing historical framework, Heidegger in his later thought abandons the project of a fundamental ontology. Sometimes, it is still said that Dasein does the projecting and chooses fundamental stances. More often, however, even this view is abandoned. There simply is a succession of fundamental frameworks. We should try to grasp the logic hidden in their succession, and prepare ourselves for a new stance by reflecting on the present one. Such is the Neo-Hegelian leitmotif in Heidegger's later thought.

This leitmotif is not without its problems, problems that are also inherent in structuralism as an ontological position. As we have seen, the Neo-Hegelian notion that real history consists of a series of all-embracing or totalitarian frameworks, which determine how people act and think in specific historical epochs, tends to swallow up its transcendental foundation in the fundamental ontology of Dasein. If it is really the case that *everything* we conceive of is determined by a contingent historical framework, this must be true for transcendental philosophy as well. Heidegger's Kantianism inevitably turns into Neo-Hegelianism. The Neo-Hegelian theme constitutes the final victory of historical relativism over essentialism in Heidegger's works. It implies that no theory in science or mathematics and no philosophical doctrine can be called "true" independently of a specific historical framework or fundamental stance. Truth becomes relativized to a totalitarian projected framework. Does it not follow that Neo-Hegelian historical relativism also swallows itself? Is it not landed in a weak version of the paradox of the liar? Why should we believe that Neo-Hegelian historicism is a true view, if it implies that all views, itself included, can be true only in relation to a contingent totalitarian framework? The same paradox is involved in Marxism: if it is true that all thought is determined by economic relations of production, this thought itself is also determined by such relations. If so, why should we accept it? Finally, the paradox is also inherent in Nietzsche's doctrine of the will to power, according to which something is called "true" only because it serves a specific will to power.

There seems to be only one solution to the paradox of the liar as it is involved in Heidegger's Neo-Hegelian theme: to reintroduce something that is immune to historical relativism. This is one of the functions of the postmonotheist leitmotif in the question of being. Before introducing this fifth and final leitmotif, I will briefly compare Heidegger's Neo-Hegelian theme to Hegel's own philosophy.

C. Heidegger's Inversion of Hegel

Hegel was not a historical relativist. Although he held that theories and doctrines that were developed in a specific historical period of the past could never be entirely true because they were somehow relative to that period, he also held that these doctrines and theories were aspects of one, final, all-inclusive Truth. Hegel indeed introduced something in his philosophy that is immune to historical relativism. Underlying the various stages of historical development, Hegel thought, is the Absolute, the Idea, or God, and historical stages are merely phases in God's own development. According to Hegel's—or Schelling's—grandiose metaphysical narrative, at first the Absolute is *an sich* (in itself) in an abstract manner, after which it externalizes itself in nature. In a third phase, the Absolute slowly comes back to itself again in a long historical process, the process of Western civilization, until it discovers that nature and history are aspects of its own self-realization. Hegel's philosophy is the culmination point of this ontotheogony, in which the Absolute becomes fully conscious of itself. At last, it is not only *in* itself but also *for* itself (*an und für sich*). As Hegel's Absolute is One and unique, we might call this theme the monotheist leitmotif in Hegel's thought.

Hegel's philosophy was influenced by Proclus, Jacob Böhme, and Spinoza. It is a mystic kind of pantheism, with extravagant rationalist pretensions, because Hegel held that the real is the rational, the real being God's own development. In order to understand Hegel's thought, however, it will not do to trace historical influences. We should rather attempt to reconstruct his philosophy as a solution to certain philosophical or theological problems. One of these problems, the problem of creation, was produced by the attempt to reconcile a Greek or Hellenistic notion of God with creationism. A second problem became urgent during the scientific revolution: What are we to think of God's revelation in the Bible, if the Bible is incompatible with scientific theories?

The problem of creation arose because the later monotheist Greeks had the tendency to conceive of God in terms of autarky. Aristotle's God, for instance, is as a Greek nobleman wanted to be: he merely reflects himself and does not need the world, even though he is the world's *telos*. This Aristotelian notion of God is incompatible with creationism, and Aristotle did not believe that the world is created. Why should a God who does not need anything except himself create a world external to himself? Hegel's solution, which is essentially also Spinoza's, is that creation is God's autodevelopment. The created world is nothing but an aspect of God, and everything is in God. This theory strongly resembles Neo-Platonism as it was conceived of by Plotinus and Proclus. Neo-Platonism held that the world is not created: it has emanated from the One.

What is the origin of the problem of revelation? When science advanced in the sixteenth, seventeenth, and eighteenth centuries, it increasingly contradicted cosmological and other doctrines expressed in the Bible. How to resolve this contradiction between science and revelation? Philosophers such as Descartes and Spinoza, who wanted to vindicate both religion and science, argued that God adapted his revelation in the Bible to the historical stage of civilization of the time. As a consequence, we should not interpret the Bible literally, but have faith in rational theology as a clue to biblical teachings, for God reveals himself also in nature and in human thought. A next step, taken by Lessing and many others, was to consider God's revelation as a historical process, an "education of the human race," which progresses from revelation in images and parables to rational comprehension. Hegel's system is the result of combining Spinoza's pantheism with Lessing's doctrine of *revelatio continua*. According to Hegel, the creation of the world is God's externalization in matter, whereas human history is God's progressive self-revelation, culminating in the philosophy of the Absolute.

Hegel's philosophy consists of two parts. First, the individual human being should become conscious, by means of a great number of dialectical steps, of the fact that he is *in* God. This individual journey to the Absolute is sketched in Hegel's *Phänomenologie des Geistes* (*Phenomenology of Spirit*). Once arrived at God's point of view, the philosopher is able to develop the logic of God's autodevelopment, which is also dialectical, as it was in Plotinus and Proclus. This logic is sketched in Hegel's *Wissenschaft der Logik* (*Science of Logic*). Although Hegel's philosophy is usually considered as representing German romanticism, Hegel was a philosopher of the Enlightenment as well, because he believed in rational progress. According to Hegel, human history is progress, culminating in the identity of human consciousness and God's consciousness.

We are now able to see why Heidegger's Neo-Hegelian leitmotif, although it is a reversal of Marx's reversal of Hegel, is yet not identical with Hegel's philosophy. On the contrary: it is a reversal of Hegel in its own way. Heidegger's narrative of productionist metaphysics turns Hegel's optimism into pessimism. While the history of metaphysics according to Hegel is a history in which God progressively reveals himself, Heidegger holds that the history of productionist metaphysics is a continuing regression into Darkness, fully consummated by the era of technology, in which man errs, the earth is destroyed, human action becomes meaningless, and Being withdraws itself. How to explain Heidegger's reversal of Hegel's optimism about God's revelation into pessimism?

It seems to me that there is only one answer to this question. Between Hegel and Heidegger stands Nietzsche, and Nietzsche proclaimed the death of God. We will see that Heidegger, like Hegel, backed up historicism by a monotheist leitmotif. However, because Heidegger's later thought is a meditation on the death of God, his monotheist theme is in reality a postmonotheist leitmotif.

§ 11. The Postmonotheist Theme

Apart from Heidegger's commitment to National Socialism, which I will discuss in the next chapter, there is at least one other aspect of his life that is relevant to the interpretation of his works: Heidegger's complex and ever changing relation to Catholicism and to Christianity in general. In his judicious biography, Hugo Ott evokes Heidegger's Catholic youth in Meßkirch, near Konstanz in Baden, and the religious controversies of the time.[364] Let me relate one telling episode by way of an upbeat to the theme "Heidegger and religion."

Heidegger's parents belonged to the poorer part of the population of Meßkirch, and they accepted the dogmatic decisions on papal infallibility of the First Vatican Council of 1870. The more liberal and mostly richer *Altkatholiken* rejected these dogmas, so that during Heidegger's youth the small town of Meßkirch was divided by heated religious controversies. When the latter party, supported by the Baden government, obtained the right to use the Church of St. Martin in 1871, the loyal Roman Catholics decided to abandon their preaching-house. In 1875 they founded a temporary church in a barn, and it was here that Heidegger's father served as a sacristan and that young Martin was baptized in 1889. Six years later, in 1895, the Church of St. Martin was restored to the Catholic community. On the first of December there was a festive entry of the congregation. It must have made a deep impression on little Martin Heidegger that the Old Catholic sacristan, who was reluctant to meet his successor, handed the key not to Martin's father Friedrich Heidegger but to him, a six-year-old boy.[365] Perhaps this story should be regarded as an omen of Heidegger's later philosophical development.

Martin Heidegger received the education typically given to a talented boy from a modest background: he was predestined to a religious career. How to explain, then, that Heidegger became the philosopher of Being instead of a Catholic bishop, as his mother once hoped?[366] One might say that he broke away from the Church of Rome because of his independence of mind, even though in his first publications of 1910–11, suppressed in the *Collected Works* and not mentioned on official lists, the young student of theology forcefully defended the authority of the Church against the modern *Weltanschauung*.[367] Apart from Heidegger's mental independence, other factors may have been influential. At first, Heidegger wanted to become a Jesuit. On 30 September 1909, he entered the novitiate of the Jesuits in Tisis, near Feldkirch (Vorarlberg). But after the initial test period of two weeks he had to leave, probably because he complained about heart troubles. In other words, the Societas Jesu had turned him down by reason of its strict health requirements.[368] Heidegger now applied for a place in the Collegium Borromaeum in Freiburg, in order to study theology at the university. In 1911, however, he had to abandon his theological studies on the advice of his superiors, once again because he suffered from nervous heart troubles, and the road to priesthood was blocked forever.[369] From 1911–12 on, when he studied mathematics, philosophy, and physics, Heidegger intended to become a Catholic philosopher. Having got his doctorate *summa cum laude* in 1913, he hoped to get the chair of Christian (Catholic) philosophy in Freiburg. The choice of a Scholastic topic for his habilitation, suggested by Heinrich Finke, was determined both by this ambition and by the fact that there was a grant available for Thomist studies. However, after Heidegger's habilitation in 1915, which qualified him for the chair, the committee decided to nominate Josef Geyser from Münster as the only candidate.[370] This decision was a crucial blow to Heidegger. One might say that in June 1916, Catholicism had thwarted his ambitions for a third time.[371]

In this same summer of 1916, Heidegger acquired another motive for moving away from Catholicism. After some other love affairs, he met Elfride Petri, a student of economics from a Prussian officer's family, who belonged to the evangelical-Lutheran church, and whom he married in March 1917. Nearly two years later, on 9 January 1919, Heidegger wrote a much quoted letter to his friend Father Engelbert Krebs, saying that "epistemological insights that pass over into the theory of historical knowledge have made the *system* of Catholicism problematic and unacceptable to me—but not Christianity and metaphysics, although I take the latter in a new sense." Heidegger had studied Schleiermacher's *Reden über die Religion* (*Discourses on Religion*) in the summer of 1917, and was acquainted with Luther's thesis of the perverting influence of Greek metaphysics on Christianity, an influence that came to its apogee in (Neo)-Scholastical philosophy. He ended the letter by stating the conviction that he had an "inner call to philosophy" and that by fulfilling this "call to the eternal vocation of the inner man" he could "justify his existence before God"—surely quite a Lutheran formula.[372]

Heidegger's rupture with Catholicism was but a first step in his gradual disengagement from Christianity, a step motivated by the three disillusionments described above, by his mixed marriage, by his studies of Schleiermacher, Dilthey, and Luther, and finally by Husserl's influence from 1916 on. After the debacle of the religious chair, Heidegger tried to obtain Husserl's support, and Husserl strongly disapproved of external constraints in philosophy, such as an official religious commitment.[373] As we will see, this movement away from Christianity would eventually lead to a variety of atheism in 1933.

At least at this stage in Heidegger's career, life and works are intimately related. It is not difficult to trace Heidegger's personal religious development in his early writings and courses.[374] In the conclusion of his *Habilitationsschrift*, written in 1916, Heidegger already claims that the most authentic vocation of philosophy is to go beyond the theoretical attitude, so that the "living spirit" may aim at a "breakthrough to true reality and real truth."[375] Whereas he held at the time that the mystic experience of medieval Christianity and Scholastic philosophy complement each other, these Eckhartian lines announce Heidegger's rejection of Scholasticism at the end of the First World War.[376] Heidegger came to endorse the Lutheran thesis that Greek metaphysics had contaminated the Christian "life of the spirit."[377] In his course on the phenomenology of religion during the winter semester of 1920–21, interpreting Paul's letters, Heidegger attempted to evoke and analyze the life-experience of early Christianity, which had been obscured and buried by the Scholastic tradition. In a Lutheran manner, the course aimed at reawakening the life of the spirit, an authentic Christian religiosity that "lives temporality as such," in contradistinction to the easy life of those who are absorbed in the world. St. Paul pressed his followers to the point of despair in order to make them understand their situation of decision between these two modes of life, each alone and already "before God." Similarly, Heidegger conceived of philosophy as the attempt to restore life to its essential temporality, insecurity, and distress, a conception that he still expressed in his *disputatio* with Cassirer in 1929.[378]

The course on Paul's letters may be regarded as a first attempt to develop a hermeneutical analysis of human life, taking early Christianity as a *formale Anzeige* (formal indication) of life's existential structures. In contrast, the next lecture course on Augustine and Neo-Platonism (summer semester of 1921) aimed at a "destruction" of Greek influences that would have contaminated the pure self-understanding of the early Christians.[379] Whereas Paul's letters exhort us to stay awake in this world and to be always prepared for Christ's second coming, which will occur unexpectedly as "a thief in the night" (1 *Thessalonians* 5:2), St. Augustine's Neo-Platonic notion of a God as the *summum bonum* leads easily to quietism and to an attempt to find peace in an eternal Deity. The Greek conception of God as an eternal substance would have been alien to the early Christian experience of life, which stressed life's insecurity and its finite temporality, and understood human existence as a preparation for the second coming.[380]

Heidegger's development from his habilitation in 1916 to the ontology of Dasein in *Sein und Zeit* (1927) was determined by four cardinal motives, as is evident from his courses and seminars.[381] In the first place, there is the religious "Eckhartian" impulse toward an intensification of life, which might bring us before God. Second, Heidegger wanted to fulfill Dilthey's intentions aiming at an ontology of human life, at a hermeneutical interpretation of human existence that provides a foundation to the historical sciences. In the third place, Heidegger tried to radicalize Husserl's project of a phenomenological description of the natural attitude and of the manner in which entities are constituted by the transcendental subject. He did so by substituting concrete historical Dasein for Husserl's ahistorical transcendental ego. Finally, when Heidegger turned to Aristotle in 1921, this was originally motivated by the Lutheran thesis that Aristotelian philosophy had perverted the Christian experience of life. Accordingly, Heidegger proposed a "destruction" of Aristotle's philosophy, in order to restore religious life to its original meaning and intensity, an objective that clearly inspired the Natorp essay of 1922.[382] To his astonishment, Heidegger discovered in Aristotle a wealth of phenomenological descriptions of human existence, and he even came to see Aristotle as a more "original" phenomenologist than Husserl. This explains the predominance of the fourth, Aristotelian motive in the analysis of Dasein in *Sein und Zeit*.[383] As Kisiel showed, the transcendental leitmotif, which originally derived from Husserl, was considerably strengthened in the very final draft because of Heidegger's readings of Kant in his seminars.[384]

The analysis of Dasein in *Sein und Zeit,* we may conclude, originated in part from religious impulses, and in this respect a study of Heidegger's life might illuminate his works. Heidegger hinted at the relevance of theology and religion to his philosophy when he wrote in 1953–54 that "without this theological past [*Herkunft*], I would never have got on the road of thinking." And he added significantly: "but the past constantly remains future [*Zukunft*]."[385] It is less clear, however, which specific interpretation of his works is implied by Heidegger's Catholic origins. With regard to *Sein und Zeit*, for instance, we might argue that existentialia of Dasein such as *Sorge* (concern), *Angst* (anxiety), or the opposition between the falling of Dasein (*Verfallen*) and authenticity (*Eigentlichkeit*), are derived from Christian sources. Indeed, *Sorge* and *Angst* can be traced back to St. Augustine, *Sein-zum-Tode* to Luther, and the opposition between falling and authenticity reminds us of Paul's dichotomy between the life of the world and the life of the Spirit, and also of Augustine's analysis of temptation in *Confessiones*, book X.[386] Yet this genealogy of Heidegger's technical terms does not specify what they mean. In *Sein und Zeit*, Heidegger stresses several times that one should not interpret his existentialia in a religious or theological manner. The existential of *Verfallen*, for example, points to a specific structure of human existence, to the fact that primarily and mostly we are absorbed in worldly affairs, and it does not refer to the biblical Fall, a hypothetical event in the past of which a phenomenological ontology of Dasein can have no experience.[387] In general, one might say that influences or origins can never determine the meaning or interpretation of a philosophical text. To think that they can would be a genetic fallacy, because the text is an autonomous and organic whole, a free creation by its author, which should not be reduced to the sources that the author used. The studies of the genesis of *Sein und Zeit* by Kisiel, Van Buren, Thomä, Greisch, and others may contain valuable clues for an interpretation of that book, but they can never be a substitute for such an interpretation.

In the case of *Sein und Zeit,* there are three more specific reasons for resisting the temptation of a too facile religious interpretation. First, the project of a fundamental ontology of Dasein aims at specifying structural and transcendental characteristics of human life, which pertain to our existence in all cases, whether we are religious or not. This means, second, that where Heidegger derived notions from Christian sources such as St. Paul, St. Augustine, Eckhart, Luther, Pascal, or Kierkegaard, he took these notions not in their original religious sense, but as formal pointers (*formale Anzeigen*) to the phenomenon of human life as such, to the ontological constitution of humans.[388] Finally, the ontological stance seems to imply that *Sein und Zeit* is religiously neutral, or rather, as Heidegger said in the Natorp essay, that philosophy is *fundamentally atheistic*: it is the attempt to restore human life to its most authentic possibilities by describing its inner tendency, so that philosophy cannot rely on something external, such as a religious revelation. Being the "real explicit performance of the tendency in life to interpret its fundamental movement," philosophy must be atheistic, Heidegger wrote in 1922.[389]

But this notion of a fundamental atheism in philosophy is a slippery one. It is instructive to quote a footnote to the Natorp essay of 1922, in which Heidegger explains what he means:

"Atheistic" not in the sense of a theory such as materialism or the like. All philosophy that understands itself in what it is, that is, as the factical manner in which life interprets itself, must know that from the religious point of view the act of violently throwing back life to life itself, which philosophy performs, is an insurrection against God. Only in this way philosophy stands honestly before God, that is, in keeping with the possibilities that are at its disposal to the extent that it is philosophy. "Atheistic" means here: liberating oneself from the tempting and anxious tendency of merely talking about religion.[390]

We might call the attitude Heidegger describes here methodological atheism. Philosophy interprets human life out of itself, counteracting life's tendency to obscure its most authentic possibilities. It thereby "throws life back into the harshness of its destiny," as Heidegger said in 1929 during his *disputatio* with Cassirer. Doing so, philosophy should not talk about God, because it is not a *philosophical* possibility to reach God. In order to stand honestly before God, the philosopher should merely interpret human life and not try to theorize about God. Philosophy should be altogether pretheoretical. The footnote is explained entirely by Heidegger's Lutheran conception of faith as grace, which he expresses also in section 3 of *Sein und Zeit*. Because faith is a gift from God, and because God is revealed to us in faith only, a philosopher who longs for God but has not received this gift is not entitled to talk about God at all. Yet, analyzing the human condition without mentioning God is a blasphemy or an "insurrection against God."

It follows that this kind of methodological atheism is nothing else than what is usually called the religious quest for God by opening one's heart for his graceful coming. By making man understand thoroughly the harshness of his condition, philosophy would restore him to his most authentic possibility, the possibility of standing before God, whereupon God might perhaps bestow his grace on man. Philosophy, as Heidegger conceived it in 1922, purported to be more authentically religious than Scholastic theology, which yielded to the temptation to talk about God. Heidegger's early distinction between philosophy and theology does not coincide with a distinction between areligious thought and religious thought. On the contrary, philosophy is more authentically religious than traditional theology.

Is *Sein und Zeit* atheistic in this deeply religious sense? The book was read in this manner by friends of Heidegger such as Bultmann and Löwith, but the text itself does not allow us to solve the problem in a decisive way.[391] On the one hand we might think that in some passages, such as the one I quoted in section 10C, where Heidegger says that the universality of being has to be sought "higher up," the term "being" is another word for what Christians call God. The ultimate quest for being supposedly is the quest for God, and *Sein und Zeit* prepares us for this quest. A footnote to "Vom Wesen des Grundes" (1929) points in the same direction. The ontological interpretation of Dasein as being-in-the-world does not decide against or in favor of a possible being-to-God, Heidegger says. Yet the elucidation of the transcendence of Dasein provides us with a notion of Dasein sufficient for raising the question as to what the relation of Dasein to God might be ontologically.[392]

On the other hand, Heidegger criticizes traditional Christianity in a number of crucial passages. In section 10, for instance, he rejects the Christian notion of a transcendence of man, which means that man transcends himself toward God, because "Christian dogmatics . . . can hardly be said to have made an ontological problem of man's being."[393] For the same reason, Heidegger repudiates the traditional notion of man as God's creature. He traces the concept of being as having been produced back to Greek Antiquity, and calls it a "baleful prejudice," because Dasein's mode of being is very different from that of tools or artifacts.[394] By implication, God cannot be conceived of as a creator either. One might think that this critique of the Christian notion of God as a creator still belongs to Heidegger's early Lutheran project of cleansing Christian religion from the contamination by Greek metaphysics. In fact, it partly destroys traditional Christianity itself, because the notion of God as a creator is also present in the *Old Testament*. According to the book of *Genesis*, God created first the heavens and the earth, and then he created the animal kingdom and man. The idea that God created man "after His own likeness" (*Genesis* 1:26–27), and that man is an image of God, is central to Christianity. Should one not infer that Heidegger's analysis of Dasein in *Sein und Zeit* is a thoroughly secular ontology of human existence, even though it bears a structural resemblance to traditional Christian anthropology in many respects?

Let me draw some conclusions from this preliminary discussion, and state the problem of interpretation that I want to solve in this section. (1) One cannot deny that there is a strong religious impetus in Heidegger's early works. (2) The fact that *Sein und Zeit* is a nontheological and even antitheological book[395] does not exclude its being deeply religious in the sense of Heidegger's methodological atheism as defined in 1922. (3) But the text of *Sein und Zeit* does not (yet) enable us to decide whether Heidegger's intentions in writing the book were purely ontological, as they seem to be, or rather ontological and religious. Even if Heidegger in 1927 still had the religious objectives that he adopted in 1922, these objectives were not stated in the text. This fact explains that *Sein und Zeit* could be interpreted both as a preparation for the jump to religion (Bultmann) and as an atheist ontology (Sartre). (4) Heidegger's critique of a creationist conception of man in *Sein und Zeit* implies a critique of a creationist conception of God, even though Heidegger does not draw this conclusion in 1927. In other words, the traditional Christian notion of God is implicitly "destroyed" by Heidegger's question of being. Finally, (5) it seems that we can only decide about the ultimate religious or nonreligious intentions of *Sein und Zeit* by studying Heidegger's later works. Heidegger conceived of the analysis of Dasein in *Sein und Zeit* as a *way* to the aim of working out the question of being, that is, as a preparation for asking the question of being in the appropriate manner.[396] Does it not follow that we may be able to discover what *Sein und Zeit* was ultimately aiming at only by investigating the way in which Heidegger worked out this question later?[397]

How are we to interpret Heidegger's question of being in the later works? One strand in this question, I argued in the previous section, is the Neo-Hegelian theme. But this theme leaves unexplained a large number of sayings on being that Heidegger repeats a great many times in these works. He says, for instance, that being is one (*einzig*), that it summons us by its soundless voice (*lautlose Stimme*), that it is concealed from us and even conceals or withdraws itself (*Verbergung*), that it is a mystery (*Geheimnis*), that it gives itself, that the truth of being is the being of truth, that we should await the coming (*Ankunft*) of being, and the like. It is very difficult to understand what these phrases mean, even in their contexts, until one notices that they are structurally similar to traditional Christian sayings about God.[398]

This insight has triggered a host of interpretations. At the far right of the spectrum we find the straightforward proposal that one should read "God" instead of "being" in the relevant passages, and that Heidegger is a somewhat idiosyncratic theologian in the Eckhartian tradition.[399] For Eckhart, Being (*ens, esse*) and God (*deus*) are the same, and creatures share in God's being. Being in this sense is hidden in all beings, and the religious philosopher has the task of revealing Being in beings. At the far left is the position that Heidegger's "theological" locutions should be taken metaphorically, because Heidegger himself stresses that being is not identical with God, and that Heidegger's later question of being merely tries to evoke the "wonder of wonders" that beings *are*, the amazing fact that there is something rather than nothing, a fact for which we will be grateful if only we pay proper attention to it.[400] Between these extremes, we find interpretations that argue either that Heidegger's later question of being resembles specific religious views, such as negative theology, Mahayana Buddhism, and Taoism, or that Heidegger's later work was influenced by religious views, such as Neo-Platonism and medieval mysticism, especially Eckhart and Aquinas, or, finally, that Heidegger's texts both resemble and are influenced by these religious conceptions.[401]

One cannot say that interpretations of this kind are incorrect. Surely Heidegger was influenced by a great number of religious authors, mainly Paul, Plotinus, Augustine, Eckhart, Luther, Pascal, Schleiermacher, and Kierkegaard, and one might find resemblances (and also differences) between his writings and any religious view one prefers. An immense domain of possible scholarly exercises opens up for our eyes: What about Heidegger and Zen, Heidegger and Lao Tsu, Heidegger and Dogen, Heidegger and Vedanta, Heidegger and Nagarjuna, Heidegger and Proclos, or Heidegger and Carl Braig?[402] Yet comparative studies of resemblances and influences are unsatisfactory, because they remain at the surface of Heidegger's thought. In his interpretations of Paul and Augustine, Heidegger attempted to revive the inner tendency or fundamental movement of the experience of life (*Grundbewegtheit*) that informs their writings. Should we not attempt in a similar way to capture the *Grundbewegtheit* of Heidegger's later works? The problem that I want to solve in this section is as follows: How are we to explain the "religious" theme in the later Heidegger with reference to the "fundamental movement" of his thought?

According to my interpretative hypothesis, this *Grundbewegtheit* is what I call the postmonotheist leitmotif, which sprang from Heidegger's early yearning to become an authentic Christian. In the following three subsections, I will (A) develop the postmonotheist theme, (B) explore the parallelisms between Heidegger's later discourse on being and traditional Christianity, and (C) show the explanatory power of my hypothesis by giving a survey of the topics in the later Heidegger that become intelligible if understood in terms of the postmonotheist leitmotif. In order to convince the reader of the adequacy of my interpretation, I substantiate it by a wealth of quotations in the notes.

A. The Lutheran Model

Let me start my exposition of the postmonotheist theme by giving three clues that indicate the nature of Heidegger's philosophical *Grundbewegtheit*. The first clue is extracted from a letter that Heidegger wrote to his pupil and friend Karl Löwith on 19 August 1921.[403] According to Kisiel, this letter is a "confession" to Löwith, which "provides a revealing self-portrait of his fundamental orientation during this entire phase of religious concerns of 1915–1921."[404] We will see later how Heidegger's early orientation, that is, his *Herkunft*, was fulfilled in his later works, that is, his *Zukunft*. At least two passages in this letter are crucial for understanding Heidegger's deepest intentions. In a first passage, Heidegger stresses that he is a "Christian theo*logian*":

> I work concretely and factically out of my "I am," out of my intellectual and wholly factical origin, milieu, life-contexts, and whatever is available to me from these as vital experience in which I live. . . . To this facticity of mine belongs what I would in brief call the fact that I am a "Christian theo*logian*."[405]

Kisiel plausibly explains the underscoring of the suffix "-logian" as hinting at Heidegger's focus of that time: the philosophical foundations of theology in the fundamental experiences that phenomenology aims to explore.[406] In the second passage, Heidegger stresses that for him philosophy is a personal quest, and that the specific kind of objectivity pertaining to philosophy is something "proper to oneself":

> You each [to wit: Oskar Becker and Karl Löwith] consider a different aspect of me as essential, what I do not separate . . . , namely, the life of research—working with theoretical concepts—and my own life. The essential way in which my facticity is existentially articulated is research, done in my own way. Accordingly, the motive and goal of philosophizing is for me never to add to the stock of objective truths, since the objectivity of philosophy, as I understand it . . . is something proper to oneself.[407]

This second passage is illuminated by the definition of philosophy Heidegger gave in the Natorp essay of 1922: philosophy is the explicit actualization of a tendency implicit in human life, the tendency to interpret our existence with regard to its most authentic possibilities. The objectivity of philosophy is the conceptualization of life, so that it is at the same time radically subjective. My first clue suggests that for Heidegger philosophy was a personal quest, analogous to or even identical with a religious quest, and not just an objective scientific undertaking like any other, as it was for a philosopher such as Carnap. Indeed, the difference between philosophy or "thinking" and the sciences is a constant theme in Heidegger's writings, from his early to his last works.[408]

One might think that this *Grundbewegtheit* of Heidegger's philosophy that characterizes his early lectures around 1920 transmuted later, and that for Heidegger philosophy had become a secular and scientific (*wissenschaftlich*) affair when he published *Sein und Zeit* in 1927. Indeed, *Sein und Zeit* is marked by echoes of the scientific rhetoric that we find in Husserl, and phenomenology is defined as a fundamental science.[409] However, my second clue shows that Heidegger's *Grundbewegtheit* did not transmute at all. Impressed by the fact that Nietzsche combined his philosophical development with continuous autobiographical reflections, Heidegger wrote in 1937–38 a brief autobiographical sketch entitled "Mein bisheriger Weg" ("My Way Up to This Moment"), which was published in 1997 in *Besinnung* (*Gesamtausgabe*, vol. 66). From this important text, in which Heidegger describes his philosophical development starting with his dissertation on the doctrine of judgment in psychologism (1913) up to *Beiträge zur Philosophie* (1936–38) I quote the most revealing passages:

> But who would want to deny that on this entire road up to the present day the discussion [*Auseinandersetzung*] with Christianity went along secretly and discretely [*verschwiegen*]—a discussion which was and is not a "problem" that I picked up, but both the way to safeguard my ownmost origin—parental home, native region [*Heimat*], and youth—and painful separation from it, both in *one*. Only someone who has similar roots in a real and lived catholic world may guess something of the necessities that were operative like subterranean seismic shocks [*unterirdische Erdstöße*] on the way of my questioning up to the present day . . .
>
> It is not proper to talk about these most inner confrontations [*innersten Auseinandersetzungen*], which are not concerned with questions of Church doctrine and articles of faith, but only with the Unique Question, whether God is fleeing from us or not and whether we still experience this truly, that is, as creators [*als Schaffende*] . . .
>
> What is at stake is not a mere "religious" background of philosophy either, but the Unique Question regarding the truth of Being, which alone decides about the "time" and the "place" which is kept open for us historically within the history of the Occident and its gods . . .
>
> But because the most inner experiences and decisions remain the essential thing, for that very reason they have to be kept out of the public sphere [*Öffentlichkeit*].[410]

We are entitled to infer from this text not only that Heidegger's *Grundbewegt-heit* was a religious quest even in 1936–37, that is, after his explicit rejection of Christianity in 1933–35, but also that this religious quest is identical with the question of Being. Furthermore, Heidegger affirms here what pupils such as Lö-with have always held but could never prove: that the most fundamental theme that informs everything which Heidegger said is something he kept silent about: the religious leitmotif.[411]

My third clue is a telling piece of information given by another pupil and friend of Heidegger, Hans-Georg Gadamer. According to Gadamer, Heidegger once said that his life's goal was "to be a new Luther."[412] We know that Heidegger had the reputation of being a great connoisseur of Luther's writings.[413] But obviously, he not merely wanted to know what Luther wrote; he wanted to be in the twentieth century what the young Luther was in the sixteenth century: a religious innovator. My thesis is that Heidegger's *Grundbewegtheit* was informed by what I call a *Lutheran model*, and that the "religious" aspect of his later works can be explained as a radicalization of Luther. In this sense, the later works fulfilled Heidegger's early intentions. But what is a Lutheran model? And how is the Lutheran model related to the postmonotheist leitmotif?

The young Luther reacted to a deep crisis in the Christian religion of his time, a crisis provoked by the Renaissance and by extravagant practices of the Roman Church such as selling indulgences. Luther exposed these practices, which substituted outer actions for the inner repentance demanded by the New Testament. Theologically, the main question Luther asked was how a man can be justified before God. Whereas the Church held that good works and the sacraments helped justify man, Luther stressed that God's righteousness cannot be conceived in terms of a transaction in which satisfaction is made to God. He returned to Paul's conception that it is only God's grace that transforms and makes man righteous before God. As a consequence, human activity no longer has a part in the ultimate determination of man's destiny. Grace alone decides. This position seriously undermined the claims of the Catholic Church and the function of the sacraments. According to Luther, our relation to God is a personal one that does not really need the tradition of the Church (the apostolic succession) as an intermediary.

We will see that many elements of Luther's theology, such as the notion that human destiny is not of our own making but is "sent" to us (*Geschick*) and that grace is crucial, have their counterparts in Heidegger's later discourse on being. What I call the Lutheran model, however, is the *form* rather than the *content* of Luther's thought. Let me specify this form in three tenets. First, Luther held that there is an original revelation of God in Christ and in the Bible. Second, he assumed that the tradition of theology that transmitted God's revelation to us in fact betrayed the revelation, because it tried to cast the original message in the concepts of Greek philosophy, which are incompatible with it. Luther's railings against Aristotle are well known. In chapter 3.25 of his *Appeal to the Ruling Class of German Nationality* (1520), he wrote for instance about Aristotle: "It pains me to the heart that this damnable, arrogant, pagan rascal has seduced and fooled so many of the best Christians with his misleading writings. God has made him a plague to us on account of our sins."[414] Luther's idea is not only that the Scholastic tradition betrays or conceals the original Christian message, but also that this concealment is "sent" to us by God. Third, if tradition is a falling away from the origin, one has to *destroy* the tradition, that is, Scholastic philosophy, in order to revive the original message.[415]

Heidegger applied this Lutheran model of tradition as apostasy or as falling away from an origin in three phases of his development. In a first phase, around 1916 to 1922, he simply rediscovered Luther and used him to break away from his Catholic past. We saw that Heidegger came to accept Luther's thesis of the corrupting influence of Greek metaphysics on Christian religion, and that he wanted to revive the original experience of temporality in early Christian life. This is why, in his course on the phenomenology of religion in 1920–21, he focused primarily on the earliest Christian document, Paul's first letter to the Thessalonians. Heidegger then turned to Aristotle in order to "destroy" his contaminating influence on Christianity. However, when he discovered in Aristotle a wealth of insights in the structure of human life, Heidegger's use of the Lutheran model entered its second phase, which culminated in *Sein und Zeit*: the model was formalized into the idea that the philosophical tradition had fallen away from *its* origins in Plato and Aristotle. The question of being, raised by these thinkers, had "subsided from then on as a theme for actual investigation." What Plato and Aristotle achieved "was to persist through many alterations and 'retouchings' down to the 'logic' of Hegel. And what they wrested with the utmost intellectual effort from the phenomena, fragmentary and incipient though it was, has long since become trivialized."[416]

In fact, Heidegger distinguishes in *Sein und Zeit* two kinds of falling away (*Verfallen*). The first consists in the tendency of human existence to get absorbed in the world and to interpret itself in its terms, by reflection so to say. The Aristotelian interpretation of humans in terms of matter and form is a product of falling in this sense, because the notions of matter and form are derived from the domain of artifacts. A destruction of Aristotle is needed in order to show that human life has to be conceptualized in terms of a very different set of categories (the existentialia). The second kind of falling is conceived on the Lutheran model. Tradition made the Aristotelian concepts overfamiliar to us and it conceals their original source in specific "fundamental experiences." This is why we have to destroy the tradition of philosophy.[417] In other words, the tradition of philosophy is interpreted as a kind of falling, which conceals another falling: the fact that human existence was alienated from itself to begin with.

I now come to Heidegger's later works and to the third phase of Heidegger's application of the Lutheran model. As we saw in section 10, above, Heidegger in these works interprets the history of metaphysics as a continuing regression into Darkness, a falling away from an original disclosure (*Eröffnung*) of being. My hypothesis is that Heidegger's initial metaphysical attempt to bring man before God by methodological atheism as defined in 1922, an attempt that should be located in the years 1928–30, when Heidegger started to use the word "metaphysics" in a positive sense, failed. This failure would explain the growing influence of Nietzsche on his thought after 1930. Heidegger already read Nietzsche before the First World War and he discusses Nietzsche's views on history in section 76 of *Sein und Zeit*.[418] But Nietzsche's influence grew from 1930 on, culminating in Heidegger's choice to become a Nazi in 1933, and, afterwards, in Heidegger's lectures on Nietzsche from 1936 to 1940.[419] In his account of the years 1933–34, Heidegger says that during 1930–32 he discussed Ernst Jünger's works *Die Totale Mobilmachung* and *Der Arbeiter* when they appeared in a small circle with his assistant Brock, and that he tried to show how Jünger's writings express an "essential understanding" of Nietzsche's metaphysics, which enables us "to see through the present and to foresee the future of the West" (see §§ 14 and 15, below).[420]

Nietzsche proclaimed the death of God. Heidegger quoted this statement in his *Rektoratsrede* of 27 May 1933. Within the context of the rectoral address, the quote illustrated Heidegger's thesis that the Greek origin of science in philosophy had been betrayed afterwards by "the Christian-theological interpretation of the world and by the later mathematical-technical thought of the modern epoch."[421] Clearly the Lutheran model is applied here, for Heidegger claims that an original Beginning is betrayed by a later tradition, and that we have to renew this Beginning by destroying the tradition. What Heidegger argues is that the Germans in 1933 have to renew the Greek origin of science as a "innermost determining center of the whole national Dasein of the people."[422]

It is important to see that Heidegger's application of the Lutheran model in the rectoral address is an inversion of this model. According to Luther and Heidegger in 1920–21, the Christian God had died in human hearts because the Scholastic tradition had interpreted the God of Abraham, Isaac, and Jacob in terms of Aristotelian Being. God had become an Eternal and unchanging Substance. How can such a God become manifest to us in time? Greek thought had contaminated our notion of God by interpreting him in terms of Being. This is why we have to go back to early Christianity and to destroy the tradition of the Schools.[423] In 1933, however, Heidegger reverses his early Lutheran thesis. He now claims that the *Greek* origin, which reveals the totality of beings, has been contaminated by the later *Christian* interpretation of the world. Being, Heidegger would say some years later, had been concealed by the fact that it was interpreted as *a* being, such as the Christian God.[424] The death of God was then diagnosed as the death of a mistaken interpretation of Being. By implication, Heidegger in 1933 advocated the destruction of the *Christian* element in the tradition instead of a destruction of the *Greek* element. The later evangelical minister Heinrich Buhr describes how in the fall of 1933, during one of his *Wissenschaftslager* (camps of science) in Todtnauberg, Heidegger gave a violent speech against Christianity, Christian theology, and the Christian interpretation of life.[425] Clearly, Heidegger had become a virulent atheist and anti-Christian by 1933.

Is it possible to give a rational reconstruction of this reversal of Luther? Or should we explain Heidegger's attempts at a destruction of Christianity in his National Socialist years by appealing to psychological factors, such as his early resentment against the Catholic Church, and by reference to his objective of bringing his philosophy into the Party line? The National Socialist propaganda, exploiting the German yearning for a strong leader they had lacked since the days of Bismarck, also used the notion of a transcendent power that had sent Hitler to save the Germans, a power that was not identical to the Christian God. Hitler himself often referred to Providence in his speeches, even after he had foresworn Catholicism and Christianity in 1937.[426]

We saw that *Sein und Zeit* implies at least one possible reason for discarding the traditional Christian conception of God: if human existence cannot be understood in terms of a created entity, then God cannot be conceived of as a creator. The traditional Christian God is essentially a creator, a perfect and almighty being (*Seiendes*).[427] Perhaps it was Eckhart who inspired Heidegger to substitute Being (*Sein*) for God, and to attribute the "death of God" to the fact that Being had been misconceived of as *a* being, namely, God. In Heidegger's later writings, Being (*das Sein*, or *das Seyn*) is often used in the sense of a mysterious transcendent agent or event, which sends (*schickt*) us our fate (*Geschick*), just as did Luther's God. I will write the word "Being" with an uppercase initial whenever it is used in this manner. A destruction of the Christian tradition would show that the *transcendens schlechthin* is Being and not the personal God of Christianity. In this manner, the later Heidegger used the Lutheran model against Luther and against Christianity itself. Christianity was now interpreted as a falling tradition, which betrayed and obscured an original revelation of Being in Greek thought.[428] However, because of the very fact that Heidegger's thought remained Lutheran in a sense, it could not really do justice to Greek philosophy. In interpreting the Greeks, Heidegger projected Lutheran themes into their writings, as we will see below.

Heidegger's reversal of Luther explains the structural aspects of his later discourse on Being, aspects that are formally identical with the structures specified at the end of section 6, above. For Luther, the relation to God is the essential core of human beings. Similarly, Heidegger held in his later works that "man dwells only in his essence if he is addressed by Being."[429] Accordingly, (1) the *question of Being* is the most fundamental question for man. This question of Being is in fact a quest for Being. (2) Dasein has an understanding of this question (*Seinsverständnis*), for Dasein is essentially transcendence toward Being. However, (3) in the ontotheological tradition of metaphysics, Being is misconceived as *a* being, that is, as God, so that the tradition falls away from its origin. We live in oblivion of being (*Seinsvergessenheit*), because (4) we do not acknowledge the crucial distinction (*ontological difference*) between Being and beings. We endorse (5) the ontology of presence: we think that we might represent Being as an eternally present entity or a personal God, whom we might manipulate. As we saw, Luther thought that God had sent to us the Aristotelian misinterpretation of Christianity as "a plague on account of our sins." Similarly, Heidegger held in his later works that Being concealed itself in the history of metaphysics, and that the fate (*Geschick*) of the stages of metaphysics was sent to us (*geschickt*) by Being. It would be the task of the thinker (6) to wrest us from the oblivion of Being by (7) raising the question of Being anew and by (8) retrieving the tradition of metaphysics as a concealment of Being. Only in this manner (9) would man turn in upon his essence and origin again.

I call Heidegger's inverted application of the Lutheran model in his later works the postmonotheist leitmotif in the question of being. The leitmotif is "postmonotheist" in two complementary senses. First, it is *post*monotheist because Heidegger claims that the monotheist tradition is done with. God is dead, as Nietzsche said. Heidegger fully endorsed this statement from 1933 on, even though he made occasional tactical genuflexions for Christianity after the war. Heidegger's later discourse on Being comes after (*post*) monotheism. In the important lecture series *Einführung in die Metaphysik* (*Introduction into Metaphysics*) of the summer semester of 1935, which Heidegger published in 1953 because it was "particularly appropriate to make visible a stretch of the way from *Sein und Zeit* (1927) to the latest publications," we clearly recognize Heidegger's inversion of Luther and his destruction of Christianity.[430] Heidegger starts with the question "why there is something rather than nothing," the very question with which he had concluded his inaugural lecture of 1929. He talks about the "hidden power" of this question, which might strike us in moments of "great despair" or "jubilation of the heart."[431] And he argues that the question is the most fundamental one, because it opens up the possibility of transcending the totality of beings to their "ground" (*Grund*), namely, Being, whereas the question is only a real one in a "leap" (*Sprung*) and *as* leap.[432]

This sounds very similar to traditional Christian metaphysics. But at this point Heidegger starts his destruction of the Christian view. "Someone for whom the Bible is divine revelation and truth, already has the answer before he even starts asking the question 'why is there something rather than nothing.' "[433] In other words, a (Christian) believer cannot really *question*.[434] Both echoing and reversing Paul's statement that "God made foolish the wisdom of the world" (i.e., Greek philosophy), Heidegger claims that the philosophical question of Being "is folly in the eyes of faith." The believer is not really able to sustain Heidegger's philosophical questioning, and Christian philosophy is like a wooden iron.[435] What is more, Christianity itself is but Platonism for the people, Heidegger proclaims, echoing Nietzsche.[436] Hugo Ott was the first to see that *Einführung in die Metaphysik* is among other things an implicit polemics with the Christian philosopher Theodor Haecker, whose book *Was ist der Mensch?* had a great success after its publication in 1933.[437] Haecker's book was an undisguised and passionate Catholic critique of National Socialism, nationalism, and racism, a very untimely book indeed, and Haecker got in trouble with the Nazis. Heidegger claims in *Einführung in die Metaphysik* that philosophy is untimely.[438] In fact, he did the very timely job of demolishing Christian philosophy, probably because it dared to oppose the National Socialist revolution.[439]

Heidegger's later thought is *post*monotheistic, then, because Heidegger had to destroy the Christian tradition in order to inaugurate his thinking about Being.[440] In a second sense of the expression, it is also post*monotheistic*. What I mean is that Heidegger's later discourse on Being retains many structural parallelisms with traditional Christian theology. What is more, to the extent that this discourse on Being is intelligible at all, it derives its intelligibility from these structural parallelisms with Christianity. Putting together the two aspects of postmonotheism, we might define the postmonotheist theme as *the attempt to replace the Christian religion by a different variety of religious discourse*, the meaning of which is parasitic upon the monotheist Christian discourse that it intends to destroy.[441] Like a real parasite, Heidegger's discourse of Being lives on the blood of the religious tradition of Christianity, and it aims at destroying this tradition by arguing that Christianity belongs to the metaphysical era of *Seinsverlassenheit*. Somewhat more sympathetically, one might say that Heidegger's postmonotheist leitmotif is an attempt to rescue religion after the death of God. Religion is saved by arguing that the God of Christianity is a mere entity among entities, an idol, so to say, and that his death was merely the death of a fallen tradition that obscured Being as it really is.[442] Although God is dead, Being itself is as living as ever, even though it is concealed by the metaphysical and theological tradition. Yet in telling us about Being, Heidegger inevitably falls back on the very structures of Christianity, although he abstracts from the Christian contents.

In the next subsection I will give an impression of the astonishing range of structural parallelisms between Heidegger's later discourse on Being and an Eckhartian-Lutheran version of Christian monotheism. Being is One. It reveals itself in the Beginning. The tradition has fallen away from this Origin, and in fact, Being has concealed itself in traditional metaphysics. The thinker has to destroy the tradition in order to inaugurate a return or "step back" (*Schritt zurück*) to the Beginning, and to prepare a Second Coming (*Ankunft, anderer Anfang*) of Being. There is, however, one obvious difficulty for such an inverted Lutheran scheme. Luther could rely on the conviction, shared with his Catholic opponents, that the Bible is a revelation of and by God, and that God manifested himself in Christ. Because he perverts or inverses Luther, Heidegger discards the Bible as a revelation of Being. But this raises a problem for the application of a Lutheran model of tradition: Where should we look for the original revelation of and by Being, or the Beginning of real history, from which the tradition has fallen away?

In *Einführung in die Metaphysik* of 1935, Heidegger tries to move from the question concerning beings to the question of Being.[443] Traditional metaphysics would not ask this latter question, for it seeks the ground of beings in another being, God. This holds also for Aristotle, so that Aristotle already lived in "oblivion of Being" (*Seinsvergessenheit*).[444] Asking the question of Being "means nothing less than to retrieve the beginning of our historical-spiritual Dasein and to transform it into the other beginning."[445] Heidegger claims that the saying of Being (*Sagen des Seins*) by thinkers and poets "founds" (*Gründen und Stiften*) the historical Dasein of a people.[446] Consequently, only the philosopher and the poet may know about the "inner greatness" of the National Socialist movement.[447] The German people, which finds itself in the middle, so that it has most neighbors and is most endangered, is also the metaphysical people, which has to decide to renew the Greek beginning of Being.[448] But again, where should the German people find the original revelation of Being, if even Plato and Aristotle did not ask Heidegger's question of Being as distinguished from the question concerning beings? In *Einführung in die Metaphysik* Heidegger discovers the original Beginning mainly in Parmenides' saying that *noein* ("to think") and *einai* ("to be") belong together.[449] Having elucidated this saying by means of a comparison with Sophocles' *Antigone*, he concludes that in Parmenides' vision, the essence of man is grounded in the opening (*Eröffnung*) of the Being of beings.[450] Dasein as such is the place (*das Da*) where Being reveals itself.[451] Being reveals itself by means of the original distinction between Being and beings, which is the source of history. After Parmenides and Heraclitus, Greek thought allegedly has fallen away (*Abfall*) from this original revelation of Being, and Heidegger sees Plato and Aristotle both as the End of the Beginning and as the Beginning of the End.[452] In the process of falling away from the original revelation of Being, human thought would have gained supremacy over Being. Consequently, Being became concealed. The question of Being aims at restoring Being to its primacy.

Ten years later, in a publication of 1946, Heidegger sought the original revelation of Being even earlier, and found it in a fragment of Anaximander, the oldest text of Western thought. This text is "Greek," Heidegger says, in the sense of the "early fate" (*die Frühe des Geschickes*), "as which Being itself lights up in beings and claims an essence of man."[453] But the very fact that beings appear to Dasein conceals the "light of Being." Being withdraws in the very act of revealing itself in beings.[454] A Christian theologian might argue that God's creation of the world obscures God himself, because man tends to be absorbed in the created world and to forget about its Creator. Similarly, Heidegger claims that the original revelation of Being is obscured by beings, so that it is inherent in the Beginning that the Beginning is forgotten. For this reason, aberration (*die Irre*) or forgetfulness of Being is "the essential space of history."[455]

The historian of ancient philosophy will object that Heidegger's interpretation of the pre-Socratics violates the texts, and that it is a projection of his postmonotheology into the extant fragments of Anaximander, Parmenides, and Heraclitus. Indeed, Heidegger's postmonotheistic discourse on Being is altogether alien to the atmosphere of Greek thought, which never turned Being into a historical process of revelation. Heidegger is the first to admit this violence in his interpretations.[456] However, with the unflappable boldness of a theologian such as Karl Barth, who in his study of Paul's Letter to the Romans discarded historical Bible scholarship in order to find his theological Truth in the Holy Book, Heidegger set aside the standards of history and philology: "all eyes of all historians will never suffice to see the happening [*Geschehnis*] of Being."[457] The reason is that history as an academic discipline belongs itself to the history of the oblivion of Being. As a consequence, a philosophical interpretation should probe deeper into the texts than a purely historical or "scientific" exegesis is able to do:

> The authentic interpretation [*eigentliche Auslegung*] should show that which is not stated in words anymore but which yet is said. In doing so, the interpretation must necessarily use violence. The proper sense [*das Eigentliche*] should be looked for where a scholarly [*wissenschaftliche*] interpretation does not find anything anymore, although the latter stigmatizes as unscholarly [*unwissenschaftlich*] everything that transcends its domain.[458]

Clearly, the inverted application of the Lutheran model compelled Heidegger to construe an anti-Christian postmonotheistic *mythology*, which linked a fictional Greek Origin of Being to a new German Beginning.[459] As in the rectoral address of 1933, Heidegger in the summer of 1935 summoned the Germans to renew the Greek revelation of Being. The "inner truth and greatness" of the National Socialist movement would consist in this renewal. Gradually, it dawned on Heidegger that the actual National Socialist revolution would never effectuate the rebirth of the Greek beginning, and that Germany would lose the war. The postmonotheist theme turned out to be as flexible as the Christian tradition that it meant to replace. The Second World War, provoked by the National Socialist totalitarian state, could be interpreted as a consequence of our oblivion of Being, rather than as a refutation of Heidegger's ontological myth. If the German Renewal of the Greek Beginning had led to disaster and ignoble destruction, it had not been a real renewal after all. According to Heidegger's later insight into our historical fate (*Geschick*), the World Wars announced the elimination of the very distinction between war and peace. This elimination was inevitable when the truth of Being failed to come.[460] Although Heidegger turned out to be a false prophet of Being in 1935, Being continued to reveal itself to him. To prepare us for a second coming of Being was Heidegger's contribution to what has been called the myth of the twentieth century (see § 14C).

B. Analogies with Christian Monotheism

The flexibility of Heidegger's postmonotheist theme excuses us from the task of tracing its development in his later writings, although this might be an interesting scholarly investigation in its own right: the subtle and often opportunist transformations of the postmonotheist leitmotif reflect Heidegger's attitude to the changing fate of Germany before, during, and after the war (see § 14C). Nearly all the later works contain the postmonotheist leitmotif in some form, and the general structure of the leitmotif remains the same from 1935–38 on. Its most impressive development is to be found in *Beiträge zur Philosophie*, Heidegger's second *chef d'oeuvre*, written in the years 1936–38. This manuscript, which Heidegger did not publish, must be regarded as the hidden source from which Heidegger's later publications flowed forth.

Instead of analyzing each text in detail, I substantiate my postmonotheist interpretation of the later Heidegger in two ways. In the present subsection I explore the parallelisms between Heidegger's later discourse on Being and traditional Christian theology, drawing on a wide range of texts. In the next subsection I discuss a number of doctrines of the later Heidegger that should be viewed against the background of the postmonotheist theme.

1. The Uniqueness of Being. We have wondered many times why Heidegger places so much stress on the unity of being, to the point of identifying the question of being with a quest for a unique (sense of) "being" underlying the multiplicity of senses and beings. The Aristotelian leitmotif, the phenomenologico-hermeneutical theme, and the Neo-Hegelian leitmotif did not provide a solution to this problem, whereas the transcendental solution turned out to be a partial one only, because it could not explain all texts.[461] I am claiming that the hypothesis of a postmonotheist leitmotif is the best explanation for Heidegger's assumption that there is a unique sense of the word "being." In this sense, the word "being" (*das Sein*, or *das Seyn*) refers to postmonotheist Being. Whereas the texts do not allow us to decide unambiguously whether Heidegger was already referring to postmonotheist Being at the time of *Sein und Zeit*, he does clearly so from 1935 on. The first parallel between traditional Christian theology and Heideggerian postmonotheism, then, is that Heidegger in the later works stresses the uniqueness of Being (*das Sein*) in contrast to the multiplicity of beings (*die Seienden*). As he says in "Die Kehre" ("The Turn"), Being has no rival.[462]

Heidegger uses a great number of German expressions and phrases to highlight the uniqueness of Being.[463] Being is the Singularity of beings (*das Einzigartige des Seienden*), the unique one, which transcends itself to itself, so that it is the *transcendens schlechthin*.[464] This formula reminds us of Anselm's celebrated definition of God, as does the phrase that "Being is more being [*seiender*] than each and every being."[465] Furthermore, Being not only is the being of beings, as it was according to the phenomenological conception. The question of being rather aims at Being itself in *its* being.[466] Being is the One Mystery (*Geheimnis*),[467] the Singular (*das Einzige*), which conceals itself.[468] Being is not God, it is not a foundation of the world (*Weltgrund*), and when we ask what being is, we can only answer: it is *itself*. Compare the passage in the Old Testament where Yahweh says to Moses: "I am who I am" (*Exodus* 3:14). Being is nearer to us than all beings, although this nearness remains farthest from us.[469] Surely this is a variation on Augustine. Being is Truth, and the Truth of Being is the Clearing (*Lichtung*) in which we stand, expressions that recall the biblical idea of truth as God's revelation in Christ.[470] When we say in German: *es gibt das Sein*, the *es* that "gives" Being, is Being itself.[471] This reminds us of the metaphysical notion of God as *causa sui*.[472] Being is simple (*einfach*) and Being is the Same as Nothingness (*das Selbe mit dem Nichts*).[473] Nothingness is also called the veil of Being (*die Schleier des Seins*), an expression current in mystical writings.[474] Being is light (*Licht*); it is the Wholly Other (*das ganz Andere*) to beings, it is the Incalculable (*das Unberechenbare*) and the Indestructible (*das Unzerstörbare*).[475] Being is *the* topic (*Sache*) of thinking.[476]

The number of expressions Heidegger uses for postmonotheist Being exceeds by far the number of names for and attributes of God in the Bible. There would be no point in compiling a complete enumeration of Heidegger's definite descriptions of Being. In the text "Aus einem Gespräch von der Sprache" (1953–54), for instance, Heidegger refers to Being by means of thirteen different expressions: *der Sach-Verhalt* (literally: state of affairs; here: the conduct [*das Verhalten*] of the topic [*die Sache*]), *das Anfangende* (the Incipient), *das Unbestimmbare* (the Indeterminable), *das lichtende Verhüllen* (that which veils while shining), *das Ungesagte* (the Unsaid), *das eigentlich Tragende* (that which really supports), *Nichts* (Nothingness), *Leere* (Emptiness), *Ohne Namen* (that which does not have a name), *das unbestimmte Bestimmende* (the indeterminate Determiner), *die Zwiefalt aus der Einfalt* (the Duplicate from the Simple, that is, the distinction between Being and beings that springs from Being itself), *das anfänglich Vertraute* (that which has been familiar from the beginning), and *das ganz Andere* (the wholly Other).[477] Even an incomplete list will suffice to show that in the later works Heidegger incessantly celebrates the uniqueness of Being. He is not a postpolytheist but a postmonotheist thinker.

2. Creation and Revelation. Being is not God, and we saw that Heidegger argued already in *Sein und Zeit* that the traditional notion of creation is ontologically inadequate. Nevertheless, Heidegger's postmonotheology admits of an analogue of the creation myth. Heidegger says that Being is putting forward (*entbergen*) beings, and that in the process of putting forward entities, Being conceals itself.[478] Being is clearing or shining forth (*Lichtung*); it pro-jects beings and sends humans into the existence of Da-sein.[479] Being is opening up (*Eröffnung, Offenheit*); it gives itself in the open, and the original mystery for all thought is that Being *is*.[480] Being is also a deliverance or a handing over (*das Einhändigen des Anwesens*), which hands over presence to things present.[481] Being gives each entity the warrant of being, and without Being each and every being would remain "beingless."[482] In giving being to entities, Being gives itself.[483] Heidegger's message seems to be that we should reject the traditional notion of a God as a creator, which dispels our sense of wonder about the fact that beings *are*. Instead, we should accept the notion of Being as the wonderful process of revealing entities to us. We might be inclined to identify Heidegger's Being with the mere fact or event that entities are, and sometimes Heidegger seems to do so. But mostly

Heidegger's later grammar of Being suggests that Being is an agent, the agent that inaugurates and sustains the fact that beings are. In other words, there is postcreationism in Heidegger's postmonotheism.

This postmonotheist analogue of the creation myth has an additional religious advantage. Monotheistic religions could never really cope with the problem of the plurality of religions. Should one denounce competing gods as idols, mere products of human fantasy? In that case it becomes difficult to sustain the claim that one's own God is not such a product. Or should one admit that they have some religious value, pretending, for instance, that the other gods are somewhat misleading representations of the God of, say, Christian monotheism? This solution will not do either, for why should the Christian God put such misleading images in people's minds? In *Beiträge zur Philosophie*, Heidegger offers a radical solution to the problem of the plurality of religions. Postmonotheist Being is at the origin of all gods, including the Christian one and including a possible God who is perhaps bound to arrive. Being sends gods to humans in order to save them, for instance, so that all gods have an equal status.[484] It follows that no god is the only true one; no god is unique. But postmonotheist Being is unique and without rivals. This is why Heidegger asks one unique question only: the question of Being.[485]

3. The Fall, History, and Eschatology. As in traditional Christianity and Christian Neo-Platonism, Heidegger assumes that the autodistinction by Being between Being and beings (*der Unter-schied*), that is, his analogue for creation or emanation, is a historical process with a beginning and an *eschaton* (end of the present world). It is the history of Being. Although some Greek philosophers, Plato, for instance, admitted of a beginning of the world, the notion of history as *eschatology* is lacking in ancient Greek thought.[486] Again, Heidegger projects a Judeo-Christian pattern back into Greek philosophy. Playing with the Greek term *epochē* (abstinence of judgment) and the German word *Epoche* (epoch), he says that in sending out (*schicken*) historical epochs (*Epoche, Geschick*), Being withholds itself (*epochē*). Real world history (*eigentliche Weltgeschichte*) is the succession of these epochs, and this succession is Time. When the history of Being is gathered in its end, this gathering is the "eschatology of Being." "Being itself is as a fateful sender [*geschickliches*] in itself eschatological."[487] Like in Christianity, there is in Heidegger's postmonotheology a Beginning and an End of Time.

At this point the postmonotheist leitmotif and the Neo-Hegelian theme merge. The Neo-Hegelian history of being (*Seinsgeschichte*) becomes a series of epochs that are sent to us (*geschickt*) by Being as a transcendent agent (*Seinsgeschick*). Real history (*eigentliche Geschichte*) is a fate (*Geschick*) that Being sends (*schickt*) to us, Heidegger repeats again and again with an adroit (*geschickt*) pun on the German root *schick*.[488] No wonder that the coherence of Heidegger's thought is lost upon English readers, because his wordplays do not survive translation. No wonder, too, that Heidegger says about Hegel that he was "the only thinker of the West who experienced the history of thought in a thinking way."[489]

Both Hegel and Heidegger interpret the history of metaphysics as a permanent revelation of and by Being. However, between Hegel and Heidegger stands Nietzsche, who proclaimed the death of God. Hegel could still conceive of history as a progressive self-revelation by the Absolute, culminating in its complete self-transparency. Heidegger, on the contrary, claims that the history of metaphysics is a history of Being's progressive self-concealment, beginning with Plato's substitution of Ideas for Being and ending with the death of God and the destruction of the earth by technology. This is why humans inevitably go astray or why they are insane (*irren*). Each epoch of world history is an epoch of erring or madness (*die Irre*). From the viewpoint of the history of Being (*Seynsgeschichte*), the earth is the wandering planet (*Irrstern*).[490]

According to Heidegger, then, history is not progress, but a falling away from the origin, as the inverted Lutheran model implies. In the process of revealing entities in history-shaping ways, Being conceals itself more and more. If metaphysics articulates the ways in which the totality of beings is revealed in each epoch, as the Neo-Hegelian theme has it, metaphysics is also a concealment of Being, because in thinking the totality of beings, Being is forgotten.[491] Yet, because beings cannot become manifest without the Light of Being, the history of metaphysics is also a revelation of Being. Being reveals itself in the history of metaphysics in its very concealment.[492] The history of metaphysics contains a trace (*Spur*) of Being, because beings cannot emerge in their totality without Being. But, Heidegger says, this trace was erased when Being was conceived of as a highest being, as a transcendent entity.[493] In other words, the last trace of Being was destroyed when Being became conceived of as God. The notion of God annuls the crucial difference between Being and beings (the ontological difference), because it *represents* Being, which cannot be represented, as an omnipresent entity, *a* being. Consequently, we have to destroy the Christian monotheist or ontotheological tradition in order to turn back to Being. But if the metaphysics of Christian monotheism is a fate (*Geschick*) sent to us by Being, how can we destroy it?

4. Predetermination. The notion of real history (*eigentliche Geschichte*) as fate or destiny (*Geschick*) sent to us (*geschickt*) by Being is Heidegger's postmonotheistic equivalent of Luther's notion of predetermination. The fundamental way in which the totality of entities is revealed to us in a specific epoch of Being, such as the world as a creation by God, or the reign of technology (*das Wesen der Technik*), cannot be changed by human effort.[494] Dasein exists in the throw (*Wurf*) of Being, which sends us our fate.[495] Being, not man, decides how entities appear to us in a specific epoch. Being decides how truth as openness will *be*.[496] The truth or openness (*das Wesen der Wahrheit*) in which beings become manifest to us, is a *diktat* by Being.[497]

5. Deus absconditus. "Truly, thou art a God who hidest thyself, O God of Israel, the Saviour," says *Isaiah* 45:15. Especially when it claims that God is transcendent to nature, monotheism tends to conclude that God is invisible, and it becomes a disturbing problem how we might come to know God. Because God is almighty, this invisibility must be explained by the alleged fact that he hides himself. In Heidegger's later discourse on Being, the postmonotheist analogue of this theme of the hidden God (*deus absconditus*) expresses itself in a great many ways, which a reader of the later Heidegger will easily recognize. Being is forgotten (*Seinsvergessenheit*) because it conceals itself (*Seinsverborgenheit*).[498] This means that Being has abandoned us (*Seinsverlassenheit*) so that we live in abandonment by being and are homeless.[499] Being withdrew itself (*Entzug*) in the beginning of the history of Being, and it refuses itself to us.[500] Being is hidden, it is like a shadow, so that we are doomed to err (*Irre*) and our life is meaningless.[501] Being is not a ground (*Grund*), but an abyss (*Abgrund*), which hides the real ground.[502] It is a mystery, which does not betray itself.[503] It turns away from us.[504] Yet, Being is *das Fragwürdigste*, both in the sense that it is the most problematical (*fragwürdig*), because it is hidden, and in the sense that it is the most worthy (*würdig*) aim of our quest (*Fragen*).[505] Nowhere in the history of Western metaphysics do we find an experience of Being itself.[506] The history of Being necessarily began with forgetfulness of and by Being.[507]

6. Mourning about Metaphysics as Repentance. We have seen that in Heidegger's later writings there is a postmonotheist analogue of creation (2) and a postmonotheist analogue of the Fall (3, 5). The Fall is the moment at which God turns away from man and makes him "homeless." From a narratological perspective, we might say that creation or paradise and Fall are the first two stages in a mythological scheme that is common in religions. The scheme has two further stages: repentance and redemption by grace. These four stages constitute what the theologian calls the cycle of paradise, apostasy and enslavement, repentance, and deliverance. We will now see that there is also a postmonotheist analogue for the latter two stages of the mythological scheme in Heidegger's later works: repentance and grace or deliverance. The theme of repentance is connected to Heidegger's later conception of metaphysics.

From the mid-1930s on, Heidegger conceived of metaphysics as a series of doctrines on the totality of beings, each of which defines the fundamental attitude of a historical epoch (the Neo-Hegelian leitmotif; see § 10, above). According to the postmonotheist theme, these doctrines articulate ways in which beings are revealed to us by Being, ways that are sent to us (*Geschick*, see point 3, above).[508] Because Being conceals itself when it reveals beings (*Deus absconditus*), metaphysics is also the tradition of forgetfulness of Being. In metaphysics, the totality of beings is articulated in each historical (*geschichtlich*) period, and this very articulation conceals Being.[509] Metaphysics is a veil of Being, which Being itself sends to us. It is Being's disguise, in which the difference between beings and Being is absent, because Being is misinterpreted as *a* being: God.[510]

However, if this is the case, the history of metaphysics should be reappropriated in a new way. It should be read as a series of hints (*Winke*) or traces (*Spuren*), which Being sends us even though it conceals itself in these very traces.[511] The overcoming of metaphysics (*Überwindung*), a desideratum of *Sein und Zeit*, now becomes a mourning for metaphysics, a coping with the fact that Being withdrew from us in metaphysics and a getting over Being's withdrawment (*Verwindung*). The postmonotheist analogue of repentance is this *Verwindung*. Like in the process of mourning for a dead beloved one, we have to retrieve the past in order to get over the absence of Being. The point of Heidegger's later elucidations of the metaphysical tradition is that this tradition is now interpreted *as* abandonment by Being.[512] Heidegger tries to show that no metaphysician thought of Being as such, that is, Being in Heidegger's sense.[513] Reading the metaphysical tradition in this manner means contemplating the Absence of Being. Only by getting over (*verwinden*) metaphysics, contemplating Being's absence, may we prepare an overcoming (*Überwindung*) of metaphysics, that is, a new advent of Being.[514] For this new advent of Being, it is necessary to overcome metaphysics, because metaphysics prevents us from thinking the question of Being.[515] Clearly, Heidegger's proclamation of the End of Metaphysics, or the End of Philosophy, should be read in the light of the inverted Lutheran model.[516] His retrieval of metaphysics as self-concealment of Being is a postmonotheist analogue of Christian repentance, and the idea that Being withholds itself in the history of philosophy, thereby condemning man to an aimless ramble (*Irre*), is an analogue of God's wrath, by which we are punished for the fact that we do not acknowledge Him. It would be a serious misunderstanding to interpret Heidegger's elucidations of the metaphysical tradition from Anaximander to Nietzsche as contributions to historical scholarship in philosophy. They are attempts to read his postmonotheist mythology into the philosophical tradition.[517]

7. Preparing: The Theme of John the Baptist. According to the Gospels of Matthew (3) and Luke (3), John the Baptist confronted the Jewish people with their need to repent. In this manner he prepared the advent of the Son of man, and he understood himself as a forerunner of this advent (cf. Luke 3:15–18; John 1:19–28). Similarly, Heidegger in his later years thought that the task of the thinker is to prepare a new advent of Being (*Ankunft des Seins*).[518] This is yet another striking parallel between Heidegger's postmonotheist discourse on Being and traditional Christianity. We might call it the subleitmotif of John the Baptist. In "Nietzsche's Wort 'Gott ist tot,' " Heidegger clearly defines this notion of thinking as preparation: "what matters to preparatory thinking is to light up [*lichten*] the space [*Spielraum*] in which Being itself might put man, as far as man's essence is concerned, into an original relation to It again. To be preparatory is the essence of such a thinking."[519] What Heidegger's thinking aims at preparing is an "openness for Being."[520] It is an attempt to make man ready for the call or demand (*Anspruch*) of Being.[521] Before 1945, Heidegger addressed himself primarily to the German *Volk* (people). This *Volk* would be unique in its origin and its destiny, because it relates to unique Being.[522] After Germany's defeat, Heidegger was prudent enough to include Europe, and even mankind as a whole, in the audience of his postmonotheist message.

8. The Decision. Preparing us for a new advent of Being must consist in exhorting us to make a decision (*Entscheidung*), for we have to decide to open our existence to Being.⁵²³ Because modern science and technology constitute the End of metaphysics in the sense that they complete the concealment of Being—in the eyes of the modern naturalistic *Weltanschauung*, Heidegger's quest for Being is absurd—the decision to open our existence to Being also involves a decision about science and technology.⁵²⁴ Heidegger stresses that he is not against science or technology. To be "against" science and technology would be incongruous with Neo-Hegelian postmonotheism, because in their essence (*Wesen*) science and technology belong to the fate (*Geschick*) of modern metaphysics, which was sent to us (*geschickt*) by Being itself.⁵²⁵ Yet, by reflecting on the essence (*das Wesen*) of science and technology, we should understand that they *are* such a predetermined fate or destiny, something from Being (*Wesung*), and that there is a truth deeper than that of science, the Truth of Being. In this sense, Heidegger's decision to open up existence to Being is antinaturalist: it denies that science provides us with the deepest truths there are. According to Heidegger, the modern epoch of the Enlightenment and of science, in which there is an ever-increasing progress in human knowledge, is in its essence an epoch of regression into Darkness, the final consummation of our evil fate (*böses Geschick*) of *Seinsverlassenheit*.⁵²⁶

However, when we make the decision to open ourselves to Being, we will squander ourselves (*verschwenden*) as a sacrifice (*Opfer*) out of a gratitude (*Dank*) that appreciates the clemency (*Huld*) or grace (*Gunst*) of Being.⁵²⁷ The decision to open ourselves to Being presupposes another decision: Being's decision to refuse or to give itself to us.⁵²⁸

9. Grace, Deliverance, Second Coming. According to Paul and Luther, the grace of God is not an obligation God has toward us, provided that we do what is required by the laws of religion. On the contrary, grace is a free gift of God. We are never justified before God by our works or by the sacraments, but only by God's grace. Similarly, Heidegger says that accomplishments and works may perhaps prepare our sacrifice, but will never fulfill it.⁵²⁹ Human activity can never counter the danger of being deaf to the call of Being.⁵³⁰ The sacrifice is brought home only by the Event (*das Ereignis*) of Being, and we can never predict, manipulate, or calculate this Event.⁵³¹ When the Event, the "unprethinkable advent of the Inevitable" occurs, our thinking becomes "obedient to the voice of Being." Hearing (*hören*) and being obedient to (*gehorchen*) the voice of Being, our thinking will seek the Word, which helps the truth of Being to its expression. Only when human language springs from the Word does it stand upright.⁵³²

Heidegger expresses his postmonotheist analogue of the second coming of Christ with his usual richness and variation of linguistic invention. He speaks of *das Ereignis* (the Event), *Ankunft* (Advent), *Geschehen*, *Geschehnis* (Happening), *Gabe*, *Geschenk* (Gift), *Rettung* (Salvation), *Gunst* (Favor), *Augenblick* (Instant), *Kairos*, *Parousia* (the appropriate moment; personal presence), *Wandel des Seins*

(Change in Being), *Kehre im Ereignis* (Turn in the Event), and *der andere Anfang* (the Other Beginning).[533] Again, there is no point in trying to compile a comprehensive list of Heidegger's expressions for the second coming. In his later philosophy, Heidegger always says the same, albeit each time in different words.[534] The reader of the later works will easily recognize this postmonotheist theme of grace, if only he keeps in mind the framework of the postmonotheist interpretation.

10. Thinking as Devotion. It will by now dawn on us what the later Heidegger means by *Denken* ("thinking") and its substitutes *Andenken* ("remembering," in German a noun, but Heidegger uses it as a verb; *Andenken* is related to the German *Andacht*, devotion, a word that Heidegger usually avoids and yet suggests to the German ear), and *Besinnung* (reflecting-on-the-sense-of; *Besinnung* contains the word *Sinn*).[535] Let me first state what Heideggerian thinking is not. Heidegger contrasts thinking with scientific thought (*Wissenschaft*), with religious faith (*Glaube*), and with common sense (*der gesunde Menschenverstand*).

He bluntly declares that the sciences "do not think".[536] Scientific thought is characterized as calculating or computing (*rechnen*), even though in the usual sense of these terms computation is only a fraction of scientific thought.[537] "To calculate" (*Rechnen*) gets a negative connotation in Heidegger's texts. It is linked to being *calculating* and calculating is seen as the attempt to master, dominate, and manipulate things. Calculating turns to destruction of the earth; it uses and wears out (*verbrauchen*) beings.[538] In the modern era, man does not let beings be what they are, but he assaults them.[539] Science and technology are interpreted as the final realization of Nietzsche's metaphysics of the will to power. Each and every entity in our epoch has become an object to be dominated by calculation.[540] Heidegger plays down the sincere longing for understanding the world, life, and humanity, which motivates a real scientist. He claims that the scientific attitude precludes our openness to Being.[541] The epoch of science and technology is the era of the consummation of meaninglessness.[542] In conformity with the antinaturalist stance of *Sein und Zeit*, Heidegger repeats that science is not "an original happening of truth."[543]

Heidegger's pejorative descriptions of science and technology fit in well with the tradition of religious critique of science, which started with Paul's condemnation of Greek science and philosophy as "folly" in 1 *Corinthians* 1:20. This tradition was intensified by German romantics such as Schlegel, Hölderlin, Novalis, and the young Schleiermacher, who reacted against the scientific worldview of the Enlightenment and wanted to reenchant the world by a renewal of religion. Yet Heidegger also distinguishes his notion of thinking from the concept of religious faith (*Glaube*). As in the case of science, he interprets faith in a pejorative sense. According to Heidegger, faith is not the questioning and restless quest for God, which it is for many modern Christians. On the contrary, faith is seen as the presumption of knowing the answer to all questions concerning the meaning of life. The believer is not really able to question things (*fragen*), Heidegger said in the spring of 1935.[544] Both science and faith are seen as a falling away from thinking, a falling away that is the evil fate (*Geschick*) sent by Being.[545] There is an abyss between faith and thinking.[546] According to Heidegger's inverted Lutheran scheme, Christian faith betrays Being because it conceives of Being as *a* being: God. It forgets about the crucial ontological difference between Being and beings. This is why "someone who has experienced theology and faith from its Origin must be silent about God in the domain of thinking."[547]

According to the school of ordinary-language philosophy, which flowered in the 1960s and 1970s, philosophy is different both from scientific thought and from faith, because it is close to common sense. But Heidegger sharply distinguishes philosophical thinking (*Denken*) from common sense as well.[548] From the point of view of common sense (*das alltägliche Vorstellen, der gesunde Menschenverstand*), philosophical thought is something mad (*etwas Verrücktes*). Playing with the German word *verrückt*, Heidegger says that one can effectuate this madness or shift (*Verrückung*) in one's attitude only by one jerk (*Rück*), that is, all at once.[549] Heidegger does not like common sense. It is "the refuge of those who are envious of thinking" and it "has never thought about anything from its Beginning."[550] Common sense allegedly is not as sensible as it seems; it is a mere trivialized product of the Enlightenment. Surely, it is not capable of judging about "that which really is: Being."[551]

Apart from the image of madness, Heidegger often uses that of a *Sprung* (leap). Only by a leap we can arrive in the *Ortschaft des Denkens* (locality of thinking).[552] What Heidegger means is that we can never prove what thinking yields, nor argue for it.[553] In thinking something becomes manifest which "manifests itself while it hides itself at the same time," that is, Being.[554] Although thinking is beyond the realm of argument and discussion, and indeed beyond the conceptual, it has its own rigor or strictness (*Strenge*), which is "stricter" than the strictness of exact conceptual thought. This rigor is achieved when "saying remains pure in the element of Being."[555]

The images of madness and of a leap remind us of respectively Paul and Kierkegaard. According to Paul, God turned the wisdom of the world into folly. Conversely, faith will appear foolish or mad when it is seen from the point of view of common sense. Kierkegaard held that only a leap can bring us to faith, because there is an abyss between finite human beings and the Infinite. Should we not suppose, then, that *thinking* in the sense of the later Heidegger is a postmonotheist analogue of the search for God in faith?[556] This hypothesis is amply confirmed by the positive ways in which Heidegger characterizes his notion of thinking.

The leap of thinking brings us into our "belonging to Being," and it is a precondition for the *Er-eignis* (the event by which we become ourselves) of this belonging.[557] Thinking is essentially *fragen* (asking, questioning, wondering) and Heidegger calls questioning the "piety of thinking."[558] Thinking is a way toward that which is worthy of our quest (*das Fragwürdige*).[559] When we ask the question of Being properly, we question ourselves, so that we become problematical and worthy of inquiring about (*fragwürdig*) in our relation (*Bezug*) to Being, and open ourselves to it.[560] Questioning is in fact a kind of responding, that is, responding to the call of Being, which by its soundless voice (*lautlose Stimme*) determines us (*uns be-stimmt*) so that we may become determinate or get in the right mood (*Stimmung*) for the possibility to experience Being. Being is not a product of thinking, but real thinking is an Event of Being.[561] Whenever we ask ourselves what it is that is called "thinking" (*"was heißt Denken?"*), we should primarily interpret this question as: What is it that summons us to think (*"was ist es, das uns heißt, uns gleichsam befiehlt, zu denken"*)? And what summons us to think is the "Most Thinkworthy" (*das Bedenklichste*), that is, Being.[562] The quest for Being is the ultimate aim of our existence and of history.[563] If our thinking hears the voice of Being and is obedient to it (*hören, gehorchen*), it becomes transformed in itself (*Wandlung, Verwandlung*), and thinking (*Denken*) will turn into thanking (*Danken*).[564] However, we cannot force Being to come, so that thinking in the sense of asking requires waiting, "even a life long."[565] Waiting is not an absence of thought, but an openness for the Mystery, coupled with resignation concerning worldly matters.[566] Being itself is waiting too, Heidegger claims in good old Eckhartian style, because it *needs* us.[567] It is waiting until we will have prepared ourselves for it by deeming it worthy of attention.[568] The thoughtful attention to Being is the first Service that man has to perform.[569]

Thinking is "of Being" (*des Seins*) in two senses: Being makes thinking happen (*"Denken ist vom Sein ereignet"*) and thinking is obedient to (*gehören*) Being, giving heed to (*hören auf*) Being.[570] Thinking is essentially an anticipation of the advent of Being. Being has already sent itself to thinking (*zugeschickt*), so that Being has become historical (*geschichtlich*) in the history (*Geschichte*) of philosophical thought. Because Being became the destiny (*Geschick*) of thinking, all essential thinkers of the past are saying the same (*das Selbe*): even though Being conceals itself in their writings, they are speaking of Being.[571] The history of metaphysics is the history of the revelation of Being in its self-concealment.[572] It contains hints (*Winke*) of Being.[573]

11. Being, Dasein, and Ethics. I now come to a final aspect of Heidegger's postmonotheist discourse on Being that I want to summarize and discuss: the relation of Being to man or Dasein. Whereas in *Sein und Zeit* Heidegger tried to raise the question of being by analyzing Dasein's understanding of being (*Seinsverständnis*), in his later works he attempts to think the essence (*das Wesen*) of man as a relation (*Bezug*) to Being. Clearly this is a postmonotheist analogue to the biblical doctrine that man is essentially related to God. Heidegger's later notion of man implies both a rejection of humanism and a rejection of a naturalist or scientific conception of man. This is clearly stated in the "Brief über den 'Humanismus,' " which is in fact a letter against humanism, and in many other later works.

Heidegger adopts an idiosyncratic definition of humanism. As he says in "Platons Lehre von der Wahrheit" ("Plato's Doctrine of Truth"), humanism is essentially related to the history of metaphysics. Humanism is a conception of man according to which man occupies a central place (*eine Mitte*) within the totality of beings.[574] Because metaphysics defines the totality of beings as such, each kind of humanism, whether it be Marxist, Christian, Roman, Renaissance, or existentialist, presupposes or implies a metaphysical stance.[575] We have seen that Heidegger interprets the history of metaphysics as a history of abandonment by Being. Although in each historical epoch metaphysics conceives of the totality of beings in a sense which is sent to us by Being as our destiny, it does not reflect on Being as such. Heidegger concludes that metaphysical humanism does not inquire into the relationship (*Bezug*) between Being and man, and that it even obstructs such an inquiry.[576]

This means that we have to overcome humanism, because "man only resides in his proper essence, if he is claimed by Being."[577] Man is defined in his inner nature by his relationship with and need for (*Bezug*) Being, so that he can only be himself in this relationship.[578] Man is the shepherd (*Hirt*) of Being, who has to assume the function of a guardian (*Wächterschaft*) of Being, being a neighbor (*Nachbar*) of Being.[579] Overcoming humanism does not mean that we reject it as "false," for Being itself sent humanism to us as a fate, as indeed it sent to us all fundamental stances of metaphysics. Overcoming humanism means realizing that even the most sublime definitions of man by humanism "do not yet experience the proper dignity (*eigentliche Würde*) of man," which consist in Man's relation (*Bezug*) to Being, and in the fact that he "stands in the Truth of Being."[580] Dasein is now defined in an Eckhartian manner as the authentic level of human existence, on which man stands in the openness of Being and is appropriated by Being.[581]

According to Heidegger, the overcoming of humanism by his "thinking of Being" will not provide mankind with moral rules. Although this kind of thinking is in itself "original ethics," it does not have results and is sufficient to itself by being itself.[582] If ever there be rules and laws for man, they must come from Being itself, as assignments by Being. Only such assignments by Being will be able to bind man. Laws that are merely man-made can never be binding.[583] In other words, Heidegger's overcoming of humanism implies an overcoming of traditional ethics and morality as well. In order to read the "Brief über den 'Humanismus' " in its proper historical perspective, one should remember that it was written in the fall of 1946. Jean Beaufret had asked Heidegger whether it would be possible to give meaning to "humanism" again, a question that was probably motivated by the holocaust and the horrors of the Second World War. Heidegger answered by a letter to the effect that humanism and traditional morality should be overcome by his philosophy of Being.[584]

Heidegger's postmonotheism turns out to imply an authoritarian and heteronomous conception of ethics, according to which moral laws are not binding unless they are assignments by Being. The only difference with respect to the heteronomous notion of morality that we find in the Bible is that as yet Heidegger's Being did not issue any moral commandments. As a result, his postmonotheist conception of ethics annuls morality altogether. Is it far-fetched to wonder whether this destruction of ethics came all too timely to a philosopher who had been involved with Nazism and who never clearly and unambiguously distanced himself from it (see § 14, below)?

Finally, Heidegger's view of man as essentially related to transcendent Being implies a qualified rejection of naturalist conceptions of man. According to naturalism, mankind is a product of the biological evolution, and to grasp this fact is essential to our knowledge of man. In order to understand human beings, we should try to explain what makes man special by studying among other things man's biology, the brain in particular. Heidegger does not deny that such an investigation is possible. What he denies is that it will reveal the "essence" (*das Wesen*) of man. For it "could be that nature conceals its very essence" in the aspect which it turns to scientific inquiry, and we devaluate man's essence by conceiving it from the point of view of animal nature.[585] It is important to note that in his later works, Heidegger uses the philosophical term *Wesen* (essence) in a new and idiosyncratic sense. It is a marker of the level on which something is a *Wesung des Seyns*, that is, on which it is understood as coming from Being (*das Seyn*).[586]

Whereas the biological and paleontological studies of man discover a more or less gradual distinction between man and other higher mammals, Heidegger reaffirms the traditional Christian thesis that man is separated from the animal kingdom by an abyss.[587] The reason is that animals are never positioned freely in the Clearing of Being (*die Lichtung des Seins*). As a consequence, animals lack language.[588] Here we recognize the postmonotheist analogue of the Christian thesis that man is special because of his relation to God.

C. Postmonotheist Doctrines

I explored the parallelisms and analogies between Heidegger's postmonotheist discourse on Being and traditional Christianity at great length, among other reasons because many American interpreters, such as Dreyfus and Hall, tend to deny that religion is involved in Heidegger's philosophy (see § 6, above).[589] The Lutheran and postmonotheist interpretation of the later Heidegger has been amply corroborated. In his elucidations of the metaphysical tradition, Heidegger uses a Lutheran model, according to which the tradition has fallen away from an original revelation. The metaphysical or ontotheological tradition of the West allegedly is the veil of Being's self-concealment, and it should be retrieved as such in order to overcome metaphysics and to prepare ourselves for a second coming of Being. Heidegger's exegesis of metaphysics is not meant to be a contribution to the history of philosophy in the usual sense. It is a religious myth, which links a pre-Socratic Greek beginning to present-day (German) realities. Moreover, the meaning of Heidegger's later discourse of Being turns out to be parasitic on the Christian tradition Heidegger wanted to supersede. If Heidegger's discourse on Being has a meaning at all, this is because of its structural resemblance to traditional Christian doctrines. These Christian structures, the Christian flesh being stripped off, are then projected back into the philosophy of the pre-Socratics. Heidegger was a postmonotheist philosopher indeed, and this explains the great appeal of his later writings to those who forswear traditional Christianity and yet want to remain religious in some sense.

Heidegger's early impetus toward an authentic religion, then, was fulfilled in the later works, and his theological origin (*Herkunft*) turned out to be his future (*Zukunft*), as he himself stressed.[590] I conclude this section by briefly discussing some well-known views of the later Heidegger that cannot be explained satisfactorily unless one understands them on the basis of the postmonotheist interpretation: Heidegger's opinion on interpretation as such (see § 5, above), his critique of logic (see § 2, above), his philosophy of language, his philosophy of truth, art, poetry, and technology, and finally what I called the concealment of the question of being (§ 1, above). The fact that these Heideggerian doctrines may be explained by the postmonotheist theme is a final confirmation of the hypothesis that this leitmotif is central to Heidegger's later question of being.

1. Interpretation. Heidegger's doctrine on interpretation or elucidation has been discussed in section 5 of chapter 1. The main problem I raised was how we should explain Heidegger's counterintuitive claim that the interpreter has to add something "out of the topic [*Sache*] of the interpretation" to the content of the text, and that he has to do so covertly (*unvermerkt*). I argued that this maxim of covertness would be justified in situations of applicative interpretations of authoritative texts, where the very act of interpretation is thought to derogate from textual authority. The hypothesis that this was Heidegger's view of the texts which he was interpreting would explain the maxim of covertness. At first sight, however, my hypothesis does not account for Heidegger's maxim. Heidegger states the maxim of covertness as a preliminary remark on the interpretation of Nietzsche's philosophy. But interpretations of philosophers of the past will rarely be applicative, and their works will not carry authority in the sense in which a holy book of a revealed religion does. At first sight, then, my explanation of Heidegger's hermeneutical doctrine seemed to be altogether unconvincing.

Yet a first element of the explanatory hypothesis was corroborated by an analysis of Heidegger's views on interpretation in *Sein und Zeit*. Because understanding is said to be projective, all interpretation is applicative. What was still missing is the corroboration of the second element: that according to Heidegger the philosophical texts to be interpreted carry authority. However, this second element of my hypothesis is confirmed by Heidegger's postmonotheist conception of metaphysical texts. The later Heidegger construes the tradition of metaphysics as a revelation of and by Being in which Being conceals or withdraws itself in the very act of revealing beings in their totality. If Heidegger were right, the texts of the "essential thinkers" (*wesentliche Denker*) of the metaphysical tradition would carry the same authority for the postmonotheist thinker as the Bible does for an orthodox Christian. Moreover, it is also clear what Heidegger means when he says that the interpreter should add something to the text (*Beigabe*) out of the matter of his own concern (*Sache*). For Being is called *die Sache des Denkens* (the topic of thought) and the task of the Heideggerian interpreter is to read hints (*Winke*) of Being into the texts of the metaphysical tradition. This is why, according to Heidegger, all "essential" thinkers say one and the same thing: they speak of the advent of Being.[591]

Heidegger would not endorse the phrase "reading into the texts," which expresses a commonsensical view of his procedure.[592] He holds that it is Being itself which inspires the interpretations of metaphysical texts by the "thinking of Being."[593] In other words, Heidegger endorses a postmonotheist variety of the Lutheran doctrine of interpretation of the Scriptures, according to which God inspires the interpretation by a sincere Christian. Furthermore, the postmonotheist interpretation of metaphysics is an applicative interpretation. It has the function of preparing a new advent of Being by coping with (*Verwindung*) the fact that Being withdrew itself from us in the metaphysical era. The interpretation of metaphysics is an act of repentance, which makes us ready for Being.[594] To sum up, Heidegger's interpretation of the great metaphysical texts is a postmonotheist analogue of the Christian interpretation of the Bible, with the only difference being that the Bible explicitly speaks about God, whereas Heidegger claims that the metaphysicians of the past never speak explicitly of Being in his sense. Yet, Being spoke through them implicitly, and this ultimately explains why all essential thinkers say the same thing.[595]

2. Logic. In section 2 of chapter 1, I discussed Heidegger's rejection of logic in *Was ist Metaphysik?* I suggested a tentative interpretation, drawing a parallel with Wittgenstein's *Tractatus*, and I concluded that we need an interpretation of the question of being in order to grasp the precise meaning of Heidegger's liquidation of logic. Whereas I touched on the problem of logic several times earlier in this chapter, only the postmonotheist leitmotif fully explains Heidegger's attitude with regard to logic. Heidegger conceives of logic in a traditional Aristotelian manner, although he often mentions mathematical logic. He holds that logic presupposes a specific conception of language, according to which we say *something about something* when we make a statement.[596] Logic analyzes the inner structure of a simple statement as the attribution of a predicate to a subject.[597] Accordingly, logic assumes that language is always used to speak about (actual or possible) *beings*. As Wittgenstein said in the *Tractatus*, indicative language is used to state facts or describe possible states of affairs. Both Wittgenstein and Heidegger conclude that language, as logic sees it, does not speak of the "mystical," the "sense of the world" (Wittgenstein), or of Being (Heidegger).

However, at this point there is a crucial difference between Heidegger and Wittgenstein. According to Wittgenstein in the *Tractatus*, logic shows the essence or deep structure of language, which is the necessary structure of all possible languages. The logical conception of language is the only true conception. As a consequence, we cannot express the mystical or the sense of the world in language at all. Wittgenstein concludes that the philosopher who wants to meditate on the sense of the world cannot but remain silent. Heidegger suggests, on the contrary, that another notion of language is possible.[598] Indeed, he holds that Being implicitly expresses itself in language. Whenever we use the little word "is" and other forms of the verb "to be," we express Being, or rather, Being speaks to us.[599] If this "is" were never uttered, we would not be able to relate to beings.[600] The proposition that beings *are* is not a trivial tautology. It rather contains the fullest mystery of all thinking "in a first hint [*Wink*] of saying."[601]

Admittedly, logic gives a different interpretation of the verb "to be" as a logical expression: it means either identity, or existence, or predication. This is precisely the reason why Heidegger has to destroy logic in order to raise the question of Being.[602] From Being's point of view, Heidegger says in *Beiträge zur Philosophie*, logic is a mere illusion (*Schein*).[603] The "logical" conception of language is inherent in the metaphysical conception of the totality of beings, and it is part of the falling-away or decay (*Verfall*) of thinking. Accordingly, it is a mistake to think that one might overcome metaphysics by a logical analysis of language, as Carnap attempted to do.[604] Both logic and metaphysics are a product of our fateful abandonment by Being.[605] In order to prepare the advent of Being, we have to overcome logic and metaphysics.[606] If Heidegger raises the problem of logic in the later works, this is in order to inaugurate a new notion of language.[607] What is this new notion?

3. Language. Language became increasingly important as a theme of reflection in Heidegger's later works.[608] There are observations on language scattered throughout them, and six essays on language were edited under the title *Unterwegs zur Sprache* (*On the Way to Language*). To the extent that Heidegger's later writings are not mere commentaries but articulate his own thought, they always say the same thing in a great many different wordings. As this is also true for his writings on language, I summarize their common denominator.

In the essay "Die Sprache" ("Language"), Heidegger states the aim of his reflections on language in his usual abstruse jargon. These reflections serve the purpose "of coming into the speaking of language in such a manner, that this speaking happens as that which provides the essence [*das Wesen*] of mortals with its residence."[609] Since Being Itself is "that which provides the essence of mortals with its residence," the reflection on language purports to "come into the speaking of language" in such a way that this speaking happens as Being's speaking. Indeed, Heidegger's objective is not to propose yet another philosophical view of language.[610] He wants to teach us to "inhabit" language as the house of Being. What does this mean?

Heidegger first criticizes the common philosophical and scientific conceptions of language, according to which human beings speak and use language as an instrument of expression and communication. These conceptions are not false, but they altogether miss the essence (*das Wesen*) of language.[611] We remember that Heidegger associates the term *Wesen* with his neologism *Wesung*: that which stems from Being. In order to come into the speaking of language in the desired manner, we should realize that *language speaks*.[612] What Heidegger means by this obscure statement, which he often repeats in his later works, is not the structuralist doctrine that language as a structure is prior to the individuals speaking that language, these individuals being raised in a common culture and into a preexisting language. He rather claims that Being speaks to us through language, so that language in its primary essence (*Wesen*) is the Word of Being.[613] Thanks to the fact that language is the advent of Being, language speaks to us, and if we listen in the right manner, we "inhabit" language as our home. Language is the House of Being, for Being provides us with language as our dwelling.[614] Animals lack a language, because they never exist "in the light or clearing of Being."[615]

Heidegger's notion of language, then, is a postmonotheist analogue of the Gospel according to John, which states that in the beginning was the Word, that the Word was with God, and that God sent the Word to us in Christ. It is an analogue only, however, because the monotheist tradition of Christianity suffers from the fate (*Geschick*) of abandonment by Being, and Heidegger criticizes the theological conception of language on the basis of John's Gospel as remaining within the traditional (metaphysical) notion of language.[616] Metaphysics not only conceals Being; it also masks the essence of language.[617] It is the aim of Heidegger's reflections on language to restore language to its proper essence as a house that Being built for us.

4. Truth, Art, and Poetry. In his celebrated essay "Der Ursprung des Kunstwerkes" ("The Origin of the Work of Art"), based on lectures of 1935–36 and published for the first time in 1950, Heidegger claims that in the work of art "the truth of beings sets itself to work." Accordingly, the essence (*das Wesen*) of art is "the truth of beings setting itself to work" (*das Sich-ins-Werk-setzen der Wahrheit des Seienden*).[618] In order to understand this formula, which sounds objectionable because art is usually associated with beauty and not with truth, we should turn to Heidegger's redefinition of "truth" in *Sein und Zeit* and in the later works.

Traditionally, truth is understood as a relation of adequacy between propositions or statements and the stated facts or the things in the world characterized by these propositions. In section 44a of *Sein und Zeit*, Heidegger argues that this traditional conception of truth as *adaequatio rei et intellectus* is problematical, and that it will remain so unless one tries to understand truth on the basis of the ontology of Dasein. The reason is that what we mean by the truth of a statement becomes clear only if this statement is *shown* to be true, as Husserl had argued in his sixth logical investigation. But it is Dasein that shows that a statement is true by discovering that the matter about which the statement says something is *as* the statement says it is. Only because Dasein is "being discovering" in relation to "discovered beings" can there be truth.[619]

From this plausible but trivial account, Heidegger in section 44b draws the drastic conclusion that truth in the most fundamental sense is this "being discovering" of Dasein, and not truth as attributed to statements. Being discovering or "being in the truth" is a mode of being or an existentiale of Dasein. Because being in the truth would enable *Dasein* also to be untrue, "Dasein is equiprimordially both in the truth and in untruth."[620] Now Dasein's capacity to discover and reveal things is also called the *Erschlossenheit* (disclosedness) of Dasein. Disclosedness is the *Da* of Dasein, as Heidegger says. The reader will remember (see § 5, above), that there are two modes of disclosedness, namely, finding-oneself-in-a-situation (*Befindlichkeit*) and understanding (*Verstehen*). What is primarily and fundamentally revealed by our *Da* is a world, in the sense of a horizon or structural whole of significant relations, in which the tools and other things that we encounter are always already situated. According to the transcendental theme in *Sein und Zeit*, this structural whole is a priori, in the sense that entities can be present for Dasein only because a world is projected (*Entwurf*).

It is but a small step from the analysis of *Sein und Zeit* to using the word "truth" for this structural whole of significant relationships itself, which allegedly enables things to be present to us. Indeed, in *Sein und Zeit* Heidegger used the term "truth" for the condition of the possibility of propositional truth, and he claimed that this structural whole or world is such a condition. For the sake of clarity, I will call this sense of "truth" transcendental, in contradistinction to propositional truth. When Heidegger uses expressions such as "truth" and "the essence of truth" (*das Wesen der Wahrheit*) in the later works, he often means historical structures of significant relationships, or worlds, which allegedly enable things to show up for us. According to the Neo-Hegelian theme, there is a series of such structures. This series is the history of being, since in each of these structures, being has a different sense. Whereas in *Sein und Zeit*, it was Dasein that projects worlds, such a transcendental agent seems to be lacking in the Neo-Hegelian theme. It is the world itself that "worlds," and it is truth itself that sets itself to work. We have seen, however, that, ultimately, Being sends (*schickt*) us a world or a truth as a fate (*Geschick*), so that there is a postmonotheist analogue of creation and revelation.

In order to understand how truth can "set itself to work" in a work of art, we have to take the term "truth" in the transcendental sense. It is a significant structure or world, which enables things to manifest themselves. Heidegger argues in "Der Ursprung des Kunstwerkes" that a work of art, such as a painting by Van Gogh or a Greek temple, has the power to unfold a whole significant structure or world, because it is *Dichtung*. The German word *Dichtung* usually means poetry or a literary work, but I suspect that in this context Heidegger links it with *dicht* (dense), and we might translate *Dichtung* as "a piece of condensed significance."[621] Being such a condensed significance, the work of art is able to open up a significant world. In "Der Ursprung des Kunstwerkes," Heidegger still uses the term *Entwurf* (projection). However, it is not Dasein, or the artist, who projects a world and in this sense sets truth to work by creating a work of art. Rather, truth, or the unconcealedness of being (*die Unverborgenheit des Seienden*) projects itself and throws itself to us.[622] Although Heidegger treats the postmonotheist theme with discretion in this essay, he nevertheless says that it is Being that lets truth happen, where "truth" has the sense of a free sphere of openness in which beings manifest themselves.[623] If this is the case, postmonotheist Being is the real author of the work of art, even though this is only hinted at in Heidegger's essay on art.[624] Such a conception would fit in well with Heidegger's later views on language and poetry.

We saw that language essentially is the Word of Being. Heidegger uses the German term for literature, *Dichtung*, in a broad and in a strict sense. In the broad sense, all art is *Dichtung*, where *Dichtung* is the happening of truth in the sense of opening up a world.[625] Because it is a piece of condensed significance (*Dichtung*), the work of art opens up a world or clearing of significant relations, which Heidegger calls truth. *Dichtung* in the strict sense of literature or poetry is only one way of such a clearing projection of truth.[626] Yet poetry is a privileged form of *Dichtung*, because in poetry language comes to itself as the "saying of the unconcealedness of Being." Language is the event (*Geschehnis*) in which beings become accessible to humans, and this is why poetry is the most original *Dichtung* in the broad sense.[627] No wonder, then, that according to the later Heidegger poetry is intimately related to thinking.[628] The poet and the thinker allegedly fulfill narrowly related functions. Poetry, opening up a world or a Truth in the sense of a structured whole of significant relations, hints at Being that sends us such a Truth.[629] Thinking aims at saying Being in a more explicit manner and at preparing the second coming of Being. Hence, thinking should never become poetry.[630] Heidegger's elucidations of poems by Rilke, Hölderlin, Trakl, or Stefan George pretend to discern such hints to and by Being, or, alternatively, to show that a poet remains within the domain of metaphysics, as is allegedly the case of Rilke. In this book, I do not go into the question as to whether Heidegger's elucidations of poetry satisfy criteria of sound literary criticism. This question is not only beyond my competence; it is also a question Heidegger would not bother about in the least. He claims that his elucidations of metaphysical texts and of poems touch on a domain that is essentially inaccessible to ordinary scholarship, the domain of Being. We may conclude that Heidegger's later philosophy of truth, art, and poetry becomes intelligible if it is integrated into the basic structures of his later thought, the Neo-Hegelian and the postmonotheist leitmotifs.

5. The Reign of Technology. This conclusion holds also for Heidegger's philosophy of technology. In his writings on technology, Heidegger is not concerned with investigating modern technology and its dangers; he is rather talking about what he calls the "essence" (*das Wesen*) of technology. As we saw in section 10, such an "essence" is a transcendental framework that discloses entities in a specific manner, a fundamental stance (*Grundstellung*) or a "way of revealing" (*Weise des Entbergens*), as Heidegger calls it in his essay on technology of 1954.[631] Heidegger claims that the essence of technology reigns in our time, so that everything is disclosed to us as raw material for, or means of, production, exploitation, and consumption.[632] "The earth now reveals itself as a coal mining district, the soil as a mineral deposit."[633] The fundamental stance of technology is expressed in Nietzsche's metaphysics of the will to power, which is the final stage of productionist metaphysics.[634] In the metaphysical stance of technology, Plato's and Aristotle's decision to conceptualize beings in terms derived from the domain of artifacts is brought to its logical conclusion.[635] According to Heidegger's inverted Hegelianism, the reign of technology is the nadir of the metaphysical fall, in which mankind is completely deaf to the voice of Being. As long as man encounters everything within the framework (*das Gestell*) of technology, the world is without salvation and all traces of the Holy are wiped out.[636]

We may be preoccupied with the dangers of technology and overpopulation. Heidegger was not really concerned with these dangers or, to the extent that he was, he considered them as symptoms of another and more "real" danger. According to the essay on technology, "the threat to man does not come in the first instance from the potentially lethal machines and apparatus of technology. The real threat has already afflicted man in his essence." This real or authentic threat is "that it could be denied to him to experience the call of a more primal truth."[637] The real danger is greatest during the reign of technology, Heidegger claims, and he quotes Hölderlin: "But where danger is, grows / The saving power too."[638]

Naïve readers of "Die Frage der Technik" will understand neither what Heidegger means by the "authentic threat" (*eigentliche Bedrohung*) of technology, nor why "the saving power grows where danger is." Yet, what Heidegger says in the essay is fully explained by the postmonotheist leitmotif, which incorporates the Neo-Hegelian theme. Fundamental stances such as the reign of technology are sent (*geschickt*) to us by Being as our fate (*Geschick*), so that technology in its essence is not man-made.[639] These stances belong to the history of metaphysics, in which Being gives entities in the open while concealing itself. During the reign of technology, all traces of Being are wiped out, because the reign of technology is the completion of productionist metaphysics. The danger of the oblivion of Being is greatest during the reign of technology, since the scientific and technological frame of mind does not admit of a notion of transcendence.[640] However, by meditating on the "essence" of technology, we may conjecture that this fundamental stance is sent or granted to us by a Mystery, and that what grants us the reign of technology is the "saving power."[641] Although Heidegger does not use the term "Being" in the essay on technology, what grants us fundamental stances (*das Gewährende*) is postmonotheist Being. Heidegger's message is that we may hope to be saved by Being if only we meditate with repentance on the essence of technology and if only we interpret this "essence" as a fate that Being sent to us.[642]

It is obvious, then, that Heidegger's philosophy of technology belongs to the genre of religious meditation. We should not expect from Heidegger any contribution to solving the pressing problems of technology and the natural environment that mankind faces. He even holds that nobody can solve these problems, because they are rooted in the fate (*Geschick*) that Being determined for us.[643] What the thinker can do is to "think ahead" and prepare the next fundamental stance, because there allegedly is a dialogue between the thinker and the "fate of the world."[644]

6. The Concealment of the Question of Being. In the first section of chapter 1, I discussed a peculiar feature of Heidegger's question of Being, which I called its concealment. Heidegger claims not only that we cannot answer the question of being, but also that we do not yet understand it, and that perhaps we are not even able to understand the question. At first sight, the concealment of the question of being frustrates any attempt to elucidate it by means of an interpretation. Why would we attempt to interpret a question raised by a philosopher if he himself claims that we are not able to understand this question? I concluded, however, that the concealment of the question of being should be taken as yet another feature of this question, which an interpretation should be able to explain. Indeed, it can be accounted for on the basis of the postmonotheist theme in two complementary ways.

First, one might explain the concealment of the question of Being by analogy with the theme of a *Deus absconditus* in traditional Christianity. In order to understand a question or a quest, we have to know what it is aiming at. The central religious question is the quest for God. But if God is hidden, as the Bible says, we will never really understand the quest for God until God bestows his grace on us. This is why believers tend to claim that unbelievers cannot even understand the very questions religious persons are asking. As Paul says in his Letter to the Romans (3:11): "no one understands, no one seeks for God." Similarly, if Being is hidden because it withdraws itself from us, as Heidegger pretends, it is difficult to understand the question of Being. Indeed, this question will be a folly to ordinary mortals. It is nearly inevitable that the question of Being is misinterpreted, Heidegger stresses repeatedly in *Beiträge zur Philosophie*.[645]

Apart from this internal explanation of the concealment of the question of Being as a postmonotheist analogue of the *Deus absconditus* theme, there is a second, external explanation that Heidegger did not and could not give himself. This explanation takes into account the strategy that a postmonotheist thinker must adopt in order to be a successful postmonotheist.

The core of the postmonotheist leitmotif is the idea that traditional monotheism died because Being was misinterpreted as *a* being, God. The postmonotheist strategy purports to destroy monotheism and to rescue religion by arguing that monotheist faith, which died, is not the true religion. True and authentic faith is the thinking of Being. This strategy faces a dilemma. One the one hand, postmonotheology should resemble traditional monotheism sufficiently for satisfying similar religious cravings. Indeed, we saw that the meaning of Heidegger's postmonotheist thought is parasitic on the Christian tradition. On the other hand, postmonotheism should not resemble traditional monotheism too closely. For in that case, it could be interpreted as just another variety of the deceased monotheist tradition, as a watered-down and more abstract version of Christianity, a substitute religion, and the postmonotheist strategy will fail altogether.

   This strategic dilemma, which is inherent in Heidegger's postmonotheism, explains why the question of Being is bound to resemble, but cannot resemble too closely, the traditional religious quest for God. It explains the constant tension in Heidegger's later works, which consists in simultaneously hinting at religious connotations and holding off such connotations. And it also explains why many interpreters feel confident in giving straightforward religious interpretations of the later works, while others feel equally confident in arguing that the later Heidegger is not a religious philosopher at all. Both types of interpretation are mistaken, for each of them highlights only one aspect of the essentially ambivalent postmonotheist theme. Heidegger sowed his postmonotheist hints thinly in his publications, thereby keeping the postmonotheist leitmotif from becoming too conspicuous. Only by listing these hints, as I did in this section, can one substantiate the postmonotheist interpretation with an overwhelming plausibility.

Synthesis

THE CENTRAL thesis of the interpretation proposed in this book is that Heidegger's question of being does not have one clearly defined meaning. It contains five leitmotifs or fundamental themes, which are multifariously interwoven in Heidegger's texts.

In chapter 2, I analyzed and developed each of these leitmotifs separately. A review of the discussion there will serve to introduce the topic of the present chapter. The first leitmotif, the meta-Aristotelian theme, provides the bipolar scheme that informs Heidegger's question. Heidegger took from Aristotle the idea that the question of being has two opposite poles, a pole of differentiation and a pole of unity. We can discover these two poles in each of the two main phases of Heidegger's thought: the earlier phase, which culminated in *Sein und Zeit* and *Kant und das Problem der Metaphysik*, and the later phase, which started between 1927 and 1938, and which lasted until Heidegger's death in 1976. In *Sein und Zeit*, the phenomenologico-hermeneutical leitmotif is the pole of differentiation. The constitution of being of entities is different in each ontological region; hence each region has its proper categorial structure. It is the task of a regional ontology to draw up the categories of a specific region by what Heidegger calls a productive logic. Dasein or man is a region of beings among others, and because Dasein's mode of being is existence, the ontological categories of Dasein are called "existentialia." They are brought to light by the hermeneutical phenomenology of Dasein. The diversity of ontological regions is unified by the transcendental leitmotif, which is the pole of unity in *Sein und Zeit*. Dasein now becomes a fundamental region or rather a transcendental agent *in* man, like Husserl's transcendental ego, which it was meant to replace. Dasein unites ontological regions because it projects a world, that is, a global structure of meaningful relations, which is a priori in relation to ordinary experience, and in which each ontological region finds its proper place.

In the later works, however, the transcendental theme mutated into a source of differentiation: the Neo-Hegelian leitmotif. According to the Neo-Hegelian theme, there is a sequence of fundamental stances or transcendental structures that constitute different historical epochs. In each of these epochs, the word "being" has a different sense. But we cannot say any more that Dasein is a transcendental subject which projects these structures, because transcendental philosophy itself belongs to one particular historical stance, the stance of modern subjectivist metaphysics. Rather, Dasein is entangled in the present fundamental structure, the reign of technology (*das Wesen der Technik*). The deep structures of historical epochs seem to succeed each other autonomously, and the Neo-Hegelian theme resembles structuralism. Yet, the diversity of fundamental structures is unified in Heidegger's later works as well, though not by a transcendent*al* agent. The unifying power is wholly transcendent to beings. It is Being itself (*das Seyn selbst*) that sends (*schickt*) us the fundamental stances of history (*Geschichte*) as our destiny (*Geschick*), concealing itself in the process. The ultimate unifying theme of Heidegger's thought turns out to be the postmonotheist leitmotif, which is the pole of unity in the later works.

This pluralist or pentafold interpretation of Heidegger's question of being explains in part the characteristic combination of richness and darkness in Heidegger's writings. The reader may be spellbound by the plethora of meanings suggested by Heidegger's question of being, a question that seems to be obscure because it is not possible to assign a single meaning to it unambiguously and in all contexts. The pluralist interpretation also explains the fact that different unitarian interpretations of Heidegger's philosophy have been proposed, each of which fails because it does not account for all texts. Finally, the pentafold interpretation explains why different types of readers, atheists such as Sartre and believing Christians such as Bultmann, could be attracted to Heidegger, and why analytic philosophers, who abhor ambiguity, generally loathe Heidegger's works.

Heidegger does not explicitly distinguish among the different leitmotifs in his question of being. Indeed, he suggests that he was stirred by one and the same question during his entire philosophical journey, although he also stresses that he explored a plurality of paths in asking this unique question. Is it possible to give some justification for this unitarian view, in spite of the plurality of leitmotifs? Can we discover a deeper unity in the "way" of Heidegger's thought? It is the aim of the present, synthetic chapter to investigate how the different leitmotifs hang together. The various themes of the question of being are interwoven in many ways, as I attempt to show in section 12, so that, paradoxically, the unification of leitmotifs is not unified in itself. Different types of unification will be distinguished. In section 13, I discuss the celebrated *Kehre* (turn). After the Second World War, Heidegger suggested that his later thought was linked directly to *Sein und Zeit* by a turn. The turn would be a mode of unification of Heidegger's *Denkweg* (way of thought), similar to a bend in a road that unites two straight stretches. Here, too, it seems that unification comes in many ways, for apparently there are different turns.

In respect to Heidegger's philosophy of the turn it has been pointed out that by linking the later works that were published after the Second World War directly to *Sein und Zeit*, Heidegger tried to divert attention from the crucial period between 1927 and 1945, thereby obfuscating the depth of his philosophical passion for National Socialism. There is a similar problem in the interpretation advanced in this book. Because I am concentrating on the fundamental structures of Heidegger's thought, as they became crystalized in *Sein und Zeit* and in the later works,

I tend to neglect the confusing intermediate period between these two main phases. It would require another book to make up for this omission, and to discuss down to the smallest detail Heidegger's perplexing quest after the tremendous success of *Sein und Zeit* until the end of the war. During this quest, Heidegger's writings, his life, and the fate of Germany were intimately connected, and the interpretation of the texts written during this epoch of great turmoil, war, and infamous crime should take into consideration the particular historical circumstances. A book on this period should be written by someone who is simultaneously a philosopher, a trained historian of the Third Reich, and a connoisseur of German literature, especially of Hölderlin. Furthermore, it should be based on an extensive investigation of the extant archives.[1]

Although I am not capable of writing such a book, I will dedicate two sections to the intermediate period. In section 14, entitled "Heidegger and Hitler," I raise questions as to the relation between the five leitmotifs and Heidegger's involvement with National Socialism. Did Heidegger derive his Nazi sympathies from the philosophy of *Sein und Zeit*, as he seems to have told Löwith in 1936? If so, what is the logical force of such a derivation? And how do the two leitmotifs in Heidegger's later works relate to his Nazi past, if ever it became really past? In section 15, the final section of my interpretation, I focus on Heidegger's philosophical encounter with Nietzsche. In the preface to the two volumes on Nietzsche that he edited from lecture materials in 1961, Heidegger says that this publication provides a view of his philosophical journey (*Denkweg*) from 1930 to 1947.[2] He stresses that other publications, such as "Platons Lehre von der Wahrheit" ("Plato's Doctrine of Truth," 1942), "Vom Wesen der Wahrheit" ("On the Essence of Truth," 1943), and *Erläuterungen zu Hölderlins Dichtung* (*Elucidations Concerning Hölderlin's Poetry*, 1951), which contains texts from 1936 to 1943, are much less significant in this respect.[3] I will claim that Heidegger's encounter with Nietzsche was of seminal and pivotal importance in the genesis of his later thought, much more so than the fascination he felt for Hölderlin.

One should not overestimate the role of philosophy in National Socialism, for most National Socialists had a plebeian contempt for intellectuals and intellectual matters. But if ever a philosopher was hailed as an intellectual father of Nazism at all, this philosopher was Friedrich Nietzsche. Indeed, Hitler had a carefully staged photograph made of himself and Nietzsche's bust. Is it far-fetched to suppose that Heidegger's encounter with Nietzsche is related to his attitudes vis-à-vis National Socialism? To do justice to its context, one should compare Heidegger's interpretation of Nietzsche to contemporary interpretations, such as those of Baeumler and Härtle.[4] My purposes in section 15 are more limited. I will investigate how Heidegger's interpretation of Nietzsche fits in with the fundamental structures of his later works, and I will venture to speculate about what Nietzsche's view of Heidegger would have been, if, *per impossibile*, Nietzsche would have had the opportunity to read Heidegger's later writings.

§ 12. FORMS OF SYNTHESIS

After my longwinded eleventh section, the reader will yearn for refreshing brevity. Fortunately, I can be brief in discussing the different manners in which the five leitmotifs are interwoven in Heidegger's writings. Once the leitmotifs are brought to light, various forms of synthesis suggest themselves, and the reader might discover them without my help. The meta-Aristotelian theme, for example, provides the bipolar structure of the question of being, as I already noted. We saw that in each of the two main phases of Heidegger's thought, there are two leitmotifs that make up the poles of this structure. Here we have a form of synthesis, which is partly chronological. Without trying to be comprehensive, I will now discuss some other forms of synthesis, which may be grouped under the headings of (A) syntactical forms, (B) semantic transformations, and (C) motivational links. Finally, I will raise the problem of translation with regard to Heidegger's works (D). We will see that a number of particularities of Heidegger's wordcraft makes it difficult to translate his texts without loss of meaning, connotation, or magic. This peculiar wordcraft turns out to be a unifying factor in its own right.

A. Syntactical Forms, Polyvalence, and Contradictions

By analogy, one might speak of a "grammar" of Heidegger's question of being. This grammar remains the same under all interpretations of the question, that is, in the different leitmotifs. At the end of section 6, above, I described the grammar of the question of being as a formal structure, consisting of nine elements. Furthermore, I argued in sections 7 to 11 that this formal structure is inherent in each of the five leitmotifs. In other words, the five leitmotifs are synthesized by a common grammar.

The first element of this grammar is the idea (1) that there is one unique and fundamental question of philosophical thought, the question of being. It is justified to call this an element of the grammar of the question of being, because a different meaning is assigned to it in each of the five leitmotifs. According to the meta-Aristotelian theme, the primacy of the question of being derives from Aristotle's foundationalist philosophy of science, even though Heidegger did not explicitly retrieve this philosophy. From the point of view of the phenomenologico-hermeneutical theme, the question of being aims at articulating the ontological constitutions proper to different regions of entities. In this sense, the question is fundamental because regional ontologies are a priori foundations of the sciences of these respective regions. In the transcendental interpretation, the question of being purports to show that the enabling condition of encountering entities, such as tools, consists in a global structure of meaningful relations, a world, projected by Dasein. Because of the temporalizing nature of Dasein, transcendental time allegedly is the horizon for encountering things as meaningful, and, indeed, for giving meaning to anything whatsoever. According to the Neo-Hegelian theme, everything that happens or manifests itself in a historical epoch is somehow determined by a fundamental structure or a sense of being. In the reign of technology, for instance, things manifest themselves as raw materials for exploitation and technical domination. When we ask the question of being, we discover what things essentially *are* in our time. Finally, the postmonotheist theme turns the question of being into a quest for Being, Heidegger's analogue of the monotheist God. This question is the primary issue for man because, in his deepest essence (*Wesen*), man is Da-sein, the open space in which Being occurs (*sich ereignet*).

In a similar way, the other syntactical elements of the question of being have a different sense in each leitmotif. Understanding of being (2, *Seinsverständnis*) is an implicit grasp of different regional constitutions of being, or a transcendental capacity of Dasein to project worlds, or an attuning to the fundamental stance of one's time, or it is an implicit understanding of absent and transcendent Being, a longing for religious fulfillment. In *Sein und Zeit*, it is also an individual Dasein's understanding of itself and its environment, its capacity to live meaningfully in a meaningful world. Forgetfulness of being (3, *Seinsvergessenheit*), in general, is our lack of attention to what we understand in understanding being, but within the framework of the postmonotheist theme it becomes Being's abandonment of us, mortals. The ontological difference (4) is either the distinction between entities and their constitution of being, or the distinction between meaningful entities and a priori transcendental structures or worlds, or the difference between the fundamental stance of an epoch and the things that manifest themselves in that epoch, or, finally, the difference between Being (*das Seyn*) and all entities, a difference that simultaneously is brought forward and concealed by Being itself when Being gives entities in the open, so that humans may apprehend them.

The nine elements of Heidegger's grammar of being, then, are polyvalent in the sense that they have different functions and different meanings, depending on each leitmotif. Let me give yet another example of this polyvalence. According to the phenomenologico-hermeneutical leitmotif in *Sein und Zeit*, the destruction and retrieval of the metaphysical tradition (element 8) is needed in order to show both that the basic concepts of Greek metaphysics still determine our ways of thinking about ourselves and that these concepts are inadequate for human life, because they were derived from the domain of artifacts and not from the domain of human existence. This destruction is needed in order to prepare a construction: the construction of a system of existentialia, which capture our ontological constitution as it really is. Within the framework of the Neo-Hegelian leitmotif, however, humans "are" differently in different historical epochs. The retrieval of metaphysics is now needed because the present epoch is the outcome of a sequence of fundamental stances. In order to understand our epoch, we should see that it is but the final stage in the development of productionist metaphysics, which started with Plato and is brought to completion in Nietzsche's philosophy of the will to power and in the reign of technology. Finally, the postmonotheist leitmotif transforms Heidegger's early overcoming (*Überwindung*) of metaphysics into a meditation of mourning and repentance (*Verwindung*). The metaphysical tradition is seen as a tradition of thinking about the totality of beings, in which Being itself is forgotten. In fact, Being itself sent us metaphysical stances, so that our forgetfulness of Being is but a corollary of Being's withdrawal from us. We should retrieve the tradition of metaphysics by interpreting it *as* the veil in which Being concealed itself, in order to experience our deepest distress (*Not*) and to prepare for a second coming of Being.

As is to be expected, the polyvalence of key grammatical elements in Heidegger's question of being easily leads to apparent or real contradictions. In section 4.4, above, I mentioned the well-known clash between two versions of Heidegger's postscript to *Was ist Metaphysik?* In the postscript of 1943, Heidegger wrote that being does act (*wohl west*) without beings. This was changed in the edition of 1949, where Heidegger now stated that being never acts (*nie west*) without beings. Several explanations of this contradiction are possible.[5] We may suppose that in the text of 1943 Heidegger had the postmonotheist leitmotif in mind, according to which it is at least conceivable that Being acts without beings. Within the framework of the other leitmotifs this is impossible, and Heidegger's correction in 1949 might be explained by supposing that he then had the Neo-Hegelian leitmotif in mind. In this case the contradiction would be apparent only. Perhaps it is more plausible to interpret Heidegger's correction as a drastic change in his postmonotheology. In 1943 it became clear to most Germans that Germany would not be able to win the war. Did this insight prompt Heidegger's desperate assumption that Being could be cut loose from the Germans altogether?[6] When he had regained some self-confidence in 1949, Heidegger returned to his usual postmonotheist and Eckhartian view that Being needs man because what Being sends has to be received by us, even though what Being sends to us may be its self-concealment in metaphysics. The texts do not allow us to prefer one interpretation over the others.

Let me now give an example of a real contradiction that is caused by a clash between two leitmotifs. According to the Neo-Hegelian theme, our present era of technology must be understood as the final consummation of the history of productionist metaphysics. The Greek decision to conceive of things in categories that were derived from the domain of artifacts led in the end to a subjectivist metaphysics of the will to power. Nietzschean metaphysics is the deep structure of the present epoch, and this allegedly explains the fact that present-day culture is dominated by technology. In order to substantiate his grandiose metaphysical narrative, Heidegger tried to show how Greek productionist metaphysics was radicalized in some main stages of philosophical history: Roman philosophy, Christian creationism, and modern subjectivist philosophy. The Neo-Hegelian leitmotif implies that there is some kind of logical order, an order of radicalized

decay or falling, between the metaphysical stances.[7] Otherwise, it would be meaningless to claim that "technology, taken as a form of Truth, is rooted in the history
of metaphysics."[8] But the notion of a logical order between the metaphysical
stances contradicts the postmonotheist idea that Being is as free and inscrutable
as a *Deus absconditus* (hidden God). If Being sends (*schickt*) us the historical
stances of metaphysics as our fate (*Geschick*), and if it is impossible to fathom
Being by means of rational and empirical methods, then the attempt to discover
an inherent order of increasing decay in the history of metaphysics must fail. In
Heidegger's postmonotheist theme, there is no answer to the question of what
determines the sequence of historical epochs or fundamental stances, because the
epochs are free gifts of hidden Being.[9]

The Neo-Hegelian theme is intimately connected to the postmonotheist leitmotif in Heidegger's later works. Indeed, the two themes are two sides of the
same coin. Both in Hegel and in Heidegger, a notion of "deep history" is related
to a (post-) monotheist notion of Being, because Being is supposed to reveal itself
in history, if only in the manner of its self-concealment. This historical revelation
is deep history, a (post-) monotheist analogue of the Christian history of grace
(*Heilsgeschichte*). As a consequence, the contradiction we noted is also a contradiction within Heidegger's postmonotheist leitmotif itself. How did this contradiction arise? We may answer the question by a schematic comparison of Heidegger and Hegel (cf. also § 10, above).

According to Hegel, historical reality is a temporal realization of Absolute
Logic, which is Hegel's philosophical and historicized version of God's mind.
The very insight that what is historically real is ultimately logical will be acquired
in history itself, when the philosopher reaches the Absolute by tracing its phenomenology. History is progress, and progress culminates at the point where we see
the logical, that is, divine nature of historical reality. At this point, our mind
coincides with the Absolute, and the Absolute coincides with itself. We saw that
Heidegger reverses Hegel's optimism. Instead of viewing history as a progression
toward an ultimate illumination, Heidegger construes metaphysical history as a
regression from Truth, as an ever deeper Fall. In the present era of science and
technology, Being is more concealed than ever, to the point that even this concealment is concealed so that we do not notice the distress (*Not*) of Being's absence
anymore. Now the question arises: How can Heidegger stick to Hegel's claim
that history is logical, and simultaneously give up Hegel's happy illusion that one
might discover this logic by identifying oneself with the Absolute? If history is a
revelation of Being, the logic of history must be Being's logic. However, if Being
is concealed, we will not be able to discover Being's logic. How, then, can one
justify the claim that there is a logic in deep history?

Heidegger was not unaware of this difficulty. In his seminar on "Zeit und Sein"
(1962), he tried to resolve it by distinguishing between the "why" and the "that"
of deep history. Although the abandonment by Being prevents us from knowing
why the sequence of fundamental stances in history is as it is, we know *that* it is

as it is, and "within this *That* . . . human thought is able to establish something like a necessity in the succession, something like lawfulness and logic."[10] This "logic" allegedly implies that the history of metaphysics is a history of increasing abandonment by Being.[11] However, this solution faces a dilemma. Perhaps Being has really abandoned us. In this case, we can never know whether the "logic" we discover in deep history is Being's logic. It might just as well be an accidental pattern, or a projection of our provincial prejudices. But then we can never know that Being has really abandoned us, because the logical pattern that Heidegger claims to have discovered is the very pattern of an increasing abandonment by Being. Or, alternatively, we are able to discover the logic of deep history, and we can know that this logic is Being's logic. In that case, however, Being has not really abandoned us, because we are able to fathom Being's logic. We must conclude that Heidegger's reversal of Hegel leads to inconsistency.[12]

B. Semantic Transformations

In a number of texts published shortly after the Second World War, Heidegger reintroduced existentialia that were central to *Sein und Zeit*, such as Dasein, *Existenz* (existence), *Sinn* (sense), *das Man* (Everyman or the One), *Lichtung* (clearing), *Entwurf* (project), *Verfallen* (falling), *Geschichtlichkeit* (historicality), being as transcendens, *Wahrheit* (Truth), and *Welt* (world). By integrating the early existential analysis into his thought after the turn, he forged a terminological bond between *Sein und Zeit* and the later works. This process of recycling existentialia took the form of an authoritative interpretation. In the "Brief über den 'Humanismus' " of 1946, and in the introduction to *Was ist Metaphysik?* of 1949, Heidegger professed to reveal the true sense of the existentialia. *Sein und Zeit* was interpreted as a preliminary stage, preparing the question of being in the sense of the later Heidegger. Forgetfulness of being (*Seinsvergessenheit*), as experienced in *Sein und Zeit*, would include the "all-sustaining conjecture" that "the connection between Being and man belongs to Being itself." But this conjecture could not become an explicit question, Heidegger says, unless the definition of man was first liberated from the notions of subjectivity and *animal rationale*. This would have been the task of *Sein und Zeit*.[13] Admittedly, the fact that the third division of part 1 had not been published made it more difficult to see that *Sein und Zeit* abandons the notion of man as a subject, because in this division "the whole is reversed." Yet, by the celebrated turn, "the thinking that was sought first arrived at the location of that dimension out of which *Sein und Zeit* is experienced." In other words, the turn that Heidegger actualized in his later works allegedly is identical with the turn as planned in *Sein und Zeit*, so that Heidegger's later philosophy is a mere fulfillment of his early intentions, and not a change of viewpoint.[14]

Heidegger's autointerpretation of the existentialia of *Sein und Zeit*, and, indeed, of the function of this book as a whole, is a special type of unification, which connects the early masterpiece to the later works. However, this unification raises serious issues. Many commentators have argued that Heidegger's later interpretation of the existentialia in fact is a reinterpretation that attributes to the existential terminology of *Sein und Zeit* a meaning very different from the one it had in that book. Löwith contends, for example, that there was indeed an important shift in viewpoint between *Sein und Zeit* and the later Heidegger. In *Sein und Zeit*, Heidegger attempted to think of *being* from the point of view of *Dasein*; later he defines *Dasein* from the point of view of *Being*. According to Löwith, Heidegger camouflaged this shift by his interpretation of the existentialia, suggesting a greater unity in his *Denkweg* than in fact there is.[15] This interpretation was confirmed by F.-W. von Herrmann's investigations, which also established that Heidegger's recycling of the existentialia involved semantic transformations. When Heidegger interpreted the existentialia in his later works, he did so from the perspective of his later philosophy, and not at all from the perspective and problematic of *Sein und Zeit*.[16] Of course a philosopher has the right to reinterpret themes of his earlier thought. But many commentators agree that Heidegger should be criticized for masquerading his drastic semantic transformations of the existentialia as a faithful interpretation.[17]

There is no doubt that Heidegger's claim in the "Brief über den 'Humanismus,'" repeated in the letter to Richardson of 1962, that in *Sein und Zeit* the question of being is set up outside the sphere of subjectivism, is plainly false as a historical interpretation of the text.[18] Although the analysis of Dasein in *Sein und Zeit* is not an anthropology, and even though traditional subjectivist metaphysics is rejected by conceiving of Dasein as being-in-the-world, *Sein und Zeit* is still subjectivist in the sense of a transcendental philosophy, according to which Dasein constitutes *Sein* by projecting a world. Because Heidegger in *Sein und Zeit* held that being (*Sein*) is constituted by Dasein's opening up a world (*Wahrheit*), he could say that "there is" being only in so far as there is Truth, and that Truth is only in so far as and as long as Dasein is.[19] I will now give some examples of Heidegger's later interpretations of existentialia, in order to show that these interpretations involve semantic transformations from the transcendental to the postmonotheist leitmotif. As these two leitmotifs are different, even contradictory, Heidegger's "interpretation" of the existentialia in fact reversed their meanings.

Nonetheless, one might wonder whether there is not a justification for Heidegger's claim that his later interpretation of the existentialia reveals their true and most profound sense. Is it not possible to suggest a motivational link between *Sein und Zeit* and the later works, which is such that it explains both the abyss and the deeper unity between the two phases of his thought? In the next subsection (§ 12C) I argue that there is such a motivational link, and that Heidegger may have derived it from the religious works of Blaise Pascal.

The existentialia in *Sein und Zeit* that best express the transcendental leitmotif are Truth (*Wahrheit*), project (*Entwurf*), world (*Welt*), clearing (*Lichtung*), and sense (*Sinn*). According to Heidegger's transcendental conception of Truth in section 44 of *Sein und Zeit*, Dasein is "Truth" in the sense of being-uncovering. Truth in this transcendental sense is a condition for the possibility of propositional truth, and the condition is "subjective" because it is an existential of Dasein. Only because Dasein exists are beings uncovered. Dasein is both a necessary and a sufficient condition for Truth in the transcendental sense. " 'There is' Truth only in so far as Dasein is and as long as Dasein is," Heidegger says in section 44c.[20]

The existential of being-uncovering is related to that of a project (*Entwurf*). Beings cannot be uncovered by Dasein unless Dasein projects a world, an a priori structure of meaningful relations. As is clear from sections 31 and 69b of *Sein und Zeit*, Dasein is the projecting agent, and the world that Dasein projects is a condition for the possibility of discovering specific entities or facts.[21] The transcendental notion of world is developed in section 69c. World as a transcendental structure of meaningful relations is projected by Dasein. For this reason, there *is* no world unless Dasein exists, and "in so far as Dasein temporalizes itself, a world *is* too."[22] Clearly, Dasein is both a necessary and a sufficient condition for a world. Accordingly, "if the 'subject' gets conceived ontologically as an existing Dasein whose being is grounded in temporality, then one must say that the world is 'subjective.' "[23] *Sein und Zeit* belongs to the subjectivist transcendental tradition in modern philosophy, even though it abandons traditional forms of subjectivism such as Kant's or Husserl's.

Finally, the existentialia of clearing (*Lichtung*) and sense (*Sinn*) have a transcendental meaning as well. *Sinn* is defined as the "upon-which" of primary projection (*das Woraufhin des primären Entwurfs*). As a consequence, what "gives" meaning to beings is the projection of being by Dasein.[24] Dasein is the ultimate light-giving source; it is the clearing (*Lichtung*), which enables things to appear and to be meaningful.[25]

In the "Brief über den 'Humanismus' " and in the introduction to *Was ist Metaphysik?* of 1949, Heidegger gives a very different, postmonotheist interpretation of these existentialia.[26] Truth is now called the "Truth of Being" (*die Wahrheit des Seins*). Being illuminates (*lichtet*) beings when it sends us a metaphysical stance. However, in metaphysics we do not think of this Truth of Being as such. To do so requires that metaphysics be overcome, and overcoming metaphysics means piously commemorating Being itself (*"Andenken an das Sein selbst"*). What is decisive is whether Being itself, out of its own truth, will establish a relationship to us humans, or whether metaphysics will prevent this relationship from shining forth.[27] Whereas in *Sein und Zeit*, Dasein was the transcendental source of Truth, in the later writings Truth is Being's self-concealing revelation.

The notion of a project (*Entwurf*) is subjected to a similar semantic transformation. According to the "Brief über den 'Humanismus,' " *Entwurf* in *Sein und Zeit* does not refer to a performance of a subject. It would be the "ec-static" relation of Dasein to the clearing of Being.[28] Flatly contradicting *Sein und Zeit*, Heidegger now says that "what throws in projection is not man but Being itself."[29] As a consequence, project (*Entwurf*) and thrownness (*Geworfenheit*) are not opposites, as they were in *Sein und Zeit*, but one and the same thing: the fact that man is thrown into ec-sistence by Being. Whereas in the earlier book, thrownness signified the fundamental contingency of man, this contingency now seems to be denied, for Being sends (*schickt*) man his fate (*Geschick*). In *Sein und Zeit*, Dasein projects being, but the "Brief über den 'Humanismus' " states that Being projects Dasein.[30] Similarly, the later Heidegger claims that world is not projected by Dasein either. On the contrary, "world" as an existential would mean the openness of Being. Being itself is *as* this openness, into which it has thrown man.[31] World is identified with clearing (*Lichtung*) and with Truth (*Wahrheit*), which both are "of Being" in the sense of a *genitivus subjectivus*.[32] Finally, sense (*Sinn*) is identified with "Truth of Being," so that Being, not Dasein, is the source of Truth and of sense.[33]

In accord with these semantic transformations, the pivotal terms Dasein, Da, and "existence" get a new meaning, which contradicts the meaning these terms had in *Sein und Zeit*. In 1927, Heidegger introduced "Dasein" as a term for that being which, in its being, is concerned with its own being. Dasein is in each case mine, and it exists in the sense that it has to effectuate its life. Dasein has to be its *Da*, where the prefix means the fundamental openness of human beings for the world, for others, and for themselves.[34] If Heidegger says in *Sein und Zeit* that Dasein is concerned with being, the term "being" refers primarily to Dasein's own being or existence.[35] The situation is very different in the "Brief über den 'Humanismus,' "[36] Now "ec-sistence" is defined as "standing in the clearing of Being." Man stands in the clearing of Being when he is claimed by Being. Only when he is claimed by Being will man "dwell in his essence" and inhabit language as the home of Being.[37] This notion of ec-sistence has nothing in common with Sartre's existentialism, which was inspired by *Sein und Zeit*.[38] Whereas in 1927 Dasein was concerned with its own being, Heidegger in 1946 opposes Being and man. Not man is essential, he says, but Being—as the dimension of the ecstasis of ec-sistence. Man ec-sists in the sense that he belongs to and obeys the Truth of Being, guarding this Truth.[39] Ec-sistence, then, is an "ecstatic dwelling in the nearness of Being."[40] The prefix Da is redefined as the Truth or clearing of Being in which Dasein stands, and the fact that there is such a thing as this *Da* is an act of providence (*Schickung*), due to Being itself.[41] In accordance with these new definitions, but clearly contradicting the analysis of *Sein und Zeit*, Heidegger says in 1949 that the term "Dasein" was introduced in *Sein und Zeit* in order to express the relation (*Bezug*) of Being to the essence of man.[42]

These examples of semantic transformations show that Heidegger not only redefines the existentialia of *Sein und Zeit*, misleadingly presenting his new definitions as reliable interpretations, but also that the new definitions flatly contradict the old ones. This fact confirms my interpretative hypothesis. For there is a contradiction between the transcendental theme and the postmonotheist leitmotif in Heidegger's question of being. According to the transcendental theme, being is projected by Dasein. The postmonotheist leitmotif implies, however, that Dasein is projected or thrown by Being.

Heidegger's recycling of the existentialia raises a serious problem for the interpreter. Why did Heidegger cover up the contradictions between his later thought and *Sein und Zeit* by means of a reinterpretation of this book? How could he affirm, in the preface to the seventh edition of 1953, that the road *Sein und Zeit* has taken "remains even today a necessary one, if our Dasein is to be stirred by the question of Being"?[43] For the fundamental themes in Heidegger's later question of being are incompatible with the fundamental themes of *Sein und Zeit*, and it is difficult to conceive that it would be necessary to approach Heidegger's later postmonotheist question of being by means of a road that flatly contradicts it. It seems that in order to endorse his later thinking about Being, one should forget about *Sein und Zeit*.

This problem of interpretation is not easily resolved. One cannot say, for instance, that *Sein und Zeit* and the later works simply describe one and the same relation between Dasein and Being from two different points of view, first from Dasein's perspective and then from Being's side. The reason is that both "Dasein" and "Being" are defined differently in the later works. Karl Löwith, who was one of the first to analyze the semantic transformations in Heidegger's recycled existentialia, having listed a great number of contradictions between *Sein und Zeit* and the later works, concludes that there is at best a psychological or *existenziell* motive that explains the leap to the primacy of Being over Dasein: Heidegger's longing to shake off the burden of existence, which he so penetratingly described in *Sein und Zeit*.[44] But this view does not explain why Heidegger deemed it necessary to reinterpret *Sein und Zeit* from the perspective of his later thought, and, indeed, why he turned the meanings of the existentialia upside down, under the pretense of an interpretation. Can we find a philosophical justification for this procedure, or should we conclude that the later interpretation of the existentialia merely served the purpose of suggesting a greater unity in Heidegger's *Denkweg* than in fact there was? This question brings us to yet another type of unification, which I call unification by motivational links.

C. Motivational Links

There are a great number of motivational links, connecting to each other the different leitmotifs in Heidegger's question of being. Some of these links are synchronic, such as the complementary relation between the Neo-Hegelian theme and the postmonotheist leitmotif. Others are diachronic, interlocking Heidegger's later thought with *Sein und Zeit* and even with earlier writings. What we are looking for is a diachronic motivational link, which not only connects the postmonotheist theme to *Sein und Zeit* but also justifies Heidegger's problematic procedure of recycling the existentialia. What motives could Heidegger have had for "interpreting" in his later work the central concepts of *Sein und Zeit* ? Let me first discuss two motives which, however, will not solve our problem.

In section 10B we discovered a motivational and conceptual link between the transcendental leitmotif and the Neo-Hegelian theme. According to the former, Dasein projects global frameworks or worlds, which determine the meaning of entities. However, if these global frameworks are really all-embracing, as Heidegger claims, the transcendental theme becomes unstable, because it presupposes that transcendental philosophy itself lies outside of the present world or framework, so that no framework is really all-embracing. This contradiction was solved by the Neo-Hegelian theme, which says that there is nothing but a sequence of holistic frameworks, without a transcendental subject. Transcendental philosophy itself would belong to one of these frameworks, the modern subjectivist tradition inaugurated by Descartes.

This motivational link suggests an interpretation of *Sein und Zeit* from the perspective of the Neo-Hegelian theme. *Sein und Zeit* will be seen as a final stage in the development of subjectivist metaphysics, so that it occupies a specific place within the logic of Neo-Hegelian *Seinsgeschichte*. Another motivational link, which I did not discuss earlier, leads to a similar result. According to the hermeneutical conception of *Sein und Zeit*, this book offers a hermeneutical interpretation of *Dasein*. The hermeneutical doctrine says that all interpretations are historical. As a consequence, the inquiry into the ontological constitution of Dasein "is itself characterized by historicality."[45] From this perspective, the hermeneutical interpretation of Dasein would become more fully conscious of itself if it understands itself as a specific historical stage in Man's self-understanding. Such a historical interpretation of the analysis of *Sein und Zeit* would be yet another spiral within the hermeneutical circle. In fact, many different historical interpretations of *Sein und Zeit* are possible, depending on the contexts that one takes into account. One might consider *Sein und Zeit* as a stage in the history of metaphysics, as Heidegger's Neo-Hegelian theme implies. One might also read the book as a typical expression of German cultural despair after the Great War, as a dadaist and expressionist philosophical manifesto, or as a secularized version of Kierkegaard's existentialism.

It is crucial to see that these and similar motives for interpreting *Sein und Zeit* do not explain Heidegger's procedure of recycling the existentialia. Admittedly, an interpretation of *Sein und Zeit* based on these motives will deepen our historical understanding of the existentialia as defined in that book. It will reveal their origins in Aristotle, St. Paul, St. Augustine, Luther, Pascal, and Kierkegaard, and it will link them with themes in the literature of the time, such as the theme of death in German expressionism. But it will never change the meanings of the existentialia. From a hermeneutical perspective, it would be illegitimate to turn the sense of the existentialia into its opposite, pretending that one is merely revealing their real meaning. However, this is precisely Heidegger's procedure in later writings such as the "Brief über den 'Humanismus' " and the introduction to *Was ist Metaphysik?* If Heidegger's procedure is justified at all—and this is denied by many commentators—there should be yet another motivational link that explains it. My hypothesis is that there is such a motivational link, and that Heidegger derived this link from Pascal's religious writings, published as *Les Pensées*.[46]

Officially, Pascal plays a minor role in Heidegger's oeuvre. Two footnotes in *Sein und Zeit* refer to Pascal, on pages 4 and 139, and there is no doubt that Heidegger read *Les Pensées* before 1927.[47] In the later works as published by Heidegger himself, we find four further references to Pascal.[48] At a crucial moment of his life, in August 1945, shortly after the breakdown of Nazi Germany, Heidegger planned to set up a small seminar in order to study one of Pascal's texts. It seems plausible to interpret this plan, which was never carried out, as a tactical maneuver to appease the French occupying authorities.[49] Could it be that Pascal provided the main motivational link, connecting *Sein und Zeit* to the later Heidegger, even though he merely plays a supporting part in Heidegger's philosophical narrative? This is the interpretative hypothesis that I want to defend.

Les Pensées is a collection of fragments written as parts of an apologetics for Christianity. Although Pascal died before he could complete his book, it is not difficult to reconstruct its apologetic strategy. As a brilliant mathematician, logician, and physicist, Pascal realized that the traditional Scholastic proofs of God's existence are both unsound and ineffective. Because the axioms of these proofs are uncertain, the proofs will not carry conviction, even if the deductions were valid. Moreover, Pascal rejected traditional philosophical theology, such as Descartes', for reasons similar to those of Luther's repudiation of Scholasticism. Traditional theology allegedly is concerned with the God of the philosophers, and not with the God of Abraham, Isaac, and Jacob. How, then, should one defend Christianity and how might one convince the unbeliever? Pascal's study of the art of persuasion taught him that he should appeal to people's hearts instead of to their minds. He invented an effective strategy, which consists of two stages.

In the first stage, Pascal provides a religiously neutral description of the human condition. The point of this description is to show that our life, as we experience it without religion, is both miserable and deeply puzzling, and it is crucial that the description is purely secular lest unbelievers will be put off. In order to convince the unbelievers who enjoy their lives, Pascal tries to show that even in our most happy moments we are on the run from ourselves. We live in diversion (*divertissement*) all the time. If we give up diversion, we will see how miserable man is, being confronted by despair, sickness, and death. Man is also puzzling. He is neither an angel nor a beast. He strives to acquire knowledge, but reflecting on the possibility of knowledge, he becomes a skeptic. In one telling fragment Pascal reveals his tactics. If man is vain and boasts about his endeavors, Pascal scorns him. If man despises himself, Pascal praises him. The aim is to make man comprehend that he is an incomprehensible monster.[50]

Having prepared the ground for Christianity by this psychological massage, Pascal proceeds to the second stage of his strategy. He now tries to show that

Christianity explains man's puzzling dual nature, because man was created in paradise and then was punished for original sin by the Fall. Christianity also makes man happy, for it forgives his sins and holds out the prospect of eternal bliss. The rational unbeliever is confronted by the famous wager argument. Although we cannot prove that God exists, it is rational to opt for the assumption that he does and to open ourselves up to his grace. This is a reasonable gamble, for we will lose nothing or at most finite goods, and gain a chance of eternal and infinite happiness. Reason, if it falls short of demonstrating the truth of Christianity, should not obstruct our conversion either. However, in order to become real Christians, we need God's grace, which will profoundly transform us.

My hypothesis is that Heidegger *mutatis mutandis* applied this two-stage strategy in his *Denkweg*, or, at least, that he unified his philosophical career from the perspective of his later philosophy by applying it. The existential analysis of Dasein in *Sein und Zeit* is the first stage. It consists of a religiously neutral ontology of human existence. Indeed, there are some striking analogies with Pascal's *Pensées*.[51] One is the analogy between Pascal's notion of diversion and Heidegger's concept of inauthenticity (*Uneigentlichkeit*). In ordinary language we use the notions of diversion and of not-being-oneself (inauthenticity) in a local way. Some of our activities are meant to divert us, and sometimes we are not ourselves (inauthentic). Both Pascal and Heidegger stretch these notions and transform them into global ones. If we may believe Pascal, everything we do is diversion, even work, and if we may believe Heidegger, nearly everything we do is inauthentic, because we are absorbed in the world and in the life of Everyman (*das Man*). When we do not divert ourselves, Pascal then argues, we realize that we are miserable, prone to illness, and bound to die. Similarly, Heidegger claims that we are authentic only when we confront our death in *Angst*, revealing our existence as a burden (*Last*). With regard to both Pascal's and Heidegger's pictures of the human condition, we might raise the question as to whether they paint it in more gloomy colors than reality justifies, in order to prepare us for a leap to religion.

Heidegger's second stage, at least in the later works, is not Christian religion but a postmonotheist worship of Being. We might say that this second stage is related to *Sein und Zeit* by means of a postmonotheist analogue of Pascal's strategy. It is inherent in this interpretation that *Sein und Zeit* itself should be religiously neutral. The text should not reveal its ultimate religious intentions, because in that case the unbeliever will not be convinced: he or she would see through the strategy at once. As a consequence, the preparatory analysis of Dasein should portray human existence as entirely independent, not relying on transcendent Being. A transcendental view of Dasein, which implies that Dasein constitutes being, thereby giving sense to beings, would suit this purpose very well. But what explains Heidegger's later "interpretation" of the existentialia, which turns their sense upside down? How can one explain Heidegger's procedure of recycling the existentialia, assuming that my interpretative hypothesis is correct? Heidegger's early notion of theology will lead us to an answer.

In 1919, Heidegger rejected the theology of the Schools because he endorsed a Lutheran view of Christianity, according to which faith is a graceful gift of God, transforming man in his inner nature. This view explains Heidegger's conception of theology in *Sein und Zeit*. In section 3 of that book, he says that theology is involved in a crisis, because it "is slowly beginning to understand once more Luther's insight that the 'foundation' on which its system of dogma rests has not arisen from an inquiry in which faith is primary." If God reveals himself in faith only, theology must seek "a more primordial interpretation of man's being toward God, prescribed by the meaning of faith itself."[52] According to this text, theology has the task of giving an interpretation of man's existence as related to God, an interpretation that is prescribed by the meaning inherent in faith. How should such a religious interpretation of man's existence be connected to the transcendental analysis of Dasein in *Sein und Zeit*?

This problem is left unresolved in Heidegger's masterpiece. In fact, Heidegger's three-story conception of knowledge points to a solution, but it is easy to see that this solution is inadequate. According to *Sein und Zeit*, the existential analysis of Dasein is fundamental ontology. Fundamental ontology yields a notion of being according to which being is a global framework of meaningful relations, projected by Dasein. This general notion of being is then diversified into different regional notions: natural being, historical being, and so on. Regional ontologies have the task of setting up a categorial framework that captures the constitution of being of specific regional entities. Each scientific discipline or "positive science" is based on a regional ontology of its domain. In short, the existential analysis of Dasein is the foundation of regional ontologies, and regional ontologies are the foundations of the sciences, because Dasein constitutes being.

Heidegger suggests in *Sein und Zeit* that theology is a positive science like any other. This would imply that the ontological sense of its object is "posited" by Dasein, as is the case with other positive sciences. If so, the fundamental ontology of Dasein would be the foundation of theology. But this view flatly contradicts the inherent meaning of faith. From the religious perspective, the ontological sense of God shines forth from God himself; it can never be posited by man. What is more, man's own existential sense is determined by God. Accordingly, the religious interpretation of Dasein's being-toward-God will contradict the existential interpretation of Dasein in *Sein und Zeit*. In what sense, then, can the latter be the foundation of the former?

Heidegger discussed this urgent problem in a crucial lecture of 1927, entitled "Phänomenologie und Theologie" (*Phenomenology and Theology*), which was published in the second edition of *Wegmarken* (*Signposts*) of 1978. In this lecture, he distinguishes between two levels of analysis: (1) the *existenziell* level of factical life (*Existenzform*) and worldview (*Weltanschauung*) and (2) the level of the sciences that conceptualize this first level. On the former level, philosophical life and faith are "deadly enemies." There is a struggle between two competing worldviews.[53] Philosophy as a form of life is "free questioning by a Dasein that stands on itself." Faith is the very opposite form of life, in which Dasein "is not in its own power," "having become a servant because it is brought before God, thereby being *re*born."[54] Dasein's rebirth in faith is a transformation (*Umstellung*) of human existence by God's mercy.[55]

If philosophy and faith are opposite and incompatible forms of life, one would expect that philosophy and theology, being the sciences that conceptualize these forms of life on the second, reflective level, are incompatible as well. How can one reconcile this conclusion with the doctrine of *Sein und Zeit*, that fundamental ontology is the philosophical foundation of theology as a positive science? How can theology be both based on and incompatible with philosophy? It is the aim of "Phänomenologie und Theologie" to solve this difficult problem.

Heidegger starts with the thesis of *Sein und Zeit* that there is an absolute difference between philosophy as the science of being and the positive sciences, which are concerned with beings. The object of a *positive* science is revealed or *posited* beforehand. Because theology is a positive science, theology is nearer to chemistry and mathematics than to philosophy.[56] Yet there is a crucial difference between theology and the other positive sciences. The objects of ordinary positive sciences are manifest to all of us. According to *Sein und Zeit*, their ontological sense is posited by Dasein. The object of theology, on the other hand, is only revealed in faith, and faith is a transformation of human existence. The aim of Christian theology is to conceptualize human existence in faith, that is, human life as determined by that in which the Christian believes when he or she has faith.[57] Because the object of theology is revealed in faith only, there is neither a motive nor a justification for theology, except faith. We can never deduce the necessity of theology as a science from the system of sciences or from philosophy. How, then, can philosophy be a foundation of theology, as Heidegger suggested in *Sein und Zeit*?

Heidegger's answer to this question is implied both by his Lutheran definition of theology as a science of human existence in faith and by his definition of philosophy as fundamental ontology. Fundamental ontology is an existential analysis of independent Dasein. Theology is an analysis of human existence as transformed by faith. Even though philosophy and faith as forms of life are "mortal enemies," philosophy and theology, as the respective sciences of these incompatible forms of life, are positively related to each other. The reason is that faith, as a rebirth or transformation (*Umstellung*) of Dasein, retains the old structure of Dasein in the manner of a Hegelian *Aufhebung*, for it is still *human existence* that is transformed by faith. As a consequence, theology will have to rely on the existential analysis of Dasein, which conceptualizes the existential structure of Dasein before its transformation by faith. Philosophy, by its regional ontology of Dasein, gives a "formal indication" of the mode of existence that will be transformed by faith. In this manner, philosophy "co-directs" the conceptual development of theology, which, however, is "directed" by faith.[58]

Heidegger's conception of the relation between theology and the phenomenology of Dasein, as expressed in his lecture of 1927, implies that the existentialia developed by philosophy will have to be reinterpreted by theology. From the perspective of faith, theology will claim to reveal the *real* meaning of these existentialia, even though this meaning often will be opposite to the definitions of the "atheist" existential analysis. In particular, theology will transform the notion that Dasein projects itself into the idea that Dasein is a project of God.

We come to the conclusion that Heidegger's paper on phenomenology and theology *prescribes the very procedure of semantically transforming the existentialia that the later Heidegger in fact applied.* Admittedly, Heidegger in his later works did not become a Christian theologian. His later thought is post-theological, and his semantic transformations of the existentialia are postmonotheist analogues of the transformations prescribed for Christian theology. We saw that "thinking," as conceived of by the later Heidegger, is a postmonotheist analogue of faith. The relation of Heidegger's later thinking to *Sein und Zeit* may now be interpreted as a postmonotheist analogue of the relation of faith-theology to philosophy as analyzed by Heidegger in 1927.

This interpretation may seem to be somewhat speculative. But it fully explains Heidegger's paradoxical reinterpretation of the existentialia, and it accounts for the unity of Heidegger's *Denkweg* on the model of Pascal's apologetic strategy. It also explains why after his postmonotheist conversion, Heidegger could still say that the road of *Sein und Zeit* remained a necessary one, if our Dasein is to be stirred by the question of Being.[59] For Pascal's apologetic strategy implies that an analysis of our human condition remains a necessary first step to faith. In short, my hypothesis yields a convincing solution to the problem of the primacy of Dasein, raised in section 4.6 above. The ontological analysis of Dasein is an indispensable preparation for asking the question of Being in the religious sense. Only an insight into the harshness of the human condition will arouse our need to ask the question of Being.[60]

There is yet another problem that is solved by the Pascalian hypothesis. As I noted in the preface to this book, the literary genre of Heidegger's writings changes after *Sein und Zeit*. Instead of a systematic philosophical treatise we now find essays, dialogues, lectures, and letters. This difference in genre of Heidegger's writings corresponds to the difference between the two stages in Pascal's strategy. Whereas we might map secular human existence in a systematic manner, Being itself eludes all attempts at systematic description because it conceals itself (theme of the *Deus absconditus*) and at best reveals itself in hints (*Winke*). It is the task of the thinker to pass these hints on to his people, and the literary genres of Heidegger's later works are adapted to this task.[61]

As my quotes in the next note show, the Pascalian interpretation of *Sein und Zeit* is fully and explicitly confirmed by *Beiträge zur Philosophie*, Heidegger's second chef d'oeuvre written in 1936–38.[62] The very structure of this latter book should be understood from the perspective of a Pascalian strategy, connected to the Neo-Hegelian and the postmonotheist leitmotifs. The same holds for the sequel to *Beiträge*, the volume *Besinnung*, which Heidegger wrote in 1938–39.[63]

This is not to say, however, that Heidegger anticipated his postmonotheism when he wrote *Sein und Zeit*. As I will argue in section 13C, he hoped for a conversion to authentic Christianity, prepared by methodological atheism as defined in the Natorp essay of 1922. A footnote to "Vom Wesen des Grundes" and a crucial letter to Elisabeth Blochmann, both of 1929, point in this direction.[64] In 1929, Heidegger thought that probably Being and God are identical, as his teacher Carl Braig had argued and as Eckhart had said long before. But methodological atheism implies that man can never decide such a question; the answer can be given only by revelation and grace. What the philosopher is able to do is merely to liberate himself from idols, and, having explored the human condition, to release himself into nothingness, hoping for grace, as Eckhart and Kierkegaard had taught. From a Pascalian perspective, this was the function of Heidegger's inaugural lecture of 1929, *Was ist Metaphysik?*[65] The atmosphere of this lecture is markedly religious, in contrast with the secular analyses of human existence in *Sein und Zeit*. If *Sein und Zeit* was a preparation for a conversion, *Was ist Metaphysik?* was Heidegger's first attempt to provoke such a conversion. This attempt failed, so we may guess, and Nietzsche taught Heidegger why it had to fail: the God of Christianity is dead. In his rectoral address of 1933, Heidegger summons his colleagues and students to take seriously Nietzsche's insight in God's death and man's abandonment amidst the totality of beings, for it implies that "our ownmost Dasein is heading for a grand transformation."[66] Heidegger now thought that this transformation was brought about, not by the Christian God, but by the National Socialist revolution, and he hoped that Nazism would take Nietzsche's insight to heart. It may be, however, that he changed his mind later, as we will see in section 15. Actual Nazism was just another kind of nihilism, and only a postmonotheist conversion could save us. Or is there a more positive relation between Heidegger's Nazism and his postmonotheist leitmotif?

D. Heidegger's Wordcraft and the Problem of Translation

In the celebrated interview in *Der Spiegel*, Heidegger said that "just as little as one can translate poems, one can translate thinking [*ein Denken*]."[67] The reason is that in both poetry and thinking, in contrast to the standardized uses of language of science or commerce, "language itself speaks of itself."[68] According to a commonsensical interpretation of Heidegger's view, most poets and some philosophers use their language in an idiosyncratic way, drawing on resources particular to that language. When one attempts to translate their work, one experiences the different powers and possibilities of expression proper to different languages, and one realizes that every translation of such a work is an interpretation.[69] However, what Heidegger really meant by his *dictum* is that when poets and thinkers use language, Being makes language speak of itself. When Being speaks of itself through a language, Heidegger seems to assume, what the language is saying cannot be translated. How is this assumption to be explained?

Heidegger's later view of translation is derived from the postmonotheist theme. Like the German romantics and Walter Benjamin, Heidegger sanctified language. Language, when it speaks of itself in the writings of the essential poets and thinkers, would be a saying of Being (*Sagen des Seins*; see § 11C.3). The genitive (*des Seins*) is both a *genitivus subjectivus* and a *genitivus objectivus*, so that Being itself speaks of itself through our language, thereby speaking to us and claiming us (*Anspruch*). According to Heidegger, the silent voice of Being is the origin of human language.[70] Is it far-fetched to suppose that Heidegger's later view on translation is a postmonotheist analogue of the human predicament after Babel, where God confused the language of the descendants of Noah, so "that they may not understand one another's speech" (*Genesis* 11:1–9)? According to *Beiträge zur Philosophie*, unique Being (*das Seyn*) is intimately related to the unique German Volk, and the essence (*Wesen*) of a people is its "voice."[71]

However this may be, it is not because I endorse Heidegger's views on this topic that I am raising the problem of translation. The reason is, rather, that many characteristics of Heidegger's wordcraft cause nearly insuperable difficulties for the translator. As a consequence, countless connotations and connections in the German text are lost in translating Heidegger, however scrupulous the translation may be. This loss will grow with the distance between German and the language into which the texts are translated. Dutch translations are closer to the original than English ones, and translations into English will be more faithful than translations into Chinese or Japanese. Yet, the distance between the German original and English translations is so great that an academic interpretation of Heidegger should be based on the German text. This justifies my practice of quoting Heidegger in German in the notes, and of presenting English quotes in the main text as mere paraphrases of the original.

There may be a global explanation for the alleged fact that it is more difficult to translate German philosophy into English than *vice versa*.[72] In Heidegger's case, there are many local causes. As some of these causes are related to particular forms of unification in Heidegger's works, I discuss the problem of translation in this section. Without trying to be exhaustive, I will list some main difficulties of translating Heidegger.

In *Sein und Zeit*, Heidegger says that it is "the ultimate business of philosophy to preserve the *force of the most elemental words* in which Dasein expresses itself, and to keep the common understanding from leveling them off."[73] Heidegger's aim in philosophy is opposite to Carnap's, for instance, and Heidegger saw Carnap as his most radical opponent.[74] Whereas Carnap wanted to make language in philosophy as unambiguous, clear, and "scientific" as possible, Heidegger wanted to restore language to its greatest expressive power. Carnap's objective was logical regimentation and scientific standardization. This objective guarantees that his texts are easy to translate. However, in order to intensify the expressive power of "the most elemental words" in which Dasein expresses itself, Heidegger had to draw on the specific resources of German, loading his texts with as many connotations as possible. In this respect, Heidegger's wordcraft is closer to theology, poetry, rhetoric, and propaganda than to science. Whereas Carnap was after an enlightened humanism in philosophy, and thought that scientific method would be able to resolve all philosophical problems, Heidegger aimed at an intensification of Dasein. This is a first, general reason why it is more difficult to translate Heidegger than it is to translate Frege, Carnap, or Reichenbach.

A second general reason is Heidegger's thesis in *Sein und Zeit* that the traditional philosophical vocabulary is not adequate for describing the ontological constitution of human life. Most existentialia are Heideggerian neologisms, or at least old terms used with more or less new meanings. The English translator should find English terms and neologisms that correspond as closely as possible to the German ones. Sometimes this is not difficult. *Alltäglichkeit* becomes "everydayness," although in this translation the German connotation of ordinariness or commonplaceness is lost. *Sein-zum-Tode* is adequately rendered by "being-toward-death." The only drawback in such cases is that German has a far greater potential for coining compound substantives than does English. Other cases are more difficult. The existentiale of *Befindlichkeit* is derived from German idioms such as "Wie befinden Sie sich heute?", and it suggests other meanings of the verb *befinden*, such as "to be located." The corresponding English idiom, "how are you today?", is different and it will not yield a substantive. The translation by "state of mind" is notoriously misleading, because it belongs to the traditional philosophical terminology that Heidegger rejects, and also because it does not at all capture what Heidegger means: the fact that we find ourselves in a situation and are attuned to this situation. Similar difficulties arise with relation to *Bewandtnis* and *Bewandtnisganzheit*.[75]

Heidegger not only coins new compound substantives from idioms. He also uses adverbs, pronouns, and relative expressions as elements for his neologisms. Thus we find, for instance, *das Auf-sich-zu*, a term which characterizes the fact that the future "comes toward us," or *das Mit-dabei-sein*, to be translated as "being-'in on it'-with-someone." By adding further verbal forms, compound substantives of baffling complexity are created, such as *das Je-schon-haben-bewenden-lassen*, a term that refers to the a priori conditions for something to manifest itself as a tool. Heidegger often uses such compounds as subjects of sentences where a personal subject would ordinarily be found. Even if the compounds can be translated into English, they cannot function as grammatical subjects. In some cases, the translator cannot do better than to quote the original German sentence in a note in order to back up an obscure and highly artificial translation. It is tempting to dissolve Heidegger's compounds in the translation, using paraphrasing sentences instead. But by this procedure, Heidegger's practice of using one term for each of his existentialia will be lost, and the tight-knit fabric of *Sein und Zeit* will fall apart.

Let me now discuss a third source of difficulties, a source that is related to a peculiar unifying strategy that Heidegger employs in the later works. This strategy consists in using one and the same morpheme or series of morphemes in many different words, thereby interlocking these words and suggesting some philosophical connection. Mostly the morpheme is a common root of the words in question or the stem of a verb. An example is the common morpheme *stim* in *Stimmung* (mood), *Stimme* (voice), *stimmen* (to tune, to be correct), *abstimmen* (to tune in on), *bestimmen* (to determine), and *Bestimmung* (purpose, destiny). The philosophical connection that Heidegger suggests is that Being, by its soundless voice (*lautlose Stimme*), determines (*bestimmen*) us in our destiny (*Bestimmung*), and that we experience this determination in fundamental moods (*Stimmungen*), which tune us in on (*stimmen, abstimmen*) what *is*. Moods, according to the later Heidegger, are fundamental because they tune us in (*stimmen*) on the voice (*Stimme*) of Being.[76] We might call this strategy a unification of themes by common morphemes. Whenever Heidegger uses a word that contains the morpheme *stim*, he intends to evoke the entire network of words that is unified by it. This type of unification is completely lost in translation, as is clear from the English equivalents listed above.

One might object that such a loss is not a loss of content. For "what value is to be attached to a line of argument which appears to depend on the fact that in a particular language two words happen to have a common root"?[77] However, the objection misses the point of Heidegger's later writings altogether. In these writings, Heidegger does not want to offer arguments, and indeed, he claims that thinking is beyond the realm of logic and discursive thought. Whenever the authentic or "essential" thinker uses words, it is language itself that speaks, and Being speaks through it. The connections in language by means of common morphemes should be viewed as hints (*Winke*) to the origin of language in Being, hints given by Being itself. Being sends (*schickt*) us these hints, as it sends us our destiny (*Geschick*). In doing so, Being happens (*gescheht*), and whenever Being happens in our Da-sein, there is deep history (*Geschichte*). If we adapt ourselves to our destiny with dexterity (*geschickt*), we will become ourselves (*eigentlich*) in the event (*Ereignis*) which is Being.

Heidegger unifies his later works not only by common morphemes, but also by using etymologies and other kinds of wordcraft. These types of unification disappear in translations. An analytical philosopher may conclude that nothing essential is lost, because logical connections do not depend on the contingent forms of words. But he should not forget that this criterion for evaluating a translation is not Heidegger's criterion. According to Heidegger's postmonotheist conception of language, Being's hints consist of verbal connections peculiar to German. Because these hints, which unify Heidegger's later works, vanish in another language, his "thinking" does not survive a translation. In 1935, Heidegger claimed that the German people (*Volk*) is the metaphysical people, which has the unique vocation of saving the fate of Europe by relating to Being.[78] Heidegger never abandoned this provincial conviction of the uniqueness of Germany. In 1966 he told *Der Spiegel* that the Germans have a special calling, which consists in a dialogue with Hölderlin. This dialogue allegedly prepares a reversal (*Umkehr*). When asked whether the Germans are specially qualified for this calling, Heidegger responded that their qualification consists in the German language, which is intimately related to the language of the Greeks. He added that the French confirm this view again and again, for "whenever they start to think, they speak German."[79] Because Heidegger decided that the interview should be published after his death and because he did not change the text after 1966, we may safely assume that during the last ten years of his life, Heidegger's conviction of a special vocation of the Germans remained unshaken. Apparently, Being chose the German language as a medium for sending its hints to mankind. Indeed, Being preferred the German language to the exclusion of all the others, for its hints do not survive translation. (In § 14B, I will try to account for this peculiar teutonic flavor of Heidegger's postmonotheism.)

§ 13. THE TURN (*DIE KEHRE*)

The celebrated turn (*die Kehre*) is an important touchstone of any interpretation of Heidegger's question of being. The reason is that the turn supposedly accounts for the transition from *Sein und Zeit* to Heidegger's later thought. In other words, the notion of the turn is the major synthesizing link between early and later Heidegger, so that the topic of the turn belongs in this chapter on synthesis.

With regard to each proposed interpretation of Heidegger's question of being we should ask: Does it allow us to make sense of *die Kehre*?[80] Unfortunately, texts on the turn in Heidegger's works are both scarce and obscure, and there are nearly as many interpretations of the turn as there are books on the later Heidegger.[81] Furthermore, there is a tendency in the secondary literature to discover ever more turns in Heidegger's philosophical career. In an essay on "Heidegger and Theology" of 1993, John Caputo describes three, and perhaps even four, turns: a first turn from Catholicism to Protestantism in 1919; a turn between 1928 and 1935, which culminated in Heidegger's "hellish endorsement of National Socialism"; a third turn after the war which can be dated back to 1936–38; and, finally, a possible return to Catholicism, testified by the fact that on request of the deceased, Bernhard Welte celebrated a Catholic Mass in the church of St. Martin's at the occasion of Heidegger's funeral in 1976.[82]

Caputo's essay is a perceptive sketch of Heidegger's philosophical journey, and we might discover even more turns in the path of Heidegger's thought. Nonetheless, multiplying the number of turns does not contribute to an interpretation of the turn (*die Kehre*). One should distinguish between the notion of the turn as it occurs in Heidegger's writings, and the quite different concept of a change in Heidegger's philosophy.[83] Even if there turn out to be many turns, these turns are not always identical with shifts in Heidegger's thought, while many shifts in his thought do not amount to a turn in the technical sense of the term. In this chapter, I will argue that what Heidegger says on the turn (*die Kehre*) can be fully explained on the basis of my interpretation. The notion of a turn fits in well with the postmonotheist and the Neo-Hegelian leitmotifs. Moreover, the hypothesis of a Pascalian strategy explains the manner in which Heidegger conceived of the relation between the turn as planned in *Sein und Zeit* and the turn as described in the later works.

Apart from an important reference to a turn in his lectures of 1928,[84] Heidegger developed his later notion of the turn in *Beiträge zur Philosophie*, written in 1936–38 and published posthumously in 1989.[85] In print, he referred to the turn for the first time in the "Brief über den 'Humanismus,' " published in 1947. The turn is discussed in two other letters, one of 18 June 1950 to a young student named Buchner, and the other to William J. Richardson, written in April 1962.[86] Furthermore, Heidegger gave four talks in Bremen on 1 December 1949, the last of which was entitled "Die Kehre." It was published in 1962 in *Die Technik und die Kehre*.[87] Heidegger seems to have been reluctant to speak publicly of the turn, and three of the four texts on the turn published during his life are letters. Should we suppose that Heidegger was inspired by Plato's example and used the genre of a letter to express his most intimate thought?[88]

Be this as it may, there are two further texts that should be taken into account when we focus on the notion of a turn, even though the term itself is not used in these texts.[89] The first text, "Vom Wesen der Wahrheit" ("On the Essence of Truth"), is a lecture Heidegger gave many times from 1930 on and which he published in 1943. According to the "Brief über den 'Humanismus,' " this text provides a certain insight in the thinking of the turn, which is characterized as a turn from "Sein und Zeit" to "Zeit und Sein."[90] In 1962, Heidegger held a lecture in Freiburg, entitled "Zeit und Sein" ("Time and Being"), which was published in 1968.[91] Even though the term *Kehre* is not used in this text either, the lecture is relevant to the turn, for its title is a reversal of the title of *Sein und Zeit*. Accordingly, we should suppose that the lecture is concerned with the turn from "Sein und Zeit" to "Zeit und Sein" to which Heidegger referred in the "Brief über den 'Humanismus.' " This assumption is confirmed by the letter to Richardson, written shortly after Heidegger held the lecture "Zeit und Sein," for in the letter to Richardson Heidegger describes the turn in these very same terms.[92] Both "Vom Wesen der Wahrheit" and "Zeit und Sein" belong to the most abstruse texts Heidegger ever wrote. I will now state my interpretation of the turn, based on the Neo-Hegelian and the postmonotheist leitmotifs, and show that it explains both all explicit texts on the turn and a number of obstinate problems. Furthermore, I will discuss two reversals that are identical with the turn: the reversal from "Being and Time" to "Time and Being," and the reversal from "the Essence of Truth" (*das Wesen der Wahrheit*) to "the Truth of Being" (*die Wahrheit des Wesens*).

The composition of this section is as follows. In (A), I will propose my global interpretation of the turn. Then (B) it will be explained why the turn is a reversal from "Being and Time" to "Time and Being." My explanation of this point raises (C) the difficult problem concerning the relation between the turn as planned in *Sein und Zeit* and the turn in Heidegger's later writings. I will argue that this problem can be solved by the hypothesis that Heidegger already applied the Pascalian strategy when he was writing *Sein und Zeit* (see § 12C). Finally (D), a discussion of the essay "Vom Wesen der Wahrheit" will clarify why the turn is also a reversal from the "Essence of Truth" (*das Wesen der Wahrheit*) to the "Truth of Being" (*die Wahrheit des Wesens*).

A. The Anatomy of the Turn

In his postmonotheist theory of history, Heidegger uses an eschatological scheme, derived from Christianity (see § 11B.3).[93] There is a first beginning, when Being started to send (*schicken*) historical stances or destinies (*Geschicke*) to humans, thereby inaugurating authentic history (*eigentliche Geschichte*). According to Heidegger, this beginning happened in ancient Greece, and each of the historical stances sent to humanity is a metaphysical deep structure that accounts for a historical epoch. In this manner the postmonotheist theme is linked to the Neo-Hegelian leitmotif. Now Heidegger holds that by the very event of sending historical destinies to humans, events that place beings in the open (cf. *Lichtung, Wahrheit, Entbergung*), Being itself is concealed, or rather conceals itself. Playing with the term "epoch," Heidegger says that in sending the epochs of history to humans, Being withholds (the Greek term *epochē*) itself. Instead of *epochē*, he also uses terms such as *Entzug* (withdrawal) and *Abkehr* (turning away from).[94] Heidegger holds, then, that at the beginning of history, Being turned itself away from humans (*Ab-kehr*). This is a first turn, and it was Being itself that turned. Because the history of metaphysics is a series of epochs sent by Being, metaphysics is the history of Being's self-concealment, in which man inevitably goes astray (*Irre*; see § 11B.6–7).

I interpreted this doctrine as a postmonotheist analogue of the Judeo-Christian idea that shortly after creation, God turned himself away from Adam and Eve. Because of the Fall, mankind became absorbed in the world, and God's creation obscured the creator. According to Heidegger, the Fall (*Abfall*) in the history of Being happened after the pre-Socratics or even earlier. In any case it was co-inaugurated by Plato, who was the first to conceive of beings according to the model of artifacts, thereby founding the history of productionist metaphysics.[95] Heidegger's postmonotheist narrative is eschatological because a second turn is anticipated. Like Christ's second coming, this second turn is another beginning (*andere Anfang*), which will be inaugurated when Being turns itself to us again. Philosophers of a certain type, such as Marx, think that a change for the better will come only after a profound crisis (cf. Marx's *Verelendung*). The later Heidegger is a thinker of this catastrophic type. He holds that the second turn, which is called *die Kehre*, will only come when the history of productionist metaphysics has been fully consummated in the epoch of technology. In this epoch, human deviation (*die Irre*) will be complete, the earth will be destroyed, and everything will have become meaningless, because our abandonment by Being has become absolute.[96] We do not experience this abandonment anymore. Our greatest distress is that we do not sense the distress of being abandoned by Being and go along happily: it is the *Not der Notlosigkeit*. As Heidegger says, the concealment of Being is itself concealed, and the forgetfulness of Being is forgotten.[97] This is why the epoch of technology is the "greatest danger."[98] However, "where danger is, grows / the saving power too," Heidegger claims, quoting Hölderlin.[99] The reason is that as soon as we grasp the danger *as* danger, we will see that the epoch of technology is sent to us by Being. If we learn to conceive of history (*Geschichte*) and our present epoch of technology (*das Wesen der Technik*) as a fate (*Geschick*), sent (*geschickt*) to us by Being, we will prepare a turn of Being toward us. Allegedly, Being will not turn toward us out of itself, because Being needs us in order to be sheltered.[100]

Heidegger uses the term *Kehre* primarily for this postmonotheist analogue of the second coming.[101] This is why he speaks of "the turn in the event" (*die Kehre im Ereignis*), since the event (*Ereignis*) is Being's happening, and the turn is the event of Being that will make humans authentic (*er-eignen*, compare *eigentlich*) and that will bring Being itself (*eigens*) to the fore.[102] The turn will arrive at the appropriate moment (*Augenblick*, *kairos*), which can neither be predicted nor calculated in advance.[103] In the letter to Richardson, Heidegger says that the turn is a *Sachverhalt*, and that it is in play within the *Sachverhalt* itself.[104] One shows a lack of sensibility for Heidegger's wordcraft if one translates the word *Sachverhalt* by "state of affairs," or simply by "matter," as Richardson does. According to Heidegger, Being is *die Sache des Denkens* (the issue for thought).[105] Apart from the component *sach*, the German term *Sachverhalt* contains *verhalt*, which is both the stem of the verb *verhalten* and related to the noun *Verhältnis*. The verb *verhalten* means among other things to behave and to hold back. *Verhältnis* means relationship, a relationship that supports or sustains (*halten*) us in our deepest being or essence: Da-sein. Accordingly, the proper translation of Heidegger's term *Sachverhalt* is "Being's-behavior-of-holding-itself-back-in-its-sustaining-relationship-to-humans." And the *Kehre im Sachverhalt* is the reversal of this behavior, that is, Heidegger's postmonotheist analogue of the second coming.

From this primary and fundamental notion of a turn, Heidegger derives a number of secondary notions, for which he mostly uses other terms, such as *Wandlung* and *Verwandlung* (change, transformation). First of all (1), each change of fundamental metaphysical stance in history is a turning (*Wandlung*), and this turning is a turn in being, where "being" is taken in the Neo-Hegelian sense. Because many of these turnings have occurred, Heidegger speaks of a wealth of (possible) transformations in being (*Wandlungsfülle des Seins*).[106] As he claims that Being will not send us a new fate (*Geschick*) unless we meditate on the sense of the present one, such a turning in being requires (2) that we turn toward Being, trying to grasp the sense of the present epoch of technology, and, indeed, the sense of history as the concealment of Being in metaphysics. This turn of humans toward Being will prepare a new fate, and it will prepare the final turn (*Kehre*) of Being toward us.[107] As we saw in section 11, above, the requirement of our turning toward Being is a postmonotheist analogue of the Christian requirement that we open our hearts to God. (3) Such a preparatory human turn toward Being is an answer to the claim (*Anspruch*) or call (*Zuspruch*) of Being, so that Being has always already turned itself to us, albeit in the paradoxical manner of turning away from us. When Being will finally reveal itself to us in the Event of the other Beginning, that is, by the turn in its primary sense, we humans will be transformed, and this is a turn in us (*Wandlung, Verwandlung*) in a fourth sense (4).[108] I interpreted the latter event as a postmonotheist analogue of the Christian transformation or rebirth of man by divine grace. Finally (5), Heidegger's notion of *die Kehre* as applied to his own development after *Sein und Zeit* must be seen as an individual instance of a turn in sense (2). For Heidegger holds that the primary *Kehre* is yet to come.

B. From "Being and Time" to "Time and Being"

Both in the "Brief über den 'Humanismus' " and in the letter to Richardson, Heidegger says that the turn in the primary and fundamental sense is a turn from "Being and Time" to "Time and Being." In the latter epistle he adds that this turn is not primarily a process in questioning thought; it belongs to the *Sachverhalt* itself, which is designated by the titles "Being and Time" and "Time and Being."[109] According to the postmonotheist interpretation, we should only expect that the turn occurs in the *Sachverhalt*, as I explained above. But why is this primary turn a turn from "Being and Time" to "Time and Being"? In order to answer this question, we should analyze Heidegger's lecture "Zeit und Sein" of 1962.

The lecture "Zeit und Sein" as published in *Zur Sache des Denkens* (*Concerning the Topic of Thought*) consists of an introduction (pp. 1–5) and three movements, one on *Sein*, one on *Zeit*, and one on *Es gibt*. The German expression *es gibt* means "there is . . . " or "there are . . . ," but it is crucial for Heidegger that *gibt* is the present tense third-person singular of the verb *geben*, which means "to give."

In the first movement of the lecture, Heidegger distinguishes two meanings of the word *Sein*, having rejected the sense of "Being" as a founding entity (*Grund*). In one sense, for which Heidegger uses *Sein* in this lecture, being is given by *Es gibt*. *Sein* in the second sense is *Es gibt* itself, and Heidegger says that in the act of giving, *Es gibt* withdraws itself in favor of *Sein*.[110] All this sounds utterly obscure, until one realizes that Being *that gives* (*Es gibt*) is postmonotheist Being (*das Seyn* in *Beiträge*), and being which *is given* is being in the Neo-Hegelian sense (*das Sein*). The first movement turns out to be yet another formulation of Heidegger's postmonotheist analogue of creation and the Fall, according to which Being (*Es gibt*) withdraws itself in favor of the fundamental stances (*Sein*), which are sent to us as epochs of history. This interpretation is confirmed by the fact that Heidegger develops the theme of authentic history in the remainder of the first movement, using his habitual puns on *schicken, Geschick, Geschichte*, and *Epoche—epochē*. It is also corroborated by Heidegger's reference to Hegel's dialectics as "the most colossal thinking of the modern era," for Heidegger's Neo-Hegelian theory of history is a reversal of Hegel's theory, as we saw in section 9C, above.[111]

In the second movement of the lecture, Heidegger claims that time has four dimensions. Apart from the three dimensions of authentic time (*eigentliche Zeit*), there is a fourth dimension, because the unity of these three dimensions is grounded in a "passing-on-to" (*Zuspiel*). This *Zuspiel* is a "handing" or "giving" (*Reichen*), and time is a gift from *Es gibt*.[112] Again, this text will seem to be abstruse, until it is clarified by the postmonotheist interpretation. What Heidegger wants to say is that time itself is administered to us by Being in the postmonotheist sense (*Es gibt*), and that by giving this very gift, Being conceals itself and remains mysterious (*rätselhaft*).

This interpretation is confirmed by the third movement, which discusses *Es gibt* itself. The verb *geben* in *Es gibt* turns out to refer to what Heidegger usually calls *schicken*, and to the *reichen* of time. Sending (*schicken*) epochs of being and handing over (*reichen*) time belong together, because the *Es* that sends and gives is the Event (*das Ereignis*) or the *Sach-Verhalt*.[113] As we already know, *Ereignis* is another term for Being or the happening of Being in the postmonotheist sense, and for its turns toward us and away from us. We are not surprised to read, then, that Heidegger's aim in the lecture is to direct our attention to Being as the Event, and that Being disappears in the Event.[114] By reflecting on Being's self-concealment, Heidegger tries to prepare for a second coming of Being.

On the basis of this postmonotheist and Neo-Hegelian interpretation of the lecture, we are now able to guess what Heidegger means when he characterizes the turn (*die Kehre*) as a turn from "Being and Time" to "Time and Being." The title "Being and Time" stands for the first turn of Being, when Being turned itself away from us, giving us the time of real history.[115] As in Hegel, history is considered as Being's revelation in, or as, time, a revelation by which Being also conceals itself. The reversal of the title to "Time and Being" points to the second turn, the turn from history to Being itself. As Heidegger says in the letter to Richardson, the turn "is inherent in the very *Sachverhalt* designated by the headings: 'Being and Time,' 'Time and Being.' "[116]

Is it far-fetched to suppose that by characterizing the second turn in this manner, Heidegger endorsed a postmonotheist analogue of the Christian doctrine of the End of Time, at which history as we know it will be substituted by something essentially better? The interval between Being's first turn and Being's second turn would be the era of metaphysics, in which Being conceals itself.[117] Metaphysics is productionist, and the stances of productionist metaphysics are as many stages in an ever-deeper Fall, which is completed in the era of technology. This era, Heidegger suggests, might last very long. But because "where danger is, the saving power grows," the end of the era of technology will be the end of time and history as we know them. There will be a turn from time or history to Being itself. The early Christians believed with Papias that after Christ's second coming, there will be a millennium during which the kingdom of the Savior will be set up in material form on the earth (Rome now considers this doctrine as a heresy). Similarly, Heidegger conceives of the second turn as a new or other beginning (*andere Anfang*). This further similarity between Heidegger's later works and (early) Christianity corroborates the postmonotheist interpretation, which accounts for the turn as described by the later Heidegger. Yet a number of difficulties remain.

C. Heidegger's Pascalian Grand Strategy

A first difficulty is concerned with the relation between two separate turns from "Being and Time" to "Time and Being." I gave a postmonotheist interpretation of the turn as portrayed in the lecture "Zeit und Sein." But this turn seems to be different from the turn from "Being and Time" to "Time and Being" that was planned in *Sein und Zeit*, a turn that I discussed in section 9C, above. At first sight, the turn as planned in *Sein und Zeit* was simply another spiraling movement in the hermeneutical circle that involves being and Dasein. From ancient Greece on, notions of being had been specified by temporal criteria.[118] It was the official aim of *Sein und Zeit* to account for this fact in two steps. In a first step, which encompasses divisions 1 and 2 and which leads from being to time, a transcendental notion of time was developed by an ontological analysis of Dasein. In a second step, which leads back from time to being, Heidegger wanted to spell out a unified notion of being within the horizon of transcendental time, and to show how specific notions of being could be developed from the unified notion, using temporal criteria. This second step would be the content of the third division of *Sein und Zeit*, entitled "Zeit und Sein." Clearly, a turn was planned in the structure of *Sein und Zeit*, and this turn might be described as a turn from "Sein und Zeit" to "Zeit und Sein." However, the third division of *Sein und Zeit* was never published, and it seems that Heidegger later substituted for this turn a very different turn, the postmonotheist turn that I interpreted above (§ 13A–B). If this is the case, how can Heidegger claim that there is only one turn, and that this turn was already anticipated in *Sein und Zeit*?[119] It seems that Heidegger illegitimately projects back his later postmonotheist notion of a turn into his earlier book. Why does he do so? Can we justify his procedure?

This first difficulty is related to a second one, that of dating the incipience of the thought of the turn in Heidegger's career (see the introduction to § 10, above).

In the letter to Richardson, Heidegger says that "the *Sachverhalt* thought in the term *Kehre* was already at work in my thinking ten years prior to 1947."[120] According to this quotation, the turn would have occurred around 1937, when he was writing *Beiträge zur Philosophie*. If this is the case, how can Heidegger claim that the *Kehre* had already been planned ten years earlier, in *Sein und Zeit*? How are we to resolve the contradiction between Heidegger's datings of the turn?

I want to suggest that these two problems may be solved by the following hypothesis. It is plausible to assume that the Pascalian strategy, which I discussed in section 12C, was not only a model that the later Heidegger used in order to unify his *Denkweg* by hindsight. He also followed this strategy when he was writing *Sein und Zeit*. This hypothesis unifies Heidegger's *Denkweg* in a radical manner. If it is correct, Heidegger's entire oeuvre, from the early courses on the phenomenology of religion in 1918–21 to the latest writings, was informed by a unified scheme, a Pascalian Grand Strategy, of which the secular phenomenology of human existence in *Sein und Zeit* was the first stage, whereas the second stage consists of the postmonotheist writings published after the Second World War.

Let me first explain how this hypothesis solves the second difficulty, that of dating the incipience of the turn. Inherent in the Pascalian strategy is a notion of faith as granted by divine grace. There is no way to merit faith or to obtain it by bargaining with God. The only manner to prepare ourselves for the grace of faith is to analyze the human condition in its harshness, and to show that mostly we try to escape from it into dispersion (first stage of the strategy). Heidegger endorsed the notion of faith as divine grace and revelation, which is also Paul's and Luther's notion, both in *Sein und Zeit* and in "Phänomenologie und Theologie" of 1927.[121]

This notion of faith implies that we can neither predict the moment of grace nor describe its content beforehand. As Paul says in his first letter to the *Thessalonians* (5:2), "the day of the Lord will come like a thief in the night"; hence we must keep awake for the Moment to come (*kairos, Augenblick*). Moreover, it might be very difficult to recognize the moment of grace when it arrives. We might think that it has arrived, try to describe the contents of this revelation (second stage of the strategy), and then feel that it simply was not it. That Heidegger's later notion of *Kehre* is a postmonotheist analogue of this Neo-Lutheran notion of grace is demonstrated by the lecture "Die Kehre" of 1949 and by the letter to Buchner of 1950. In "Die Kehre" Heidegger stresses that nobody knows when and how the turn will happen in history.[122] And Heidegger wrote to Buchner that if one attempts to hear the claim or address (*Anspruch*) of Being, it is very easy to mishear it, and that the possibility of a blind alley is greatest in the kind of thinking that wants to listen and hear.[123] Should we not assume that Heidegger describes his own experiences with the turn as anticipated in *Sein und Zeit*?

Let us suppose, then, that *Sein und Zeit* was written as an attempt to prepare us and Heidegger himself for grace by a secular analysis of the human condition (first stage). Let us also suppose that Heidegger initially thought that grace had come, and that he tried to express it in metaphysical terms, using the traditional (Eckhartian) notion of Being as God (second stage). But this attempt at expressing the turn failed, as Heidegger admits in the "Brief über den 'Humanismus.' "[124] Later, when he wrote *Beiträge zur Philosophie* in 1936–38, Heidegger found a more adequate, postmonotheist language for describing the anticipated turn.[125] This hypothesis would justify the identification of the later notion of a turn with the turn as anticipated in *Sein und Zeit*. For according to Heidegger's Lutheran conception of faith as grace, the anticipation of the turn cannot have any specific content. It is only by hindsight, after having heard the call of Being properly, that we can realize what the content of our anticipation should have been. As Heidegger wrote to Richardson, "a good number of years are needed before the thinking through of so decisive a *Sachverhalt* can find its way to the clear."[126]

Summarizing the proposed solution to the second problem, we might say that, because of Heidegger's notion of faith, the incipience of the turn cannot be dated with precision. Having completed the first stage of the Pascalian strategy by writing *Sein und Zeit*, Heidegger was waiting for grace from 1927 on. There were at least two specific attempts to receive grace, a "metaphysical" one in 1927–30, when Heidegger held his inaugural lecture *Was ist Metaphysik?* and tried to awaken our fundamental boredom (the fact that Being is hidden) in the magistral lectures of 1929–30 on the fundamental concepts of metaphysics, and a "postmetaphysical" one in 1936–38, when he wrote *Beiträge zur Philosophie*. Both attempts might be called a turn in sense (5) above (§ 13A).

Does my hypothesis also solve the first problem, that even though Heidegger's later turn from "Being and Time" to "Time and Being" is very different from the early turn to "Time and Being" as planned in *Sein und Zeit*, Heidegger identifies the two turns? Surely, it is not difficult to reinterpret the *terminus a quo* of the early turn, *Sein und Zeit*, in terms of Heidegger's later thought, using the strategy of reinterpretation prescribed in "Phänomenologie und Theologie," a strategy that Heidegger himself later applied when he recycled the existentialia (see § 12C, above). If *Sein und Zeit* is a religiously neutral description of the human condition, forming the first stage of a Pascalian strategy, one might very well say that it expresses the experience of oblivion of Being in the sense of the later Heidegger. *Sein und Zeit* is situated within the realm of historical time, in which Being withdrew from us. This is indeed what Heidegger says in *Beiträge* and the "Brief über den 'Humanismus.' "[127]

However, the difficulty was rather concerned with the *terminus ad quem* of the turn, "Time and Being." Here a reinterpretation along Pascalian lines is more problematic, because the hermeneutical reversal of "Being and Time" to "Time and Being" as planned in *Sein und Zeit* is very different indeed from Heidegger's later postmonotheist reversal. Yet there are many reasons for endorsing the hypothesis that Heidegger anticipated some kind of religious *Kehre* in *Sein und Zeit* itself. First, when discussing the reversal of *Sein und Zeit* in section 9C, above, I noted that some texts do not fit in with the hermeneutical and transcendental view of this reversal. Heidegger says, for instance, that Being is "higher" than beings, and this points to a religious meaning of "Being." If the ultimate point of *Sein und Zeit* was a religious one, Heidegger was justified in identifying the turn to "Time and Being" as anticipated in that book with his later turn. We discovered similar hints to a religious (Neo-Platonist) connotation of "Being" in Heidegger's lectures on the *Fundamental Problems of Phenomenology* of 1927, which contain an abortive sketch of the third division of *Sein und Zeit*.

Second, we should not forget that Heidegger developed the notion of methodological atheism as a preparation for grace already in the Natorp essay of 1922 (see § 11, above). Moreover, Heidegger says in a footnote to "Vom Wesen des Grundes" of 1929 that although the ontology of Dasein in *Sein und Zeit* does not contain a decision against or in favor of "a possible being-to-God," it yields a notion of Dasein on the basis of which we might *ask* what the relation of Dasein to God might be ontologically.[128] The fact that *Sein und Zeit* does not contain such a decision fits in with the Pascalian strategy and with Heidegger's notion of faith as grace. According to this Lutheran notion of faith, Dasein can never establish a relation to God by its own decision, because only God is able to decide about this relation, and the ontology of faith can be developed only from the point of view of faith.[129] In other words, Heidegger endorsed a Pascalian strategy both in 1922 and in 1929, so that it is plausible to assume that he also endorsed it while writing *Sein und Zeit*.[130] As I said before, it is no objection that the Pascalian strategy is not expressed in the book itself, for expressing it would prevent its success (see § 12C, above). It is revealing that when Heidegger describes the strategy at all, he does so in footnotes.

Third, the hypothesis that Heidegger endorsed the Pascalian strategy already in 1927 is corroborated by his lectures on Leibniz and logic of the summer semester of 1928. These lectures contain the term *Kehre* for the first time, in an appendix on the idea and function of a fundamental ontology.[131] Even if the term *Kehre* were a later interpolation—as Heidegger wanted the collected works to be an edition *aus letzter Hand*, he ruled that later additions should be integrated into the texts without critical footnotes—the notion of a religious turn is suggested by the lectures themselves. Let me merely note two salient points. In section 10 of the lectures, entitled "The Problem of Transcendence and the Problem of Being and Time," Heidegger gives a summary of the problem of transcendence as it was developed in *Sein und Zeit*. This summary differs from the book in an interesting way. The notion of *Zerstreuung* (diversion), which was marginal in *Sein und Zeit*, suddenly becomes the central idea. Heidegger even speaks of a "transcendental diversion," and claims that this diversion explains that humans are able to let themselves be supported by nature and that Dasein is able to be with others.[132] In other words, Heidegger interprets our entire worldly existence as a product of transcendental diversion. This peculiar view comes very close to Pascal, who argued in *Les Pensées* that human life in general is characterized by *divertissement*. It also reminds us of Neo-Platonism, according to which the One is diversified by the admixture of matter. In both cases, becoming conscious of our diversion is a condition for opening our hearts to God.[133]

The appendix to section 10 of the lectures, in which the term *Kehre* occurs, equally points to a religious turn. In this appendix, Heidegger construes the relations among fundamental ontology, ontology, and metaphysics along Kantian lines.[134] Metaphysics consists of fundamental ontology and "metontology."[135] Fundamental ontology embraces (1) the transcendental analysis of Dasein and (2) the analysis of the temporality of being. Metontology (meta-ontology) is concerned with being in its totality (*das Seiende im Ganzen*).[136] Now Heidegger says that there is a turn (*Umschlag*) from fundamental ontology to metontology. The reason is that Dasein, which understands and projects being, is itself part of the totality of beings. In other words, Dasein is able to understand being only because a possible totality of being is already present.[137] The problem that Heidegger raises here is inherent in transcendental philosophy from Kant to Schopenhauer and Husserl: if the transcendental subject constitutes the totality of beings, the constituting subject must be part of the constituted totality, because it is a being itself. Therefore, transcendental philosophy turns into (met)ontology. Heidegger now uses the word *Kehre* for this reversal (*Umschlag*), and says that the analysis of the temporality of being is the *Kehre* from fundamental ontology to metontology or metaphysical ontics.[138] At first sight, this *Kehre* does not have a religious connotation. But at the end of the appendix, Heidegger suddenly says that the *Kehre* transforms *the* fundamental problem of philosophy itself, which is contained in Aristotle's dual notion of philosophy as first philosophy and theology.[139] Although Heidegger rejected the philosophy of the Scholastics in 1919, he seems to have retained one crucial notion, that reflection on the totality of beings might lead us to Being.[140] If this is the case, the two possible interpretations of the turn to "Time and Being" as planned in *Sein und Zeit* are united, and the hypothesis that the ultimate intentions of that book were religious is confirmed yet again.[141]

There is a fourth and wholly explicit corroboration of the thesis that Heidegger composed *Sein und Zeit* with the Pascalian strategy in mind. On 12 September 1929, Heidegger wrote a letter to his friend Elisabeth Blochmann, apparently after an intimate stay at Heidegger's hut in Todtnauberg and a visit to the monastery at Beuron. He seems to apologize for having gone too far—or not far enough?—in their friendship during these shared summer days; the letter is not clear in this respect.[142] Then he writes about the truth of our Dasein. This is not a simple thing, he says, and our inner truthfulness has its own depth and multiplicity. It does not consist only of rational considerations made up by us. The truth of our existence needs its own day and hour, in which we "have our Dasein as a whole." Then we experience "that in all that is essential, our heart must keep itself open to grace." For "God . . . calls each of us with a different voice."[143]

It is clear from *Sein und Zeit*, sections 45–53, that we "have our Dasein as a whole" only when we authentically anticipate death. In this letter to Blochmann, Heidegger interprets such a poignant sense of our own death, which enables us to grasp Dasein as a whole, as a preparation for the leap to faith, which opens our heart to God's grace. At the end of *Was ist Metaphysik?* Heidegger also spoke of the fundamental possibilities of Dasein as a whole, and of a leap into nothingness.[144] Eckhart had taught that we have to release ourselves and to leap into nothingness in order to experience Being or God. As is the case in Pascal, it seems that Heidegger's analysis of the "wholeness" of Dasein as being-toward-death in *Sein und Zeit* should be read as an anticipation of grace. The letter to Blochmann of 12 September 1929 shows that at that time Heidegger still thought that grace would come from the Christian God, even though he makes abundantly clear that he rejects conventional Catholicism and Protestantism.[145] In the manner of mystics such as Eckhart, he speaks of the necessity of being "ready for the night," and of abstaining from barring the way to the depth of Dasein.[146]

Heidegger's lectures of 1928 imply that the turn is a turn *within* metaphysics, and metaphysics is taken in a positive sense, as it is in *Was ist Metaphysik?* of 1929 and in *Grundbegriffe der Metaphysik (Fundamental Concepts of Metaphysics)*, Heidegger's impressive course of 1929–30. This confirms what Heidegger says in the "Brief über den 'Humanismus' ": that in *Sein und Zeit* he anticipated a *metaphysical* turn, which failed.[147] I have assumed that *Sein und Zeit* was written as an attempt to find God in some metaphysical sense. As I will argue in sections 14 and 15, it is likely that the failure of this first turn motivated in part Heidegger's enthusiasm for Hitler and Nietzsche. But this voluntaristic enthusiasm for Nazism in 1932–36 led to a second failure, the failure of the rectorate. On 1 July 1935, Heidegger wrote to Karl Jaspers that he was wrestling to overcome two thorns, the fiasco of the rectorate and the religion of his origin.[148] I will argue that Heidegger's later postmonotheist philosophy of the turn was the outcome of this inner struggle (see §§ 14–15).

D. *From the Essence of Truth to the Truth of Being*

Before I do so, one more difficulty has to be removed. Thus far, I have attempted to explain why the *Kehre* may be described as a turn from "Being and Time" to "Time and Being," and I have tried to justify the fact that Heidegger identifies his later turn with the turn as anticipated in *Sein und Zeit*. There is yet another description of the turn. According to the "Brief über den 'Humanismus,' " the lecture "Vom Wesen der Wahrheit" ("On the Essence of Truth") of 1930, published after many redraftings in 1943, provides a certain insight into the thinking of the turn from "Being and Time" to "Time and Being."[149] Obviously, Heidegger meant the lecture as published in 1943, and not its first draft of 1930, which does not yet contain the later notion of the turn.[150] The problem is, however, that in this lecture, the turn is characterized as a turn from "The Essence of Truth" (*das Wesen der Wahrheit*) to "The Truth of Being" (*die Wahrheit des Wesens*), and not as a turn from "Being and Time" to "Time and Being".[151] What is the relation between this "veritative" turning and the "onto-temporal" turning that I discussed above? And what does the veritative turning mean? Let me first try to answer the second question on the basis of a summary of "Vom Wesen der Wahrheit."

The text of 1943 consists of a brief introduction, eight short sections, and a note that was added partly in 1943 and partly in 1949. In the introduction, Heidegger claims that philosophy is incommensurable with common sense, because it asks essential questions about essentials (*Wesensfragen*). Heidegger then develops the following train of thought. The traditional notion of Truth as *adaequatio rei et intellectus* (§ 1) presupposes that judgments can be adapted to things (*Angleichung*). But this presupposes in its turn that there is an open region (*das Offene eines Bezirks*) or an open comportment (*offenständiges Verhalten*) in which things are manifest. Heidegger calls this open region "the essence of Truth" (*das Wesen der Wahrheit*), in contrast to propositional truth (§ 2). He further claims that such an open comportment is based on freedom, and concludes that "the essence of Truth is freedom" (§ 3).[152]

Up to this point, Heidegger's argument in "Vom Wesen der Wahrheit" resembles section 44 of *Sein und Zeit*, in which Heidegger developed a transcendental notion of Truth as Dasein's being uncovering. Because Dasein's being uncovering is a kind of projecting (*Entwurf*), it may be said to be based on freedom, and this is what Heidegger argued in "Vom Wesen des Grundes" of 1929.[153] However, at the end of section 3 of "Vom Wesen der Wahrheit," Heidegger claims that it is a preconception to think that freedom is a property of man. What, then, is freedom?

Our preconceptions will be unsettled only if we are "prepared for a transformation in our thinking."[154] Clearly, the necessity of a turn is announced here. Freedom, Heidegger says in section 4, is "to let beings be" (*das Seinlassen von Seiendem*), and by letting beings be, freedom performs the essence of Truth in the sense of revealing beings.[155] Man does not possess freedom. Rather, freedom possesses man, because "it gives to man in safekeeping the history of the essential possibilities of historical humanity in the disclosure of beings as a totality."[156] However, when freedom attunes (*abstimmen*) our behavior to a totality of beings, a tuning that reveals itself to us in moods (*Stimmung*), this totality as such remains undetermined (*das Unbestimmte, Unbestimmbare*), so that freedom, in revealing particular beings, conceals the totality (§ 5).

This concealment preserves what is most proper to Truth as its own (*das Eigenste als Eigentum*). To the essence of Truth belongs its terrible un-essence (*Unwesen*) or authentic un-Truth (*eigentliche Un-wahrheit*), and this is the mystery (*das Geheimnis*). "But surely for those who know . . . the un- of . . . un-Truth points to the still unexperienced domain of the Truth of Being" (§ 6).[157] Un-Truth means that man is astray in errancy (*Irre*). Having turned to available and common things (*das Gangbare*), humanity is turned away from the mystery. Such is man's errancy or madness (*Irre*), which belongs to the inner constitution of Dasein.

However, when man assumes the openness of beings in its primordial essence, "resolute openness [*Ent-schlossenheit*] toward the mystery is under way into errancy as such," and the question of Being is raised. Then we will see why the

Essence of Truth is related to the Truth of Being (§ 7).[158] Accordingly, we have to wonder whether the question of the essence of Truth (*das Wesen der Wahrheit*) must not be at the same time a question concerning the Truth of Being (*die Wahrheit des Wesens*) (§ 8).[159] In the note, Heidegger adds that the question of the essence of Truth is answered by the nonpropositional saying that "*das Wesen der Wahrheit ist die Wahrheit des Wesens*," where "Wesen" means *Seyn* and "Wahrheit" means sheltering that clears (*lichtendes Bergen*) as the basic characteristic of Being. He claims that this answer is the saying of a turn within the history of Being.[160]

As the reader will agree, the lecture "Vom Wesen der Wahrheit" is no less abstruse than "Zeit und Sein" of 1962. But again, obscurity vanishes as soon as it is read in the light of the postmonotheist interpretation. It is Being itself that freely sends truths to humanity, where "Truth" means a historical epoch in which entities *are* in a certain sense. This is what Heidegger means by *das Wesen der Wahrheit*. Of course, the term "Wesen" does not mean essence in this context, even though it is commonly translated in this manner. *Wesen*, Heidegger says in *Beiträge zur Philosophie*, should be understood as *Wesung*, a neologism that means the way in which Being *is*.[161] According to Heidegger's postmonotheist theory of creation and revelation, Being conceals itself in the process of revealing entities to us, so that humanity is going astray, and *Un-wahrheit* belongs to *Wahrheit*.[162] As soon as we remind ourselves of *das Wesen der Wahrheit* in this sense, we will anticipate the insight that it stems from *Die Wahrheit des Wesens*, that is, from the true way in which Being "is," as revealing and concealing. This insight is provided by the *Kehre*, which the lecture helps prepare.

We come to the conclusion that the essays "Vom Wesen der Wahrheit" and "Zeit und Sein" describe two aspects of one and the same turn. Whereas "Zeit und Sein" focuses on the temporal aspect of Heidegger's postmonotheist analogue of creation and revelation, "Vom Wesen der Wahrheit" describes its ontological aspect. These two aspects cannot be separated and they are identical in the end. For according to Heidegger, the domain of revealed truth (*Entbergung*) is essentially temporal and historical (*geschichtlich*). It is the domain of deep or authentic history, in which beings are manifest to Dasein and Being conceals itself.

§ 14. HEIDEGGER AND HITLER

Having discussed in sections 12 and 13 the forms of synthesis that connect Heidegger's later works as published after the war to *Sein und Zeit*, I now turn to the intermediate period of 1927–46. During this period, Heidegger entangled himself in National Socialism and developed the fundamental leitmotifs of his later thought, the Neo-Hegelian theme and the postmonotheist leitmotif. It has been assumed that the genesis of Heidegger's later philosophy is unrelated to the turmoil of the time, and indeed, the development of Heidegger's thought has an inner logic, the logic of the Pascalian strategy. Nevertheless, there are at least three compelling reasons for examining possible links between Nazism and Heidegger's philosophy. In order to provide some background to the present section, I will advance these reasons before specifying the issues with which I want to deal.

The first reason is that on 22 April 1933, six years after the publication of *Sein und Zeit*, Heidegger became rector of Freiburg University, and that, having entered the National Socialist Party with great pomp on the first of May, he was instrumental in the *Gleichschaltung* (forcing into the Party line) of that university by the Nazi regime, which had seized power on 30 January 1933.[163] Many of Heidegger's pupils have depicted the episode of the rectorate as an isolated intrusion of political reality in Heidegger's apolitical life, an intrusion unconnected to Heidegger's philosophy. Like Plato's Sicilian adventure, Heidegger's rectorate would have been due to the illusions of an unworldly philosopher about political reality. The comparison with Plato is only too fitting—Heidegger lectured on Plato's notion of Truth and on the simile of the cave shortly before and during the rectorate, and he quoted Plato's *Republic* at the end of the rectoral address— but it does not show what it is meant to prove: that there is no intimate relation between the rectorate and Heidegger's philosophy.[164] On the contrary, it suggests that Heidegger had philosophical motives for becoming a rector at this crucial moment of German history.

Like Plato, Heidegger believed in 1933 that the philosopher has a deeper insight into reality than ordinary mortals, who are imprisoned in the cave, as Plato's simile says. This insight would enable the philosopher to give spiritual and political guidance to his people. The German university had to be transformed on the basis of philosophy, Heidegger argued in his rectoral address, in order to educate the "leaders and guardians of the destiny of the German *Volk*."[165] Admittedly, Heidegger's view of the essence of the German university did not coincide with the view of the anti-intellectual National Socialist movement, if only because the Nazis did not have a unified conception of universities at all, and probably wanted to downgrade the existing institutions to some kind of polytechnics. This is why Heidegger could say after the war that by becoming a rector, he had wanted to prevent the imminent supremacy of the Party within the university, and to save and stabilize what was positive.[166] Nonetheless, Heidegger thought that the destiny of the German people required for its fulfillment Hitler's dictatorship, the ruthless nature of which had become clear in April 1933, and that it required the liquidation of traditional academic freedom and the introduction of a *Führerprinzip* (principle of leadership) within the universities.[167] In his speech in Tübingen on 30 November 1933, Heidegger stated these claims clearly, and he tried to put them into practice with great zeal. He also pointed out that the real revolution within the universities had not even begun, and, paraphrasing Nietzsche, he said that the present generation of Germans was merely transitory, merely a sacrifice.[168]

Although Heidegger and Plato shared the doctrine that the philosopher should lead his people, because he is supposed to see deeper into the nature of reality than other human beings, their conceptions of philosophical leadership turn out to be rather different. Whereas Plato was horrified by the fact that Athenian democracy condemned Socrates to death, thereby sacrificing an individual for the sake of political and religious correctness, Heidegger seemed relatively unconcerned about the fate of individuals for pseudo-Nietzschean reasons. The future greatness of Germany made it necessary to sacrifice oneself, and, perhaps, others. As a rector, Heidegger wrote to the staff and faculties of Freiburg University on 20 December 1933: "the individual, wherever he stands, does not count. What counts only, is the destiny [*Schicksal*] of our people [*unseres Volkes*] in their state."[169] If this totalitarian view explains the fact that Heidegger was not bothered by the creation of concentration camps and the elimination of Jews from German academia in 1933, there are ample grounds for investigating the relations between Nazism and his philosophy.[170]

There is yet a second reason for discussing the political dimension of Heidegger's works. When he had to justify himself in 1945, and later in the interview with *Der Spiegel* and in the account on the rectorate written in 1945 and published in 1983, Heidegger concealed the extent of his involvement with the National Socialist Party. Whereas he claimed that he had no contacts with the Party and no political involvements before April 1933, Heidegger's election as a rector seems to have been carefully staged by a group of National Socialists within Freiburg University, and in private Heidegger had committed himself to Hitler as early as 1932 or perhaps even Christmas 1931.[171] Furthermore, while Heidegger claimed that as a rector he never participated in political meetings and had had no personal or political contacts with Party officials,[172] he in fact sent a telegram to Hitler about the tactics of the *Gleichschaltung* on 20 May 1933; he approved of semimilitary training of students; on 3 November 1933 he urged on the German students a blind loyalty to Hitler and a readiness to sacrifice; he publicly supported Hitler's decision to leave the League of Nations on 11 November 1933; and he denounced the outstanding chemist Staudinger on 10 February 1934.[173] Finally, whereas Heidegger suggests in his account published in 1983 that he was isolated from the National Socialists after February 1934,[174] in reality he was involved in a project for a National Socialist academy of teachers in August 1934; he destroyed the careers of his Catholic pupils Gustav Siewerth and Max Müller in 1938 on the grounds that they did not favor the National Socialist state and that a Catholic could not be a real philosopher; in spite of attacks on his philosophy by Krieck and other Nazi-ideologues, he was still considered as "a party member and champion of National Socialism" from 1934 to 1945; and in his lectures of 1942 he could still speak of "the historical uniqueness" of National Socialism.[175]

It may be thought that Heidegger's dishonesty about his political past does not compromise his philosophy. His attitude may be seen as typical of the Adenauer epoch, in which Western Germany was rebuilt as a democratic state and most Germans were not willing to dig into the horrors and moral complexities of the Nazi regime and the war. At worst, it seems, one might reproach Heidegger for not being more courageous and more sincere than the majority of his fellow countrymen, which one might expect of a philosopher who once considered himself a spiritual leader of his people and who defined leadership as "the strength to be able to go on alone."[176] Why, then, should Heidegger's apologetic strategy after the war be relevant to his philosophy?

The problem is that Heidegger himself drew his works into the ambiguous twilight of his political apologetics. In the account of the rectorate published in 1983, he spends nearly four pages on an authoritative interpretation of the rectoral address, accusing of malice those who read the address differently.[177] According to Heidegger's interpretation, the term *Wehrdienst*, for instance, did not mean military service. The stem *Wehr-* was meant in the sense of self-defense.[178] Similarly, the word *Kampf* did not refer to battle or war. It should be understood as an equivalent of the Greek *polemos* as used by Heraclitus in fragment 53, which Heidegger translates idiosyncratically as: to expose oneself to what is essential, mutually respecting each other.[179]

However, these later interpretations sound false if one tries to locate the rectoral address in the context of the German situation in 1933, when students were urged to join the SA (*Sturmabteilung*; stormtroopers) and the SS (*Schutzstaffel*; protective squadron of the Nazi Party). About the *Wehrdienst*, Heidegger said in the address that it is concerned with the obligations to "the honor and the destiny of the nation between other peoples." It would demand "the readiness for action to the last, tightened by discipline."[180] How can these phrases have referred to self-defense only? No country was menacing Hitler's Germany at that time. It may have been true that Heidegger privately thought of Heraclitus when he used the word *Kampf* in the rectoral address, although he does not mention him. But how should the audience in 1933 have known this, when Heidegger said, for instance, that "the questionable nature of Being itself forces the people to work and to fight [*Kampf*], and forces it into a state," and that "all capacities of the will and the mind, all powers of the heart, and all bodily skills must be developed *by* fight [*Kampf*], increased *in* fight, and preserved *as* fight"?[181] The audience at the time would have had associations with Hitler's *Mein Kampf*, and not with Heraclitus. Moreover, instead of referring to Heraclitus, Heidegger quoted Carl von Clausewitz immediately after this phrase on *Kampf*, and we know that he advocated Hitler's policy of including all German-speaking peoples within the German *Reich*.[182] Clearly, Heidegger put his gift for reinterpreting his own works to other uses than purely postmonotheist ones.

We should be suspicious, then, not only regarding Heidegger's later account of his political activities, but also regarding Heidegger's exegesis of his earlier political philosophy. In the case of the rectoral address, this suspicion merely concerns Heidegger's allegedly authoritative interpretations, and not the wording of the text itself, which was published in 1933. But what should we think of Heidegger's later editions of texts written between 1933 and 1945 or of the edition of the collected works?

There are at least two clear cases where Heidegger without notice changed an original text on Nazism in a later edition.[183] In his 1953 edition of *Einführung in die Metaphysik* (1935), we read that "what nowadays is offered everywhere as the philosophy of National Socialism . . . has no relation at all to the inner truth and greatness of this movement." In parentheses, Heidegger then explains that this inner truth and greatness consists in the encounter between planetary technology and modern man.[184] Heidegger claims that he endorsed this explanation already in 1935, when he delivered the lectures, for he says in the preface that what is printed between parentheses was written at the same time as the original text. However, this is not probable.[185] Heidegger developed his views on "planetary technology" after 1935. It would have been easy to verify the reliability of Heidegger's edition by collating it with the manuscript, but Otto Pöggeler discovered that the relevant page of the manuscript is missing.[186] Interestingly, the passage between parentheses was lacking in the galley proofs of the edition of 1953.[187] We can only conclude that Heidegger added the text in brackets while reading the proofs, thereby altogether reversing the meaning of the original lecture.[188] What Heidegger meant in 1935 was that his philosophy of Being was the only valid foundation of National Socialism, whereas his philosophical rivals, such as Krieck and Baumgarten, in the attempt to give a philosophical basis to Nazism could not grasp the "inner truth and greatness of this movement." Incidentally, Hitler frequently used the phrase "inner truth and greatness of the movement" when talking about the successes of his Party. The addition of 1953 means, on the contrary, that Heidegger would have considered Nazism as "a symptom of the tragic collision of man and technology." As such a symptom, Nazism would have had its greatness "because it affects the entirety of the West and threatens to pull it into destruction." At least, this was the interpretation developed by Christian E. Lewalter in reply to Habermas's letter in *Frankfurter Allgemeine Zeitung* of 25 July 1953.[189] Heidegger eagerly endorsed Lewalter's interpretation in a letter to *Die Zeit*, published on 24 September 1953, adding that there was no need to remove the passage on National Socialism, because "the lecture itself can clarify it to a reader who has learned the craft of thinking."[190] In short, Heidegger lied about the origin of the passage between parentheses, offered an interpretation of his text of 1935 that contradicts its original intentions, and accuses readers who took the text at face value of not having learned the craft of thinking.

In a second case of textual manipulation, Heidegger apparently thought that even those who master the craft of thinking would misunderstand him. From the 1971 edition by Hildegard Feick of his lectures on Schelling, given in the summer of 1936, a passage on Hitler and Mussolini was omitted, in which Heidegger said that these "two men, who launched countermovements [against nihilism] in Europe, based on the political organization of the nation, that is, of the people, were ... influenced by Nietzsche." In the text preceding the omitted passage, Heidegger discussed Nietzsche's diagnosis of the modern era, according to which this era is characterized by the rise of nihilism. Heidegger still endorsed Nietzsche's definition of nihilism as the process of devaluation of values, which causes an inner disintegration of human life. He saw Hitler and Mussolini as leaders who attempted to fight nihilism and to revitalize their peoples, inspired as they were by Nietzschean philosophy. After Karl Ulmer, a former philosophy student, had notified the public about this omission in a letter to *Der Spiegel,* the editors of the collected works could not but publish the original text.[191] It is clear why Heidegger omitted the passage on Hitler and Mussolini from the 1971 edition: it contradicts his later interpretation of Nietzsche as an *expression* of nihilism, and it would explode Heidegger's strategy of projecting this later interpretation, which he developed after 1936, back into his earlier texts (see § 15, below). Strangely enough, Ingrid Schüßler, the editor of the *Gesamtausgabe* volume 42, does not breathe a word about this difference between the two editions in her postscript to the volume.

From these examples we may conclude that not only Heidegger's later interpretations of texts published between 1932 and 1945, but also the very editions of texts that were written in this period but published after the war, may be contaminated by his attempt to launder his political past. In order to discover the extent of this contamination, we should carefully compare Heidegger's postwar editions of lecture courses delivered during the Hitler era with the editions in the collected works. Even the edition of the collected works is not beyond suspicion. Heidegger wanted the collected works to be his final authorized edition, an *Ausgabe letzter hand*, as the prospectus says. To this end, he ruled that the editors should integrate later additions into the texts themselves, adapting the style of the additions to the style of the main text. Moreover, he did not want the edition to be a critical one. There may have been many good reasons for this procedure. But how will the reader be able to know whether it did not also serve Heidegger's apologetics?

I now come to the third reason why a discussion of Heidegger's relation to Nazism is imperative, and this may very well be the most serious one. Although after the war Heidegger tried to conceal the extent of his involvement with Nazism, in 1962 Guido Schneeberger reedited a number of texts published in 1933–34, which clearly show Heidegger's Nazi convictions of the time. For instance, in an address to the German students of 3 November 1933, Heidegger incited them to participate in the National Socialist revolution, using an extremely militant rhetoric. Talents and privileges had to "prove their worth by the power of fighting action in the struggle for itself of the entire people"; the "courage to sacrifice should grow incessantly"; not maxims and ideas should be the rules of life, but "the *Führer* himself and alone *is* present-day and future German reality and its law."[192] In this text, Heidegger substitutes the authority of Hitler for the claims of morality. The third reason for discussing Heidegger's relation to Nazism is that Heidegger never officially and unambiguously retracted these and other philosophical views, which makes him co-responsible for the horrors of Nazi Germany.[193] As Herbert Marcuse wrote to Heidegger on 28 August 1947, Heidegger neither before nor after 1945 took back in public his Nazi doctrines of 1933.[194] He stayed in Nazi Germany, even though he could easily have found a post abroad. And he never condemned publicly any of the crimes committed by the National Socialist regime.[195] To Marcuse's request to express his views on the liquidation of millions of Jews, Heidegger replied that this was not worse than what the Allied countries had done to the Germans from the East, that is, to those who were expelled from East Prussia and from the parts of Germany that were handed over to the Poles after the war. In his second letter, Marcuse concluded that by giving this reply, Heidegger had placed himself outside the sphere in which intercourse between human beings is possible.[196] How could Heidegger compare the genocide of the Jews to the forced migration and incidental murder of the East Germans? And how could he assume that the responsibility for Nazi crimes might be rejected with the argument that the Allied forces had done similar things? Surely one cannot justify Heidegger's silence after the war by saying that, if Heidegger had condemned National Socialism, he would have implied a greater responsibility for its crimes than he in fact had, as Safranski argues.[197] Not only would a public condemnation have implied nothing of the sort, but, more seriously, Heidegger made himself as responsible for Hitler's crimes as a philosopher *qualitate qua* can be, by substituting Hitler's authority for the claims of morality and reason in 1933. As Paul Celan seems to have found out in 1967 and 1970, Heidegger's refusal to condemn Nazi crimes lasted until the very end. It is at least legitimate to question the extent to which this attitude regarding Nazi Germany is connected to Heidegger's later philosophy.

Given these three reasons for investigating the relations between Heidegger's philosophy and his National Socialist sympathies, it is not surprising that there is an ever-growing stream of publications, even books, on Heidegger's Nazism.[198] Let me briefly summarize some results before fixing the objectives of this section. One might distinguish four approaches in the literature. The most basic task is to establish the facts of Heidegger's Nazi past. There are a great number of expert Heidegger scholars who have invested their philosophical careers in Heidegger. For that reason they may not be eager to defile Heidegger's name. It is no wonder, then, that the most important embarrassing facts were established by philosophical outsiders such as Hugo Ott, Victor Farias, and Guido Schneeberger.[199] I have summarized some of their results just now, but probably there is still a wealth of material to be discovered in archives.

A second task is to compare Heidegger's attitude during the Hitler era with the attitude of other German philosophers and intellectuals. Hans Sluga has studied a sample of German philosophers who became members of the Nazi Party between 1932 and 1940. He concludes that when the totalitarian state was established, the strife between philosophical factions in Germany was not abolished but merely politicized. In order to survive within the system, National Socialist philosophers had to argue that their views were close to Nazism, and many philosophers claimed to have provided Nazism with philosophical foundations. Perhaps this fact puts into perspective Heidegger's contention in 1936 that his political involvement was based on the philosophy of *Sein und Zeit*.[200] But it also weakens his claim that after 1934 he was attacked by the Party: an attack by Ernst Krieck may have been nothing more than an assault by someone who competed with Heidegger in the attempt to develop a philosophy of Nazism.[201]

In the third place, we might look for passages in Heidegger's works that either straightforwardly express Nazi doctrines or in which related views are developed. As I suggested above, such an investigation should not be based on the edition of the collected works, but on the manuscripts themselves, and it should take into account all Heidegger's letters of the period. Having established a survey of the relevant texts, one might then proceed to compare Heidegger's views with those of successful Nazi ideologues such as A. Rosenberg, A. Bäumler, E. Krieck, H. Schwarz, H. Heyse, and others. It has been argued that Heidegger's philosophy has nothing in common with National Socialism.[202] But this is an unphilosophical statement: most views have something in common, and Heidegger's philosophy as expressed in 1933–45 has much more in common with the Nazi ideology as expressed in *Mein Kampf* and Hitler's speeches than with, say, Carnap's logical positivism. For instance, both Heidegger and Hitler rejected the values of the Enlightenment and preferred an authoritarian way of thinking to the tradition of free discussion and criticism. Both Hitler and Heidegger believed that they were somehow sent by Destiny, and that their personal fate was essentially linked to the destiny of the German *Volk*. Both Heidegger and Hitler talked often about heroes, struggle (*Kampf*), and sacrifice (*Opfer*), and held that the individual had to sacrifice himself or herself for the German people in their State. They both rejected democracy and endorsed the *Führerprinzip*. Hitler's revolution has been described as a revolution against reason, and Heidegger rejected logic in favor of a "turbulence of more original questioning." Both Heidegger and Hitler were revolutionaries who wanted to destroy traditional morality, Christianity, liberal bourgeois society, humanism, and Marxism.

Admittedly, there are also differences between Heidegger's (later) philosophy and Hitler's ideology. One should not expect that a trained philosopher would agree completely with a self-educated political agitator. Heidegger could not endorse Hitler's crude biologism and racism, if only because these doctrines squarely contradict the fundamental tenet of *Sein und Zeit* and the later works, that philosophy is the foundation of the sciences. Accordingly, Heidegger wanted to provide Nazism with a proper philosophical foundation at least in 1933–35. But if this philosophical foundation links revolutionary Germany to the Greeks, as Heidegger argued in the rectoral address, this is not a great departure from the official Party line. Nazi ideologues compared Germany both with Rome and with Greece, and according to the main founder of the racist doctrine, Houston Stuart Chamberlain, the ancient Greeks had been predominantly Aryan.[203] We might say that Heidegger aimed at substituting a spiritual version of Nazism for Hitler's crude Darwinist version.

Do such parallelisms imply the conclusion that Heidegger's "relentless pursuit of Being was *centrally* related to Nazism," as Tom Rockmore argued in his book on *Heidegger's Nazism and Philosophy*?[204] There are two reasons for being careful at this point. First, many of the themes I mentioned are not specific to Nazism. In fact, Hitler did not invent the ideological ingredients with which he concocted his political doctrine. Both Heidegger and Hitler drew on a long tradition of German nationalism and of romantic reactions against the Enlightenment, and this might explain the fact that their views were similar on so many points.[205] Second, we should investigate how central Heidegger's Nazi-like opinions are in relation to his philosophy as a whole. Do these opinions belong essentially to Heidegger's unique philosophical question, the question of being, so that "the concern with *Being* is itself intrinsically political," as Rockmore claims?[206] Or are they rather developments of Heidegger's philosophy that could have been different, given the fundamental structures of his thought? In order to answer this question, we need an interpretation of Heidegger's philosophy that distinguishes between fundamental structures and accidental details. Without an analysis of Heidegger's philosophy as a whole, we can never conclude that his question of being is centrally related to Nazism, instead of being peripherally related. Yet Rockmore, who purports to establish the former conclusion, claims that it can be substantiated without such a global analysis.[207]

Clearly, there is a fourth objective for secondary literature on Heidegger's relation to National Socialism: to answer the question of how central this relation is within the context of Heidegger's philosophy. For philosophers, this question will be the main issue. In the eight previous sections, I have attempted to develop an interpretation of Heidegger's philosophy. According to this interpretation, there are five fundamental leitmotifs in the question of being, which allegedly is the only and unique question of philosophy. The aim of the present section is to investigate the connections between these five fundamental themes and Heidegger's Nazism. As I developed my interpretation mostly without reference to Heidegger's entanglement with National Socialism, one will expect the negative conclusion that Nazism is not essential to the fundamental themes of Heidegger's thought. It does not follow, however, that Heidegger's adherence to Nazism was entirely accidental or peripheral. There is a spectrum of possible relations between a philosophy and a political position, relations of many different kinds and of different logical strengths, between the two extremes of "central" and "peripheral." Precisely because discussions of Heidegger's Nazism tend to be antagonistic, dividing the participants into the two camps of Heidegger-advocates and Heidegger-prosecutors, we have to be specific and avoid the trap of partisanship.

I proceed in three stages. First (A), I raise the question as to whether there is a route from the three leitmotifs in the question of being of *Sein und Zeit* to National Socialism. Second (B), I try to find out whether the postmonotheist leitmotif in

Heidegger's later philosophy, as developed from 1935 on, should be seen as a reaction against and implicit criticism of National Socialism, or as an attempt to develop an authentic Nazi religion. Finally (C), I briefly investigate the connections between the Neo-Hegelian theme and Heidegger's interpretation of Nazism before, during, and after the war.

A. *Nazism and Authenticity*

According to the interpretation proposed in this book, the question of being in *Sein und Zeit* is a symphony of three different leitmotifs, which I called the meta-Aristotelian theme, the phenomenologico-hermeneutical theme, and the transcendental theme. It seems to be clear that these leitmotifs as such do not have political implications. The question of being in the sense of the meta-Aristotelian theme purports to investigate the different meanings of "to be" and their alleged common root in one fundamental meaning. In the sense of the phenomenologico-hermeneutical theme, the question of being aims at developing regional ontologies, which conceptualize the ontological constitutions of different kinds of entities. In particular, it aims at a regional ontology of Dasein, because Heidegger claims that our own ontological constitution has been misinterpreted during the entire philosophical history of the West. Finally, the question of being in the transcendental sense purports to show that Dasein is a transcendental agent *in* human beings, which projects a world and thereby enables entities to be.

At first sight, then, one will conclude from my interpretation of the question of being that *Sein und Zeit* is an unpolitical book. This conclusion seems to be corroborated by Heidegger's distinction between an ontological level and an ontical level of analysis. The hermeneutical ontology of human beings conceptualizes the existential structure of Dasein, which is supposed to be essentially the same, regardless of however, whenever, or wherever humans in fact shape their lives.[208] The ontological or *existenzial* level should be carefully kept apart from the ontical or *existenziell* level. The former is supposed to be a priori, whereas the latter is empirical. Accordingly, the ontology of Dasein in *Sein und Zeit* should be compatible with all possible political systems, and it should not imply or favor one political ideology over another. It may be that the existential analysis of *Sein und Zeit* is contaminated by cultural vogues of the interbellum, and that Heidegger sometimes interlarded his ontology with a critique of contemporary society. One might argue, however, that such contaminations are not essential to Heidegger's project, and that one should not pay too much attention to them. It would be altogether mistaken to claim that Heidegger's concern with Being is intrinsically political.[209] *Sein und Zeit* is an unpolitical book because it is concerned with ontology. This is the received view of traditional Heideggerians.[210]

The received view has been contested by external critics such as Bourdieu, who pointed out that Heidegger's distinction between an ontological level and an ontical level of analysis is untenable, and that, in fact, theorists on human nature such as Hobbes or Rousseau designed their ontology of humans with specific political implications in mind. Heidegger's ontological stance might be an ideological device that masks his unavowed or repressed political drives. Furthermore, it has been suggested that there is a structural analogy between Heidegger's conservative revolution in philosophy, which aspired to reinstate philosophy in the fundamental position from which it had been dismissed by scientific advances in the first quarter of the twentieth century, and the conservative revolution of the National Socialists. Bourdieu concludes that Heidegger's purely philosophical choices have political implications, even if these implications were not consciously envisaged by Heidegger himself.[211]

There are two problems with this line of external critique. First, speculations about unavowed or repressed political instincts, which allegedly produce political connotations within theoretical texts, are immune to empirical assessment. Second, even if there were a structural analogy—a "homology" as Bourdieu says—between the philosophical and the political domains, this does not prove that a philosophical view that occupies a position in the philosophical domain topologically similar to the position of a specific political view in the political domain implies or suggests that political view. It is true that Heidegger tried to reinstate philosophy as a fundamental discipline as against those who reduced it to epistemology or to the theory of science. In this sense, Heidegger staged a conservative revolution in philosophy. But Husserl did likewise. If, therefore, one argues that Heidegger's conservative revolution in philosophy connoted the National Socialist conservative revolution in politics, on the sole ground that there is a structural analogy between the political and the philosophical, one should also endorse the absurdity that Husserl's transcendental philosophy connotes the Nazi ideology.[212]

In this subsection I reject both a dogmatically unpolitical interpretation of *Sein und Zeit* and an external critique that is not borne out by textual analysis. It has been argued by many authors that Heidegger's notion of authenticity points to a transition between his ontological analysis and the ontical level of factual existence. In particular, the notion of authenticity as resoluteness allegedly induces us to "resolute action," regardless of traditional moral considerations. Even though the ideal of resoluteness is formal in the sense that Heidegger does not recommend particular resolutions, it is said to predispose Heidegger and his readers to some form of political radicalism or "decisionism."[213] Let me now spell out this line of argument, which I endorse, in some detail. I will try to determine to what extent Heidegger's ideal of authenticity in *Sein und Zeit* might have been a motive for his decision to join the Nazis in 1933. It goes without saying that Heidegger may have had many extraphilosophical motives for his decision as well, but analyzing them falls outside the scope of this book.

Heidegger's notion of authenticity (*Eigentlichkeit*) has many dimensions, and I discuss the most relevant ones only. One dimension is that the notion links the ontical and the ontological levels in *Sein und Zeit*, and it does so in two directions.

First, we allegedly see our Dasein as it really is, as finite being-toward-death, only in moments of authenticity. Mostly, Heidegger claims, we divert our attention from the human condition, fleeing from it into worldly occupations, and the tendency of falling (*Verfallen*) is a structural characteristic of our mode of being. This means that the proper ontological level for analyzing Dasein is accessible only from a specific ontical stance, the stance of authenticity. Authenticity is the ontical condition for the possibility of doing ontology aright. As long as we are not authentic, we will misinterpret the existential structure of Dasein, and we will not be able to understand *Sein und Zeit*.

Second, the ontological analysis of authenticity as a possibility of Dasein refers us back to the ontical level. In section 75 of *Sein und Zeit*, for instance, Heidegger points out that without authentic resoluteness, Dasein will be dispersed and it will disintegrate into a series of disconnected experiences. The philosophical problem as to what explains the unity of our stream of consciousness, which is raised by authors on personal identity in the tradition of Locke and Hume such as Wilhelm Dilthey, allegedly is a pseudo-problem due to an inauthentic and dispersed mode of Dasein. Only by resolutely being-toward-death will we be able to get a grip on our life as a whole, and to bring about (*zeitigen*) the time of our life (*Zeit*) in the manner of "existentiell constancy" (*existenzielle Ständigkeit*).[214] These observations, if correct, are ontological results. But they imply an ideal of ontical existence: that we be resolute in our own life. The notion of resoluteness is a formal one in that an ontological analysis can never prescribe what we should decide at specific moments. As Heidegger says in section 60 of *Sein und Zeit*: "Resoluteness, by its ontological essence, is always the resoluteness of some factical Dasein at a particular time. . . . But on what is it to resolve? *Only* the resolution itself can give the answer."[215] Yet, the ontological notion of resoluteness refers us back to the actual situations of life, and encourages us to be resolute in our individual existence. As an ontological interpretation, it "liberates Dasein for its uttermost possibility of existence."[216] Technically speaking, the notion is a formal indication (*formale Anzeige*).

Heidegger developed the methodological concept of a formal indication already in 1919–21 (see § 8B).[217] But the most striking account of this slippery notion is to be found in his monumental lectures on the basic concepts of metaphysics, read during the winter semester of 1929–30, when Germany was plunged into the depths of economic crisis. The ontological concepts of the analysis of Dasein, Heidegger says, should not be taken as referring to characteristics of some actual entity. Rather, they are *formal indications* in the sense that by showing the ontological form of our existence, they indicate the necessity for us to wrest ourselves from the vulgar interpretation of being, and "to transform ourselves into the Da-sein in us." The concepts are *formal* because they will never connote the individual ontical content of the life of each of us. They are *indicative* because they point to a concrete and individual existence, inciting us to transform ourselves into authentic Dasein.[218]

The notions of authenticity and formal indication are fundamental to Heidegger's intentions in *Sein und Zeit*, even though the latter notion is not conspicuously present in the text.[219] Clearly, the ontology of Dasein is not an aim in itself. It is only a *way*, as Heidegger stresses at the end of the book in section 83. This way leads from the ontical level of our individual existence, via the reflexive detour of ontological conceptualization, back to ontical existence, which the ontological analysis purports to transform. In his religion course of 1920–21, Heidegger said that philosophy "springs from factical life experience . . . and then springs right back into factical life experience."[220] We find an echo of this statement in section 7 of *Sein und Zeit*, where Heidegger writes: "Philosophy is universal phenomenological ontology, and takes its departure from the hermeneutic of Dasein, which, as an analytic of *existence*, has made fast the guiding-line for all philosophical inquiry at the point where it *arises* and to which it *returns*."[221] These considerations lead us to an important result. If the guiding line of all philosophical inquiry not only begins at the ontical level of our individual existence, but also returns to this level, Heidegger's distinction between the ontological and the ontical cannot be used for arguing that *Sein und Zeit* is a theoretical book that is not related to Heidegger's life. On the contrary, the point of the book, and, indeed, of philosophy in Heidegger's sense, seems to be that one becomes more authentic in one's individual existence. If this is the case, it is perfectly legitimate to ask whether Heidegger's ideal of authenticity in *Sein und Zeit* predisposes one to Nazism.

Let us admit, then, that the ultimate objective of Heidegger's ontological enterprise in *Sein und Zeit* is practical, or rather *existenziell*: to become more authentic in one's actual life. According to Rockmore, it automatically follows that "fundamental ontology is basically political." However, this conclusion can be deduced only if one takes the term "political" in an unusually wide sense. As Rockmore writes: "*Being and Time* . . . is not political in the sense of . . . Machiavelli's *The Prince* or Hobbes's *Leviathan*. . . . But it is political in another, more basic sense, concerning the realization of human being in the human context."[222] Even so, we are not interested in this more basic sense of the term "political." What we want to know is whether there is a possible link between the notion of authenticity in *Sein und Zeit* and Heidegger's Nazism. His decision to become a Nazi was political in the ordinary sense of the term: Heidegger became member of the National Socialist Party; he had certain ideas, however vague, about what kind of state the German people needed in order to actualize their "destiny"; and he thought that the philosopher should guide the party by providing a philosophical foundation to Nazism. By introducing an ambiguity into the term "political," Rockmore avoids rather than solves the problem as to the relation between *Sein und Zeit* and Heidegger's Nazism. Even worse, the ambiguity leads to a fallacy of equivocation if one infers from the political nature of *Sein und Zeit* in Rockmore's idiosyncratic sense that the book is political in the usual sense. Rockmore actually commits this fallacy where he writes that "Heidegger's conception of ontology commits him, as a condition of thinking through the problem of the meaning of 'Being', to a political understanding of human being, that is, to an idea of the person as mainly inauthentic but as possibly authentic in a concrete fashion. The very concern with fundamental ontology requires a political turn."[223] Rockmore suggests here that Heidegger in *Sein und Zeit* endorses the Platonic idea that a really good (authentic) man can only exist in a good (authentic) political body, and that our personal authenticity would require a political revolution. However, it is not at all clear that this was Heidegger's opinion when he wrote *Sein und Zeit*.

Heidegger develops his notion of authenticity in sections 40, 53, 60, and 62 of the book, analyzing the four dimensions of *Angst*, being-toward-death, conscience, and resoluteness. He constantly opposes authenticity to Dasein's impersonal mode of existence, Everyman or the One (*das Man*). Whereas usually One flees *Angst*, authentic Dasein confronts *Angst*, thereby acquiring "the freedom of choosing itself and taking hold of itself" (§ 40). Similarly, One tries to forget one's mortality, whereas authentic Dasein, by anticipating death as its ownmost possibility, which nobody else can actualize in its place, may wrench itself away from the One or the They, and project itself on its ownmost potentiality-for-being (§ 53).[224] The possibility of authentic existence discloses itself to us in the call of conscience, and authentic resoluteness means to be summoned out of one's lostness in Everyman (§ 60).[225] Finally, authentic resoluteness enables us to grasp our Dasein as a whole, whereas One experiences life as fragmented and dispersed (§ 62).

We get the impression from these sections that Heidegger's ideal of authenticity is that of a radical individualism. Heidegger consistently stresses that authenticity individualizes and isolates us (*vereinzeln*). He says, for instance, that "Anxiety individualizes Dasein for its ownmost Being-in-the-world," and that it "thus discloses it as *'solus ipse.'* "[226] Death, as understood in authentic anticipation, also "individualizes Dasein down to itself."[227] Understanding the call of conscience "discloses one's own Dasein in the uncanniness of its individualization."[228] Moreover, authentic individualization seems to be difficult to square with "worldly" calls such as that of politics: "The call of conscience passes over in its appeal all Dasein's 'worldly' prestige and potentialities. Relentlessly it individualizes Dasein down to its potentiality-for-being-guilty, and exacts of it that it should be this potentiality authentically."[229]

The unprejudiced reader cannot but conclude from these texts that according to Heidegger, authentic Dasein is individualistic in the extreme. It is resolute by making its own decisions, and, as Heidegger says, "the certainty of the resolution signifies that one holds oneself free for the possibility of taking it back."[230] Authenticity in this sense seems to be incompatible with Heidegger's unconditional surrender to Hitler's authority in 1933. The impression of an incompatibility between the idea of authenticity and Heidegger's submission to Hitler in 1933 is reinforced by the insight that Heidegger's concept of authenticity in *Sein und Zeit* is a secularized version of Kierkegaard's notion of the absolute commitment of faith.[231] Kierkegaard's notion is utterly individualistic as well, because the leap to faith that brings the individual before God presupposes that one disentangles one-self from one's involvement in worldly occupations. For Kierkegaard, political action would be counterproductive if one wants to be authentic.[232]

Admittedly, it has been argued that Heidegger introduced a contradiction into Kierkegaard's notion by secularizing it. Heidegger's and Kierkegaard's idea that one has to disentangle oneself radically from Everyman or the They and worldly occupations in order to become authentic does not make sense unless one assumes the possibility of a radically unworldly life, a possibility that Heidegger does not want to consider in *Sein und Zeit*. As a consequence, it seems that Heidegger's authenticity cannot be a choice for a possibility radically different from worldly ones, as in Kierkegaard. It can only be a radically different way of choosing for common and ordinary possibilities. Even so, Heidegger maintained Kierkegaard's individualistic rhetoric. This rhetoric is incompatible with the collectivist ideology of National Socialism, according to which "the individual, wherever he stands, does not count," and "what counts only is the destiny of our people in their state," as Heidegger told the staff of Freiburg University on 20 December 1933.

Should we then conclude that Heidegger's notion of authenticity in *Sein und Zeit*, even though it connects ontology to actual life, cannot in the least explain Heidegger's conversion to Nazism, because it is thoroughly individualistic? Should we assume that Heidegger's conversion must have been due to extraphilosophical motives only, motives similar to those which led so many Germans to vote for Hitler? Perhaps it would have been warranted to draw this conclusion, if Heidegger had not written section 74 of *Sein und Zeit*. Indeed, Heidegger told his former pupil Karl Löwith in 1936 that his choice for Hitler had been based on his notion of historicality, which is developed in section 74.[233]

In this section, on the "Basic Constitution of Historicality," Heidegger attempts to describe the way in which authentic Dasein "happens," suggesting that Dasein has a history (*Geschichte*) because of the structural way in which it happens (*geschieht*). This way is then called historicality (*Geschichtlichkeit*). Authenticity was characterized by resoluteness, and resoluteness is a projecting of oneself upon one's own being-guilty, a projecting that is reticent, ready for anxiety (*Angst*), and anticipates death. But whence, Heidegger now asks, can Dasein draw those possibilities on which it factically projects itself?[234] Authentic Dasein projects itself into the future, anticipating its death, by resolutely choosing certain possibilities. The content of these possibilities cannot be derived from the future itself, or from death as its anticipated final term, because the future and anticipated death are empty. Heidegger concludes that the content of the possibilities that we project must be derived from the past, that is, from Dasein's thrownness (*Geworfenheit*) in a specific tradition. Factical possibilities of authentic existing must be disclosed *"in terms of the heritage* which resoluteness, as thrown, *takes over."*[235] Although Heidegger writes, somewhat misleadingly, that "only being-free for death gives Dasein its goal outright and pushes existence into its finiteness," he maintains that the factical content of a specific goal is determined authentically when Dasein "chooses its hero" from a "heritage," thereby explicitly retrieving a tradition.[236] If one authentically chooses one's goal by retrieving a tradition, and if the finiteness of one's existence snatches one back from the endless multiplicity of possibilities that offer themselves as closest to one—those of comfortableness, shirking, and taking things lightly—Dasein is brought into the simplicity of its fate (*Schicksal*).[237]

Now these notions of a hero, of fate, and of a heritage do not yet bring *Sein und Zeit* much closer to Nazism. Germans often stressed their privileged relation to the Greeks, and the Greeks of Athens invented democracy. On the basis of these notions, Heidegger could have chosen a great Greek democrat as his hero, and he could have combated Nazism. However, there is one paragraph in section 74 that seems to contain a sudden intrusion of *völkisch* (popularly nationalist) ideology in *Sein und Zeit*. Let me quote the second part of this paragraph:

> But if fateful Dasein, as being-in-the-world, exists essentially in being-with others, its historizing is a co-historizing and is determinative for it as destiny [*Geschick*]. This is how we designate the historizing of the community [*der Gemeinschaft*], of a people [*des Volkes*]. Destiny is not something that puts itself together out of individual fates, any more than being-with-one-another can be conceived as the occurring together of several subjects. Our fates have already been guided in advance, in our being-with-one-another in the same world and in our resoluteness for definite possibilities. Only in communicating and in struggling [*Kampf*] does the power of destiny become free. Dasein's fateful destiny in and with its "generation" goes to make up the full authentic historizing of Dasein.[238]

Authors such as Farias and Rockmore have made much of this passage, because it seems to express the *völkisch* ideology that was an important seedbed for Nazism.[239] Yet it is a plausible thesis that the historical unity of a people and its tribulations cannot be explained by merely tracing the lives of individuals, for the simple reason that individual human beings become what they are partly by being raised within a specific culture and language. Also, the notion of a generation is a legitimate sociological and historical concept. One might distinguish between the fate (*Schicksal*) of an individual and the destiny (*Geschick*) of a people without endorsing *völkisch* ideology. But Heidegger goes further than this, for it does not follow that the full authenticity of an individual consists in melting together one's individual fate and the destiny of one's people, as he suggests when he writes that "Dasein's fateful destiny in and with its generation goes to make up the full authentic historizing of Dasein." It does not follow either that the power of a people's destiny becomes free only in struggle or fight (*Kampf*).

By connecting these notions of struggle and fateful destiny of a people with the notions of heritage and of choosing one's hero, one might concoct the following *völkisch* interpretation of Heidegger's conception of authentic history. An individual cannot be authentic unless the people to which he or she belongs is authentic. This requires that the people choose their hero on the basis of their national heritage, and that they engage in battle or struggle (*Kampf*) in order to renew the heroic possibilities of their past. Surely such an interpretation of the quoted passage seems to yield the conclusion that *Sein und Zeit* paves the way to Nazism. The Nazi movement claimed to lead Germany from the alleged apathy of the Weimar Republic to future greatness by forcing the Germans into the national unity of a *Volk*, in which the individual does not count. In order to force the Germans into the common destiny of a *Volk*, a totalitarian revolution was necessary, and one might interpret Heidegger's kairiological notion of *Augenblick*, a propitious instant or moment of vision for authentic Dasein, as prefiguring the historical moment of the National Socialist revolution in 1933. Along these lines, Rockmore concludes that "the very concern with fundamental ontology requires a political turn," and that "the concern with 'Being' is itself intrinsically political."[240] Similarly, Farias concludes that the philosophy of *Sein und Zeit* positively establishes properly fascist tenets, which lead up to the later events.[241]

There is, however, a serious problem with Farias' and Rockmore's argument. The notion of communal authenticity as developed in section 74 of *Sein und Zeit*, even if it can be stretched in the above sense, seems to be a rather isolated occurrence of *völkisch* ideology in the book. At first sight, there is no logical or other connection between the individualist notion of authenticity as developed in sections 40, 53, 60, and 62 and the communal notion of authenticity of section 74. By stressing in the former four sections that authenticity individualizes and isolates us (*vereinzeln*), Heidegger seems to deny that authenticity can be a communal way of life. Admittedly, he sketches an authentic way of being-with-others (*Mitsein*) in section 60. But this authentic being-with-others consists in mutually letting each other be (*sein lassen*) in each other's most individual possibilities of existence.[242] This ideal of authentic being-with-others fits in better with a liberal democracy, which subscribes to the Kantian dictum that one should treat others as ends in themselves and not merely as means, than with Hitler's totalitarian state, in which the individual is reduced to a mere means for realizing the historical destiny of a mythical entity, the *Volk*.

Authors such as Farias and Rockmore, then, are faced with a dilemma. Either they have merely shown that Heidegger's Nazism is related to one isolated and accidental paragraph in section 74 of *Sein und Zeit*, which contradicts the remainder of the book. An orthodox Heideggerian might argue that this passage is an unfortunate concession to *völkisch* ideas that were in vogue at the time, and that we had better disregard it. Or, alternatively, Farias and Rockmore should provide an interpretation of Heidegger's notion of authenticity according to which the two contradictory extremes of individual and *völkisch* authenticity are intimately related—so intimately related that someone who endorses the ideal of individual authenticity might end up by submitting himself or herself to an allegedly authentic destiny of the *Volk*. Neither Farias nor Rockmore provides us with such an interpretation. This is what I attempt to do now, in a very tentative spirit.

Heidegger's ideal of individual authenticity may be seen as the final stage of a historical development in philosophy, the development of ever more radical notions of an autonomous person. The notion of an autonomous person is part and parcel with the notion of an authentic philosopher, because the philosopher is supposed be autonomous and to think for himself. Somewhat schematically, we might distinguish four stages in this development, each of which expresses one of four degrees of autonomy. Human beings are raised within a particular culture, which provides habits, traditional rules of conduct, and standardized social roles. This is why, as Heidegger says, "proximally Dasein is Everyman, and for the most part it remains so."[243] The first and lowest stage of autonomy arises when an individual is not content with strict conformity to these habits, rules, and roles, but creates a pattern for himself, by applying the rules in novel ways and by changing some of the habits. On the reflective level, this lowest stage of autonomy is expressed by the discovery of the Sophists that norms and rules are not fixed by nature but by convention.

At the lowest level of autonomy, the norms and rules are still predominantly given by "the others." It is always "They" who tell me how to behave, even though I may apply the norms in a personal way. As Heidegger says, "proximally, it is not 'I,' in the sense of my own Self, that 'am,' but rather the Others, whose way is that of the 'They.' "[244] However, if autonomy means that I liberate myself from the pressure of Others in my existence, it seems that there is room for a next degree of autonomy or authenticity. In this second stage of autonomy, the philosopher will reject traditional norms and roles as valid guidelines for conduct and thought, because they are fixed by others. He will look for insight and values on a higher or a deeper level than that of tradition. Thus Plato postulated eternal forms, Descartes assumed innate ideas that were guaranteed by God, and Hume claimed to discover basic principles of human nature. Only by thinking and acting in accordance with these forms, ideas, or principles, they thought, will we be able to become really authentic.

With Immanuel Kant, the notion of authenticity as autonomy entered its third stage. Kant argued that Plato's Forms, God's ideas, or empirical principles of human nature are still external or heteronomous elements, which are not determined by ourselves, that is, by our rational choice. If autonomy means that one determines one's own rules, these rules should be freely chosen on the basis of rational insight. Kant defined freedom as the capacity to give oneself a law out of respect for this law. His categorical imperative would enable us to determine rationally which maxims deserve respect and should be elevated to the status of moral laws. Enlightened autonomy, Kant wrote in his celebrated essay *Was ist Aufklärung?* of 1784 means that we think for ourselves and decide what to do on the basis of reason alone. For Kant, philosophical authenticity in the sense of autonomy consists in a superior form of rationality.

But this notion of rational authenticity is exploded by a criticism that Nietzsche raised. Kant's allegedly rational criterion for choosing maxims as moral laws boils down to the question of whether maxims can be universalized without a contradiction. Kant argued, for instance, that the maxim "I am allowed to lie" cannot be universalized, because the conditions required for my successful lying would be destroyed if everyone lied. Therefore it is an immoral maxim. Nietzsche objects that the criterion of universalizability is not a purely rational criterion. On the contrary, the idea that moral norms should be the same for all humans is a moral norm itself, which is not at all self-evident. The norm is rejected by aristocratic cultures, and, in fact, it serves the interests of the weak in a society as against the strong. If so, Kant's principle of rational choice between maxims is a heteronomous principle, which expresses the interests of the weak in society, and it should be abandoned by an autonomous individual. The idea that we can determine what principles are morally valid by pure reason alone turns out to be an illusion.

As a consequence of this critique, the ideal of authenticity as autonomy enters its fourth stage, which is the stage of Heidegger's *Sein und Zeit*. We now see, or are supposed to see, that the autonomous person cannot rely on *any* ideas or principles in making his authentic choices. A resolute choice becomes its own "justification." Any choice is justified, if only it is a resolute one. When Heidegger raises the question on what Dasein is to resolve, he answers: "*Only* the resolution itself can give the answer."[245] By stressing the word "only" Heidegger suggests that according to his conception all moral and political norms or ideas belong to the sphere of the They, and that we should disregard preexisting norms if we want to be authentic.

The claim that this voluntarist and decisionist doctrine of authenticity is defended in *Sein und Zeit* is confirmed by Heidegger's notion of authentic truth. We remember that according to the transcendental notion of truth sketched in section 44 of *Sein und Zeit*, truth is not primarily a relation between what one asserts and reality: it is the fundamental openness (*Erschlossenheit*) of Dasein, which enables entities to "be." Because openness is characterized by projection (*Entwurf*), and authentic projection is a product of resoluteness (*Entschlossenheit*), the transcendental notion of truth gives rise to a notion of authentic truth of existence (*Wahrheit der Existenz*). In resoluteness (*Entschlossenheit*), we are disclosed to ourselves in an authentic way, and a situation is disclosed to us in which we have to act (*Situation*). This is what Heidegger calls the truth of existence (*Wahrheit der Existenz*). If Dasein is resolute, it will become clear-sighted for the situation (*Situation*) in which it has to act and for the propitious instant (*Augenblick*) at which it has to act.[246] However, if only the resolution itself determines what we should decide, the truth of existence in this sense cannot be evaluated by moral or other criteria. According to Heidegger's decisionist notion of authenticity, we are justified by resoluteness alone. The situation in which we act authentically "gets disclosed in a free resolving that has not been determined beforehand." The certainty of the truth of existence purely consists in that Dasein "maintains itself in what is disclosed by the resolution."[247]

It has been argued that Heidegger's decisionist notion of authenticity is, as it were, a negative condition for the possibility of Nazism. By relegating moral and political norms to the domain of inauthenticity (*das Man*), Heidegger destroyed all possible moral obstacles to a totalitarian choice.[248] But this negative condition is not sufficient for arguing that *Sein und Zeit* predisposed Heidegger to Nazism. It remains true that his concept of authenticity, as developed thus far, is utterly individualistic, and that it is difficult to reconcile this concept with the *völkisch* notion of authenticity that emerges in one isolated paragraph in section 74 of the book. Is there a relation between these two concepts of authenticity? This is the main question that my interpretation intends to solve.

In order to answer it, two insights are essential. On the one hand, Heidegger's notion of authenticity is the fourth and most extreme stage of development of the concept of autonomy. If moral rules are all heteronomous, they cannot restrict our authentic and autonomous freedom. Consequently, nothing guides free resolute choices. Although it is finite in the sense of being-toward-death, our freedom is a "supreme power," as Heidegger says in section 74.[249] On the other hand, such a supreme power of freedom is also a form of "powerlessness," because in it, Dasein is left entirely to its own devices, and cannot rely on the culture that sustains it in its inauthentic life.[250] Whereas "Dasein in its everydayness is disburdened [*entlastet*] by the They," authentic resoluteness destroys the disburdening function of the culture that supports us, and thereby reveals our Dasein as a burden.[251]

Now I want to suggest that the burden of authentic resoluteness as Heidegger sees it is in principle unbearable. It is simply impossible to be resolute without relying somehow and to some extent on preexisting cultural roles and norms. This is why Heidegger's individualistic notion of authenticity, according to which Dasein has to liberate itself from common moral rules in order to choose one's hero freely, tends to collapse into a collectivist notion, according to which the choice is not made by an individual at all, but is predetermined by the destiny of the *Volk* to which one belongs. Once Dasein has become authentic by liberating itself from standard morality, life becomes unbearable, and the liberated individual will seek to shake off the burden of radical individuation (*vereinzelung*) by joining a collectivist mob.

Heidegger did not analyze this collapse as such. According to him, we might attain the ideal of individual authenticity at least in some privileged instants. I am suggesting the interpretative hypothesis that this collapse of the individualistic ideal of authenticity into a collectivist notion is what is *happening* in the crucial paragraph of section 74, of which I already quoted the second half. Heidegger starts this paragraph by the observation that the superior power of authentic freedom is simultaneously a form of powerlessness, because Dasein is left to its own devices. Assuming this powerless supreme power, "Dasein becomes clairvoyant for what happens to devolve upon it in the situation that has been disclosed."[252] Heidegger then develops his notion of Dasein's fateful destiny within the commu-

nity of a *Volk,* and claims that individual fates are "guided" by the power of a
common destiny, which "becomes free in communication and struggle."

We may conclude, then, that the relation between Heidegger's individualistic
notion of authenticity and his *völkisch* notion is not one of logical implication but
at best a psychological one. Because of the very fact that individual authenticity
as Heidegger sees it is unendurable, Dasein, which has liberated itself from preexisting morality in its attempt to become authentic, will tend to subject itself to the
first collectivist movement that comes along, provided that this movement claims
to actualize the national Destiny. The philosophical destruction of traditional culture in *Sein und Zeit,* which was in accord with many trends of "cultural despair"
in Germany during the interbellum, created an absolute void or "nothing" for the
individual who longs for authenticity, and, psychologically speaking, this void
generated the temptation of a leap to faith or to a totalitarian movement.

In this sense, *Sein und Zeit* prefigures Heidegger's appeal to the German students of 3 November 1933, a text in which we find the same characteristic collapse
of his notion of authenticity into authoritarianism. In accordance with the ideal
of authenticity of *Sein und Zeit,* Heidegger first claims that "not maxims and
'ideas' should be the guidelines" of the students' lives. In order to be authentic,
the students should make their own resolute decision. But because the individual
fates had already been determined by the destiny of Hitler's revolution, the "full
authentic historizing of Dasein" for Germans in 1933 could only consist in an
unconditional submission to Hitler.[253] As Heidegger wrote: "the *Führer* himself
and alone *is* the present and future German reality and its law."[254]

B. An Authentic Nazi Religion?

One might object to the somewhat speculative argument I developed thus far that
it does not cohere with my global interpretation of *Sein und Zeit.* From the fact
that authenticity in Heidegger's sense of a resolute and radical autonomy is unendurable, I concluded that it tends to collapse into totalitarianism. This tendency
would explain both the transition to the notion of *völkisch* authenticity in section
74 of *Sein und Zeit* and Heidegger's own transition to Nazism in 1931–33, at least
to the extent that the latter can be explained by intraphilosophical motives. But the
hypothesis of such a tendency to collapse is a *psychological* one only. Logically
speaking, other solutions are available to the authentic individual who experiences
life as an unbearable burden. One of these solutions is the leap to religion.

In sections 12C and 13C, above, I argued that *Sein und Zeit* must be interpreted
as the first stage of a Pascalian strategy. According to this strategy, an analysis of
the human condition should reveal that authentic existence is an unbearable burden, from which we try to escape into forms of inauthenticity or diversion. Such
an analysis of the human condition would prepare the second stage of the strategy:
the leap to faith. This interpretation removes the contradiction within Heidegger's
notion of authenticity to which I referred above: that it would not make sense to

postulate that an authentic individual should be radically independent of existing culture if there were no possibility of existence independently of this culture. According to the Pascalian strategy, there is such a possibility, the existence in faith, so that the contradiction disappears. However, if *Sein und Zeit* was intended to prepare a leap to faith, can it be meant to prepare a revolutionary transition to a totalitarian state?[255] In order to solve this problem in my interpretation, we have to raise the following question: How does the postmonotheist theme relate to Heidegger's Nazism? I will briefly sketch my answer and then, equally briefly, discuss the relation between Heidegger's Nazism and the Neo-Hegelian leitmotif. A full treatment of these topics would require another book.

If *Sein und Zeit* is the first stage of a Pascalian strategy, where, in Heidegger's subsequent writings, do we find the second stage, which urges us to make the leap to faith? The early Heidegger conceived of faith as a grace of God, a conception that is clearly expressed in the lecture on phenomenology and theology of 1927. It follows that the leap to faith, to the extent that we humans are capable of it, is in fact a leap into nothingness, and that we may only hope that nothingness will reveal itself as identical to Being or God. Heidegger urges us "to release ourselves into nothingness" at the end of *Was ist Metaphysik?*, his inaugural lecture of 1929. We should "liberate ourselves from those idols everyone has," and we should "let the sweep of our suspense take its full course," so that it "swings back into the basic question of metaphysics that nothingness itself compels: Why are there beings at all, and why not rather nothing?"[256] These admonitions have a clear religious meaning. The traditional metaphysical answer to the question as to why there are beings and not rather nothing is: because God sustains them. If the Pascalian interpretation of *Sein und Zeit* is correct, the analysis of Dasein in that book leads us back to traditional metaphysics in the sense of a quest for Being or God. It prepares us for a turn, and, according to my interpretation, *Was ist Metaphysik?* tries to invite Being to turn toward us. Heidegger's inaugural lecture is the second stage of his Pascalian strategy, and the fact that this markedly religious text was written two years after the publication of *Sein und Zeit* confirms the Pascalian interpretation of Heidegger's masterpiece (see §§ 12C and 13C, above).

Heidegger elaborated this second stage in his impressive lecture series on the *Fundamental Concepts of Metaphysics* of 1929–30, which, as he wrote to Elisabeth Blochmann, was meant to make an entirely new start.[257] The objective of this series is to transform Dasein. We should "find ourselves in such a way that we are *given back* to ourselves." In order to prepare us for this transformation, Heidegger tries to arouse the fundamental mood of boredom.[258] Boredom in the deepest sense allegedly consists in an inner emptiness, in the fact that "the *mystery* is lacking in our Dasein." As a consequence, "the inner dread does not come, which each mystery brings with it, and which gives to Dasein its inner greatness." The deepest and most essential deprivation in our Dasein is not that we are plagued by particular pressing needs, but that an essential deprivation is refused to us, and that we do not even hear of it.[259] In an influential paper, Winfried Franzen interpreted section 38 of these lectures as prefiguring the National Socialist contempt for civilized bourgeois life. The section would express a yearning for hardness and gravity (*Härte und Schwere*), which, even though it is a philosophical theme in the lectures, would predispose Heidegger to political involvement with the Nazis.[260] However, one should read Heidegger's yearning for hardship primarily in a religious sense, rather than as an anticipation of Nazism. Heidegger's lectures of 1929–30 are akin to Kierkegaard's essay on *The Present Age*. When Heidegger rejects as superficial the needs of his time, which were urgent during the depression of 1929, he does so because a preoccupation with these needs suppresses what is according to him our real need: to acquire again the knowledge of "what it is that makes us possible."[261] Heidegger does not and cannot tell us what it is that makes us possible, except that Dasein has to become authentic. What makes us possible can only reveal itself to us in grace. Therefore, we have to wait, in order to hear essential things, when we tune in on (*stimmen*) the fundamental mood (*Grundstimmung*) of boredom.[262] The lectures on the fundamental concepts of metaphysics of 1929–30 aim at preparing us for a religious conversion, as did *Was ist Metaphysik?* and Kierkegaard's *The Present Age*.

This interpretation of the lectures is consonant with the Pascalian view of *Sein und Zeit*. But it gives a special urgency to the objection I raised. If Heidegger was heading for religious grace even in 1930, how should we explain the fact that he opted for Hitler only two years later? A first possible answer to this question is speculative but simple. Heidegger tells us in the "Brief über den 'Humanismus' " that the turn as envisaged in *Sein und Zeit* could not be expressed in the language of metaphysics.[263] What he meant is, one might suggest, that religious grace, conceived of as an answer by Being to our metaphysical quest, did not arrive in 1929–32. If it is indeed true that Heidegger's entire philosophical enterprise from the Natorp essay of 1922 to the lectures of 1929–30 is a preparation for metaphysical grace by means of methodological atheism, this must have been a terrible deception. The turn to Nazism can now be explained, at least in part, as the product of a religious disappointment. Heidegger discovered that man is abandoned in the midst of beings. I argued that Heidegger's ideal of authenticity predisposed him to some kind of absolute and radical solution, because authenticity in Heidegger's sense makes life unbearable. As the religious solution (the grace of faith) turned out to be unavailable, the only alternative left was a totalitarian movement, which would radically relieve the burden of autonomous existence. In short: Heideggerian authenticity plus atheism yields totalitarianism.

That this hypothesis is not altogether implausible is shown by the central role of Nietzsche in Heidegger's rectoral address of 1933. In this speech, Heidegger urged the audience to take seriously Nietzsche's dictum that God is dead. If I am right, Heidegger discovered the truth of this statement during the years between 1929 and 1933. Because God is dead, our Dasein is placed before a great transformation (*vor einer großen Wandlung*). Dasein is exposed without any protection to what is hidden and uncertain. Questioning remains the highest form of knowledge. The truly spiritual world (*geistige Welt*) of the German people will become a world of most inner and most extreme danger (*innersten und äußersten Gefahr*). Whereas Heidegger defines spirit (*Geist*) as being resolute concerning the essence of being (*Entschlossenheit zum Wesen des Seins*), he claims that the spiritual world of a people is the "power of most intensely proving the worth of its forces of blood and soil" (*"die Macht der tiefsten Bewahrung seiner erd-und bluthaften Kräfte"*). It is the power of the most intimate arousal and most encompassing disruption of its Dasein (*"Macht der innersten Erregung und weitesten Erschütterung seines Daseins"*), which guarantees greatness to a people.[264] In this passage, Heidegger seems to move directly from Nietzsche's discovery that God is dead to the necessity of a German revolution, rooted in *Blut und Boden* (blood and soil).

Heidegger turned to Nietzsche, we might conclude, because Nietzsche's diagnosis of his epoch explained the fact that metaphysical grace did not come in 1929–32, and Nietzsche seemed to justify the transition to Nazism by showing that spirit is rooted in blood and that Dasein is struggle for power. As I have already mentioned, Heidegger suggests that Ernst Jünger influenced him in this respect. For he tells us in his account of the rectorate written in 1945 that he discussed Jünger's essay *Die totale Mobilmachung* (1930) and his book *Der Arbeiter* (1932) in a small circle with his assistant Brock when they appeared, and that he tried to show how in Nietzsche's metaphysics "the history and present of the Occident was clearly seen and predicted." He adds that Nietzsche's metaphysics, as interpreted by Jünger, was corroborated by the facts, and that in our time everything, whether it be communism, fascism, or democracy, belongs to the universal rule of the will to power.[265]

If this interpretation is acceptable, there is no direct relationship between the ideal of authenticity in *Sein und Zeit* and Heidegger's turn to Nazism. The unbearable burden of authentic life can be relieved in two ways: by a leap to faith and by a totalitarian commitment. Only when the first solution seemed to be ruled out did Heidegger jump to the second. Nietzsche's thesis of God's death explained why the first solution was not available, and the metaphysics of the will to power paved the way to a second solution: Nazism.

This second solution did not work very well either, at least on the practical level, for Heidegger's rectorate ended in a failure. On 1 July 1935 Heidegger wrote to Karl Jaspers that his solitude was nearly complete, and, with a reference to 2 *Corinthians* 12:7, that there were two thorns (in his flesh): the clash with the faith of his background and the failure of the rectorate. He added that these two thorns were enough of those things that should be really overcome.[266] How, we might ask, did Heidegger overcome the two thorns in the following years? He attempted to do so by developing his postmonotheist theme, that is, by creating a new religious idiom, which was intended to replace the theist and metaphysical idiom of Christianity. I discussed this new idiom in section 11, above, in detail. Heidegger sketched the postmonotheist theme for the first time in the voluminous *Beiträge zur Philosophie*, which he wrote during the years 1936–38. Only if we understand, so he says in that manuscript, how uniquely necessary Being is, even though Being is not present as God, and only if we are tuned in on the abysses between man and Being, and between Being and gods, will preconditions for a future "history" become real.[267]

We may conclude that there are three turns in Heidegger's philosophical journey between 1927 and the later works. From the first stage of a Pascalian strategy in *Sein und Zeit* Heidegger turned to the miscarried metaphysical and theist conversion of 1929–30. The failure of this conversion, and Nietzsche's explanation of it, made him turn to Nazism. And the failure of the rectorate in 1934 motivated the final turn in 1936–38 to the postmonotheist theme, which rejects metaphysical *Sein* in favor of postmonotheist *Seyn*.

One might infer that if the postmonotheist theme was developed as an attempt to surmount the failure of the rectorate, it should be considered as an implicit critique of the National Socialist movement.[268] But in fact, things are more ambiguous than that. Authors such as Paul de Lagarde (1827–91), who became popular as a *praeceptor Germaniae* during the Nazi period, argued that Germany needed a proper German religion, which could provide a new German state with a spiritual basis. As Lagarde said, being German is not a matter of the blood, but of the spirit.[269] Lagarde's belief that contemporary Christianity was dead, and that religion was indispensable to a new Germany, received widespread assent after the First World War.[270] Many groups in the interbellum shared Lagarde's heritage: the desire to convert Christianity into a polemical, anti-Semitic, nationalistic faith that would supplant the old and decadent tenets of a perverted and universal Christianity.[271] The research program of developing a national religion was also supported by the Nazis. As Vermeil wrote, "the Nazi German seeks to identify his personal religion with his membership of the Reich, with a Reich that is never completed and eternally in process of creation."[272] Might one not interpret Heidegger's postmonotheism as a form of spiritual Nazism, as an attempt to fulfill the desideratum of a proper German religion?

It is striking that Heidegger seeks an original revelation of Being in the writings of pre-Socratics such as Anaximander and Parmenides, and not in the Old Testament. Even though the eschatological structure of Heidegger's postmonotheist religion is not Greek but markedly Judeo-Christian, Heidegger in his postmonotheist interpretation of Western metaphysics painstakingly eliminates the references to Jewish influences.[273] In accordance with Nazi ideology, he merely stresses the Greek-German axis. During the interview with *Der Spiegel* in 1966, which was published posthumously in 1976, Heidegger was asked whether he saw a special role for the Germans in the domain of thought. He answered in the affirmative, and claimed that the Germans were qualified for this role because their language had a specially intimate affinity with the language of the Greeks.[274]

Should we say, then, that Heidegger's postmonotheist theme is a continuation of Nazism with other, spiritual means? And, conversely, was Heidegger's Nazism perhaps continuous with his longing for a religious conversion, instead of being an alternative to it? This is at least an interesting hypothesis for further research, and it is a second answer to the objection that I raised in this subsection.

This second answer is more credible than it may seem to contemporary scholars who ignore the spiritual history of the Third Reich. It is well known among historians, for instance, that the *Schutzstaffel* (SS) of the NSDAP (*National-sozialistische Deutsche Arbeiterpartei*) was not only a political and military organization, but also a militant religious—some would prefer to say pseudoreli-gious—order, with its own idea of the Absolute, its rituals, and its credo. Although the SS confession remained in a state of flux until the end of the war—Himmler considered this as a virtue; adult men had to be able to fight without fixed doctrinal forms—it always contained some fundamental articles of faith, such as a belief in one God, one country (Germany), and one leader (Hitler). This God was not the God of Christianity, and the Cross was replaced by the swastika. Hitler saw himself as the founder of a new and modern religion, as a historical figure on a par with Jesus, and the new religion allegedly created a new type of man, superman (*der Übermensch*). In the *Über-religion* (super-religion) of Hitler and Himmler, all Judeo-Christian elements were to be replaced by proper German content, and Hitler repeatedly told his intimates that Christianity had to be de-stroyed in Germany. The Christian teaching of the infinite value of individual human beings was supplanted by the "liberating doctrine of the nullity and insig-nificance of the individual and his life in contrast to the visible immortality of the Nation," and the dogma of the "life and actions of the law-giving *Führer*, which releases the faithful masses from the burden of taking decisions," was substituted for the Christian creed of Christ's suffering and death for humanity, Hitler boasted during one of his conversations.[275] As there cannot be two elected peoples, the Jewish people had to be destroyed, for the Germans are God's people. The Ger-man God was not a God of Love but a God of Strife, and although he intervened in history at rare moments, he remained hidden most of the time. The new German religion had to be the foundation of a new morality. It would replace the Christian ethics of love with a morality of power and war, partly derived from social Darwinism.[276]

Neither Himmler nor Hitler succeeded, however, in working out this new theol-ogy. Their many practical tasks did not leave them time for such lofty occupations. May we not suppose that Heidegger, after the debacle of the rectorate, took leave from the practice of Nazism only in order to concentrate on the much more funda-mental task of developing a Nazi religion? This hypothesis would explain a great number of features of Heidegger's later postmonotheism. For instance, Heideg-ger's Being is never associated with love but often with strife (between earth and world, etc.) and in *Beiträge zur Philosophie*, the uniqueness of Being is related to the uniqueness of the German people.[277] According to Pöggeler, *Beiträge* is

Heidegger's attempt to "save" the Nazi revolution, whereas this book informs Heidegger's entire later oeuvre.[278] Even though the structures of his later thought are derived from the Judeo-Christian tradition, the Jewish and Christian contents are rejected. The Christian God belongs to the metaphysical tradition of ontotheology, a tradition that should be overcome. Finally, whereas authentic existence in *Sein und Zeit* is still predominantly individual, in the later works Heidegger is not concerned anymore with our individual salvation. What should be saved is an entire epoch, Europe, or the West. Heidegger endorsed Hitler's doctrine of the nullity of the individual in 1933, when he wrote to the staff of Freiburg University that "the individual, wherever he stands, does not count" and that "what counts only, is the destiny of our people in their state."[279] Is Heidegger's rejection of humanism and traditional morality after the war not in accordance with this perverse doctrine? Does he not suggest in the "Brief über den 'Humanismus,' " that Being will issue new moral commandments? As I said, the hypothesis that Heidegger's later thought aimed at developing a Nazi religion deserves further investigation on the basis of all available documents from the years 1934–45. At present, these documents are still locked up in the *Deutsche Literatur Archiv* in Marbach, and Heidegger ruled that scholars are not allowed to investigate his unpublished papers.

C. Deciphering Deep History

Let me now turn to the final question I want to deal with in this section. What is the relation between the Neo-Hegelian theme and Nazism? According to the Neo-Hegelian leitmotif in Heidegger's question of being, there is such a thing as authentic or deep history, which consists of the series of fundamental metaphysical stances in which Being has disclosed the totality of beings to mankind (see § 10, above). The "essential" philosopher, who is able to acquire an insight into deep history, will discern the metaphysical significance of what happens in his time. He is able to grasp what *is*. Inspired by Ernst Jünger, Heidegger discovered between 1930 and 1933 that the metaphysical significance of his epoch may be expressed by the catchwords of God's death, nihilism, and the will to power. The notion that God is dead means that the very idea of a transcendent realm loses its hold on humanity. Because human values were supposed to derive from this transcendent realm, these values are increasingly weakened, a process that Nietzsche called nihilism. Nietzsche further argued that ultimate reality, at least the ultimate nature of life, is will to power. Heidegger used these notions not only in 1933, but also in 1945. As we will recall, he insisted in 1945 that "everything nowadays is part of the reality of the will to power, whether it is called communism, fascism, or democracy."[280] This statement shows that Heidegger used Nietzsche in the same manner as the Nazis did: as an instrument for destroying moral distinctions. The claim of humanism and democracy that they are morally superior to fascism and Nazism allegedly is a mere tactical move in a struggle for power. If this were true, it would become impossible to condemn Nazism from a moral point of view.

The Neo-Hegelian theme, if valid, would justify Heidegger's claim in his lectures on metaphysics of 1935 that he is able to discern the "inner truth and greatness" of the National Socialist movement, that is, its real metaphysical significance. But Heidegger's interpretation of this significance shifted considerably between 1935 and 1953, when the lectures were published. Even though the Neo-Hegelian leitmotif remained formally the same, its content changed as a function of the vicissitudes of Germany's destiny. This fact weakens the credibility of Heidegger's epistemic claim that he is able to intuit deep history as it really is. Let me briefly mention some of the most important shifts, in order to substantiate this criticism.

In the course on Schelling of 1936, Heidegger saw Mussolini and Hitler as leaders of a countermovement to nihilism. If nihilism was the process of devaluation of values, which enfeebles humanity, fascism and Nazism revitalized the respective peoples of Italy and Germany by endorsing Nietzsche's doctrine of the will to power.[281] Like fascism, Nazism was in accord with the fundamental metaphysical stance of the modern epoch. This is what Heidegger may have meant in 1933, when, stressing the verb "is," he said that Hitler "*is* present-day and future German reality and its law."

In 1940, Heidegger still held a similar view. Nietzsche distinguishes between incomplete and complete nihilism. Whereas incomplete nihilism seeks to retain current values in a weaker form, complete nihilism accelerates the collapse of decaying values that are devoid of credibility. Socialism allegedly is a form of incomplete nihilism, because it retards the resolute rejection of Christian values, accepting them in some weaker and secularized version. Complete nihilism, on the other hand, turns into active nihilism if it acknowledges the will to power as the basis of all evaluations. Active nihilism sets the stage for a reevaluation of all values (*Umwertung aller Werte*), and it is a countermovement to incomplete and passive nihilism.[282] It seems that in 1940 Heidegger regarded Nazi Germany as the personification of active nihilism. Having argued that Nietzsche's metaphysics of the will to power radicalized Descartes' philosophy, he allows himself a reference to contemporary events, that is, to Germany's victory over France, during a course that is at first sight strictly concerned with a philosophical interpretation of Nietzsche.

These days, he says in 1940, we witness "a mysterious law of history," namely, "that one day a people [the French] is no longer up to the metaphysics that arose from their own history [Cartesian metaphysics], at the very moment in which this metaphysics transformed itself to the unconditional" (by Nietzsche's doctrine of the will to power). As Nietzsche saw, so Heidegger claims in Jüngerian fashion, the modern machine economy requires a "new humanity, which moves beyond present-day man." "It is not sufficient to have armored cars, aeroplanes, and wireless sets. . . . What is needed is a humanity that is fundamentally up to the unique basic essence of modern technology and its metaphysical truth, that is, a humanity that lets itself be mastered entirely by the essence of technology, with the very purpose of directing and using the particular technical processes and possibilities." Only superman (*der Übermensch*) is equal to this task, and, conversely, superman needs the machine economy in order "to establish an unconditional mastery of the earth."[283] In other words, the victorious German army represents a new humanity, *der Übermensch*, which is up to the essence of technology because it is able to use technical warfare in order to establish an unconditional rule over the earth (*unbedingte Herrschaft über die Erde*). Germany's victory over France has a Nietzschean metaphysical significance, and it is only a prelude to Germany's hegemony over the world.

It is obvious that in 1940 the *Wehrmacht*'s first heady victory went to Heidegger's head. One notes how different this philosophy of technology sounds from the pessimistic view which Heidegger once held and which he came to adopt again after Germany's defeat, that is, after the German *Übermensch* had been technologically outwitted by the Allied forces. Heidegger in these lectures on Nietzsche develops again his doctrine that the history of metaphysics is the history of the oblivion of Being. But he also gives his metaphysical blessing to the successes of the *Wehrmacht* (the German army), arguing that only when metaphysics is on the verge of being completed is an uninhibited domination of beings possible, and that the "motorization" of the *Wehrmacht* is "a metaphysical act, which surpasses in depth the abolition of 'philosophy.' "[284] The completion of metaphysics by a German hegemony would then prepare a new advent of Being.

During the summer semester of 1942, Heidegger still thought that a German victory was metaphysically necessary. He argued that America's decision to enter the war could not lead to a destruction of "Europe, that is, the *Heimat*, and the origin of the Occident," because "what is at the origin cannot be destroyed." Consequently, America's decision was "only the last American act of . . . self-destruction," and the hidden spirit (*verborgene Geist*) of the origin will not even have a "glance of contempt" to spare for this self-destructive process.[285] With his characteristic modesty, Heidegger in 1942 identified Germany with Europe, anticipating the fulfillment of Hitler's dreams.

It will by now be clear that Heidegger's intuitions about metaphysical deep history were not immune to the vicissitudes of the war. Whereas Heidegger initially saw Germany's victories as a prelude to a new metaphysical beginning, based on a victorious German will to power, the Battle of Stalingrad in 1942–43 probably changed his views on the will to power and technology. They now turned out to be forces that endangered Being, and the real question became: "How should beings be saved and rescued within the free space of their essence, if the essence of Being is . . . forgotten?"[286] The question was, in less metaphysical clothing: How could the Germans be saved and rescued within the boundaries of the space that belonged to them essentially, if they did not pay heed to Heideggerian Being? As Losurdo observes: "from this moment on, Germany no longer represents active nihilism, which fights for a different configuration of Being. . . . The German combatant is no longer the *Übermensch* capable of mastering technology better than his enemies; instead, he is . . . the desperate custodian of the truth of Being."[287] It is no accident that Heidegger in his postscript to *Was ist Metaphysik?* of 1943 urged that metaphysics, including the metaphysics of the will to power, should be overcome, thereby reversing the meaning of the original lecture. In order to acquire the mysterious possibility of experiencing Being, we should have the lucid courage to admit *Angst*. If we have this courage, we recognize in the abyss of dread the domain of Being.[288] Furthermore, we should be ready for sacrifice, that is, "the farewell to beings on the way to safeguarding the favor of Being."[289] In 1943, we may conclude, Heidegger saw Germany as the custodian of Being, which might save Being by sacrificing itself. Being, he now said, might dwell without beings, a statement that was corrected after the war.[290] The philosopher could not only discern the metaphysical meaning of a German victory. Even a German defeat turned out to have a metaphysical significance: by bidding farewell to beings, Germany might safeguard the favor of Being.[291] It seems that during the Battle of Stalingrad, the fate of Heidegger's Germany transubstantiated into a postmonotheist analogue of Christ's sufferings on the cross.

After the war, Heidegger stressed more than before that both nihilism and the will to power are metaphysical positions that man has to overcome. One might think that by this last interpretation of deep history, Heidegger distanced himself from Nazism. Although he still published the phrase on the inner truth and greatness of the National Socialist movement in 1953, he now added that this greatness consisted in the confrontation of technology and modern man.[292] This confrontation, he implied, could carry man to destruction, and we should reflect on the metaphysical stance of technology in order to prepare its disappearance. Like so many German conservatives, Heidegger blamed technology for the German defeat, and developed a despondent philosophy of the technical era.[293]

There is a deep ambiguity in Heidegger's later evaluation of Nazism. If Nazism belonged to the metaphysical stance of technology and the will to power, which has to be overcome in order to prepare a new advent of Being, democracy belongs to this very same metaphysical stance.[294] Heidegger's metaphysical curse on Nazism—if any—condemns democracy as well, and even in the interview with *Der Spiegel* of 1966, Heidegger expressed doubts about democracy as a political system.[295] Furthermore, we will remember that all metaphysical stances are sent to us by Being; hence Nazism posthumously received Heidegger's postmonotheistic fiat.[296] National Socialism is simply part of the Destiny that Being prepared for us, so that nobody is personally responsible for it. Because we still live in the era of technology, Heidegger says in 1952, the Second World War did not decide anything. A true and sufficient reflection on the essential destiny of man on earth will be prohibited if one thinks in terms of "moral categories, which are always inadequate and too narrow-chested."[297] In short, Nazism is a historical destiny, part and parcel of the modern technological era to which democracies also belong, and it would be narrow-minded to draw moral distinctions between these systems, which are metaphysically the same.[298]

I conclude that the two leitmotifs of Heidegger's later thought, the postmonotheist and the Neo-Hegelian theme, are much more intimately connected to Heidegger's Nazism than the three leitmotifs of *Sein und Zeit*, although even here the connection does not amount to a logical implication. Heidegger's Neo-Hegelian presumption to fathom deep history enabled him to invest National Socialism with a metaphysical significance which, although it changed over the years, never became unambiguously negative. And the postmonotheist theme fits in well with the Nazi attempt, rooted in the writings of Lagarde and others, to invent a proper German religion, which would eliminate all Jewish content. For these reasons, it is profoundly mistaken to interpret Heidegger's later philosophy as a critique of Nazism. Heidegger never clearly rejected National Socialism. Arguably, his later philosophy should be seen as an attempt to continue Nazism on a spiritual level.

Hitler and Heidegger belonged to the same generation: they were both born in 1889. In the light of the later Heidegger, the claims in section 74 of *Sein und Zeit*, that "only in communication and struggle does the power of destiny become free," and that "Dasein's fateful destiny in and with its 'generation' goes to make up the full authentic historizing of Dasein," acquire an ominous weight.[299] Even after the destruction of Germany and after Hitler's unheroic suicide in 1945, Heidegger did not unambiguously part company with the *Führer* of his generation.

§ 15. HEIDEGGER AND NIETZSCHE

On 30 March 1933, Heidegger wrote to his friend Elisabeth Blochmann about the hidden mission of the German *Volk* in Western history. The events of the time—Heidegger meant Hitler's revolution—inspired him with a "rare power of concentration" (*eine ungewöhnliche sammelnde Kraft*), and they reinforced his will and conviction to work in the service of a great task. In order to build a world grounded on the *Volk*, one had to expose oneself to *Being* itself (*dem Sein selbst*) in a new way, and had to confront both the antispirit of the communist world (*dem Widergeist der kommunistischen Welt*) and the moribund spirit of Christianity (*dem absterbenden Geist des Christentums*).[300] We have seen that in 1933 Heidegger was deeply inspired by Nietzsche. Indeed, from Nietzsche's point of view, moribund Christianity and the communist world amount to the same thing: they are incomplete forms of nihilism. Even in 1937, Heidegger still thought that Nazism was a countermovement to incomplete nihilism. It was an active nihilism, based on the doctrine of the will to power, which would prepare a new beginning by destroying old values.

I argued in the previous section that Nietzsche paved the way to Nazism for Heidegger between 1931 and 1933.[301] However, Heidegger's enthusiasm for Nazism led to the disastrous rectorate, and after 1934, Heidegger adopted a more distanced view of the actual regime. The revolution of 1933 had never been carried out on the fundamental, philosophical level that Heidegger had envisaged. In the years 1936–38, Heidegger developed the postmonotheist leitmotif in *Beiträge*, perhaps in order to provide Nazism with a spiritual and religious basis. But the postmonotheist theme conflicts with Nietzsche's philosophy. As a consequence, Heidegger had two important motives for attempting to digest and overcome Nietzsche. First, it was Nietzsche who, reinforced by Jünger and the pre-Socratics, pushed Heidegger toward actual Nazism and caused the "thorn in his flesh" of the rectorate. Second, Nietzsche's philosophy seemed to condemn beforehand Heidegger's later postmonotheist thought as a mere shadow of the dead Christian God.[302] The confrontation with Nietzsche is more important for understanding Heidegger's later thought than his philosophical exploitation of Hölderlin. Whereas the latter was part and parcel of the postmonotheist leitmotif, Nietzsche stood in the way of postmonotheism. Heidegger admitted the importance of Nietzsche for his spiritual career when he wrote in the preface to the 1961 edition of his courses on Nietzsche that this publication provided a view of the philosophical path (*Denkweg*) that he followed between 1930 and 1947, whereas the book on Hölderlin of 1951 merely gives some indirect knowledge of this path.[303] For this reason I decided to discuss Heidegger's interpretation of Nietzsche and to leave out a similar section on Hölderlin.

In reality, Heidegger's 1961 edition of the Nietzsche courses masks the first part of the path that he followed between 1930 and 1947. It does not contain texts that show that Nietzsche was instrumental to Heidegger's conversion to Nazism, for it starts with the lectures on *The Will to Power as Art* of 1936–37.[304] Furthermore, Heidegger expurgated the text and left out all passages about Nazism and the war. When he discusses his editorial principles in the preface, he forgets to tell us that the edition is a bowdlerized version. The two volumes on Nietzsche of 1961, then, show to the initiated eye traces of Heidegger's apologetics.[305] Yet they are a reliable guide to the second part of Heidegger's philosophical trail between 1930 and 1947. They demonstrate that Heidegger's later interpretation of Nietzsche increasingly had the objective of surmounting Nietzsche. This holds in particular for the latest text of the second volume, called "Die seinsgeschichtliche Bestimmung des Nihilismus" ("The Destiny of Nihilism within the History of Being"), which was written during the years 1944–46.

In this section, I first discuss in subsection (A) Heidegger's interpretation of Nietzsche on the basis of his *Nietzsche* of 1961 and of texts such as "Nietzsches Wort 'Gott ist tot' " (1943, "Nietzsche's Thesis 'God Is Dead' ") in *Holzwege*, *Was heisst Denken?* (*What Means Thinking?*), Heidegger's lecture course of 1951–52, and "Wer ist Nietzsches Zarathustra?" (1953, "Who Is Nietzsche's Zarathustra?"), published in *Vorträge und Aufsätze*. I will try to show that Heidegger's interpretation of Nietzsche is informed by the two leitmotifs that I attribute to his later works, the Neo-Hegelian theme and the postmonotheist leitmotif, and that it is a reversal of Nietzsche's own views. As a consequence, I am contradicting the opinion, shared by most French Heidegger specialists, that Heidegger "is the author of the most decisive interpretation of Nietzsche's thought put forth to this day."[306] A reversal of Nietzsche's views can hardly be called the "most decisive interpretation" of Nietzsche.

What would Nietzsche have thought of such a reversal? What would have been his assessment of Heidegger's philosophy as a whole? These questions are at least as interesting as Heidegger's view of Nietzsche, and in the second subsection (B) I attempt to derive from Nietzsche's works a Nietzschean perspective on Heidegger.

A. Heidegger's Reversal of Nietzsche

Heidegger's interpretation of Nietzsche aims at answering two questions: (1) What is Nietzsche's fundamental stance (*Grundstellung*) within the history of Western metaphysics? and (2) Did Nietzsche ask the proper question of philosophy and, if not, why could he not do so?[307] Question (1) clearly belongs to the Neo-Hegelian leitmotif in Heidegger's later works. We remember from section 10 that my reconstruction of this leitmotif consists of nine theses. The most important ones are that, according to Heidegger, each cultural epoch is based on a *Grundstellung*, which is an all-embracing way in which entities are disclosed to us and in which we are manifest to ourselves. Fundamental stances are expressed by systems of metaphysics, because metaphysics attempts to characterize the totality of what there is. Real or authentic history consists of the series of fundamental stances, as expressed by the history of Western metaphysics. The Heideggerian philosopher has access to real history without relying on ordinary history as an academic discipline, and indeed, without relying on academic disciplines of any kind. In this sense, philosophy is fundamental.

According to the postmonotheist theme, the history of metaphysics is a history of fundamental stances that Being sent (*schicken*) to us as our destiny (*Geschick*).[308] But in the act of disclosing beings, Being conceals itself. This is why the question regarding Being, which allegedly is the proper question of philosophy, is not raised within metaphysics. The history of metaphysics is a veil of Being, and Heidegger's meditation on this history purports to interpret the sequence of metaphysical systems *as* the history of Being's self-concealment. Such a meditation prepares a new beginning, in which Being will disclose itself to us unconcealed. Clearly, Heidegger's second question (2) fits in with this postmonotheist theme. It is not difficult to predict Heidegger's argument: he will argue that Nietzsche did not and could not ask the proper question of philosophy and that, therefore, we have to overcome Nietzsche. I now briefly discuss Heidegger's answers to questions (1) and (2), in this order.

1. Nietzsche's Fundamental Stance. According to Heidegger, a metaphysical fundamental stance has two aspects. It posits *what* beings are in their totality (*das*

Seiende im Ganzen), and it posits *how* they are in their totality.[309] In his lectures on Nietzsche of 1936–37, 1937, and 1939, Heidegger argued that Nietzsche's doctrine of the will to power (*Wille zur Macht*) specifies the *what* of a metaphysical fundamental stance, and that the idea of the eternal recurrence of the same (*Ewige Widerkunft des Gleichen*) specifies the *how*.[310] In other words, Nietzsche held that the fundamental nature of all entities is will to power, and he postulated that everything exists in the manner of an eternal recurrence of the same. Perhaps this is a plausible interpretation of the later Nietzsche, and one might say that Nietzsche developed a fundamental metaphysical stance in this limited sense.[311]

Somewhat more questionable is Heidegger's view of metaphysical stances in general, as applied to Nietzsche. Heidegger held that metaphysical stances cannot be argued for by appealing to neutral facts, because they constitute a specific, all-embracing disclosure of beings, so that facts only emerge on the basis of a metaphysical stance. As a consequence, metaphysics is fundamental to scientific disciplines, and scientific or other arguments for metaphysical stances are impossible.[312] However, in the years 1885–88 Nietzsche developed a "scientific" proof of the eternal recurrence of the same, expressed in fragments 1062–1067 of *Wille zur Macht* (*The Will to Power*), a selection from the unpublished papers that Peter Gast and Nietzsche's sister Elisabeth published in 1906. Both according to Heidegger and to the Nazi ideologist Alfred Baeumler, *Wille zur Macht* is Nietzsche's main book.[313] But if Nietzsche tried to develop a scientific proof of eternal recurrence, he would perhaps not have endorsed Heidegger's conception of a metaphysical fundamental stance. Conversely, in order to interpret Nietzsche's philosophy as a metaphysical stance in his own sense, Heidegger has to play down the importance of Nietzsche's arguments for the eternal recurrence and stress other aspects of this thought: that it functions as a test and selection instrument for those who attempt to conceive it.[314] Because Nietzsche's fundamental metaphysical stance cannot be argued for, Heidegger would claim, it cannot be criticized by argument either, and this too holds for metaphysical stances in general. The reason is that, as the postmonotheist theme says, Being sends (*schickt*) us metaphysical stances as our destiny (*Geschick*).[315]

That the notion of a metaphysical or fundamental stance (*Grundstellung*) is external to Nietzsche may be shown in yet another manner, which requires a summary of Nietzsche's global strategy. Nietzsche developed his mature philosophical position as a counterattack against what he called "nihilism." Nihilism in Nietzsche's sense is both an existential attitude and a historical process. As an attitude, it is the conviction that human life is worthless and without value. According to Nietzsche, the attitude of nihilism is becoming more and more prevalent in Western culture. This complex historical process is called "nihilism" as well, and the term now refers to the cultural phenomenon of a gradual devaluation of the highest values.[316] At the origin of this process, Nietzsche claims, are Platonism and Christianity. The latter, which is merely a vulgar form of the former, and Platonism itself argued that values originate from a transcendent and perfect source, God or the idea of the good.[317] A transcendent and eternal being was postulated as the standard of value for our mortal and transitory life on earth. Platonism and Christianity also inspired a love of truth, Nietzsche says, and this love of truth made Western man discover that the transcendent and higher reality is nonexistent. As a consequence, the values that allegedly were derived from it gradually lost their authority, and human life became without a moral orientation. The historical process of nihilism, then, begins because a "nothing" (*nihil*), to wit, a transcendent authority, is posited as a "being," and it advances because the imaginary nature of such a transcendent authority is gradually brought to light. As human values were thought to be derived from this authority, values become destitute of their meaning-bestowing power, and nihilism as an attitude is the result. In his *Zur Genealogie der Moral* (*Genealogy of Morals*), Nietzsche argued that Christian values in fact originated in ancient Mediterranean societies from the resentment of the weak against the strong, and that the underlying classes used the notion of a suprasensible moral authority as a powerful ideology, which undermined the self-confidence of the masters. The values that were allegedly derived from a higher, transcendent reality did in fact originate from low and mean motives: the power instincts of slaves and the weak.

Nietzsche understands his own philosophy as a reversal of Platonism.[318] Whereas Plato and Christianity posited a transcendent, timeless world, which would be more real than the actual and temporal world, Nietzsche holds that the actual changeable world is the only one there is. Most contemporary philosophers will agree with Nietzsche on this point. But they will not endorse Nietzsche's metaphysical view of the world, according to which its nature is will to power, and its manner of being is an eternal recurrence of the same. Nietzsche's metaphysics of the will to power and the eternal recurrence is posited as an anti-Christian principle of valuation, which will necessitate a radical reevaluation of all values (*Umwertung aller Werte*). If power is the only principle of valuation, Christian morality will be superseded by the right of the mighty and the gifted, that is, by those who are able to affirm life as it is. In order to test whether one has such an *amor fati* (love of one's destiny), Nietzsche revived the ancient notion of an eternal recurrence of the same. Only if one is able to endure the thought that even the most trivial details of life will recur infinitely many times exactly as they are now will one affirm life in a Nietzschean manner. The type of human being who endures this thought is superman (*der Übermensch*), and Nietzsche's protagonist Zarathustra is the teacher who rejected a moral view of the world, which had been the old Iranian Zoroaster's view, and teaches the doctrines of the will to power and the eternal recurrence. Teaching them means learning to endure these doctrines and to become a superman oneself.

Because Nietzsche conceived of the history of Western thought as the history of Platonism and nihilism, he saw his reversal of Platonism as the *end* of Western metaphysics and as a new beginning. He claimed to have overcome metaphysics by his doctrine of the will to power. Even so, Nietzsche did not limit the validity of this doctrine to a special historical period. The doctrine allegedly is valid for all times, the eternal recurrence being an eternal return of power configurations. This is the second point at which we can see that Heidegger's notion of a fundamental metaphysical stance is alien to Nietzsche. When Heidegger says that Nietzsche's philosophy is the end of the metaphysical tradition, he seems merely to repeat what Nietzsche himself claims. However, what he means is very different: that Nietzsche's philosophy is the last fundamental stance in a series of stances, and that it is valid as a metaphysical foundation only for Nietzsche's metaphysical epoch, in which, Heidegger claims, we are still living. The merit of Heidegger's interpretation is that he unifies the five fundamental themes of Nietzsche's later philosophy—nihilism, will to power, eternal recurrence, reevaluation of values, and superman—into a coherent metaphysical position, which I sketched just now. But he does so on the basis of a notion that is external to Nietzsche, the Neo-Hegelian notion of a fundamental stance (*Grundstellung*). This notion introduces historical relativity into a doctrine that Nietzsche meant as an absolutely valid one.

It follows that Heidegger's notion of the end of metaphysics is at odds with Nietzsche's notion. Whereas Nietzsche claims to have overcome metaphysics in the sense of a doctrine of transcendent being, Heidegger argues that Nietzsche's philosophy is the final stage of metaphysics. It is the end of metaphysics in the special sense that metaphysics is fully consummated by Nietzsche.[319]

2. The End of Metaphysics and the Question of Being. Why, according to Heidegger, is Nietzsche's philosophy the end of metaphysics in this special sense? Heidegger advances three reasons for this claim, reasons which, taken together, constitute an answer to the second question (2) his interpretation was meant to resolve.

In the first place (a) Nietzsche's philosophy as the end of metaphysics allegedly still belongs to metaphysics because it merely reverses the metaphysical position that was at the beginning of the metaphysical tradition: Platonism. Instead of saying that the sensible world is unreal and the suprasensible world is real (Platonism), Nietzsche says that the suprasensible world is unreal and only the sensible world is real. Such a reversal leaves intact the very terms of the original position. For this reason, Heidegger says, it still belongs to the tradition of metaphysics.[320] Allegedly it is the end of this tradition in the sense of its final stage, because by Nietzsche's reversal of Platonism all possibilities of metaphysics have been exhausted.[321]

Second (b), Nietzsche's philosophy is the end of metaphysics, Heidegger asserts, because Nietzsche unites in a synthesis the two contradictory doctrines with which metaphysics began. Parmenides answered the metaphysical question of what being is (*was das Seiende sei*) by saying: being is. Heraclitus answered: being becomes. According to Nietzsche, being is an eternally recurring becoming, in which each time a will to power fixes the stream of becoming, so that it becomes stable being.[322] Again, Nietzsche's synthesis of Parmenides and Heraclitus supposedly is the end of metaphysics because it does not leave us any further meta-physical possibilities, that is, possibilities of distinguishing or uniting being and becoming.[323]

Finally (c), Heidegger claims that Nietzsche is the end of metaphysics for the reason that his philosophy of the will to power is the most radical variety of an idea that informed Western metaphysics from the beginning: the idea that being should be understood as being produced. This notion originated in the works of Plato and Aristotle, who derived their fundamental ontological concepts, such as matter and form, from the domain of artifacts. It was fundamental to the medieval view of the world as created *ex nihilo* by an omnipotent God. Since Descartes the idea of being as being produced has been radicalized, because entities were conceived of as posits, produced by a subject. Nietzsche's view that subjects are volitional forces that posit stable objects as conditions for increasing their power is the final stage of this radicalization.[324] According to Heidegger, we saw in section 10, above, Nietzschean metaphysics expresses the fundamental stance of the reign of technology (*das Wesen der Technik*), in which all entities are regarded as means and raw materials for production.[325]

As the reader will notice, these arguments for Heidegger's thesis that Nietzsche's philosophy is the end of metaphysics are not very convincing. In the first argument (a), Heidegger assumes that one might only overcome metaphysics by changing the very concepts in which metaphysical positions are expressed. Why should this be the case? Moreover, Heidegger presupposes both in the first and the second arguments (a, b) that metaphysics has exhausted its possibilities by Nietzsche's reversal of Plato, or by the Nietzschean synthesis of Parmenides and Heraclitus. How should we know that this is true? Surely we are unable to survey either the future or the possibility space of metaphysics.[326] In his third argument (c), Heidegger assumes that the final metaphysical position must be "productionist" in the sense that all entities are interpreted as posits. Even though this is true of some modern metaphysical systems, such as the one Quine proposed in *Word and Object*, it is not true of most modern varieties of naturalism, ac-cording to which the evolution of the universe and life on earth are not posited by a subject at all. It seems that contemporary metaphysics and science refute the third argument. How could Heidegger believe, then, that his arguments are convincing?

The answer to this question is a simple one. The arguments are inconclusive unless one endorses Heidegger's postmonotheist conception of (the essence of) metaphysics. According to this conception, metaphysics says what and how *be-ings* are in their totality, but it never raises the fundamental question concerning (postmonotheist) *Being* (see § 11B.3 and 6). Because Being is not *a* being (an entity), one cannot really overcome metaphysics as long as one goes on using traditional metaphysical concepts, which are concepts denoting entities (argument a). Nietzsche's reversal of Platonism exhausts the possibilities of metaphysics because it completes the Fall that began with Plato. Heidegger claims that Plato, or rather his followers, betrayed the original revelation of Being in pre-Socratic thought by interpreting Being as an eternal entity, as an *idea*.[327] With Plato begins the history of metaphysics as oblivion of Being, because transcendent *Being* is conceived of as a transcendent eternal *entity* such as the Idea of the Good or the Christian God. This reification of Being allegedly suppresses the possibility of its manifestation in our temporal life, because Being is not *a* being (ontological difference). Nietzsche's philosophy completes the Fall of metaphysics by eliminating reified and eternal Being again (the death of God), thereby erasing the last trace of Being within metaphysics (argument b).[328] For this reason, the doctrine of the will to power is the expression of the fundamental stance of the modern technological era, in which all traces of transcendent Being are wiped out (argument c).[329] As Heidegger says in *Beiträge*, Nietzsche's philosophical preoccupations are far away (*weit entfernt*) from the question of Being.[330]

Heidegger claims that postmonotheist Being (*das Seyn*) is the source of meaning (*Sinn*) in our life, and that Being is transcendent in relation to all beings. In a celebrated text, which Heidegger often discussed, Nietzsche describes how a madman seeks God and discovers that we murdered him. The madman tells the audience that this crime is greater than we can bear. He wonders how man was capable of committing such a superhuman crime.[331] Heidegger retorts that *Being* was murdered because metaphysics conceived of Being as an entity, God. The death of God, he implies, is only a belated consequence of a more original sin: that we did not open ourselves to Being as it is, but tried to conceive of it as an entity. This entity, God, would have died because it was not living Being to begin with. Nietzsche conceived "being" (*Sein*) as a value or entity posited by a will to power. This made him guilty, Heidegger says, of an especially "deadly" kind of thinking. Because Nietzsche holds that everything there is has been posited by a subject, he allegedly prevents Being from coming into "its living nature" (*die Lebendigkeit seines Wesens*).[332] The reason is that we cannot posit, conceive of, or otherwise master Being. Because transcendent Being is the source of meaning, Nietzsche's metaphysics inaugurates the epoch of completed meaninglessness by abolishing transcendent or suprasensible Being.[333] And because Nietzsche's metaphysics holds that the essence of all beings is will to power, it expresses the fundamental stance of the epoch of technology.[334]

We now see clearly that Heidegger answers his second question (2) in the negative. Nietzsche did not raise the fundamental question of philosophy, the question of Being.[335] Nietzsche could not raise this question because he only recognizes beings, claiming that beings are a will to power, whereas Heideggerian Being is transcendent in relation to all beings (ontological difference), and cannot be posited, calculated, or otherwise controlled by power. We have to admit, then, that Nietzsche's philosophy excludes Being in Heidegger's sense. For when Heidegger claims that Nietzsche did not raise the question of Being, he means postmonotheist Being. This exegesis illuminates two theses that are central to Heidegger's interpretation of Nietzsche: that Nietzsche was a metaphysician who did not grasp the *essence* of metaphysics (*das Wesen der Metaphysik*), and that Nietzsche combated nihilism without ever coming to terms with the *essence* of nihilism (*das Wesen des Nihilismus*).[336]

As we will remember, Heidegger uses the expression "the essence of" (*das Wesen des . . .*) as a marker, which indicates the Neo-Hegelian and postmonotheist level at which things *are* in their relation to Being. The essence of technology (*das Wesen der Technik*), for instance, is not technological itself: it is the fundamental stance in which everything is disclosed to us as raw material for production and domination, a stance or epoch that Being sent (*schickte*) to us as our destiny (*Geschick*).[337] Likewise, the essence of truth (*das Wesen der Wahrheit*) is Being's free act of sending us such a fundamental stance or destiny. The essence of metaphysics is Being's self-concealment in the act of revealing beings in their totality. Finally, the essence of nihilism is the fact that Being counts for nothing during the history of metaphysics. According to Heidegger's postmonotheist and Neo-Hegelian notion of metaphysics, metaphysics is essentially nihilistic, because within metaphysics, the question of Being is never raised.[338]

Of course Heidegger is right when he claims that Nietzsche did not grasp the essence of nihilism and of metaphysics in this Heideggerian sense. However, it is misleading to suggest that there was something there for Nietzsche to grasp, which he then failed to do. The situation is rather that Nietzsche had a conception of metaphysics and of nihilism that was very different from Heidegger's. Heidegger claims that although Nietzsche pretended to have surmounted metaphysics and nihilism, he failed to do so. Nietzsche's victory over metaphysics would have been a final entanglement in metaphysics.[339] This "interpretation" is doubly misleading. First, Heidegger here substitutes *his* notions of (the essence of) nihilism and metaphysics for Nietzsche's notions. But surely Nietzsche never claimed that he purported to surmount metaphysics and nihilism in *Heidegger's* sense. Second, Heidegger's definitions of nihilism and metaphysics are the very opposites of Nietzsche's definitions, so that Heidegger, in stating that Nietzsche did not overcome nihilism and metaphysics, paradoxically admits that Nietzsche did what he claimed to do. If we spell this out briefly, we will see that Heidegger's "interpretation" of Nietzsche is in fact a reversal of Nietzsche's doctrines.

Nietzsche defined metaphysics as Platonism, and "Platonism" is a label for all doctrines that devaluate the sensible world of bodily life by postulating something "higher," a suprasensible source of values.[340] Nihilism is the process in which these values lose their force, because the very idea of a suprasensible realm becomes more and more dubious. Nietzsche surmounted metaphysics and nihilism by arguing that the real source of values is life itself, and he thought that this insight would prompt a reevaluation of values because he conceived of life, and indeed of beings in their totality, as will to power. Heidegger, on the contrary, defined metaphysics as the set of doctrines that say what beings are in their totality without meditating on transcendent Being. And he defined (the essence of) nihilism as the idea that transcendent Being counts for nothing. It follows that

Nietzsche's attempt to overcome metaphysics and nihilism in *his* sense by radically rejecting any transcendent authority and by conceiving of beings in their totality as will to power is precisely a metaphysical and nihilist move in *Heidegger's* sense, because according to Heidegger it is "metaphysical" and "nihilistic" to reject transcendent Being. Heidegger said in the "Brief über den 'Humanismus' " that transcendent Being is the only source of morality there is.[341] Accordingly, when Heidegger in his turn claims that he surmounts metaphysics and nihilism, and that he does so by listening to transcendent Being, this is a metaphysical and nihilist move in *Nietzsche's* sense of the terms.[342] Whereas Nietzsche's victory over metaphysics consisted in abolishing each and every transcendent authority, celebrating the vitality of life on earth, Heidegger wanted to surmount metaphysics by reintroducing a transcendent authority, postmonotheist Being.

As a consequence, Heidegger's interpretation of Nietzsche is in reality a reversal of Nietzsche, which exploits the ambiguity of the term "metaphysics." Nietzsche claims to surmount metaphysics as a doctrine of transcendence (Platonism), and he does so by developing a metaphysics in the sense of a doctrine on beings in their totality (ontology). Heidegger, on the contrary, purports to overcome metaphysics as a mere doctrine on the totality of beings (ontology) by raising the question of Being, a question that is metaphysical in the sense that it transcends the realm of sensible reality, and, indeed, the realm of entities altogether.

It is not altogether honest, then, that Heidegger presents his reversal of Nietzsche as an interpretation or elucidation.[343] The term "confrontation" (*Auseinandersetzung*), which he also uses, is a more apt description of what he is doing. But we should not forget what Heidegger says about interpretation or elucidation. In section 5, above, I quoted a text on elucidation from "Nietzsches Wort 'Gott ist tot,' " in which Heidegger claims that in interpreting a text, we should covertly add something (*Beigabe*) derived from the topic (*Sache*) of the elucidation.[344] For Heidegger, the topic of interpretation and thought (*die Sache des Denkens*) is transcendent Being itself. What he means is that in interpreting a text belonging to the history of metaphysics, we should read it *as* a manifestation of Being's self-concealment.[345]

This is what Heidegger does in interpreting Nietzsche, when he claims that Nietzsche did not really surmount nihilism and metaphysics. I observed in a note to section 5 that the German word *Beigabe* has yet another meaning than that of something added. The word can also be used to refer to funeral gifts. My suspicion that by adding something of Being to the interpretation of Nietzsche, Heidegger in fact aimed at carrying Nietzsche to the grave, has been confirmed by the result that Heidegger's interpretation of Nietzsche is a reversal of the latter's intentions. Whereas Nietzsche wanted to annul each and every transcendence, Heidegger annulled this annulment, and raised the question of transcendent Being.

One might object that the transcendence that Nietzsche rejected was that of transcendent *entities*, and that the transcendence that Heidegger restored is not one of entities but the transcendence of *Being*. Could one not argue, as Heidegger does, that the nihilism that Nietzsche experienced is in reality a symptom of our abandonment by Being, so that Nietzsche and Heidegger are very near to each other, after all?[346] Did they not agree that the metaphysical God is dead? And did Heidegger not fulfill Nietzsche's intentions by arousing a new sense of transcendence? I do not think that Nietzsche would have been impressed by this rejoinder. He would easily have recognized Heidegger as a philosopher of a specific type: the type which, by doing philosophy, really is longing for theology. It is time to surmise what Nietzsche's view of Heidegger would have been.

B. A Nietzschean Perspective on Heidegger

We have seen that Heidegger's interpretation of Nietzsche is a reversal of Nietzsche's intentions. No two philosophers are more antithetically related than Nietzsche and Heidegger.[347] Whereas Nietzsche rejected transcendence and celebrated the vitality of life in this world, Heidegger believed that human existence is meaningless unless it is related to transcendent Being. According to Heidegger, Nietzsche remained embroiled in metaphysics and nihilism instead of overcoming them, for he merely reflected on beings in their totality without paying heed to transcendent Being. By presenting this external critique of Nietzsche as an inner conflict in Nietzsche's thought, exploiting the ambiguity of the words "metaphysics" and "nihilism," Heidegger attempted to destroy Nietzsche's philosophy from within. He claimed that in elucidating metaphysical texts, we should add a *Beigabe*: the idea that the history of metaphysics is Being's self-concealment. In Nietzsche's case, this *Beigabe* turned out to be a funeral gift. Like the sniper's bullet, it had to go unnoticed in order to be effective.

Heidegger's elucidation of Nietzsche focused on Nietzsche's metaphysical position, which, Heidegger says, was only partially developed in sketches for a *chef d'oeuvre* that Nietzsche in his final lucid years planned to write. Accordingly, Heidegger pretends that Nietzsche's real philosophy lies buried in the *Nachlaß*.[348] From a critical point of view, however, the metaphysical bias of Heidegger's interpretation is an unfortunate one. Nietzsche's metaphysics and epistemology of the will to power are self-defeating positions. Because Nietzsche holds that truths are mere instruments that a will to power posits in order to augment its power, he compromises the claim that his own philosophy of the will to power is true. In other words, Nietzsche's metaphysics and epistemology are caught in a weak version of the paradox of the liar. This is not a criticism Heidegger raises. According to Heidegger, metaphysical fundamental positions can be neither criticized nor supported by argument. However, it is a reason for not taking Nietzsche's metaphysics and epistemology too seriously. Nietzsche was at his best as a psychologist of religion and morals. Before it became universalized into an untenable metaphysical system, the doctrine of the will to power was a powerful psychological tool, which Nietzsche used in his genealogy of morals and religion.[349] If I am raising the question of what Nietzsche's view of Heidegger would have been, I am not interested in Nietzsche the metaphysician but rather in Nietzsche the psychologist.

There are good reasons for trying to give a psychological account of Heidegger's philosophical career. Heidegger held that one can neither argue for nor criticize metaphysical stances. He also held that philosophical thought (*Denken*) in his own special sense of the word is beyond rational evaluation. *Denken* is supposed to be a receptiveness to an authority that transcends discursive thought, the authority of Being. In section 11, I contended that Heidegger's *Denken* is a postmonotheist analogue of Christian faith, and I attempted to reconstruct the inner dynamics of Heidegger's postmonotheism. Apart from such an immanent philosophical reconstruction, the psychologist will claim, there is room for a psychological explanation of Heidegger's later philosophy. The fact that someone holds views for which he does not and cannot adduce reasons calls for a psychological account. I want to speculate briefly about the psychological analysis that Nietzsche would have given of Martin Heidegger's later philosophy. As far as method is concerned, I will proceed as follows. We know that Heidegger was deeply inspired by Luther and St. Paul, and that he wanted to become a new Luther. Obviously, Heidegger identified himself to some extent with these religious authors. May we not suppose that he did so because, from a psychological point of view, his religious strategy resembled that of Paul and Luther? If this is the case, we might apply Nietzsche's insightful psychological observations on Paul and Luther to Heidegger as well. I will first summarize Nietzsche's psychological analysis, and then argue that there are striking resemblances between Paul and Luther on the one hand and Heidegger on the other.

Nietzsche's most extensive psychological account of St. Paul is to be found in section 68 of *Morgenröte* (*Sunrise*). On the basis of data contained in the New Testament, Nietzsche tries to reconstruct Paul's psychological makeup. He reads the New Testament not as a revelation inspired by the Holy Spirit, but with his "own, reasonable and free spirit," and claims that Christianity would have long since belonged to the past if all readers read the Bible in this manner. Before his conversion, Paul was called Saul. He was a fanatic Jew, who wanted to practice the Jewish Law as perfectly as possible, and who fiercely persecuted the Christians. According to *The Acts of the Apostles* (8:3–4), Saul destroyed the Christian community in Jerusalem; "ravaging the church, and entering house after house, he dragged off men and women and committed them to prison." He consented to the death of Christian Jews, and was "breathing threats and murder against the disciples of the Lord." Yet, this violent persecutor of Christians became the founder of Christianity. He was responsible for the fact that an insignificant Jewish sect, the leader of which was crucified in spite of the expectations of his followers, gave rise to one of the great religions of the world. According to the New Testament, this should be explained by the fact that God converted Saul, and elected him as an "instrument to carry My name before the Gentiles and kings and the sons of Israel" (*Acts* 9:15). But how should one explain psychologically Saul's conversion and his role as a founder of Christianity? This is the question Nietzsche tries to answer in section 68 of *Morgenröte*.

Saul's fanaticism in persecuting the Christians, Nietzsche says, is a symptom of his deep veneration for the Jewish Law. Saul would have attempted to satisfy the requirements of the Law with an uncompromising zeal. Unfortunately, the moral demands of the Jewish Law were so strict that it was impossible to comply with them. Again and again, Saul felt a tendency in himself to violate the commandments, and he became convinced of the "weakness of the flesh." In the end, he started to hate the Law. It was as if by its sublime and implacable nature, the Law itself seduced him to violate its decrees. The Law became as a cross to which Saul had been nailed. The more he failed to satisfy the moral commandments, the more he hated the Law.

According to *Acts* 9:3–6, Saul fell to the ground during his conversion, and he heard a voice saying to him: "Saul, Saul, why do you persecute me?" Nietzsche interprets this event as an epileptic attack, which may have been provoked by the mental tensions to which Saul was exposed. During the attack, Saul formed in his mind the thought that would save his life, by showing a way out of the *aporia* into which he had maneuvered himself. Was it not utterly stupid to persecute the followers of this Jesus of Nazareth? Is Jesus not the one who could release Saul from his obsession with the Law? Could Jesus not be used as a revenge on the Law for the fact that the Law had become Saul's personal cross? Had Jesus not liberated Saul already from his guilt, because Jesus had died for him on the cross?

Whereas initially the Crucifixion had been Saul's main motive for not believing that Jesus was the Messiah, his epileptic delusion gave rise to a radical reinterpretation of Christ's death on the cross, an event that had shocked Jesus' followers so deeply. Christ died on the cross, Saul now thought, in order to deliver us from our sins and in order to destroy the Jewish Law that gave rise to these sins. It was the psychological mechanism of resentment and revenge, then, which caused the conversion of Saul the Jew into Paul the founder of Christianity.

In section 68 of *Morgenröte*, Nietzsche draws a parallel with Luther. He suggests that Luther had also attempted to become perfect and justified according to the standards of traditional religion, Catholicism in his case. Luther did not succeed, and started to hate the spiritual ideal, the pope, the saints, and the whole clergy with a deadly hatred, a hatred that he did not dare confess. He then rationalized his hate, and became a reformer. In another text, section 358 of *Die fröhliche Wissenschaft* (*The Gay Science*), Nietzsche adds that Luther was also motivated by a hatred against the "higher type" of human being that the Roman Church had tried to promote. The Reformation was a plebeian revolt of a farmer's son against the spiritual aristocracy of Rome.[350] Luther tried to fulfill the exacting demands of the Augustinian order with as much zeal as Saul applied in trying to live up to the Jewish Law, and like Saul, Luther was harassed by deep feelings of guilt when he failed to do so.

Nietzsche's psychological interpretations of Paul and Luther are somewhat speculative, for at least in Paul's case we do not possess much biographical knowledge. The situation is different with regard to Heidegger. Is it possible to construe Heidegger's conversions to Nazism and to postmonotheism on a Nietzschean model, as a product of resentment against and revenge on the "religion of his origins" (Glaube der Herkunft)?[351] In section 11, I hinted at Heidegger's strict Roman Catholic upbringing, and I described how the Catholic Church thwarted the ambitions of young Martin three times. In 1909, Heidegger was rejected as a novice by the Jesuits; in 1911, he was forced to abandon his studies in theology; and in 1916, the chair for Catholic philosophy in Freiburg was given to Josef Geyser, even though Heidegger was a much more talented candidate. The rejection of 1911 seems to have thrown Heidegger into a deep crisis, from which he emerged only after a recovery process of several months.[352] The reason is clear: Heidegger's education had been paid for by the Church, and it seemed to be the very sense of his life that he would become a Catholic priest or even a bishop. In February 1911, however, the way to priesthood was blocked forever. Nevertheless, Heidegger got a grant from a Catholic foundation for writing his Habilitationsschrift, and in 1915, asking for a renewal of this grant, Heidegger wrote that his work would be devoted to the struggle for the Catholic ideals of life.[353] The historian Heinrich Finke had raised expectations that Heidegger could get the chair of Catholic philosophy in Freiburg, and because of Finke's influence, the ministry postponed making an appointment until Heidegger got his Habilitation. It is still unclear why Finke finally changed his mind. However, without any doubt the fact that Geyser was proposed as the only candidate convinced Heidegger that Catholics could not be trusted, and it threw him into an existential crisis for the third time.

When we add to these deceptions the harsh life Heidegger had led from the age of fourteen until the end of his Gymnasium education in the Catholic Konradihaus in Konstanz, we begin to suspect that Heidegger may have had many motives for resentment and wrath against the Church of Rome, motives stemming from his financial dependence on the Church and from his frustrated ambitions.[354] It is not difficult to document the fact that Heidegger gradually developed a fierce hatred for the Jesuits and the Catholic Church, and even for Christianity in general, similar to the hatred that Nietzsche attributed to Paul and Luther. There is a well-known passage, for instance, in a letter that Heidegger wrote to Elisabeth Blochmann on 22 June 1932, where he says that if communism is perhaps terrible (grauenhaft), Jesuitism is devilish (teuflisch).[355] Furthermore, there are many invectives against Christian faith and philosophy in Heidegger's lectures and in Beiträge zur Philosophie.[356] Finally, there is the violently anti-Catholic letter that Heidegger wrote as a rector to the Reichsführer of the German students, Oskar Stäbel.[357] One cannot doubt, it seems to me, what Nietzsche's view on Heidegger would have been. Like Paul and Luther, Heidegger started to hate the religion of his origins because he was not able to live up to its demands. One of his reasons for becoming a Nazi may have been that he saw in Nazism and in Nietzsche's notion that God is dead a cross on which he could nail Christianity. The most effective way to destroy Christianity was to develop a new and anti-Christian religion. This, Nietzsche would have said, was the psychological point of Heidegger's later Neo-Hegelian and postmonotheist works.

Critique

BECAUSE OF their abstruseness Heidegger's works are highly resistant to criticism. Indeed, Heidegger seems to have felt that an attempt to express clearly what he wanted to say would shipwreck his philosophical project, for in *Beiträge zur Philosophie* he wrote: "to make oneself understood is suicidal to philosophy."[1] My analysis of Heidegger's postmonotheist leitmotif explains why this is the case for a postmonotheist philosopher. As soon as the postmonotheist strategy is overtly expressed, it will fail to be effective (see § 11C.6: *The Concealment of the Question of Being*). The *Grundbewegtheit* (fundamental drive) of Heidegger's philosophy turned out to be a religious quest, an attempt to become an authentic believer, ultimately by overcoming the Christian tradition. However, as Heidegger wrote in "Mein bisheriger Weg" ("My Way Up Until the Present Moment") of 1937–38, a text published posthumously only in 1997, the very fact that the "most inner experiences and decisions remain the essential thing" implies that "they must be kept far from the public domain."[2] Heidegger admits here that his philosophical writings are informed by a hidden religious agenda, and this fact explains why they are so excessively difficult to understand. In another posthumously published text from 1937–38, "Beilage zu Wunsch und Wille" ("Supplement to Wish and Will"), Heidegger asserts that those who read his lecture courses on philosophers of the past, such as Plato, Hegel, or Nietzsche, as historical accounts and contributions to historical scholarship *"have understood nothing at all."*[3] The reason is that these lectures are essentially a "groping for the truth of Being and its founding in Da-sein," which is "disguised in other thoughts."[4] Heidegger explicitly affirms in 1937–38 that groping for the truth of Being or asking the question of Being is nothing but asking "the unique question whether God is fleeing from us or not."[5]

There seems to be only one fruitful method for evaluating Heidegger's works. As I argued in sections 5 and 6 of this book, one should first try to give a purely historical interpretation of his thought, which is as clear and as charitable as possible. A critique of Heidegger's philosophy should then aim at his texts *as* clarified by the interpretation. An advocate of Heidegger may still feel that the critic does not understand what Heidegger wanted to say. But now the burden of proof lies with him or her, and not with the critic. The Heideggerian has to show what is wrong with the interpretation on which an evaluation is based, and or she or he has to demonstrate this in detail by providing an alternative account of the texts.

In this chapter, I attempt to assess the fundamental themes in Heidegger's question of being. In order to exhibit what is interesting, fruitful, and true in Heidegger's question of being, one has to separate it from the false, the misleading, and the sterile. In doing so, one inevitably uses one's own criteria, which are not necessarily Heidegger's standards. Indeed, one may wonder whether Heidegger endorsed any standards in evaluating philosophers other than the assumed truth of his grandiose philosophical narrative. As we saw, he rejected the canons of scientific procedure and of historical scholarship, and he despised common sense. He even repudiated logic and the requirements of clarity. All this he gave up in favor of "thinking," that is, in favor of an attempt to relate to "Being."

I argued in section 2 of this book that one cannot repudiate logic and yet continue to speak or write meaningfully. Refusing to be clear has perhaps the advantage that what one says will never be unambiguously refuted. However, it has the disadvantage that one will not really know what one is saying, and that one will never learn, because one learns only when one is prepared to put to a test what one asserts, and testing one's assertions requires clarity. This is also true in relation to thinking about our own lives. Heidegger's works are fascinating to many because they are concerned with human existence. It is often supposed that in this domain one cannot have the same demands for clarity as in science. Philosophers who are preoccupied with lucidity are inclined to infer that in order to be clear, one has to be scientific and impersonal. This is a mistake, which Walter Kaufmann once dubbed the pedantic fallacy.[6] There is no reason why one should not try to be clear and precise in thinking about human existence. Wittgenstein wrote to Norman Malcolm in 1944: "what is the use of studying philosophy if all that it does for you is to enable you to talk with some plausibility about some abstruse questions of logic . . ., and if it does not improve your thinking about the important questions of everyday life."[7] Improving our thinking means, among other things, learning to think more lucidly. In assessing the fundamental leitmotifs of Heidegger's question of being I will use the criteria of consistency, conceptual clarity, and general academic method.

There is probably no intellectual tradition that has contributed as much to undermining the virtues of clarity and critical discussion as the tradition of dogmatic theology, and it is easily explained why this is the case. From an intellectual point of view, the contemporary Christian theologian, for example, finds himself faced with a difficult dilemma. Modern man will not be able to endorse numerous assertions made in the *New Testament* as they were originally intended. Should the theologian officially reject these statements? Then it will seem arbitrary that he sticks to others, and the claim that the Bible contains a divine revelation, and, indeed, that it has some special authority at all, will be seriously undermined. Or should the theologian resort to the device of "interpreting" the statements in such a way that they become acceptable to the modern believer? This is the procedure usually adopted, but it violates the canon of method for historical interpretation. When a modern theologian interprets a biblical text, he usually reads into this text what he himself wants to believe, discarding its original meaning. Such an interpretation is purely applicative and it does not aim at historical adequacy.

We have seen that Heidegger applies this theological procedure in interpreting the tradition of Western philosophy. He objects to criticizing philosophers of the past.[8] Instead, he interprets the "essential" thinkers and pretends that they all express the same elusive thought, the thought of Being. Yet the essential thinkers did not think this thought explicitly, for doing so is to be Heidegger's prerogative.[9] As we saw in sections 5 and 11C.1, Heidegger insists that in interpreting great philosophers, one should covertly add something out of the topic (*Sache*) of the interpretation. This is indeed what he is doing, for allegedly Heidegger's Being is the topic of thought. I prefer not to apply this dubious procedure. By projecting one's cherished ideas into the writings of philosophers, one does not do justice to their intentions. The "violence" in his interpretations, of which Heidegger seems to be proud, is in fact nothing but a refusal to take authors seriously as human beings. Philosophers of the past are used as a mere means for telling one's own philosophical narrative; they are not considered as "ends in themselves" and as real partners in an ongoing debate.

Instead of reinterpreting philosophers until they supposedly say what one wants them to say, one ought to take them at their word by carefully testing one's interpretative hypothesis, and to discuss critically what they are in fact contending. Critical discussion and conceptual analysis are the primary media of philosophy, not applicative interpretation or hermeneutics, procedures that belong primarily to the traditions of theological and legal thought, in which there are texts that carry authority. According to Heidegger, the advance of science and critical discussion in the Western tradition is in reality a decline, fall (*Abfall*), or regress into Darkness. To the liberating tradition of critical discussion and independent research he prefers, at least from the early 1930s on, a style of thought that is both authoritarian and obscure, mythical and reactionary.[10] I am afraid that I cannot agree with Heidegger on this crucial point, and I will not have much patience with the two fundamental leitmotifs of Heidegger's later works, the Neo-Hegelian and the postmonotheist themes. I criticize them briefly in section 16 without trying to be exhaustive, because I do not think that, once they are brought to light and exposed clearly, they will be accepted by any sensible person.

Heidegger's Neo-Hegelian and postmonotheist leitmotifs are forms of anti-naturalism and anti-intellectualism. The fundamental stances of deep history, and postmonotheist Being that sends us these stances, are said to be beyond the domain of reason and empirical research. Yet they are supposed to be more fundamental than what is accessible to science and reasoning. Heidegger's philosophy allegedly prepares us for a choice between science and logic on the one hand, and "thinking of Being" on the other hand.[11] It is the upshot of my argument in section 16 that if there is a choice on this point, it is the choice between intellectual honesty and obscurantism. If we must make this choice, as Heidegger argues, it seems obvious to me that we ought to reject the alternative that Heidegger himself prefers.

The philosophy of *Sein und Zeit*, which I discuss in section 17, is also antinaturalist. As we saw in section 9A, Heidegger adopts a variety of transcendentalism in order to show that science rests on an all-embracing and optional projected framework, which fails to do justice to the world as it really is. I argue that this transcendental leitmotif does not stand up to critical scrutiny. There is yet a second antinaturalist stratagem in *Sein und Zeit*, and this is the conviction, which Heidegger inherited from Aristotle and Husserl, that the totality of beings is neatly carved up into ontologically distinct regions that each have their a priori essence, so that ontology logically precedes the ontical sciences. Applied to Dasein, this thesis of the regionality of being implies that discoveries made in biology, for example, can have no bearing on what we think about the ontological constitution of human existence. In *Sein und Zeit*, Heidegger already accepted by implication what he proclaims explicitly in the "Brief über den 'Humanismus' "—that what scientific disciplines discover about humans cannot be essential to Dasein.[12] We will have good reasons to reject Heidegger's notion of regional ontologies as well, and, indeed, to reject his very distinction between the ontical and the ontological.

What, then, is fruitful and positive in *Sein und Zeit*? Not Heidegger's assumption that in order to analyze the various meanings of "to be" we must use a phenomenological method, for Heidegger's principle of referentiality as applied to the verb "to be" is false. We should also reject Heidegger's conviction, derived from Aristotle's philosophy of science, that philosophy is somehow more fundamental than the sciences. What is fruitful and novel, however, is Heidegger's attempt to give a philosophical or structural account of how we understand ourselves in ordinary life. His thesis that our daily understanding of life (*Alltäglichkeit*) is very different from what many traditional philosophers supposed it to be, when they applied categories such as substance or matter and form to it, is plausible indeed. Quotidian human self-understanding neither can be reduced to, nor should it be eliminated in favor of, a scientific account of humans and their brains. To this extent Heidegger's antinaturalism is correct. But he was mistaken in believing that our common self-understanding and science are necessarily incompatible, and, therefore, equally misguided in believing that he had to relegate science to an inessential position in order to rescue the "meaningfulness" of human existence.

If I accept the philosophical project of *Sein und Zeit* to some extent, I do not approve of it as it stands. The project was ruined not only by a muddled method, the method of hermeneutical phenomenology, but first of all by Heidegger's Pascalian objectives. The analysis of *Angst* and death was meant to persuade readers that the pathological state of anxiety is the hallmark of authenticity, and that death is "Dasein's ownmost possibility."[13] These statements, if they are meaningful at all, fly in the face of common sense, and their only possible point is that they prepare a leap to religion and afterlife. I argue in section 18 that the philosophical project of preparing man for the leap to religion by a secular analysis of the human condition is incoherent. If the analysis is not religiously biased, it will not induce us to make leaps of any sort. In order to provide a compelling motive for a leap into nothingness and for raising the question of Being, Heidegger had to distort our common understanding of the human condition.

The composition of this critical chapter is informed by the idea that in order to perceive what is valuable in Heidegger's contribution to philosophy, we have first to remove "some of the rubbish that lies in the way to knowledge," as Locke once said. This is the reason why I start with discussing the two leitmotifs that constitute the question of being in Heidegger's later works, the Neo-Hegelian and the postmonotheist themes (§ 16). According to my opinion, there is nothing in these leitmotifs that withstands criticism. The same idea structures section 17, in which I assess the transcendental leitmotif and the phenomenologico-hermeneutical theme in *Sein und Zeit*. By carefully peeling off the indigestible integuments of Heidegger's ontology of Dasein, I try to penetrate into its nourishing and fruitful core. Finally, section 18 aims at substantiating my assessment of *Sein und Zeit* by an analysis of what Heidegger says about two special and crucial topics, death and the multitude (*das Man*).

I decided to omit a separate assessment of the meta-Aristotelian theme, which provides the bipolar structure of the question of being in the two main phases of Heidegger's thought. As we saw in section 7, Heidegger's idea that the question of being is the most fundamental question man can ask is probably not derived from the meta-Aristotelian theme; rather, it is informed by the transcendental and the postmonotheist leitmotifs. Furthermore, the meta-Aristotelian theme turned out to be based on a foundationalist philosophy of science that is now generally rejected, so that an assessment of this leitmotif would contribute nothing new and merely repeat well-known critiques of foundationalism in the philosophy of science. Accordingly, I merely assess the four leitmotifs that give real content to Heidegger's question of being.

I must confess that my evaluation of Heidegger's philosophy of being comes out more negatively than I anticipated when I started working on this book. I console myself with the thought that truth is more important than allegiance to a philosophical movement or loyalty to a particular thinker. Moreover, the reader will remember that I merely assess the fundamental structures or leitmotifs of Heidegger's philosophy. Even if these leitmotifs are not acceptable, Heidegger's writings contain many striking and provocative thoughts that may inspire us.

Some readers will object to my assessments of Heidegger's philosophy of being that I often use arguments developed by other philosophers, such as Wittgenstein or Strawson, and that for this reason my criticisms are external rather than internal. Indeed, many hermeneutical authors have a marked preference for internal criticisms or "deconstructions" of philosophers, criticisms that merely use ideas put forward by the thinker whose works are under scrutiny. We saw that Heidegger himself has this internalist preference, but that his allegedly internal evaluations of philosophers such as Aristotle or Nietzsche are in fact attacks from the outside disguised as tensions within Aristotle's or Nietzsche's works (see §§ 7A and 15A).

It is preferable to be open and above board in one's dealings with other philosophers. Moreover, there is no good reason for preferring internal to external critique. By limiting oneself to internal criticisms, one at best establishes the (in)consistency of a doctrine, never its truth or the falsity of specific theses. But consistency and inconsistency are important only because two mutually inconsistent statements cannot both be true; hence the ultimate rationale of internal criticism or deconstruction must be to determine whether a doctrine is true or false. Since a merely internal critique never suffices for doing so, the champion of internal criticism is internally incoherent. The important question is not whether critical arguments are internal or external; it is whether they are sound or mistaken. Only if one believes that authority is decisive in the domain of thought will one think that it is relevant to the validity of an argument who its author was.

§ 16. THE LATER WORKS

According to the interpretation submitted in this book, there are only two fundamental themes in Heidegger's later works, the Neo-Hegelian and the postmonotheist leitmotifs. These themes are narrowly related, because Being in the postmonotheist sense is conceived of as a transcendent and hidden Event or Actor, which sends (*schickt*) us history-shaping epochs (*Geschicke*) in which beings are disclosed in specific ways or senses of "being." Postmonotheist Being dispatches Neo-Hegelian fundamental stances and conceals itself in this process.

As we have seen in section 12A, there is a contradiction between the postmonotheist theme and the Neo-Hegelian leitmotif; hence they cannot both be true. Heidegger claims that the sequence of fundamental stances that constitute deep history is lawful or logical. He assumes that there is an ever-deeper Fall from an original Beginning, a continuing regression into Darkness. In our epoch of technology, Being in the postmonotheist sense allegedly is more concealed than ever. I argued that this view faces a dilemma, which Heidegger was unable to resolve. Either Being is really concealed, as the postmonotheist leitmotif has it. In that case we can never know whether the logic of the Neo-Hegelian leitmotif is Being's logic, and this latter leitmotif as a whole is illegitimate. Or, alternatively, we are able to fathom the logic of Neo-Hegelian deep history. But now Being is not really concealed, contrary to what Heidegger claims in the postmonotheist leitmotif.

It seems, then, that there are inconsistencies in Heidegger's later writings, which arise because the two leitmotifs are not always compatible. However, I will not pursue this line of criticism further, because I propose that we reject both the Neo-Hegelian and the postmonotheist themes. Reversing the order in which I presented them, I now first assess the postmonotheist leitmotif (A) and then discuss the Neo-Hegelian theme (B). Finally (C), I make some comments on Heidegger's use of rhetoric in the later works, arguing that it is intimately connected with these leitmotifs.

A. *Postmonotheism Repudiated*

The postmonotheist leitmotif may be criticized for reasons of two different kinds, religious and philosophical ones. Let me briefly explore possible religious motives for repudiating this theme, taking John Caputo's work as an example of such criticisms, before going into philosophical reasons.

In an instructive paper on Heidegger and Eckhart, Caputo discusses a number of parallelisms between these two authors.[14] Both Eckhart and Heidegger reject a merely anthropological or secular account of mankind and they claim that man must be understood in relationship to something that transcends beings. They both hold that the greatness of man is nothing purely human; it rather rests in the alleged fact that man is a privileged place in which the transcendent comes to pass. This place is what Heidegger calls Dasein in the later works, and we might add to Caputo's essay that Heidegger follows Eckhart where he exhorts us to "transform ourselves into our Dasein." Moreover, both Eckhart and Heidegger claim that we run the risk of forgetting about the hidden place (*Da*) in us, because we engage in worldly occupations. According to Heidegger, this Fall (*Verfallen, Abfall*) has become complete in the era of technology. Furthermore, they both stress that Being and Dasein belong together to the point that they are nothing but two poles of a relationship. In a true mystical fashion, the belonging together of Being and man is even conceived of as an identity.[15] There are many other parallelisms, such as between Heidegger's and Eckhart's views on language, on grace or gift, and on resignation (*Gelassenheit*). Finally, both Eckhart and Heidegger think that Being is present in all beings. God penetrates his creatures, says Eckhart, and man should learn to discover him in them. Similarly, one might add, Heidegger claimed already in *Sein und Zeit* that Being is a "hidden phenomenon" in all beings, the phenomenon *par excellence*, which phenomenology should uncover.[16] In Heidegger's hands, phenomenology becomes a "method" of discerning something that does *not* show itself to us, the nonphenomenon of Being. As I said in section 11, Eckhart played a crucial role in Heidegger's career, not only in his early years but also in shaping the postmonotheist theme. This hypothesis is amply confirmed by Caputo's work on Eckhart and Heidegger.

Having discussed parallelisms between the two German masters, Caputo raises the question of where Heidegger really differs from Eckhart.[17] The differences that he discusses give rise to religious criticisms of what I have called the postmonotheist theme. First, Eckhart's God is a God of love, so that the relationship between God and the soul is one of loving trust. In Heidegger's case, the situation is radically different. Because Heideggerian Being is not *a* being, it cannot have a will, let alone a good and loving will. Heidegger concurs with Eckhart that humans must be released to Being. But, in the second place, if they are so released, they will discover that although Being is a ground (*Grund*), this ground is also an abyss (*Abgrund*). In other words, Being is not a principle of intelligibility, as was the Christian God, but it is unintelligible. Whereas Hegel identified Being with Absolute Reason, so that the real is rational and the sequence of historical epochs is regulated by a principle of unfolding rationality, Heidegger holds that we must acknowledge the inscrutability of Being. The Event of Being, Heidegger says, is a play (*Spiel*). Deep history is the history of the play of Being, of its "fluctuating retreat and advance, revelation and concealment," as Caputo says. This explains that where Eckhart can speak of peace, Heidegger likes to talk about a venture, a wager on the outcome of a portentous, dangerous game.[18] Accordingly, Dasein does not trust; it can only hope for and prepare by thought a future advent of Being.[19] But, Caputo wonders, if Heidegger has undermined all possible grounds for trust, how can there be grounds left for a reasonable hope? In the third place, by denying that Being is *a* being, Heidegger has divorced Being from any possible personalist conception. There is no talk of father, son, and giving birth, as there is in Eckhart. In Caputo's view, this must be counted as the most decisive difference between Eckhart and Heidegger.

These dissimilarities between Eckhart and Heidegger, and indeed, between the Christian tradition and Heidegger's postmonotheism, may give rise to serious religious objections. If there is nothing in Heidegger's Event (*Ereignis*) to love and almost everything to fear and mistrust, Caputo says, "it is hard to see how the 'releasement' for which Heidegger asks can continue to make any sense." The reason is that this releasement "is detached from its religious context, . . . from its relationship to a loving God."[20] Admittedly, Heidegger says that Being gives being, and that Dasein thanks Being for it. But in Heidegger's model of Being, giving and thanking cannot mean what they mean in a relation between persons. As Caputo writes: "there is nothing benevolent about the giving of the Event; there is no gratitude in the thanking of Dasein."[21]

Caputo's criticisms may be interpreted in two ways. A first interpretation is purely religious. I said in section 11C.6 that the champion of postmonotheism faces a dilemma of strategy. On the one hand, what he says has to resemble monotheism sufficiently for satisfying the same religious cravings. On the other hand the postmonotheist doctrine should not resemble monotheist religions too closely. For in that case it will be interpreted as yet another watered-down version of Christianity, and the postmonotheist strategy of saving religion after the death of the Christian God will founder. One way of interpreting Caputo's objections is that Heidegger, eager to avoid the second horn of the dilemma, impaled himself on the first. His postmonotheist discourse differs too much from traditional religion. For that reason it cannot satisfy the religious needs that Christianity satisfied, the longings of the human heart for eternal love and peace.

However, such a religious criticism of the philosophy of Being is problematic for two reasons. Heidegger might reply that his religious needs were different from the Christian ones. This reply reduces Caputo's criticisms to a matter of religious taste. As we have seen, there are reasons to suppose that Heidegger's religious cravings were not the same as those of Roman Catholics. According to the tentative hypothesis that I put forward in section 14B, Heidegger tried to develop an authentically German religion in *Beiträge zur Philosophie*, and this unpublished book informed his entire later oeuvre. Hitler and Himmler wanted to replace the Christian God of love with a German God of strife and war, to which individual Germans might be willing to sacrifice themselves. Heidegger's Being is a plausible candidate for this job, for Heidegger talks repeatedly about strife (*Streit*) and sacrifice (*Opfer*). If my hypothesis can be substantiated by further research in the Heidegger archives, Heidegger's later works are a continuation of Nazism by other means.

A second objection might be that the pragmatic question about which religious cravings are satisfied by a specific doctrine is *toto coelo* different from the question as to the truth and meaningfulness of this doctrine. One may believe in a doctrine because it is satisfactory to do so, even though this doctrine is false or meaningless. Conversely, one might reject Heidegger's postmonotheism because it does not satisfy one's religious needs and yet the doctrine might be true.

This rejoinder brings me to a second interpretation of Caputo's criticisms. At some points he seems to be arguing that what Heidegger says about Being is not true or false, because it is devoid of sense. Heidegger's notion of authenticity (*Eigentlichkeit*) in *Sein und Zeit,* according to which death is man's deepest and most individual possibility, is replaced in the later works by the Event (*Er-eignis*) of Being, whereby the Truth of Being is disclosed to us. "Nonetheless," Caputo observes, "one wonders whether this is anything more than a merely verbal maneuver." "What possibilities for man lie in the 'Event'? The whole notion in the later Heidegger of a 'higher' humanism has a tendency to slip into a rather vacuous play on words."[22] Again, speaking about Heidegger's notion of releasement (*Gelassenheit*), Caputo says: "It is hard to see how the 'releasement' for which Heidegger asks can continue to make sense once it is detached from its religious context, . . . from its relationship to a loving God."[23] Finally, Caputo seems to suggest that Heidegger's notion of thinking as thanking is devoid of meaning as well, for it "rests not on any personalistic overtones of the Event but on the kinship—etymological or otherwise—of '*Denken*' and '*Danken*.' "[24] What can it mean to thank if one cannot thank somebody? There is, Caputo says, no gratitude in the thanking of Dasein.[25] But a notion of thanking that does not involve gratitude is nonsensical.

The charge of meaninglessness is not a typically religious criticism of Heidegger; it is a philosophical objection. Moreover, in the hands of a religious author such as Caputo the charge is not without risks, because it might backfire on traditional monotheism. Let us therefore leave the domain of religious strife, and turn to philosophical reasons for rejecting Heidegger's postmonotheism.

Heidegger stresses again and again that "essential thinkers" will not be able to argue for their views or to support them by empirical evidence. Heideggerian thinking or questioning, we saw in section 11B.10, just means authentically believing, and authentically believing seems to be defined implicitly as believing what Heidegger asserts about Being.[26] What can be said, the reader might ask, in favor of a belief *vis-à-vis* Heidegger? It may be that we will endorse Heidegger's sayings on Being as soon as we are talked into a specific fundamental mood (*Grundstimmung*). Is being in a mood a good reason to believe what Heidegger contends? We might pursue two separate lines of criticism here, a semantic and an epistemological line, which may be combined into the following dilemma.

Religious belief, including postmonotheist faith, either transcends the domain of reason and scientific discourse altogether or it may be evaluated by reasonable criticism and discussion. The first horn of this dilemma, which Heidegger accepts, might be called the doctrine of faith transcending reason.[27] If faith transcends reason, the believer is not allowed to say anything about the object of faith that might possibly conflict with present or future empirical findings. This requirement implies that it becomes very hard to say something meaningful about the object of one's belief. All possible developments in the empirical world must be compatible with a faith that transcends reason. The truth or falsity of the religious doctrine cannot make any difference which is detectable by empirical or rational means. If one endorses even a weak verificationist principle in the theory of meaning, one must conclude that religious doctrines that transcend reason are meaningless. And if one rejects all versions of the verification principle, one still has to explain how the believer is able to give meaning to his doctrines if he cannot point to any empirical implication of what he believes.

It seems that Heidegger does not succeed in doing so. He says for instance that Being acts in various ways: it sends epochs and conceals itself. How can it make sense to attribute actions to Being if one denies that Being is an entity? Only entities like persons can meaningfully be said to be agents. Indeed, the grammatical role of the term "Being" in Heidegger's discourse on Being, as a subject in action sentences, is incompatible with Heidegger's denial that there is an entity called Being. Furthermore, Heidegger claims that we will be saved by the Event (*Ereignis*) of Being. What can it mean to be saved, if being saved will not have any detectable influence on our lives, since the discourse of Being is claimed to be beyond the province of reason and empirical inquiry? If Heidegger's discourse of Being transcends this province, it must be mere rhetoric, and we simply have no idea what Heidegger means.

We come to the conclusion that if the first horn of the dilemma is true, this implies that it must be false, and therefore it is false. For if the doctrine that belief transcends reason implies, via a train of reasoned thought, that a belief which transcends reason cannot be expressed in meaningful language, then the doctrine implies that a belief which satisfies it is not a belief at all, because there are no beliefs without there being something which *is* believed. As this conclusion is established by reasoning, the doctrine that belief transcends reason is self-refuting.

Heidegger has to admit, then, that if his discourse of Being has any semantic content, it can be submitted to critical discussion. This discussion might proceed as follows. Religious believers, whether polytheist, monotheist, or postmonotheist, tend to claim that they have specific religious experiences that must be explained by supposing that their religious doctrine is true. The fact that they believe in God, they hold, has to be accounted for by the supposed facts that God exists and that he gave them faith in him by his grace. Similarly, Heidegger contends that if he speaks of Being, it is in reality Being that is speaking, and he assumes that specific fundamental moods (*Stimmungen*) attune one (*stimmen*) to the voice (*Stimme*) of Being. However, the explanation of faith or of religious experiences or moods by supposing that religious doctrines are true faces a second dilemma, which is fatal to such attempted explanations. This dilemma arises because of the plurality of religions.

As there are many religions, one must *either* admit that each of them has to be explained by supposing that the religious doctrine which it embraces is true. Consequently, one has to posit innumerable gods and supernatural beings, including Heideggerian Being. Religious people will find this result unacceptable, because they claim that only their own religious doctrine is completely true, so that religions are mutually incompatible. Even if they stress, like the Church of Rome, that there is much truth in other religions, they cannot hold that all religious doctrines are true simultaneously and entirely, for different religions contradict each other on many points.[28] The result of this first horn of the dilemma is equally unacceptable from a scientific point of view. It violates, among other standards of scientific reasoning, the principle of economy (Occam's razor), which implies that we should try to explain the phenomena of religious belief by one explanatory theory only, and not accept as many theories as there are religions.

Or believers might suppose that only their own religious doctrine has explanatory value in accounting for the psychological presence of faith in them, and explain the existence of other religions by a psychological theory of projection. But this second horn of the dilemma would be a case of special pleading. I do not think that the believer can provide a reasonable solution to the dilemma. This is why, if religious belief is open to critical evaluation, we should always try to explain its existence by adopting a secular theory of projection, which, in principle, is able to account for all forms of religion by means of one and the same set of hypotheses. In other words, we should not assume that religious doctrines are true in order to explain the fact that people believe in them.

I conclude that we ought to reject Heidegger's postmonotheist doctrine of Being in any case. If it transcends reason, it will be meaningless. If it does not transcend reason, it is shipwrecked by the dilemma of the plurality of religions.

Sometimes Heidegger claims that the philosophy of Being cannot be expressed in propositions, that is, in assertions that are true or false.[29] If this were the case, what Heidegger says would be neither true nor false and, indeed, he would not be *saying* or asserting anything, even though he misleads us by using the grammatical form of assertions in his discourse on Being. It is up to the Heideggerians to explain what kind of speech acts Heidegger is performing if he does not make assertions and yet appears to do so. Let it be sufficient here to observe that, if Heidegger did not assert anything, there is nothing to discuss either. Because to believe that *p* means: believing that *p* is true, we cannot even *believe* what Heidegger says if he does not assert anything, that is, if he does not make claims to truth. I argued in section 11 that Heidegger's postmonotheology appears to make sense because it bears structural resemblances to traditional Christian monotheism. We now see that it only *appears* to make sense. In fact, it is an empty play with words, which appeals to us because we like to think that there is more to human life than in fact there is, *even though we realize that no meaningful description of this "more" can be true.*

B. An Assessment of the Neo-Hegelian Leitmotif

The Neo-Hegelian theme in Heidegger's question of Being is a reversal of Hegelian *Heilsgeschichte*. Instead of being a progressive development of the Absolute, deep history is claimed to be a regression into the Darkness of the technological age, in which all traces of postmonotheist Being are wiped out. We may suppose that the notion of a history of grace (*Heilsgeschichte*) was invented by Christianity in order to account for the fact that the second coming did not occur soon after Christ's death, as the early Christians expected. In order to give meaning to this delay, Christians supposed that the Holy Spirit is active in history, slowly preparing the second coming, and this is still the doctrine of the Catholic Church. Heidegger's notion of a hidden history is a postmonotheist version of this view, and it is of the catastrophic type. He describes the age of technology in apocalyptic terms and holds that the saving Event will arrive only when danger is greatest.

The Neo-Hegelian leitmotif is also a variety of historicized Kantianism. Each historical epoch allegedly is determined by a fundamental stance (*Grundstellung*) or a transcendental framework, a holistic structure that determines how things appear to man in that epoch. Fundamental stances of the past are expressed in metaphysical systems, and the present era of science and technology is based on Nietzsche's metaphysics of the will to power. Because fundamental stances are a priori in relation to experience, to empirical science, and to a culture as a whole, the Neo-Hegelian theme restores metaphysics to the lofty position that it had lost in the first quarter of the twentieth century as a consequence of scientific revolutions and of the logical positivist's critique of metaphysics. The Neo-Hegelian theme is meant to bring about a conservative revolution in philosophy, for the metaphysician allegedly is able to grasp how and what things fundamentally *are* in a historical epoch.

As in the case of the postmonotheist leitmotif, there are ample reasons to suspect that Heidegger has not succeeded in giving a clear meaning to his Neo-Hegelian doctrine. It has been argued that the very idea of a comprehensive scheme or framework is difficult to understand.[30] In order to discern what it means, we would have to specify separately what is contained *in* the scheme and what is processed or organized *by* the scheme. Such a specification seems to be impossible if the scheme is really comprehensive. The problem is well illustrated by the paradoxes of Kantianism. Kant assumed that the transcendental framework contains the forms of space and time, and also categories such as substance and causality. This would explain why the world as perceived in terms of the scheme is a spatial and temporal world, which contains causally interacting substances. However, if the scheme is so comprehensive that it contains time, space, causality, and the other categories, how are we supposed to specify what is organized by the scheme? Kant answered that what is organized is a pure manifold of sensations, which arises because a world in itself impinges on our senses. This answer contradicts the idea that space, time, causality, and substance are structural features of the transcendental scheme, and cannot be ascribed to the input that is processed by the scheme. To speak of a manifold, for instance, is not justified unless we are able to say what kind of items the manifold consists of. A pack of cards taken as cards is a manifold, but taken as a pack it is only one. Saying this presupposes the categories of substance, property, and relation, which belong to the Kantian transcendental scheme, so that we cannot say what the input of the scheme is without using this very scheme: we cannot even say meaningfully that the input is a pure manifold. What is left, then, of the notion that there is such a thing as a comprehensive scheme, which organizes or structures something neutral that precedes it? Notoriously, the same paradox arises concerning causality. If causality belongs to the transcendental framework, we are allowed to apply the category of causality within the phenomenal world only. This excludes Kant's view that there is an input organized by the scheme, an input that arises because the world in itself impinges on our nerve endings. For clearly, "input" and "impinges" are causal terms.

Quine's watered-down version of Kantianism in *Word and Object* is paradoxical for similar reasons.[31] According to Quine, comprehensive linguistic structures are created in order to cope with a manifold of stimuli. In order to account for the stimuli that we receive and in order to predict their future course, we invented a language. Quine thinks that a language is a collection of sentences, and that a collection of sentences is a theory. The language we invented is said to be the simplest possible theory that accounts for the stimuli, and the objects we speak about by using the language allegedly are *posits*, entities postulated by the theory in order to explain and predict stimuli. Stimuli, Quine holds, are not sense data but rather triggerings of sensory receptors at the surface of our bodies. There are many things wrong with this view. For instance, languages such as English or French are neither collections of sentences nor theories. A language as such, which consists of a grammar and a vocabulary, does not assert or explain anything, although we *use* a language in asserting something in order to explain things.[32] But what interests us here is the fact that as soon as Quine has adopted the notion of a comprehensive conceptual scheme, he cannot specify without inconsistency what is organized or processed by the scheme. The notion of a stimulus will not do the job, because, as stimuli are not given to us as raw data in perception, they must be *posits* too, so that nothing remains which could motivate the invention of language in the first place.

Quine's doctrine of a comprehensive conceptual scheme that organizes or explains a manifold of stimuli is as incoherent as Kant's notion of a transcendental framework that organizes a manifold of sensations. The comprehensive scheme, we saw, tends to swallow what it was supposed to organize or explain. Quine has a liking for Neurath's image of a boat. Scientists and philosophers alike would be sailing in the boat of knowledge over a wide ocean, reconstructing their boat at sea. The image of the boat suggests that it is somewhat arbitrary where we start our reconstructions. As an epistemologist, Quine chooses stimuli as a starting point of his rational reconstruction of knowledge, for stimuli are the links where the causal chains between external objects and knowledge enter the body.[33] However, if external objects turn out to be posits, the causal chains must be posits as well, and so are the stimuli, so that Quine's empiricism evaporates during the rational reconstruction, leaving the residue of an incoherent linguistic idealism. Quine could have learned from Heidegger's *Sein und Zeit* on this point. If we are beings-in-the-world, we could just as well start our reconstruction of knowledge with ordinary objects in the world, such as chairs and tables. If we do so, the doctrine that these objects are *posits* cannot be justified, and it becomes clear that Quine's starting point was not arbitrary, because it produced the incoherent idealist result.

In the later works, Heidegger propounds a view similar to Kant's and Quine's, notwithstanding the deep differences among these three thinkers, for Neo-Hegelian fundamental stances are like a Kantian transcendental scheme and like a Quinean conceptual framework in that they are supposed to determine *as what* we will experience things. In contradistinction to Kant and Quine, Heidegger does not attempt to tell us what is organized by a Neo-Hegelian fundamental stance. Indeed, his view does not even leave real room for the very notion of a scheme that organizes or processes an input. The reason is that Heidegger rejects the scientific account of perception that is presupposed by Kant and Quine, an account that gives some plausibility to the picture that an input is processed by a transcendental framework, and that by processing an input the framework makes ordered experience possible. Heidegger either did not specify the content of his Neo-Hegelian doctrine at all, or he relied on some postmonotheist version of the creation myth, according to which the world is created differently in different eras.

In both cases, we ought to reject the Neo-Hegelian leitmotif: in the first case because it is empty; in the second case because we ought to reject postmonotheism

Heidegger claims that in different historical eras, things *are* in a different sense. Neo-Hegelian "being" would mean one thing in, say, the year 1300 and it would mean another thing in the era of technology. In the medieval epoch, Heidegger says, "being" meant being created by an omnipotent God, whereas in our times, "being" allegedly has the meaning of showing up for us as raw materials for production or consumption. But even if we assume that in the medieval epoch everyone believed that God created the world, it is difficult to see how such a belief could function as a transcendental condition for the possibility of experience. Surely medieval men did not need their religious convictions in order to see that there were trees and mountains and animals around. We should rather say that their religious beliefs somehow "colored" some of their perceptions. In modern times the exploitation of nature is much more advanced than it used to be, and sometimes it has disastrous effects. But is the notion that we might exploit nature a transcendental condition for being able to perceive trees and rivers, as Heidegger suggests?

In *Sein und Zeit*, Heidegger argued that seeing something *as* something is more fundamental than seeing something. Put in his terminology, understanding (*Verstehen*) would be more fundamental than perception (*Anschauung*).[34] On the basis of this premise, he might conclude that a thirteenth-century monk lived in another world than we do. The monk would perceive everything *as* created by God, and we would perceive everything *as* possible raw materials for production and consumption. Heidegger suggests that the two epochs are incommensurable for this reason. However, if perceiving *as* were really more fundamental than perceiving *tout court*, and if cultures were incommensurable, it would be impossible to learn to understand another culture, whereas the Neo-Hegelian leitmotif assumes that we are able to do so, for it speaks of different comprehensive frameworks and tries to specify their contents. It is both more plausible and more coherent to assume that humans have approximately the same perceptual world because they have approximately the same discriminatory capacities, and that cultural differences in perceiving *as* are secondary, built on a common perceptual world.[35] It is incoherent, then, to claim that the medieval belief in God's creation, or our tendency to exploit nature, are transcendental conditions for the possibility of experience, and it is implausible to pretend that perceiving *as* is more fundamental in this sense than perceiving.

These are not the only reasons why Heidegger's Neo-Hegelian leitmotif does not make sense. Heidegger sometimes suggests that what is true is relative to a fundamental stance. The truths of science allegedly are true only on the basis of the modern "mathematical" framework and there would be no neutral facts on which science can be established.[36] Both truth and facts would be relative to a conceptual scheme or fundamental stance. Heidegger embraced relativism concerning truth in order to substantiate his antinaturalism. But Heidegger's relativism concerning truth is a muddled position. Admittedly, it is correct to say that in order to express true statements, we need the concepts that are required for doing so. The ancient Greeks could neither express nor grasp the truths of quantum mechanics because they did not possess the relevant concepts. Concepts are relative to a conceptual scheme in the trivial sense that they are part of it. Yet it does not follow, and it is indeed misleading to say, that the truths of quantum mechanics are relative to a conceptual scheme. What is said, when something is said by using the terminology of quantum mechanics, is true if things are as they are said to be. If it is true, it is true *simpliciter*. What makes the statement true is something in the world, not something in the world plus a conceptual framework. To assert that truths are relative to a conceptual framework either means that we need such a framework in order to formulate statements that are true or false, which is trivial, or it means that one and the same statement might be true relative to one framework and false relative to another. This idea is incoherent, as I will argue in section 17A.

It is often claimed that what was true for the ancient Greeks is not true for us.[37] This is correct if one merely means that the Greeks believed things that we now reject. Here one uses "to be true for" in the sense of "to believe." It was true for Aristotle that the earth is located in the middle of a spherical universe, because this is what Aristotle believed. But if one infers that it is somehow *true* that the earth is located in the middle of a spherical universe, namely, true-for-the-Greeks, and that, therefore, it cannot be false at the same time, except *for us*, so that truth is relative to a culture, one is taken in by the misleading form of the words "true for x." It was introduced in the sense of "x believes," and surely what someone believes may be false. Aristotle was simply wrong in believing that the earth occupies the center of a spherical universe. Heidegger argues that the ordinary concept of truth is superficial, and he replaces it by transcendental and postmonotheist conceptions. If he had analyzed the ordinary notion of truth more carefully, he would have avoided the incoherent view that truth is relative. This view is not only incoherent; it also undermines itself. For if it is true that truth is relative, relative to which conceptual scheme would *this* truth be true (see §§ 16C.4 and 17A, below, for further discussion)?[38]

Heidegger's Neo-Hegelian theme, we may conclude, is infected by meaninglessness and incoherence. One point that I have not yet discussed is his use of terms such as "technology" and "information," where he says that we live in the era of technology or of information.[39] What he means by this is that nowadays everything manifests itself to us as raw materials for production and exploitation, or as information. These claims are faced by a dilemma. If we take the terms "production," "exploitation," and "information" in their usual sense, Heidegger's claim is plainly false. We simply do not perceive our fellow humans, for example, as raw materials for exploitation, even though perhaps some Nazis did. If we nevertheless want to say that everything in our time appears as F, where F is some predicate, then we can do so only at the price of depleting F of its meaning. By including everything in the extension of F, we will reduce the intension to zero. This holds also for Nietzsche's use of the expression "will to power." The statement that everything is will to power is either plainly false or meaningless. What Nietzsche and Heidegger suggest is that it is true in some deep metaphysical sense. As is often the case, such metaphysical claims are a symptom of the misuse of words.

Apart from semantic objections to Heidegger's Neo-Hegelian theme, there are epistemological and moral objections. Let me mention first some epistemological problems. Heidegger claims that deep history cannot be discovered by the methods of historical scholarship and empirical research. Fundamental stances would be a priori. How are we supposed to know what the fundamental stance of our epoch consists in? It is no use to say that metaphysicians are able to discern it, for we now want to know what this ability of the metaphysicians looks like. If metaphysicians discover fundamental stances by being in specific moods, we will wonder how we might distinguish between fundamental moods and other moods. The difficulty is that Heidegger does not provide a criterion for doing so. Sometimes he claims that he has a specific epistemic gift for discerning what Being sends us, and he compares those who do not have this gift to people who are color-blind.[40] Unfortunately, this analogy with color-blindness does not withstand critical scrutiny. Color-blindness can be explained by specific defects in our visual apparatus, whereas I suppose that the inability to grasp what Heidegger claims to be discerning cannot be so explained. Heidegger relies on a epistemic model derived from theology, and assumes that he is the recipient of some kind of revelation.

This model is destroyed by what I call the sectarians' dilemma. If two philosophers, say Heidegger and anti-Heidegger, put forward conflicting claims about the fundamental stance of the present age, they each have two possibilities. They might either hold that both opposing claims are of equal epistemic value. If so, the claims are of no value whatsoever, because they contradict each other. Or they might each pretend that their own claim is somehow superior to the rival claim. Heidegger admits that this pretension cannot be substantiated by reasoning or empirical research, and he does not make clear how it can be substantiated otherwise. What Heidegger counts on, then, is that we will simply believe what he says. He uses a number of authoritarian rhetorical stratagems in order to obtain this perlocutionary effect, and he is remarkably successful in securing it, especially on the European Continent and in Japan, where analytical training in philosophy is sometimes less thorough than one should wish (see § 16C, below).

A little reflection suffices to reach the conclusion that the Neo-Hegelian leitmotif, if it makes sense at all, must be false. The idea that the history of Western civilization can be explained by the Heideggerian hypothesis of deep history, a sequence of homogeneous, simple, and comprehensive transcendental frameworks, which succeed each other with sudden breaks (*jäh*), cannot be squared with history as it actually is, because, among many other reasons, there are no clear empirical boundaries between historical epochs.[41] Heidegger's idealistic mo-nocausal explanation of history fares no better than other monocausal explana-tions, such as Marx's, and his metaphysics of history seems to be nothing but a hypostatization of textbook classifications of history in periods. As Franzen ar-gued convincingly, it is not an attempt to confront history, but an escape from historical realities.[42]

These epistemological criticisms are related to weighty moral objections. If one believes, as the Neo-Hegelian theme has it, that everything in our time is determined by the fundamental stance of technology, one will have to endorse a doctrine of global false consciousness. As long as we are not under the spell of Heideggerian thought, we will deny that everything appears to us as Heidegger claims that it does, namely, as raw materials for production and consumption. The Heideggerian will reply that this does not refute his doctrine, because supposedly we are not yet authentically attuned to the present fundamental stance: we do not yet grasp what *is*. The doctrine of a global false consciousness, whether it be Heideggerian, Marxist, or Nietzschean, implies that objections are not taken seri-ously; they are interpreted as confirmations of the very doctrine to which the critic objects. As a consequence, the person who objects is not taken seriously as a rational and critical interlocutor. In Marxist states, critics used to be imprisoned in psychiatric hospitals for this reason. One wonders what would have happened if Heidegger had been successful in his attempt to become a leading Nazi ideolo-gist. It may be that only his lack of success saved him from Nuremberg.

This first moral point is related to a second one. Heidegger's Neo-Hegelian doctrine that we should be attuned to the fundamental stance of our epoch implies that a moral critique of what happens is meaningless or inessential, an implication that Heidegger explicitly endorsed.[43] We saw that in 1933 Heidegger embraced Nazism without any moral reservations, claiming that we should not be guided in our existence by maxims and ideas, because "the *Führer* himself and alone *is* the present and future German reality and its law."[44] Heidegger italicized the word "is" in this statement in order to stress that Hitler was in accord with the funda-mental stance of Germany and of Europe in 1933. What the statement suggests is that *because* Hitler is in accord with the fundamental stance of 1933, he is the only moral authority that one should accept if one wants to be in accord with the times. The Neo-Hegelian theme resembles the Marxist notion of an objective historical necessity, to protest against which is not only useless but also immoral. Even in 1942, Heidegger saw Nazism as an inevitable expression of the reigning Neo-Hegelian fundamental stance.[45]

It may seem that Heidegger's postwar theme of technology refutes this criti-cism. Like many German conservatives, Heidegger developed a despondent cri-tique of technology after the war. He cast his philosophy of technology in terms of the Neo-Hegelian leitmotif, and he appeared to be extremely critical of technol-ogy. During the reign of technology (*das Wesen der Technik*), the earth will be destroyed and life will become meaningless. However, Heidegger's critique of technology cannot lead to fruitful action or critical discussion; it can only lead to quietism. Heidegger claims that the age of technology is a fate, so that it would be naïve to think that we could avert destruction and meaninglessness by any concrete measures.[46] The only thing that he advises us to do is to wait and to attempt to relate to Being by thought. Heidegger's seemingly "deep" critique of technology is nothing but pseudo-religious quietism disguised as a radical critique. The morally undesirable effect of this critique is that it condemns all real and fruitful criticisms of technology as superficial, naïve, and insufficiently radical.[47]

Finally, we saw in section 14C that Heidegger used the Neo-Hegelian theme in order to give a metaphysical fiat to Nazism. National Socialism allegedly was a metaphysical necessity, because it expressed the fundamental stance of the modern times. If Nazism was indeed metaphysically inevitable, Germans cannot be held responsible for its horrors, so that the Neo-Hegelian theme has an exculpating function. This function is not annulled by the fact that Heidegger calls the fundamental attitude of the modern epoch a ramble in which we go astray (*Irre*).[48] He claims that we cannot help going astray, and democracy is said to be part of this wrong track as well.[49]

Apart from metaphysically justifying Nazism as something inevitable, the Neo-Hegelian theme destroys the notion of morality in two more specific ways. First, Heidegger suggests that all events which occur within the framework of the modern fundamental stance are *morally* the same because they are *metaphysically* the same. In an unpublished lecture on technology of 1949, called "Das Ge-Stell" ("The Frame"), Heidegger said that "Agriculture is now a mechanized food industry, in essence the same as the manufacturing of corpses in gas chambers and extermination camps."[50] It seems to be the rhetorical point of this revealing text, which Heidegger wisely suppressed in the printed version of "Die Frage nach der Technik," that because the Holocaust is "essentially" or metaphysically the same as mechanized agriculture, to wit, an expression of the reign of technology, and because we accept mechanized agriculture without moral qualms, we should have no moral qualms about the Holocaust either.

Second, the Neo-Hegelian theme destroys morality because of Heidegger's specific view of our fundamental stance in the modern era. Heidegger holds that our present fundamental stance is expressed by Nietzsche's philosophy of the will to power. Now the doctrine of the will to power says that everything is will to power, including moral convictions. Christian morality allegedly is nothing but a strategic instrument of the will to power of the weak, and Heidegger suggests in 1945 that democratic morality is also a mere instrument of power.[51] But if moral judgments are reduced to a will to power, their inherent moral quality is denied. The doctrine of the will to power is a license for a ruthless struggle for power, and it was used in this way by the Nazis, who claimed that moral condemnations of their regime were nothing but propaganda by the Allies. We must conclude that Heidegger used the doctrine of the will to power in the very same way as the

National Socialists, in order to destroy moral discourse and to wipe out moral criticisms.

I argued in section 14A that Heidegger's destruction of morality began in *Sein und Zeit*. By relegating moral and political norms to the domain of inauthenticity, Heidegger destroyed all possible moral obstacles to a totalitarian regime. Whereas in 1927 authentic and free Dasein seemed to be its own moral justification if only it made resolute decisions, in 1933 Heidegger invested Hitler with a moral monopoly. Hitler allegedly was Germany's only reality and law. In section 14A, I developed a somewhat speculative hypothesis in order to explain Heidegger's *volte face* from radical autonomy to radical heteronomy in ethics. Investing Hitler with supreme and exclusive moral authority was an ominous move, which heralded Heidegger's ultimate destruction of morality. His final solution came in two phases: a first one when in the mid-1930s Heidegger introduced the idea that the will to power is the present fundamental stance, thereby reducing moral convictions to mere instruments of power; and a second phase in 1946, when Heidegger made Being into the unique heteronomous source of morality, claiming that laws cannot be binding if they are made by humans only.[52] It might be argued that Being is a better candidate for this role than Hitler, but we cannot be sure of that. Heidegger admits that Being has not yet issued moral commandments, so that the heteronomous ethical doctrine of the "Brief über den 'Humanismus' " destroys existing morality in the name of an unknown morality yet to come. What Heidegger says about ethics, both in *Sein und Zeit* and in the later works, is perverse and destructive. One ought to reject the Neo-Hegelian theme and the postmonotheist leitmotif, if only because of their implications for morality.

C. Heidegger's Rhetoric

"Who thinks grandly, must err grandly," Heidegger once wrote.[53] That he wrote "must" instead of "might" expresses his Neo-Hegelian and postmonotheist doctrine that man is doomed to err, so that our choice is at best between erring in a grand way and erring in a less majestic manner. In subsections A and B, I argued on semantic, epistemological, and moral grounds that Heidegger erred in proposing a postmonotheist and a Neo-Hegelian leitmotif. Heideggerians often quote Heidegger's statement about erring and go on being Heideggerians, as if erring were inevitable and acceptable. This is a regrettable mistake. If a philosopher erred, one ought to reject his errors. What one should repudiate first of all is Heidegger's gloomy and erroneous Neo-Hegelian doctrine that erring is inevitable, because it is nothing but a postmonotheist variety of the notion of an original sin.

We have seen that according to Heidegger no reasons can be adduced for endorsing his later philosophy. Thinking is beyond the domain of reason and empirical evidence. Why, then, we might wonder, are so many philosophers and men of letters impressed by what Heidegger says? Part of the explanation is that Heidegger's later discourse on Being is structurally parallel to traditional Christian discourse. Heidegger treats the parallelisms in a discrete manner, interspersing them in his long-winded exegeses of the philosophical tradition. They become obvious only when one lists them on the basis of a large sample of textual evidence, as I have done in section 11. However, the parallelisms are perlocutionarily effective because of the very fact that they are concealed in the texts and not stated as such. By means of these hidden powers, the texts will persuade those who reject traditional Christianity and yet want to remain religious in a more diffuse sense. Indeed, Heidegger is often praised as a thinker who tries to make us aware of our dependence on something "higher than ourselves." Another part of the explanation is Heidegger's clever use of rhetoric. Even those who are trained in analytical philosophy may be mesmerized by the extraordinary expressiveness and rhetorical power of Heidegger's later writings. I will now briefly discuss eight characteristic rhetorical stratagems that are often used by Heidegger and Heideggerians, most of which are rooted in the Neo-Hegelian and postmonotheist leitmotifs.[54]

1. The Stratagem of the Fall. If the Neo-Hegelian and postmonotheist doctrines were true, modern man would be fated to err. Heidegger erred grandly, because he erred in accordance with the present fundamental stance of the will to power. His opponents, however, err in petty ways, because, disagreeing with Heidegger, they do not acknowledge what *is* in our times, even though they are unwittingly determined by the present fundamental stance. Heidegger holds that logic is bound up with a false metaphysics that conceals Being, and that language in its ordinary uses blinds us to the light of Being as well. For this reason, opponents of Heidegger's philosophy who try to state their objections clearly and pay heed to the principles of logic, need not be refuted: the very medium of their thought is condemned beforehand, because they have fallen from the House of Being. Christians sometimes held that everything, from language to inanimate matter, had been corrupted by the Fall. Similarly, Heideggerians suggest that all ways of philosophizing other than their own are contaminated, and that one does not need to show this in detail. These ways of philosophizing simply belong to the "reign of technology" (*das Wesen der Technik*), or to the "era of information," to "logocentrism," or to whatever other pejoratively labeled comprehensive category Heideggerians may invent. All philosophers are in Plato's cave, except the Heideggerians.[55]

2. The Stratagem of the Radical Alternative. If everything that human beings do or think is contaminated by the Fall, redemption must consist in an alternative that is radically different from anything we are able to conceive of: an entirely new Beginning.[56] The conjunction of stratagems (1) and (2) puts the Heideggerian in a comfortable, because unassailable, "position": he may condemn all other philosophical doctrines and movements in the name of an alternative that is ineffable because it is radically different: the Saving Event. One will be tempted by the stratagem of the radical alternative until one perceives that the unassailable position is attained at the price of emptiness and that the way to this position is a way to nowhere. The stratagem is particularly damaging in relation to the problems of technology. It is vital for mankind to develop new types of technology that are ecologically stable, so that humanity will be able to last longer without destroying its ecosystem. Heideggerians will condemn and depreciate attempts to find such solutions to the problems of technology and overpopulation for not being sufficiently radical and for remaining within the "reign of technology."[57] As I said, this means that they advocate quietism under the guise of radical criticism.

3. The Stratagem of Undifferentiating Abstraction. Heidegger tries to characterize the fundamental stance of the present epoch by stretching indefinitely the extension of nouns such as "technology" and "information." We have seen that these nouns become meaningless by such an abstraction, even though Heidegger pretends that he is still using them meaningfully. I call this type of abstraction *undifferentiating* because Heidegger suggests that differences between items within the extension of these empty terms do not really matter and are indifferent. In 1935 he said that Russia and the United States are "metaphysically the same"; in 1945 he contended that communism, fascism, and democracy belong to one and the same metaphysical reality of the will to power; and in 1949 he ventured the opinion (which I quoted already) that "agriculture is now a mechanized food industry, in essence the same as the manufacturing of corpses in gas chambers and extermination camps."[58] We will not agree with Heidegger that there is no interesting difference between Stalin's Russia and Franklin Roosevelt's America, or between mechanized agriculture and extermination camps. Nonetheless, Heidegger's rhetoric suggests that the metaphysical deep structure that they allegedly have in common is infinitely more important than the differences between them. I commented above on the moral implications of this stratagem.

4. The Stratagem of Persuasive Redefinition. Theologians are masters of persuasive redefinition. It used to be the case that believing Christians were not allowed to doubt religious dogmas, but as soon as doubting the literal truth of the New Testament became widespread, theologians such as Paul Tillich were quick to point out that "real" faith does not exclude doubt. One has "faith" as long as one has an "ultimate concern" in life.[59] Nearly all core concepts of Christianity have been redefined in the course of Western history, because religious dogmas had become unacceptable in their original sense. Heidegger often uses this strategy of persuasive redefinition, and he applies it not only in the later works.

In section 44 of *Sein und Zeit*, for instance, he considers the common notion of truth, according to which it is true to say something if things are in fact as they are said to be. He argues that this notion of truth is not "fundamental." We establish that an assertion is true if we discover that things are as the assertion says. From this trivial premise, Heidegger infers that *being true* means *being discovering*. The truth of an assertion would consist in its being discovering, whereas false assertions conceal reality. Because it is primarily Dasein that discovers, Dasein, and not propositions, would be primarily "true." Heidegger concludes that "Truth, in the most primordial sense, is Dasein's disclosedness," and that Truth is an existentiale of Dasein.[60]

Heidegger's argument is a *non sequitur*, as a logical analogy shows. If a (transcendental) condition for being F should be called F "in a more primordial sense," mastering a language should be called "lying" in a more primordial sense because one cannot lie without mastering a language. In section 44 of *Sein und Zeit* Heidegger merely redefines the word "true." But he presents this redefinition as a deep discovery, claiming that he is "preserving the *force of the most elemental words* in which Dasein expresses itself." He pretends to "keep the common understanding (of these words) from leveling them off to that unintelligibility that functions as a source of pseudo-problems." The definition of "Truth" as being-uncovering would "not be a mere explanation of a word"; allegedly it emerges from an analysis of those ways in which *Dasein* comports itself, "which we are accustomed in the first instance to call 'true.' "[61] In reality, meanings of words do not emerge from an analysis of phenomena. Phenomena do not determine the rules of language, but we decide how we want to use a word, if we do not simply accept its current meaning. There is no deep revelation, then, in what Heidegger says about truth. Indeed, the facts that humans often discover whether something is true or not and that they are "openness" to the world in the sense that they are equipped for making such discoveries, is perfectly trivial. Heidegger confers the appearance of depth on his redefinition of the word "true" by presenting it misleadingly as a significant philosophical finding.

Initially we may wonder why Heidegger would want to redefine the word "true" and what the rhetorical point of disguising his redefinition as a discovery is, but my last quotation points the way to an answer. Heidegger claims that there are ways in which Dasein comports itself, "which we are accustomed in the first instance to call 'true.' " These ways are what he labels "Truth of Existence." He writes: "*authentic* disclosedness shows the phenomenon of the most primordial Truth in the mode of authenticity," and he adds that "the most primordial, and indeed the most authentic, disclosedness in which Dasein, as a potentiality-for-Being, can be, is the *Truth of Existence*."[62] Heidegger's play of redefinitions has brought us from the commonplace notion of propositional truth to a very different and much more nebulous notion, that of existential Truth. If my Pascalian interpretation of *Sein und Zeit* is correct, Heidegger assumes that we live in existential Truth whenever the Truth of Being is revealed to us, or, at least, when we open ourselves to grace by authentically being-toward-death. The potentiality-for-Being of which Heidegger speaks here must be our potentiality to receive Being's grace, that is, our potentiality to *be* in the full Eckhartian sense.

We saw in section 13D that Heidegger introduces in his later works two further persuasive redefinitions of the word "truth." The "essence" of Truth (*das Wesen der Wahrheit*) is the series of historical epochs that Being sends to humans, epochs in which entities *are* in a specific sense, whereas the Truth of Being (*die Wahrheit des Wesens*) is the way in which postmonotheist Being itself *is*, revealing beings

and concealing itself. Ultimately, then, the rhetorical point of Heidegger's stratagem of persuasive redefinition as applied to the word "truth" is a double one.
We should understand "truth" as the true way to live, that is, as paying heed to
postmonotheist Being and to Neo-Hegelian truths. This is the Truth of Existence.
And we should not worry too much about the truth of what Heidegger is telling
us, because the notion of propositional truth is superficial and ontologically derivative. Real questioning would not consist in critically discussing the claims that
Heidegger puts forward; it consists rather in blindly believing what he says and
in adopting a piously questioning attitude. If only we were to fathom the *essence*
of Truth, we would hold in proper contempt the question of whether Heidegger's
philosophy is true in the vulgar sense of propositional truth. In this manner, Heidegger purports to destroy the mental independence of his readers.

   5. Strategies of Immunization. Heidegger's notion of thinking as questioning
is one strategy of immunization among others. Heideggerians often claim that
criticism of what Heidegger says must be due to misunderstandings. This is a
time-honored theological strategy: if the Bible is God's word and if God is infallible, we will never criticize the Bible as long as we understand it well. Similarly,
if what Heidegger says is in fact what Being gives us to understand, and if Being
is the only source of Truth, as Heidegger suggests, then we should not criticize
Heidegger's later writings. I do not want to deny that criticisms may be unfair;
surely they might be due to misunderstandings. But this cannot be the a priori
predicament of all possible criticisms, unless Heidegger's postmonotheist doctrine of being is true and unless Heidegger is infallible. It is at this very doctrine
that my criticisms are aimed.

   Heidegger stressed repeatedly that we do not yet understand his question of
Being (see § 1, above). What he might mean by this puzzling statement is that
modern man is not attempting to hear the voice of Being, because he is preoccupied with mastering the world. Or perhaps Heidegger meant that Being itself does
not yet respond to our questioning. In that case we would not be able to understand
what the proper object of the postmonotheist quest is, because we will know this
only when Being reveals itself to us. According to Heidegger's Lutheran conception of faith, we will not really understand our religious quest until the moment
of grace has arrived. These claims presuppose that Heidegger's question of Being
has the postmonotheist meaning that I attributed to it. If one denies that this
interpretation is correct, hence that I have misunderstood Heidegger's question
of Being, one has the obligation to provide a better interpretation of the great
number of texts that seem to substantiate it.

   Yet another strategy of immunization is to denounce and to decry the very
notions of criticism and critical discussion. This is a venerable rhetorical move,
practiced by most traditional religions and in all totalitarian states. Heidegger
expressed his contempt for critical discussion many times. He said that by busily
wanting to refute, one will never be able to attain the way (*Weg*) of a thinker, and
that the urge to criticize belongs to those expressions of small-mindedness that

the general public needs for its entertainment.[63] In the "Brief über den 'Humanismus' " he wrote: "All refutation in the field of essential thinking is foolish," and in lectures of 1951–52 he said that the urge to be clear and unambiguous belongs to the reign of technology.[64] One might answer such claims with a shrug and view them as a desperate attempt by Heidegger to protect his highly questionable thought from criticism. Most philosophers in the Anglo-Saxon world agree that critical discussion is one of the essential methods of clarifying and testing ideas. It seems, however, that on the European Continent, Heidegger's rhetorical move of denouncing critical discussion has been effective. Seen from a properly philosophical perspective, the influence of Martin Heidegger in European philosophy resembles the destructions of the Second World War on the Continent of Europe. The birthplace of the Enlightenment has been invaded by a revolutionary and yet reactionary power, which aims at replacing the open and critical mind of the Enlightenment by totalitarian and authoritarian thought.

  6. *Stratagem of the Obedient Ear.* Heidegger's postmonotheist philosophy claims to be inspired by the voice of Being. By tuning in (*stimmen, abstimmen*) on the voice (*Stimme*) of Being and by getting in the appropriate mood (*Stimmung*), we would be able to let our thinking be determined (*bestimmen*) by Being. Heidegger seems to claim that his later thought is Being's thought, and that his later discourse on Being is in fact Being's discourse, as we saw in section 11C. This doctrine abolishes the personal responsibility of Martin Heidegger for what he said, and he behaved accordingly.[65] I tried to show in section 14C that Heidegger interpreted Neo-Hegelian deep history in different ways during the crucial years of 1939–46, adapting himself to Germany's changing fortunes in the war. But he never admitted that he had misinterpreted deep history at an earlier moment when he changed his interpretation afterwards. Similarly, when he published in 1953 his introduction to metaphysics of 1935, including the notorious phrase on "the inner truth and greatness of this movement," that is, of National Socialism, accompanied by a clarifying note, he did not say that he had changed his mind on the metaphysical nature of Nazism. All "turns" in Heidegger's thought are supposed to be due to turns in Being, and they would never mean that Heidegger rejected his former opinions.[66] This rhetorical strategy implies that Heidegger could not be held accountable for what he said or wrote. It was only consistent that after the war Heidegger refused to withdraw his Nazi pronouncements or to express regrets or grief about the Holocaust, because presumably Being was responsible for these instances of erring. Heidegger's radically heteronomous conceptions of morality and thought destroy the very notion of personal responsibility in both domains. Heidegger claimed, however, that this heteronomy is the highest form of responsibility, because it is responsiveness to Being.[67]

  7. *Stratagem of the Forest Trails (Holzwege).* In section 11C.6, I have analyzed the strategic dilemma that the postmonotheist thinker has to face. If his postmonotheist doctrine resembles traditional Christianity too closely, it will be seen through as nothing but a watered-down version of monotheist religion, and the

postmonotheist strategy of rescuing religion in the age of God's death will be shipwrecked. If, on the other hand, the postmonotheist doctrine does not resemble traditional monotheism sufficiently, it will not satisfy the traditional religious yearnings and it will lose its appeal. This dilemma implies that the postmonotheist philosopher cannot argue his case openly. He has to fight a spiritual guerrilla war against scientific and critical thought, and he can never reveal where he really stands. His troops move along forest trails; they will not advance into the clearing of a battlefield.

The stratagem of the forest trails includes a number of different rhetorical moves. First, Heidegger sprinkled the clues to postmonotheism thinly in his texts. On many pages of impressive and often scholarly interpretations of earlier thinkers, one finds only a few paragraphs in which Heidegger's own objectives emerge, and they rarely emerge clearly. The force of these rhetorical tactics should not be underestimated. The reader will be impressed by Heidegger's scholarship, and he will swallow the postmonotheist hints without examining them critically. Second, Heidegger never argues clearly against his adversaries—the spirit of the Enlightenment, scientific thought, and common sense. He says, for instance, that he has no objections against science and technology, but that he only wants to fathom their essence (*Wesen*). As we have seen, however, Heidegger's notion of *Wesen* is bound up with the antiscientific doctrines of Neo-Hegelianism and postmonotheism; *Wesen* means the level "of Being" at which things are.[68]

Third, Heidegger often uses the fallacy of poisoning the well instead of sound philosophical analysis, especially if he wants to denounce his main enemy, common sense. In 1920, Heidegger said that philosophy is nothing but the battle against common sense.[69] How did he fight this battle? His lectures on *Was heisst Denken* of 1951–52 give an impression of his methods. He says that common sense is "the refuge of those who are envious of thinking," and that it is "a mere trivialized product of the Enlightenment," not at all "as sound and natural as it pretends to be."[70] One finds no interesting analysis of what common sense is or of how it works, merely a stream of abuse. It is Heidegger's objective to intimidate those who want to raise commonsensical objections to his authoritarian doctrines, and to bully them into abandoning common sense altogether.

8. Stratagem of the Elect. One will wonder how Heidegger could claim that he was able to raise and understand the question of Being, if Being is concealed and the Fall has been completed. How could he gain access to the impenetrable and hidden place from where he was able to experience the Truth of Being, if this truth remains concealed to ordinary mortals? Heidegger lectured repeatedly on Plato's simile of the cave, and Plato's simile provided him with the solution to this problem. Heidegger belonged to the elect, to those favored by Being, who were destined to hear Being's voice. In *Beiträge zur Philosophie*, the theme of the elect occurs again and again. Perhaps it had to overcompensate for Heidegger's isolation and lack of success in the Nazi movement. Heidegger was writing, he says, for "the few" or "those rare ones," who possess "the highest courage to solitariness" that is needed in order to think "the nobility of Being."[71] Heidegger claims that it was a mistake to assume that an essential revolution can be understood by everyone from the start: "only a few stand always in the blazing light of this lightning."[72] Another mistake would be to think that one might introduce a "principle of the people" (*völkisches Prinzip*) if one had not before achieved a "highest rank of Being." In other words, the German revolution that had started in 1933 had to be directed by select individuals such as Heidegger, because "the people [*das Volk*] will only become a real people when the most unique ones come and when they start to have premonitions."[73] A people is only a real people if it receives its historical fate by finding its God. But how, Heidegger asks, should the German people find its God if there were not secluded individuals who seek God on its behalf, individuals who may seem to stand over against a people that is not yet a people?[74] Without Heidegger's new German religion, he suggests, the German people (*Volk*) could not become a real people. This claim corroborates my interpretation of Heidegger's postmonotheist leitmotif, to wit, that it was meant to be essential to a new German authenticity. Heidegger stresses again and again that only great and secluded individuals will be able to create the silent space in which the God may come to pass.[75] After the Second World War, Heidegger used the same rhetorical move, but as the French had now become his main philosophical public, he was shrewd enough to weaken the emphasis on Germany.

The stratagem of the elect is a powerful rhetorical weapon because Heidegger intimates to his readers that they will belong to the few elect human beings if only they adhere to his philosophy. The craving to be part of an elite is one of the many needs that traditional Christianity satisfied. God the Almighty would take an infinite interest in each Christian believer, however humble and insignificant he or she is. Similarly, the illusion of belonging to the mental aristocracy that understands and endorses Heidegger's thought might raise one's self-esteem. If there is one traditional religious craving that Heidegger's postmonotheism satisfies, it is the craving to belong to the inner circle of the elect.

§ 17. AN EVALUATION OF *SEIN UND ZEIT*

Sein und Zeit was first published as volume 7 of Husserl's *Jahrbuch für Philosophie und phänomenologische Forschung*, and Heidegger presented his masterpiece as an exercise in phenomenological ontology.[76] In 1913, Husserl had defined phenomenology as a presuppositionless science of transcendental consciousness and its intentional correlates. According to Husserl, the principle of presuppositionlessness was necessary because phenomenology had to solve the problem of the external world by a study of consciousness, that is, by investigating the sphere of what is indubitably given. Husserl's philosophical program implies that one can make no assumptions about what is not phenomenally present in or to consciousness; such assumptions would make the solution to the problem of the external world circular. Husserl's starting point inevitably led him to a variety of subjectivism: transcendental idealism.[77]

One might read *Sein und Zeit* as a radical critique of this Husserlian program. Heidegger argued that Husserl's notion of phenomenology as a presuppositionless science was in fact contaminated by presuppositions that originated with Descartes. The idea that the sphere of consciousness and its intentional correlates is indubitably given and that, therefore, it had to be the starting point of philosophy, was implied by Cartesian doubt concerning the external world. This doubt had been made possible by the scientific conception of the world in the seventeenth century.[78] Descartes' view of the material world as a closed mechanical system that logically excludes mental events or properties implied the necessity of the notion of consciousness as a separate substance that allegedly could exist apart from matter. Only if consciousness is a separate substance, that represents matter on the basis of its immanent sensations, is Cartesian doubt concerning the external world possible.

Heidegger argued in *Sein und Zeit* that the assumptions that inform Husserl's notion of phenomenology are mistaken. Human beings do not consist of two substances, matter and consciousness, and it is nonsensical to doubt the existence of the external world. As Husserl's Cartesian presuppositions are concerned with the way in which the human ego *is*, Heidegger claimed that the question of *being*, not the problem of consciousness and its intentional correlates, is the fundamental issue of phenomenology, and, indeed, of philosophy. Because the notion of epistemology as first philosophy, which Husserl endorsed, was based on questionable ontological presuppositions, ontology is more fundamental than epistemology. Heidegger claimed that philosophy must be phenomenological ontology, which raises the question of being. Phenomenology consists in a hermeneutical investigation of the phenomenon of being, and the phenomenon of being is concealed by the philosophical tradition. Moreover, phenomenology is not at all presuppositionless, as Husserl thought; it is involved in the hermeneutical circle.

I think that this Heideggerian critique of Husserl's phenomenology is largely correct. But Heidegger elaborated his criticism in two dubious ways. First, he argued that the ontology of Dasein is somehow primary in working out the project of a phenomenological ontology. The ontology of Dasein would be fundamental ontology; it would be the philosophical basis of all other ontologies, such as the ontology of nature.[79] I argued in section 4.6 that Heidegger provides no convincing arguments for this priority of Dasein in the introduction to *Sein und Zeit*. Perhaps one may regard the priority thesis as a residue of Husserl's doctrine that transcendental consciousness is ontologically fundamental. Although Heidegger rejected Husserl's notion of transcendental consciousness as an independent substance on which the world depends, and although he argues that Dasein is in-the-world, he failed to draw the conclusion that the human subject cannot be ontologically fundamental. However, this reading of Heidegger is not charitable, and we need another interpretative hypothesis that explains Heidegger's assertion that Dasein is ontologically primary.

In this book I have argued that Heidegger's question of being contains five different leitmotifs. Two of them, the transcendental and the postmonotheist theme, provide an explanation of the alleged primacy of Dasein. In sections 12C and 13C, I argued that *Sein und Zeit* is linked to the later works as the first phase of a Pascalian strategy in an apologetics of Christianity to its second phase. In order to raise the question of Being in a monotheist or postmonotheist sense, we have to analyze the human condition, because only such an analysis provides us with a motive to open our hearts to grace, that is, to raise the question of Being, or, as Heidegger says in *Sein und Zeit*, to grasp our most authentic possibility. By rejecting the postmonotheist theme in section 16A, I implicitly repudiated this argument for the primacy of Dasein.

We still have to investigate the validity of the other possible justification for the primacy of Dasein: the transcendental theme. According to the transcendental theme, Dasein has understanding of being (*Seinsverständnis*) in the sense that it projects holistic transcendental frameworks, which are conditions of the possibility of encountering entities in the world. As a transcendental philosopher, Heidegger claims that these conditions for encountering entities are also conditions for the very *being* of these entities. Because the former conditions are inherent in Dasein, the ontology of Dasein is more fundamental than other ontologies, which explore the latter conditions. I rejected the very notion of a transcendental framework in criticizing the Neo-Hegelian leitmotif. I will also reject it as it figures in *Sein und Zeit*, pursuing a similar line of critique. This is the topic of subsection (A).

There is a second dubious way in which Heidegger expanded his assessment of Husserl's transcendental idealism. Heidegger argued not only that the Cartesian categories of matter and consciousness are inadequate if we want to characterize the manner in which we humans *are*. His thesis is more radical. He held also that all other traditional philosophical categories are inadequate if we want to elaborate an ontology of human existence. This radical thesis explains the dual composition of *Sein und Zeit* as it was originally planned: a construction of new categories for human existence, the so-called *existentialia*, is coupled with a destruction of traditional categories. The destruction focused ultimately on traditional notions of time, because Heidegger held that finite transcendental temporality (*Zeitlichkeit*) is the most fundamental "condition of the possibility of Dasein."[80]

If we ask Heidegger how he can be so sure that no traditional set of philosophical categories is appropriate for characterizing Dasein, he answers by making two complementary assertions. First, he claims in section 1 of *Sein und Zeit* that the categories that philosophers traditionally used and are still using are trivialized versions of the categories that Plato and Aristotle "wrested with the utmost effort of thought from the phenomena."[81] I will not examine this dubious historical thesis, but one may wonder whether the philosophers of the seventeenth century, who rejected Aristotelian essences and final causes, fully remained within the tradition of Plato and Aristotle. What interests me here is Heidegger's second claim. He says in section 6 of *Sein und Zeit* that Descartes inherited medieval categories, particularly the category of *ens creatum*, and that "createdness in the widest sense of something's having been produced, was an essential item in the structure of the ancient conception of Being."[82] What Heidegger suggests in this passage is a thesis that he elaborated in his early courses on Plato and Aristotle: that "the phenomena from which these thinkers wrested their categories" were of a specific kind; these phenomena belonged to the ontological region of tools or "readiness-to-hand" (*Zuhandenheit*). Heidegger claims that because they have been derived from the ontological domain of artifacts and tools, the traditional philosophical categories are inappropriate for analyzing the mode of being of Dasein.[83] The reason is that artifacts are created in the sense of manufactured, whereas Dasein is not.

It is primarily this second claim that motivates Heidegger's project of constructing new categories for Dasein, the existentialia. But this claim presupposes a dogma which, ironically, is ultimately derived from Aristotle: the dogma that the totality of beings is neatly carved up into ontological regions, each of which has its own "essence."[84] Only if this dogma of the regionality of being were true could Heidegger be confident about the philosophical soundness of his philosophical enterprise in *Sein und Zeit*. If it is not true, then it is not clear a priori that categories derived from phenomena other than Dasein do not apply to Dasein as well, and one would have to show this in each specific case. One should note that Heidegger's thesis of the regionality of being is more extreme than Aristotle's. Aristotle assumed that the category of *ousia* (substance) applies to all particulars, so that there is a common ontological structure of entities that belong to very different ontological regions, such as artifacts, plants, and humans, for example. Heidegger denies this in *Sein und Zeit*. How else can he assume without further argument that categories derived from the domain of artifacts do not apply to Dasein? Heidegger's notion of the regionality of being belongs to what I have called the phenomenologico-hermeneutical leitmotif. According to this leitmotif, "being" means the constitution of being of entities in a specific ontological region. I discuss the phenomenologico-hermeneutical leitmotif in subsection (B), without pretending that it is the only possible source of Heidegger's strong notion of the regionality of being. Heidegger's conviction that Dasein is entirely *sui generis*, so that no categories derived from other domains can possibly apply to Dasein, probably is at least as much inspired by Christianity as by Aristotle. For Christianity held that only man was created "in God's own image."[85]

Both the transcendental leitmotif and the dogma of the regionality of being are antinaturalist themes that I reject. Yet a major objective of my critique is to find out to what extent Heidegger's antinaturalism is correct. Is the way in which human beings understand life and the world, that is, their "understanding of being" (*Seinsverständnis*) in one of the many senses of this term, not a proper object of philosophical analysis? Should we not defend the thesis that this understanding of being is somehow irreducible, and refute the attacks of scientistic philosophers such as Quine or the Churchlands? If it is indeed irreducible, by what method we will be able to study our everyday understanding of life becomes an urgent philosophical question. I will argue in subsection (B) that Heidegger's idea of a phenomenologico-hermeneutical method was muddled and untenable. The proper philosophical method for investigating our "understanding" of our own being is a linguistic analysis of the conceptual structures in which this understanding is articulated. There are other methods for investigating it, but these are not properly philosophical: historians, cultural anthropologists, sociologists, psychologists, and novelists also explore human "understanding of being."

If we reconstruct *Sein und Zeit* in this sense, how much of the book will turn out to be philosophically sound and how much defective? In section 18, I argue that Heidegger's secular analysis of human self-understanding was biased by his religious objectives. His notions of the They (*das Man*) and of authenticity, for instance, and the related conception that death is our "ownmost possibility," are patently absurd, unless they are meant to prepare for the "leap" into Nothingness that is required by Heidegger's Lutheran and Eckhartian conception of faith. This means that the analysis of Dasein cannot be maintained as it stands, even if it is put on a methodologically sound basis. Heidegger's ideal of authenticity marred his book in serious ways, so that it was not what he claimed it to be: a necessary prerequisite for an adequate ontological analysis of human existence.

We may wonder what remains of Heidegger's question of being after this critical onslaught. The attack, I hold, will have annihilated the question of being not only in its postmonotheist and Neo-Hegelian senses, but also in the sense of the transcendental leitmotif. Moreover, the phenomenologico-hermeneutical question of being will not survive unless it is put on a new methodological footing. It is misleading to maintain that this question is concerned with "being." We should rather say that it aims at a philosophical elucidation of the conceptual structures in which everyday human life expresses itself. Such an elucidation is an important philosophical task, and, apart from Heidegger, many philosophers have contributed to it, philosophers such as Ludwig Wittgenstein, Gilbert Ryle, and Peter Strawson. We should not adopt a denigratory stance toward these conceptual structures by calling them "folk psychology," for example. This would suggest that there is a better conceptual structure in the making for expressing our life, such as the conceptual structure of the sciences of the brain. Heidegger was right in arguing that our everyday understanding of life is irreducible because it is constitutive of what it is to be human, and that it cannot be eliminated in favor of something essentially better. If this is the case, scientistic philosophers such as Quine and the Churchlands suffer from a lack of reflection. They argue that we could do without our everyday conceptual structures but they fail to show convincingly how we would be able to live and to remain fully human without them, while they cannot but continue to use in their daily lives the very structures that they reject in theory.[86] Having these conceptual structures, which comprehend the intricate conceptual networks of moral, aesthetic, legal, and everyday practical discourse, is indeed part of what it is to be human in a more than purely biological sense.

A. *Heidegger's Transcendentalism*

The transcendental theme is one possible explanation for the primacy of Dasein with regard to the question of being. Transcendental arguments consist of two steps. It is first argued that specific conditions are necessary for encountering entities, and then it is argued that these very same conditions are necessary for entities in order to *be*. *Sein und Zeit* is a treatise of transcendental philosophy because Heidegger holds that a global framework of referential relations, the *world* in his special sense, is a transcendental condition both of understanding entities as tools or as objects of science and for the very *being* of tools or of objects of science. As the world is an existentiale of Dasein, the ontology of Dasein is basic to all other ontologies. This is why Dasein is the primary topic of investigation if we want to answer the question of being by developing regional ontologies.

In section 9 of this book, which was devoted to the transcendental leitmotif in *Sein und Zeit*, I tried to define Heidegger's specific variety of transcendentalism by discussing two questions. Kant argued that his transcendental theory is the only solution to the problem of how synthetic a priori propositions are possible. As Heidegger does not raise this problem in *Sein und Zeit*, and since he plays down its importance for understanding Kant in his book on Kant of 1929, we should wonder what motivated Heidegger's transcendental turn. This was my first question. In sections 15–18 of *Sein und Zeit*, Heidegger professes to discover by a purely phenomenological analysis of tools that they cannot be encountered and used without an *a priori* global framework of referential relations, an equipmental context that he then calls the *world*. However, this alleged discovery does not follow from his phenomenological descriptions. A hammer "refers" to nails and wooden planks, and the hammer, nails, and planks may be used to build a hut on a mountain, which "refers" in its turn to the needs and projects of a human being. But why should there be an a priori and global framework of referential interrelations, which is a transcendental condition both for encountering tools and for tools *being* there? The transcendental philosopher must hold that the transcendental conditions for the possibility of x have an ontological status different from x's ontological status. This is indeed what Heidegger claims.[87] But why is it not possible to explain the fact that tools exist by the empirical fact that humans use things as tools, without postulating a transcendental framework? As the text of *Sein und Zeit* does not convincingly answer my first question, I proposed an explanatory hypothesis that provides a rationale for Heidegger's transcendental turn.

I argued in section 9A that Heidegger went transcendental in *Sein und Zeit* because transcendentalism enabled him to provide an antinaturalist solution to a philosophical problem that arose during the scientific revolution, the problem of the manifest and the scientific image. Many philosophers thought, and many still do even now, that the modern scientific view of the world is incompatible with the commonsense view of the world and of human life as somehow "meaningful." My hypothesis is that Heidegger endorsed this incompatibility thesis and that he wanted to save the "significance" of the world by relegating science to a secondary domain. He first argued, in sections 15–18 of *Sein und Zeit*, that the way in which entities are in themselves (*an sich*) is what he calls readiness-to-hand (*Zuhandenheit*).[88] Because this mode of being is characterized by significance (*Bedeutsamkeit*) and familiarity (*Vertrautheit*), the world of things as they are in themselves is familiar and meaningful.[89] He goes on to argue, in sections 19–21 and 69b, that the scientific view of the world skips (*überspringt*) the world as it really is, that it is impoverished and derivative, and that it is based on a projected transcendental framework, the framework of the world as "mathematical." There allegedly is no possible justification of scientific theories on the basis of things as they really are, for Heidegger claims that we cannot establish scientific facts unless we project the scientific transcendental framework first.[90] He suggests that this framework is optional, because it is due to a project (*Entwurf*). As a consequence, the scientific view of things cannot be forced on us. It would be perfectly reasonable to reject it as a conception of how things really are. Heidegger's transcendental argument is incompatible with his postmonotheist question of Being. Yet it is an excellent preparation for asking the question of Being in the postmonotheist sense, for postmonotheists also reject the idea that the sciences are able to discover things as they really are.[91]

Even though Heidegger did not raise Kant's problem of the synthetic a priori, his transcendental theory resembles Kant's transcendental philosophy. Like Heidegger, Kant argued that the world as it is in itself is the home of those things which he cherished most: religion and morality. Like Heidegger, he held that the world as science sees it is secondary, a phenomenal world only, because it is based on a transcendental framework. But there is an important difference between Kant and Heidegger on this point, which motivated the second question that I discussed in section 9. Kant is a transcendental idealist. He could think that the phenomenal world is based on a transcendental scheme because, as contemporary cognitive scientists would say, he endorsed an information-processing theory of perception. The input of the perceptual mechanism, caused by a world in itself that impinges on our senses, is processed by a transcendental framework which is inherent in the transcendental subject, and which adds new information in the act of processing (space, time, and the categories). As a consequence, the phenomenal world inherits the characteristics that the framework adds to the input, and this supposedly explains the possibility of a priori propositions that are also synthetic in the sense that they contain information about the (phenomenal) world. Kant's solution to the problem of synthetic a priori propositions works only if the phenomenal world is constituted by the transcendental ego, hence ontologically dependent on it, and this view is called transcendental idealism. The empirical world, which is constituted by the transcendental subject, cannot be the world in itself in which the subject exists and which impinges on its sense organs. Conversely, the world in itself in which the transcendental subject exists, cannot be constituted by a transcendental framework.

In *Sein und Zeit*, Heidegger rejected transcendental idealism and information-processing theories of perception. He called the transcendental subject Dasein and held that Dasein is essentially in-the-world, where "world" is defined as the significant world of everyday life. How can one be a transcendental philosopher, I queried in section 9B, without being a transcendental idealist? If phenomenal entities are not constituted by a transcendental subject, what might it mean to say that the subjective conditions for encountering them are also conditions for these entities to *be*? A trivial answer to this question consists in saying that "being" just *means* "being encountered by Dasein." The two stages of a transcendental argument collapse into one, and the result is what I called weak transcendentalism. Weak transcendentalism identifies the conditions for encountering entities with the conditions for entities being there by simply redefining the verb "to be." I argued on the basis of textual evidence that this is what Heidegger is doing in *Sein und Zeit*. He seems to hold that "being" (*Sein*) is nothing but the *significance* that Dasein projects on preexisting entities.

This view would have been indistinguishable from the commonplace conviction that entities do not have any significance unless we humans bestow significance on them, if Heidegger had not put forward the Neo-Kantian idea that individual entities cannot be encountered *as* they are, for instance, as objects of scientific research, unless Dasein projects an encompassing framework on all entities. Indeed, this idea of a global framework is crucial to Heidegger's antinaturalism. Only by arguing that the things which science pretends to discover simply are not there *as such* apart from an optional transcendental framework is Heidegger able to reject the claim that science discovers things as they really are.

There are many difficulties in Heidegger's weak transcendentalism, and each of the three objections that I will discuss is sufficient to reject his antinaturalism.

1. The World-an-sich a Projection? Let me first raise an internal difficulty in *Sein und Zeit*. Heidegger develops his notion of the world *an sich* (in itself) as the significant world of everyday life in sections 15–18 of the book, long before he introduces his notion of project (*Entwurf*) and projected frameworks in sections 31 and 69b. The very idea that Dasein essentially exists in a meaningful world *an sich* would not make sense, of course, if this meaningful world were a projected world as well and if the projected framework were as optional as the projected framework of science. The very notion of a world *an sich* seems to have a meaning only in contrast with the notion of a transcendentally projected world or framework. What Heidegger appears to be arguing, then, is that the world of science is based on a transcendental projection by Dasein, whereas the significant world of everyday life is not: it is the world as it is in itself, the world in which Dasein as a transcendental subject exists. This is what he has to argue if he wants to be an antinaturalist in a strong sense.

Regrettably, such a line of argument conflicts with Heidegger's view of understanding as expressed in section 31 of *Sein und Zeit*. According to Heidegger's theory of understanding, we saw in section 5, above, all understanding is projective. This implies that even the meaningful world in itself, as defined in sections 15–18 of *Sein und Zeit*, must be a projected world. Indeed this is what Heidegger argues in a number of crucial passages. In section 40, for instance, he suggests that the meaningful world as such is annihilated in the experience of *Angst*. "It collapses into itself," he says, and he adds that "the world has the character of completely lacking significance."[92] In this latter sentence, Heidegger uses the term "world" in the sense of the totality of beings, and not in the sense as defined in section 18 of *Sein und Zeit*, where he said that the very worldliness of the world consists in being a significant whole of referential relations.[93] For if this significant world collapses into itself, no world in Heidegger's special sense of the word survives: we are confronted by a meaningless totality of entities. We might say that in the experience of *Angst*, Dasein is without any projective understanding, and this very fact would reveal that the world as a meaningful structure is nothing but Dasein's projection.[94] This interpretation is confirmed by section 43c, where Heidegger says that if Dasein did not exist, there would not be a world in itself either.[95]

However, if even the world as a meaningful structure is Dasein's projection, Heidegger's claim that readiness-to-hand (*Zuhandenheit*) is the way in which entities are in themselves (*an sich*), whereas the scientific projection skips entities as they really are, becomes unjustified, and his antinaturalism collapses. We might try to save Heidegger's claim in various ways, but none of them works. For instance, we might say that even though both the meaningful world of everyday life and the world of science are projections of Dasein, the first is somehow a more fundamental projection than the second. But more fundamental in which sense? Heidegger might mean that there has been a stage in human culture in which humans used tools without possessing any objective knowledge about the universe. This is an implausible claim, and he does not try to substantiate it. Or Heidegger might mean that the meaningful world of readiness-to-hand is semantically prior to the scientific enterprise, because the concepts of science are derived from everyday concepts. Again, this is not a claim that he tries to make plausible, and the failure of logical positivist reductionism of theoretical concepts has shown that it must be false. One might wonder, moreover, whether most everyday concepts do not belong both to the world of tools and the world of objective knowledge, so that Heidegger's distinction between two different global projections collapses. The notion of a stone, for instance, does not essentially belong to a framework of readiness-to-hand, although it might function within the context of such a framework. Finally, Heidegger might argue that the scientific framework is secondary because its genesis is motivated by difficulties within the framework of readiness-to-hand. Indeed, this is the view that Heidegger promises to substantiate where he writes in section 13 of *Sein und Zeit*: "If knowing is to be possible as a way of determining the nature of the present-at-hand by observing it, then there must first be a *deficiency* in our concernful dealings with the world."[96] But we saw in section 9A, above, that Heidegger did not succeed in showing that this is the case. We come to the conclusion that if both the meaningful world of everyday life and the world of science are projections of Dasein, they must be equiprimordial, and this conclusion refutes Heidegger's antinaturalism.

Another attempt to save Heidegger's claim that the significant world of everyday life is more fundamental than the world that objective perception and science reveal is Dreyfus's interpretation of *Sein und Zeit*, according to which the claim means that all revealing and all knowledge are ultimately rooted in meaningful and shared social practices.[97] But this interpretation does not rescue Heidegger's view either. From the trivial point that scientific research is a social practice it does not follow that the things that science discovers depend on a social practice or "projection." Moreover, it is simply not true that human capacities of perception always depend on social practices: they are innate biological capacities, without which humans would not be able to engage in social practices to begin with.

2. The Very Idea of a Comprehensive Scheme. The second problem is, of course, whether the picture of a Dasein that might project the worlds of both readiness-to-hand (*Zuhandenheit*) and presence-at-hand (*Vorhandenheit*) is an intelligible picture. With regard to the Neo-Hegelian leitmotif, I argued that the very idea of a comprehensive framework is incomprehensible because, if the framework is really comprehensive, we cannot specify anymore what is framed by the framework. As Heidegger rejects transcendental idealism, he cannot say, like Husserl in *Ideas* I, that the *entities* in the world are constituted by the transcendental subject. Entities are not dependent on Dasein, Heidegger declares at the end of section 44 of *Sein und Zeit*, but *being* is.[98] I interpreted this obscure claim by supposing that what Heidegger means by "being" (*Sein*) here is the significance that Dasein supposedly bestows on entities by projecting a global framework. One might wonder how Dasein can bestow significance on entities unless these entities already exist and are perceived by Dasein. Should we not suppose that both Dasein and other entities must be present in the first place, and that this presence is an empirical condition for the possibility of the transcendental projection of an encompassing framework? We saw that Heidegger could not avoid saying such things when, in section 40, he claimed that "the world has the character of completely lacking significance" whenever Dasein stops projecting frameworks of significance. If Heidegger cannot avoid saying such things, he destroys his claim that being-present (*Vorhandenheit*) is always due to the projection of a transcendental scheme, thereby demolishing the very basis of his antinaturalism. Furthermore, if Heidegger's transcendental view implicitly presupposes a naïve realism regarding Dasein and other entities, his assertion that the problem of the external world is a pseudoproblem that has to be rejected is disingenuous: in fact, Heidegger endorses one of the traditional solutions to the problem. Heidegger's transcendental philosophy is as incoherent as the transcendental views of Kant, Husserl, or Quine, and it is incoherent for similar reasons.[99]

This does not imply that Heidegger's notion of a projection (*Entwurf*) is illegitimate in all contexts. As is the case with many *existentialia*, Heidegger uses the technical term *Entwurf* in different senses, which he does not explicitly distinguish. When Heidegger introduces the term in section 31 of *Sein und Zeit*, he uses it primarily in order to capture the future-directedness of Dasein. Because it *is* in a sense its possibilities, Dasein always pro-jects a possible course of life into the future. The term *Entwurf* expresses the familiar fact that we understand ourselves partly in terms of our possibilities of future existing and, according to Heidegger, such an understanding is our potentiality-for-being itself.[100] There is a second sense of *Entwurf* which, Heidegger argues, is linked up with the first. We always project our life into the future within a space of possibilities that is inherent in the cultural matrix into which we were "thrown." Heidegger suggest that this possibility space, and indeed the entire matrix of significant relations which he calls the world, is also projected by Dasein, instead of admitting that the possibility space belongs to an existing culture and is, for that reason, largely independent of individual Dasein. Heidegger identifies this second projection (*Entwurf*) of a possibility space with a transcendental framework in the Kantian sense.[101] Clearly one might reject Heidegger's notion of a transcendental projection of an a priori framework and yet admit that the term *Entwurf* expresses the valid insight that we understand ourselves partly in terms of our possibilities of future existing.

3. Problems of Relativism. I now come to my third main objection to Heidegger's transcendental theory. Heidegger's transcendental leitmotif leads to relativism concerning facts and truth, as did his Neo-Hegelianism. In section 69b of *Sein und Zeit*, Heidegger claims that "only in the light of a nature that has been projected in this fashion" (of mathematical physics, for instance) "can anything like a 'fact' be found," and that "the 'grounding' of 'factual science' was possible only because the researchers understood that in principle there are no 'bare facts.' " He adds that the projection of nature in this sense discloses an a priori.[102] This passage is convoluted. It is true that without the technology of measuring and without the conceptual structures of mathematics and of physical theories, we would not be able to discover certain facts or features of the world. But this does not imply that *what* is discovered does not exist independently of our conceptual structures. Without Newtonian mechanics, the planet of Pluto would never have been discovered. Yet Pluto is not a product of Newtonian mechanics, something that *is* only relative to an a priori framework. To use Heidegger's jargon, it is correct to say that only in the light of a projected nature could Pluto be found, but it is a mistake to conclude that the grounding of the thesis that Pluto exists out there is possible only because there are no bare realities. On the contrary, the claim that Pluto exists is "grounded" or justified only if Pluto is in fact present in space apart from our projections. If Pluto did not exist independently of Dasein, the claim that there is a planet out there would be false. From the fact that a scientific hypothesis is a "projection," it does not follow that testing it is a mere projection as well. Philosophers and historians of science, such as Kuhn and Feyerabend, have argued for a relativism concerning facts and experience similar to Heidegger's. They hold that all perception is theory-laden to the point that without theory there would be no perception at all. I think that their arguments are mistaken, but I will not examine them here.[103] Heidegger does not adduce arguments for his relativistic transcendentalism. He erroneously believes, or professes to believe, that it follows from his phenomenological descriptions.

What Heidegger says about truth is equally confused, as I began to argue in section 16B and C.4. Having claimed in sections 44a and 44b of *Sein und Zeit* that there is a deeper meaning of the term "Truth" than propositional truth, to wit, Dasein's being-discovering as a transcendental condition for the possibility of propositional truth, Heidegger draws some conclusions concerning propositional truth in section 44c. He says, for instance, that " 'there is' truth only in so far as Dasein *is* and so long as Dasein *is*." This would imply that "Newton's laws, the principle of contradiction, any truth whatever—these are only true as long as Dasein *is*." Before Newton's laws were discovered, Heidegger claims, they were not "true." But of course they were not false either. Before Newton, he concludes, Newton's laws just were neither true nor false. This does not mean that before Newton there were no such entities as have been uncovered and pointed out by using these laws. It means that through Newton the laws became true; with him, entities became accessible in themselves to Dasein. Heidegger concludes that all truth is relative to Dasein. This allegedly does not make truth subjective in the sense that it is left to the subject's discretion, because Dasein's being uncovering "brings the uncovering Dasein face to face with entities themselves."[104]

In section 44c, Heidegger correctly rejects the notions of eternal truths and of truths "in themselves" that we find in Leibniz, Bolzano, Frege, Husserl's *Logische Untersuchungen*, the early Russell, and in Neo-Kantians. But he makes the opposite mistake by saying that propositional truth is somehow temporal, as temporal as Dasein itself. He concludes, misleadingly, that Newton's laws were neither true nor false before Newton, became true due to Newton, and, as Heidegger forgets to add, became false in 1919 because of Einstein and Eddington. This is a misleading account of the notion of propositional truth because it is ungrammatical to say that a law of physics became true at a certain point of history. What one should say is that at that point of history, the law was held or discovered to be true (or false). It may be that Heidegger fell victim to his own confusing redefinition of the word "true," because if "true" means being discovered, then it would at least make sense to say that Newton's laws became true because of Newton, for it was Newton who formulated the laws. What is a platitude if "truth" is used in Heidegger's idiosyncratic sense of the word, seems to be an intriguing philosophical discovery if one mixes up this Heideggerian sense with the ordinary sense of the word "true," propositional truth. This is precisely what Heidegger does, and the result is conceptual confusion presented as a deep philosophical discovery.

Propositions such as Newton's laws do not become true at particular times, nor do they stop being true when it is discovered that they are not true. These observations are grammatical remarks in Wittgenstein's sense of the phrase. The word "true" in the ordinary sense of propositional truth does not admit of a time index, so that what Heidegger says here is nonsensical and not false. Neither does it make sense to say that Newton's laws became true due to, or through, Newton.[105] Perhaps Newton formulated these laws for the first time, but whether they are true or not depends on nature, not on Newton. By his celebrated dictum, "there is truth only as long as Dasein *is*," Heidegger may have wanted to express the trivial insight that in order to state, or think of, a truth, one needs a language, and that there is no living human language without Dasein.[106] Conceptual structures are dependent on Dasein, and we need conceptual structures for formulating propositions that may be true or false. But it is misleading to say that, therefore, truth in the sense of propositional truth depends on Dasein, because whether an empirical proposition is true or not depends on the world only, even though human beings may discover whether it is indeed true or not (see § 16B). Clearly, Heidegger's transcendental notion of truth was confusing even to himself, because he was unable to keep it separate from the ordinary notion of propositional truth.

The transcendental doctrine that facts and truths are relative to an encompassing framework seems to suggest that what is true relative to framework A may be false relative to framework B. This notion of relative truth is incoherent, as philosophers of science from Aristotle to Newton Smith have argued. It will suffice here to summarize one of their arguments. What the relativist says is that for some x, x may be true relative to A and false relative to B. Can we find some one candidate for x, the truth of which can vary, giving us a substantial version of relativism without lapsing into incoherence? If one supposes that x is a *sentence* in the sense of a string of material signs, then we do not get a substantial variety of relativism. Whether a sentence is true—assuming counterfactually that it makes sense to ascribe truth to sentences—depends both on what it means and on how the world is. Accordingly, if x is a sentence, its truth value might vary because of the fact that its meaning or reference varies, so that we do not get a substantial version of relativism. On the other hand, if x is supposed to be a proposition, the assumption that x can vary in truth value given one and the same world leads to incoherence, because propositions are individuated in terms of truth conditions. If the proposition that the sun has nine planets is true, this very same proposition cannot be false as well, relative to some framework, for then it would not be the same proposition. As a consequence, there is no candidate for *x* that gives us a substantial version of relativism without lapsing into incoherence.

This point might be explained in yet another way. Suppose that members of a philosophical tribe whose language we do not understand, let us call them the Heideggerians, utter a declarative sentence S in making a statement. They obviously think that they are saying something true. In order to know what they mean, we have to translate S into a sentence of our own language, say T. Now it may be that we hold T to express a true proposition, so that we agree with the Heideggerians. If we do not hold T to be the expression of a true proposition, we must conclude either that the Heideggerians are mistaken or that T is not a correct translation for S. It would be incoherent to suppose both that T expresses a falsehood, that T is a correct translation of S, and that, nevertheless, the Heideggerians are right in believing that S expresses a true proposition. In other words, it is incoherent to suppose that one and the same proposition is expressed both by S and by T, if we believe that T expresses a false proposition and also suppose that the Heideggerians correctly believe that S expresses a true proposition. Relativism concerning truth is as incoherent as relativism with regard to facts. Because this type of relativism is inherent in Heidegger's transcendental leitmotif, this leitmotif is incoherent as well.[107]

Let me end with a comment on the slippery expression "condition for the possibility of," which transcendental philosophers often use. Heidegger suggests in *Sein und Zeit* that what he calls being (*Sein*) is the condition for the possibility of beings (*Seiendes*), and I interpreted him as claiming that without an a priori comprehensive framework entities can neither be significant nor show up for us. I argued that this transcendental notion of a comprehensive scheme is incoherent. But Heidegger often uses the expression "conditions for the possibility of" in contexts where he might mean either that something is merely an empirical condition for the possibility of something else, or that two things are conceptually related under a specific description. Because he does not distinguish these different senses of the phrase "condition for the possibility of," and indeed, because he does not define any of them clearly, he often seems to think that claims about conditions for possibilities that may be true in the empirical or the conceptual sense support his transcendental views. It may be true, for instance, that time is a condition for the possibility of concern (*Sorge*), because "concern" *means* that we are concerned with our future life and that our existence is an issue for us.[108] But this condition is a conceptual one, and it does not substantiate a deep transcendental theory. Moreover, it may be true that in some cases we have to turn toward an object in order to perceive it, for instance, when we want to see an object that is behind our backs, but this is a trivial empirical truth and not a profound, transcendental one.[109] In many cases, the claim that we have to turn toward something in order to perceive it is plainly false, for example, in most cases of hearing or smelling.

B. Is a Phenomenology of Being Possible?

A critical evaluation of Heidegger's phenomenologico-hermeneutical leitmotif in *Sein und Zeit* has to address two problems, which I discuss in the present subsection. Heidegger claims in the introduction to *Sein und Zeit* that the question of being is not only concerned with the many ways in which we use the verb "to be," but also and primarily with the phenomenon of being. The phenomenon of being allegedly is the phenomenon *par excellence*, the phenomenon of phenomenology, and this phenomenon is said to be hidden in all empirical phenomena.[110] The contention that being is hidden in each empirical phenomenon may mean at least four different things, and my two problems are linked up with two of these four meanings.

Heidegger's claim about the omnipresent phenomenon of being might be an echo of Eckhart's doctrine that Being in the sense of God is hidden in all creatures. If so, phenomenology in Heidegger's hands turns into a pseudo-phenomenological theology, and the attempt to discover the phenomenon of Being in each and every entity is akin to the religious endeavor to "let be" things what they really are: traces of Being. If this is what Heidegger means, we should reject the idea of a phenomenon of Being for the reasons that I adduced in criticizing Heidegger's postmonotheist theme. Second, the notion of a hidden phenomenon of being may have a transcendental sense, and this is what Heidegger most clearly suggests in section 7 of *Sein und Zeit*.[111] I rejected the idea that there is a hidden phenomenon of being in this second sense as well, both in its Neo-Hegelian and in its Neo-Kantian varieties. The two problems that I want to discuss now are implied in the third and the fourth senses of a "phenomenon of being."

Heidegger's claim that there is a hidden phenomenon of being in all empirical phenomena is at least in part derived from Husserlian assumptions about meaning, as I argued in section 8A. Husserl's principle of referentiality says that all meaningful expressions are referring expressions, even though meaning and reference are distinguished as different aspects of expressions. If there can be no meaning without reference, simple expressions such as "to be" cannot have gotten a meaning unless there is a phenomenon of being. Because we use the verb "to be," in the different senses of existence, predication, and identity, with regard to all entities, the phenomenon of being must be present in all entities. Furthermore, Husserl's principle of acquaintance says that in order to elucidate the meaning of simple expressions we have to study the phenomena to which they refer. It follows that we have to investigate the phenomenon or phenomena of being in order to elucidate the meanings of the verb "to be," and this is the third sense of Heidegger's claim that there is a phenomenon of being. The question of being in so far as it is concerned with the meaning or meanings of "to be" has to be answered by the phenomenological method. My first problem (1) is whether the principles of referentiality and of acquaintance are correct, and whether they hold for the verb "to be." If not, Heidegger's claim that one and the same question of being is not only concerned with the meanings of a verb but also with a phenomenon is misguided. In order to trace the meanings of "to be" we have to practice linguistic analysis and not phenomenology.

Finally, Heidegger's thesis that a phenomenon of being is concealed in all entities might mean that each entity belongs to a particular region of being, and that each region has its own essence. Phenomenology has the task of constructing a regional ontology for each region by "grounding" the "fundamental concepts" for this region on a descriptive exploration of the relevant domain. This would "signify nothing else than an interpretation of those entities with regard to their basic structure of being" (*Grundverfassung seines Seins*). A regional ontology is said to be a priori in relation to the empirical science of its domain, because its concepts express the essence of that domain.[112] In accord with his notion of a regional ontology, Heidegger claims that his phenomenological descriptions of Dasein have an a priori generality and that they do not stand in need of being justified by empirical or ontical research.[113] Heidegger's very contention that he is doing ontology instead of pursuing merely ontical research is based on the Husserlian assumptions that there are essences and that ontology is a study of essences. My second problem (2) is whether this claim can be maintained, and whether it is consistent with Heidegger's view that the phenomenology of Dasein is *also* hermeneutics. I now discuss both problems in this order, and I argue that we must reject the phenomenologico-hermeneutical leitmotif.

1. The Principle of Referentiality and the Verb "to Be." Husserl defends the principles of referentiality and acquaintance for all expressions, and in particular for all logical words, such as "and," "all," "some," "if . . . then," "or," "not," and "is" in its various logical uses. As we saw in section 8A, he argues for these principles on the basis of a theory of meaning according to which meanings of words are due to object-directed or "intentional" acts. However, as the best and indeed the only way to trace the meanings of words consists in studying how these words are actually used, we should investigate how the logical words of our language are used instead of starting from a dogmatic theory of meaning. Are the logical words really employed in order to refer to something, as Husserl holds? We will see that this view leads us into absurdities.

Husserl was trained as a mathematician and, like many mathematicians, he was tempted to think that mathematical objects exist out there, waiting to be discovered. In his first book, the *Philosophie der Arithmetik* of 1891, he argued that numbers should be interpreted as sets and he raised the question as to what holds the elements of a set together.[114] He answered that a mental act of collecting, counting, or conjoining makes entities into the elements of a set, and that, therefore, the concept of a set is a second-order concept, abstracted from a mental act of collecting, which is based on perceptual mental acts. This view was rejected in section 44 of Husserl's sixth *Logical Investigation*, on the ground that reflection and abstraction based on the mental acts of collecting or counting yields the concepts of collecting and counting and not the concepts of a set and of number. Husserl concluded that the notion of a set is abstracted from an objective phenomenon, not from a subjective mental act but from its objective "intentional correlate," and he argued that this objective phenomenon is the phenomenon referred to by the word "and." This is why Husserl discusses the word "and" in his fourth *Investigation*, and it explains the peculiar fact that he discusses it as a syncategoreumenon linking names, instead of treating the conjunction as a junctor of propositions.[115]

However, we use the word "and" primarily as a junctor of propositions, and in this case it is patently absurd to think that it is a referring expression. If I say truly "the sun is shining" and I say truly "the fridge is empty," I may also say truly "the sun is shining *and* the fridge is empty." There can be no objective counterpart in reality to the word "and," a counterpart that is required for the truth of the third assertion, because in that case the truth of the third assertion would not logically follow from the truth of the first two assertions. That logical constants are not used as referring expressions becomes even clearer in the cases of "not" and "or." First, every assertion of the form "p or q" is logically equivalent to an assertion of the form "not (not p and not q)." But if "or" and "not" were referring expressions, assertions of the first form would be made true by situations structurally different from the situations that make assertions of the second form true, and logical equivalence would be excluded. Moreover, an assertion of the form "p or q" is true if one of its disjuncts is true. Suppose that there is a situation that makes the first disjunct true. What does the word "or" refer to? If "or" is a junctor, it should refer to a relation between two situations, and a relation exists only if its relata exist. For this reason, Husserl's assumption that "or" is a referring expression implies the absurd doctrine that for an assertion of the form "p or q" to be true, it is not sufficient that things are as "p" says that they are. It would also be required that things are as "q" says that they are. But then "or" would mean the same as "and."

The absurdity of the principle of referentiality as applied to logical expressions can be demonstrated most convincingly in the case of "not." If an assertion of the form "p" is true, "not-not-p" is true as well. How can this be the case if "not" refers to something? If the word "not" were a referring expression, the situation that makes "not-not-p" true would necessarily be richer than the situation that makes "p" true, so that the truth of "not-not-p" would not follow from the truth of "p." Similar arguments show that the "is" of predication cannot be a referring expression. From the proposition that the brown horse runs in the meadow, it follows that a running horse in the meadow *is* brown. This could not follow logically if the expression "is" refers, for in that case the situation that makes the second assertion true must be richer than the situation that makes the first assertion true. Husserl would reply that the "is" of predication is implicitly present in the attributive uses of adjectives. Clearly this is an *ad hoc* assumption adduced in order to save his theory.

The "is" of existence is not a referring expression either. Imagine that we want to give a description of an imaginary entity, call it E, and then add that E exists. The claim that E exists goes beyond the description we first gave: it says that there *is* something which is E. Should we suppose that the expression "is" in the sense of existence is a referring expression? In that case, the claim that E exists would attribute a feature to E that E as originally described lacks, so that the existing entity cannot be E as originally described. This is patently absurd, for giving a description of some entity E and then going on to claim that this very same entity exists, is something we can do. The claim that E exists says that we may use the description of E in order to refer successfully to something, namely, E; it does not say that E has a specific feature that we have to add to our original description, the feature of existence. David Hume used an argument of this kind in order to show that "existence" is not an idea, and Kant concluded that because a hundred existing *Thaler* are not more *Thaler* than a hundred imaginary *Thaler*, existence is not a real predicate. Heidegger discusses Kant's thesis many times and he admits that "to be" in the sense of "to exist" does not refer to a property. Yet he seems to assume that "to exist" refers to some other kind of feature of entities, as if existence were a kind of action. Being would be a phenomenon, to be investigated by phenomenology. But to say this is to commit the very same mistake that Hume and Kant repudiated. There may be superficial grammatical similarities between action verbs and the verb "to exist," but these similarities should not mislead us into thinking that action verbs and "to exist" are logically similar, so that "to exist" refers to a specific kind of action or activity, the activity of existing.

Finally, it is clear that "is" in the sense of identity, as in "the Evening Star is the Morning Star," is not a referring expression either. To discover that the Evening Star is the Morning Star is to discover that the entity we refer to by the expression "the Evening Star" is the same entity as the one to which we refer by the expression "the Morning Star." Apart from the discovery that these two expressions are used to refer to the same thing, the planet Venus, we do not discover a new feature of this entity, the feature of identity. Some philosophers think that we can say both meaningfully and truly of each entity that it is identical to itself. Should we not conclude that the "is" of identity refers to a feature that each entity possesses, and that we know a priori that all entities have this feature? We should beware of drawing this conclusion, for these philosophers are confused. If we say that this is A and we add "A is A," we do not add new information about A. Moreover, we do not have a use for the expression "A is A"; the word "is" is used vacuously here, and this explains the misleading suggestion that we utter an a priori truth. At best, we might say, the phrase "A is A" expresses a rule of language: the rule that if we have decided to use the name "A" for an entity, we must go on using it for that entity.

Let me come back to "is" in the sense of existence, for this is the most interesting case. When we claim that a specific number exists, what we claim is different from what we claim when we say that there is a bottle of wine in the fridge, and we adduce different kinds of grounds in order to substantiate each of these claims. Some philosophers have concluded that there are different senses of "to exist," and they distinguish the timeless existence of numbers from the spatiotemporal existence of bottles. Other philosophers, such as Quine, argue that the difference between these cases is entirely due to the difference between the predicates "bottle" and "number," and that the verb "to exist" is used in one sense only, the sense specified by the use of variables bound by quantification.[116] Heidegger thought, as Husserl did, that these issues are among the deepest problems of philosophy, and that phenomenology is the correct method for solving them. At some point, I have reconstructed what Heidegger says as raising the problem as to whether we are justified in assuming that logical constants are topic-neutral. This is an interesting issue, and it is a pity that Heidegger did not elaborate his philosophy of logic instead of suggesting that logic is somehow flawed altogether.

We must conclude from the above considerations that phenomenology is not the correct method for answering the question of being, to the extent that this question is concerned with the different uses of the verb "to be." In section 7C of *Sein und Zeit*, Heidegger makes the puzzling claim that *being* is the phenomenon that phenomenology has to investigate because "it is something that proximally and for the most part does not show itself at all: it is something that lies hidden, in contrast to that which proximally and for the most part does show itself."[117] We may now explain this puzzling contention as follows. Heidegger started with a mistaken assumption that he inherited from Husserl, the assumption that the verb "to be" is used as a referring expression. This assumption then produced the illusionary impression that there has to be a phenomenon of being in each and every entity. Because he could not find such a phenomenon, Heidegger concluded that the phenomenon of being must be hidden, and that phenomenology has the task of bringing this hidden phenomenon to light. A mistaken view on language, the principle of referentiality, created the illusion of an enigmatic and occult phenomenon, which has intrigued Heideggerians for three quarters of a century.

2. Heidegger's Phenomenologico-Hermeneutical Method: Essences and Categories. I now come to the second problem implied by Heidegger's phenomenologico-hermeneutical leitmotif, which is concerned with the fourth sense of Heidegger's puzzling claim that there is a phenomenon of being concealed in every entity. Heidegger asserts that each entity belongs to an ontological domain or region and that each region has its own essence. The world is neatly carved up into essentially different domains, and philosophy has the task of exploring regional essences in order to construct regional ontologies, which are a priori in relation to the sciences. The ontology of Dasein is such a regional ontology, and its method is phenomenological and hermeneutical. Regional ontologies allegedly draw fundamental concepts or "categories" from the source of the phenomena themselves. In the case of the ontology of Dasein, these concepts are called existentialia, in order to distinguish them from the categories of other domains. Heidegger's question of being now gets the sense of a question that aims at investigating regional essences, or, as he also says, "the fundamental constitution of being" of each region.[118] The contention that in *Sein und Zeit* Heidegger is doing ontology as opposed to ontical or empirical anthropology is based on the idea that there are regional essences. My second problem is concerned with this doctrine, and it splits up into three different questions. If there are essences, does Heidegger convincingly explain how we may know them (a)? Are there essences at all (b)? Finally, if there are no essences, what are we to think of Heidegger's radical claim that the philosophical tradition was wrong in applying to human beings categories that also apply to other kinds of entities (c)? Let me discuss these questions in this order, starting with the first, epistemological one.

(a) In his second *Logical Investigation*, Husserl argued at great length that there are essences, and he tried to show in later works, such as his lectures on phenomenological psychology and in *Erfahrung und Urteil* (*Experience and Judgment*), how we might know essences by what he called eidetic variation.[119] Heidegger does nothing of the sort. He neither argues that essences exist, nor does he explain how we might know them. On the one hand, he seems simply to rely on Husserl's authority at this point, but on the other hand he mars Husserl's conception by claiming that the phenomenology of Dasein is hermeneutical. I will argue that Heidegger's conception of philosophical method is utterly confused, and that he fails to explain convincingly how knowledge of essences is obtained.

In the first draft of *Sein und Zeit,* the Natorp essay of 1922, Heidegger still advocated a purely hermeneutical method. It is the task of philosophy to interpret human life. Historical investigations are crucial to philosophy because a confrontation between past and present interpretations of human life may reveal decisive possibilities of existing. Indeed, Heidegger says in 1922 that the philosophical interpretation of human life is historical through and through, so that "in each time only . . . the perspective of one's own time and generation is the real object of investigation."[120] Hermeneutics is concerned with what is historical and unique, and in 1922 there is no claim to essential generality. Historical interpretation is a method of disciplines such as history, and although there are many interesting methodological problems here, there is no reason to reject this method. However, it will never yield statements of essential and a priori generality. The historian may interpret the way in which the Greeks understood themselves and the world or he may interpret the self-understanding of his own time; he will not be able to understand human self-understanding as such, as Heidegger purports to do in *Sein und Zeit*. To the extent that Heidegger practices hermeneutics as defined in 1922, his research is ontical and not ontological.

If one abstracts from the transcendental leitmotif, Heidegger's claim in *Sein und Zeit* that he is doing ontology in contradistinction to ontical research may be justified only by the Husserlian idea that phenomenology discerns essences. One would expect Heidegger to explain how we might grasp essences in the method-ological section 7 of the book, but he does even start giving an explanation. He stresses that the notion of phenomenology is a methodological concept, and he defines phenomenology as the endeavor "to let that which shows itself be seen from itself in the very way in which it shows itself from itself."[121] This formula fits human activities as widely disparate as doing botany and showing someone paintings in the Louvre. Heidegger denies this. He says that when he claims that phenomenology is descriptive, the term "description" "does not signify such a procedure as we find, let us say, in botanical morphology." In the context of phenomenology, "the term has rather the sense of a prohibition—the avoidance of characterizing anything without . . . exhibiting it directly and demonstrating it directly."[122] But the botanist would accept this prohibitive sense of description as well, so that Heidegger has done nothing to show how a phenomenological description of essences is possible, and what distinguishes phenomenological de-scription from the descriptions in other descriptive disciplines such as botany, geography, or anthropology.

We must conclude that Heidegger's characterization of his phenomenologico-hermeneutical method gets bogged down in evasive and sweeping statements. Moreover, the phenomenological claim to essential generality is contradicted by what Heidegger said about hermeneutics in 1922, that it can be concerned with human self-understanding at a specific historical period only. There is yet another contradiction between the "methodologies" of phenomenology and hermeneutics, as I argued in section 8C. Whereas hermeneutics claims that understanding is presuppositional, phenomenology pretends to be presuppositionless. Heidegger endorses both contradictory claims, the first in sections 31–32 of *Sein und Zeit* and the second in section 7C. It seems that Heidegger is faced with a dilemma with respect to philosophical method. Either he uses the hermeneutical technique of interpreting the way in which humans understand themselves and the world. Then his results will be limited to specific cultural epochs, and the job of the philosopher cannot be very different from that of the novelist, the historian, or the cultural anthropologist. In particular, the philosopher cannot pretend to knowl-edge that is fundamental and a priori. Or, if the philosopher wants to stick to the latter claim, he has to substantiate it by a convincing methodological argument, which Heidegger does not provide.

It is not sufficient to say, for instance, that we can construct an ontology of ourselves because Dasein already understands itself anyway, so that it *is* ontologi-cal.[123] Heidegger first has to prove that this statement itself has essential generality, instead of being an empirical or a purely conceptual truth, and he also has to prove that human self-understanding in all periods of history concerns features that have essential generality. For it might be that what we understand in under-standing ourselves is always limited to specific historical periods, whereas the essentially general features, if they exist at all, escape us. Or it might be the case that even though our self-understanding is concerned with general features, these features have empirical generality only.

If Heidegger cannot substantiate his claim that he is able to discern essential structures, and if he does not elaborate a methodology for discerning such structures in opposition to the methodology of empirical anthropology, he has to abandon his distinction between the ontical and the ontological. As we will see, the distinction is untenable, and it has the undesirable rhetorical function of enabling Heidegger to present his private and time-bound view of human existence as an essential insight which is a priori, thereby making it immune to empirical criticisms. Yet there seems to be more to *Sein und Zeit* than this conclusion suggests. At many points, the reader has indeed the impression that what Heidegger says about Dasein is not merely empirically true, but essentially so. In order to explain this impression, I will proceed to the second question, the question as to whether essences exist.

(b) Husserl postulated in 1901 that there must be essences because he thought that this assumption is the only way to avoid psychologism in logic and mathematics.[124] If logic and mathematics are either about essences or about mental occurrences, and if the latter view implies the incoherent and skeptical position of psychologism, as Husserl argued in *Prolegomena*, then we have a strong *prima facie* case in favor of essences. Furthermore, as there is no doubt that we possess logical and mathematical knowledge, Husserl concluded that we must be able to know essences. Generalizing this conclusion, he held the doctrine that knowledge of essences is also possible in other, "material" domains. Even though his arguments purporting to prove the existence of essences and the possibility of knowing them are not convincing, we might give Husserl and Heidegger the benefit of the doubt if it is true that we have to choose between essences or skepticism.

Unfortunately, there is no good reason to adopt Husserl's disjunctive premise, because it is based on a misleading assumption. Logic and mathematics are not *about* a domain of objects. These disciplines do not consist of descriptions, but rather specify how we may infer from specific descriptions of objects or events other descriptions of objects or events. Accordingly, Husserl did not have a good *prima facie* case in favor of essences, and Heidegger was wrong in relying on Husserl's authority. That there is such a thing as a "material a priori" is not a discovery of Husserl's, as Heidegger suggests in his lectures of 1925 on the history of the concept of time, but it is a philosophical theory.[125] I will argue along Wittgensteinean lines that this theory is mistaken.

Let us assume that there are essences. Then true statements about these essences cannot be mere conceptual truths, which express the rules for using words. In traditional philosophical jargon we might say that truths about essences cannot be analytic; they have to be synthetic a priori. Let us suppose further that "nothing can be green and red all over" expresses such a truth about the essences of green and red. If this truth is synthetic, it must be meaningful to say that something is green and red all over, even though it is excluded by the essence of green and red that this statement is true of something. A synthetic statement is characterized by bipolarity. As far as its meaning is concerned, it may be true and it may be false, whereas to suppose that an analytic statement is false would yield a contradiction.

In other words, if there are essences, these essences would rule out a priori a situation that is conceptually possible and that can be described meaningfully, to wit, that something is red and green all over. The problem is that we have no idea what it means to say that something is red and green all over. When we learned the meaning of color words by samples, there was no sample called "red and green all over," and the uses of "red" and "green" were learned with regard to very different samples. However, if we are not able to describe what would be the case if the statement "nothing is red and green all over" were false, then this statement cannot be synthetic. As a consequence, it cannot be about essences. In the ordinary sense of the word "true" it is not true either, for it expresses a rule for using the words "red" and "green."

If one thinks that expressions of rules for the usage of words, such as "nothing can be both round and square," are true in the ordinary sense of corresponding with some reality, one will conclude that these statements are essentially true. Is it not a priori excluded that something exists that would refute them? And if this is a priori excluded, it must be excluded by something that is not purely contingent, the essence of round and square. However, expressions of rules of language are not true at all, or at best true in a very special sense only, the sense in which we say that it is true that a king in a game of chess can move one square a time. This is true in the sense that it expresses a rule of chess and not because it corresponds to an essence. What we call a king in chess is a piece that may be moved according to a set of rules, and this rule belongs to the set. Similarly, when we say that something cannot be round and square, we do not exclude a possibility that a round object would otherwise have and that we could meaningfully describe, namely, to be square. We only exclude a form of words, and forms of words are excluded by the very rules for using these words. When we say that something cannot be round and square, what we are saying is that it would not make sense to describe something as round and square. We are not claiming that it would make sense but that this possibility is excluded by essences. Essences are shadows that language casts on reality.[126]

This criticism, which Wittgenstein elaborated in great detail for the reason that it applied to his *Tractatus*, leads to devastating conclusions with regard to Heidegger's philosophical method. Many statements in *Sein und Zeit* may seem to be necessarily true. If this is the case, it is not because Heidegger managed to discover the essence of human existence, but because in these statements he is merely expressing rules for the usage of words. He is not describing a phenomenon, or the essential constitution of being of an entity, but he is exploring the meanings of expressions, laying down new rules for the usage of his neologisms, or stating the implications of the rules that he laid down. As Heidegger was convinced that he was not merely analyzing the meaning of words, but rather that he was trying to describe the essential structures of a phenomenon, he confusedly mixed descriptions in his conceptual analyses, descriptions that are either empirically true of all human beings, or merely true of some human beings, or even false. He had the tendency to present his idiosyncratic views of human life as essential truths, for instance, when he argued in section 58 of *Sein und Zeit* that human beings are essentially guilty. The illusion of doing eidetic phenomenology produced a great number of secondary illusions, which a rational reconstruction of *Sein und Zeit* has to dispel.

Ideally, such a rational reconstruction first has to determine the logical status of all sentences in *Sein und Zeit*. With regard to each and every sentence, we have to ask: Does it express an existing rule of language? Or is it rather like a stipulative and persuasive redefinition of existing expressions, as I argued with regard to Heidegger's transcendental notion of truth? Or is it perhaps a stipulation for the use of a new expression, or a statement of the implications of such a stipulation? Or, finally, does it express an empirical truth or an empirical falsehood? I predict that the result of such a rational reconstruction will be that Heidegger confusingly mixed expressions of all these logical kinds, and that this confusion invalidates his arguments. In section 18, I attempt to substantiate this diagnosis by an analysis of what Heidegger says about Everyman or the They (*das Man*), death, and authenticity.

In a second stage of the rational reconstruction, one might try to rewrite *Sein und Zeit* in order to put the book on a sound methodological basis. There are three different ways of doing so. *Sein und Zeit* may be read as an essay in cultural criticism. The passages on the They, for instance, may be reconstructed as a diagnosis and critique of German bourgeois life during the *interbellum*, when the Great War had seemed to make so many bourgeois values pointless and unauthentic. However, as an essay in cultural criticism, *Sein und Zeit* is much too abstract. The book would gain in strength if concrete analyses of cultural phenomena were added. Cultural criticism is blind without a careful empirical underpinning. The same holds for the second type of rational reconstruction. *Sein und Zeit* may also be read as a hermeneutical interpretation of the understanding of life and the world of Heidegger and his generation, in accord with Heidegger's conception of hermeneutics in 1922. These two types may be combined into one. The hermeneutical interpretation of German Dasein in the interbellum was informed by a specific ideal of "authentic" existence, which explains that Heidegger devaluated bourgeois life as exemplifying the They from the point of view of authenticity as a passionate freedom-toward-death.

Third, we might reconstruct *Sein und Zeit* as an essay in conceptual analysis. The conceptual structures of everyday life are complex, intricate, and subtle. Many philosophers suffer from confusion with regard to these structures, for instance, because they mix up everyday and specialists' uses of words. Dogmatic philosophical theories about man, often inspired by scientific disciplines such as physics, biology, or cognitive psychology, tend to distort our views of ordinary language. Descartes' picture of a human being, according to which the vocabulary of the mental is used to refer to processes of a separate mental substance, and his theory of perception, which says that the colors and other secondary qualities of objects are mere dispositions in these objects to cause sensations in the mind, is an illustration of this point. We might reconstruct Heidegger's critique of the Cartesian ontology and his new ontology of Dasein as an attempt to trace the rules for the everyday use of those words that are somehow of central importance if we want to express ourselves as human beings. Because our capacity to use these words correctly and with subtlety is part of what it is to be human in a more than biological sense, this project of conceptual analysis is linked to the attempt to preserve standards of being human. The connection between the ontology of Dasein and authenticity, which is stressed again and again in *Sein und Zeit*, has an equivalent even in this third rational reconstruction of the book.

Each of these rational reconstructions of *Sein und Zeit* is a worthwhile endeavor, but none of them will substantiate the extravagant claim that the philosopher is able to construct a priori ontologies that are fundamental to the sciences. Heidegger's distinction between the ontical and the ontological levels has to be abandoned in any case. The attempt at a hermeneutical interpretation or a critique of one's culture is not essentially different from similar attempts by journalists, novelists, historians, sociologists, or literary critics. If one wants to avoid empty abstractions, one has to study the empirical cultural phenomena in detail. A critique of technology, for instance, will have to be based on an extensive investigation of the historical, economic, ecological, and psychological aspects of specific technological developments. Instead of "founding" empirical disciplines, the philosopher will have to acquire thorough knowledge of the relevant empirical investigations, provided that he wants to avoid engaging in pretentious idle talk.

On the other hand, the analysis of everyday conceptual structures, even though it can perhaps do without empirical investigations, will not yield a priori knowledge either, except in the humble sense that it provides us with overviews of the rules of our language. Making such an overview has a philosophical point whenever confusion about rules for using words produces philosophical problems. By reminding us what rules we were supposed to use, and by showing how we got confused, the philosopher will be able to dissolve conceptual entanglements. This philosophical task is not easy, and it is clearly distinguished from what empirical scientists, journalists, historians, novelists, and cultural critics are doing most of their time. If one looks for a method and a task proper to philosophy, one will opt for the third rational reconstruction of *Sein und Zeit*. But one should not engage Heidegger as a teacher in this method, for he himself gets entangled in conceptual confusions again and again. Its paradigmatic practitioners are Wittgenstein, Austin, Ryle, Strawson, and many other figures in the analytical tradition, such as Norman Malcolm, Arthur Prior, Alan White, Bede Rundle, Anthony Kenny, and Peter Hacker.

(c) We are now prepared to answer my third and final question. Heidegger claimed in *Sein und Zeit* that traditional philosophical categories do not apply to Dasein, because they were derived from the domains of artifacts or inanimate things. This claim explains the dual task that Heidegger set himself: to "destroy" traditional categories and to construct new ones for Dasein, the existentialia. Heidegger's claim presupposes the doctrine of essences. If the totality of beings is carved up into essentially different domains, concepts that fit one domain will be essentially unfitting for another domain. I have argued, however, that the doctrine of essences is mistaken. Can Heidegger's claim be justified apart from this erroneous doctrine? Was Heidegger right in assuming that categories that apply to artifacts and inanimate things cannot apply to Dasein?

The answer to this question will depend on one's notion of a category. It is not easy to develop a coherent notion of a category, as the analytical tradition in philosophy shows.[127] Apart from his rudimentary doctrine on essences, Heidegger did not express an interesting view of what categories are.[128] In his early writings, such as his paper on "Categories" of 1938 and "Philosophical Argument" of 1946, Gilbert Ryle tried to explain the concept of a category in terms of the logical powers of propositions. But such an attempt must fail, because formal logic abstracts from all differences in subject matter. If Ryle meant "logical powers" in the sense of formal logic, this notion cannot be of any help in elucidating that of a category. If, on the other hand, he meant the expression "logical powers" in a different sense, as yet to be defined, he was trying to elucidate the obscure by the unknown.

A more promising attempt to define the notion of a category starts with examples of category mismatch. In the simple case of a singular subject-predicate proposition, we have such a mismatch when the individual item specified by the subject expression is of such a sort that both the affirmation and the denial of the predicate in question of that individual are a priori rejectable.[129] When we say, for instance, that the number four is blue, or that my idea of democracy has the temperature of 21 degrees Celsius, we produce examples of category mismatch or category mistakes. Skipping all sorts of technicalities, we may now define what categories are, both in the case of categories of individuals and in the case of categories of predicates.

Two individuals belong to some one *relative* category of individuals if there is a predicate or set of predicates such that that predicate or every member of that set of predicates can be predicated without category mismatch of both items. Socrates and my dog belong to at least one relative category in this sense because, for instance, they are both stubborn. They do not belong, however, to one and the same *absolute* category, for we may define absolute categories of individuals by saying that two items belong to the same *absolute* category if and only if they have all their relative categories in common.[130] Because it makes sense to say of Socrates that he is a Greek or that he is not a Greek, whereas this does not make sense in relation to my dog, Socrates and my dog do not belong to one and the same absolute category.

Do all human beings belong to one and the same absolute category of individuals? This seems to be a minimum requirement for Heidegger's philosophical program to make sense, since he assumes that all Dasein is of one and the same category or ontological region. But clearly this requirement is not met. There are predicates, such as "being a Nazi," so that it and its negation can meaningfully be predicated of one human being, for instance, Martin Heidegger, whereas it does not make sense to ascribe it or its negation literally to another human being, such as René Descartes. Heidegger seems to be faced with a dilemma with regard to categories of individuals. On the one hand, all human beings fall under many common relative categories of individuals, but the notion of a relative category is too weak as a rational reconstruction of Heidegger's concept of an ontological region: human beings will have relative categories in common with many other kinds of entities. The notion of an absolute category of individuals, on the other hand, is too strong. It may be that no two human beings belong to one and the same absolute category.

Examples of category mistakes also give rise to a definition of a category of predicates. If both the affirmation of a predicate and its denial are a priori rejectable with regard to an individual specified by a subject expression, there will be, in general, a more abstract predicate that is a priori rejectable for that individual under all definite descriptions of it, whereas its denial is true of that individual. We will then take the a priori rejectability of this more abstract predicate as an explanation of the category mismatch, and the abstract predicate may be called a categorial predicate or a category of predicates.[131] For instance, when we say that the word "table" is neither red nor not-red, we may explain this by saying that words are not colored, and the relevant categorial predicate is being-colored. On this definition, some of Heidegger's existentialia, such as being-in-a-mood (*Befindlichkeit*), would count as categorial predicates, whereas others, such as falling (*Verfallen*), would not. Moreover, it is questionable whether categories in this sense are an interesting class of concepts. The category skeptic might argue that with regard to any individual under a specific description, category mismatches may be construed, and that usually the relevant categories are philosophically uninteresting. Clouds in the air are neither cheap nor expensive, because they do not have a price. Bikes have neither much nor minimal horsepower, because bikes do not have engines. Is "having-a-price" or "having-an-engine" a category in any interesting sense of the word?

It seems to be better, then, to restrict the notion of a category to very abstract concepts, such as that of a state, a disposition, an occurrence, an event, or a property, even though we do not have a substantial theory or a definite list of such categories. But if these concepts are called categories, it is clear that the same categories may apply to humans and to many other kinds of entities. A glass is brittle; it has the disposition to break. In the very same sense of the word "disposition," I may be said to have the disposition to be cheerful or despondent. We must conclude that in this intuitive sense of the term "category" Heidegger was wrong in claiming that the same categories cannot apply both to inanimate things or tools and to Dasein, whereas we did not succeed in finding another sense of "category" that would make Heidegger's claim plausible. As a consequence, *there simply is no interesting philosophical program of constructing specific categories for human life.* A philosopher might explore a great number of concepts in which human beings express their understanding of life. But it is not fruitful to claim that some of these concepts are categories or "existentialia," whereas others are not. In other words, there is no distinction left between the ontological and the ontical if Heidegger's theory of essential structures is discarded.

Yet there is a successor program to Heidegger's philosophical project of *Sein und Zeit*. It is an interesting and difficult question under which categories psychological concepts should be subsumed, in the last and loose sense of "category." It is often said, for instance, that if A believes that p, A is in a mental *state*, which might be identical to a brain state, or it is said that A has a propositional *attitude* to the proposition "that p." Quite often these categorizations of psychological concepts function as premises for philosophical theories, such as the identity theories of the mind. However, it may plausibly be argued that to believe "that p" is neither to have an attitude nor to be in a state, so that these theories of the mind are nonsensical.[132] Let me now briefly elaborate such an argument in order to show that this successor program to the philosophical project of *Sein und Zeit* is both important and substantial.

Attitudes. Paradigmatic attitudes are having sympathy for someone, hating someone, favoring something, or trusting someone. Believing *in* someone is an attitude, but believing that p is not an attitude toward the proposition p. For one may believe what one fears or hopes, namely, that p, but one cannot fear or hope a proposition. Moreover, "that p" is not the name of something, so that believing that p cannot be an attitude toward something. A relational assertion of the form "aRb" is true only if a and b exist, so that if "A believes that p" expressed an attitude to something, *that p* would have to exist in order that someone may believe that p. But it does not make sense to say that *that p* exists. Finally, if *what* we believe when we believe that p were a proposition, what is believed would not be what is the case if one's belief is true, for it is nonsense to say that a proposition is the case. This is absurd, because if I believe that p, my belief is true precisely if it is the case that p.

States of mind. States of mind, on the other hand, are things one is *in*. One is in a state of anxiety or elation. Now I may have believed that p since last year, but it is certainly not the case that I have been in one and the same state of mind since last year. I may believe many things at a time, but does it make sense to say that I am in many different states of mind at the time, namely, believing that p, believing that q, and so on? I may be unsure in what state of mind I am, and I may try to read off this state of mind, say depression, from my behavior.

However, it does not make sense to say that I am unsure of what I believe, if in fact I believe something. "I don't know what I believe" rather means "I don't know what to believe," and this does not express uncertainty about a state of mind I am in, but rather about the question whether I have sufficient grounds to believe that p rather than that q. If it is difficult to believe that p, this does not mean that it is not at all easy to get oneself into a specific state of mind. What is meant is rather that it is improbable that p, given the evidence. States of mind have duration. They are interruptible, as when I am concentrating on my writing and the telephone rings, and they are terminated by sleep, for one does not feel elated or depressed while one is asleep. But it makes no sense to say that my belief that p was interrupted, or that my falling asleep terminated my belief that p, which resumed when I woke up. The "grammar" of believing that p is very different from that of mental states, hence one cannot meaningfully say that believing that p is a mental state.

Dispositions. Nor is believing something a disposition, for dispositional verbs do not typically take an intentional accusative ("that p"). Dispositions are defined by what they are dispositions to do or to suffer, for instance, to break or to feel frightened, but believing that p is not so defined. Although A's saying "p" is a criterion for thinking that A believes that p, A's believing that p is not a disposition to say "p," for dispositions are tendencies to do something frequently or always under specific conditions, while A may believe that p without ever saying so. If we say that A is timorous, we attribute the disposition of feeling frightened to A and this says something about A's character. But if we say that A believes that p, we do not attribute a character trait to A. Explaining behavior by reference to a disposition is explaining it as instantiating a regularity. However, if A believes that p, for instance, that Yeltsin will win the elections in Russia, we may have no idea at all what A will do if he acts on his belief, and probably he will not act on this belief at all. Again, if the grammar of "belief" is different from the grammar of dispositions, it is nonsensical to say that beliefs are dispositions.

These considerations are meant to show two things. First, Heidegger's thesis that each region of entities has different categories is unconvincing, not only because there are no essences, but also because categories in the most intuitive sense of this term will apply to entities of very different kinds. Second, it is a difficult philosophical task to determine under which categories we should subsume other concepts. If belief is neither an attitude, nor a state or a disposition, most philosophical accounts of belief are mistaken or confused. We must conclude that Heidegger's conception of his philosophical task in the published two divisions of *Sein und Zeit* was misguided—there are no specific categories of human existence in any substantial sense of 'categories'—and that there is an interesting philosophical task that he neglected, the task of categorizing the concepts that we use in describing and expressing ourselves by studying the "logical grammar" of words.

We have seen that Heidegger's thesis of the essential regionality of being is not only mistaken, but that it led him astray in his conception of philosophy. One final reason for rejecting this thesis is derived from the history of science. The notion of essences was abandoned during the scientific revolution because it had led to sterile plays with words and to intellectual stagnation. Heidegger's notion of regional ontologies as a priori underpinnings of the empirical sciences would lead to stagnation as well. If the empirical sciences have to remain within the conceptual space created by regional ontologies, and if these regional ontologies are constructed with the concepts of everyday life because they precede empirical research, the evolution of science would be hampered by historically contingent and myopic classifications, and the unification of science would be precluded. A whale would still have to be considered as a fish, because it was classified as belonging to the region of fishes many centuries ago. Husserlian essentialism is difficult to square with other, more Kuhnian elements of Heidegger's conception of science. We have ample reason, then, for rejecting Heidegger's essentialism, and with it his distinction between the ontical and the ontological.

§ 18. DEATH AND THE MULTITUDE

If the idea that there are essences is a philosophical illusion, produced by the shadows that language casts on reality, Heidegger's phenomenological project in *Sein und Zeit* collapses. There cannot be such a thing as a regional ontology of Dasein, which is a priori in relation to the sciences of man. Heidegger's phenomenological descriptions do not possess "essential generality." They consist either of empirical generalities or of rules for the uses of words, disguised as descriptive statements, or, finally, of a mixture of these two kinds, interlarded with images and metaphors. Nonetheless, one might try to save what is philosophically fruitful in *Sein und Zeit* by reconstructing the book as an essay in conceptual analysis. In this section I try to substantiate these general criticisms, raised in section 17B, by reviewing in part what Heidegger says (A) about Everyman, the They or the One (*das Man*), and (B) about authenticity and death. I argue that Heidegger's analysis of these phenomena is biased, and that the specific nature of his bias can be explained by the hypothesis that *Sein und Zeit* was conceived as the first stage of a Pascalian strategy (see §§ 12C and 13C).

A. *The Incoherence of "Authenticity"*

Heidegger's concept of the They or the One was introduced in the third section of this book. I argued that the concept is confused, because Heidegger runs together two very different notions. On the one hand, the concept of Everyman or the They expresses the insight that our personal identity is to a large extent due to the cultural matrix into which we were born and raised, so that we live always already in a shared and public cultural world. Because in a sense we are what we do, and because in our daily life we mostly act according to preexisting roles and patterns, Heidegger says that the real subject of our everyday life is the One. We behave in a situation as *One* is supposed to behave in that situation. Without such conformity, language and a shared cultural world cannot exist. On the other hand, when Heidegger identifies the concept of the One with that of inauthenticity, he confuses conformity with conformism, which is a specific attitude vis-à-vis the common cultural background.

I will now review sections 25–27 of *Sein und Zeit* in more detail and develop my explanatory hypothesis regarding this surprising confusion in Heidegger's concept of the They. For in order to understand *Sein und Zeit*, it is not sufficient to point out that there is such a confusion. We should also be able to explain why and how it came about. Before developing the hypothesis, the textual problem must be constructed carefully.

In the chapter on Everyman or the They Heidegger wants to answer the question: "*Who* is it that Dasein is in its everydayness?"[133] As it stands, this question may seem to be underdetermined. We have no idea what Heidegger is hinting at, and we might happily answer: well, *we all* lead our daily life, individually and with each other. However, Heidegger intends his question as an ontological one, and he explains in section 25 of *Sein und Zeit* that it derives its point from the view that he rejects: that of the Cartesian tradition in general and Husserl's transcendental idealism in particular. According to Husserl's *Ideas I*, both language and the world depend ontologically on a transcendental ego, which constitutes a meaningful language and a world by interpreting its sense data. For Husserl, the transcendental ego is the ultimate source of meaning, significance, and the world. This theory resembles the doctrine that Quine put forward in *Word and Object*; the main difference being that Quine substituted stimuli for sense data and a material subject for Husserl's spiritual substance. The problem that theories of this type have to face is how they can account for the existence of an intersubjective world. Neither Husserl nor Quine was able to solve this problem.

Rather than solving it, Heidegger tries to *dissolve* the problem of intersubjectivity and of other minds. In section 26 of *Sein und Zeit,* he does so by putting forward the following two theses. First, the public cultural world is not constituted by individual egos; it is a primary phenomenon. The world is always shared with other human beings, whom we meet obliquely, as it were, in coping with our environment. For instance, tools refer to possible users. If we walk along the edge of a field instead of crossing it, we do so because it is owned by someone else. The book we are reading was bought at so-and-so's shop.[134] Second, Heidegger concludes that being-with-others (*Mitsein*) is an essential mode of being or existentiale of Dasein, which it has always and essentially, even if it is alone. We can only be alone and miss someone, he argues, because we are essentially with-others, and our being-with-others cannot be explained by supposing that each of us is a separate substance that knows other persons by empathy (*Einfühlung*).

Admittedly, Heidegger's rather dogmatic statements in this section do not suffice to dissolve the traditional problem of other minds. Husserl could easily have acknowledged the phenomena that Heidegger describes, and he could have tried to argue that these phenomena are constituted by transcendental egos. But the issue in which I am interested is a different one: What is the logical and epistemic status of Heidegger's statements, if his claim that they are a priori truths about essential structures is mistaken? There are two possible reconstructions of what Heidegger says in section 26 of *Sein und Zeit*.

First, one might argue that the primacy of the social and cultural world for human beings, and the intersubjective dimension of human life, are very general empirical features of *Homo sapiens*. Because human behavior is only partially determined by instinct, there is both room and need for culture, and since we are born and raised in a specific culture, our personal identity is to a large extent determined by the culture into which we happened to be born. Furthermore, it is true that we can only miss someone if we are with others in the first place.[135] Again, this point may be interpreted as an empirical statement. We will not miss John if we did not know him first, and our general capacity to miss and to need persons is due to our empirical nature of a gregarious animal.

There is yet a second, more philosophical account of what Heidegger says, and this is the interpretation that Dreyfus prefers in his commentary on *Sein und Zeit*. We might reconstruct section 26 of *Sein und Zeit* along Wittgensteinean lines as making conceptual points about the public nature of rules and the connection between rules and forms of life. For example, we might say that a piece of equipment embodies a norm for its use, and that this norm or rule may be followed by anyone. Because rules are public in this Wittgensteinean sense and cannot exist without shared practices, the world that consists of equipment, houses, schools, roads, and the like is a public world. Dreyfus claims that Heidegger coined the term *das Man* in order to refer to the normal user of equipment.[136] Similarly, Heidegger's point that we cannot miss someone unless we are with others might be reconstructed as a conceptual gloss on the verb "to miss": it is nonsensical to say that you miss John and to add that you do not know someone of that name.

Up to this point, one might accept Heidegger's analysis in one of its two possible reconstructions. But irrespective of how we reconstruct section 26 of *Sein und Zeit*, we will not be able to swallow its conclusion, which Heidegger develops in section 27. This conclusion is that "Dasein, as it is absorbed in the world of its concern—that is, at the same time, in its being-with toward others—*is not itself*."[137] If Dasein in its daily life is not itself, Heidegger argues in section 27, it must be the case that its being has been *taken over* by someone else, Everyman or the They (*das Man*).[138] Dasein is not itself, he says, but "its being has been taken away by the others."[139] These others are not specific other human beings, but indefinite others. "What is decisive is just that inconspicuous domination by others that has already been taken over unawares by Dasein as being-with."[140]

Heidegger claims that because we behave as everyone else in our daily life, when, for instance, we use public transport or read the papers, "this being-with-one-another dissolves one's own Dasein completely into the kind of being of 'the others.' "[141] In short, in everyday life we are not-ourselves or inauthentic; our existence has been usurped by the others or the They, which "deprives the particular Dasein of its responsibility" and of its independence, and which closes it off from itself.[142]

What Heidegger says here squarely contradicts his earlier analysis of the public world in both of its reconstructions. According to the empirical and anthropological reconstruction, our personal identity is largely determined by our national and local culture and by the rules and roles that it provides. That Martin Heidegger was a German university professor from a modest social and a specific local background is part of Heidegger's personal identity. But if our "self" is to such an extent a social construct, one cannot go on to claim that when we behave according to the roles and rules of our culture, we are *not* ourselves but inauthentic. As I argued in section 3 of this book, Heidegger's notions of the They and of authenticity suffer from internal contradictions.

Similarly, Heidegger's statements in section 27 of *Sein und Zeit* fly in the face of what he is supposed to be saying according to the Wittgensteinean reconstruction. If Heidegger coined the expression *das Man* in order to refer to the normal user of words and equipment, as Dreyfus claims, it would be misleading to translate this expression by "the They." Such a translation suggests that *I* am distinguished from *them*, whereas according to Dreyfus "Heidegger's whole point is that the equipment and roles of a society are defined by norms that apply to anyone," including ourselves.[143] However, if this was indeed Heidegger's whole point, how can he identify *das Man* with indefinite *others*, who have taken over my existence and deprived it of its responsibility? How can he conclude that when we act according to rules and roles, we are *not ourselves*, because our existence is taken away and usurped by *others*? The point is especially clear with regard to language. In speaking a language, I have to follow the common and public rules for using words. Why should this imply that I am not myself? It seems to be a mystery for which reasons Heidegger draws this conclusion. Yet one thing is obvious. If Heidegger claims in section 27 that *das Man* is identical with the *others* as opposed to my real *self*, the English neologism "the They" captures precisely what he means, and Dreyfus's criticism of the translation is unjustified. An even better translation would be "the multitude." Heidegger belongs to the large number of intellectuals of his generation who tried to distance themselves from the masses by arguing that their real self was not part of them.[144]

The easiest way out of the problem is to conclude that Heidegger was utterly confused, and this is what Dreyfus argues. On the one hand, Heidegger is supposed to be making a Wittgensteinean point: that public rules cannot exist if most of us do not behave most of the time according to them. Without conformity in behavior there can be no rules, and without rules there can be no "significant" world in Heidegger's sense. Ultimately, then, the source of the intelligibility of the world and of language consists in the average public practices that we share, and not in a transcendental ego à la Husserl. But pointing to the constitutive function of shared practices is very different from pointing out the dangers of conformism. As Dreyfus says, Heidegger, "influenced by Kierkegaard's attack on the public in *The Present Age*, does everything he can to blur this important distinction."[145] Because "Heidegger does not distinguish . . . constitutive *conformity* from the evils of *conformism*," the chapter on the They in *Sein und Zeit* is "not only one of the most basic in the book, it is also the most confused."[146]

However, this solution cannot be the end of the matter. If Heidegger ran together two different notions that may be easily distinguished, one should wonder what explains the fact that he did "everything to blur this important distinction." Why did Heidegger argue that we are not ourselves if we behave according to common rules and roles? Dreyfus's answer to this question is interesting, but it will not do as an interpretation of *Sein und Zeit*. He argues in the main body of his commentary that we are authentic in Heidegger's sense if we own up to what we really are, rather than covering up features of ourselves. This is why one has to be authentic in order to develop an adequate analysis of Dasein. According to Dreyfus, Heidegger's interpretation of the average and everyday intelligibility of life (*Alltäglichkeit*) in *Sein und Zeit* reveals that this intelligibility is rooted in shared practices. Yet, Dreyfus says, there is something that the average intelligibility of our daily life tends to cover up, "that it is *merely* average everyday intelligibility" (my italics). We tend to think that the way we do things is the correct way, not only in the sense that we behave in accordance with the rules that we happen to have, but also because we suppose that these rules and practices are based on some deeper foundation, such as God, human nature, or solid good sense. Dreyfus claims that, for Heidegger, inauthenticity consists in the illusion that there is such a foundation to our common practices. We allegedly become authentic as soon as we realize, with Dreyfus's Wittgensteinized Heidegger, that common practices are groundless. "The only deep interpretation left is that there is no deep interpretation."[147] In other words, inauthentic persons behave according to roles and rules under the illusion that there is some foundation to their common practices, whereas the authentic individual behaves according to these very same rules and roles, realizing, however, that they are contingent and without foundation. Because Dasein cannot avoid behaving according to cultural roles, authenticity can only mean that Dasein "just takes them over differently," that is, with resoluteness and accepting their contingency.[148] In Dreyfus's hands, Heidegger's authentic individual becomes a Californian multiculturalist. As we will see, there is more to Heidegger's notion of authenticity than Dreyfus seems to think.

In order to make sense of Heidegger's texts, I propose a solution that takes Kierkegaard's influence more seriously than Dreyfus is prepared to do even in his appendix.[149] I suggest that in *Sein und Zeit*, Heidegger wanted to prepare us for the traditional religious view that, even though Dasein is "in-the-world," our real "self" is not *of* this world at all. This is why, having stressed that we always already live in a public world, Heidegger goes on to claim that we are not ourselves or inauthentic as long as we do so. In order to become ourselves, we have to grasp our worldly life as a whole and see that death opens the possibility to an afterlife in which we can be really ourselves. Only when we realize that our real "self" is not *of* this world, even though Dasein is being-*in*-the-world, can we be authentic. This message of *Sein und Zeit*, I submit, is not explicitly expressed in the text, because Heidegger intended the book as the first stage of a Pascalian strategy. I argued in sections 12C and 13C that the first stage of such a strategy consists in a secular description of the human condition, which nevertheless prepares the reader for the leap to faith. It does so by suggesting that in our worldly life we are dispersed and not really ourselves, so that, in order to be authentic, we must be prepared to leave this world and be ready for death. Because a purely secular analysis can never substantiate this notion of a transcendent self, Heidegger's notion of (in)authenticity was bound to be incoherent.

On the one hand, Heidegger argued that Dasein cannot avoid being absorbed in the world with others. On the other hand he claimed that if one is absorbed in the world with others, one is inauthentic, and this is the result of what he calls fallenness or falling (*Verfallen*).[150] This notion of a Fall makes sense in a Christian account of man. The traditional Christian will claim, as Kierkegaard and Pascal did, that our real self is an eternal spirit. Life on earth is only temporary, and when we cling to earthly things, we betray our real self and commit the sin of falling. In order to overcome falling, we have to meditate on the finite and death-bound nature of our being-in-the-world. This will prepare us for the leap to an absolute religious commitment. In Kierkegaard, the account is explicitly religious. He argues by means of a subtle dialectic that all attitudes in life are contradictory and that, if we realize the contradictions, we will work our way up toward absolute religious commitment, by which we will finally identify with ourselves as spirits. But in order to use it as the first stage in a Pascalian strategy, Heidegger had to secularize Kierkegaard's account of (in)authenticity, with the inevitable result that he ran into contradictions. For it does not make sense to argue that Dasein is necessarily absorbed in the world and then to condemn Dasein's daily life in the world as inauthentic, unless there is another life, which is *not* of this world.

At first sight, it may seem that Heidegger wanted to develop a *purely* secular account of authenticity. To be authentic consists in facing up to the contingent and finite nature of Dasein, abandoning the illusion that being-in-the-world is somehow justified. Authentic individuals admit the anxiety that contingency, freedom, and death inspire in them, and, being opened up for the situation in which they happen to find themselves, they choose their possibilities with resolution. These possibilities cannot be different from the possibilities chosen by inauthentic Dasein, because according to Heidegger's secular account of authenticity, there are no other possibilities than those that are prefigured by culture and history. If follows that authenticity can only be distinguished from inauthenticity as a special way or style of choosing the same possibilities—not as choosing different possibilities. The authentic individual, Heidegger says, anticipates death without illusions, and acts resolutely with a sober understanding of what factically the basic possibilities of Dasein are. Being authentic in this sense gives us an unshakable joy.[151]

Many Heideggerians claim that Heidegger's secularized account of authenticity, including what he says about resoluteness, anxiety, anticipating death, guilt, conscience, and authentic historicality, is a coherent account, which spells out a possible attitude in life, and this is what Dreyfus and Rubin argue in the appendix to Dreyfus's commentary. But they add, correctly to my mind, that if Heidegger's description of authenticity is successful, its very success makes his account of inauthenticity incoherent.[152] If secular authenticity is a possible attitude, which gives us an unshakable joy, how can Heidegger pretend that inauthenticity and fallenness are inevitable? Heidegger's analysis of authenticity and inauthenticity faces a dilemma. Either his analysis is consistently secular. Dasein is finite being-in-the-world, and it is inevitable for Dasein to be absorbed in worldly affairs. Authenticity consists in facing up without illusions to what Dasein really is. If this is the case, there can be nothing wrong with being-absorbed-in-the-world, and it does not make sense to say that one is inevitably inauthentic and prey to *Verfallen*. Or, on the other hand, Heidegger might argue that there is something deeply unsettling about our daily life in the world, and that if one acquiesces in this worldly existence, one is inauthentic and prey to falling. But this makes sense only in the context of a straightforwardly religious account of authenticity, which holds out the hope for another existence which is not in-the-world, or at least for a non-worldly dimension of our existence-in-the-world.

My hypothesis is that Heidegger did not want to make this choice consistently, because his Pascalian strategy implies that he had to hint at the second horn of the dilemma by developing the first. On the one hand, he had to pretend that he was giving a purely secular account of (in)authenticity in order to convince the unbeliever of the truth of his descriptions. On the other hand, he had to intimate that our secular life in the world backslides inevitably, because, as long as we are absorbed in the world, we do not face the kind of being we really are. To suggest this was necessary in order to prepare the reader for a leap to faith, as the first stage of the Pascalian strategy is supposed to do. I am claiming, then, that the confusions and contradictions in Heidegger's analysis of *das Man*, *Verfallen*, and (in)authenticity are not accidental or due to careless writing on Heidegger's part. Rather, they are inherent in Heidegger's Pascalian strategy.

B. Authenticity and Death

Let me now try to corroborate this hypothesis by reviewing in detail what Heidegger says in sections 46–53 of *Sein und Zeit* about authenticity in relation to death. I first summarize Heidegger's pronouncements on death and I subject them to a critical analysis. Having shown that what Heidegger contends regarding authentic being-toward-death is paradoxical and cannot be justified from a secular philosophical perspective, I then argue that the hypothesis of a Pascalian strategy fully explains Heidegger's text.

Of the various dimensions of Heidegger's notion of authenticity, what he calls being-toward-death seems to be the most important one.[153] For Heidegger claims (1) that death is "Dasein's *ownmost* [*eigenste*] possibility." As death is our ownmost possibility, we become ourselves or authentic (*eigentlich*) by relating properly to our own death.[154] These are surprising statements, and one will want to know why Heidegger thinks that death is our ownmost possibility. He answers by claiming (2) that "by its very essence, death is in every case mine." The reason is that one Dasein cannot represent another in dying, whereas we can represent each other in performing many functions in life. *"No one can take the other's dying away from him,"* Heidegger writes in italics, and he concludes that dying is a unique possibility that every Dasein itself must take on itself.[155]

How, then, does Dasein relate to its own death? Or, to use a more Heideggerian locution, how does my own death "enter into my Dasein as a possibility of my being"?[156] Heidegger calls our relation to our own death "dying" (*Sterben*), and he claims accordingly (3) that "factically, Dasein is dying as long as it exists," because it allegedly relates to its death as soon as it has been born, even if it does not yet know that it is bound to die.[157] If dying is in reality the way in which we relate to our death from the beginning of our life on, one will not be surprised to hear that, according to Heidegger, we cover up this horrendous fact in daily life. Not being able to face dying all the time, we pretend that death is an event at the end of life, which, when we are not yet very old, probably will occur in a relatively distant future. We admit that there is an empirical certainty that all humans die, but as long as it is not our turn, our own death does not really concern us most of the time. Heidegger stigmatizes this stoic and commonsensical attitude to death as inauthentic. Having this attitude, we allegedly reassure ourselves about death and try to escape from the anxiety that being-toward-death inspires, thereby covering up the fact that we are dying permanently.[158] In order to become authentic, we have to face up to permanent dying as our relation to death. Because death is our ownmost possibility, we will become ourselves when we open up to this possibility by letting anxiety take hold of us.

What does it mean to relate authentically to death and to acknowledge that we are dying as long as we live? According to Heidegger, we first have to admit (4) that our death "is possible at any moment."[159] Whenever we realize that this is the case, "the possibility of death is not weakened," as in the inauthentic attitude to death, but it is "understood as a possibility, cultivated as a possibility, and endured as a possibility."[160] Heidegger calls authentic understanding of death as our own possibility "running on ahead toward the possibility" (*Vorlaufen in die Möglichkeit*). He makes extravagant claims for such an understanding, for instance (5), that if we run ahead toward our own death, we are able to *be* ourselves *as a whole,* because in anticipating death, we also anticipate all possibilities of existing that will precede it.[161] In running ahead toward death, "Dasein opens itself to a constant threat arising out of its own 'there,' " the threat of dying. Furthermore, the "fundamental mood that holds open the utter and constant threat to itself, which arises from Dasein's ownmost individualized being, is anxiety."[162] Because death is essentially individual, anxiety enables me to be myself and frees me from the bonds of the They, so that being-free-for-death is the same thing as being free to become myself.[163] Heidegger stresses that death is final. It is "the possibility of the impossibility of any existence at all," because "death, as a possibility, gives Dasein nothing to be 'actualized,' nothing which Dasein . . . could itself *be.*" If we relate to death in the manner of running ahead toward it, this possibility "becomes ever greater." Death reveals itself to be such that "it knows no measure at all," because it "signifies the possibility of the measureless impossibility of existence." It is the last and uttermost possibility.[164] And yet, Heidegger points out (6) that his ontological analysis of death does not imply that there is no life after death. That there is a life after death is a mere ontical and metaphysical possibility, about which a phenomenological ontology can tell us nothing. What is even more, "only when death is conceived in its full ontological essence can we have any methodological assurance even in *asking* what *may be after death*; only then can we do so with meaning and justification."[165]

Many existentialist philosophers have acclaimed Heidegger's analysis of being-toward-death in *Sein und Zeit* as one of the most profound and sharp-witted pieces ever written by a philosopher. I will now briefly examine the seven theses that I numbered in my summary, making use of Paul Edwards' refreshing book on the topic.[166] We will find that Heidegger's allegedly deep analysis of death does not contain significant philosophical insights. It is a mesmerizing play with words, a masterly piece of rhetoric. When we see through his artifice, we will wonder what its point is, a question that I try to answer at the end of this subsection.

1. Death as My Ownmost Possibility. Is there a sense in which it is both true and interesting to say that "death is my ownmost possibility"? Heidegger intends this claim as a statement of essential generality, which is necessarily true of each of us. But is it true at all? The problem is, clearly, that the words "death," "possibility," and "ownmost" may have many meanings. One thing that Heidegger seems to mean by "ownmost" is that when a person dies, he or she is "most on his or her own," that is, alone. He says, for instance, that when Dasein is face to face with death, "all its relations to any other Dasein have been undone." And he claims that "the nonrelational character of death . . . individualizes Dasein down to itself."[167] The argument seems to be that because we all die alone, anticipating our death "wrenches us away from the They" and teaches us to be an authentic individual.[168] If we adopt the hypothesis that the word "ownmost" means "most on our own" or "alone," the word "death" clearly cannot have the meaning of being dead, for it does not make sense to say that a corpse is or is not alone. It follows that, on this reading of "ownmost," Heidegger must mean by "death" the terminal phase of one's life, the phase of dying, and not the state of being dead. Now we may ask: Is it an interesting truth to say that when we die, we are most on our own or alone?

Even this statement is not unambiguous. There are three senses in which someone may be said to die alone, and in each of these senses it is plainly false to say that everyone dies alone. In a first sense, someone dies alone if no other human being is present when he or she dies. A mountaineer may climb a mountain on his own, without being accompanied. Ten thousand feet above the last village or hut, he is forced by a snowstorm to pass the night and he freezes to death. It is clearly false to say that each and every Dasein dies on its own in this sense. Very often, other people are present when someone dies. Second, someone may be said to die alone when he or she feels mentally isolated during the terminal phase of life. Napoleon spent his final six years in Saint Helena. His second wife, Marie Louise of Austria, sent no word to him, nor did he have any news from his son, the former king of Rome. After he fell ill in 1817, doctors who were thought to be well-disposed to Napoleon were dismissed. His illness lasted from the end of 1817 until 5 May 1821, when he died. Napoleon, we may suppose, felt completely isolated during his final years, and in this sense he died alone. But again, some people do not feel psychologically isolated when they are dying and are on their deathbed surrounded by family and friends. Finally, the phrase "dying alone" might mean that one dies when no one else dies at the same time and place. One does not die alone, in this sense of being the only one who dies, if one is on a plane that is blown up by a bomb. All passengers are killed, so that one does not die on one's own. This very example proves that not everyone dies alone in this third and somewhat stretched sense either. We should conclude that in all three senses of "dying on one's own," it is not true that we all die on our own.

How, then, can Heidegger claim that, as a matter of necessity, Dasein dies on its own? One possibility is that he implicitly redefined the phrase "dying on one's own" so as to be equivalent to "dying." Now it becomes logically impossible that someone does *not* die on one's own, and the claim that death is our ownmost possibility becomes a true general statement. However, this statement does not express an interesting philosophical insight. It just means that we all die, and this we knew all along. Heidegger's thesis that death is our ownmost possibility, if interpreted as the claim that we all die alone, sounds like the expression of a deep philosophical insight. This rhetorical effect is obtained in the following manner. On the one hand, the thesis suggests an informative interpretation: we die alone when we are completely isolated, high up in the mountains, for instance. In this interpretation, it is false that we all die alone. On the other hand, the thesis is true in a trivial sense, for it can be made true by definition. The reader who swallows Heidegger's text without analysis does not realize that one cannot have it both ways: it is impossible to interpret Heidegger's statement as both true and informative.

It may be that the rhetorical effect is also obtained by other confusions, for instance between dying and being dead. It is trivially true to say that when Dasein is dead, "all its relations to any other Dasein have been undone," for it does not make sense to say that a corpse relates to a human being. But it would be informative, though empirically false, to claim that when people are in the terminal phase of their life, it is always the case that their relations to other human beings have been undone. Again, the impression of a deep philosophical insight arises when we overlook the fact that one cannot interpret Heidegger's statement so that it is both informative and true. Furthermore, we might be taken in by misleading pictures. The image of falling asleep is often used as a euphemism for dying. We say "he fell asleep peacefully," instead of "he died peacefully." Of course, we do not mean that a dead person is really sleeping, because one cannot be asleep unless one is alive. If a dead person were really asleep, and woke up after the entombment, he or she would feel both physically and mentally isolated, if at least we assume that there is no stowaway in the coffin. A Heideggerian might conclude that a dead person is alone, and that death is our ownmost possibility. But clearly, death is not like sleep at all and it is nonsense to say that a corpse is alone. Similar considerations apply to other euphemisms for death, such as "to depart" or "to disappear." When we read in French newspapers that "Mitterand a disparu," we might imagine that he is hiding in a place where, essentially, he cannot be found by other human beings, the Province of Death. Because Mitterand has disappeared, leaving his dead body behind, we cannot get in touch with him anymore, so that he must be terribly lonely. This is just another misleading image, unless we really believe that there is some kind of life after death. But this is something Heidegger cannot claim, officially at least, because his phenomenological ontology of death can only interpret death as a phenomenon *in* human life.[169]

Let me now turn to a very different interpretation of Heidegger's claim that "death is our ownmost possibility." By "ownmost possibility" Heidegger might mean a possibility *in* our life which is, if it is actualized, the moment of our highest fulfillment. He suggests this interpretation where he writes that death is an *excellent* possibility of Dasein (*ausgezeichnete Möglichkeit des Daseins*), a possibility that is distinguished from all other possibilities by its excellence.[170] Many followers of Heidegger have claimed that death is the culmination of human life, a golden opportunity, the crown of our existence.[171] Again, there are different interpretations of this claim, depending on what one understands by "death" and by "possibility." It would be perverse to say that, in general, *being dead* is an excellent possibility for man. One would not say this unless one were a misanthropist to the point of wishing that the human species, including oneself, is wiped out. Except when in the midst of a depression or of beastly suffering, we do not regard being dead as something desirable. Also, being dead is not a possibility *in* life at all, so that it is not false but meaningless to suggest that death in the sense of being dead could be our crowning achievement. Heidegger does not fare better if "death" is interpreted as dying. When Achilles refused to fight, Patroclus took his armor and heroically risked his life in order to throw back the Trojans. Like Ares he rushed forward, killing twenty-seven men. Then he was wounded by Euphorbus's lance and was killed by Hector. One might think that, in this case, dying was the moment of Patroclus's highest fulfillment, because he fell for his people. However, this is a perverse view, which Homer does not endorse. It may be that fighting like Ares and risking his life were Patroclus's crowning achievements, but the fact that he was wounded and killed was a piece of bad luck, so bad that Homer tried to explain it by supposing that Apollo interfered and unbuckled Achilles' armor. For most people, heroically risking their life is certainly not their highest achievement. It may be that the Nightwatch is Rembrandt's masterpiece, so that painting it was the crowning success of his life as a painter. Yet Rembrandt probably did not risk his life while he was painting. Moreover, it usually is not the case that there is *one* crowning achievement of a human life. In most cases, Heidegger's suggestion that there is one possibility or opportunity in our life that is the most distinguished or excellent one, simply does not make sense.

Under point (3), I will make some further comments on Heidegger's claim that death is a possibility for us, for it is not at all clear in which sense of the term "possibility" he thinks that this is the case. As far as thesis (1) is concerned, we come to the conclusion that what Heidegger says is utterly confused, and that there is no interpretation under which it is both interesting and true. The best I can make of Heidegger's statements that death is Dasein's ownmost possibility, and that, by relating properly to death, we become ourselves or authentic, is that when we think about our own death, we realize that life is short and that we have to use it well. When Wittgenstein was on holiday in Norway with David Pinsent in 1913, he was convinced that he was going to die soon. As Pinsent recorded in his diary, Wittgenstein was frightfully worried not to let the few remaining moments of his life be wasted. There was no good reason to suppose that Wittgenstein would not live a long life, and in fact he died in 1951. Nevertheless, the illusion that he would die soon may have been useful for Wittgenstein. If this is what Heidegger means, I would agree, but it is not an original thought. The notion of *memento mori* is a classical one. Also, Heidegger seems to deny that this is what he means. For he writes in section 53 of *Sein und Zeit* that authentic being-toward-death is not the same thing as thinking about one's own death.[172]

2. Nobody Can Die in My Place. If Heidegger's claim that my death is more mine than anything else, and that it is my "ownmost possibility," is nonsensical, false, or trivially true, we will wonder what Heidegger's grounds for putting it forward are. These grounds are to be found in the second half of section 47 of *Sein und Zeit*, where Heidegger argues that in the matter of death, no human being can substitute for another. He first stresses that we can represent each other in daily life in many ways. If I am ill, a colleague can substitute for me and give my lectures, and if I am very busy on the day of the elections, my wife can vote in my place.[173] Heidegger claims that representability is not only possible in everyday life, but that it is "even constitutive for our being with another."[174] This fits in well with Dreyfus's Wittgensteinean interpretation of being-in-the-world in terms of shared background practices. For these practices are governed by rules, and rules are public in the sense that in principle anyone may follow them. The notions of a rule and a social role are related to a generalized notion of representability or substitutivity. As a consequence, this notion of substitutivity is also inherent in the concept of Everyman or the They, to the extent that this concept is explained in terms of social roles and rule-governed practices.[175]

Having explained the notion of representability, Heidegger then argues for the thesis that my death is more mine than anything else, so that I will not become really myself unless I relate properly to my death. His argument consists of three propositions, which he seems to regard as equivalent. Heidegger first claims that:

(a) the possibility of substitution breaks down completely with regard to death.[176]

He then adds in italics a second claim, as if it were equivalent to the first:

(b) *no one can take the other's dying away from him.*[177]

Finally, he seems to admit that proposition (a) is false. For he writes that "of course someone can 'go to his death for another.' " But he adds that this kind of substitution, when one sacrifices oneself for the other in some definite affair, is not what he meant by (a). The reason is that "such 'dying for' can never signify that the other has thus had his death taken away in even the slightest degree." Dying, he says, is something that every Dasein itself must take on itself at the time.[178] In other words:

(c) by its very essence, death is in every case mine, in so far as it "is" at all.[179]

I think that proposition (a) is indeed false if we take the notion of representing in the sense in which Heidegger explained it. When during the Second World War the Dutch resistance blew up a counting register or a bridge, the Germans reacted by executing a fixed number of political prisoners. One prisoner could then volunteer to die instead of another, and this happened in some cases. It is not true, then, that "the possibility of representing breaks down completely" with regard to death. Instead of admitting this honestly, Heidegger now redefines (a) so as to mean (b).

Proposition (b) is of course true, but trivially so. That we cannot take someone's dying away from him is true in the sense that we cannot *ultimately* deliver a human being from death. This is not an interesting philosophical insight; it is an empirical platitude. It just means that we all are going to die in the end, and that no doctor can prevent this. But Heidegger's wording of this empirical truth is very misleading. By saying that nobody can take my dying away from me, he suggests that my death is some kind of possession, like a priceless treasure, which nobody is able to steal, because it is so utterly *mine*. This brings me to proposition (c).

To say that, by its very essence, my death is mine, seems to be a deep metaphysical statement, a statement about essences. However, the illusion that there are essences is produced by the shadows that grammar casts on reality, as I argued in section 17. Statement (c) is true in a sense, and it is as trite as (b), but for a different reason. That the death which will end my life is *my* death is not an empirical truth, but a rule for the use of words. What we *call* "my death" is simply the death that will end *my* life. Similarly, the pain that I feel in my body is *my* pain, and not someone else's pain, and this is true by definition. We might express these rules of language differently by saying, for instance, that someone else cannot have my pain and that someone else cannot die my death. The illusion that these statements express deep metaphysical truths arises when we misinterpret them as factual or synthetic statements, and then realize that they are somehow necessarily true. One construes "you cannot die my death" analogously to "you cannot drive my car," that is, as the negation of an empirical possibility. This is what Heidegger does when he suggests that (c) is equivalent to (a), which in fact denies an empirical possibility, though falsely. It then seems that this empirical possibility is *necessarily* excluded, because (c) is conceptually true. And it seems that only the essence of my death can exclude with necessity the empirical possibility that someone dies in my place.

In reality nothing is excluded by (c) except meaningless forms of words. It is not empirically or metaphysically false, but simply nonsensical to say that when Mitterand died, he in fact died the death of Maria Callas, except if we mean that they both died from a similar cause, such as cancer. That I cannot die someone else's death has nothing to do with empirical, metaphysical, or ontological limitations; it is a matter of grammar. When I tell someone about Mitterand's death, and then add that he died *his own* death, I am not stating an extra fact over and above the fact that Mitterand died. What I was adding was merely an explicit statement of a rule of language. Now such a statement is not always trivial. It may be crucial to remind one how certain words are used if confusions arise because people do not follow the rules for the use of words consistently. In the present case, however, an explicit statement of the rule is trivial indeed, for there are no reasons to suppose that anybody has ever been tempted to violate the rule in question. Who would be inclined to say, when Mitterand died, that he in fact died the death of, say, President Kennedy? We come to the conclusion that Heidegger's thesis (2) of the unsubstitutability of death is a confused mixture of an empirical falsehood (a), a trivial empirical truth (b), and a trite rule of grammar (c). Because Heidegger thinks that (a) and (b) are equivalent, he mistakenly assumes that (a) is true, and because he thinks that (a) is equivalent with (c), he concludes erroneously that (a) is necessarily true, a statement of ontological necessity.

If it is a mere matter of grammar that the death which will end my life is *my* death, my death is not *more* mine than the thoughts that I have, or the pain I feel in my body. It follows that thesis (2), in the sense in which it is true, does not justify Heidegger's claim that I can become myself or authentic only by relating to my death, because my death is allegedly *more mine* than anything else. However, one might try to defend Heidegger on this point by arguing that there is more to proposition (a) than I have said up until now. There is a limit to substitutability with regard to death that perhaps does not exist in other cases of substitution. I may imagine that someone else gives not just one lecture in my place, but represents me in all my lectures. For some reason, I keep my chair nominally, even though I do not lecture anymore, and year after year until my retirement, the course description says that Professor Y's lectures will be given by Mr. X. In the case of death, however, it is difficult to imagine that always when I am about to die, someone else dies in my place, for it is an empirical fact that all human beings eventually die.

We now might reconstruct Heidegger's argument for the connection between death and authenticity as follows. He assumes that we are not ourselves as long as we behave according to rules or roles. Roles and rules are conceptually connected with substitutability in a wide sense. Heidegger concludes that we become ourselves whenever the possibility of substitution breaks down. Furthermore, he implies that this possibility breaks down at one point only: death. As a consequence, we become ourselves by relating properly to our own death. If this is indeed Heidegger's argument, is it sound? Does substitutability break down at one point only, namely, death?

It is easy to see that this is not the case. If it is true that (b) nobody can take away my death, because I will ultimately die, then it is equally true that nobody can eat in my place. Admittedly, someone else might go to a dinner party instead of me, but there is a limit to substitutability in the case of eating as well. For empirical reasons, my hunger will not be appeased when someone else eats in my place. Similarly, my bladder will not be emptied when someone else goes to the lavatories, and my muscles will not be trained when someone substitutes for me in a rugby team. All these limits to substitutability have to do with our body, and we begin to suspect that there is an explanation of the fact that substitution breaks down in the case of death. Substitution is not possible if what we do or suffer is primarily related, under a specific description, to our body instead of to social roles or rules. Because Heidegger focuses on death, and omits a discussion in *Sein und Zeit* of the human body in everyday life, he does not see that what holds for death is true for eating, breathing, and sports as well. We must conclude that death is not *more mine* in the sense of unsubstitutability than breathing, eating, or playing tennis. Lucullus might rejoice and claim that to be authentic is to eat well. This claim, in its turn, is no more justified than Heidegger's contention that we have to relate to our own death in order to become authentic.

The fact that Heidegger omits a discussion of the human body in *Sein und Zeit* seriously distorts his analysis of everyday life.[180] He argues in section 26 of his chapter on the They that one's identity in everyday life is constituted by the roles one is assuming and the rules one is following. As Heidegger says, we are what we pursue.[181] Because rules and roles may be followed and played by anyone, he concludes that the real subject of everyday life is *das Man*, anticipating the structuralist philosophers of the 1970s. However, my identity in everyday life is not merely determined by the roles that I assume and by the cultural matrix into which I was born. My genetic structure, my bodily constitution, and my personal history are determining factors of equal importance. If one takes these factors into account, Heidegger's thesis that we are not really ourselves in everyday life becomes even more implausible than it already is.

In his commentary on *Sein und Zeit*, Dreyfus proposes an ingenuous interpretation of Heidegger's thesis that one becomes authentic by relating to death. But in this interpretation, the thesis is open to a similar criticism. According to Dreyfus, the only way "the possibility of dying could have existential meaning would be as what Kant calls an *analogon*," that is, "as a concrete example that stands for something else that cannot be represented." When we anticipate death, we anticipate the possibility that there are no possibilities left for us. As Heidegger says, "death, as possibility, gives Dasein nothing to be 'actualized,' nothing which Dasein, as actual, could itself *be*." Death is the impossibility of all possibilities.[182] According to Dreyfus, death might become an analogon for living lucidly in such a way that I am constantly owning up to the fact that Dasein can make no possibilities its own. Death, as the condition in which there are no possibilities of living left to me, might be a symbol of the true condition of life, because in life *no possibility can become really my own*.[183] Because Dreyfus interprets Heideggerian authenticity as owning up to what Dasein essentially is, he has to conclude, paradoxically, that I become myself or authentic by realizing that no possibility in life can really become my own possibility.

Why is it the case, according to Heidegger as interpreted by Dreyfus, that no possibility can be really my own possibility? The reason seems to be that everyday life, as he sees it, is fully determined by preexisting roles. As roles imply substitutability, no possibility in life is supposed to be exclusively my own, except death, where "the possibility of substitution breaks down completely." We have seen, however, that if substitutability breaks down in the case of death, it breaks down as well in all cases where my behavior is primarily related to the body rather than to social roles and institutions. Moreover, if my behavior is not only determined by rules and roles, but also by the idiosyncratic features due to my genetic structure and my personal history, there seems to be no convincing argument for the view that no possibility of existing can be exclusively my own. Even when I am fulfilling public functions that other people are able to fulfill as well, the specific way in which I am behaving will be personal, so that death is not a convincing "analogon" of the human condition.

3. Being-toward-the-End: We Are Dying Continuously. Heidegger claims that death is not simply the end of life. This commonsensical view, which most philosophers endorse, he condemns as inauthentic, a product of fleeing and falling. If death is the end of life, it is the "end" in a very special sense. My death is not being-at-its-end (*Zu-Ende-sein*) of my Dasein, but a being-toward-the-end (*Sein zum Ende*).[184] Heidegger calls this being-toward-the-end "dying" (*sterben*), and he draws the startling conclusion that we are dying as long as we live.[185] Again, we will wonder how he derives this conclusion, and his main argument is to be found in section 48 of *Sein und Zeit*. In this section, Heidegger raises the question "in what sense, if any, death must be conceived as the ending of Dasein."[186] He discusses several senses of "end" and "ending," such as being ripe (of a fruit), ceasing (of rain, of a road), completion (of a building or a painting), and being used up (bread), and he claims that by none of these modes of ending can death be suitably characterized as the "end" of Dasein.[187] Heidegger's reason for this dogmatic assertion is his thesis of the regionality of being, which he stresses in the opening paragraphs of section 48. Because the totality of beings is carved up into ontological regions that are essentially different from each other, the category of "end" is bound to have a different meaning with regard to each region. Accordingly, death cannot be the end of life in the sense in which, for instance, rain ends when it stops, where "to end" means "to cease."[188] This result does not yet give us a clue in which sense of the word "end" death is indeed the end of Dasein, so that Heidegger needs yet another premise. The lacking premise is a thesis that he propounded in section 31 of *Sein und Zeit*, the thesis that Dasein *is* in a sense its future or its possibilities, namely, in the sense that it projects possibilities of existing and is concerned with its future life.[189] On the basis of this premise, Heidegger proposes a baffling syllogism: (a) Dasein is its possibilities; (b) death is a possibility of Dasein; therefore, (c) Dasein *is* its death, or, in other words, death is a mode of existing.[190] Because the only sense in which death can be a mode of existing is death as dying, as opposed to death as being-dead, this syllogism directly yields Heidegger's conclusion that we are dying as long as we live.

Heidegger does not present his argument in such a transparent way. As Edwards writes, he announces his doctrine with the kind of fanfare that is usually reserved for a major contribution to human knowledge, whereas in fact both his argument and his conclusion merely state familiar facts, couched in pretentious and fantastically misleading language.[191] Heidegger's thesis of the regionality of being is false, as I argued in section 17. Furthermore, the syllogism he proposes contains a fallacy of ambiguity. And the conclusion that we are dying all the time is nothing but a persuasive redefinition of the word "dying." I will argue these three points briefly.

Nobody denies that human beings are different from animals and inanimate things. It does not automatically follow, however, that a category applicable to other entities than Dasein is not in the same sense applicable to it. The sense of "disposition" in which my dog has a disposition to wag its tail when I prepare its food is the very same sense of the word "disposition" in which I may be said to have the disposition of cheering up when I am going to a dinner party. Now it is perfectly clear except to Heidegger and the Heideggerians, that when I am dead, I will have ceased to exist, in the very same sense in which a house has ceased to exist when it is destroyed by fire. Being dead, predicated of humans, animals, or plants, just means having ceased to live, and this is what "ending" means when one says that death ends life. Admittedly, a house and I are very different kinds of entities. But this fact does not imply that an expression such as "will come to an end" is predicated of a house and of me in different senses.

One might of course redefine "end" so as to mean *concern about* our end, and this is what Heidegger does when he says that "the 'ending' that we have in view when we speak of death does not signify Dasein's being-at-its-end but rather being-toward-the-end."[192] One is free to redefine an existing expression as one pleases, as long as one clearly distinguishes the new sense from the habitual one. But Heidegger's redefinition is a perverse verbal trick for two reasons. First, he presents his stipulative redefinition as a description of what we meant all along and should always mean. Second, he still needs the words "end" and "death" in their usual senses in order to express his new definition, so that it is patently false that these words can *only* have the new stipulated sense if used with regard to human beings. In Heidegger's neologism "being-toward-the-end," the component "end" cannot mean "being-toward-the-end" as well, on pains of an infinite regress in his definition. Similarly, if Heidegger redefines "death" as being-toward-death, the component "death" in this latter expression just means what the word meant all along.

That Heidegger's syllogism contains a fallacy of ambiguity is not difficult to discover. When he calls death a possibility of Dasein, the word "possibility" has a very different sense from that in which he claimed in section 31 of *Sein und Zeit* that Dasein *is* its possibilities. In this latter, existential sense of the term, a possibility is neither a mere logical possibility, nor an empirical possibility. It is a *possible course in life* that I might take or fail to realize, and I have possibilities in this existential sense because I am "thrown" into a specific situation. A possibility in Heidegger's special sense is an alternative in life that I know myself capable of choosing. Being a decent democratic citizen of the Weimar Republic or being a Nazi revolutionary are examples of such possibilities, which are possible projects of life within a specific historical setting. When Heidegger calls death a possibility of Dasein, he must mean something very different, for death is clearly not a possible course in life. Admittedly, I can choose to commit suicide, but if I am successful, my act will end my life, so that even in this case death is not a possibility in Heidegger's existential sense. Incidentally, Heidegger stresses that what he means by death as a possibility is not that we might commit suicide.[193] It follows that the term "possibility" in premise (a) has a different meaning from "possibility" in premise (b), so that the conclusion (c) does not follow.

As a consequence, there is no reason to believe that we are dying all the time. This proposition sounds like the result of a spectacular discovery. We all thought that human beings die only at the end of their life, but now, thanks to Dr. Heidegger, we know that people are dying all the time and start to die as soon as they are born. It is as if a mysterious new and fatal disease has been identified, a disease from which all human beings suffer during their entire life. Heideggerians have indeed hailed Heidegger's thesis as a deep ontological insight, which refutes the commonsense conception of death. But the appearance is deceptive. One cannot make such discoveries sitting behind one's desk in a hut in the mountains. What Heidegger did was simply redefine the word "dying" to mean knowing that one will die in the end and being concerned with one's death. No conception of death has been refuted, because one cannot refute a view by redefining words.

It may be that there is yet another argument for Heidegger's thesis that we are dying all the time, and this argument is based on considerations about phenomenological method. Phenomenology is a description of phenomena that excludes all speculations about what is not really exhibited. We have to describe the phenomena exactly as they manifest themselves to us, and their manner of manifestation has to be described as well.[194] If one wants to embark on a phenomenology of death, there seems to be a serious methodological problem: In what sense is death a phenomenon? Heidegger discusses this problem in section 47 of *Sein und Zeit*, and the argument of section 47 prepares the considerations about the notion of end in section 48, which lead to Heidegger's conclusion that my death should not be conceived of as my being-at-the-end, but rather as my being-toward-my-end. One may reasonably suppose, then, that this conclusion is partly based on Heidegger's methodological considerations.

The project of a phenomenology of death seems to be faced with an insuperable difficulty. Let me explain the problem in Heidegger's own words. It is impossible that I experience my own death, because "when Dasein reaches its wholeness in death, it simultaneously loses the being of its 'there.' By its transition to no-longer-Dasein, it gets lifted right out of the possibility of experiencing this transition and of understanding it as something experienced."[195] Because I cannot experience anything anymore when I am dead, I cannot experience my death, and my death is not a possible phenomenon for me that I might investigate phenomenologically. The solution seems to be that a phenomenology of death investigates the death of *other* persons. However, Heidegger rejects this solution, since when we experience the death of other human beings we do not experience "the actual having-come-to-an-end of the deceased." This is because "death does indeed reveal itself as a loss, but merely as a loss such as is experienced by those who remain." Heidegger's point is, then, that "in suffering this loss (of someone else), we have no access to the loss of being as such, which the dying person 'suffers.' "[196] A phenomenology of someone else's death will never reveal "the ontological meaning of the dying of the person who dies, as a possibility of being that belongs to *his* being."[197]

An ontological explorer less astute than Heidegger might have given up the project of a phenomenology of death at this point. If neither the death that ends my own life nor the deaths of others can be the phenomenon to be investigated, what is this phenomenon supposed to be? Heidegger rejects such a *tertium non datur*. The most important phenomenon of death has been overlooked, and this is death as something *in* our life: death in the sense of being-toward-death. Because we are dying as long as we are living, a phenomenology of death is possible after all.

In spite of what he claims, Heidegger did not solve the methodological problem that he so ably conjured up, as my earlier comments on his conclusion show. To assert that we are dying during our entire life boils down to a redefinition of "to die"; it is not the discovery of a new phenomenon, death in life. Heidegger simply confuses our attitude toward our own death with death itself. We may phenomenologically study our *concern* about our own death, but this is not the same thing as a phenomenology of death. Without a doubt, the best phenomenology of our own death was given by Epicurus, when he said that as long as I am there, my death is not there, and when my death will have arrived, I will not be there anymore. One might object that phenomenology has to describe *the manner in which things show up* for us, so that a phenomenology of death should investigate the way in which my own death is "given" to me. However, it does not follow that my death, as distinguished from concern about my death, is somehow present in my life, as Heidegger seems to think. Epicurus observed correctly that in my concern about death, my own death is given to me *as something absent*, as an event in the future that will put an end to my life.

Not only Heidegger's solution to his methodological problem is mistaken; the problem itself is a sham. He seems to think that a phenomenology of death should investigate "the loss that the dying person suffers" as opposed to the loss suffered by those who remain. This suggests that what should be studied is the experience of someone who has lost her or his life already, the experience of being dead. Such a phenomenological project is nonsensical, because one cannot experience or "suffer" anything when one is dead. Heidegger misconceives death as an inner state of the dead person, whose dead body is the outer appearance of her or his death. He imagines this inner state as one of bereavement, as if the dead person is bereaved of herself or himself. The others, who remain, have no access to this inner state of death. They can only see the dead body. And the deceased person, although he or she has the inner state of having suffered the loss of his or her life, is strangely unable to conduct phenomenological investigations: he or she is dead after all. One is bound to be mystified if one thinks about death in this confused manner.

4. Authentic Being-toward-Death as Running-Ahead-in-the-Possibility. I now come to Heidegger's characterization of authentic being-toward-death. If we are-toward-our-own-death, he says, we realize that death is possible at any moment, and, instead of weakening this possibility, we understand death as a possibility and cultivate it as such.[198] I already argued that death cannot be a possibility in the technical sense of the term, which Heidegger explained in section 31 of *Sein und Zeit.* However, Heidegger does not warn the reader that he is using the word "possibility" in a new and undefined sense. At times, he even seems to be unaware of the change of meaning himself, and this explains why he commits the fallacy of ambiguity that I discussed above. We now have to ask what Heidegger might mean when he says that death is a possibility that has to be cultivated if we want to be authentic. Having written thirty pages about death as a possibility, Heidegger finally realizes in section 53 of *Sein und Zeit* that he has to explain what he means. By saying that death is possible at any moment, Heidegger does not mean, as we would, that it is logically or empirically possible that I die at any given moment. The first of these alternatives is true but trivial; the second is true or false, depending on one's background assumptions. Heidegger intends to say something really deep. He wants to reveal how we may relate authentically to our own death. What he means by death as a possibility becomes clear in his discussion of four different ways of "being toward a possibility" on pages 261–262 of *Sein und Zeit*.

Heidegger rejects three possible attitudes toward a possibility as inauthentic with regard to my own death. First, we may relate to a possibility in the sense of *trying to actualize* it. Heidegger rejects this attitude in the case of death, because by actualizing a possibility, we annihilate it as such, whereas authentic being-toward-death consists in cultivating and enduring the possibility of death. As a consequence, an authentic attitude toward death cannot consist in committing suicide, because, "if this were done, Dasein would deprive itself of the very ground for an existing being-toward-death."[199]

Second, we might merely *think about* death instead of seeking to actualize it. Heidegger rejects this attitude as inauthentic as well, because, when brooding over death, we allegedly weaken death as a possibility, calculating how we might have it at our disposal. Heidegger is unfair here. There are many ways of thinking about death, and calculating is only one of them. In his zeal to say something profound, he wants to avoid the impression that he is merely recommending that we think about death. It may seem, in the third place, that the proper attitude toward death is that of *expecting*. But Heidegger says, correctly, that when we expect something possible, what we expect is the realization of the possibility. He concludes that in expecting death we also "weaken death as a possibility."

In order to cultivate death as a possibility instead of weakening it, we have to adopt a fourth attitude toward our death, which Heidegger calls "running ahead into the possibility" (*Vorlaufen in die Möglichkeit*), and this is authentic being-toward-death. Heidegger does not clearly explain what he means by "running-ahead-into-the-possibility," nor what "possibility" means in this context. Clearly he is under the spell of the following image. If we run ahead toward a macroscopic phenomenon such as a crevasse or a house on fire, it will appear to become greater and more impressive when we approach it. Heidegger seems to think that we may run ahead toward death as a possibility in a similar way, for he writes that "as one comes closer understandingly, the possibility of the possible just becomes greater," and "as one runs forward into this possibility it becomes 'greater and greater,' that is to say, the possibility reveals itself to be such that it knows no measure at all."[200] He also seems to think that if we run ahead *toward* a possibility, we run *away* from an actuality. This is shown by phrases such as the following: "the closest closeness that one may have in being-toward-death-as-a-possibility, is as far as possible from anything actual."²⁰¹ Heidegger mis-leadingly pictures possibility and actuality as scalar magnitudes, in fact, as the limits of a scale on which we might run to and fro. When we near the pole of possibility as closely as possible, we are farthest removed from the pole of actual-ity. Conversely, when we run toward actuality, we get away from death as a possi-bility. Now what do we perceive when we have the closest closeness to death as a possibility? How is it to have a close-up of this "boundless possibility " of death? Heidegger's answer to this question is clear and definitive. "The more unveiledly this possibility gets understood, the more purely does the understand-ing penetrate into it *as the possibility of the impossibility of any existence at all.* Death, as possibility, gives Dasein nothing to be actualized, nothing which Dasein, as actual, could itself be. It is the possibility of the impossibility of every way of comporting oneself toward everything, of every way of existing."²⁰² In other words: a close-up of death as a *possibility* reveals that this possibility cannot contain any *actuality.*

There is a lot of dramatizing going on in section 53 of *Sein und Zeit.* Heideg-ger's image of running ahead toward death is fantastically misleading, not only because possibilities and actualities are not spatial objects that one might ap-proach or avoid by running, but most of all because Heidegger suggests that he is not merely using a metaphor: he pretends to be describing a specific attitude vis-à-vis our own death. However, when we unpack the metaphors, what Heideg-ger says is sensible enough, though not at all new. He is claiming that death is absolutely final. Death does not leave us anything to be actualized. Every way of comporting ourselves will be impossible. Our death is a total annihilation of ourselves. The dramatizing has the function of suggesting that Heidegger is saying something radically new and that he is revealing the possibility of a new attitude toward death, the authentic attitude. But this is an illusion. Everyone who does not believe in an afterlife will agree that death is absolutely final. Instead of staging with so many theatrical effects the idea that there is one authentic attitude in relation to one's own death, Heidegger might have done better to list the con-vincing scientific arguments against the doctrine of afterlife. For it is an illusion to think that there is only one attitude which corresponds to the insight that death is final. This insight may inspire many different attitudes. It might give us regret because we would have liked to enjoy life more than we do, and we know that when it will have ceased, all our opportunities will be destroyed. It might also make us sad because we enjoy life very deeply and do not want it to stop. The knowledge that death is absolutely terminal may inspire revolt, longing, anxiety, or heroic equanimity. In section 51 of *Sein und Zeit,* Heidegger condemns equa-nimity as inauthentic, and he holds that anxiety is the authentic mood in which to envisage death. But there is no logical or "essential" connection between anxi-ety and the insight that death is final. As a consequence, Heidegger's claim that anxiety is the authentic mood in relation to my death and that equanimity is inauthentic is nothing but a depraved insinuation without any logical or phenomenological justification.

We now see in what sense Heidegger calls death a "possibility." Death is a *possibility* in the sense that being dead is the total absence of all *actualities*, that is, a complete absence of experiences and behavior, because our death is an integral annihilation of ourselves. We "diminish" or "weaken" this possibility if we imagine that we somehow go on living in spite of our death, in some kind of afterlife. By doing so, we illegitimately smuggle some *actuality* into the measureless possibility of death. We "cultivate" and "endure" death as a pure possibility if we realize that no actuality will be left for us when we die. To use the word "possibility" in this unprecedented and idiosyncratic sense is, as Edwards says, carrying the misuse of language to the ultimate degree.[203] For it is neither the sense of the word that Heidegger defined in section 31 of *Sein und Zeit*, nor is it what we mean by the word in any of its usual senses. Also, this use of the word is highly paradoxical and totally superfluous, for to grasp death as a *possibility* means, according to Heidegger, to see that our death is the *im*possibility of any future life, and this we may very well express without using the term "possibility" at all. Heidegger's strange use of the word "possibility" is easily overlooked, because death may also be called a possibility in the habitual sense of something that may happen. Heidegger emphatically denies that this is what he means, for this sense of "possibility" corresponds to the allegedly inauthentic attitude of expecting death.

Heidegger may have had several reasons for misusing the word "possibility." One is his insatiable urge to give the impression that he is saying something spectacular and profound, although he is merely stating that death is final so that there is no afterlife. This requires verbal fireworks such as "death is the possibility of the impossibility of all possibilities," in which the word "possibility" is used in three different senses. There is a second reason of a more logical nature. Heidegger seems to think that if something is not actual, it must be possible. Hence, if our death cannot contain any actuality, because when we are dead we can have no actual experiences, death must be "a possibility without measure." There are two logical blunders in this argument. First, something may be neither actual nor possible, because it is impossible, so that the absence of actualities in death does not imply that death is a possibility. Second, although death excludes actuality in the sense that it is a total absence of all experiences and behavior, it may be actual in another sense. When someone is dead, his or her death has actually occurred. For these two reasons, it is not true that everything which is not actual must be possible, so that there is no justification left for Heidegger's thesis that death is a "possibility" in any profound sense, and that, in order to be authentic, we have to cultivate and endure it as such a "possibility."

5. Existing as a Whole. That Heidegger misleads himself and his readers by his metaphor of running-forward-toward-death becomes even more clear in the remainder of section 53 of *Sein und Zeit*. Heidegger claims that, by running forward toward death, we are able to exist *as a whole*. This wholeness is important for Heidegger, and the problem of how we can exist as a whole is one of the main problems that he wants to solve in the second division of *Sein und Zeit*. In section 45, he explains the problem of wholeness as follows. In order to study a phenomenon ontologically, we have to make sure that we envisage the phenomenon as a whole.[204] This requirement sounds plausible enough, for if we overlook a large part of the entity we are investigating, our ontological analysis will be incomplete. Heidegger does not warn us, however, that there are so to speak different dimensions of wholeness. If someone asks me whether I am living in my house as a whole, I may answer in the affirmative, because I am using all the rooms and do not rent out part of the house. I am not implying, however, that I am living in the house from the time it was built until the moment of its destruction; I am talking about synchronic wholeness rather than diachronic wholeness. When Heidegger raises the problem of wholeness in section 45, however, what he seems to mean is diachronic wholeness. He stresses that human beings exist between birth and death. As long as Dasein exists, it is *not yet* something, and as soon as Dasein has completed its life, it does not exist anymore. Heidegger concludes that the nature of Dasein essentially resists the possibility that it grasp itself as a whole.[205] It is never the case that my entire life, from birth to death, is a *phenomenon* for me. How, then, is an adequate phenomenology of Dasein possible? Because Heidegger does not distinguish between synchronic and diachronic wholeness, he overlooks the simple fact that the problem of diachronic wholeness is not unique to a phenomenology of human existence. Indeed, it arises with respect to a phenomenology of all entities which last in time and which are, for that reason, present to us as a phenomenon only as long as their existence is not yet at its end. If it were considered to be a real problem, phenomenology would be impossible, for the difficulty is insuperable.[206]

As in the case of the phenomenological problem of death, Heidegger claims to have succeeded in the dashing exploit of having solved an insoluble problem. Whenever we run ahead toward death, this running ahead "discloses also all the possibilities that precede this last possibility, which is not to be outstripped." For this reason, running ahead toward death gives us the possibility of existing as a whole potentiality-for-being.[207] If I understand Heidegger, he is using here the image of running ahead in sense very different from the way he used it in relation to death as a possibility that becomes greater and greater as we approach it. What he is suggesting with regard to wholeness is rather that we might run ahead toward death *as the very last event of life*, and survey all the future phases of our life on the way, in the same manner as we might run ahead of our companions to the end of a road, and, having run back, tell them about what is still in front of them. Used in this way, the image of running ahead is even more misleading than it was with regard to death as a possibility. We cannot literally run ahead in time, as if we could already live in the year 2025 while the rest of mankind is lagging behind in the year 1998. Admittedly, we might run ahead of this moment in a figurative sense, when we think about our future life and our death to come. But this will not do in order to solve Heidegger's original problem, the problem of how we can grasp (*erfassen*) our life as a whole phenomenon. What Heidegger needs in order to solve it is literally running ahead in time, and there is no such thing. Again, we see that Heidegger has not discovered with his notion of running-ahead-toward-death a new and authentic attitude with regard to death. In fact, there is no coherent notion at all, and the only thing Heidegger has "discovered" is a confused and misleading metaphor. The sense in which we might grasp our life as a whole by running ahead toward death is to *imagine* how our future life will be. That we can do this is a platitude, but it will not put us in front of our future life *as a real phenomenon*. Our real future life may be very different from what we imagined. Heidegger's obscure metaphor of running ahead toward death enables him to masquerade as an audacious ontological explorer, who brings to light precious gems from the hidden caverns of human existence, whereas in fact he is either stating platitudes or uttering sheer nonsense.

6. Afterlife and the Finality of Death. As we have seen, Heidegger stresses that death is final. My death does not leave me anything to actualize, and this is why Heidegger called death a "possibility" in his strange and idiosyncratic sense. When I will be dead, nothing will be left of me, and there will be nothing that I can *be* as an actual self.[208] My death is a total extinction of myself. Clearly this implies that there is no afterlife, even though Heidegger offers no arguments for this conclusion, and does not state it explicitly. To our great astonishment, however, Heidegger also claims that his ontological analysis of death *leaves the question of afterlife entirely open*. In section 49 of *Sein und Zeit,* he explains how the existential analysis of death is demarcated from other interpretations of this phenomenon. He argues that his existential analysis of death is fundamental in relation to a biology, psychology, theodicy, or theology of death.[209] This view fits in both with the transcendental theme, according to which the existential analysis discovers a priori conditions for the possibility of all factual existents, and with the phenomenologico-hermeneutical theme, which claims that a regional ontology of Dasein is the foundation of all sciences of man. Having read section 53 of *Sein und Zeit*, in which Heidegger states that death does not leave us any possibilities of behavior, experience, and existing, we might expect that he will go on to deny the legitimacy of all doctrines of survival after death. What he writes is the very opposite. If death is defined as the end of Dasein as being-in-the-world, "this does not imply any ontical decision whether 'after death' still another mode of being is possible, either higher or lower, or whether Dasein 'lives on' or even 'outlasts' itself and is 'immortal.' "[210]

There is, it seems, a straightforward contradiction between section 49 and section 53 of *Sein und Zeit*. If Heidegger wants to leave open the question of an afterlife in his ontology of death, he has no right to claim that "death . . . gives Dasein nothing to be actualized, nothing which Dasein, as actual, could itself *be*."[211] If, on the other hand, he wants to stress that my death is a total annihilation of all my possibilities of being, he has no right to pretend that his analysis of death is compatible with a doctrine of survival after death. There are two ways in which one might try to resolve this contradiction, but neither of them works.

First, one might stress that ontology is about essential structures, whereas the possibility of an afterlife is an ontical possibility. Heidegger suggests this way out when he writes that the problem of afterlife asks for an "ontical" decision. Now it is true that essential possibilities need not be actualized in fact, so that, if Heidegger's ontology of death left open the possibility of an afterlife, it might nevertheless be the case that no afterlife exists. But the converse is not true. If it belongs to the essence of death that death does not leave us any possibilities of existing, as Heidegger says in section 53, then an afterlife is essentially or ontologically excluded, and what is ontologically excluded cannot be ontically possible. Obviously, Heidegger was not well versed in modal logic.

Second, one might stress that Heidegger's analysis of death is merely concerned with Dasein as being-*in-the-world*. When he asserts in section 53 that death is final, he might merely mean that death does not leave us any possibilities of existing *in this world*. One might add that a phenomenology of Dasein cannot do more, and that it would be unwarranted to make phenomenological claims about a possible life in another realm. This solution is shipwrecked by two difficulties. The first is that Heidegger's statements about the terminal nature of death in section 53 are entirely unqualified. What he says is not that death does not leave us any possibilities of existing *in this world*; he says that death does not leave us any possibilities of existing *tout court*. Moreover, by studying our being in this world, we can discover many conclusive grounds for rejecting the doctrine of an afterlife. Our mental life turns out to be dependent on bodily functions, so that, when our body rots away or is destroyed by fire after death, no possibility of mental life can remain. We must conclude that the contradiction between sections 49 and 53 of *Sein und Zeit* cannot be resolved.

Dreyfus and Rubin claim in the appendix to Dreyfus's commentary on *Sein und Zeit* that Heidegger successfully secularized Kierkegaard's notion of religiousness by developing his concept of authenticity.[212] It will by now be clear that this cannot be the case. Heidegger's concept of authenticity can hardly be called successful, if its central dimension of being-toward-death contains so many confusions and contradictions. We have seen that if Heidegger's statements are interpreted so that they are true, what he says is trivial and not very interesting. Furthermore, not everything that Heidegger asserts can be true, for he contradicts himself. The appearance of novelty and profoundness was produced by a spectacular apparatus of verbal fireworks and hocus pocus, which dazzles the reader and tends to paralyze the capacity for lucid thought.

It is of course misleading from the start to suggest that there is a global disjunction between two pervasive attitudes in life, the inauthentic one and the authentic one. The concept of being not oneself, as it is used in everyday language, is a specific and local notion. To say that one was not oneself or inauthentic in a determinate situation means that one was not in one's normal bodily or mental condition, for instance, because one was shy or drunk. In everyday use, the negative expression of being *not* oneself is common parlance. We never say, "I am really myself now," because *not* being oneself is the exception and being oneself is the rule.[213] The reason is that "being not oneself" just *means* that we are not in our normal condition and that we do not behave as we usually do. Heidegger perversely puts this ordinary notion on its head. He is claiming that in our everyday life, we are usually *not* ourselves, and that the only moments where we are ourselves are moments of anxiety and dread in the face of death as a total annihilation. We now have to ask why Heidegger is putting forward this depressing claim.

The explanation is that Heidegger did not secularize Kierkegaard's notion of religiousness at all. He merely pretended to secularize it, because he was cleverly using Kierkegaard's notions of dread and nothingness within the framework of a Pascalian strategy. Kierkegaard claimed that in everyday life we are not really ourselves, because we do not seek to identify with the eternal spirit that is our real self. In order to identify with it, we have to live in a completely different manner and become what we are not yet. The *not yet* presents itself to us as *nothing*, because it is different from all our worldly occupations, and this nothing haunts us and produces dread. In our everyday existence, we try to escape from dread and to suppress it. If we face up to dread, we realize that our worldly life is not our true life, and we will venture the leap to an absolute religious commitment.

In order to apply Pascal's strategy for leading people toward Christianity, Heidegger had to divide Kierkegaard's apologetic exercise into two distinct phases. First, by a purely secular analysis of the human condition he had to convince his readers that everyday life is inauthentic, and that authenticity consists in anticipating death with dread, in facing up to existential guilt, and in many other unpleasant things. The ontological analysis of Dasein had to be secular in order to convince the unbeliever, and it had to paint life in this world in dark and gloomy colors in order to arouse the craving for religion. The second phase was to satisfy this religious craving by explicitly metaphysical writings such as *Was ist Metaphysik?* This hypothesis illuminates and explains everything that Heidegger says about death and authenticity.

In the first place, it explains the contradiction concerning the afterlife. In his analysis of Heidegger on death, Paul Edwards avows being "endlessly astonished that many Christians, Catholics as well as Protestants, are followers of Heidegger and have expressed their total acceptance of his teachings on death." These Christians appear to see no inconsistency in endorsing Heidegger's view that death is a total absence and their Christian faith in eternal life after death.[214] Admittedly, Christian followers of Heidegger will not be able to explain how it is possible to maintain both that death means a total annihilation and that we will live on forever after death, if this means to show how a contradiction might be true. What may very well be shown is, however, that this contradiction is inherent in the rhetoric of Christian apologetics.

According to traditional Pauline Christianity, God sent his son Christ to us in order that, if we believe in him, we may obtain eternal bliss. The promise of eternal bliss is the most important treasure that Christianity has to offer. Perhaps modern Protestants do not believe anymore in an afterlife, but that there is such a thing is still the doctrine of the Catholic Church, as the present pope, John Paul II, has stressed repeatedly. In order to convince the unbeliever that he must risk the jump to faith, the defender of Christianity has to impress him with the doctrine of eternal bliss. Unfortunately, there are no convincing arguments in favor of this doctrine. On the contrary, everything seems to speak against it. This is why an apologetics of Christianity will not be triumphant unless it succeeds in drowning reasonable thought by arousing very forceful feelings. In order to make the doctrine of eternal salvation attractive, death has to be imagined as something absolutely horrible, something to which we can only relate authentically by feeling dread. To this end, Heidegger argues that death is total destruction, and he condemns a calm acceptance of death as inauthentic. Paradoxically, the defender of Christianity has to stress that death is final and that, therefore, it has to be envisaged with anxiety, in order to prepare the grounds for the belief that it is not final after all because there is an afterlife for those who risk the jump to faith. This paradox explains the contradiction with regard to afterlife in *Sein und Zeit,* and it accounts for the fact that Heidegger presents his ontological analysis of death as a necessary preparation for raising the issue of an afterlife: "only when death is conceived in its full ontological essence can we have any methodological assurance in even asking what may be after death; only then can we do so with meaning and justification."[215]

The hypothesis of a Pascalian strategy also accounts for the remaining five points that I discussed above. If death is the entrance to eternal bliss, it can be called with justification (1) my *most distinctive* possibility. Because by dying I will become identical with my true self, death is also the possibility that is *most my own.* Death will truly individualize me, for my true individuality is my metaphysical self, not my everyday life with the others in the world. No one (2) can represent me in the case of death, because no one else will become my true self when dying. Supposedly, God has reserved a most individual eternal life of bliss for each of us. Afterlife is individual; we will not merge into a spiritual soup after death, as Buddhists believe. Because life on earth is a sorry business, and its only point is to prepare eternal bliss by properly relating to death, Heidegger can say (3) that Dasein is dying as long as it exists in the world. Life in the world is like death or permanent dying if compared to the bliss of afterlife. Furthermore, (4) we have to be prepared at each moment of our life to give up everything by imagining death as a total annihilation, because, as Paul says in his first letter to the *Thessalonians*, "the day of the Lord will come like a thief in the night." Finally, by running toward death as the entrance to eternity, (5) our life in the world will appear as a limited whole, which is of no great value compared to eternal happiness. If we grasp life as such a limited whole, we will be prepared to release it and to risk the leap into nothingness.

We come to the following conclusion. The hypothesis that Heidegger applied a Pascalian Grand Strategy in *Sein und Zeit* not only allows us to give a unified interpretation of his entire "way of thought" (§§ 12C and 13C, above). It also illuminates what Heidegger says on inauthenticity, death, and authenticity in *Sein und Zeit* itself, and a similar analysis may be given of Heidegger's discussions of other topics in that book, such as existential guilt and the call of conscience. I am not claiming that Heidegger openly expresses Christian doctrines in his philosophical *chef d'oeuvre*. This is precisely what he should avoid if he is pursuing the Pascalian strategy. What I am claiming is, first, that the doctrines which he is expressing are utterly incoherent and confused if they are naïvely interpreted in the way in which Heidegger presents them, namely, as purely secular analyses of the phenomenon of human existence. Second, I hold that these doctrines become more coherent as soon as one supplies the Christian views at which they are hinting implicitly. We might say that Heidegger was a Neo-Pascalian theologian rather than a philosopher. Arguably he was the most creative religious writer of the twentieth century, who outwitted both official theologians and many philosophers by going underground and by concealing his religious message in secular philosophical garments.

CONCLUSION

MARTIN HEIDEGGER held that one single question is central to his thought, which, indeed, is the fundamental question of philosophy: the question of being. He suggests that the history of philosophy from the pre-Socratics to Hegel and Nietzsche was informed by this question, but unfortunately no one before Heidegger himself succeeded in adequately expressing it. Philosophers had formulated questions about beings, but they had never managed to raise the question of being. Yet, what Heidegger himself says about the question is notoriously difficult to understand. Heidegger stressed repeatedly that no one really grasps the question of being. And this seems to be true, for one does not find in the vast secondary literature on Heidegger a book that clearly and satisfactorily solves the following two problems: What does Heidegger's question of being mean, and what should we think of it? In order to fill this gap, I have attempted to write such a book.

From a methodological point of view, interpretation must precede evaluation and criticism. In order to make sure that criticisms hit the target instead of a phantom produced by the critic's imagination, the interpretation must be based on a meticulous analysis of the German texts and it has to meet the usual standards of philological and historical scholarship. It is not true, as is sometimes suggested by philosophers of the hermeneutical and deconstructivist schools, that "anything goes" in interpretation, or that the attempt to establish with a maximum of objectivity what texts meant in the historical circumstances in which they were produced is a priori futile. Too many interpreters of Heidegger's texts, especially in the United States, prematurely associate his thought with that of other philosophers, such as Wittgenstein or Dewey, in an attempt to make Heidegger *salonfähig* in contemporary academic circles. What interests me is the historical Heidegger as he really was, not recent intellectual projections.

This does not imply that one might derive a substantial interpretation of Heidegger's question of being from the texts alone, by induction, so to speak. One may go on indefinitely summarizing and collating Heideggerian texts without ever reaching clarity about the question of being, since one will encounter the same obscurities again and again. This is the reason why I have adopted a hypothetico-deductive method of interpretation. Heidegger himself claims that in interpreting philosophical texts, we have to add an extra, and that we have to do so covertly. I have preferred to add an extra openly, and to formulate an interpretative hypothesis that, I claim, accounts for all texts on the question of being and for Heidegger's oeuvre as a whole. In order to invent such a hypothesis, one has to have a firm grasp of the many problems of interpretation concerning Heidegger's question of being. In the first, introductory chapter, I formulated a number of these problems, such as the problem of how Heidegger can claim to raise a question that nobody understands (§ 1), the issues created by Heidegger's rejection of logic (§ 2), problems concerning the notion of authenticity (§ 3), the problem of why Heidegger thinks that there is a phenomenon of being to which the verb "to be" refers, problems concerning the ontological difference and the transcendence of being, and the crucial difficulties concerning the ontological priority of the question of being and the primacy of Dasein in raising this question (§ 4). Other problems are concerned with Heidegger's notions of interpretation and elucidation (§ 5).

In scientific methodology it is required that a hypothesis which was invented in order to solve a specific set of problems has the capacity to provide solutions to problems of a different set. If the hypothesis lacks such a capacity, it is written off as *ad hoc*. Because theories in science incorporate laws which, logically speaking, are completely general, the set of new problems by which a theory is to be tested may be very large or even infinite. Although in my view the methodology of historical interpretation is globally the same as that of the sciences—it should be hypothetico-deductive—there is an interesting difference on this point: the corpus of texts to be interpreted in a given case may be large, as large as Heidegger's *Gesamtausgabe*, but it is never infinitely so. It follows that it is possible in principle to design an interpretative hypothesis with *all* relevant problems of interpretation in mind. In such a case, the distinction between *ad hoc* hypotheses and legitimate hypotheses collapses. This does not imply that the hypothesis, if adequate, is illegitimate, but that it can be ultimately justified only by comparing it to rival hypotheses.

In this book I have tried to avoid *ad hoc*-ness by developing my hypothesis with a specific set of problems on my desk and by testing it against a different set of problems. My hypothesis concerning the question of being explains, for instance, what Heidegger says about topics as widely diverse as poetry, language, thought (*Denken*), truth, freedom, logic, technology, the turn (*die Kehre*), and interpretation. It also accounts for Heidegger's interpretations of historical philosophers, such as Anaximander, Parmenides, Aristotle, Plato, Descartes, Schelling, Hegel, and Nietzsche, and for his elucidations of poems by Rilke, Trakl, Hölderlin, and others.

Furthermore, my hypothesis enables us to solve two crucial problems that have obsessed Heidegger scholars for the past fifty years. What is the relation between *Sein und Zeit* and the later works? And how could Heidegger legitimately claim in writings such as the "Brief über den 'Humanismus' " (1946) and the introduction to *Was ist Metaphysik?* (1949) that he is revealing the *true meanings* of existentialia such as existence, clearing (*Lichtung*), project (*Entwurf*), there (*Da*), truth, and world, whereas in fact what he is saying is the very opposite of his definitions in *Sein und Zeit*? This problem was raised by Müller in 1949 and by Löwith in 1953, and in his dissertation of 1964 Von Herrmann solidly established the fact that after the war Heidegger reinterpreted the existentialia of *Sein und Zeit*. But these writers did not come up with a clear and satisfactory answer to the question of why Heidegger claimed after the war that he was revealing the *true* meanings of the existentialia whereas in fact he was reinterpreting them. My hypothesis saves Heidegger on this point from the unjustified accusation that he was trying to manipulate his readers or to juggle with his own texts. Yet I do not think that it is possible to save Heidegger from accusations of this type in all cases. After the war, he clearly corrupted earlier passages concerning Nazism.

There are two other ways of avoiding *ad hoc*-ness in interpretation. One is the strategy of convergence, which consists in analyzing different aspects of texts, such as grammar, literary form, and content, and in investigating whether the results of these aspect-analyses corroborate the central hypothesis. It is a striking fact about Heidegger's oeuvre that whereas *Sein und Zeit* is a systematic treatise in the grand manner of German philosophy, with pretensions so high as Germany had not seen since Hegel's *Phänomenologie des Geistes*, the later publications are mostly modest and short: essays, talks, letters, little dialogues, and lectures. My hypothesis on the question of being, and more in particular the hypothesis of a Pascalian strategy in conjunction with Heidegger's Lutheran notion of faith, account for this drastic shift in the literary genre of Heidegger's publications. Another aspect of Heidegger's philosophy is his shrewd use of rhetoric, and I argued in section 16C that the specific rhetorical strategies that Heidegger uses in his later works fit in with my interpretative hypothesis.

The second way of avoiding *ad hoc*-ness is comparing one's interpretative hypothesis with those of others. In historical interpretation, as in science, comparing different hypotheses with an eye on the data to be accounted for is one of the best methods of testing and it should always be applied. Nevertheless, I have tried to avoid the mistake committed by Hans Vaihinger in his monumental book on Kant's first *Critique*, the mistake of commenting not only on a philosophical text but also on all commentaries on that text. Vaihinger's fate was instructive: in his two massive volumes he does not manage to go beyond Kant's transcendental aesthetics. Accordingly, I relegated most discussions of secondary literature to the notes and I have invited other authors on Heidegger to the front stage only if this seemed to be useful from a didactic point of view. In doing so, I have preferred substantial interpretations such as Dreyfus's Wittgensteinean interpretation of *Sein und Zeit* to authors who mainly offer learned summaries of Heidegger's oeuvre, such as Pöggeler, Von Herrmann, Grondin, Richardson, Werner Marx, Kockelmans, and Kisiel. This is not to say that books by these latter authors are useless. On the contrary, they are indispensable for getting an overview of Heidegger's works and they often draw one's attention to details that one would have overlooked oneself. Yet, if the name of the game is substantial historical interpretation, such books are less instructive than full-blooded interpretative hypotheses such as the one Dreyfus argues for in his commentary on *Sein und Zeit*.

In comparing interpretative hypotheses and in evaluating them, one has to apply criteria similar to those that are used in the sciences. One should wonder, for instance, which hypothesis accounts best for most texts and for the greatest number of interpretative problems, and which hypothesis is more likely, given the historical circumstances and the personal history of the author. This does not mean that each criterion for theory evaluation in the sciences has its analogue in the field of historical interpretation. The criteria of prediction and mathematical precision do not apply here, and, whereas in science there are good reasons for adopting criteria of simplicity, it seems to me that simplicity is perhaps not a valid criterion for evaluating interpretations at all. Could it not be the case that the author of a corpus of texts aspires to maximum complexity in his thoughts, so that a simple interpretation would be utterly inadequate? Although, broadly speaking, the methodology of historical interpretation is similar to scientific methodology, one should never forget that explaining and predicting empirical phenomena on the one hand, and attributing meaning to texts on the other hand, remain two different activities, so that specific methodological devices and rules will be different in each case.

The standard objection to my method of interpretation is that interpretation essentially involves a hermeneutical circle and that, for this reason, the method of interpretation is fundamentally different from scientific method. I argued in section 5 that this objection is based on an outdated inductivist conception of scientific research. Science does not proceed from a presuppositionless investigation of neutral data to laws and theories. On the contrary, without some hypothesis we will not know which data to collect, and often the data are interpreted within the framework of received theories and against an implicit background of scientific practices. As a consequence, we find in science something like the hermeneutical circle or the projective structure of interpretation, as Heidegger also calls it. I criticized Heidegger for not having clearly distinguished two different "circles" in interpretation, the presuppositional circle and the holistic circle. The first circle is inevitable because we cannot start reading and interpreting texts from a neutral vantage point. We are always already shaped by the culture in which we are living, and we inevitably start by projecting the preconceptions of this culture into the texts we are reading. The holistic circle is different. This second circle is inevitable because the details in a text are illuminated by an understanding of the whole, whereas understanding the whole in its turn is impossible without grasping the details. Both circles are in reality spiral movements. In the holistic spiral, we start by reading parts of the text until we get an overview. Then we reread unclear passages in order to interpret them as functions of the whole, and we reinterpret the whole in view of our enriched understanding of the details, and so on and on. Another holistic spiral is concerned with different aspects of a text, such as the linguistic aspect, the historical circumstances in which it was produced, the literary genre to which it belongs, the personal history of its author, the rhetoric or logical structure, and its content. Again, the interpretation of each of these aspects may depend on an understanding of other aspects, so that here too a spiral movement is inevitable. In the presuppositional spiral, finally, we start reading texts with the assumptions embedded in our present culture. But whenever we notice that the texts do not make sense in this light, we become conscious of these assumptions as such and of the cultural and historical distance between us and the texts we are studying. The result should not be, as Gadamer sometimes seems to claim, that our cultural horizon and the cultural horizon of the text melt into each other (*Horizontverschmelzung*), so that cultural distance is annihilated, but rather that this cultural distance is appreciated as such.

Both the presuppositional spiral and the holistic spiral have their analogues in scientific method, so that the existence of these spirals in hermeneutics does not prove that the method of interpreting texts must be fundamentally different from the scientific method. The pernicious effect of being obsessed by the hermeneutical circle is that one concentrates too much on the context of discovery and neglects the context of justification. In section 5, we saw that Heidegger does not develop a method of testing interpretations. Indeed, his conviction that the projective structure of interpretation is the same as the projective structure of human life precludes developing such a method. Because it does not make sense to "test" a human life-project in terms of truth, plausibility, or adequacy, Heidegger tends to think that objectively testing historical interpretations of texts is somehow impossible too. Under the influence of Heidegger, Gadamer, and Derrida, the craft of interpretation has often degenerated into a completely arbitrary and pointless activity of "dissemination."

Reflection on the methods of interpretation is imperative for someone who is interpreting Heidegger's texts. Yet it was the aim of my book to develop a substantial interpretation of Heidegger's question of being and not to write a treatise on hermeneutics. I argued in section 6 that such a substantial interpretation has to be pluralistic, because Heidegger's question of being has several distinct meanings instead of one. Using a terminology borrowed from musical theory, I claimed that there are five distinct *leitmotifs* in the question of being. This thesis dictates the structure of my interpretation. In the second, analytical chapter, I distinguished the five different leitmotifs and developed them in detail. The third chapter was concerned with synthesis; it purported to show how the five leitmotifs hang together and that, in spite of the plurality of leitmotifs, there is also a unity in Heidegger's question of being.

As Heidegger claimed in later life that he was inspired by Brentano's dissertation on Aristotle when he developed the question of being, I studied Heidegger's relation to Aristotle in section 7. I argued that Heidegger's question of being is different from Aristotle's, so that there is not an Aristotelian but rather a meta-Aristotelian leitmotif in Heidegger's question of being. Yet there are also similarities. Heidegger claims, as Aristotle did, that the question of being is the most fundamental question of human thought, and Heidegger's question has two poles, a pole of unity and a pole of differentiation, as was the case with Aristotle's question. The meta-Aristotelian leitmotif provides the formal framework for both major phases in Heidegger's philosophical development. In both phases, there are two material leitmotifs, which figure each as a pole of differentiation or as a pole of unity.

In *Sein und Zeit*, the phenomenologico-hermeneutical leitmotif is the pole of differentiation and the transcendental leitmotif is the pole of unity. The point of sections 8 and 9, in which I discussed these two leitmotifs, is not primarily to trace historical influences on Heidegger, influences of Husserl, Dilthey, Kierkegaard, Kant, Lask, and Rickert, for instance. Not only is the fact that Heidegger was influenced by these and many other philosophers a historical platitude, but it also does not help us very much in interpreting Heidegger's works. Heidegger modified Husserl's conception of phenomenology and he tried to meld together phenomenology and hermeneutics. The questions that I am asking are rather: Why did Heidegger modify Husserl's conception? For what reasons does Heidegger claim that Husserl's sixth *Logical Investigation* formed a breakthrough in the question of being? Why did Heidegger reject Husserl's notion of formal ontology as a possible answer to the question of being? And did Heidegger succeed in amalgamating phenomenology and hermeneutics?

Heidegger derived from the philosophical tradition of Aristotle and Husserl the idea that reality is carved up into separate ontological regions, and that phenomenology has the task of developing a priori ontologies of these regions. In these regional ontologies, the specific constitution of being of the relevant entities is revealed. The question of being in the phenomenological sense aims at developing a specific set of categories for each region. If this is the case, there is no reason to think that Dasein is the primary topic to investigate if one wants to raise the question of being. One possible explanation of the primacy of Dasein in *Sein und Zeit* is the transcendental leitmotif, which I discussed in section 9. Again, the point of my discussion was not to stress that Heidegger was influenced by Kant and by Neo-Kantians such as Rickert and Natorp, but rather to give a precise interpretation of Heidegger's specific variety of transcendentalism. Three major questions informed my elucidations of Heidegger's transcendental philosophy in *Sein und Zeit*. First, why did Heidegger go transcendental if, in his interpretation of Kant, he plays down Kant's own arguments for the necessity of a transcendental philosophy? Second, how can one be a transcendental philosopher without being a transcendental idealist? I argued that Heidegger's variety of transcendental philosophy is very different from Kant's and Husserl's. It is a variety of weak transcendentalism as opposed to strong transcendentalism, because Heidegger does not have a constitution theory concerning the entities of the empirical world. Although *being* is transcendentally projected by Dasein, *entities* do not depend on Dasein at all. Yet the ultimate point of Heidegger's transcendental philosophy is the same as in the cases of Kant and Husserl: it is a bulwark against philosophical naturalism. Finally, I argued that not all texts on the transcendence of being in *Sein und Zeit* can be interpreted in the transcendental sense, so that the transcendental theme seems to transcend itself. My third question as to the meaning of this nontranscendental transcendence in *Sein und Zeit* is answered in section 11.

From 1933 on, Heidegger's transcendental leitmotif mutated into Neo-Hegelianism. Instead of assuming, as he did in *Sein und Zeit*, that Dasein is a transcendental agent that remains essentially the same throughout history, Heidegger now claims that deep history consists of a sequence of fundamental frameworks, which determine how things and Dasein are experienced in the different epochs of history. I interpreted this Neo-Hegelian leitmotif, which is discussed in section 10, as a reversal of Hegel's notion of *Heilsgeschichte* (history of salvation). Whereas Hegel thought that deep history is a dialectical progression toward the culminating point of an absolute *parousia*, Heidegger sees deep history as a Fall, a continual regression into darkness that reaches its bottomless pit in the present age of technology. Heidegger's view of history is of the catastrophic type. Although he holds out the hope of an ultimate salvation, he claims that salvation will be possible only "when danger is greatest." Heidegger's despondent philosophy of history and of technology fits in well with the atmosphere of German conservative thought after the World Wars, in which very often technology was blamed for Germany's defeat.

According to the Neo-Hegelian theme, the philosopher is in possession of rare powers of vision. He is able to see what really *is* in a historical epoch, whereas ordinary mortals are confined to Plato's cave. In this manner, Heidegger saw in 1933 that "the *Führer* himself and alone *is* the present and future German reality and its law." Heidegger's capacities for metaphysical clairvoyance survived the destruction of Europe by the Second World War and they also survived Germany's defeat. From the 1940s on, Heidegger developed his diagnosis of the present historical epoch as the reign of technology, and his thought became a major source of inspiration for deep ecology.

The Neo-Hegelian theme in Heidegger's later question of being depends logically on a fifth strand in this question, which I called the postmonotheist leitmotif. It has often been noticed that Heidegger's later thought bears striking resemblance to Christian religion. Yet it is obvious that Heidegger was not, and did not want to be, a monotheist theologian or metaphysician. Traditional metaphysics and ontotheology had to be overcome (*Überwindung*), he claimed, and the tradition of metaphysics was interpreted as the history of the "oblivion of being." Philosophy in the traditional sense had arrived at its end by exhausting its possibilities, Heidegger contended. After the end of metaphysical theology and philosophy, our task is "thinking" in a new Heideggerian sense. What are we to make, then, of the striking parallelisms between Christianity and Heidegger's later thought? And why does Heidegger say that we have to interpret and cope with (*Verwindung*) the tradition of metaphysics from the pre-Socratics to Nietzsche, if this tradition has to be surmounted?

My answer to these questions is that Heidegger applied to Christianity itself the idea of tradition that Luther used in order to dismantle or "destroy" Scholasticism.

According to Heidegger, the Christian metaphysical tradition is a fallen-off tradition that conceals an original source of significance and transcendence instead of keeping it open. Nietzsche diagnosed the modern condition by establishing the fact that "God is dead." Heidegger retorts that God died because the Christian God was a lifeless idol to begin with, the product of "deadly thinking," because it conceived of *Being* as an entity: God. Thus, by not paying heed to the "ontological difference" between Being and beings, the metaphysical tradition of ontotheology became the tradition of the oblivion of Being. Heidegger deems it to be an important task to interpret the tradition of metaphysics *as* the tradition of the oblivion of Being, and many continental scholars have followed Heidegger in this respect. But they rarely realize, I argued in section 11, what the real point is of this Heideggerian undertaking. Interpreting the history of metaphysics *as* the history of oblivion of Being is not primarily a contribution to historical scholarship in philosophy. Rather, it is an act of repentance, which is needed to prepare a new "event" or advent of Being. Heidegger's entire later philosophy is an attempt to rescue religion in an age of atheism.

The religion that Heidegger wants to rescue, or rather to inaugurate, is not that of Christianity. The application of a Lutheran model of tradition to Christianity as a whole implies that the Bible and Christ cannot be the original source of revelation and meaningfulness that a destruction of the tradition purports to uncover. Rather, Heidegger seeks this original and hidden source of significance in the writings of the pre-Socratics. His religion is not monotheistic but postmonotheist, in the sense that it comes *after* monotheist metaphysics and yet structurally resembles monotheism, because Being is said to be One and Unique. My discussion of Heidegger's postmonotheist leitmotif in section 11 aimed at corroborating this interpretative hypothesis by a large sample of textual evidence. The parallelisms with Christianity were developed in detail, and I argued that the postmonotheist theme explains what Heidegger says about topics as widely different as language, technology, poetry, truth, interpretation, and thought.

One may wonder what motive propelled Heidegger into developing the specific variety of postmonotheism that we find in his later works. For instance, why did he eliminate meticulously traces of Jewish influence in his interpretation of Western metaphysics? And why did he reconstruct the development of Western philosophy as a rectilinear movement from Greek antiquity to Nietzsche? In section 14, I proposed the speculative hypothesis that in his later writings from *Beiträge zur Philosophie* on, Heidegger tried to realize an old *desideratum* of German religious nationalists such as Paul de Lagarde, Hitler, and Himmler: that of developing an authentic German religion. This hypothesis explains the disregard of Jewish influences in the history of metaphysics, and it accounts for the fact that the Christian God of Love is replaced by belligerent Being. Rather than giving love and eternal life to human beings, Heidegger's postmonotheist Being sends them strife or struggle (*Streit*) and demands sacrifices (*Opfer*). If this hypothesis is correct, Heidegger was more or less in line with the National Socialists when he developed his postmonotheist theme from 1936 on, and he did not reject Nazism as such, contrary to what Silvio Vietta and other authors have argued. In accordance with a great many Nazi intellectuals, Heidegger claimed that Nazi Germany had to retrieve the greatness of the Greeks and cleanse German spirituality from Jewish and Christian influences. Paraphrasing Carl von Clausewitz, I contended that Heidegger's postmonotheist leitmotif was a continuation of Nazism by other, philosophical means.

My analytical second chapter shows that in Heidegger's question of being, the word "being" means at least four different things. According to the phenomenologico-hermeneutic leitmotif, *being* is the regional ontological constitution of specific entities, such as animals, humans, or tools, which has to be conceptualized a priori by regional ontologies. Within the framework of the transcendental leitmotif, *being* is a holistic transcendental structure, projected by Dasein, without which particular entities cannot show up for us. The Neo-Hegelian leitmotif implies that *being* is the history-shaping manner in which entities disclose themselves in a historical epoch, and each epoch has its own sense of being. Finally, according to the postmonotheist leitmotif, *Being* is a transcendent agent or event, which sends (*schickt*) us historical epochs as our destiny (*Geschick*), and conceals or withdraws (*epochē*) itself in the process. The metaphysical tradition is the history of this continuing withdrawal, and Heideggerian thinking aims at preparing a new advent (*Ankunft*) of Being in the epoch in which danger is greatest because Being is entirely concealed: the present epoch of technology.

The third chapter, on synthesis, had to show how the five different leitmotifs in Heidegger's question of being hang together. There are many different forms of synthesis and I discussed the most important ones, mainly in section 12. First, we saw that the meta-Aristotelian theme provides a formal framework for each of the two main periods in Heidegger's thought, the phase of *Sein und Zeit* and the phase after the war. In each of these two phases, there is a pole of differentiation and a pole of unity. In *Sein und Zeit*, the phenomenologico-hermeneutic theme is the pole of differentiation, because there are many ontological regions, whereas the transcendental leitmotif provides unification. The pole of differentiation in the later works is the Neo-Hegelian leitmotif and the postmonotheist theme is the pole of unity because Being is the One and Unique source of historical diversity. Second, the five leitmotifs are unified by a common formal idiom, which I discussed in section 6. This idiom consists of nine different elements, such as the "oblivion of being" or the "ontological difference," which are present in each of the leitmotifs, although they adopt a different meaning in each case. Third, Heidegger reinterprets the existentialia of *Sein und Zeit* in his postwar writings, so that there is a diachronic unification by means of semantic transformations of key notions.

These semantic transformations are then explained by a fourth type of unity, the motivational link of the Pascalian Grand Strategy, which connects *Sein und Zeit* to the later works. In his apologetics of Christianity, Pascal first gave a religiously neutral analysis of the human condition, which showed that without Christ human beings are wretched and incomprehensible. In a second stage the Christian religion is presented as the only solution to the problems of man's existential predicament. I argued in sections 12 and 13 that the secular ontology of Dasein in *Sein und Zeit* (1927) was meant to be the first stage of such a Pascalian strategy, which aims at preparing man for the leap to religion, a leap that Heidegger sketched for the first time in *Was ist Metaphysik?* (1929). Because Heidegger interprets faith in a Lutheran fashion as the product of grace and revelation, and because grace did not come as Heidegger expected, the second stage of Heidegger's Pascalian strategy went through three different phases: a metaphysical phase in the years 1929–31, a Nietzschean and atheist phase in the years 1932–35, and a final postmonotheist phase from 1935 on. Heidegger's reinterpretation of the existentialia belongs to the third phase, and it is explained by an analogical application of his views on theology of 1927, as expressed in "Phänomenologie und Theologie." This third phase provides yet another type of unification, the fifth type, which consists in unification by means of wordplays. I discussed the structure and the point of Heidegger's wordplays in section 12D, showing how they are related to Heidegger's views on translation and to his postmonotheism.

Apart from these five types of unification of leitmotifs, chapter 3 contains a discussion of three issues that are central for understanding the unity of Heidegger's thought: the problem of the so-called turn (*die Kehre*), Heidegger's Nazism, and Heidegger's relation to Nietzsche. In section 13, I argued that my interpretative hypothesis accounts for Heidegger's texts on the turn and that it explains both the turn from "being and time" to "time and being" and the turn from "the being of truth" to "the Truth of Being." Section 14 on Heidegger and Hitler starts with a summary of some historical facts and then raises the issue whether there are possible links between *Sein und Zeit* and Heidegger's Nazism. I tentatively construed such a link in a critical discussion with Farias and Rockmore. My argument here is speculative and the logical force of the link between *Sein und Zeit* and Nazism is not very strong. Stronger links exist between Nazism and the two leitmotifs of Heidegger's later philosophy, as I argued in the last two subsections of section 14. In section 15 on Heidegger and Nietzsche I attempted to show that Heidegger's celebrated interpretation of Nietzsche is in fact a reversal of Nietzsche's intentions, produced by a clever play with two different notions of metaphysics, and that this interpretation is based on the two leitmotifs of Heidegger's later works. I argued that after 1934 Nietzsche gradually became Heidegger's greatest philosophical enemy, who had to be destroyed by an "interpretation." In order to redress the balance, the section ends with an attempt to formulate a Nietzschean interpretation of Heidegger, based on Nietzsche's psychological account of religious revolutionaries such as Paul and Luther.

Whereas the first three chapters of the book purport to determine what Heidegger's question of being means, the fourth and final chapter aims at evaluating it. What should we think of the five leitmotifs that constitute the question of being?

In section 16, I argued on semantic, epistemological, and moral grounds that we should wholly reject the Neo-Hegelian and the postmonotheist leitmotifs. Indeed, no sensible person would have accepted these leitmotifs if Heidegger had stated them more clearly. However, speaking in riddles was Heidegger's deliberate strategy, as is shown by a passage in *Beiträge zur Philosophie*, where Heidegger says that "to make oneself understood is suicidal to philosophy." My analysis of the strategical dilemma for a postmonotheist philosopher in section 11C.6 shows why this is correct in Heidegger's own case. I hope that as soon as it has become clear what Heidegger was up to, the project of his later philosophy will lose its appeal altogether.

Many readers who loathe Heidegger's later writings have a great admiration for *Sein und Zeit*. But is the philosophy of *Sein und Zeit* more viable than the later works? In section 17, I attempted to refute the idea that there is a phenomenon of being in all entities, and I rejected the transcendental leitmotif as well. Moreover, the notion that there are regions of being which each have their own essence is mistaken, so that Heidegger's distinction between the ontical and the ontological collapses. Heidegger's description of a phenomenologico-hermeneutic method is shown to consist of evasive statements, and in reality the methodological claims of phenomenology and of hermeneutics cannot be reconciled. It follows that *Sein und Zeit* is a disaster area as far as method is concerned. But, one might object, does Heidegger's masterpiece not contain deep philosophical insights, which may be saved by a rational reconstruction of the book?

I considered three possible reconstructions of *Sein und Zeit*, one as an essay in the hermeneutics of contemporary self-understanding, one as an attempt at cultural criticism, and one as an exercise in linguistic analysis. The third type of rational reconstruction is the most "philosophical" one, but I argued in section 18 on *death and the multitude* that Heidegger is the worst possible teacher in linguistic analysis. Although he announces his views on death with the fanfare that is usually reserved for great scientific discoveries, what he says is a confusing mixture of empirical falsehoods, linguistic rules masquerading as metaphysical insights, trivial truths, and misleading images. The same point could be argued with regard to other chapters of *Sein und Zeit*. What Heidegger says on death is not a sound philosophical analysis. Rather, it is a spectacular piece of rhetoric, which fits in well with my Pascalian interpretation of the book.

I have deemed it superfluous to pursue this onslaught on Heidegger's philosophy any further, for instance, by a critical analysis of the meta-Aristotelian theme. Aristotle thought that the question of being is the most fundamental question of philosophy and science. I argued in section 7 that this view depends on a philosophy of science that is now generally rejected. It may be that Heidegger tacitly endorsed this philosophy of science and I adduced some reasons for supposing that he did. But there is not much credit to be gained by criticizing Heidegger's philosophy of science because, as I claim in section 4.5, this part of Heidegger's thought is sketchy and incoherent anyway.

We may conclude that Heidegger's question of being should be rejected completely as it stands. Nevertheless, there are two successor questions to the question of being, which are each of considerable philosophical interest. One is concerned with the conceptual structures in which everyday Dasein expresses itself in everyday life and without which Dasein would not be "human." How should we describe and classify these structures? By way of an example, I argued in section 17B.2 that a belief is neither a state of mind nor a disposition or an attitude, contrary to what is commonly assumed. Under what category, if any, has belief to be subsumed? Research in this area is both difficult and badly needed. Rather than Heidegger, we should adopt Wittgenstein, Ryle, Austin, and Strawson as our teachers here. The other successor question is concerned with the verb "to be." As it is a mistake to think that there is a phenomenon of being, this question should be tackled by linguistic analysis as well, and not by phenomenology.

The English verb "to be" has many uses, which are interrelated in interesting ways. What are these uses and what are their interconnections? Logicians and linguists have done much work in this area, but many obscurities remain. For instance, is the verb "to be" simply ambiguous, or are its various uses related by means of a family resemblance? A third possibility would be that the different uses are connected by an interrelation based on paradigm cases. Each of these views runs into difficulties with regard to the verb "to be," so that it remains an open question as to what the specific nature of the interrelations between its various uses is. In the philosophical tradition, important issues such as the question concerning the ultimate constituents of reality or the question regarding the proper objects of knowledge were formulated in terms of the verb "to be." This was not an illegitimate move, even though it implied the risk of conceptual confusion in view of the many different uses of "to be." For this reason, analytical work on the verb "to be" and its Indo-European cognates may have great philosophical relevance, and philosophers should read the publications by Charles Kahn and others on this topic. There is no reason to think, however, that this second successor question is narrowly related to the first. Hence no special unifying bond exists between the two successor questions of Heidegger's question of being.

The following abbreviations are used for Heidegger's works. They are listed in alphabetical · order. In the case of published lectures or works published during Heidegger's lifetime, the year in which the lectures were given or the year of the first edition of a published work if a later edition is listed is cited parenthetically immediately after the title. Mostly, references to volumes of the collected works (GA) are specified in the notes by the number of the volume and not by an abbreviation of its title; hence there is no need to list these volumes here.

AED *Aus der Erfahrung des Denkens.* Pfullingen: Neske, 1954.

Antwort *Antwort. Martin Heidegger im Gespräch.* Edited by Günther Neske and Emil Kettering. Pfullingen: Neske, 1988.

B *Besinnung.* GA, vol. 66 (1997).

Beiträge *Beiträge zur Philosophie (Vom Ereignis).* GA, vol. 65 (1989).

BT *Being and Time.* Translated by John Macquarrie and Edward Robinson. Oxford: Blackwell, 1962.

BW *Basic Writings.* Edited by David Farrell Krell. Revised and expanded edition. London: Routledge, 1993.

D *Denkerfahrungen 1910–1976.* Frankfurt a/M.: Klostermann, 1983.

EHD *Erläuterungen zu Hölderlins Dichtung* (1951). 4th ed. Frankfurt a/M.: Klostermann, 1971.

EM *Einführung in die Metaphysik* (1935). 3rd ed. Tübingen: Niemeyer, 1966.

EuPh Europa und die deutsche Philosophie. Lecture held in the Bibliotheca Hertziana, Rome, 8 April 1936. In *Europa und die Philosophie.* Schriftenreihe Martin Heidegger Gesellschaft, vol. 2. Edited by Hans-Helmuth Gander. Frankfurt a/M.: Klostermann, 1992.

FD *Die Frage nach dem Ding* (1935–36). 2nd ed. Tübingen: Niemeyer, 1975.

FS *Frühe Schriften.* GA, vol. 1 (1978).

G *Gelassenheit* (1959). 10th ed. Pfullingen: Neske, 1992.

GA *Gesamtausgabe.* Edition of Heidegger's collected works. Frankfurt a/M.: Klostermann, 1975– .

GAAH *Martin Heidegger Gesamtausgabe. Ausgabe letzter Hand.* Prospectus of GA. Frankfurt a/M.: Klostermann, November 1991. Cf. also the prospectus of September 1994.

GAP *Die Grundbegriffe der Antiken Philosophie* (1926). GA, vol. 22 (1993).

GbM *Die Grundbegriffe der Metaphysik. Welt—Endlichkeit—Einsamkeit* (1929–30). GA, vol. 29/30. 2nd ed. (1992).

GP *Grundprobleme der Phänomenologie* (1919–20). GA, vol. 58 (1993).

GPh *Die Grundprobleme der Phänomenologie* (1927). GA, vol. 24. 2nd ed. (1989).

Hei/Blo Martin Heidegger and Elisabeth Blochmann, *Briefwechsel 1918–1969.* Edited by Joachim W. Storck. Marbach am Neckar: Deutsche Schillergesellschaft, 1989.

Hei/Ja   Martin Heidegger and Karl Jaspers. *Briefwechsel 1920–1963.* Edited by Walter Biemel and Hans Saner. München and Frankfurt a/M.: Piper & Klostermann, 1992.

HW   *Holzwege* (1950). 4th ed. Frankfurt a/M.: Klostermann, 1963.

ID   *Identität und Differenz.* Pfullingen: Neske, 1957.

KM   *Kant und das Problem der Metaphysik* (1929). 4th ed. Frankfurt a/M.: Klostermann, 1973.

Logik   *Logik. Die Frage nach der Wahrheit* (1925–26). GA, vol. 21 (1976).

N I; N II   *Nietzsche* (1936–46). 2 vols. 2nd ed. Pfullingen: Neske, 1961.

NWK   *Nietzsche: Der Wille zur Macht als Kunst* (1936–37). GA, vol. 43 (1985).

PGZ   *Prolegomena zur Geschichte des Zeitbegriffs* (1925). GA, vol. 20. 2nd ed. (1988).

PhrL   *Phänomenologie des religiösen Lebens* (1918–21). GA, vol. 60 (1995).

PIA   Phänomenologische Interpretationen zu Aristoteles (1922). In *Dilthey-Jahrbuch für Philosophie und Geschichte der Geisteswissenschaften* 6 (1989): 235–269 References are to both *Jahrbuch* and manuscript pages.

PIA/EPF   *Phänomenol. Interpretationen zu Aristoteles/ Einführung in die phänomenol. Forschung* (1921–22). GA, vol. 61 (1985).

Richardson Letter to W. J. Richardson, April 1962. Edited as a preface to Richardson's book *Through Phenomenology to Thought.* Den Haag: Martinus Nijhoff, 1963.

Schelling   *Schelling. Abhandlung über das Wesen der menschlichen Freiheit (1809)* (1936). Tübingen: Niemeyer, 1971.

SD   *Zur Sache des Denkens.* Tübingen: Niemeyer, 1969.

SdU   *Die Selbstbehauptung der deutschen Universität; Das Rektorat 1933/34: Tatsachen und Gedanken.* Edited by Hermann Heidegger. Frankfurt a/M.: Klostermann, 1983.

Sprache   *Unterwegs zur Sprache* (1959). 4th ed. Pfullingen: Neske, 1971.

SvGr   *Der Satz vom Grund.* Pfullingen: Neske, 1957.

SZ   *Sein und Zeit* (1927). 11th ed. Tübingen: Niemeyer, 1967.

TK   *Die Technik und die Kehre* (1962). 8th ed. Pfullingen: Neske, 1991.

VA   *Vortraege und Aufsaetze* (1954). 5th ed. Pfullingen: Neske, 1985.

VS   *Vier Seminare.* Frankfurt a/M.: Klostermann, 1977.

W   *Wegmarken.* Frankfurt a/M.: Klostermann, 1967.

WhD   *Was heisst Denken?* (1951–52). Tübingen: Niemeyer, 1971.

WW   *Vom Wesen der Wahrheit* (1931–32). GA, vol. 34 (1988).

WiM   *Was ist Metaphysik?* (1929). With introduction (1949) and postscript (1943). 10th ed. Frankfurt a/M.: Klostermann, 1969.

WiPh   *Was ist das—Die Philosophie?* (1955). Pfullingen: Neske, 1956.

N O T E S

PREFACE

1. Wittgenstein (1921), no. 6.52.

2. SZ, § 62, p. 310: "Aber liegt der durchgeführten ontologischen Interpretation der Existenz des Daseins nicht eine bestimmte ontische Auffassung von eigentlicher Existenz, ein faktisches Ideal des Daseins zugrunde? Das ist in der Tat so. Dieses Faktum darf nicht nur nicht geleugnet und gezwungenerweise zugestanden, es muß in seiner *positiven Notwendigkeit* aus dem thematischen Gegenstand der Untersuchung begriffen werden. Philosophie wird ihre 'Voraussetzungen' nie abstreiten wollen, aber auch nicht bloß zugeben dürfen." As the final sentence shows, this passage is a polemic with Husserl's principle of presuppositionlessness, which was essential to Husserl's epistemological conception of philosophy. Cf. SZ, § 4, p. 13: "Die existenziale Analytik ihrerseits aber ist letztlich *existenziell* d. h. *ontisch* verwurzelt" (Heidegger's italics).

3. Cf. Husserl's letter to Ingarden of 2 December 1929, in Husserl (1968), p. 56.

4. KM, p. 263: "und daß die Philosophie die Aufgabe hat, aus dem faulen Aspekt eines Menschen, der bloß die Werke des Geistes benutzt, gewissermaßen den Menschen zurückzuwerfen in die Härte seines Schicksals." I did not like, however, the harshness of this formula itself, which seems to express both the influence of Pauline theology and a petty bourgeois resentment against the cultured classes, to which Cassirer belonged.

5. In *Beiträge*, § 259, pp. 433–434, Heidegger comments on such an interpretation: "So aber ist denn alles aus der Bahn der Seinsfrage herausgefallen."

6. WiM, p. 40: "weil das Sein selbst . . . sich nur in der Transzendenz des in das Nichts hinausgehaltenen Daseins offenbart." Cf. KM, §§ 41 and 43.

7. Cf. WiM, pp. 46–47, 50.

8. WiM, pp. 36–37: "Wenn so die Macht des Verstandes im Felde der Fragen nach dem Nichts und dem Sein gebrochen wird, dann entscheidet sich damit auch das Schicksal der Herrschaft der 'Logik' innerhalb der Philosophie. Die Idee der 'Logik' selbst löst sich auf im Wirbel eines ursprünglicheren Fragens."

9. Cf. Hühnerfeld (1961), pp. 7–18, and Kisiel (1993), p. 287. According to Kisiel, the quotation is used by Heideggerians to justify their lack of interest in Heidegger's life.

10. As Barash (1988) observes: "Heidegger . . . was highly secretive about his past. His collected works, which will eventually comprise as many as eighty volumes, are characterized by an unusual lack of autobiographical detail, by the deliberate omission of some of his most significant early course lectures, as well as of all but the most scant correspondence. All of the material that has been held back is kept locked in the *Deutsches Literaturarchiv* at Marbach, where only librarians and Heidegger disciples have been given the right of entry" (p. 8). Cf. also Heidegger, N I, p. 19: "Aber wie alles Biographische ist auch diese Veröffentlichung großen Bedenken ausgesetzt."

11. See SdU. According to Zimmerman (1990), note 19 on pp. 279–280, there are four waves. See that note for references. Habermas's essay has been reprinted in Habermas (1971), pp. 67–75.

12. Ott (1988), p. 7.

13. Löwith (1986), p. 57: "weil ich [Löwith] der Meinung sei, daß seine Parteinahme für den Nationalsozialismus im Wesen seiner Philosophie läge. Heidegger stimmte mir ohne Vorbehalt zu und führte mir aus, daß sein Begriff von der 'Geschichtlichkeit' die Grundlage für seinen politischen 'Einsatz' sei. Er ließ auch keinen Zweifel über seinen Glauben an Hitler; nur zwei Dinge habe er unterschätzt: die Lebenskraft der christlichen Kirchen und die Hindernisse für den Anschluß von Österreich. Er war nach wie vor überzeugt, daß der Nationalsozialismus der für Deutschland vorgezeichnete Weg sei; man müsse nur lange genug 'durchhalten.' "

14. Ott (1988), pp. 201–213.

15. Ott (1988), pp. 160, 232: "Der Führer selbst und allein *ist* die heutige und künftige deutsche Wirklichkeit und ihr Gesetz" (Heidegger's italics). Herbert Marcuse saw in such phrases a symptom of a humiliating genuflection of philosophy before politics; see the *Zeitschrift für Sozialforschung* 3 (1934), pp. 193–194, quoted by Ott, p. 162. Heidegger's phrase is quoted from the "Aufruf an die Deutschen Studenten" ("Appeal to the German Students") of 3 November 1933, published in the *Freiburger Studentenzeitung* 8, no. 1 (1933), p. 1. See Schneeberger (1962), pp. 135ff., and Martin (1989), p. 177.

16. SZ, p. v: "Die in den bisherigen Auflagen angebrachte Kennzeichnung 'Erste Hälfte' ist gestrichen. Die zweite Hälfte läßt sich nach einem Vierteljahrhundert nicht mehr anschließen, ohne daß die erste neu dargestellt würde. Deren Weg bleibt indessen auch heute noch ein notwendiger, wenn die Frage nach dem Sein unser Dasein bewegen soll."

17. See Kisiel (1992) and Kisiel (1993), pp. 2–4, on the many problems inherent in Heidegger's *Gesamtausgabe*. In his 1993 work, p. 544, note 2, Kisiel even speaks of the "paramilitary assaults on scholarship by Heidegger's literary executors."

18. Edwards (1979), p. 71, note 168.

19. Ott (1988), pp. 8–9.

20. In paraphrasing *Sein und Zeit*, I have usually remained close to the standard translation of BT.

CHAPTER I
INTRODUCTION

1. Cf. FD, p. 24: "Alle bisherigen Überlegungen haben vermutlich zu nichts anderem geführt, als daß wir jetzt mit dem Ding weder aus noch ein wissen und nur ein großes Wirbeln im Kopf haben. Gewiß—das war auch die Absicht."

2. Dreyfus (1991), p. 10. See for the historical background of this Wittgensteinian interpretation of *Sein und Zeit*: Philipse (1992), pp. 251–258.

3. Sheehan (1981a), pp. viii and xvi; cf. Sheehan in Guignon (1993), p. 82.

4. Zimmerman (1990), p. xv. According to p. 116, Heidegger's term "being" "named the self-concealing presencing in light of which entities revealed themselves in various ways." On pp. 224–226, Zimmerman stresses an ambiguity in Heidegger's notion of being (*das Sein*) as *physis*: *physis* is defined both as the event of self-emergence of an entity and as the appearing or showing forth of an entity. He does not discuss what these various formulas mean or how they hang together.

5. Okrent (1988), p. 7; cf. pp. 125–129 and 205–218.

6. This is Dreyfus's case. Zimmerman's interpretation is especially instructive for the later Heidegger, whereas Okrent provides a pragmatist and verificationist rational reconstruction of Heidegger's thought rather than a comprehensive historical interpretation.

7. This is one of the problems with Sheehan's interpretation. There are other problems too. For instance, the doctrine of the *analogia entis* goes back to Aristotle. Heidegger refers briefly to this answer to the question of being in section 1 of SZ. Is it really plausible to assume that Heidegger's own articulation of the meaning of being is nothing more than a new variety of the *analogia entis* doctrine, as Sheehan in fact assumes? Because Zimmerman (1990) focuses on Heidegger's philosophy of technology and art and its cultural context, we should not expect to find a highly sophisticated interpretation of the question of being in this instructive book.

8. Such summaries may be useful, and I advise everyone who lacks the time to study Heidegger's writings in chronological order to read, for instance, Pöggeler (1963). Richardson (1963) is less useful as an introduction because of its length, but it provides, perhaps, more attempts at an interpretation. However, this interpretation is entirely internal in the sense of section 5, below, and it lacks critical distance with regard to Heidegger's thought. A special case of an internal summary is Kisiel's (1993) monumental work, in which he scrupulously traces the genesis of *Sein und Zeit* from 1915/1919 to 1927. The interest of this book lies in the fact that Kisiel uses documents (letters, lecture notes, etc.) that are still unpublished, and the book is a *must* for the specialist. Even though it offers a great number of data that are crucial for interpreting Heidegger's thought, it does not aim at a critical interpretation itself. The nonphilosopher will profit most from Safranski (1994), a masterly narrative of Heidegger's life and philosophical development, situated in its historical and intellectual setting.

9. I say "seems to be," because one might be critical concerning Heidegger's later reconstructions of his *Denkweg*, such as "Mein Weg in die Phänomenologie." Kisiel (1993) comments cynically on "the old Heidegger's autobiographical statements" as follows: "We are . . . treated repeatedly to the story of his boyhood years in the gymnasium and the gift of Brentano's dissertation . . . , which has triggered a small industry of articles analyzing this text in its relation to Heidegger's thought. Such work demonstrates the eagerness of scholars for reliable biographical clues to Heidegger's development more than the actual relevance of Heidegger's selective reading of his own life to the main lines of his thought. Why this attempt in his old age to revive the ties with his Catholic past . . . ? Why do we hear absolutely nothing about those dark war years of 1917–19 . . . , when he broke with his Catholic past?" As I will argue in sections 11 and 15B, Heidegger's ever-changing relation to his Catholic upbringing is crucial for interpreting his thought. But so is his relation to Aristotle (see § 7, below). Cf. also Greisch (1994), pp. 2–4ff., who argues that the question of being originated only in 1923.

10. Cf. Ott (1988), p. 54; Brentano (1862).

11. "Mein Weg in die Phänomenologie" (1963), SD, p. 81. Cf. the *curriculum vitae* that Heidegger wrote at the occasion of his accession to the Academy of Sciences of Heidelberg: "Im Jahre 1907 gab mir ein väterlicher Freund aus meiner Heimat, der spätere Erzbischof von Freiburg, Dr. Conrad Gröber, Franz Brentanos Dissertation in die Hand: *Von der mannigfachen Bedeutung des Seienden nach Aristoteles* (1862). . . . Die damals nur dunkel und schwankend und hilflos sich regende Frage nach dem Einfachen des Mannigfachen im Sein *blieb* durch viele Umkippungen, Irrgänge und Ratlosigkeiten hindurch der unablässige Anlaß für die zwei Jahrzehnte später erschienene Abhandlung *Sein und*

Zeit" (Heidegger's italics). See *Sitzungsberichte der Heidelberger Akademie der Wissenschaften* 1957–58, pp. 20–21 (quoted by Ott [1988], p. 54). Cf. also *Richardson*, pp. ix–xi.

12. Cf. Aristotle, Met. XI, 2, 1060b: 4; Top. IV, 6, 127a: 28; Met. III, 3, 998b: 20; Met. V, 11, 1018b: 32; Met. X, 2, 1053b: 20.

13. Cf. Aristotle, Met. IV, 1, 1003a: 21, and 2, 1003b: 21. Cf. for first philosophy as a science of the first principles: Met. I, 1, 981b: 28; Met. XI, 7, 1064b: 3–4.

14. Cf. Aristotle, Met. VII, 1, 1028b: 2.

15. Cf. Aristotle, Met. IV, 2, 1003a: 33; Met. V, 7, 1017a: 7; Met. VI, 2, 1026a: 33; Met. VII, 1, 1028a: 10; Met. IX, 10, 1051a: 34.

16. SD, p. 81: "Unbestimmt genug bewegte mich die Überlegung: Wenn das Seiende in mannigfacher Bedeutung gesagt wird, welches ist dann die leitende Grundbedeutung? Was heißt Sein?" Cf. *Richardson*, p. xi: "Welches ist die alle mannigfachen Bedeutungen durchherrschende einfache, einheitliche Bestimmung von Sein?"

17. SZ, § 3, p. 11: "Ontologisches Fragen ist zwar gegenüber dem ontischen Fragen der positiven Wissenschaften ursprünglicher. Es bleibt aber selbst naiv und undurchsichtig, wenn seine Nachforschungen nach dem Sein des Seienden den Sinn von Sein überhaupt unerörtert lassen. Und gerade die ontologische Aufgabe einer nicht deduktiv konstruierenden Genealogie der verschiedenen möglichen Weisen von Sein bedarf einer Vorverständigung über das, 'was wir denn eigentlich mit diesem Ausdruck 'Sein' meinen.' "

18. Cf. SZ, p. 1: "Die konkrete Ausarbeitung der Frage nach dem Sinn von 'Sein' ist die Absicht der folgenden Abhandlung. Die Interpretation der *Zeit* als des möglichen Horizontes eines jeden Seinsverständnisses überhaupt ist ihr vorläufiges Ziel" (Heidegger's italics).

19. SZ, p. 19.

20. SZ, p. 19.

21. SZ, § 83, p. 437: "Es gilt, einen *Weg* zur Aufhellung der ontologischen Fundamentalfrage zu suchen und zu *gehen*" (Heidegger's italics).

22. G, p. 35: "Wir sollen nichts tun sondern warten."

23. EM, p. 157: " 'Sein und Zeit' meint bei solcher Besinnung nicht ein Buch, sondern das Aufgegebene. Das eigentlich Aufgegebene ist Jenes, was wir nicht wissen und das wir, sofern wir es *echt* wissen, nämlich *als* Aufgegebenes, immer nur *fragend* wissen. Fragen können heißt: warten können, sogar ein Leben lang" (Heidegger's italics). Cf. GbM (GA vol. 29/30), Heidegger's lectures of 1929–30, p. 273: "In der recht entfalteten Frage liegt das eigentliche metaphysische Begreifen. Anders gesagt, die metaphysischen Fragen bleiben ohne Antwort—im Sinne der Mitteilung eines erkannten Sachverhaltes."

24. TK, p. 36: "Denn das Fragen ist die Frömmigkeit des Denkens."

25. WiM, pp. 18–19: "Einen deutlicheren Beleg für die Macht der Seinsvergessenheit, in die alle Philosophie versunken ist, die aber zugleich der geschickhafte Anspruch an das Denken in S.u.Z. geworden und geblieben ist, konnte die Philosophie nicht leicht aufbringen als durch die nachtwandlerische Sicherheit, mit der sie an der eigentlichen und einzigen Frage von S.u.Z. vorbeiging. Darum handelt es sich auch nicht um Mißverständnisse gegenüber einem Buch, sondern um unsere Verlassenheit vom Sein."

26. *Antwort*, pp. 23–24: "es ist ein *Entzug des Seins*, in dem wir stehen. Das am meisten charakteristische Merkmal für die Seinsvergessenheit—und Vergessenheit ist hier *immer* zu denken vom Griechischen her, von der *lethe*, d. h. vom Sich-Verbergen, vom sich-Entziehen des Seins her-, nun, das charakteristischste Merkmal des Geschicks, in dem wir

stehen, ist—soweit ich das überhaupt übersehe—die Tatsache, daß die *Seinsfrage*, die ich stelle, noch nicht *verstanden* ist" (Heidegger's italics).

27. Cf. Löwith (1965), p. 20: "In der Tat wird niemand behaupten können, er habe wissentlich verstanden, was das Sein, dieses Geheimnis ist, von welchem Heidegger redet."

28. Cf. N I, p. 9: " 'Nietzsche'—der Name des Denkers steht als Titel für *die Sache* seines Denkens" (Heidegger's italics).

29. See for a survey of these texts: Fay (1977), Mohanty (1992), and Borgmann (1978).

30. WiM, p. 24.

31. WiM, p. 39: " 'Das reine Sein und das reine Nichts ist also dasselbe.' Dieser Satz Hegels (*Wissenschaft der Logik* I. Buch, WW III, S. 74) besteht zu Recht." It is important to see, however, that Heidegger endorsed this proposition for reasons very different from Hegel's. According to Heidegger, being and nothingness belong to each other because being manifests itself to Dasein if the latter is exposed into nothingness. Cf. WiM, pp. 39–40: "Sein und Nichts gehören zusammen, aber nicht weil sie beide—vom Hegelschen Begriff des Denkens aus gesehen—in ihrer Unbestimmtheit und Unmittelbarkeit überein-kommen, sondern weil das Sein selbst im Wesen endlich ist und sich nur in der Transzen-denz des in das Nichts hinausgehaltenen Daseins offenbart." Cf. also "Vom Wesen des Grundes," preface of 1949, W, p. 21: "Das Nichts ist das Nicht des Seienden und so das vom Seienden her erfahrene Sein"; and "Brief über den 'Humanismus,' " W, p. 191: "Das Nichtende im Sein ist das Wesen dessen, was ich das Nichts nenne. Darum, weil es das Sein denkt, denkt das Denken das Nichts."

32. WiM, p. 33: "Die für unsere Absicht zunächst allein wesentliche Antwort ist schon gewonnen, wenn wir darauf achthaben, daß die Frage nach dem Nichts wirklich gestellt bleibt. Hierzu wird verlangt, daß wir die Verwandlung des Menschen in sein Da-sein, die jede Angst mit uns geschehen läßt, nachvollziehen, um das darin offenkundige Nichts in dem festzunehmen, wie es sich bekundet."

33. WiM, pp. 36–37.

34. WiM, pp. 25–26. The idea is that man's openness to the world is a precondition of worldly entities being themselves, an idea that reminds us both of Kant's transcendental philosophy and of Genesis 2:19, where the Lord God forms beasts and birds out of the ground and brings them to the man to see what he will call them. As usual, Heidegger's prose is difficult to translate. He writes, for instance: "Der aufbrechende Einbruch verhilft in seiner Weise dem Seienden allererst zu ihm selbst" (WiM, p. 26).

35. WiM, pp. 26–27. The crucial passages are: "Aber merkwürdig—gerade in dem, wie der wissenschaftliche Mensch sich seines Eigensten versichert, spricht er von einem Anderen. Erforscht werden soll nur das Seiende und sonst—nichts; das Seiende allein und weiter—nichts; das Seiende einzig und darüber hinaus—nichts. Wie steht es um dieses Nichts? . . . Die Wissenschaft will vom Nichts nichts wissen. Aber ebenso gewiß bleibt bestehen: dort, wo sie ihr eigenes Wesen auszusprechen versucht, ruft sie das Nichts zu Hilfe. Was sie verwirft, nimmt sie in Anspruch. Welch zwiespältiges Wesen enthüllt sich da? . . . Wie steht es um das Nichts?"

36. Carnap (1931), pp. 219–241. See especially section 5.

37. According to the verification principle, the meaning of a word is determined only if (1) its syntax is specified (explicitly or implicitly) and (2) it is specified how simple sentences containing the word are verified or tested, that is, how their truth or falsity might be discovered. See Carnap (1931), p. 221.

38. Heidegger's use of the word "beings" in this context violates logical grammar as well, for he uses the term as if it were a predicate such as "horses," whereas, from a logical point of view, "beings" expresses an object-variable and a quantifier.

39. Carnap and Heidegger met during the "Davoser Hochschulkurse" (from 17 March until 6 April 1929), and discussed philosophy. We may assume that *Was ist Metaphysik?*, Heidegger's inaugural lecture that was held on 24 July 1929, is in part an implicit polemics against Carnap.

40. WiM, p. 28: "Die gemeinhin beigezogene Grundregel des Denkens überhaupt, der Satz vom zu vermeidenden Widerspruch, die allgemeine 'Logik,' schlägt diese Frage nieder."

41. WiM, p. 28: "Weil uns so versagt bleibt, das Nichts überhaupt zum Gegenstand zu machen, sind wir mit unserem Fragen nach dem Nichts schon am Ende—unter der Voraussetzung, daß in dieser Frage die 'Logik' die höchste Instanz ist"; "Doch ist es so sicher, was wir da voraussetzen? . . . Gibt es das Nichts nur, weil es das Nicht, d. h. die Verneinung gibt? Oder liegt es umgekehrt? . . . Das ist nicht entschieden, noch nicht einmal zur ausdrücklichen Frage erhoben. Wir behaupten: das Nichts ist ursprünglicher als das Nicht und die Verneinung."

42. WiM, p. 34: "Das Nichts selbst nichtet." Krell translates: "The nothing itself nihilates" (BW, p. 103). The verb nichten does not exist in German; Heidegger formed it from the negation *nicht*.

43. WiM, p. 34: "In der hellen Nacht des Nichts der Angst entsteht erst die ursprüngliche Offenheit des Seienden als eines solchen: daß es Seiendes ist—und nicht Nichts."

44. WiM, p. 35: "Da-sein heißt: Hineingehaltenheit in das Nichts," and "Das Nichts ist die Ermöglichung der Offenbarkeit des Seienden als eines solchen für das menschliche Dasein." It has often been remarked that Heidegger's description of *Angst* is very similar to descriptions by psychiatric patients suffering from depression and depersonalization, and that the experience of irreality and meaninglessness in *Angst* is followed by a very intense experience of reality, as if the former is a precondition of the latter.

45. WiM, pp. 36–37: "Das Nicht entsteht nicht durch die Verneinung, sondern die Verneinung gründet sich auf das Nicht, das dem Nichten des Nichts entspringt. . . . Hierdurch ist in den Grundzügen die obige These erwiesen: das Nichts ist der Ursprung der Verneinung, nicht umgekehrt. Wenn so die Macht des Verstandes im Felde der Fragen nach dem Nichts und dem Sein gebrochen wird, dann entscheidet sich damit auch das Schicksal der Herrschaft der 'Logik' innerhalb der Philosophie. Die Idee der 'Logik' selbst löst sich auf im Wirbel eines ursprünglicheren Fragens." Heidegger invented the noun *das Nicht* and the verb *nichten*, and his prose offends German ears. To maintain this perlocutionary effect, which was doubtless intended by Heidegger, I translate *das Nicht* by "the not," and *nichten* by "to not" (instead of "to negate" or the Latin-inspired neologism "to nihilate," which Krell uses).

46. Wittgenstein (1921), no. 5.4: "Hier zeigt sich, daß es 'logische Gegenstände,' 'logische Konstante' (im Sinne Freges und Russells) nicht gibt." Cf. for the importance of this assumption for Heidegger's question of being: Philipse (1992) and section 8A, below.

47. Cf. Philipse (1983), pp. 111–151.

48. Cf. SZ, § 33, p. 160: "Vorläufig galt es nur . . . deutlich zu machen, daß die 'Logik' . . . in der existenzialen Analytik des Daseins verwurzelt ist."

49. Russell adhered to the referential conception of logical and mathematical constants in his early works, and indeed, to the idea of a philosophical foundation of logic and

mathematics that we find also in Husserl. Thus he wrote in the preface to *The Principles of Mathematics* (1903): "the explanation of the fundamental concepts which mathematics accepts as indefinable. This is a purely philosophical task. . . . The discussion of indefinables—which forms the chief part of philosophical logic—is the endeavour to see clearly, and to make others see clearly, the entities concerned, in order that the mind may have that kind of acquaintance with them which it has with redness or the taste of a pineapple" (Russell [1937], p. xv). In the introduction to the second edition of 1937, Russell explains how he came to abandon this view. He concludes: "Logical constants, therefore, if we are able to say anything definite about them, must be treated as part of the language, not as part of what the language speaks about. In this way, logic becomes much more linguistic than I believed it to be at the time when I wrote the *Principles*" (p. xi). Nevertheless, Russell continued to look for the *psychological* origin of the meaning of logical words (a Lockean research program that Husserl abandoned in 1901), and the theory that the disjunction "or" expresses, or corresponds to, a state of hesitation, which arises when we feel two incompatible impulses, is to be found in *An Inquiry into Meaning and Truth* of 1940 (Russell [1962], pp. 79–80, and passim). In SZ, § 33, Heidegger discusses the foundations of logic, in particular of the copula "is," and concludes that they must be traced by the existential analysis of Dasein, a research program that resembles strikingly Russell's later view.

50. Surprisingly, Heidegger discussed this manner of refuting the skeptic in his lectures on logic in the winter semester of 1925–26. See *Logik* (GA 21), § 4.

51. Fay (1977), pp. 113–114. Fay refers to *Tractatus,* nos. 2.172, 2.174, 4.003, 4.12, and 4.121.

52. Fay (1977), p. 111.

53. WiM, p. 29: "Wenn wir uns aber durch die formale Unmöglichkeit der Frage nach dem Nichts nicht beirren lassen und ihr entgegen die Frage dennoch stellen, dann müssen wir zum mindesten dem genügen, was als Grunderfordernis für die mögliche Durchführung jeder Frage bestehen bleibt. Wenn das Nichts, wie immer, befragt werden soll—es selbst— dann muß es zuvor gegeben sein. Wir müssen ihm begegnen können." This requirement is inherent to Husserl's program of a foundation of logic by means of an analysis of the "origin" of its basic concepts.

54. Cf. WiM, p. 32. Here again, Heidegger seems to violate logical grammar, because from the fact that *Angst* is not concerned with particular things, it does not *follow* that it is concerned with something called nothingness. Cf. Tugendhat (1970), p. 155. But there is a more charitable interpretation: Heidegger chose the term "nothingness" (*das Nichts*) to refer to a positive phenomenon, that is, the universal meaninglessness we experience in *Angst*, so that nothingness is a descriptive term. And the reason he opted for the term "nothingness" is the very fact that in *Angst* we are not concerned with particular things (with no-things). He might have chosen another term, as Tugendhat observes.

55. WiM, pp. 39–40: "Sein und Nichts gehören zusammen, aber nicht weil sie beide— vom Hegelschen Begriff des Denkens aus gesehen—in ihrer Unbestimmtheit und Unmittelbarkeit übereinkommen, sondern weil das Sein selbst im Wesen endlich ist und sich nur in der Transzendenz des in das Nichts hinausgehaltenen Daseins offenbart."

56. Another difficulty is, of course, that Heidegger himself links the meaning of "not" as a logical constant to the experience of nothingness in *Angst*, because the latter allegedly is the source or empirical basis of the former. Surely Heidegger cannot be acquitted on the charge of misleading verbal manipulations.

57. Wittgenstein (1921), no. 6.41.

58. One might argue that there is at least one decisive difference between the mysticisms of the early Wittgenstein and of Heidegger's WiM (cf. Philipse [1992], note 2). Whereas Wittgenstein holds that we cannot speak about the mystical (*Tractatus*, no. 7, and Wittgenstein [1965]), Heidegger's quest seems to be concerned with another kind of language, which is not dominated by logic and in which we might ask the question of being. However, in his discussion of Heidegger, probably of *Was ist Metaphysik?*, on 30 December 1929, Wittgenstein not only interpreted Heideggerian *Angst* as running up against the limits of language. He also seemed to repudiate his earlier thesis that one must pass over in silence what one cannot speak about. For the relevant entry in Waismann's notebook ends with a quotation from Augustine: "What, you swine, you want not to talk nonsense! Go ahead and talk nonsense, it does not matter!" See Wittgenstein (1979), p. 69. He did not repudiate, of course, his distinction between sense and nonsense.

59. SZ, p. v.

60. Apart from his doctoral dissertation and his *Habilitationsschrift*, Heidegger published only some papers before *Sein und Zeit* appeared in 1927. See FS, GA, vol. 1, for an incomplete edition of the early works.

61. See also Dreyfus's answer to this question: (1991), pp. 1–9.

62. He misleadingly labeled the published part of *Sein und Zeit* as "First Half." This designation was omitted from the seventh edition (1953) on, because "after a quarter of a century, the second half could no longer be added unless the first were to be presented anew" (SZ, p. v).

63. According to GPh (GA 24), p. 1, footnote, Heidegger intended to give in this lecture course of 1927 a new elaboration of the third division of part 1 of SZ. But the original plan of the course (see § 6) was not carried out. Of its three main parts, only part 1 and the first chapter of part 2 were actually written. Moreover, part 1 covers materials that belong to the second, destructive part of SZ, and not to the division on *Zeit und Sein*. Apart from the historical analyses, there is not much that is new in GPh compared to what we already know from SZ.

64. I should stress again that all translations are my own, even translations of Heidegger's titles. It would be inadequate to translate "Zur Sache des Denkens" by "Discourse on Thinking," for instance, because Heidegger's title says that the book is about the topic or the subject matter of "thinking," not on "thinking" itself.

65. SD, p. 91: "Der Verfasser war damals einer zureichenden Ausarbeitung des im Titel 'Zeit und Sein' genannten Themas nicht gewachsen. Die Veröffentlichung von *Sein und Zeit* wurde an dieser Stelle abgebrochen." Cf. "Brief über den 'Humanismus,' " W, p. 159: "Der fragliche Abschnitt wurde zurückgehalten, weil das Denken im zureichenden Sagen dieser Kehre versagte und mit Hilfe der Sprache der Metaphysik nicht durchkam."

66. The great majority of the French philosophical virtuosos of this period, such as Foucault and Derrida, were deeply influenced by the later Heidegger. As Foucault acknowledges, "my entire philosophical development was determined by my reading of Heidegger" (quoted by Dreyfus [1991], p. 9). Jean Beaufret, who has been a teacher of many present-day French philosophers, claims that Heidegger is as important as Plato in philosophy: Beaufret (1984), p. 57. Cf. on the theme of Heidegger and French philosophers: Rockmore (1995).

67. SZ, § 3. The examples are Heidegger's; see SZ, p. 9. Heidegger often repeats that these ontologies are a priori: SZ, pp. 11, 44 ("liegt a priori die Struktur der Existenzialität"),

50 (see especially footnote), 53 ("Diese Seinsbestimmungen des Daseins müssen nun aber a priori auf dem Grunde der Seinsverfassung gesehen und verstanden werden"), 85, 111, 131 ("existenzialen Apriori der philosophischen Anthropologie"), and 199–200. For Husserl, see *Ideen* I, §§ 1–17. Both Husserl and Heidegger assume that essential generalization is possible on the basis of a specific kind of *experience*, eidetic experience: SZ, p. 50, footnote, and Husserl, loc. cit. Heidegger's distinction between essence and fact is particularly clear in his lectures of the summer semester of 1928, GA 26, § 11, p. 217: "Es gilt demnach grundsätzlich und scharf auseinanderzuhalten: 1. Die faktische Existenzaussage, daß dieses bestimmte Dasein jetzt existiert. . . . 2. die metaphysische Wesensaussage, daß zum Wesen des Daseins, mag es faktisch existieren oder nicht, das In-der-Welt-Sein als Verfassung gehört."

68. See, for instance, SZ, p. 235, footnote, on Kierkegaard, and SZ, pp. 46–47 on Dilthey.

69. Cf. SZ, § 10, especially p. 50: "Andrerseits muß aber immer wieder zum Bewußtsein gebracht werden, daß diese ontologischen Fundamente nie nachträglich aus dem empirischen Material hypothetisch erschlossen werden können." In other words, the ontology of Dasein is a priori in relation to the empirical sciences of man.

70. SZ, pp. 16–17: "An dieser [i.e., everyday human existence] sollen nicht beliebige und zufällige, sondern wesenhafte Strukturen herausgestellt werden, die in jeder Seinsart des faktischen Daseins sich als seinsbestimmende durchhalten." Cf. pp. 52 ("echte Wesenserkenntnis") and 231 ("Wesen des Daseins").

71. SZ, p. 199: "Die existenzial-ontologische Interpretation ist der ontischen Auslegung gegenüber nicht etwa nur eine theoretisch-ontische Verallgemeinerung. . . . Die 'Verallgemeinerung' ist eine *apriorisch-ontologische*. Sie meint nicht ständig auftretende ontische Eigenschaften, sondern eine je schon zugrunde liegende Seinsverfassung" (Heidegger's italics).

72. SZ, pp. 85, 199, and passim: "Bedingung der Möglichkeit."

73. Cf. SZ, p. 10: "die Grundverfassung seines Seins."

74. Cf. SZ, § 4, p. 12; § 14, p. 63: "Die Beschreibung bleibt am Seienden haften. Sie ist ontisch. Gesucht wird aber doch das Sein. 'Phänomen' im phänomenologischen Sinne wurde formal bestimmt als das, was sich als Sein und Seinsstruktur zeigt"; cf. pp. 84, 120, 135, 179–180, 182, 184–185, 199–200, 221, 246, 247–248, 260, 311, 356–357, and 382. One should note that "facticity" (*Faktizität*) is an ontological characteristic of Dasein, the characteristic that Dasein is "thrown" into being (SZ, § 29), and one should not confuse this facticity with what is ontical. I use "factual" for *tatsächlich* or *ontisch*, and "factical" or "facticity" for *faktisch* or *Faktizität*.

75. Cf. SZ, § 10.

76. SZ, § 4, p. 12: "Dasein . . . ist . . . dadurch ontisch ausgezeichnet, daß es diesem Seienden in seinem Sein *um* dieses Sein selbst geht. Zu dieser Seinsverfassung des Daseins gehört aber dann, daß es in seinem Sein zu diesem Sein ein Seinsverhältnis hat. Und dies wiederum besagt: Dasein versteht sich in irgendeiner Weise und Ausdrücklichkeit in seinem Sein. Diesem Seienden eignet, daß mit und durch sein Sein dieses ihm selbst erschlossen ist. *Seinsverständnis ist selbst eine Seinsbestimmtheit des Daseins.* Die ontische Auszeichnung des Daseins liegt darin, daß es ontologisch *ist*" (Heidegger's italics). Heidegger also seems to assume that we will be able to generalize ontological self-understanding by *Wesensschau* or eidetic intuition: PGZ, §§ 6–7 and SZ, § 10, p. 50, footnote 1.

77. This claim is similar to the pretension of some analytical philosophers that they are able to do conceptual-linguistic analysis without relying on empirical linguistics. The argument is that they already master the rules of their language, and that their linguistic competence makes empirical investigations into their language superfluous. Similarly, Heidegger pretends that our competence in *living* enables us to interpret the structures of human life, and that we do not need the empirical investigations of anthropology, psychology, or biology in order to do this. Heidegger's thesis that we might discover *universal* structures of human life by exploring our own life is similar to the analytical philosopher's claim that he might discover universal and a priori conceptual structures by exploring the conceptual structures of *his own* language. I critically discuss Heidegger's claim in chapter 4, section 17B.2.

78. SZ, p. 12: "Die ontische Auszeichnung des Daseins liegt darin, daß es ontologisch *ist*" (Heidegger italicizes *ist* because he is referring to a characteristic of our constitution of being).

79. SZ, § 9, p. 42: "*Das 'Wesen' des Daseins liegt in seiner Existenz*" (Heidegger's italics).

80. As Heidegger says in SZ, § 4, p. 12: "weil die Wesensbestimmung dieses Seienden nicht durch Angabe eines sachhaltigen Was vollzogen werden kann, sein Wesen vielmehr darin liegt, daß es je sein Sein als seiniges zu sein hat, ist der Titel Dasein als reiner Seinsausdruck zur Bezeichnung dieses Seienden gewählt."

81. In SZ, Heidegger also endorses the much stronger thesis that finite temporality is the horizon for understanding the mode of being of *all* types of beings. Cf. SZ, p. 1: "Die Interpretation der *Zeit* als des möglichen Horizontes eines jeden Seinsverständnisses überhaupt ist ihr [namely, of SZ] vorläufiges Ziel" (Heidegger's italics). Cf. also GPh (GA 24), part 2. It would be more proper to call this stronger thesis the first main thesis of SZ. The problem of the relation between the stronger thesis and the weaker thesis is related to the crucial problem of SZ: How does the analysis of Dasein relate to the question of being *tout court*? See for this problem sections 4.6, 9, 12C, and 13C, below.

82. Cf. SZ, § 5, pp. 15–16: "Das Dasein hat vielmehr gemäß einer zu ihm gehörigen Seinsart die Tendenz, das eigene Sein aus *dem* Seienden her zu verstehen, zu dem es sich wesenhaft ständig und zunächst verhält, aus der 'Welt.' Im Dasein selbst und damit in seinem eigenen Seinsverständnis liegt das, was wir als die ontologische Rückstrahlung des Weltverständnisses auf die Daseinsauslegung aufweisen werden" (Heidegger's italics); and § 6, p. 21: "das Dasein hat nicht nur die Geneigtheit, an seine Welt, in der es ist, zu verfallen und reluzent aus ihr her sich auszulegen, Dasein verfällt in eins damit auch seiner mehr oder minder ausdrücklich ergriffenen Tradition." As a consequence, Dasein, although it is ontically nearest to itself, is ontologically furthest removed from itself (SZ, § 5, p. 15; cf. pp. 132 and 311).

83. Cf. SZ, § 4, p. 12: "Die Frage der Existenz ist immer nur durch das Existieren selbst ins Reine zu bringen. Das *hierbei* führende Verständnis seiner selbst nennen wir das *existenzielle*. Die Frage der Existenz ist eine ontische 'Angelegenheit' des Daseins. Es bedarf hierzu nicht der theoretischen Durchsichtigkeit der ontologischen Struktur der Existenz. Die Frage nach dieser zielt auf die Auseinanderlegung dessen, was Existenz konstituiert. Den Zusammenhang dieser Strukturen nennen wir die *Existenzialität*" (Heidegger's italics). I follow Macquarrie's and Robinson's translation (BT, p. 33) in rendering Heidegger's *existenzial* and *existenziell* by "existential" and "existentiell" in English.

84. Luther uses *destruere* in his *Heidelberger Disputation*. Cf. Van Buren (1994), pp. 167–168 and 172.

85. Cf. SZ, § 6, p. 21: "Die hierbei zur Herrschaft kommende Tradition mach zunächst und zumeist das, was sie 'übergibt,' so wenig zugänglich, daß sie es vielmehr verdeckt. Sie überantwortet das Überkommene der Selbstverständlichkeit und verlegt den Zugang zu den ursprünglichen 'Quellen,' daraus die überlieferten Kategorien und Begriffe z. T. in echter Weise geschöpft wurden."

86. SZ, § 6, p. 21.

87. Cf. SZ, p. 22: "*Destruktion* des überlieferten Bestandes der antiken Ontologie auf die ursprünglichen Erfahrungen, in denen die ersten und fortan leitenden Bestimmungen des Seins gewonnen wurden" (Heidegger's italics).

88. Cf. on Destruktion also the crucial texts of GPh (GA 24), § 5, and of PIA, p. 249/20. The first text reads: "*Destruktion*, d. h. ein kritischer Abbau der überkommenen und zunächst notwendig zu verwendenden Begriffe auf die Quellen, aus denen sie geschöpft sind" (GPh, p. 31). In his lectures of the summer semester of 1920, Heidegger stressed that destruction should not overlook the wider context of the meanings involved. See Kisiel (1993), pp. 125–127.

89. SZ, p. 24; PIA, p. 253/26–27; GPh (GA 24), pp. 146–148ff.

90. Cf. GPh (GA 24), pp. 417–418: "weshalb auch die ontologische Interpretation des Seins im Anfang der Philosophie, in der Antike, sich in der Orientierung am Vorhandenen vollzieht. Diese Interpretation des Seins wird philosophisch unzureichend, sobald sie sich universal erweitert und versucht, am Leitfaden dieses Seinsbegriffs auch die Existenz zu verstehen." Heidegger could just as well have written *Zuhandenen* instead of *Vorhandenen*; cf. SZ, § 6, p. 24: "Geschaffenheit aber im weitesten Sinne der Hergestelltheit von etwas ist ein wesentliches Strukturmoment des antiken Seinsbegriffes."

91. SZ, § 6, p. 22: "Die Destruktion hat ebensowenig den *negativen* Sinn einer Abschüttelung der ontologischen Tradition. Sie soll umgekehrt diese in ihren positiven Möglichkeiten, und das besagt immer, in ihren *Grenzen* abstecken."

92. Cf. Searle (1992), p. 90.

93. Kisiel (1993), p. 62. This is what Heidegger says in 1919 about Lotze and Emil Lask, but according to Kisiel, it applies to Heidegger as well. It is a further question, of course, whether "meaning" is compatible with the (or rather a specific) scientific worldview or not. Heidegger argued already in *Sein und Zeit* that the scientific worldview cannot be fundamental or even true, if meaning is to be possible. Contemporary philosophers such as McDowell argue that because the logical space of reasons cannot be reduced to, or otherwise accommodated in terms of the framework of causes and natural law, the scope of this latter framework has to be restricted. Cf. McDowell (1994), pp. 70–86. This is also what Heidegger does, but his restriction is a more radical one. See section 9A, below.

94. Dreyfus (1991), p. vii.

95. See for a detailed reconstruction of this tradition: Philipse (1994).

96. Locke introduced the expression "secondary quality" for empirical properties that should not be attributed to the corpuscular entities that were postulated to explain them. The secondary color-qualities (red, blue, etc.), for instance, had to be explained by mechanisms (rotating light particles in Descartes' case, or wavelengths) which have "primary" qualities only, that is, theoretical properties that physics uses in its explanations. Secondary quality terms were now interpreted as standing for (1) the phenomenal quality that supposedly is an "idea in the mind" and (2) the material disposition in the observable object to cause

such ideas in the mind. Accordingly, Locke had to assume that secondary quality words are systematically ambiguous.

97. See Carnap (1928).

98. Heidegger's diagnosis in section 43a merely identifies a necessary condition for the genesis of the problem of the external world and not a sufficient one. He does not explain what I tried to elucidate very briefly, that is, why the problem of the external world arises in the seventeenth century only, and not within the context of the Aristotelian tradition. There is no discussion of the corpuscular philosophy and its consequences for the theory of perception in Heidegger's oeuvre. In sections 21 and 69b of SZ, and in B.I.§ 5 of FD, Heidegger attempts to account for modern epistemology and metaphysics on the basis of the rise of the "mathematical" conception of the world in the seventeenth century. Heidegger stipulatively defines "mathematical" as a priori, and in SD (p. 69) he argues that Newton's principle of inertia is "mathematical" in this sense. However, his argument is vitiated by an implicit and naïve empiricist philosophy of science, and Heidegger's derivation of Cartesian doubt concerning the external world from wordplays with *Satz* and *setzen* on pp. 71 and 80 of SD does not offer any historical insight.

99. Cf. SZ, p. 52 (§ 11, *in finem*). Of course, Heidegger redefined the term "world," so that one may wonder whether he succeeded in diffusing the problem of the external world.

100. SZ, § 9, pp. 41–42: "Das Seiende, dessen Analyse zur Aufgabe steht, sind wir je selbst. Das Sein dieses Seienden ist *je meines*. . . . Das *Sein* ist es, darum es diesem Seienden je selbst geht" (Heidegger's italics). This is not an ontical statement, as if Heidegger proclaims universal egotism; it was meant to be an ontological claim. Each of us has to "act out" his own life, even if he does so altruistically. Nor is it a proclamation of solipsism. Heidegger's point is merely "that the kind of Being which belongs to Dasein is of a sort that any of us may call his own" (cf. BT, p. 67, note 1).

101. Both (common) translations of *das Man* may be misleading. "The They" (BT) suggests that we are not part of *das Man*, and "the One" (Dreyfus) perhaps suggests Neo-Platonic connotations. Heidegger derived the neologism *das Man* from German idioms such as "Man sagt . . ," "So etwas tut man nicht" (cf. in English: "One should do one's duty"). I will often use the common translations in order to link up my discussions with the existing secondary literature, and sometimes insert my pet-translation "Everyman."

102. SZ, § 27, p. 126: "das Dasein steht als alltägliches Miteinandersein in der *Botmäßigkeit* der Anderen. Nicht es selbst *ist*, die Anderen haben ihm das Sein abgenommen. Das Belieben der Anderen verfügt über die alltäglichen Seinsmöglichkeiten des Daseins" (Heidegger's italics).

103. SZ, § 9, p. 43: "Aus dieser Seinsart heraus und in sie zurück ist alles Existieren, wie es ist."

104. SZ, § 27, p. 129: "Das Selbst des alltäglichen Daseins ist das *Man-selbst*, das wir von dem *eigentlichen*, das heißt eigens ergriffenen *Selbst* unterscheiden" (Heidegger's italics). I am relying on an *a contrario* interpretation of this passage.

105. SZ, § 27, p. 126: "Dieses Miteinandersein löst das eigene Dasein völlig in die Seinsart 'der Anderen' auf. . . . In dieser Unauffälligkeit und Nichtfeststellbarkeit entfaltet das Man seine eigentliche Diktatur."

106. SZ, p. 127: "Das Man ist überall dabei, doch so, daß es sich auch schon immer davongeschlichen hat, wo das Dasein auf Entscheidung drängt. Weil das Man jedoch alles Urteilen und Entscheiden vorgibt, nimmt es dem jeweiligen Dasein die Verantwortlichkeit ab."

107. SZ, p. 129: "Als Man-selbst ist das jeweilige Dasein in das Man *zerstreut* und muß sich erst finden" (Heidegger's italics).

108. Interestingly, Heidegger stresses that the word "falling" (*Verfallen*) does not express any negative evaluation (SZ, § 38, second paragraph), even though the phenomena that constitute the falling are characterized in unambiguously negative terms.

109. It would have been much clearer if Heidegger had distinguished the common cultural background from various (authentic, inauthentic, and perhaps neutral) ways of coping with it. Even though he distinguishes among authenticity, inauthenticity, and a "modal indifference" (SZ, p. 232), he tends to identify the everyday undifferentiated mode of existence with inauthenticity. I try to explain this tendency of Heidegger in chapter 4, section 18A. From a sociological point of view, one might be tempted to say that Kierkegaard's and Heidegger's doctrine according to which living like the others is inauthentic is an expression of lower-middle-class anxieties about the rise of democracy. Cf. on this topic Carey (1992). However, the philosophical explanation is a different one (cf. § 18A–B).

110. SZ, p. 129: "Das Selbst des alltäglichen Daseins ist das *Man-selbst*, das wir von dem *eigentlichen*, das heißt eigens ergriffenen *Selbst* unterscheiden" (Heidegger's italics).

111. There is yet another ambiguity in Heidegger's notions of *das Man* and of authenticity. Heidegger suggests that being authentic implies both that one somehow distinguishes oneself from the mob and that one sees life as it really is. The assumption is, of course, that mostly we do not see life as it is. For an explanation of this assumption, see section 18, below.

112. SZ, § 40, p. 187: "Die Angst benimmt so dem Dasein die Möglichkeit, verfallend sich aus der 'Welt' und der öffentlichen Ausgelegtheit zu verstehen. Sie wirft das Dasein auf das zurück, worum es sich ängstet, sein eigentliches In-der-Welt-sein-können. Die Angst vereinzelt das Dasein auf sein eigenstes In-der-Welt-sein, das als verstehendes wesenhaft auf Möglichkeiten sich entwirft."

113. SZ, § 40, p. 188: "Die Angst vereinzelt und erschließt so das Dasein als 'solus ipse.' "

114. Cf. SZ, § 74, p. 385.

115. SZ, § 53, p. 266: "*selbst aber in der leidenschaftlichen, von den Illusionen des Man gelösten, faktischen, ihrer selbst gewissen und sich ängstenden* Freiheit zum Tode" (Heidegger's italics and emphasis).

116. Cf. GPh (GA 24), § 19, for an elaborate discussion of these points.

117. According to Dreyfus (1991), p. 6, it is likely that Heidegger was exposed to American pragmatism through Emil Lask. In any case, American pragmatism was well known in Germany before the Great War; cf. Safranski (1994), pp. 51ff. See for other pragmatist interpretations of Heidegger: Okrent (1988) and Rorty (1991).

118. Cf. Dewey (1929), p. 296: "Man as a natural creature acts as masses and molecules act; he lives as animals live, eating, fighting, fearing, reproducing."

119. In his later works, Heidegger explicitly rejected pragmatism. See, e.g., "Brief über den 'Humanismus,' " W, p. 183: "Die Herrschaft dieses Bezirkes (des homo animalis) ist der . . . Grund für die Verblendung und Willkür dessen, was man als Biologismus bezeichnet, aber auch dessen, was man unter dem Titel Pragmatismus kennt." In his transcendental, verificationist, and pragmatist interpretion of Heidegger's thought, Okrent tries to account for this text. See Okrent (1988), pp. 221–222. Yet Okrent's rational reconstruction of Heidegger leaves out too many crucial ingredients of Heidegger's philosophy; hence it fails as a historically adequate interpretation.

120. SZ, § 74, pp. 384–385: "Wenn aber das schicksalhafte Dasein als In-der-Welt-sein wesenhaft im Mitsein mit Anderen existiert, ist sein Geschehen ein Mitgeschehen und bestimmt als *Geschick*. Damit bezeichnen wir das Geschehen der Gemeinschaft, des Volkes.... In der Mitteilung und im Kampf wird die Macht des Geschickes erst frei. Das schicksalhafte Geschick des Daseins in und mit seiner 'Generation' macht das volle, eigentliche Geschehen des Daseins aus" (Heidegger's italics).

121. Schulz (1953–54), p. 76: "Demgegenüber sei hier zu zeigen gesucht, daß die in *Sein und Zeit* aufgeworfene Frage nach dem Sinn von Sein ... fragt nach dem Sinn dieses Daseins und nach gar nichts anderem." Cf. p. 212: "Sein und Nichts können ja ... deswegen nicht in der Weise des gegenständlichen Erkennens erfaßt werden, ... weil sie mein nicht zu vergegenständlichender Seinssinn sind."

122. Dreyfus (1991), p. 10: "what Heidegger has in mind when he talks about being is the intelligibility correlative with our everyday background practices."

123. In *Sein und Zeit*, Heidegger uses the word *Sinn* in many senses, which are not explicitly distinguished. Apart from the official sense of Sinn as "das ... Woraufhin des Entwurfs" (SZ, p. 151), he speaks of an "Abgrund der Sinnlosigkeit" (p. 152), of the *Sinn* of a word, and so on. Cf. Franzen (1975), p. 9.

124. SZ, § 1, p. 4.

125. SZ, § 1, first paragraph, p. 2.

126. See for Heidegger's discussion of the first prejudice SZ, § 1, fourth paragraph, p. 3.

127. We say, for instance, that Socrates *is* a man (substance), that he *was* older than Plato (relation), or that it *is* five o'clock (time). The verb "to be" is used in all categories, and everything may be said to be a "being."

128. SZ, § 7, p. 38: "Das Sein als Grundthema der Philosophie ist keine Gattung eines Seienden, und doch betrifft es jedes Seiende. Seine 'Universalität' ist höher zu suchen. Sein und Seinsstruktur liegen über jedes Seiende und jede mögliche seiende Bestimmtheit eines Seienden hinaus. *Sein ist das transcendens schlechthin.* ... Jede Erschließung von Sein als des transcendens ist *transcendentale* Erkenntnis" (Heidegger's italics). Cf. GPh (GA 24), p. 23: "Wir übersteigen das Seiende, um zum Sein zu gelangen. Bei diesem Überstieg versteigen wir uns nicht wiederum zu einem Seienden, das etwa hinter dem bekannten Seienden läge als irgendeine Hinterwelt."

129. Having discussed the question as to whether Heidegger uses *Sein* in SZ in any of the traditional senses (*esse* as *principium formale* in the Thomist sense, as *existentia*, as *essentia*, etc.), Franzen (1975) concludes that the question of being in SZ is a misleading flag that obscures Heidegger's real intentions: to show the difference between human existence and the realm of objective entities (*Vorhandenes*), and to correct the tendency of the scientific tradition to interpret the former in terms of the latter. According to Franzen, Heidegger would have done better to avoid the term "being" altogether, even though the very obscurity of this term would have been partly responsible for the success of SZ (pp. 8–16). Although Franzen's is one of the most perceptive books ever written on Heidegger, one should reject his verdict on Heidegger's question of being for methodological reasons. If one plays down the importance of this question, which Heidegger considered as the only question of philosophy, one gives away a great number of clues for interpreting Heidegger's works, clues that link Heidegger to the metaphysical tradition from Plato and Aristotle on. Because Franzen underplayed the importance of the question of being, he came to consider Heidegger merely as an antimodernist critic of his time, who tried to escape from actual history by postulating a deeper "history."

130. Cf. SZ, § 69c, p. 365: "Sofern Dasein sich zeitigt, *ist* auch eine Welt" (Heidegger's italics).

131. SZ, § 1, p. 4.

132. The possibility of defining terms by genus and difference depends on the fact that some attributes are "complex," and that attributes may form a hierarchy in which complexity decreases upwards. If we define "triangle" as a polygon having three sides, we mention the attribute that is next higher in the hierarchy than triangle, namely, polygon, and the difference that distinguishes triangles from other polygons, namely, that they have three sides. Obviously, "being" cannot be defined by this method, because "being" does not denote a complex attribute; indeed, it does not denote an attribute at all.

133. SZ, § 1, p. 4: "gefolgert kann nur werden: 'Sein' ist nicht so etwas wie Seiendes."

134. The expression "ontological difference" is used for the first time in 1927. See GPh (GA 24), part 2.

135. Cf. SZ, pp. 11 ("die Seinsart dieses Seienden [Mensch]"), 15 ("gemäß einer zu ihm, d. h. Dasein, gehörigen Seinsart"), 16 ("Seinsart des Daseins"), 43 ("Seinsart der Alltäglichkeit"), 55 ("Seinsart des In-Seins"), and pp. 57, 61, 87, and so on.

136. See, for example, SZ, § 2, p. 6: "und Sein besagt Sein von Seiendem"; § 3, p. 9: "Sein ist jeweils das Sein eines Seienden"; § 7, p. 37: "Sein aber je Sein von Seiendem ist."

137. WiM, p. 46: "daß das Sein nie west ohne das Seiende, daß niemals ein Seiendes ist ohne das Sein." This phrase reads in the fourth edition as follows: "daß das Sein wohl west ohne das Seiende, daß niemals aber ein Seiendes ist ohne das Sein." See Löwith (1965), pp. 40–43 for comments on this text. Cf. also Safranski (1994), pp. 382–383; Franzen (1975), p. 169, note 64; and Schulz (1953–54), pp. 211–213.

138. SZ, § 1, p. 4: "Allein diese durchschnittliche Verständlichkeit demonstriert nur die Unverständlichkeit," and so on.

139. SZ, § 5, p. 19. Cf. section 1, above.

140. SZ, § 2, p. 6: "*Das Gefragte* der auszuarbeitenden Frage ist das Sein, das, was Seiendes als Seiendes bestimmt, das, woraufhin Seiendes, mag es wie immer erörtert werden, je schon verstanden ist" (Heidegger's italics).

141. As the BT translation has it. The German expression is "sachlich-wissenschaftliche Vorrang." One should always remember that *Wissenschaft* embraces more than "science," and that, in Heidegger's terminology, there is a difference between *sachlich* and *objektiv.*

142. SZ, p. 9: "Mann kann aber zu wissen verlangen, wozu diese Frage dienen soll. Bleibt sie lediglich oder *ist* sie überhaupt nur das Geschäft einer freischwebenden Spekulation über allgemeinste Allgemeinheiten—*oder ist sie die prinzipiellste und konkreteste Frage zugleich?*" (Heidegger's italics); as the context makes clear, Heidegger holds that the second, italicized, alternative is correct.

143. For a conscientious study of Heidegger's notion of science, see Bast (1986b).

144. Cf. Husserl, *Ideen* I, §§ 1–17. Heidegger, who had a passion for German purism, sometimes uses the term *vorgängig* instead of *a priori.* See especially the sixth paragraph of section 3, and "Vom Wesen des Grundes," W, pp. 29–30.

145. Cf. SZ, p. 10: "Ihre echte Ausweisung und 'Begründung' erhalten diese Begriffe demnach nur in einer entsprechend vorgängigen Durchforschung des Sachgebietes selbst." As I argued before, Heidegger in *Sein und Zeit* endorsed Husserl's program of an

Ursprungsanalyse, a grounding of fundamental concepts by analyzing (the experiences of) their referents.

146. SZ, p. 10: "Solche Grundlegung der Wissenschaften unterscheidet sich grundsätzlich von der nachhinkenden 'Logik', die einen zufälligen Stand einer Wissenschaft auf ihre 'Methode' untersucht. Sie ist produktive Logik in dem Sinne, daß sie in ein bestimmtes Seinsgebiet gleichsam vorspringt, es in seiner Seinsverfassung allererst erschließt und die gewonnenen Strukturen den positiven Wissenschaften als durchsichtige Anweisungen des Fragens verfügbar macht."

147. SZ, p. 9: "Die eigentliche 'Bewegung' der Wissenschaften spielt sich ab in der mehr oder minder radikalen und ihr selbst durchsichtigen Revision der Grundbegriffe. Das Niveau einer Wissenschaft bestimmt sich daraus, wie weit sie einer Krisis ihrer Grundbegriffe *fähig* ist" (Heidegger's italics). Kuhn would probably object that the "level" a science has reached should rather be measured by the extent to which it is capable of *normal* research, in which progress seems more obvious and assured, although his notion of scientific revolutions as shifts in worldviews comes dangerously close to Heidegger. Cf. Kuhn (1970), p. 163.

148. In the parallel passage in *Logik* (GA 21, pp. 16–17), Heidegger refers to Einstein. Heidegger's "Kassel lectures" on "Wilhelm Dilthey's Research Work and the Present Struggle for a Historical Worldview" (16–21 April 1925) suggest that Heidegger reconciled the Husserlian and the "Kuhnian" elements of his philosophy of science by claiming that a science may have different "relationships" to its subject matter, and that a revolution in its fundamental concepts occurs when the scientist alters this relationship. Cf. Kisiel (1993), p. 359. This solution is also suggested in GbM of 1929–30 (GA 29/30), p. 277: "Jede Wissenschaft ist geschichtlich, weil wechselnd und wandelnd in der Grundstellung der Wissenschaft zu ihrem Gebiet, in der Fassung des Gebietes überhaupt." Such a fundamental stance (*Grundstellung*) would be a priori in the sense that it necessarily grounds empirical research and, indeed, experience, but not in the Kantian sense that it is necessarily true. This solution implies that Heidegger abandoned Husserl's notion of the a priori and anticipated Kuhn.

149. SZ, p. 11: "Ontologisches Fragen ist zwar gegenüber dem ontischen Fragen der positiven Wissenschaften ursprünglicher. Es bleibt aber selbst naiv und undurchsichtig, wenn seine Nachforschungen nach dem Sein des Seienden den Sinn von Sein überhaupt unerörtert lassen. . . . Die Seinsfrage zielt daher auf eine apriorische Bedingung der Möglichkeit nicht nur der Wissenschaften, die Seiendes als so und so Seiendes durchforschen und sich dabei je schon in einem Seinsverständnis bewegen, sondern auf die Bedingung der Möglichkeit der vor den ontischen Wissenschaften liegenden und sie fundierenden Ontologien."

150. See for an interpretation of Husserl's transcendental idealism: Philipse (1995).

151. *Sein und Zeit* may be read as an implicit polemic against Husserl, as many commentators have observed. When Heidegger attacks Descartes, he always has Husserl in mind as well, because Husserl explicitly situated his work within the Cartesian tradition. One reason for not assailing Husserl openly was that *Sein und Zeit* was written in order to enable Heidegger to become *Ordinarius* in Marburg, and that Husserl was Heidegger's main supporter. However, Heidegger gives a great number of hints that betray his real intentions. In the first paragraph of section 3, for instance, he uses Husserl's term *Fundamentalbetrachtung*, saying that a series of fundamental considerations is needed for work-

ing out the question of being. This implies that Heidegger rejects Husserl's *Fundamentalbetrachtung* of *Ideas* I.

152. Philipse (1995).

153. On 12 December 1926, Heidegger wrote to his friend Karl Jaspers on *Sein und Zeit*: "Wenn die Abhandlung 'gegen' jemanden geschrieben ist, dann gegen Husserl, der das auch sofort sah, aber sich von Anfang an zum Positiven hielt" (Hei/Ja, p. 71).

154. Husserl was somewhat sloppy in his terminology. He used "formal ontology" and "formal logic" also in the wide sense of the totality of the formal disciplines.

155. SZ, p. 38: "das transcendens schlechthin."

156. SZ, p. 9: "Sein ist jeweils das Sein eines Seienden"; p. 6: "und Sein besagt Sein von Seiendem."

157. SZ, p. 6: "Sofern das Sein das Gefragte ausmacht, und Sein besagt Sein von Seiendem, ergibt sich als das *Befragte* der Seinsfrage das Seiende selbst. Dieses wird gleichsam auf sein Sein hin abgefragt" (Heidegger's italics). However, as Heidegger says in the same paragraph: "Aber 'seiend' nennen wir vieles und in verschiedenem Sinne." In other words, there are many regions of being, and the entities of these regions *are* in different senses of the term.

158. Remember that Heidegger mentions Dasein in section 3 as an example of an ontological region or domain (SZ, p. 9).

159. SZ, p. 24: "Geschaffenheit aber im weitesten Sinne der Hergestelltheit von etwas ist ein wesentliches Strukturmoment des antiken Seinsbegriffes."

160. SZ, p. 6: "Aber 'seiend' nennen wir vieles und in verschiedenem Sinne."

161. SZ, p. 8: "Mit dem bisher Erörterten ist weder der Vorrang des Daseins erwiesen, noch. . . . Wohl aber hat sich so etwas wie ein Vorrang des Daseins gemeldet."

162. SZ, § 4, p. 14: "Das Dasein enthüllte sich hierbei als das Seiende, das zuvor ontologisch zureichend ausgearbeitet sein muß, soll das Fragen ein durchsichtiges werden," and so on.

163. SZ, p. 11: "Wissenschaft überhaupt kann als das Ganze eines Begründungszusammenhanges wahrer Sätze bestimmt werden. Diese Definition ist weder vollständig, noch trifft sie die Wissenschaft in ihrem Sinn."

164. SZ, p. 11: "Wissenschaften haben als Verhaltungen des Menschen die Seinsart dieses Seienden (Mensch). Dieses Seiende fassen wir terminologisch als *Dasein*" (Heidegger's italics).

165. SZ, p. 13: "Wissenschaften sind Seinsweisen des Daseins, in denen es sich auch zu Seiendem verhält, das es nicht selbst zu sein braucht. Zum Dasein gehört aber wesenhaft: Sein in einer Welt. Das dem Dasein zugehörige Seinsverständnis betrifft daher gleichursprünglich das Verstehen von so etwas wie 'Welt' und Verstehen des Seins des Seienden, das innerhalb der Welt zugänglich wird. Die Ontologien, die Seiendes von nicht daseinsmäßigem Seincharakter zum Thema haben, sind demnach in der ontischen Struktur des Daseins selbst fundiert und motiviert, die die Bestimmtheit eines vorontologischen Seinsverständnisses in sich begreift. Daher muß die *Fundamentalontologie*, aus der alle andern erst entspringen können, in der *existenzialen Analytik des Daseins* gesucht werden" (Heidegger's italics).

166. I argue in section 9, below, that there is an interpretation of the quoted passage that makes Heidegger's argument valid. But it is impossible to develop this interpretation on the mere basis of the introduction to *Sein und Zeit*.

167. "Brief über den 'Humanismus,' " W, p. 145 (BW, p. 217).

168. Whereas the Greek term *hermeneia* was used for translating the signs of the gods into human language, the Greeks used another word, *exēgēsis*, for the interpretation of obscure texts.

169. Cf. *Sprache*, pp. 121–122, where Heidegger suggests that this notion is crucial for understanding his own (later) conception of hermeneutics.

170. In philosophy, the term "hermeneutics" is commonly used for (the theory of) interpretation in general, and I will stick to this use. Theologians, however, often draw a contrast between hermeneutics and historical interpretation. They use the term "hermeneutics" for one type of interpretation only: the attempt to interpret sacred texts in such a way that they illuminate our present existence. Hermeneutics in this special sense is akin to what I will call applicative interpretation.

171. SZ, p. 37: "Phänomenologie des Daseins ist *Hermeneutik* in der ursprünglichen Bedeutung des Wortes, wonach es das Geschäft der Auslegung bezeichnet. Sofern nun aber durch die Aufdeckung des Sinnes des Seins und der Grundstrukturen des Daseins überhaupt der Horizont herausgestellt wird für jede weitere ontologische Erforschung des nicht daseinsmäßigen Seienden, wird diese Hermeneutik zugleich 'Hermeneutik' im Sinne der Ausarbeitung der Bedingungen der Möglichkeit jeder ontologischen Untersuchung" (Heidegger's italics).

172. Searle on the one hand claims that consciousness is a feature of the brain, so that it is material. On the other hand he asserts that consciousness is not ontologically reducible. The first assertion undermines the traditional material/mental dichotomy, because it says that the mental is in fact material without ceasing to be mental (see Searle [1992], pp. 13–16, 28). The second assertion (1992: ch. 5) seems to restore the traditional dichotomy. Indeed, it is difficult to see how Searle's view differs from property dualism.

173. Cf. Pöggeler (1963); Richardson (1963); Schulz (1953–54); Kockelmans (1984).

174. See Pöggeler (1963) for an overview, and PhrL (GA 60).

175. Pöggeler (1963), p. 37: "Heideggers Denken ist und bleibt von der Vermutung getragen, daß jenes Denken dem Verderben nicht entflieht, das sich den Bezug zur unverfügbaren Zukunft dadurch verstellt, daß es die Zeit berechnet und sich verfügbaren, 'objektiven' Gehalten zuwendet." Cf. Heidegger, PhrL (GA 60) for his lectures on Paul and Augustine of 1920–21. See for an English summary of these lectures Kisiel (1993), pp. 151–219.

176. Cf. SZ, p. 15: "Das Dasein ist zwar ontisch nicht nur nahe oder gar das nächste—wir *sind* es sogar je selbst. Trotzdem oder gerade deshalb ist es ontologisch das Fernste" (Heidegger's italics); cf. pp. 43, 132, 311. According to Heidegger, the traditional ontological alienation of Dasein from itself is rooted in an ontological structure of Dasein, the *falling* of Dasein.

177. "Nietzsches Wort 'Got ist tot,' " HW, p. 197: "Jede Erläuterung muß freilich die Sache nicht nur dem Text entnehmen, sie muß auch, ohne darauf zu pochen, unvermerkt Eigenes aus ihrer Sache dazu geben. Diese Beigabe ist dasjenige, was der Laie, gemessen an dem, was er für den Inhalt des Textes hält, stets als ein Hineindeuten empfindet und mit dem Recht, das er für sich beansprucht, als Willkür bemängelt. Eine rechte Erläuterung versteht jedoch den Text nie besser als dessen Verfasser ihn verstand, wohl aber anders. Allein dieses Andere muß so sein, daß es das Selbe trifft, dem der erläuterte Text nachdenkt." Cf., for a similar passage, N II, pp. 262–263: "In dem folgenden Text sind Darstellung und Auslegung ineinandergearbeitet, so daß nicht überall und sogleich deutlich wird, was den Worten Nietzsches entnommen und was dazugetan ist. Jede Auslegung muß frei-

lich nicht nur dem Text die Sache entnehmen können, sie muß auch, ohne darauf zu pochen, unvermerkt Eigenes aus *ihrer* Sache dazugeben können. Diese Beigabe ist dasjenige, was der Laie, gemessen an dem, was er ohne Auslegung für den Inhalt des Textes hält, notwendig als Hineindeuten und Willkür bemängelt" (Heidegger's italics). Interestingly, the term *Beigabe* is also used for funeral gifts. We will have occasion to wonder, with regard to Heidegger's interpretation of Nietzsche, to what extent this interpretation is meant to carry Nietzsche to the grave. Cf. section 15A, below. Related passages are to be found in many later writings. See, for instance, EM, p. 124: "Die eigentliche Auslegung muß Jenes zeigen, was nicht mehr in Worten dasteht und doch gesagt ist. Hierbei muß die Auslegung notwendig Gewalt brauchen. Das Eigentliche ist dort zu suchen, wo die wissenschaftliche Interpretation nichts mehr findet, die alles, was ihr Gehege übersteigt, als unwissenschaftlich brandmarkt"; cf. p. 134; "Der Spruch des Anaximander," HW, p. 343.

178. That the extra should stem from the concerns *of the interpreter* (Heidegger says: of the interpretation) is clearer in the parallel passage in N II, pp. 262–263.

179. Zimmerman (1990), p. 106. Cf. p. 113: "One is never sure whether Heidegger or Hölderlin is speaking, although Heidegger would have asserted that 'the matter itself' (*die Sache selbst*) was speaking."

180. Zimmerman (1990), p. 189. Löwith offers one of the best critiques of Heidegger's interpretation of Nietzsche in (1965), chapter 3.

181. "State of mind" is commonly used as a translation of *Befindlichkeit*, for instance, in BT. Cf. for similar criticisms Dreyfus (1991), pp. 168–169. Macquarrie (1994), pp. 23–24, comments on the translation in BT, and Kisiel (1993), p. 293, glosses on the origin of the notion of *Befindlichkeit* in Aristotle.

182. SZ, p. 137: "*Die Stimmung hat je schon das In-der-Welt-sein als Ganzes erschlossen und macht ein Sichrichten auf . . . allererst möglich*" (Heidegger's italics). Cf. on the translation of *Stimmung*: Dreyfus (1991), p. 169.

183. Cf. SZ, § 31, p. 143: "Im Verstehen liegt existenzial die Seinsart des Daseins als Sein-können . . . Dasein ist . . . primär Möglichsein," and so on, and pp. 143–144: "Die Möglichkeit als Existenzial dagegen ist die ursprünglichste und letzte positive ontologische Bestimmtheit des Daseins." *Possibility* in this sense is the mode of being of Dasein, and not a mere logical possibility. Cf. GbM (GA 29/30), p. 426: "Das Dasein verstehen meint: sich auf das Da-sein verstehen, Da-sein können."

184. One should remember that in the nineteenth-century debate on the relation between science and humanities (*Geisteswissenschaften*), *Verstehen* was often opposed to scientific *Erklären*. See Barash (1988) for the historical background of Heidegger's analysis of *Verstehen* and historicity. Heidegger's existential notion of a possibility, and of the primacy of existential possibility over actuality, is derived from Kierkegaard.

185. SZ, § 31, p. 145: "Das Entwerfen hat nichts zu tun mit einem Sichverhalten zu einem ausgedachten Plan, gemäß dem das Dasein sein Sein einrichtet, sondern als Dasein hat es sich je schon entworfen und ist, solange es ist, entwerfend." The German word *Entwurf* literally means outline, sketch, design, blueprint, or draft, and it is misleading as to what Heidegger wants to express as its standard translation "project." Sometimes I have hyphenated the word "project" ("pro-ject") in order to remind the reader that Heidegger uses the German words *Entwurf* and *entwerfen* in a special philosophical sense. Of course, Heidegger would say that planning in the ordinary sense is possible only because Dasein is fundamentally projective.

186. SZ, § 63, p. 313: "Keineswegs. Die formale Anzeige der Existenzidee war geleitet von dem im Dasein selbst liegenden Seinsverständnis," and so on; and: "Die angesetzte Existenzidee ist die existenziell unverbindliche Vorzeichnung der formalen Struktur des Daseinsverständnisses überhaupt."

187. SZ, § 32, p. 150: "Die Auslegung kann die dem auszulegenden Seienden zugehörige Begrifflichkeit aus diesem selbst schöpfen oder aber in Begriffe zwängen, denen sich das Seiende gemäß seiner Seinsart widersetzt." Cf. p. 153: "In ihm [dem Zirkel des Verstehens] verbirgt sich eine positive Möglichkeit ursprünglichsten Erkennens, die freilich in echter Weise nur dann ergriffen ist, wenn die Auslegung verstanden hat, daß ihre erste, ständige und letzte Aufgabe bleibt, sich jeweils Vorhabe, Vorsicht und Vorgriff nicht durch Einfälle und Volksbegriffe vorgeben zu lassen, sondern in deren Ausarbeitung aus den Sachen selbst her das wissenschaftliche Thema zu sichern." Cf. also pp. 314–315: "Oder hat dieses Voraus-setzen den Charakter des verstehenden Entwerfens, so zwar, daß die solches Verstehen ausbildende Interpretation das Auszulegende *gerade erst selbst zu Wort kommen läßt, damit es von sich aus entscheide, ob es als dieses Seiende die Seinsverfassung hergibt, auf welche es im Entwurf formalanzeigend erschlossen wurde?*" (Heidegger's italics).

188. Heidegger blurs many important distinctions that should be taken into account, such as the distinction between a conceptual structure and what is or can be expressed in terms of this structure.

189. SZ, § 63, pp. 311–312: "Charakter einer *Gewaltsamkeit*. Dieser Charakter zeichnet zwar die Ontologie des Daseins besonders aus, er eignet aber jeder Interpretation, weil das in ihr sich ausbildende Verstehen die Struktur des Entwerfens hat" (Heidegger's italics).

190. I am touching here on complex issues, because one cannot read anything into a text for the sake of applicative interpretation. Especially in criminal law, historical interpretation will determine the boundaries within which applicative interpretations are allowed, because "nullum crimen, nulla poena, sine previa lege poenali." In the case of tapping electricity, one will try to determine historically, for instance, whether the legislator would have included the case in his definition of theft had he known of the phenomenon of electricity.

191. Heidegger's pupil Hans-Georg Gadamer has elaborated this project in his voluminous *Wahrheit und Methode*, first published in 1960. Starting with an analysis of interpreting art, he argues against the historical school that application is inherent in all interpretation, even in purely historical and objective interpretations. However, I have not been able to discover one valid and noncircular argument substantiating this thesis in Gadamer's long-winded book. Gadamer assumes that the aim of interpretation is *agreement* with what the text says, instead of merely understanding it (Gadamer [1975], p. 277). Because he nevertheless says that what is determined in interpretation is the textual meaning (*Sinn*), he concludes that the real meaning (*der wirkliche Sinn*) of the text must be constituted ever anew by each reader or generation of readers (pp. 280, 282), and that the meaning of the text does not exist in itself (p. 269). His conception implies, as Heidegger also says, that interpreting a text is, and should be, understanding it *differently* from the way its author understood it (pp. 280, 292, 295, and passim). In interpretation there would be a fusion between the cultural horizon of the interpreter and that of the text (*Horizontverschmelzung*: pp. 289, 290, and passim). What Gadamer says is true for applicative interpretations. But his argument that what is true for applicative interpretations is necessarily true

for all interpretations is as defective as Heidegger's argument from which it derives. The *vitium originis* of Gadamer's doctrine is the absurd idea that the objective of historical interpretation is *agreement* with what the text says, and this assumption betrays the decisive influence of the tradition of religious Bible interpretation on Gadamer's views. In historical interpretation, we merely want to know what the meaning of the text was in its historical circumstances. We do not seek agreement with what Homer says on the Greek gods, for instance. Cf. Hirsch (1967), especially Appendix II, for a well-known critique of Gadamer's doctrine.

192. Cf. Löwith (1965), chapter 3, and Hirsch (1967) for similar critiques of the fashionable doctrine that it is impossible to understand what an author wants to say, and that, therefore, the meaning of texts has to be constituted by an interaction between the text and the projects or preconceptions of the reader or interpreter. Unfortunately, Hirsch's arguments are vitiated by a Cartesian or Husserlian conception of what it is to be an author. As a consequence, his views imply the very skeptical problems concerning knowledge of an author's intentions that they were meant to refute.

193. This sentence is a quote from Hirsch (1967), p. 57, who also insists on this distinction between textual meaning and significance.

194. I am using Wittgenstein's term *Lebensform* in order to stress a continuity in Austro-German thought.

195. SZ, p. 150: "Auslegung ist nie ein voraussetzungsloses Erfassen eines Vorgegebenen. Wenn sich die besondere Konkretion der Auslegung im Sinne der exakten Textinterpretation gern auf das beruft, was 'dasteht,' so ist das, was zunächst 'dasteht,' nichts anderes als die selbstverständliche, undiskutierte Vormeinung des Auslegers, die notwendig in jedem Auslegungsansatz liegt als das, was mit Auslegung überhaupt schon 'gesetzt,' das heißt in Vorhabe, Vorsicht, Vorgriff vorgegeben ist."

196. As Nuchelmans (1990) argued, theories of interpretation should start from the normal case in which we understand each other in actual conversation. There is no doubt that in this case the aim of understanding is to grasp what our interlocutor wants to say. If we fail to do so, we will ask him to make himself clear. There is no reason at all why the aim of understanding should be different when we read texts, even though it will be more difficult, and sometimes impossible, to attain this aim.

197. SZ, p. 153: "Das Entscheidende ist nicht, aus dem Zirkel heraus-, sondern in ihn nach der rechten Weise hineinzukommen."

198. According to Husserl, scientific philosophy should try to be presuppositionless, and one reason why Heidegger stresses so often the presuppositional nature of all understanding and knowledge is that he wanted to criticize Husserl. However, like Gadamer, Heidegger often tends to identify Husserl's conception of science and scientific philosophy, which derives from Descartes and ultimately from Aristotle, with science as it really is. Contemporary philosophers of science would reject Husserl's ideal of presuppositionlessness as profoundly mistaken.

199. SZ, p. 152: "Das Verstehen betrifft als die Erschlossenheit des Da immer das Ganze des In-der-Welt-seins. In jedem Verstehen von Welt ist Existenz mitverstanden und umgekehrt. Alle Auslegung bewegt sich ferner in der gekennzeichneten Vor-struktur. Alle Auslegung, die Verständnis beistellen soll, muß schon das Auszulegende verstanden haben."

200. Cf. SZ, § 2, p. 8. Cf. on this use of vagueness: Quine (1960), § 26, p. 127: "vagueness is an aid in coping with the linearity of discourse. An expositor finds that an understanding of some matter A is necessary preparation for an understanding of B, and yet that A cannot itself be expounded in correct detail without, conversely, noting certain exceptions and distinctions which require prior understanding of B. Vagueness, then, to the rescue. The expositor states A vaguely, proceeds to B, and afterward touches upon A, without ever having to call upon his reader to learn and unlearn any outright falsehood in the preliminary statement of A."

201. SZ, § 32, p. 152, third paragraph, from "Alle Auslegung bewegt sich ferner in der gekennzeichneten Vor-struktur" to "Sofern man dieses Faktum des Zirkels im Verstehen nicht wegbringt, muß sich die Historie mit weniger strengen Erkenntnismöglichkeiten abfinden."

202. SZ, p. 152, last sentence: "Idealer wäre es freilich auch nach der Meinung der Historiker selbst, wenn der Zirkel vermieden werden könnte und Hoffnung bestünde, einmal eine Historie zu schaffen, die vom Standort des Betrachters so unabhängig wäre wie vermeintlich die Naturerkenntnis."

203. SZ, § 32, p. 153. One should read this whole page, beginning with the italicized statement: "*Aber in diesem Zirkel ein vitiosum sehen und nach Wegen Ausschau halten, ihn zu vermeiden, ja ihn nur als unvermeidliche Unvollkommenheit 'empfinden,' heißt das Verstehen von Grund aus mißverstehen.*" I paraphrased the following two sentences in the text: "Dieser Zirkel des Verstehens ist nicht ein Kreis, in dem sich eine beliebige Erkenntnisart bewegt, sondern er ist der Ausdruck der existenzialen *Vor-struktur* des Daseins selbst" (Heidegger's italics), and: "Seiendes, dem es als In-der-Welt-sein um sein Sein selbst geht, hat eine ontologische Zirkelstruktur." Heidegger suggests that the ideal of objectivity is a consequence of a *verlaufen*, that is, of being lost: "Nicht darum geht es, Verstehen und Auslegung einem bestimmten Erkenntnisideal anzugleichen, das selbst nur eine Abart von Verstehen ist, die sich in die rechtmäßige Aufgabe einer Erfassung des Vorhandenen in seiner wesenhaften Unverständlichkeit verlaufen hat" (SZ, p. 153). In other words, the ideal of objectivity pertains to natural science, which investigates "meaningless" natural phenomena. But how can Heidegger claim both that the scientific enterprise is legitimate and that it has gone astray (*verlaufen*)?

204. SZ, § 32, p. 153: "Der Zirkel darf nicht zu einem vitiosum und sei es auch zu einem geduldeten herabgezogen werden. In ihm verbirgt sich eine positive Möglichkeit ursprünglichsten Erkennens, die freilich in echter Weise nur dann ergriffen ist, wenn die Auslegung verstanden hat, daß ihre erste, ständige und letzte Aufgabe bleibt, sich jeweils Vorhabe, Vorsicht und Vorgriff nicht durch Einfälle und Volksbegriffe vorgeben zu lassen, sondern in deren Ausarbeitung aus den Sachen selbst her das wissenschaftliche Thema zu sichern." But when the conceptual structures are developed on the basis of the things themselves, can they still be called a *Vorgriff* in the sense of Heidegger's projective theory of interpretation?

205. I stress again the term *verlaufen*: to go astray.

206. Kisiel (1993) overstates the case where he says (p. 6) that "the state of Heidegger scholarship . . . is still very much like that of our factual knowledge of the pre-Socratics."

207. I also used texts published elsewhere, such as the "Natorp essay" (PIA), the materials published by Schneeberger (1962), and the summaries of unpublished materials by authors such as Kisiel (1993).

CHAPTER II
ANALYSIS

1. I am quoting from Dreyfus and Hall (1992a), p. 4; cf. section 6, below, for discussion. I have argued elsewhere that Hall's interpretations of Husserl's transcendental idealism suffer from a tendency to substitute wishful thinking for interpretation. This is a danger concerning the interpretation of Heidegger's oeuvre as well. See Philipse (1995), pp. 239–242.

2. Dreyfus (1991), p. 10; cf. pp. xi, 4, 7, 11, 32, 343, note 3, and passim.

3. Dreyfus (1991), p. 11. Cf. for a similar interpretation: Okrent (1988).

4. Cf. Dreyfus and Hall (1992a), p. 2: "Thus, like Ludwig Wittgenstein, Heidegger finds that the only ground for the intelligibility of thought and action that we have or need is in the everyday practices themselves, not in some hidden process of thinking and of history." Dreyfus seems to be conscious of the somewhat forced nature of his interpretation. For on p. 144 he writes: "Up to this point in my commentary, my Wittgensteinian interpretation of being-in-the-world in terms of shared background practices may seem an alien imposition on Heidegger. In this chapter, however, my interpretation and Heidegger's statements converge." It is hardly sufficient for an adequate interpretation that it is supported by the interpreted texts in one chapter only.

5. Cf. Dreyfus (1991), p. 6: "in this sense Heidegger can be viewed as radicalizing the insights already contained in the writings of such pragmatists as Nietzsche, Peirce, James, and Dewey"; and Okrent (1988), pp. 280–281: "With the possible exception of the emphasis on temporality, the principal doctrines of the early Heidegger concerning the primarily practical character of intentionality are hardly unique in the twentieth century. A whole series of philosophers, including John Dewey, the late Wittgenstein, and the contemporary American neo-Pragmatists—who arise out of a strictly analytic context—have made very similar points."

6. Dreyfus (1991), p. 343, note 3. Cf. Okrent (1988), part 2, for a pragmatist reading of the later Heidegger.

7. Cf., for instance, WiM, *Nachwort* (1943), p. 46.

8. Dreyfus and Hall (1992a), pp. 3–4, in Dreyfus and Hall (1992). After I wrote this chapter, Dreyfus published a paper in Guignon (1993), in which he acknowledges the religious dimension in the later Heidegger, thereby implicitly cancelling his earlier interpretation (1991).

9. Löwith (1965), p. 111: "Was aber allem von Heidegger je Gesagten hintergründig zugrunde liegt und viele aufhorchen und hinhorchen läßt, ist ein Ungesagtes: das *religiöse Motiv*, das sich zwar vom christlichen Glauben abgelöst hat, aber gerade in seiner dogmatisch ungebundenen Unbestimmtheit um so mehr diejenigen anspricht, die nicht mehr gläubige Christen sind, aber doch religiös sein möchten" (Löwith's italics). I count Löwith's among the unitarian interpretations because he assumes that there is *one* fundamental notion that is the basis of everything Heidegger wrote, the religious theme, although Löwith is sharply aware of the various transformations in Heidegger's philosophy.

10. After having written this section, I discovered that several authors hinted at a patchwork view. Kisiel (1993) writes, for instance, that his book about the genesis of SZ "now becomes the inside story of the movement of drafts and redrafts, the shuffling of texts . . . still bearing signs of incomplete integration, with the gaps sometimes still showing" (etc.,

pp. 312–313). Franzen (1975) concludes on p. 112: "In Heideggers Seinsbegriff sind offenbar Elemente von verschiedenster Herkunft eingegangen. . . . Um eine Synthese, gar um eine gelungene, handelt es sich dabei freilich nicht." Finally, Bast (1986a) explicitly argues that SZ is a patchwork. However, he does not grasp the nature of the burden of proof for the patchwork theorist.

11. See Kisiel (1993) for a survey.

12. For example, in SZ, § 31, where Heidegger writes phrases such as: "Die mit der Erschlossenheit des Da existenzial seiende Sicht *ist* das Dasein gleichursprünglich nach den gekennzeichneten Grundweisen seines Seins . . . als Sicht auf das Sein als solches, umwillen dessen das Dasein je ist, wie es ist" (p. 146, Heidegger's italics). This "being as such," for the sake of which Dasein is as it is, is Dasein itself.

13. Franzen (1975) concludes that Heidegger's attempt to express his philosophical concerns in terms of "being" was altogether unfortunate (pp. 8–16).

14. Cf. Bast (1986a) for two other examples of contradictions in SZ.

15. Zimmerman (1990), p. 70.

16. Zimmerman (1990), p. 99. Heidegger agreed with Hitler that art and polis have a direct relationship, but he saw this relationship differently (ibid., pp. 99–100). See for Hitler's speech of 11 September 1935 in Nürnberg: Domarus (1973), vol. 1, pp. 527–528.

17. Zimmerman (1990), p. 94. One should not forget that by 1935 nearly all important German novelists had emigrated from Germany, being more conscious of the criminal and abject nature of Hitler and his minions than Heidegger, the philosopher of authenticity, ever became. Within the domain of literature, there was nobody left to effectuate Hitler's and Heidegger's ideas on art. This was different in architecture, and Hitler held his yearly *Kunstrede* on 11 September 1935 after having laid the first stone of a colossal conference hall. Incidentally, Zimmerman's summary of Hitler's speech is misleading. Hitler did not say that Nazism would lead the German people out of the wasteland of modernity (as if Hitler had read T. S. Eliot!). He rather argued that a great people founding a nation that will last a thousand years needs great and monumental art.

18. EM, pp. 28–29: "Dieses Europa, in heilloser Verblendung immer auf dem Sprunge, sich selbst zu erdolchen, liegt heute in der großen Zange zwischen Rußland auf der einen und Amerika auf der anderen Seite. Rußland und Amerika sind beide, metaphysisch gesehen, dasselbe; dieselbe trostlose Raserei der entfesselten Technik und der bodenlosen Organisation des Normalmenschen. . . . Wir liegen in die Zange. Unser Volk erfährt als in der Mitte stehend den schärfsten Zangendruck, das nachbarreichste Volk und so das gefährdetste Volk und in all dem das metaphysische Volk."

19. Jünger (1932) and (1930). Cf. Heidegger, SdU, p. 24: "Im Jahre 1930 war Ernst Jüngers Aufsatz über 'Die totale Mobilmachung' erschienen; in diesem Aufsatz kündigten sich die Grundzüge des 1932 erschienenen Buches *Der Arbeiter* an. In kleinem Kreis habe ich damals mit meinem Assistenten Brock diese Schriften durchgesprochen und zu zeigen versucht, wie sich darin ein wesentliches Verständnis der Metaphysik Nietzsches ausspricht."

20. Zimmerman (1990), pp. 46–93.

21. Farias (1987), pp. 111–112ff., 133ff., 152ff., 156ff., 200, and 202ff. Sluga (1993) shows that many German philosophers aspired to the role of official Party philosopher. The National Socialist revolution politicized the strife between philosophical factions in Germany, but it was not in the interest of the Party to resolve this strife. That Heidegger was disillusioned by Nazism after the Röhm purge in 1934 had been suggested already by

Gerhard Ritter, at the occasion of the *Bereinigungsausschuß* for which Heidegger had to justify himself on 23 July 1945. See Safranski (1994), p. 388.

22. Zimmerman (1990), p. 104.

23. Cf., again, Zimmerman (1990), chapter 6, and SdU, p. 24.

24. Safranski (1994), chapter 23; cf. Herf (1984).

25. Cf. Heidegger, "Bauen Wohnen Denken" (1952), in VA.

26. Zimmerman (1990), p. 239.

27. Zimmerman (1990), pp. 239–240. Cf. Heidegger, "Das Ding" (1951), in VA.

28. Neither was Nietzsche. It might be argued that Nietzsche's ethics of the *Übermensch* reflects the martial morality of the Prussian military class, which became a dominant power in the unification of Germany under Bismarck. In EM (p. 6), Heidegger claims that the philosopher is necessarily untimely: "Alles wesentliche Fragen der Philosophie bleibt notwendig unzeitgemäß."

29. As Zimmerman (1990) observes, "in regard to many thinkers to whom Heidegger was greatly indebted, he had the tendency either to discount their influence upon him or to show that he had thought more deeply than they had about a given topic" (p. 83).

30. Philipse (1994a).

31. Bourdieu (1988) aptly comments on what he calls Heidegger's polyphonic talent: "Ce qui donne à la pensée de Heidegger son caractère exceptionnellement polyphonique et polysémique, c'est sans doute son aptitude à parler harmoniquement dans plusieurs registres à la fois" (p. 69; cf. p. 58).

32. SD, p. 81, and section 1, above.

33. SZ, § 1. This is an astonishing claim, because most key concepts of Aristotle's ontology were rejected during the scientific revolution, especially the notions of Form and of a final cause. Some philosophers even rejected the notion of substance.

34. Only if the primacy of the question of being can be established by philosophical arguments will we be able to refute skeptics regarding Heidegger's question of being. The skeptic will claim, for instance, that "Existence" and "Being," as they occur in traditional metaphysics, are hypostatized forms of certain meanings of "is." Because these occurrences of "is" are in fact wholly unnecessary, and do not appear in symbolic logical languages, the skeptic will regard Heidegger's question of being as a specimen of teutonic obscurantism. Cf. Russell (1962), p. 61.

35. SZ, § 7, pp. 38–39.

36. Cf. for the notion of *Wiederholung*: SZ, §§ 68b and 74; PGZ (GA 20), pp. 187–188; KM, p. 198.

37. See GA 61, 62, 17, 18, 19, 21, 22, and 24, respectively.

38. See Kisiel (1993), appendix B and part 2.

39. PIA, see postscript by the editor. According to the editor, the manuscript counts fifty-one pages (PIA, p. 273). According to Sheehan (1981b), p. 11, there are forty pages, whereas Heidegger wrote to Karl Jaspers on 19 November 1922 that there were sixty pages (Hei/Ja, p. 34). Cf. Kisiel (1993), pp. 248–271 for an English summary of the essay, and Michael Baur, *Man and World* 25 (1992), pp. 355–393 for a translation.

40. Sheehan (1981b), p. 12.

41. PIA, p. 270; *Sprache*, p. 95: "im Sommer 1923. Damals begann ich die ersten Niederschriften zu *Sein und Zeit*."

42. According to Kisiel (1993), this is the first manuscript with this structure that Heidegger wrote (p. 249). Kisiel also stresses the importance of the Natorp essay: "Just as the

extraordinary semester of 1919 is the zero-point of Heidegger's entire career of thought, in like fashion, this version of the *Einleitung* is the zero-point of the specific project of BT" (p. 250); "The importance of this seminal text thus cannot be overestimated" (p. 251). Kisiel (1993) appeared after I wrote chapter 2 of my book, and his work is an important confirmation of many points of my interpretation.

43. PIA, p. 238/3: "Der Gegenstand der philosophischen Forschung ist das menschliche Dasein als von ihr befragt auf seinen Seinscharakter"; GA 60, p. 8: "Das Problem des Selbstverständnisses der Philosophie wurde immer zu leicht genommen. Faßt man dies Problem radikal, so findet man, daß die Philosophie der faktischen Lebenserfahrung entspringt. Und dann springt sie in der faktischen Lebenserfahrung in diese selbst zurück. Der Begriff der faktischen Lebenserfahrung ist fundamental" (text of the fall of 1920). Cf., however, GA 63, p. 60, where Heidegger defines philosophy as "ontologische Phänomenologie."

44. PIA, pp. 238–239/3–5. Cf. also p. 246/15: "die Philosophie (ist) . . . der genuine explizite Vollzug der Auslegungstendenz der Grundbewegtheiten des Lebens, in denen es diesem um sich selbst und sein Sein geht." Heidegger developed this notion of philosophy also during his course of the winter semester 1920–21 and the course of the winter semester 1921–22. See Kisiel (1993), pp. 152–156, and GA 63, p. 2.

45. This is one aspect of Heidegger's notion of retrieval (*Wiederholung*) in SZ (§§ 68b, 74). Heidegger's idea seems to be that we can derive the contents of our most authentic projects from the past only, so that we have to "choose our hero" on the basis of an explicit retrieval of a heroic past. Obviously, Heidegger was influenced by Nietzsche's notion of a monumental history, developed in Nietzsche (UB II).

46. PIA, p. 248/18: "In der Idee der Faktizität liegt es, daß je nur die *eigentliche*— im Wortsinne verstanden: *die eigene*—die der eigenen Zeit und Generation der genuine Gegenstand der Forschung ist" (Heidegger's italics). I suppose that an expression such as "factical life" or "perspective" is missing in this sentence. Here we recognize the historicist conception of authenticity I referred to in section 6, above.

47. PIA, pp. 248–249/19–21. As Heidegger says, "*Die Hermeneutik bewerkstelligt ihre Aufgabe nur auf dem Wege der Destruktion*" (PIA, p. 249/20, Heidegger's italics).

48. There are crucial differences, however. In PIA, the indication of the hermeneutical situation aims at elucidating our present situation, whereas Heidegger in SZ endorsed Husserl's essentialism: the fundamental ontology of Dasein claims to elucidate "essential structures," which are not limited to a particular historical situation. Cf. section 8C, below, *in finem*.

49. PIA, p. 261/39, last paragraph: "Den Weg, auf dem Aristoteles überhaupt den Zugang zu dem Phänomen des reinen Verstehens gewinnt, und die Art der Auslegung derselben; beide sind charakteristisch für den Grundsinn der 'Philosophie.' "

50. PIA, p. 262/40. Heidegger is not very precise in his analysis of Aristotle's text. In particular, he does not comment on the important fact that Aristotle characterizes *sophia* by means of an analogy: just as the third degree of knowledge, *technē*, is better than the second degree, *empeiria*, because in the third degree we come to know the causes of a phenomenon, so the fifth degree, *sophia*, is better than the fourth, *epistēmē*, because *epistēmē* assumes first principles that *sophia* knows. But if the argument is one by analogy only, one cannot say that Aristotle's notion of *sophia* is the ultimate stage of a series of degrees of knowledge that is essentially practical.

51. PIA, p. 262/40–41: "In seiner Tendenz auf das Mehr an Hinsehen kommt das faktische Leben dazu, die Sorge der Verrichtung aufzugeben. Das Womit des verrichtenden Umgangs wird zum Worauf des bloßen Hinsehens." In a similar way, Heidegger tries to trace the genesis of *Vorhandenheit* from *Zuhandenheit* in SZ, § 69b.

52. PIA, p. 263/42: "Aristoteles gewinnt also den Sinn der 'Philosophie' *durch Auslegung einer faktischen Sorgensbewegtheit auf ihre letzte Tendenz.* Dieser rein hinsehende Umgang erweist sich aber als ein solcher, der in seinem Worauf gerade das Leben selbst, in dem er ist, nicht mehr mit sieht" (Heidegger's italics).

53. PIA, p. 263/42: "Die Idee des Göttlichen ist aber für Aristoteles nicht in der Explikation eines in religiöser Grunderfahrung zugänglich gewordenen Gegenständlichen erwachsen, das *Theion* ist vielmehr der Ausdruck für den *höchsten* Seinscharakter, der sich in der ontologischen Radikalisierung der Idee des Bewegtseienden ergibt" (Heidegger's italics).

54. PIA, p. 263/42: "Das besagt aber: Die entscheidende Seins-Vorhabe, das Seiende in Bewegung, und die bestimmte ontologische Explikation *dieses* Seienden sind die Motivquellen für die ontologischen Grundstrukturen, die späterhin das göttliche Sein im spezifisch christlichen Sinne (actus purus), das innergöttliche Leben (Trinität) und damit zugleich das Seinsverhältnis Gottes zum Menschen und damit den eigenen Seinssinn des Menschen selbst entscheidend bestimmen. Die christliche Theologie und die in ihrem Einfluß stehende philosophische 'Spekulation' und die in solchen Zusammenhängen immer mit erwachsende Anthropologie *sprechen in erborgten, ihrem eigenen Seinsfelde fremden Kategorien*" (Heidegger's italics).

55. PIA, p. 246/16: "Die Problematik der Philosophie betrifft das *Sein* des faktischen Lebens. Philosophie ist in dieser Hinsicht *prinzipielle Ontologie*, so zwar, daß die bestimmten einzelnen welthaften regionalen Ontologien von der Ontologie der Faktizität her Problemgrund und Problemsinn empfangen" (Heidegger's italics). Cf. SZ, § 4, p. 13: "Die Ontologien, die Seiendes von nicht daseinsmäßigem Seinscharakter zum Thema haben, sind demnach in der ontischen Struktur des Daseins selbst fundiert und motiviert, die die Bestimmtheit eines vorontologischen Seinsverständnisses in sich begreift. Daher muß die *Fundamentalontologie*, aus der alle andern erst entspringen können, in der *existenzialen Analytik des Daseins* gesucht werden" (Heidegger's italics).

56. Cf. Met. II.1, 993b: 27–30 (*alēthestatos*); Met. IV.3, 1005b: 12ff. (*diapseusthēnai adunaton*; *gnōrimōtatos*; *anangkaios*). According to Met. I.2, first philosophy is theoretical and not practical.

57. Cf. Reiner (1954).

58. They are *ta malista katholou*: Met. I.2, 982a: 7ff. and 22ff.

59. Met IV.1. The term "ontology," derived from the Greek expression *to on hēi on*, was introduced by Goclenius in 1613.

60. Met. IV.2, 1003b: 5–20; Met. VII.1, 1028a: 15ff.; Met. VIII.1, 1042a: 5; Met. XII.1, 1069a: 18ff.

61. Met. VI.1 and Met. XI.7.

62. Natorp (1888).

63. Jaeger (1923); cf. Routila (1969), pp. 27ff., and Patzig (1960–61), pp. 185–187.

64. GAP (GA 22), p. 180: "Doppelbegriff der Fundamentalwissenschaft ist nicht eine Verlegenheit oder das Zusammenbestehen zweier verschiedener Ansätze, die nichts zu tun haben miteinander, sondern immer sachliche Notwendigkeit des Problems, das Aristoteles nicht bewältigte, als solches auch nicht formulierte, weshalb es künftig auch völlig in Vergessenheit geriet." Because Heidegger defines philosophy in these lectures as the criti-

cal discipline that distinguishes (*krinein*) between beings and being (§§ 3–4), and because he tries to show that Greek philosophy never succeeded in making this distinction clearly, even though it implicitly aimed at doing so, I assume that the problem to which Heidegger refers in the quotation is the problem of the ontological difference.

65. An. post. I.10; cf. Heath (1925), pp. 117–124.

66. Heidegger explicitly endorses these two theses in his lecture on "Phenomenology and Theology" of 1927, W (2nd ed.), p. 48.

67. SZ, § 3; "Vom Wesen des Grundes," W, pp. 29–30; "Phänomenologie und Theologie," W (2nd ed.), pp. 43–78.

68. SdU, p. 12: "Wissenschaft ist das fragende Standhalten inmitten des sich ständig verbergenden Seienden im Ganzen."

69. SdU, pp. 15–16. After having dealt with *Arbeitsdienst, Wehrdienst,* and *Wissensdienst* on p. 15, Heidegger concludes on p. 16: "Das mithandelnde Wissen um das Volk [i.e., *Arbeitsdienst*], das sich bereithaltende Wissen um das Geschick des Staates [i.e., *Wehrdienst*] schaffen in eins mit dem Wissen um den geistigen Auftrag [i.e., *Wissensdienst*] erst das ursprüngliche und volle Wesen der Wissenschaft" (elucidations mine). See for discussion: section 10A, below.

70. SdU, p. 11: "Alle Wissenschaft ist Philosophie, mag sie es wissen und wollen— oder nicht. Alle Wissenschaft bleibt jenem Anfang der Philosophie verhaftet," and so on.

71. HW, p. 70: "Worin liegt das Wesen der neuzeitlichen Wissenschaft? Welche Auffassung des Seienden und der Wahrheit begründet dieses Wesen? Gelingt es, auf den metaphysischen Grund zu kommen, der die Wissenschaft als neuzeitliche begründet."

72. "Der Ursprung des Kunstwerkes," HW, p. 50: "Wieder eine andere Weise, wie Wahrheit wird, ist das Fragen des Denkens, das als Denken des Seins dieses in seiner Fragwürdigkeit nennt. Dagegen ist die Wissenschaft kein ursprüngliches Geschehen der Wahrheit, sondern jeweils der Ausbau eines schon offenen Wahrheitsbereiches."

73. SD, p. 65: "Indes reden die Wissenschaften bei der unumgänglichen Supposition ihrer Gebietskategorien immer noch vom Sein des Seienden. Sie sagen es nur nicht. Sie können zwar die Herkunft aus der Philosophie verleugnen, sie jedoch nie abstoßen. Denn immer spricht in der Wissenschaftlichkeit der Wissenschaften die Urkunde ihrer Geburt aus der Philosophie." Cf. WhD, p. 90: "Die Philosophie läßt sich weder auf die Historie, d. h. auf die Geschichtswissenschaft, noch überhaupt auf eine Wissenschaft gründen. Denn jede Wissenschaft ruht auf Voraussetzungen, die niemals wissenschaftlich begründbar sind, wohl dagegen philosophisch erweisbar. Alle Wissenschaften gründen in der Philosophie, aber nicht umgekehrt."

74. See section 4.5, above, and SZ, § 3. Cf. also PGZ (GA 20), § 1, pp. 3–6. Heidegger argues in this section of PGZ that the fact of scientific revolutions (*Krisis der Wissenschaften*) shows that philosophy must ground the sciences anew, because opening up a region of beings requires a type of experience and exploration *fundamentally different* from those that dominate the sciences (PGZ, p. 4). In other words, Heidegger uses the fact of scientific revolutions to justify the Aristotelian conception of science in its Husserlian variety, whereas most philosophers of science consider the fact of scientific revolutions as a *refutation* of this conception.

75. Perhaps Carl Braig's book, *Vom Sein—Abriß der Ontologie* (1896), was the first philosophical book that Heidegger studied. See "Mein Weg in die Phänomenologie," SD, p. 81, and Richard Schaeffler, "Heidegger und die Theologie," in Gethmann-Siefert and Pöggeler (1988). The motto of Braig (1896), which was taken from Bonaventura's *Itinera-*

rium mentis in Deum (V, 3.4), sounds astonishingly similar to what Heidegger later says on the "ontological difference": "Sed sicut oculus, intentus in varias colorum differentias, lucem, per quam videt cetera, non videt, et si videt, non advertit: sic oculus mentis nostrae... assuefactus ad tenebras entium et phantasmata sensibilium, cum ipsam lucem summi *esse* intuitur, videtur sibi nihil videre," and so on (pp. v–vi). In other words, we do not see *Being* (God) itself because we are blinded by the habit of perceiving *beings*. Braig's work (1896) reaches its climax in section 30, where he argues that the totality of beings must have an *Urgrund* (ultimate foundation) in the *Ureine* (the ultimately One), who by its *absolute Selbstunterscheidung* (absolute autodistinction) creates the totality of beings. See Braig (1896), p. 157.

76. Cf. An. post. I.10.

77. In Greek: *"to on legetai pollachōs."* See Met. IV.2, 1003a: 33; Met VI.2, 1026a: 33–34; Met. VII.1, 1028a: 10; Met. VIII.2, 1042b: 26–1043a: 2; Met. XI.3, 1060b: 33 and 1061b: 13–14; and Met. XIV.2, 1089a: 7–10. The *pollachōs*-dictum usually opens a chapter and introduces a pivotal passage. Aristotle does not distinguish between propositions about the *term* "being" and propositions about beings, because he assumes a harmony between reality and thought, so that beings show themselves as they are in the ways in which we speak about them. For this reason, I will not consistently distinguish between these two kinds of propositions in my summary of Aristotle's doctrine either.

78. See Met. VI.2–3.

79. See Met. VI.4.

80. One should raise the question as to whether these differences are not due to the predicates or subject-expressions rather than to the copula. In his logic, Frege absorbs the copula into the predicate, which is treated as (the expression of a) function. Quine accuses of "false predilections" those philosophers who hold that "to be" in the sense of existential quantification is "used in many ways," depending on ontological regions. Philosophers who indulge in such "philosophical double talk" allegedly want to repudiate an ontology (say of abstract objects) while enjoying its benefits. See Quine (1960), § 49; and Heidegger, EM, pp. 68–69.

81. Cf. Ackrill (1963), p. 71.

82. Cf. Patzig (1975), pp. 40–41, and Patzig (1979), p. 40. Cf. Frege (1892), and De Rijk (1988), p. 6: "On this interpretation the semantic element is a crucial factor in the search for *ousia*. When things are introduced into discourse it is always their categorization that determines what precisely will be the speaker's (or hearer's) focus of interest. Naming things and things as named such and such are under discussion, not things themselves irrespective of the way they are designated."

83. I am glossing over three problems of interpretation here. Aristotle does not use the Greek word *pollachōs* in the text of *Categories* I, but I am assuming that in fact he is giving a classification of ways in which something may be named, and that both homonymy and paronymy are cases of names used *pollachōs* (in different ways). Furthermore, I am identifying paronymy with the *pros hen* relation of *Metaphysics*. This identification is somewhat hypothetical, for although in *Categories* I, Aristotle defines paronymy as the case in which we derive the name of one thing from the name of another thing by giving a new form to the original name, as in "grammarian," which is derived from "grammar," he does not use the expression *pros hen*. Nevertheless, I think that this hypothesis is plausible. Finally, I am assuming that in *Metaphysics*, Aristotle applied his analysis of names of

the *Categories* to the expression *to on*, so that he treated this expression as a name in the loose sense of the word.

84. I am following Routila (1969) in this respect.

85. The notion of analogy was developed originally in Greek mathematics. Three different notions of analogy were distinguished: the "arithmetical" analogy of differences (the difference between 10 and 6 is analogous to or the same as the difference between 6 and 2); the "geometrical" analogy between fractions (8:4 = 4:2); and the "harmonical" analogy, which combines the first two analogies: 9 is related to 6 as 6 is related to 4, because 6 is two-thirds of 9 and 4 is two-thirds of 6. In all cases of analogy, there is a similarity (or even identity) between *relations*. For this reason, it is confusing to call paronymy a case of analogy, as the Scholastics used to do. This misnomer is responsible for the conceptual obscurities in the medieval doctrine of the *analogia entis*, which is a case of paronymy and not of analogy: creatures are called "good" or "beings" because "good" and "being" apply primarily to their creator, God, who *is* par excellence. There is at least one text in which Aristotle uses the term "analogy" for the relation of paronymy: Met. V.6, 1016b: 33–34.

86. Cf. GAP (GA 22), § 55, where Heidegger identifies without further ado the unity of analogy with the unity of what Aristotle calls *pros hen*. What Aristotle means by *pros hen* is paronymy. Clearly, Heidegger is influenced by the Thomist tradition on this point.

87. Cf. Met. IX.6, 1048a: 31–1048b: 7. Cf. for these distinctions Routila (1969).

88. Met. V.6, 1016b: 33–34.

89. Met. XIV.6, 1093b: 16–18.

90. An. post. I.10, 76a: 37–40; cf. An. post. I.11, 77a: 26ff.

91. According to Ackrill (1963), pp. 77–81, there are two ways of interpreting Aristotle's categories, both suggested by the text of Cat. 4 and by Top. I.9, the only other early text in which Aristotle lists the ten categories. One is that the categories are highest genera, the other that they are classes of ways of saying something of a concrete particular. Cf. on this issue also De Rijk (1980) and (1988); I profited considerably from De Rijk's comments on the penultimate draft of this section.

92. Met. XI.3, 1060b: 31–1061 a: 10; and Met. XII.1, 1069a: 18–27.

93. GAP (GA 22), p. 180. Cf. Aristotle, Met. VI.1, 1026a: 23–33; Met. XI.7, 1064b: 7–14.

94. Routila (1969).

95. Met. XII.6, 1071b: 5–12.

96. As Aristotle says in Met. XII.9, 1075a: 2–5, the act of thinking and the object of thought are not different in the case of things that contain no matter.

97. PIA, pp. 238/2–239/5, and 246/15–16. Cf. GA 60, p. 15: "Die faktische Lebenserfahrung verdeckt immer wieder selbst eine etwa auftauchende philosophische Tendenz durch ihre Indifferenz und Selbstgenügsamkeit," and so on.

98. See PIA, the instructive footnote on p. 246/15: " 'Atheistisch' nicht im Sinne einer Theorie als Materialismus oder dergleichen. Jede Philosophie, die in dem, was sie ist, sich selbst versteht, muß als das faktische Wie der Lebensauslegung gerade dann, wenn sie dabei noch eine 'Ahnung' von Gott hat, wissen, daß das von ihr vollzogene sich zu sich selbst Zurückkreißen des Lebens, religiös gesprochen, eine Handaufhebung gegen Gott ist. Damit allein aber steht sie ehrlich, d. h. gemäß der ihr als solcher verfügbaren Möglichkeit vor Gott; atheistisch besagt hier: sich freihaltend von verführerischer, Religiosität lediglich beredender, Besorgnis." Heidegger endorsed this "atheist" conception of philosophy still in 1925, as is clear from PGZ (GA 20), pp. 109–110: "Philosophische Forschung ist und

bleibt Atheismus, deshalb kann sie sich die 'Anmaßung des Denkens' leisten," and so on. See section 11 for discussion.

99. PIA, pp. 252–253/25–26: "Die führende Frage der Interpretation muß sein: *Als welche Gegenständlichkeit welchen Seinscharakters ist das Menschsein, das 'im Leben Sein' erfahren und ausgelegt*? Welches ist der Sinn von Dasein, in dem die Lebensauslegung den Gegenstand Mensch im Vorhinein ansetzt? Kurz, in welcher *Seinsvorhabe* steht diese Gegenständlichkeit? Ferner: Wie ist dieses Sein des Menschen begrifflich explizitiert, welches ist der phänomenale Boden der Explikation und welche Seinskategorien erwachsen als Explikate des so Gesehenen? Ist der Seinssinn, der das Sein des menschlichen Lebens letztlich charakterisiert, aus einer reinen Grunderfahrung eben dieses Gegenstandes und seines Seins genuin geschöpft, oder ist menschliches Leben als ein Seiendes innerhalb eines umgreifenderen Seinsfeldes genommen, beziehungsweise einem für es als archontisch angesetzten Seinssinn unterworfen? Was besagt überhaupt Sein für Aristoteles, wie ist es zugänglich, faßbar und bestimmbar?" (Heidegger's italics).

100. Cf. PIA, p. 260/38: "Sein ist *Fertigsein*, das Sein, in dem die Bewegung zu *ihrem Ende* gekommen ist" (Heidegger's italics). Cf. p. 253/26: "Sein besagt *Hergestelltsein* und, als Hergestelltes, auf eine Umgangstendenz relativ Bedeutsames, Verfügbarsein" (Heidegger's italics); p. 268/50: "Denn der Sinn von Sein ist ursprünglich *Hergestelltsein*" (Heidegger's italics). Cf. also SZ, § 6, p. 24: "Geschaffenheit aber im weitesten Sinne der Hergestelltheit von etwas ist ein wesentliches Strukturmoment des antiken Seinsbegriffes."

101. Cf. PIA, pp. 248–254/18–28; 260/37–38.

102. Like Husserl and Heidegger, Aristotle thought that reality is carved up into ontological regions (genera) that would be the domains of different sciences. But whereas Aristotle assumed that genera such as *plant*, *man*, and *animal* are all species of the highest genus of *substance*, Heidegger denied that the traditional category of substance applies to Dasein.

103. PIA, p. 268/49–50.

104. PIA, p. 246/16: "Die Problematik der Philosophie betrifft das Sein des faktischen Lebens. Philosophie ist in dieser hinsicht *prinzipielle Ontologie*, so zwar, daß die bestimmten einzelnen welthaften regionalen Ontologien von der Ontologie der Faktizität her Problemgrund und Problemsinn empfangen" (Heidegger's italics). Cf. SZ, § 4.

105. PIA, p. 263/41–42.

106. PIA, p. 244/12–13: "Im *zugreifenden* Haben des *gewissen* Todes wird das Leben an ihm selbst sichtbar. Der so seiende Tod gibt dem Leben eine Sicht und führt es ständig mit vor seine eigenste Gegenwart und Vergangenheit, die in ihm selbst anwachsend hinter ihm herkommt. . . . Der als bevorstehend gehabte Tod . . . ist als Konstitutivum der Faktizität zugleich das Phänomen, aus dem die spezifische *'Zeitlichkeit'* menschlichen Daseins explikativ zu erheben ist. Aus dem Sinn dieser *Zeitlichkeit* bestimmt sich der Grundsinn des *Historischen*" (Heidegger's italics).

107. Cf. SZ, § 27, p. 129: "Daß auch die traditionelle Logik angesichts dieser Phänomene versagt, kann nicht verwundern, wenn bedacht wird, daß sie ihr Fundament in einer überdies noch rohen Ontologie des Vorhandenen hat"; § 33, pp. 157–159; § 34, pp. 165–166. This doctrine explains in part Heidegger's rejection of logic in WiM. Cf., however, section 11C.2, below, for a final elucidation of this point.

108. Originally, an edition of this course, entitled *Einleitung in die Phänomenologie der Religion*, was not planned in the *Gesamtausgabe*, at least according to the brochure of

1991. See for a summary of its contents Kisiel (1993), pp. 149ff., and Pöggeler (1963), pp. 36ff. But in 1995 the course was edited on the basis of notes of students in GA 60.

109. Cf. Pöggeler (1986–87), pp. 142–143: "So konnte die Vorstellung aufkommen, Heidegger habe durch ständiges Meditieren über die Metaphysik des Aristoteles von der Analogie des Seins aus zur Frage nach dem Sinn von Sein gefunden. Was wir von Heideggers frühen Vorlesungen wissen, widerlegt diese Vorstellung . . . mit dem Interesse für die Scholastik . . . geht das Interesse für die Mystik zusammen."

110. SD, p. 81; see section 1, above.

111. Because traditional ontology would fit "occurrent" or "present" things (*Vorhandenes*) only, Heidegger speaks of the ontology of presence (*Ontologie der Vorhandenheit*).

112. In section 7B, I explained why this is the case in Aristotle. But Heidegger does not explicitly give that explanation, whereas he hints at another, which I will develop in the main text.

113. SZ, § 7C, p. 35: "Was ist es, was in einem ausgezeichneten Sinne 'Phänomen' genannt werden muß? . . . das *Sein* des Seienden. . . . Der phänomenologische Begriff von Phänomen meint als das Sichzeigende das Sein des Seienden, seinen Sinn, seine Modifikationen und Derivate" (Heidegger's italics).

114. I argued this point extensively in Philipse (1992).

115. SZ, § 2, pp. 6–7: "Aber 'seiend' nennen wir vieles und in verschiedenem Sinne. Seiend ist alles, wovon wir reden, was wir meinen, wozu wir uns so und so verhalten, seiend ist auch, was und wie wir selbst sind. Sein liegt im Daß-und Sosein, in Realität, Vorhandenheit, Bestand, Geltung, Dasein, im 'es gibt.' "

116. Cf., for instance, GPh (GA 24), § 16.

117. SD, p. 81: "Wenn das Seiende in mannigfacher Bedeutung gesagt wird, welches ist dann die leitende Grundbedeutung? Was heißt Sein?" Cf. also KM, p. 217.

118. See Philipse (1992), p. 258, for discussion and references.

119. SZ, pp. 94–95: "Hinter diesem geringfügigen Unterschied der Bedeutung verbirgt sich aber die Unbewältigung des grundsätzlichen Seinsproblems. Seine Bearbeitung verlangt, in der *rechten Weise* den Äquivokationen 'nachzuspüren'; wer so etwas versucht, 'beschäftigt sich' nicht mit 'bloßen Wortbedeutungen,' sondern muß sich in die ursprünglichste Problematik der 'Sachen selbst' vorwagen, um solche 'Nuancen' ins Reine zu bringen" (Heidegger's italics).

120. SZ, § 1, p. 4: "Allein diese durchschnittliche Verständlichkeit demonstriert nur die Unverständlichkeit."

121. SD, pp. 81–87.

122. SD, p. 82. "Mein Weg in die Phänomenologie" was first published in a festschrift on the occasion of Hermann Niemeyer's eightieth birthday (16 April 1963), and this fact might also explain Heidegger's reference to the typography and title page of *Logische Untersuchungen*, which Niemeyer had published.

123. SD, p. 86: "Als ich seit 1919 selbst lehrend-lernend in der Nähe Husserls das phänomenologische sehen einübte und zugleich im Seminar ein gewandeltes Aristoteles-Verständnis erprobte, neigte sich mein Interesse aufs neue den *Logischen Untersuchungen* zu, vor allem der sechsten in der ersten Auflage. Der hier herausgearbeitete Unterschied zwischen sinnlicher und kategorialer Anschauung enthüllte sich mir in seiner Tragweite für die Bestimmung der 'manigfachen Bedeutung des Seienden.' "

124. VS, p. 116. Cf. Philipse (1992), p. 267, for other quotes.

125. PGZ (GA 20), pp. 97–98: "Mit der Entdeckung der kategorialen Anschauung ist zum erstenmal der konkrete Weg einer ausweisenden und echten Kategorienforschung gewonnen." Cf. p. 109.

126. In Philipse (1992), I called it the "Augustinian picture of language."

127. See Philipse (1994b) for clarifications. Husserl rejects one aspect of Platonism, the tenet that Forms are paradigms (see § 32 of the first *Logical Investigation*). But he maintains, like Plato, that Forms or "ideal species," as he calls them in 1900–1901, exist independently, apart from their instances. See first *Logical Investigation*, §§ 30–35, and the second *Logical Investigation*.

128. LU II, p. 54: "In der Bedeutung constituirt sich die Beziehung auf den Gegenstand. Also einen Ausdruck mit Sinn gebrauchen und sich ausdrückend auf den Gegenstand beziehen (den Gegenstand vorstellen) ist einerlei. Es kommt dabei gar nicht darauf an, ob der Gegenstand existiert."

129. See section 5 of the first investigation.

130. Husserl's principle is a sophisticated principle of referentiality, for he does not identify meaning with reference. The thesis that Heidegger endorsed Husserl's principle of referentiality is corroborated by many texts. Cf., for instance, EM, pp. 66–67: "Mag also das Wort 'Sein' eine unbestimmte oder auch eine bestimmte Bedeutung . . . haben, es gilt, über das Bedeutungsmäßige hinaus zur Sache zu kommen. Aber ist 'Sein' eine Sache wie Uhren, Häuser und überhaupt irgendein Seiendes? Wir sind schon oft darauf gestoßen, wir haben uns genug daran gestoßen, daß das Sein nichts Seiendes ist und kein seiendes Bestandstück des Seienden. . . . Dem Wort und der Bedeutung 'Sein' entspricht mithin keine Sache. Aber daraus können wir nicht folgern, daß das Sein nur im Wort und seiner Bedeutung bestehe . . . Vielmehr meinen wir im Wort 'Sein', in dessen Bedeutung, durch sie hindurch, das Sein selbst, nur daß es keine Sache ist, wenn wir unter Sache ein irgendwie Seiendes verstehen"; and SvGr, p. 204: "Das Wörtchen 'ist' nennt, jeweils vom Seienden gesagt, das *Sein* des Seienden" (Heidegger's italics).

131. Misleadingly, because Husserl's principle of acquaintance is not meant to be an explanation of the actual origin of meaning in perception: it does not belong to genetic or explanatory psychology, but to descriptive psychology. Cf. for Husserl's principle: first investigation, § 15.4 (LU II, p. 56), and *Prolegomena*, LU I, § 67, pp. 244–245.

132. LU I (*Prolegomena*), §§ 63 and 66; cf. § 43, in finem, p. 167.

133. LU I (*Prolegomena*), § 71.

134. LU II, introd., § 2, p. 7: "So erwächst die große Aufgabe, *die logischen Ideen, die Begriffe und Gesetze, zu erkenntnistheoretischer Klarheit und Deutlichkeit zu bringen.* Und hier setzt die *phänomenologische Analyse* ein" (Husserl's italics).

135. LU I (*Prolegomena*), § 67, pp. 243–244.

136. Cf. section 39 of the sixth investigation for these and other distinctions, and Tugendhat (1967) on Husserl's notion of truth and its influence on Heidegger's conception of truth.

137. See Philipse (1992), p. 275.

138. For a comparison of Husserl, Heidegger, and Wittgenstein, see Philipse (1992).

139. Sixth investigation, §§ 40, 42; LU II, p. 602: "Das Prototyp für die Interpretation des Verhältnisses zwischen Bedeuten und Anschauen wäre also das Verhältnis der Eigenbedeutung zu den entsprechenden Wahrnehmungen. Wer *Köln* selbst kennt und demgemäß die wahre Eigenbedeutung des Wortes *Köln* hat"; in the first paragraph of section 42, Husserl calls this "prototype" of the relation between meaning and perception "einen leit-

enden Gedanken für ihre [i.e., der Schwierigkeiten] mögliche Überwindung" (Heidegger's italics).

140. LU II, sixth investigation, §§ 60–62.

141. *Ideen* I, §§ 10 and 13.

142. SZ, § 7, pp. 31, 35.

143. Sixth investigation, § 44, LU II, p. 613: "Gilt uns Sein als *prädicatives* Sein, so muß uns also irgendein *Sachverhalt* gegeben werden" (Husserl's italics).

144. Cf. SZ, § 2, pp. 6–7: "Sofern das Sein das Gefragte [der Seinsfrage] ausmacht, und Sein besagt Sein von Seiendem, ergibt sich als das *Befragte* der Seinsfrage das Seiende selbst. Dieses wird gleichsam auf sein Sein hin abgefragt. . . . Aber 'seiend' nennen wir vieles und in verschiedenem Sinne. Seiend ist alles, wovon wir reden, was wir meinen, wozu wir uns so und so verhalten, seiend ist auch, was und wie wir selbst sind" (Heidegger's italics); § 7C, p. 37: "Weil Phänomen im phänomenologischen Verstande immer nur das ist, was Sein ausmacht, Sein aber je Sein von Seiendem ist, bedarf es für das Absehen auf eine Freilegung des Seins zuvor einer rechten Beibringung des Seienden selbst," and so on.

145. Sixth investigation, § 40, LU II, p. 603: "Und wiederholt sich diese Form nicht auch, obschon verborgener bleibend, bei dem Hauptwort Papier? Nur die in seinem 'Begriff' vereinten Merkmalbedeutungen terminiren in der Wahrnehmung; auch hier ist der ganze Gegenstand als Papier erkannt, auch hier eine ergänzende Form, die das Sein, obschon nicht als einzige Form, enthält."

146. Cf. Philipse (1992), p. 281.

147. PGZ (GA 20), pp. 64, 77, 81, 83, 95.

148. SZ, p. 35: "Was ist es, was in einem ausgezeichneten Sinne 'Phänomen' genannt werden muß? . . . Offenbar solches, was sich zunächst und zumeist gerade *nicht* zeigt, was gegenüber dem, was sich zunächst und zumeist zeigt, *verborgen* ist. . . . Was aber in einem ausnehmenden Sinne *verborgen* bleibt oder wieder in die *Verdeckung* zurückfällt oder nur 'verstellt' sich zeigt, ist nicht dieses oder jenes Seiende, sondern, wie die voranstehenden Betrachtungen gezeigt haben, das *Sein* des Seienden" (Heidegger's italics). However, there are other, Kantian and Eckhartian interpretations of this passage, which will emerge in sections 9 and 11, below.

149. Heidegger explains Husserl's notion of the categorial as the formal in PGZ (GA 20), § 6, without criticizing it.

150. Kisiel (1993), pp. 170, 172. Kisiel is too pessimistic on this point, for what Heidegger says about formalizing and generalizing in his lectures of November 1920 (GA 60, *Einleitung in die Phänomenologie der Religion*, §§ 12–13, pp. 57–65) is a more or less faithful summary of what Husserl wrote on this topic in *Ideen* I, § 13.

151. I am quoting from Kisiel (1993), p. 172. Cf. GA 60, p. 339, where the editors quote a sentence from Oscar Becker's lecture notes—"Infolge von Einwänden Unberufener abgebrochen am 30. November 1920"—and add that they have not been able to find out the nature of these objections or complaints.

152. Cf., e.g., SZ, §§ 3–4, and EM, pp. 68–69.

153. See Quine (1960), § 49, pp. 241–242.

154. Cf., for instance, FD, § A.9. Russell also made the connection between ontology and logic, but his order of explanation was the other way around. He explained the ontologies of Spinoza and Leibniz by arguing that traditional logic could not handle relations, so that, ontologically, relations had to be conceived as properties.

155. Cf. SZ, § 27, p. 129: "Daß auch die traditionelle Logik angesichts dieser Phänomene versagt, kann nicht verwundern, wenn bedacht wird, daß sie ihr Fundament in einer überdies noch rohen Ontologie des Vorhandenen hat. Daher ist sie durch noch so viele Verbesserungen und Erweiterungen grundsätzlich nicht geschmeidiger zu machen"; and GA 21 (lectures on logic, 1925–26) p. 415: "Die Aussagen als das Aussagen des Vorhandenen gründen im Gegenwärtigen. Die Logik ist die unvollkommenste aller philosophischen Disziplinen," and so on.

156. GA 60, p. 8: "Das Problem des Selbstverständnisses der Philosophie wurde immer zu leicht genommen. Faßt man dies Problem radikal, so findet man, daß die Philosophie der faktischen Lebenserfahrung entspringt. Und dann springt sie in der faktischen Lebenserfahrung in diese selbst zurück. Der Begriff der faktischen Lebenserfahrung ist fundamental"; and p. 15: "Bisher waren die Philosophen bemüht, gerade die faktische Lebenserfahrung als selbstverständliche Nebensächlichkeit abzutun, obwohl doch aus ihr gerade das Philosophieren entspringt, und in einer—allerdings ganz wesentlichen—Umkehr wieder in sie zurückspringt." Cf. Kisiel (1993), pp. 153–154.

157. SZ, p. 38. The German text is much more violent than the English translation of BT. It reads: "Philosophie ist universale phänomenologische Ontologie, ausgehend von der Hermeneutik des Daseins, die als Analytik der *Existenz* das Ende des Leitfadens alles philosophischen Fragens dort festgemacht hat, woraus es *entspringt* und wohin es *zurückschlägt*" (Heidegger's italics). Cf. SZ, p. 436: "Philosophie ist universale phänomenologische Ontologie, ausgehend von der Hermeneutik des Daseins, die als Analytik der *Existenz* das Ende des Leitfadens alles philosophischen Fragens dort festgemacht hat, woraus es *entspringt* und wohin es *zurückschlägt*" (Heidegger's italics).

158. Cf. GA 60, p. 3: "Es besteht ein prinzipieller Unterschied zwischen Wissenschaft und Philosophie"; p. 8: "Mit der Bezeichnung der Philosophie als erkennendes, rationales Verhalten ist gar nichts gesagt; man verfällt so dem Ideal der Wissenschaft"; and pp. 9, 13, 15, 62, and passim.

159. GA 60, p. 15: "Die faktische Lebenserfahrung verdeckt immer wieder selbst eine etwa auftauchende philosophische Tendenz durch ihre Indifferenz und Selbstgenügsamkeit. In dieser selbstgenügsamen Bekümmerung fällt die faktische Lebenserfahrung ständig *ab* in die Bedeutsamkeit. Sie strebt ständig der Artikulation zur Wissenschaft und schließlich einer 'wissenschaftlichen Kultur' zu" (Heidegger's italics).

160. Cf. GA 60, p. 15: "Bisher waren die Philosophen bemüht, gerade die faktische Lebenserfahrung als selbstverständliche Nebensächlichkeit abzutun, obwohl doch aus ihr gerade das Philosophieren entspringt, und in einer—allerdings ganz wesentlichen—Umkehr wieder in sie zurückspringt."

161. GA 60, p. 9: "Wir vertreten die These: Wissenschaft ist prinzipiell verschieden von Philosophie"; and especially pp. 57–65. For an English summary of the lectures, see again Kisiel (1993), pp. 153ff., especially pp. 166–170.

162. LU I, pp. 236–239.

163. I am quoting Kisiel's summary of (mainly) Becker's lecture notes: Kisiel (1993), p. 154. Cf. also pp. 166–167 and p. 529, note 3, where Kisiel explains how he reconstructed this unpublished course. Cf. also GA 60, p. 9: "Die Auffassung, als seien Philosophie und Wissenschaft objektive Sinngebilde, abgelöste Sätze und Satzzusammenhänge, muß beseitigt werden. . . . Man muß die konkreten Wissenschaften selbst in ihrem *Vollzug* erfassen; der Wissenschaftsprozeß als historischer muß selbst zugrunde gelegt werden," and so on (Heidegger's italics); cf. also pp. 56–57, where Heidegger summarizes Husserl's view.

164. SZ, § 4, p. 11: "Wissenschaft überhaupt kann als das Ganze eines Begründungszu-sammenhanges wahrer Sätze bestimmt werden. Diese Definition ist weder vollständig, noch trifft sie die Wissenschaft in ihrem Sinn. Wissenschaften haben als Verhaltungen des Menschen die Seinsart dieses Seiende (Mensch). Dieses Seiende fassen wir terminologisch als *Dasein*" (Heidegger's italics). Cf. GA 60, p. 9 (quoted above).

165. GA 60, *Einleitung in die Phänomenologie der Religion*, §§ 12–13, pp. 57–65.

166. GA 60, *Einleitung in die Phänomenologie der Religion*, § 12, p. 57: "Wir wollen versuchen, diese Unterscheidung [zwischen Generalisierung und Formalisierung] weiter-zubilden und in dieser Weiterbildung den Sinn der formalen Anzeige zu erklären."

167. GA 60, p. 58: "Die formale Prädikation ist sachhaltig nicht gebunden, aber sie muß doch irgendwie motiviert sein. Wie ist sie motiviert? Sie entspringt dem *Sinn des Einstellungsbezuges* selbst" (Heidegger's italics). Cf. pp. 58–59: "So entspringt die For-malisierung aus dem Bezugssinn des reinen Einstellungsbezugs selbst."

168. GA 60, p. 61: "Der Sinn von 'Gegenstand überhaupt' besagt lediglich: das 'Wo-rauf' des theoretischen Einstellungsbezugs," and p. 63: "Präjudiziert nun für diese Aufgabe der Phänomenologie die formal-ontologische Bestimmtheit etwas? . . . gerade, weil die formale Bestimmung inhaltlich völlig indifferent ist, ist sie für die Bezugs—und Vollzugs-seite des Phänomens verhängnisvoll—weil sie einen theoretischen Bezugssinn vorschreibt oder wenigstens mit vorschreibt. Sie verdeckt das *Vollzugs*mäßige" (Heidegger's italics).

169. GA 60, p. 63: "Wie kann diesem Präjudiz, diesem Vorurteil vorgebeugt werden? Das leistet gerade die *formale Anzeige*" (Heidegger's italics).

170. GA 60, p. 59: "Hat in der Rede von der 'formalen Anzeige' das Wort 'formal' die Bedeutung des Formalisierten oder gewinnt es eine andere? Das Gemeinsame von Formalisierung und Generalisierung ist, daß sie in dem Sinn von 'allgemein' stehen, währ-end die formale Anzeige mit Allgemeinheit nichts zu tun hat. Die Bedeutung von 'formal' in der 'formalen Anzeige' ist *ursprünglicher*" (Heidegger's italics).

171. GA 60, pp. 63–64: "Warum heißt sie 'formal'? Das Formale ist etwas Bezugs-mäßiges. Die Anzeige soll vorweg den Bezug des Phänomens anzeigen—in einem nega-tiven Sinn allerdings, gleichsam zur Warnung! Ein Phänomen muß so vorgegeben sein, daß sein Bezugssinn in der Schwebe gehalten wird. Man muß sich davor hüten, anzuneh-men, sein Bezugssinn sei ursprünglich der theoretische. Der Bezug und Vollzug des Phäno-mens wird *nicht* im Voraus bestimmt, er wird in der Schwebe gehalten. Daß ist eine Stellungnahme, die der Wissenschaft auf das Äußerste entgegengesetzt ist," and so on (Heidegger's italics).

172. GA 60, p. 64: "die formale Anzeige ist eine *Abwehr*, eine vorhergehende *Siche-rung*, so daß der Vollzugscharakter noch frei bleibt. Die Notwendigkeit dieser Vorsichts-maßregel ergibt sich aus der abfallenden Tendenz der faktischen Lebenserfahrung, die stets ins Objektmäßige abzugleiten droht und aus der wir doch die Phänomene herausheben müssen" (Heidegger's italics).

173. LU II, *Einleitung*, § 6, third *Zusatz*, p. 18.

174. In section 6 of the introduction to LU II, phenomenology is identified with descrip-tive psychology; in section 2 it is claimed that phenomenological analysis has the task of elucidating the fundamental concepts of logic (LU II, pp. 18, 7, respectively).

175. Philipse (1995), §§ ix–xv.

176. Cf. Husserl, *Ideen* I, §§ 49–55. See also Philipse (1995) for a substantiation of this interpretation of Husserl's transcendental idealism.

177. Husserl, *Ideen* I, § 49. Cf. Philipse (1995) for an analysis of this section.

178. Husserl, *Ideen* I, § 27. Cf. Heidegger, PGZ (GA 20), §§ 10b–13.

179. Cf. SZ, §§ 19–21, and PGZ (GA 20), §§ 11–12. In PGZ, § 12, Heidegger admits that Husserl had answered the traditional question of being, and had determined the modes of being or ontological constitutions of different kinds (regions) of entities. What he objects to is that Husserl answered the question in a scientific manner. Cf. PGZ, p. 155: "*Die Seinsfrage ist also gestellt, sie ist sogar beantwortet.* Nur haben wir es mit dem eigentlich *wissenschaftlichen Weg einer Beantwortung* zu tun" (Heidegger's italics).

180. SZ, p. 34: "Das was sich zeigt, so wie es sich von ihm selbst her zeigt, von ihm selbst her sehen lassen."

181. SZ, pp. 31, 35. Paradoxically, Heidegger criticizes Aristotle for not having realized that phenomena are always "given to" *someone*, whereas in § 7A–B of *Sein und Zeit* he implicitly criticizes Husserl for bringing the (transcendental) subject into play in his definition of a phenomenon and of truth. As Heidegger says in "Mein Weg in die Phänomenologie": "Was sich für die Phänomenologie der Bewußtseinsakte als das sich-selbst-Bekunden der Phänomene vollzieht, wird ursprünglicher noch von Aristoteles und im ganzen griechischen Denken und Dasein als *alētheia* gedacht, als die Unverborgenheit des Anwesenden, dessen Entbergung, sein sich-Zeigen" (SD, p. 87). In this manner, Husserl is used against Aristotle and Aristotle against Husserl.

182. Cf., for instance, SZ § 3, p. 9: "Sein ist jeweils das Sein eines Seienden"; cf. § 7C, p. 37: "Sein aber je Sein von Seiendem ist."

183. Cf. section 3, above. Heidegger clearly endorses the claims that phenomenology is the method of ontology (SZ, p. 27: "Die Abhebung des Seins vom Seienden und die Explikation des Seins selbst ist die Aufgabe der Ontologie. . . . Mit der leitenden Frage nach dem Sinn des Seins steht die Untersuchung bei der Fundamentalfrage der Philosophie überhaupt. Die Behandlungsart dieser Frage ist die *phänomenologische*"), that phenomenology is purely descriptive (SZ, p. 35), and that it analyzes essential structures (SZ, pp. 17: "wesenhafte Strukturen," p. 52: "echte Wesenserkennnis," pp. 199–200, 231: "Wesen des Daseins").

184. SZ, § 7C, p. 37: "Phänomenologie des Daseins ist *Hermeneutik* in der ursprünglichen Bedeutung des Wortes, wonach es das Geschäft der Auslegung bezeichnet" (Heidegger's italics).

185. SZ, § 3, p. 10.

186. SZ, § 5, pp. 16–17: "An dieser sollen nicht beliebige und zufällige, sondern wesenhafte Strukturen herausgestellt werden, die in jeder Seinsart des faktischen Daseins sich als seinsbestimmende durchhalten."

187. Cf. Löwith (1965), chapter 2.

188. SZ, § 3, p. 10.

189. GAP (GA 22), §§ 3–4; GPh (GA 24), §§ 3 and 22b.

190. SZ, § 4, p. 13: "Daher muß die *Fundamentalontologie*, aus der alle andern erst entspringen können, in der *existenzialen Analytik des Daseins* gesucht werden" (Heidegger's italics).

191. Cf. Okrent (1988), for a transcendental and pragmatist interpretation of the question of being.

192. SZ, § 7A, p. 31: "Im Horizont der Kantischen Problematik kann das, was phänomenologisch unter Phänomen begriffen wird, vorbehaltlich anderer Unterschiede, so illustriert werden, daß wir sagen: was in den Erscheinungen, dem vulgär verstandenen Phänomen je vorgängig und mitgängig, obzwar unthematisch sich schon zeigt, kann thematisch

zum Sichzeigen gebracht werden und dieses Sich-so-an-ihm-selbst-zeigende ('Formen der Anschauung') sind Phänomene der Phänomenologie. Denn offenbar müssen sich Raum und Zeit so zeigen können."

193. SZ, § 3, p. 11: "Die Seinsfrage zielt daher auf eine apriorische Bedingung der Möglichkeit"; § 31, p. 145: "Ist es Zufall, daß die Frage nach dem *Sein* von Natur auf die 'Bedingungen ihrer *Möglichkeit*' zielt? . . . *Kant* setzt dergleichen vielleicht mit Recht voraus. Aber diese Voraussetzung selbst kann am allerwenigsten in ihrem Recht unausgewiesen bleiben" (Heidegger's italics).

194. Kant, KdrV, A 111; A 154–158; B 193–197. Cf. Okrent (1988), p. 6, and Stroud (1968).

195. SZ, § 43c, p. 212: "Allerdings nur solange Dasein *ist*, das heißt die ontische Möglichkeit von Seinsverständnis, 'gibt es' Sein," and so on (Heidegger's italics); § 44c, p. 230: "Sein—nicht Seiendes—'gibt es' nur, sofern Wahrheit ist. Und sie *ist* nur, sofern und solange Dasein ist" (Heidegger's italics).

196. Cf., for instance, the first paragraph of SZ, § 4, p. 11: "Wissenschaften haben als Verhaltungen des Menschen die Seinsart dieses Seienden (Mensch). Dieses Seiende fassen wir terminologisch als *Dasein*" (Heidegger's italics). Usually, Heidegger introduces the term "Dasein" as a *terminus technicus* for "the being that we are ourselves," as in SZ, § 2, p. 7: "Dieses Seiende, das wir selbst je sind und das unter anderem die Seinsmöglichkeit des Fragens hat, fassen wir terminologisch als *Dasein*" (Heidegger's italics). Perhaps we should conclude, however, that the diverse ways in which Heidegger introduces the term "Dasein" are not symptoms of sloppiness, but rather of the fact that there is yet another leitmotif in *Sein und Zeit*, which I will call the postmonotheist theme (see § 11, below). Moreover, Heidegger's identification of Dasein with one regional entity, human being, is not misleading at all within the framework of the phenomenologico-hermeneutical leitmotif.

197. KM, pp. 219, 222, 227, 255: "das Dasein im Menschen." Cf. on anthropology KM, §§ 37–38. In SZ, § 10, Heidegger also argues that the ontology of Dasein is not an anthropology. But here, his argument is based on the phenomenologico-hermeneutical distinction between the ontical and the ontological, rather than on the transcendental leitmotif. The ontology of Dasein investigates "das Sein des Menschen," in the sense of "die Grundverfassung seines Seins" (cf. SZ, p. 10), whereas anthropology is an empirical (ontical) discipline that presupposes the ontology of Dasein.

198. SZ, § 7C, p. 37: "Sofern nun aber durch die Aufdeckung des Sinnes des Seins und der Grundstrukturen des Daseins überhaupt der Horizont herausgestellt wird für jede weitere ontologische Erforschung des nicht daseinsmäßigen Seienden, wird diese Hermeneutik zugleich 'Hermeneutik' im Sinne der Ausarbeitung der Bedingungen der Möglichkeit jeder ontologischen Untersuchung."

199. See SZ, § 8, p. 40: "*Kants* Lehre vom Schematismus und der Zeit als Vorstufe einer Problematik der Temporalität" (Heidegger's italics). As I explained in section 3, above, part 2 and the third division of part 1 of *Sein und Zeit* never appeared.

200. KM, § 44, p. 232: "Die fundamentalontologische Grundlegung der Metaphysik in *Sein und Zeit* muß sich als Wiederholung verstehen. Die Stelle aus Platons *Sophistes*, die die Betrachtung eröffnet, dient nicht zur Dekoration, sondern als Hinweis darauf, daß in der antiken Metaphysik die Gigantomachie über das Sein des Seienden entbrannt ist. . . . Sofern aber in dieser Gigantomachie die Seinsfrage allererst als solche erkämpft und *noch nicht* in der gekennzeichneten Weise als Problem der inneren Möglichkeit des Seinsver-

ständnisses ausgearbeitet wird, kann weder die Auslegung des Seins als solchen noch gar der hierzu notwendige Horizont der Auslegung als solcher ausdrücklich ans Licht kommen" (Heidegger's italics). But Kant of course *did* conceive the question of being as a transcendental question concerning the possibility of understanding being. He conceived of the horizon of entities as an understanding of being. See, for instance, KM, IIIB, p. 134: "Vielmehr macht der in der transzendentalen Einbildungskraft gebildete Horizont der Gegenstände—das Seinsverständnis."

201. KM, §§ 26–35; see also § 38, p. 208: "Was hat sich aber im Geschehen der Kantischen Grundlegung eigentlich ergeben? . . . daß Kant bei der Enthüllung der Subjektivität des Sujektes vor dem von ihm selbst gelegten Grunde zurückweicht."

202. SZ, § 6, pp. 23–24.

203. Cf. KM, IV, introduction, p. 198: "Unter Wiederholung eines Grundproblems verstehen wir die Erschließung seiner ursprünglichen, bislang verborgenen Möglichkeiten, durch deren Ausarbeitung es verwandelt und so erst in seinem Problemgehalt bewahrt wird. Ein Problem bewahren, heißt aber, es in denjenigen inneren Kräften frei und wach halten, die es als Problem im Grunde seines Wesens ermöglichen." Cf. on Heidegger's retrieval of Kant's transcendental philosophy also GPh (GA 24), § 4, p. 23: "Wir können die Wissenschaft vom Sein als kritische Wissenschaft auch die *transzendentale Wissenschaft* nennen. Dabei übernehmen wir nicht ohne weiteres den Begriff des Transzendentalen bei Kant, wohl aber seinen ursprünglichen Sinn und die eigentliche, Kant vielleicht noch verborgene Tendenz. Wir übersteigen das Seiende, um zum Sein zu gelangen" (Heidegger's italics).

204. A *Vorgriff* is a conceptual structure applied in advance. On the notion of a *Vorgriff*, see SZ, § 32, p. 150, and section 5, above.

205. KM, p. xiv: "So kam die Fragestellung von *Sein und Zeit* als Vorgriff für die versuchte Kantauslegung ins Spiel. Kants Text wurde eine Zuflucht, bei Kant einen Fürsprecher für die von mir gestellte Seinsfrage zu suchen." However, as I observed above, we should be careful with Heidegger's statements about his earlier works. Maybe Heidegger in 1973 was not honest at all, and only repudiated his interpretation of Kant because in the meantime he had come to reject a transcendental conception of the question of being itself, a conception that he clearly endorsed in *Sein und Zeit*.

206. A transcendental interpretation of some sort is endorsed by many authors, such as Brelage, Von Herrmann, Müller, Sinn, Schulz, Wiplinger, Franzen, Okrent, Jung, and so on, but often the precise variety of Heidegger's transcendentalism is left unspecified. For attempts to pin down Heidegger's transcendentalism, see Blattner (1994), Cerbone (1995), Frede (1986), and Schatzki (1992). One of the objectives of this section is to determine the specific nature of Heidegger's transcendental philosophy in SZ. For an assessment of the doctrine, see section 17A, below.

207. See Philipse (1994) and (1995).

208. Kant, KdrV, B 25; cf. A 12.

209. Cf. SZ, § 7C, p. 38: "Sein und Seinsstruktur liegen über jedes Seiende und jede mögliche seiende Bestimmtheit eines Seienden hinaus," and so on. Cf. for the expression "transcendence" in this sense also KM, pp. 40 ("Transzendenz des vorgängigen Seinsverständnisses"), 67 ("Sich im vorhinein in solchem Spielraum halten, ihn ursprünglich bilden, ist nichts anderes als die Transzendenz, die alles endliche Verhalten zu Seiendem auszeichnet"), 101 ("In der Transzendenz geschieht das Gegenstehenlassen des sich

anbietenden Gegenständlichen"), and passim. Cf. also GPh (GA 24), § 20e, and "Vom Wesen des Grundes," W, pp. 31–36.

210. SZ, § 69; GPh (GA 24), § 20e, pp. 423ff., 460. Cf. also "Vom Wesen des Grundes," W, p. 35.

211. KdrV, B, pp. 352–353 (= A pp. 295–296).

212. For detailed discussion, see "Vom Wesen des Grundes," W, p. 49.

213. SZ, § 7C, p. 38: "*Sein ist das transcendens schlechthin*" (Heidegger's italics).

214. SZ, § 83, p. 436: "Die Herausstellung der Seinsverfassung des Daseins bleibt aber gleichwohl nur *ein* Weg. Das *Ziel* ist die Ausarbeitung der Seinsfrage überhaupt" (Heidegger's italics). In BT, Macquarrie and Robinson translate ein Weg by "one way," thereby suggesting that Heidegger in *Sein und Zeit* did not conceive of the way via the analysis of Dasein as the only way to working out the question of being. I do not think that this interpretation is borne out by an overall exegesis of the book. Heidegger in SZ, §§ 2 and 4, argues that the question of being *must* be worked out by a preliminary analysis of Dasein. The German *ein* is ambiguous between "a" and "one," so that from a linguistic point of view both translations are possible.

215. See Kant's *Metaphysische Anfangsgründe der Naturwissenschaft* of 1786.

216. I am assuming here, as Kant did, that information processing *transforms* information. If processing merely serves to decode information, and if it does so successfully, we also perceive the world as it is, and this is a more charitable reading of Gibson's view.

217. Cf. section 7, above, and Kant (1786), preface.

218. Cf. Philipse (1994) for a reconstruction of the development of the philosophy of science before Kant.

219. There is only one passage on mathematical physics in KM, § 2, p. 11, which serves to play down the importance of Newtonian physics for Kant's problem: "Die mathematische Naturwissenschaft gibt eine Anzeige auf diesen grundsätzlichen Bedingungszusammenhang zwischen ontischer Erfahrung und ontologischer Erkenntnis. Darin erschöpft sich aber ihre Funktion für die Grundlegung der Metaphysik." Apparently, Heidegger refuses to see that Kant identified general metaphysics or the ontology of matter with the synthetic a priori foundations of Newtonian physics. There is no reference to Kant's *Metaphysische Anfangsgründe der Naturwissenschaft* in KM. Heidegger even says that according to Kant "die Ontologie primär überhaupt nicht auf die Grundlegung der positiven Wissenschaften bezogen ist" (KM, § 2, p. 12).

220. KM, § 3.

221. KM, § 3, pp. 16–17: "Die Absicht der *Kritik der reinen Vernunft* bleibt demnach grundsätzlich verkannt, wenn dieses Werk als 'Theorie der Erfahrung' oder gar als Theorie der positiven Wissenschaften ausgelegt wird. Die Kritik der reinen Vernunft hat mit 'Erkenntnistheorie' nichts zu schaffen"; § 41, p. 224: "Dieses Wort [namely, Kant's Brief to Herz of 1781] schlägt jeden Versuch, in der *Kritik der reinen Vernunft* auch nur teilweise eine 'Erkenntnistheorie' zu suchen, endgültig nieder."

222. KM, §§ 4–6, and passim.

223. See, for instance, KM, § 16, pp. 68–69: "Wenn sonach unser Erkennen als endliches ein hinnehmendes Anschauen sein muß, dann genügt es nicht, dies nur einzugestehen, sondern jetzt erwacht erst das Problem: was gehört denn notwendig zur Möglichkeit dieses keineswegs selbstverständlichen Hinnehmens von Seiendem? Doch offenbar dieses, daß Seiendes von sich aus begegnen, d. h. als Gegenstehendes sich zeigen kann. Wenn wir aber des Vorhandenseins des Seienden nicht mächtig sind, dann verlangt gerade die

Angewiesenheit auf das Hinnehmen desselben, daß dem Seienden im vorhinein und jederzeit die Möglichkeit des Entgegenstehens gegeben wird," and so on. Cf. § 19, p. 86: "Ein endliches Wesen muß das Seiende, gerade wenn dieses als ein schon Vorhandenes offenbar sein soll, hinnehmen können. Hinnahme verlangt aber zu ihrer Ermöglichung so etwas wie Zuwendung, und zwar keine beliebige, sondern eine solche, die vorgängig das Begegnen von Seiendem ermöglicht." Cf. also pp. 111, 113ff., 117, 145, 149, and 159–160.

224. See Philipse (1994), for a reconstruction of the history of modern philosophy on the basis of this problem.

225. Cf. Philipse (1990); Searle (1992). According to the eliminative materialist, the fact that we perceive colors is produced by our perceiving the world in terms of an antiquated theory. By changing our theory, we might stop perceiving colors. In Philipse (1990) I argued that such a notion of absolute theory-ladenness of observation is incoherent, and that it leads to absurd consequences.

226. Russell (1962), p. 13. Cf. for this historical reconstruction: Philipse (1994).

227. Quine in *Word and Object* (1960) rejects sensations as an epistemological basis of knowledge, and substitutes the notion of material stimuli for that of sensations. The objects of the commonsense world and the theoretical entities of physics would be "posits," assumed by us on the basis of the maxim of simplicity, in order to explain our stimuli. Because different systems of posits would be compatible with the same set of stimuli, the existence of the external world in which we believe is doubtful, even though Quine suggests that one cannot raise this doubt "from the inside." Moreover, Quine cannot be a real empiricist, for the simple reason that the stimuli as he defines them are not given to us. By rejecting the myth of given sensations, Quine implicitly rejects empiricism as well. Quine endorses Neurath's metaphor of a boat, which can be transformed only on open sea, as a simile for the growth of our knowledge. In other words, we cannot radically reject the conceptual scheme and the posits we happen to assume. This means that Quine is an internal realist, like Rorty in *Philosophy and the Mirror of Nature*. Difficulties arise for Quine as soon as one raises questions as to the theoretical status of stimuli. On the one hand, they are thought of as the primary data, which should be explained by a system of posits. On the other hand, they clearly are posits themselves, because in ordinary perception, we do not perceive stimuli but rather entities of the commonsense world. This contradiction is an illustration of Davidson's argument against the very notion of a conceptual scheme: if one holds that nothing can be thought of except within a conceptual scheme, one can no longer define the notion of a conceptual scheme in opposition to a "given" of some kind. See Davidson (1984), essay 13.

228. Cf. SZ, § 18. The relation between *Welt* and *Bewandtnisganzheit* is not as clear as one should wish, and some interpreters postulate a difference between the world as an ultimate global horizon and more specific equipmental contexts. But this point is immaterial for my interpretation of Heidegger's transcendentalism.

229. SZ, § 13, p. 61: "Damit Erkennen als betrachtendes Bestimmen des Vorhandenen möglich sei, bedarf es vorgängig einer *Defizienz* des besorgenden Zu-tun-habens mit der Welt" (Heidegger's italics).

230. SZ, § 13, p. 62: "im Erkennen gewinnt das Dasein einen neuen *Seinsstand* zu der im Dasein je schon entdeckten Welt."

231. SZ, § 69b, p. 357: "welches sind die in der Seinsverfassung des Daseins liegenden, existenzial notwendigen Bedingungen der Möglichkeit dafür, daß das Dasein in der Weise wissenschaftlicher Forschung existieren kann?"

232. SZ, § 69b, p. 357: "Es liegt nahe, den Umschlag vom 'praktisch' umsichtigen Hantieren, Gebrauchen und dergleichen zum 'theoretischen' Erforschen in folgender Weise zu charakterisieren: das pure Hinsehen auf das Seiende entsteht dadurch, daß sich das Besorgen jeglicher Hantierung *enthält*" (Heidegger's italics).

233. SZ, § 69b, p. 358: "Und wie der Praxis ihre spezifische Sicht ('Theorie') eignet, so ist die theoretische Forschung nicht ohne ihre eigene Praxis," and so on.

234. See SZ, § 16, p. 73.

235. Heidegger's account of the relation between daily concern with the world (*besorgen*) and the scientific attitude as developed in SZ, § 69b, is very different from what one expects after having read sections 13–18. In section 69b Heidegger is unable to substantiate the doctrine of section 13 that scientific knowledge is possible only on the basis of a deficiency of our concerned involvement with the world. Cf. SZ, § 13, p. 61: "Damit Erkennen als betrachtendes Bestimmen des Vorhandenen möglich sei, bedarf es vorgängig einer *Defizienz* des besorgenden Zu-tun-habens mit der Welt" (Heidegger's italics). In section 69b, Heidegger does not find such a deficiency.

236. SZ, § 69b, p. 361: "*Das Seinsverständnis*, das den besorgenden Umgang mit dem innerweltlichen Seienden leitet, *hat umgeschlagen*" (Heidegger's italics).

237. SZ, § 69b, p. 362: "die Entstehung der mathematischen Physik. Das Entscheidende für ihre Ausbildung liegt weder in der höheren Schätzung der Beobachtung der 'Tatsachen,' noch in der 'Anwendung' von Mathematik in der Bestimmung der Naturvorgänge—sondern im *mathematischen Entwurf der Natur selbst.* . . . Erst 'im Licht' einer dergestalt entworfenen Natur kann so etwas wie eine 'Tatsache' gefunden . . . werden" (Heidegger's italics). Cf. FD, § B.I.5.e.

238. KM, § 2, p. 11: "Frage nach der Möglichkeit dessen, was ontische Erkenntnis ermöglicht. Das ist aber das Problem des Wesens des vorgängigen Seinsverständnisses"; § 3, p. 16: "Transzendentale Erkenntnis untersucht also nicht das Seiende selbst, sondern die Möglichkeit des vorgängigen Seinsverständnisses, d.h. zugleich: die Seinsverfassung des Seienden"; and passim. In KM, knowledge of the Kantian a priori structures of experience is called knowledge of "the being of beings." Cf. § 16, p. 67: "Um jedoch als das Seiende, das es ist, begegnen zu können, muß es im vorhinein schon überhaupt als Seiendes, d.h. hinsichtlich seiner Seinsverfassung, 'erkannt' sein," and pp. 42, 48, 52, 119, 196–197, 221–222, 228, and 232. Cf. also "Vom Wesen des Grundes," W, pp. 29–31, 35. According to GPh, the being of an entity is contained in the intention directed toward that entity. Cf. also Okrent (1988), pp. 182–185.

239. SZ, § 21, pp. 95, 100; cf. § 69b and FD, pp. 71–72 and p. 31, where Heidegger says about science and technology: "Hier ist das Wissen und Fragen an Grenzen gekommen, die zeigen, daß eigentlich ein ursprünglicher Bezug zu den Dingen fehlt."

240. SZ, § 15, p. 71: "*Zuhandenheit ist die ontologisch-kategoriale Bestimmung von Seiendem, wie es 'an sich' ist*" (Heidegger's italics); § 18, p. 87: "*Das Dasein ist in seiner Vertrautheit mit der Bedeutsamkeit die ontische Bedingung der Möglichkeit der Entdeckbarkeit von Seiendem, das in der Seinsart der Bewandtnis (Zuhandenheit) in einer Welt begegnet und sich so in seinem An-sich bekunden kann*" (Heidegger's italics); p. 88: "Dieses 'Relationssystem' als Konstitutivum der Weltlichkeit verflüchtigt das Sein des innerweltlich Zuhandenen so wenig, daß auf dem Grunde von Weltlichkeit der Welt dieses Seiende in seinem 'substanziellen' 'An-sich' allererst entdeckbar ist"; § 23, p. 106: "*Das umsichtige Ent-fernen der Alltäglichkeit des Daseins entdeckt das An-sich-sein der 'wahren Welt', des Seienden, bei dem Dasein als existierendes je schon ist*" (Heidegger's italics);

§ 26, p. 118: "Das verankerte Boot am Strand verweist in seinem An-sich-sein auf einen Bekannten"; § 43b, p. 209: "In diesem Zusammenhang wird auch erst der Charakter des An-sich ontologisch verständlich," that is, in relation to the phenomena of World and Concern. Heidegger never uses the expression *an sich* with reference to *Vorhandenheit*.

241. SZ, § 69b and FD, § B I 5.

242. SZ, § 31, p. 145: "Das Entwerfen hat nichts zu tun mit einem Sichverhalten zu einem ausgedachten Plan."

243. FD, § A.3, p. 8: "*Mit unserer Frage möchten wir die Wissenschaften weder ersetzen noch verbessern.* Indes möchten wir an der Vorbereitung einer Entscheidung mitwirken. Diese Entscheidung lautet: Ist die Wissenschaft der Maßstab für das Wissen, oder gibt es ein Wissen, in dem erst der Grund und die Grenze der Wissenschaft . . . sich bestimmen?" This question may be read as a hint to a transcendental foundation of science. It might also hint at what I will call the postmonotheist theme (cf. § 11, below).

244. Cf. SZ, §§ 10–24 and 43. Heidegger says in *Richardson* about Husserl's transcendental idealism: "Gegen diese Position setzte sich die in *Sein und Zeit* entfaltete Seinsfrage ab" (p. xv). Cf. also his letter to Jaspers of 26 December 1926, Hei/Ja, p. 71: "Wenn die Abhandlung [namely, SZ] 'gegen' jemanden geschrieben ist, dann gegen Husserl, der das auch sofort sah, aber sich von Anfang an zum Positiven hielt."

245. Cf. Philipse (1995), §§ iv, vi–vii, xiii–xvi, xxi.

246. Cf. Husserl, *Ideen* I, §§ 40, 43, 48, 52, 143, and 148. Cf. also Philipse (1995), § xiii.

247. SZ, § 15, p. 71: "*Zuhandenheit ist die ontologisch-kategoriale Bestimmung von Seiendem, wie es 'an sich' ist*" (Heidegger's italics). Cf. sections 16, 18, and 43.

248. KM, § 5, p. 30: "Das Seiende 'in der Erscheinung' ist dasselbe Seiende wie das Seiende an sich, ja gerade nur dieses. . . . Die doppelte Charakteristik des Seienden als 'Ding an sich' und als 'Erscheinung' entspricht der zweifachen Art, gemäß der es zum unendlichen und endlichen Erkennen in Beziehung stehen kann: das Seiende im Entstand und dasselbe Seiende als Gegenstand." Cf. "Vom Wesen des Grundes," W, p. 44.

249. *Ideen* I, §§ 49–55. Cf. Philipse (1995).

250. *Ideen* I, §§ 51 (*Anmerkung*) and 58. It is clear from Husserl's letters that Husserl was a monotheist, and that he thought that human life cannot be meaningful without a reasonable God. Although he attempted to separate strictly his philosophy, which pretended to be a rigorous science, from his religious convictions, he did not entirely succeed in doing so, as these texts from *Ideen* I show. Indeed, the religious *telos* was the concealed motivation for much of Husserl's mature philosophy.

251. There is an alternative reading of this passage (SZ, § 43c, pp. 211–212), according to which the claim that real entities do not depend on Dasein must be read as a claim *internal* to the framework of occurrentness (*Vorhandenheit*). It would be the ontological sense of occurrent or extant entities that they are "independent of Dasein," whereas tools and pieces of equipment (*Zuhandenes*) as such are dependent on Dasein's purposeful behavior. But this interpretation is refuted by the parallel passage in SZ, § 39, p. 183, where Heidegger states in general, after having discussed all ontological frameworks (*Zuhandenheit, Vorhandenheit, Dasein*), that "Seiendes ist unabhängig von Erfahrung, Kenntnis und Erfassen, wodurch es erschlossen, entdeckt und bestimmt wird. Sein aber 'ist' nur im Verstehen des Seienden, zu dessen Sein so etwas wie Seinsverständnis gehört" (Heidegger's italics). Clearly, Heidegger's affirmation of the independence of entities in relation

to Dasein is not an expression of a mere empirical realism: it amounts to a rejection of transcendental idealism and an endorsement of transcendental realism.

252. SZ, § 43c, pp. 211–212: "Daß Realität ontologisch im Sein des Daseins gründet, kann nicht bedeuten, daß Reales nur sein könnte als das, was es an ihm selbst ist, wenn und solange Dasein existiert. Allerdings nur solange Dasein *ist*, das heißt die ontische Möglichkeit von Seinsverständnis, 'gibt es' Sein," and so on (Heidegger's italics); p. 212: "Die gekennzeichnete Abhängigkeit des Seins, nicht des Seienden, von Seinsverständnis, das heißt die Abhängigkeit der Realität, nicht des Realen, von der Sorge"; § 39, p. 183: "Seiendes *ist* unabhängig von Erfahrung, Kenntnis und Erfassen, wodurch es erschlossen, entdeckt und bestimmt wird. Sein aber 'ist' nur im Verstehen des Seienden, zu dessen Sein so etwas wie Seinsverständnis gehört. Sein kann daher unbegriffen sein, aber es ist nie völlig unverstanden" (Heidegger's italics); § 44c, p. 230: "Sein—nicht Seiendes—'gibt es' nur, sofern Wahrheit ist. Und sie *ist* nur, sofern und solange Dasein ist" (Heidegger's italics).

253. SZ, § 2, p. 6: "das Sein, das, was Seiendes als Seiendes bestimmt, das, woraufhin Seiendes, mag es wie immer erörtert werden, je schon verstanden ist."

254. SZ, § 31, p. 147: "Die Erschlossenheit des Da im Verstehen ist selbst eine Weise des Seinkönnens des Daseins. In der Entworfenheit des Seins auf das Worumwillen in eins mit der auf die Bedeutsamkeit (Welt) liegt Erschlossenheit von Sein überhaupt," and so on; § 32, p. 151: "Im Entwerfen des Verstehens ist Seiendes in seiner Möglichkeit erschlossen," and so on. Cf. "Vom Wesen des Grundes," W, pp. 54–55: "Der Entwurf von Welt aber ist, imgleichen wie er das Entworfene nicht eigens erfaßt, so auch immer *Über-wurf* der entworfenen Welt über das Seiende. Der vorgängige Überwurf ermöglicht erst, daß Seiendes als solches sich offenbart. Dieses Geschehen des entwerfenden Überwurfs, worin sich das Sein des Daseins zeitigt, ist das In-der-Welt-sein. 'Das Dasein transzendiert' heißt: es ist im Wesen seines Seins *weltbildend*" (Heidegger's italics). The text of "Vom Wesen des Grundes" confirms the transcendentalist realist interpretation of *Sein und Zeit*, as does KM.

255. SZ, § 32, p. 151: "Wenn innerweltliches Seiendes mit dem Sein des Daseins entdeckt, das heißt zu Verständnis gekommen ist, sagen wir, es hat *Sinn*. Verstanden aber ist, streng genommen, nicht der Sinn, sondern das Seiende, bzw. das Sein" (Heidegger's italics).

256. SZ, § 43c, pp. 211–212: "Daß Realität ontologisch im Sein des Daseins gründet, kann nicht bedeuten, daß Reales nur *sein* könnte als das, was es an ihm selbst ist, wenn und solange Dasein existiert," and so on (my italics). In this quote, Heidegger must be using *sein* in the nontechnical and nontranscendental sense of "to exist." It follows that *sein* in Heidegger's technical sense cannot include all nontechnical meanings of this verb, as Heidegger misleadingly suggests. Cf. also SZ, § 44c, p. 230.

257. SZ, §§ 14–18. Heidegger stresses the holistic nature of understanding being (*Seins-verständnis*) also in "Vom Wesen des Grundes," W, pp. 52–53: "Das menschliche Dasein—Seiendes *inmitten* von Seiendem befindlich, *zu* Seiendem sich verhaltend—existiert dabei so, daß das Seiende immer im Ganzen offenbar ist.... Die Ganzheit ist verstanden, ohne daß auch das Ganze des offenbaren Seienden in seinen spezifischen Zusammenhängen ... erfaßt ... wäre. Das je vorgreifend-umgreifende Verstehen dieser Ganzheit aber ist Über-stieg zur Welt" (Heidegger's italics).

258. My distinction between strong and weak transcendentalism differs from Blattner's distinction. According to Blattner (1994), Heidegger is a strong transcendentalist in the

sense that Heideggerian "being" is the ontological framework that determines whether something of a specific ontological kind *is*. This projected framework depends on time and time allegedly depends on Dasein. Hence Heidegger is a temporal idealist, like Kant. But how, one might ask, is Heidegger able to avoid strong transcendentalism as I defined it, that is, the view that entities depend on Dasein because they are transcendentally constituted by it (transcendental idealism concerning entities)? If entities depend on being and being depends on Dasein, entities must depend on Dasein as well, because the relation of "depending on" is transitive. As Heidegger explicitly rejects transcendental idealism, Blattner's interpretation of Heidegger as a strong temporal idealist seems to contradict the texts. In order to solve this problem, Blattner argues on the one hand that Heidegger is a realist concerning entities *on the empirical level*: he interprets Heidegger's statement that entities do not depend on Dasein as an empirical statement within the ontological framework of occurrentness. In other words, it belongs to the ontological sense of occurrent entities that they are independent of Dasein. On the other hand, Blattner holds that the question whether entities depend on Dasein or not does not make sense *on the transcendental level*, because Heidegger's transcendentalism allegedly excludes that one attributes a truth value to statements about entities as they are apart from Dasein's *Seinsverständnis*. I reject Blattner's ingenuous interpretation for two reasons. First, it is not adequate as an interpretation of *Sein und Zeit* because Heidegger puts forward the thesis that entities exist independently of Dasein not only as a thesis *within* the framework of occurrentness or "reality" (SZ, § 43c, pp. 211–212) but also as a general thesis about the relation among Dasein, entities, and sein (SZ, § 39, p. 183). Second, Blattner's interpretation does not save Heidegger, for if it is nonsensical to raise transcendental questions concerning the relation between Dasein's *Seinsverständnis* and entities as they are in themselves, apart from *Seinsverständnis*, one must conclude that Heidegger's notion of a transcendental framework is nonsensical as well, and this is the fate of all versions of internal realism, as I will argue in section 17A, below. Incidentally, my interpretation of Heidegger as a transcendental realist and a weak transcendentalist does not save Heidegger either (see § 17A). Probably there is no interpretation of Heidegger's transcendental theory that is compatible with all texts. For instance, how to square Heidegger's thesis that the problem of the external world is a pseudoproblem (SZ, § 43a) with the fact that he solves it by giving a transcendental theory? It will neither do to reply that according to Heidegger, the problem of the external world is a pseudoproblem only within the framework of *Zuhandenheit*, for the problem has never been situated within this framework, nor can one argue that it is a pseudoproblem at the transcendental level, as Blattner does. For in that case Heidegger should not have put forward a transcendental theory at all.

259. SZ, § 3, p. 10: "Auslegung dieses Seienden auf die Grundverfassung seines Seins. Solche Forschung muß den positiven Wissenschaften vorauslaufen," and so on.

260. SZ, § 18.

261. SZ, § 2, p. 6: "*Das Gefragte* der auszuarbeitenden Frage ist das Sein, das, was Seiendes als Seiendes bestimmt, das, woraufhin Seiendes, mag es wie immer erörtert werden, je schon verstanden ist" (Heidegger's italics).

262. Alternatively, one might interpret the second phrase ("that with regard to which entities are already understood") as expressing the first phase of Heidegger's transcendental argument and the first phrase ("that which determines entities as entities") as expressing the second phase of his transcendental argument.

263. SZ, § 7 C, p. 38: "Das Sein als Grundthema der Philosophie ist keine Gattung eines Seienden, und doch betrifft es jedes Seiende. Seine 'Universalität' ist höher zu suchen. Sein und Seinsstruktur liegen über jedes Seiende und jede mögliche seiende Bestimmtheit eines Seienden hinaus. *Sein ist das transcendens schlechthin*" (Heidegger's italics).

264. SZ, § 2, p. 8: "Die wesenhafte Betroffenheit des Fragens von seinem Gefragten gehört zum eigensten Sinn der Seinsfrage. Das besagt aber nur: das Seiende vom Charakter des Daseins hat zur Seinsfrage selbst einen—vielleicht sogar ausgezeichneten—Bezug."

265. From a genetic point of view, the Christian roots of Heidegger's notion of transcendence can be found in his lectures of 1920–21 and 1925, and in his *Habilitationsschrift*, where he identifies intentionality with the transcendent relationship of the soul to God (cf. Kisiel [1993], p. 408). But of course genetic considerations fall short of establishing the meaning of what Heidegger says in SZ.

266. Cf. SZ, § 2, paragraphs 9–12, and § 63, paragraphs 11–15.

267. SZ, § 8, p. 39: "*Erster Teil*: Die Interpretation des Daseins auf die Zeitlichkeit und die Explikation der Zeit als des transzendentalen Horizontes der Frage nach dem Sein" (Heidegger's italics).

268. Cf. SZ, § 66, *in finem*: "Die Interpretation der Abwandlungen des Seins alles dessen, von dem wir sagen, es *ist*, bedarf aber einer zuvor hinreichend erhellten Idee von Sein überhaupt. Solange diese nicht gewonnen ist, bleibt auch die *wiederholende* zeitliche Analyse des Daseins unvollständig und mit Unklarheiten behaftet—um von den sachlichen Schwierigkeiten nicht weitläufig zu reden. Die existenzial-zeitliche Analyse des Daseins verlangt ihrerseits eine erneute Wiederholung im Rahmen der grundsätzlichen Diskussion des Seinsbegriffes" (p. 333); cf. pp. 7, 152, 436.

269. "Brief über den 'Humanismus,' " W, p. 159: "Der fragliche Abschnitt wurde zurückgehalten, weil das Denken im zureichenden Sagen dieser Kehre versagte und mit Hilfe der Sprache der Metaphysik nicht durchkam." Cf. "Mein bisheriger Weg," B (GA 66), pp. 413–414: "Aber der eigentliche 'systematische' Abschnitt über Zeit und Sein blieb in der ersten Ausführung unzureichend und äußere Umstände (das Anschwellen des Jahrbuchbandes) verhinderten zugleich glücklicherweise die Veröffentlichung dieses Stückes, zu der ohnehin beim Wissen um das Unzureichende kein großes Vertrauen war. Der Versuch ist vernichtet, aber sogleich auf mehr geschichtlichem Wege ein neuer Anlauf gemacht in der Vorlesung vom S.S. 1927" (this latter course is GPh).

270. "Brief über den 'Humanismus,' " W, p. 159: "Hier kehrt sich das Ganze um."

271. See GPh, §§ 19–22.

272. At least if one restricts oneself to the text of the book. But there is convincing circumstantial evidence for this interpretation, which I will adduce in sections 12 and 13.

273. The expression *ontologische Differenz* was used for the first time in the lectures of 1927, GPh (GA 24), part 2.

274. Cf. KM, § 44, where Heidegger says that temporality (*Zeitlichkeit*) is the "transzendentale Urstruktur" of *Dasein* (p. 235).

275. Heidegger distinguishes between *Zeitlichkeit des Daseins* (SZ, §§ 65–71) and *Temporalität des Seins* (SZ, § 5, p. 19).

276. Cf. SZ, § 5, paragraphs 8–14. Cf. § 21, where Heidegger shows that Descartes in his philosophy of *res extensa* and *res cogitans* assumes that "Sein = ständige Vorhandenheit."

277. Cf. Robert J. Dostal in Guignon (1993), pp. 141–167.

278. Cf. KM, § 44. Here, Heidegger first points to the fact that the traditional distinctions between regions of being are temporal distinctions. This fact is then explained by the discovery of *Sein und Zeit* that temporality is the "transzendentale Urstruktur" of Dasein.

279. SZ, § 3, p. 11: "Und gerade die ontologische Aufgabe einer nicht deduktiv konstruierenden Genealogie der verschiedenen möglichen Weisen von Sein bedarf einer Vorverständigung über das, 'was wir denn eigentlich met diesem Ausdruck "Sein" meinen.' "

280. In SZ § 44c, p. 229, Heidegger rejects the notion of eternal truths because it belongs "to those residues of Christian theology within philosophical problematics that have not as yet been radically extruded." The vehemence of the German phrase ("den längst noch nicht radikal ausgetriebenen Resten von christlicher Theologie innerhalb der philosophischen Problematik") suggests that in *Sein und Zeit* Heidegger wants to eliminate all residues of theology within philosophy. Heidegger is perhaps more specific in GPh (GA 24), § 4, p. 23: "Wir übersteigen das Seiende, um zum Sein zu gelangen. Bei diesem Überstieg versteigen wir uns nicht wiederum zu einem Seienden, das etwa hinter dem bekannten Seienden läge als irgendeine Hinterwelt." Cf. section 11, below, for discussion of the religious theme.

281. GPh (GA 24), § 19, p. 370: "Es gibt keine Naturzeit, sofern alle Zeit wesentlich zum Dasein gehört." One should note, however, that Heidegger's weak transcendentalism does not justify such claims, unless time is considered to be an aspect of *Sein*. Cf. later texts such as EM, p. 64: "Es gab doch eine Zeit, da der Mensch nicht war. Aber streng genommen können wir nicht sagen: es gab eine Zeit, da der Mensch nicht *war*. Zu jeder *Zeit* war und ist und wird der Mensch sein, weil Zeit sich nur zeitigt, sofern der Mensch ist. Es gibt keine Zeit, da der Mensch nicht war, nich weil der Mensch von Ewigkeit her und in alle Ewigkeit hin ist, sondern weil Zeit nicht Ewigkeit ist und Zeit sich nur je zu einer Zeit als menschlich-geschichtliches Dasein zeitigt" (Heidegger's italics). In this passage, Heidegger's transcendental conception of time, according to which even cosmological time depends on Dasein, seems to lead Heidegger to a strong transcendental idealism, which conflicts with his view that Dasein is *in* the world. Moreover, such a strong transcendental idealism is a solution to the problem of the external world, not a rejection of this problem.

282. GPh (GA 24), § 19aß, p. 347: "Wir sagen ganz natürlich und spontan, wenn wir auf die Uhr sehen, 'jetzt.' Es ist nicht selbstverständlich, daß wir 'jetzt' sagen, aber damit, daß wir es sagen, haben wir der Uhr schon die Zeit vorgegeben." Cf. pp. 368, 388.

283. Cf. GPh (GA 24), pp. 383–384: "Sofern die ursprüngliche Zeit als Zeitlichkeit die Seinsverfassung des Daseins ermöglicht und dieses Seiende so *ist*, daß es sich zeitigt, muß dieses Seiende von der Seinsart des existierenden Daseins ursprünglich und angemessen das *zeitliche Seiende schlechthin* genannt werden" (Heidegger's italics). Heidegger argued this point already in "Der Zeitbegriff in der Geschichtswissenschaft" (1924), FS (GA 1), pp. 415–433, where he discusses the difference between the concept of time in physics and in history.

284. Cf. GPh (GA 24), § 19, pp. 376–379: "Im Sichaussprechen zeitigt die Zeitlichkeit die Zeit, die das vulgäre Zeitverständnis allein kennt" (p. 377); "Die ekstatisch-horizontale Zeitlichkeit macht nicht nur die Seinsverfassung des Daseins ontologisch möglich, sondern sie ermöglichet auch die Zeitigung der Zeit" (p. 378).

285. See, for instance, GPh (GA 24), § 20, pp. 399–405 and at the very end of the course. The image of the cave plays a crucial role in Heidegger's later work; cf., for example, "Platons Lehre von der Wahrheit," W.

286. GPh (GA 24), § 20, pp. 398–399. This claim brings Heidegger to Plato's notion of the Good.

287. GPh (GA 24), § 22, p. 453: "Weil die Zeitlichkeit die Grundverfassung des Seienden ausmacht, das wir Dasein nennen"; and § 21, p. 436: "Die Zeitlichkeit ist in sich der ursprüngliche Selbstentwurf schlechthin."

288. In *Beiträge*, § 44, pp. 93–94, Heidegger comments on his interpretation of Kant: "Solange das 'Seyn' begriffen wird als Seiendheit . . . so lange ist das Seyn selbst in die Wahrheit des Seienden herabgesetzt, in die Richtigkeit des Vor-stellens. Weil all dies bei Kant am reinsten vollzogen wird, deshalb *kann* an seinem Werk versucht werden, ein noch Ursprünglicheres . . . ganz Anderes sichtbar zu machen auf die Gefahr hin, daß nun doch ein solcher Versuch wieder kantisch gelesen und als ein willkürlicher 'Kantianismus' mißdeutet und unschädlich gemacht wird. Die abendländische Geschichte der abendländischen Metaphysik ist der 'Beweis' dafür, daß die Wahrheit des Seyns nicht zur Frage werden könnte" (Heidegger's italics). Cf. also *Beiträge*, § 134, p. 253: "Und das ist versucht im 'Kantbuch'; war aber nur dadurch möglich, daß gegen Kant Gewalt gebraucht wurde . . . diese Kantauslegung ist '*historisch*' unrichtig, gewiß, aber sie ist *geschichtlich*, d. h. auf die Vorbereitung des künftigen Denkens und nur darauf bezogen, wesentlich, eine geschichtliche Anweisung auf ein ganz Anderes" (Heidegger's italics). See section 11, below, for the meaning of these passages.

289. Cf. GPh (GA 24), § 22a, p. 454: "Der Unterschied von Sein und Seiendem *ist*, wenngleich nicht ausdrücklich gewußt, latent im Dasein und seiner Existenz *da*. Der Unterschied *ist da*, d. h. er hat die Seinsart des Daseins, er gehört zur Existenz. Existenz heißt gleichsam 'im Vollzug dieses Unterschiedes sein' " (Heidegger's italics). Cf. section 11, below, for an (Eckhartian) interpretation of such texts.

290. Cf. GPh (GA 24), § 22a, p. 454: "Der Unterschied von Sein und Seiendem ist *vorontologisch*, d. h. ohne expliziten Seinsbegriff, *latent in der Existenz des Daseins da*. Als solcher kann er zur *ausdrücklich verstandenen Differenz* werden" (Heidegger's italics).

291. Cf. GPh (GA 24), § 5, p. 29: "*Für uns* bedeutet die phänomenologische Reduktion die Rückführung des phänomenologischen Blickes von der wie immer bestimmten Erfassung des Seienden auf das Verstehen des Seins (Entwerfen auf die Weise seiner Unverborgenheit) dieses Seienden" (Heidegger's italics).

292. Cf. GPh (GA 24), § 22b, p. 458: "In der faktischen Existenz des Daseins, sei es in der wissenschaftlichen oder vorwissenschaftlichen, ist Sein bekannt, aber das faktische Dasein ist bezüglich des Seins desorientiert," and so on. See also § 22c, p. 463: "Allein, zufolge des Aufgehens, des Sichverlierens im Seienden, sowohl in sich selbst, im Dasein, als im Seienden, das das Dasein nicht ist, weiß das Dasein nichts davon, daß es Sein schon verstanden hat. Dieses Frühere hat das faktisch existierende Dasein vergessen."

293. See the GA edition of SZ, GA 2, p. 582, and "Mein bisheriger Weg," B (GA 66), p. 413.

294. Between 1928 and 1945, Heidegger lectured at Freiburg University on the following topics: Introduction to Philosophy (WS 1928–29, GA 27); German Idealism and the Present Philosophical Situation (SS 1929, GA 28); The Fundamental Concepts of Metaphysics: World, Finiteness, Solitude (WS 1929–30, GA 29/30); On the Essence of Human Freedom (SS 1930, GA 31); Hegel's *Phenomenology of Spirit* (WS 1930–31, GA 32); Aristotle: *Metaphysics* IX (SS 1931, GA 33); On the Essence of Truth: Plato's Simile of the Cave and the *Theaetetus* (WS 1931–32, GA 34); The Beginning of Occidental Philosophy: On Anaximander and Parmenides (SS 1932, GA 35); Fundamental Questions of Phi-

losophy (SS 1933, GA 36); On the Essence of Truth (WS 1933–34, GA 37); On Logic as a Question concerning Language (SS 1934, GA 38); Hölderlin's Hymns "Germanien" and "Der Rhein" (WS 1934–35, GA 39); Introduction to Metaphysics (SS 1935, GA 40); The Question concerning the Thing. On Kant's Doctrine of Transcendental Principles (WS 1935–36, GA 41); Schelling: *On the Essence of Human Freedom* (SS 1936, GA 42); Nietzsche: The Will to Power as Art (WS 1936–37, GA 43); Nietzsche's Metaphysical Fundamental Position in Occidental Thought: The Eternal Recurrence of the Same (SS 1937, GA 44); Fundamental Questions of Philosophy: Selected Problems of Logic (WS 1937–38, GA 45); Nietzsche's Second "Unzeitgemäße Betrachtung" (WS 1938–39, GA 46); Nietzsche's Doctrine of the Will to Power as Knowledge (SS 1939, GA 47); Nietzsche on European Nihilism (second term of 1940, GA 48); Schelling: On the New Interpretation of *The Essence of Human Freedom* (first term of 1941, GA 49); Fundamental Concepts (SS 1941, GA 51); Nietzsche's Metaphysics (announced for WS 1941–42 but not delivered, GA 50); Hölderlin's Hymn "Andenken" (WS 1941–42, GA 52); Hölderlin's Hymn "Der Ister" (SS 1942, GA 53); Parmenides (WS 1942–43, GA 54); Heraclitus 1, The Beginning of Occidental Thought (SS 1943, GA 55); Heraclitus 2, His Doctrine of Logos (SS 1944, GA 55); and Introduction to Philosophy: Thinking and Writing Poetry (WS 1944–45, GA 50).

295. SdU, p. 10: "Der Wille zum Wesen der deutschen Universität ist der Wille zur Wissenschaft als Wille zum geschichtlichen geistigen Auftrag des deutschen Volkes als eines in seinem Staat sich selbst wissenden Volkes."

296. SdU, p. 16: "die schärfste Gefährdung des Daseins inmitten der Übermacht des Seienden." Heidegger also uses his pet-word "being" (Sein) in this context. He continues: "Die Fragwürdigkeit des Seins überhaupt zwingt dem Volk Arbeit und Kampf ab und zwingt es in seinen Staat, dem die Berufe zugehören." As Safranski (1994) points out (ch. 12), Heidegger's three "services" correspond to the three classes of citizens of Plato's *Republic*.

297. SdU, p. 16: "Das mithandelnde Wissen um das Volk, das sich bereithaltende Wissen um das Geschick des Staates schaffen in eins mit dem Wissen um den geistigen Auftrag erst das ursprüngliche und volle Wesen der Wissenschaft."

298. The German universities had been in a crisis since the Great War, and Heidegger had wanted to revolutionize them for some time, using the Platonic Academy and medieval monasteries as an example. Probably he thought that he could use the National Socialist revolution as an occasion for doing so. Cf. Martin (1989), pp. 14–50.

299. Heidegger, "Die Universität im nationalsozialistischen Staat," *Tübinger Chronik* of 1.XII. 1933, also published in Martin (1989), pp. 178–183. Heidegger said, for instance: "Mit der Gefolgschaft wird Dozent und Student hineingebunden in den Staat. . . . Wir können nicht mehr von einem Verhältnis zum Staat sprechen, weil die Universität selbst Staat geworden, ein Glied der Staatsentfaltung. Damit verschwindet der bisherige Charakter der Universität, sie ist die leere Insel eines leeren Staates. Wir Heutigen stehen in der Erkämpfung der neuen Wirklichkeit. Wir sind nur ein Übergang, nur ein Opfer" (p. 183). See for Jaspers' opinion on the rectoral address his letter to Heidegger of 23 August 1933, in Hei/ Ja, p. 155. It is interesting to compare Heidegger's speech in Tübingen with what Heidegger says in "Das Rektorat 1933/34. Tatsachen und Gedanken" (1945), published in 1983. There Heidegger writes differently about his intentions in 1933: "Niemals war es meine Absicht, nur Parteidoktrinen zu verwirklichen und der 'Idee' einer 'politischen Wissenschaft' gemäß zu handeln" (SdU, p. 26). With regard to the rectoral address he writes: "In all

dem liegt die entschiedene Ablehnung der Idee der 'politischen Wissenschaft,' die vom Nationalsozialismus verkündet wurde" (SdU, p. 28). Yet Heidegger made the following statement concerning academic freedom in the rectoral address: "Die vielbesungene 'akademische Freiheit' wird aus der deutschen Universität verstoßen; denn diese Freiheit war unecht, weil nur verneinend" (SdU, p. 15).

300. Heidegger, "Aufruf an die Deutschen Studenten," *Freiburger Studentenzeitung* VIII, no. 1, 3 November 1933, reprinted in Schneeberger (1962), pp. 135ff. and in B. Martin (1989), p. 177. The quote is from the end of this piece: "Nicht Lehrsätze und 'Ideen' seien die Regeln Eures Seins. Der Führer selbst und allein *ist* die heutige und künftige deutsche Wirklichkeit und ihr Gesetz. Lernet immer tiefer zu wissen: Von nun an fordert jedwedes Ding Entscheidung und alles Tun verantwortung. Heil Hitler" (Heidegger's italics). Cf. Ott (1988), pp. 160, 232.

301. Schneeberger (1962), no. 132; Ott (1988), pp. 196–197. See Schneeberger (1962) for other texts of this period.

302. Ott (1988), p. 234. Ott shows that Heidegger's motive for giving up the rectorate was that, according to him, the National Socialist revolution was not sufficiently radical (pp. 234–246).

303. See Ott (1988), p. 133, for a description of the nature of this journal.

304. "Hölderlin und das Wesen der Dichtung," EHD, pp. 33–48.

305. "Wege zur Aussprache" was published in *Alemannenland: Ein Buch von Volkstum und Sendung*, Dr. Franz Kerber, ed., Stuttgart, 1937, and reprinted in Schneeberger (1962), pp. 258–262.

306. The full title of the lecture as delivered on 5 December 1930 was "Philosophieren und Glauben. Das Wesen der Wahrheit." Cf. Schulz (1953–54), p. 89. It is also significant that Heidegger omits mention of this title in his notes on the sources of the texts in W, p. 397. Cf. Grondin (1987), p. 28. This omission fits in with what I call the Pascalian strategy (§§ 11C.6, 12C, and 13C).

307. Cf. on the notion of a "last-hand" edition Kisiel (1992) and GA 5, *Nachwort*. The official label of a last-hand edition is misleading because the editions of lecture notes are often based on collating Heidegger's autographs with lecture notes by his students. More seriously, however, the very idea of a last-hand edition is an essentially ahistorical principle: instead of editing Heidegger's autographs as they were at the time in which they were originally written, the editors of the *Gesamtausgabe* insert Heidegger's later additions and corrections into the original texts, adapting their style. As a consequence, the *Gesamtausgabe* seriously obstructs any attempt to trace Heidegger's *Denkweg* in a purely historical manner. This is one of the reasons why in this book I chose the works that Heidegger published during his lifetime as a primary basis for my interpretation, although even in this case we sometimes encounter the same problem (see § 14, below).

308. One may object that Heidegger planned a second monumental book and wrote a draft of it in the years 1936–38 under the title *Beiträge zur Philosophie (Vom Ereignis)* (*Contributions to Philosophy [On the Event]*). However, Heidegger clearly says in the explanation of this title that *Beiträge* is not meant to be a philosophical treatise in the traditional sense: all false claims to being a treatise in the style of traditional philosophy must be kept away (*Beiträge*, GA 65, p. 3).

309. W, p. 159: "Diese Kehre ist nicht eine Änderung des Standpunktes von *Sein und Zeit*, sondern in ihr gelangt das versuchte Denken erst in die Ortschaft der Dimension, aus der *Sein und Zeit* erfahren ist."

310. *Richardson*, p. xvii.

311. "Brief über den 'Humanismus,' " W, p. 159; *Richardson*, p. xvii. Cf. also SZ, preface to the 7th ed. of 1953, p. v: "Deren [namely, of SZ, first half] Weg bleibt indessen auch heute noch ein notwendiger, wenn die Frage nach dem Sein unser Dasein bewegen soll."

312. Löwith (1986), p. 57.

313. *Richardson*, p. xxiii.

314. Cf. Löwith (1965), p. 12: "Darum sagt Heidegger im Grunde stets ein und dasselbe und, obschon auf komplizierte Weise, ein Einfaches." Cf. Heidegger, "Brief über den 'Humanismus,' " W, p. 193: "Diese bleibende und in ihrem Bleiben auf den Menschen wartende Ankunft des Seins je und je zur Sprache zu bringen, ist die einzige Sache des Denkens. Darum sagen die wesentlichen Denker stets das Selbe."

315. *Grundlinien der Philosophie des Rechts*, 1st ed. (1821), pp. xxi–xxii: "so ist auch die Philosophie, *ihre Zeit in Gedanken erfaßt*" (Hegel's italics); see Hegel (1955), p. 16.

316. Or, for that matter, a Neo-Fichtean leitmotif. Like Heidegger, Fichte postulated a difference between a priori and a posteriori history, and claimed that he was able to grasp the fundamental traits (*Grundzüge*) of his time. There are also striking analogies between Schelling and Heidegger, which I will not explore in this book.

317. Rorty (1980), p. 5: "It is against this background that we should see the work of the three most important philosophers of our century—Wittgenstein, Heidegger, and Dewey. Each tried, in his early years, to find a new way of making philosophy 'foundational'—a new way of formulating an ultimate context for thought. . . . Each of the three, in his later work, broke free of the Kantian conception of philosophy as foundational, and spent his time warning us against those very temptations to which he himself had once succumbed. Thus their later work is therapeutic rather than constructive, edifying rather than systematic." Ten years later, Rorty changed his mind, without telling the readers that he did. In "Heidegger, Contingency, and Pragmatism," he wrote that Heidegger "was never able to shake off the philosophy professor's conviction that everything else stands to philosophy as superstructure to base"; Dreyfus and Hall (1992), p. 225; also in Rorty (1991), p. 49. I criticized Rorty's interpretation of Western philosophy in Philipse (1994) and argued that one should distinguish between different notions of foundationalism.

318. FD, p. 33: "Grundstellungen, die das geschichtliche Dasein inmitten des Seienden im Ganzen zu diesem einnahm und in sich aufnahm. Nach diesen Grundstellungen aber fragen wir"; "Die Zeit des Weltbildes," HW, p. 96: "Das Wesentliche einer metaphysischen Grundstellung umfaßt: 1. die Art und Weise, wie der Mensch Mensch und d. h. er selbst ist . . . ; 2. die Wesensauslegung des Seins des Seienden; 3. den Wesensentwurf der Wahrheit; 4. den Sinn, demgemäß der Mensch hier und dort Maß ist," and so on; N I, pp. 448–462; N II, p. 25 ("die geschichtsgründende Wahrheit der Metaphysik"); B (GA 66), § 15, p. 75, and passim in the later works.

319. FD, p. 50: "Der Wandel der Wissenschaft. . . gründet dabei auf einem zweifachen Grunde: 1. auf der Arbeitserfahrung, d. h. auf der Richtung und Art der Beherrschung und Verwendung des Seienden; 2. auf der Metaphysik, d. h. auf dem Entwurf des Grundwissens vom Sein, auf dem das Seiende wissensmäßig sich aufbaut. Arbeitserfahrung und Seinsentwurf sind dabei wechselweise aufeinander bezogen und treffen sich immer in einem Grundzug der Haltung und des Daseins."

320. As Heidegger says in "Die Frage nach der Technik," it is "eine Weise des Entbergens" (VA, p. 16, and passim).

321. Cf. "Die Zeit des Weltbildes," HW, p. 69: "Die Metaphysik begründet ein Zeitalter, indem sie ihm durch eine bestimmte Auslegung des Seienden und durch eine bestimmte Auffassung der Wahrheit den Grund seiner Wesensgestalt gibt. Dieser Grund durchherrscht alle Erscheinungen, die das Zeitalter auszeichnen," and p. 101: "kann sich nichts entziehen"; "Wozu Dichter?", HW, p. 272: "Als ob es für das Wesensverhältnis, in das der Mensch durch das technische Wollen zum Ganzen des Seienden versetzt ist, noch in einem Nebenbau einen abgesonderten Aufenthalt geben könne, der mehr zu bieten vermöchte als zeitweilige Auswege in die Selbsttäuschungen"; "Die Frage nach der Technik," VA, pp. 19–21, 28: "Das Wesen der modernen Technik bringt den Menschen auf den Weg jenes Entbergens, wodurch das Wirkliche überall, mehr oder weniger vernehmlich, zum Bestand wird," and p. 31: "Wo dieses herrscht, vertreibt es jede andere Möglichkeit der Entbergung."

322. Cf. "Überwindung der Metaphysik," § xxvi, VA, p. 88: "In diesen Prozeß ist auch der Mensch einbezogen, der seinen Charakter, der wichtigste Rohstoff zu sein, nicht mehr länger verbirgt. Der Mensch ist der 'wichtigste Rohstoff,' weil er das Subjekt aller Vernutzung bleibt"; N II, p. 387: "Daß sogar, im Prozeß der unbedingten Vergegenständlichung des Seienden als solchen, das zum Menschenmaterial gewordene Menschentum dem Roh—und Werkstoffmaterial hintangesetzt wird." Finally, there is the baffling text in the unpublished paper "Das Ge-Stell" of 1949, where Heidegger said that "Agriculture is now a mechanized food industry, in essence the same as the manufacturing of corpses in gas chambers and extermination camps, the same as the blockade and starvation of nations, the same as the production of hydrogen bombs," first published by Schirmacher (1983), p. 25. I am quoting Rockmore's (1992) translation (p. 241).

323. "Die Frage nach der Technik," VA, pp. 19–20: "Er ist, was er jetzt als Strom ist, nämlich Wasserdrucklieferant, aus dem Wesen des Kraftwerks. . . . Aber der Rhein bleibt doch, wird man entgegnen, Strom der Landschaft. Mag sein, aber wie? Nicht anders denn als bestellbares Objekt der Besichtigung durch eine Reisegesellschaft, die eine Urlaubsindustrie dorthin bestellt hat"; cf. BW, p. 321.

324. "Die Frage nach der Technik," VA, p. 21: "Der Forstwart, der im Wald das geschlagene Holz vermißt und dem Anschein nach wie sein Großvater in der gleichen Weise dieselben Waldwege begeht, ist heute von der Holzverwertungsindustrie bestellt, ob er es weiß oder nicht." Cf. BW, p. 323.

325. "Die Zeit des Weltbildes," HW, p. 69: "In der Metaphysik vollzieht sich die Besinnung auf das Wesen des Seienden und eine Entscheidung über das Wesen der Wahrheit. Die Metaphysik begründet ein Zeitalter, indem sie ihm durch eine bestimmte Auslegung des Seienden und durch eine bestimmte Auffassung der Wahrheit den Grund seiner Wesensgestalt gibt. Dieser Grund durchherrscht alle Erscheinungen, die das Zeitalter auszeichnen"; "Nietzsches Wort 'Gott ist tot,' " HW, p. 193: "Metaphysik ist im folgenden überall als die Wahrheit des Seienden als solchen im Ganzen gedacht, nicht als Lehre eines Denkers. Dieser hat jeweils seine philosophische Grundstellung in der Metaphysik. . . . In jeder Phase der Metaphysik wird jeweils ein Stück eines Weges sichtbar, den das Geschick des Seins in jähen Epochen der Wahrheit über das Seiende sich bahnt"; FD, p. 50; SvGr, p. 198: "So bestimmt dann die gekennzeichnete Herrschaft des Satzes vom Grund das Wesen des modernen, technischen Zeitalters"; N I, pp. 448–462; N II, p. 343: "Denn die Metaphysik bestimmt die Geschichte des abendländischen Weltalters"; cf. B (GA 66), § 15.

326. Cf. FD, B.I, § 5f.

327. "Das Ende der Metaphysik und die Aufgabe des Denkens," SD, p. 63: "Das Ende der Philosophie ist der Ort, dasjenige, worin sich das Ganze ihrer Geschichte in seine äußerste Möglichkeit versammelt"; cf. on p. 63 also this passage: "Durch die ganze Geschichte der Philosophie hindurch bleibt Platons Denken in abgewandelten Gestalten maßgebend. Die Metaphysik ist Platonismus. Nietzsche kennzeichnet seine Philosophie als umgekehrten Platonismus. Mit der Umkehrung der Metaphysik, die bereits durch Karl Marx vollzogen wird, ist die äußerste Möglichkeit der Philosophie erreicht. Sie ist in ihr Ende eingegangen"; N II, p. 201 and passim.

328. Cf. "Das Rektorat 1933/34. Tatsachen und Gedanken," SdU, p. 24: "Im Jahre 1930 war Ernst Jüngers Aufsatz über 'Die totale Mobilmachung' erschienen; in diesem Aufsatz kündigten sich die Grundzüge des 1932 erschienenen Buches *Der Arbeiter* an. In kleinem Kreis habe ich damals mit meinem Assistenten Brock diese Schriften durchgesprochen und zu zeigen versucht, wie sich darin ein wesentliches Verständnis der Metaphysik Nietzsches ausspricht, insofern im Horizont dieser Metaphysik die Geschichte und Gegenwart des Abendlandes gesehen und vorausgesehen wird." Cf. also Zimmerman (1990), pp. 46–93.

329. SZ, § 29, p. 137: "*Die Stimmung hat je schon das In-der-Welt-sein als Ganzes erschlossen und macht ein Sichrichten auf . . . allererst möglich*" (Heidegger's italics).

330. Cf. GbM (GA 29/30), §§ 17–18; *Beiträge*, § 6, p. 21: "Alles wesentliche Denken verlangt, daß seine Gedanken und Sätze jedesmal neu wie Erz aus der Grundstimmung herausgeschlagen werden. Bleibt die Grundstimmung aus, dann ist alles ein erzwungenes Geklapper von Begriffen und Worthülsen. . . . Allein, die Grundstimmung *stimmt* das Dasein und damit das *Denken* als Entwurf der Wahrheit des Seyns im Wort und Begriff" (Heidegger's italics; in order to understand this quote fully, one should read my § 11, below); N I, p. 62: "Ein Gefühl ist die Weise, in der wir uns in unserem Bezug zum Seienden und damit auch zugleich in unserem Bezug zu uns selbst finden; die Weise, wie wir uns zumal zum Seienden, das wir nicht sind, und zum Seienden, das wir selbst sind, gestimmt finden"; cf. N I, pp. 118–120, 125–126; WiPh, p. 28: "Wir versuchen, auf die Stimme des Seins zu hören. In welche Stimmung bringt sie das heutige Denken? . . . Vermutlich waltet eine Grundstimmung. Sie bleibt uns aber noch verborgen." Heidegger speaks also of *Grunderfahrungen* (fundamental experiences); cf. B (GA 66), § 57; cf. § 90, p. 320: "Die Stimmung gehört zur Er-eignung; als Stimme des Seyns stimmt sie das Er-eignete (zur Gründung der Wahrheit des Seyns Be-stimmte) in eine Grundstimmung— Stimmung, die zum Grunde wird einer Gründung der Wahrheit des Seyns im Da-sein," and so on.

331. WhD, p. 90: "Die Philosophie läßt sich weder auf die Historie, d. h. auf die Geschichtswissenschaft, noch überhaupt auf eine Wissenschaft gründen. Denn jede Wissenschaft ruht auf Voraussetzungen, die niemals wissenschaftlich begründbar sind, wohl dagegen philosophisch erweisbar. Alle Wissenschaften gründen in der Philosophie, aber nicht umgekehrt"; N I, pp. 371–375; "Die Kehre," TK, p. 46; "Wer ist Nietzsches Zarathustra?", VA, p. 115: "Aber das Einzige, was jeweils ein Denker zu sagen vermag, läßt sich logisch oder empirisch weder beweisen noch widerlegen."

332. Bourdieu (1988), chapter 3. I do not endorse, however, Bourdieu's facile claim that because of a "homology" between the domains of philosophy and of politics, a conservative revolution in philosophy somehow denotes a conservative revolution in politics (pp. 73, 79, 83, and passim). Husserl's transcendental turn is also a conservative revolution in philosophy (in the sense that it reinstalls philosophy as the fundamental discipline), but

Husserl cannot be accused of being a conservative revolutionary in politics. To the extent that Bourdieu practices sociology of knowledge, it is armchair sociology *à la française*.

333. Cf. Zimmerman (1990), pp. xv, xxii, 116, 225ff., who takes this as *the* meaning of "being" in Heidegger's works. This is related to the way in which Heidegger reinterprets the term *Wesen* (essence). *Wesen* in the phrase "Das Wesen der Technik" refers to "eine geschickhafte Weise des Entbergens," that is, a history-shaping way in which entities are disclosed to us. See "Die Frage nach der Technik," VA, p. 33.

334. FD, p. 82: "Diese Umkehrung der Bedeutungen der Worte subiectum und obiectum ist keine bloße Angelegenheit des Sprachgebrauches; es ist ein grundstürzender Wandel des Daseins, d. h. der Lichtung des Seins des Seienden, auf Grund der Herrschaft des *Mathematischen. Es ist eine dem gewöhnlichen Auge notwendig verborgene Wegstrecke* der eigentlichen Geschichte, die immer die der Offenbarkeit des Seins—oder gar nichts ist" (Heidegger's italics); EM, p. 70: "Demgemäß hat das 'Sein' jene angezeigte . . . Bedeutung, eine Bestimmtheit . . . die . . . unser geschichtliches Dasein von altersher beherrscht. Mit einem Schlage wird so unser suchen nach der Bestimmtheit der Wortbedeutung 'Sein' ausrücklich zu dem, was es ist, zu einer Besinnung auf die Herkunft unserer *verborgenen Geschichte*" (Heidegger's italics); N II, p. 386: "Geschichte als Sein, gar aus dem Wesen des Seins selbst kommend, bleibt ungedacht." Cf. B (GA 66), § 62, p. 167: "Im Beständnis der Wahrheit des Seyns müssen wir jene ursprüngliche Geschichtlichkeit erreichen, durch die alle Historie überwunden ist."

335. FD, p. 33: "Grundstellungen, die das geschichtliche Dasein inmitten des Seienden im Ganzen zu diesem einnahm und in sich aufnahm. Nach diesen Grundstellungen aber fragen wir, nach dem Geschehen in ihnen und nach den geschehenden Grundbewegungen des Daseins"; and: "Was wir durchschnittlich als Vergangenheit kennen und zunächst vorstellen, ist meist nur das vormalige 'Aktuelle,' das, was damals ein Aufsehen erregte oder gar den Lärm besorgte, der immer zur Geschichte gehört, aber nicht die eigentliche Geschichte ist."

336. Margolis (1983), p. 294, quoted in Zimmerman (1990), p. 258.

337. The expression is Zimmerman's. See Zimmerman (1990), chapter 11.

338. "Brief über den 'Humanismus,' " W, p. 171: "Als eine Gestalt der Wahrheit gründet die Technik in der Geschichte der Metaphysik. Diese selbst ist eine ausgezeichnete und die bisher allein übersehbare Phase der Geschichte des Seins."

339. PIA, p. 268/49–50: "Der Ursprung der 'Kategorien' liegt weder im *logos* als solchen, noch sind sie an den 'Dingen' abgelesen; sie sind die Grundweisen eines bestimmten Ansprechens des bestimmten *aussehensmäßig* in der Vorhabe gehaltenen Gegenstandsfeldes der in *Verrichtung* besorgbaren Umgangsgegenstände. . . . Denn der Sinn für Sein ist ursprünglich *Hergestelltsein*" (Heidegger's italics); cf. pp. 252–253, 260, 266. SZ, § 6, p. 24: "Geschaffenheit aber im weitesten Sinne der Hergestelltheit von etwas ist ein wesentliches Strukturmoment des antiken Seinsbegriffes."

340. Cf. "Die Zeit des Weltbildes" of 1938, in HW.

341. "Überwindung der Metaphysik," §§ xxvi–xxviii, VA, pp. 87–95; N II, p. 20: "Dann und damit beginnt das Zeitalter der *vollendeten Sinnlosigkeit*" (Heidegger's italics).

342. Cf. N II, p. 343: "Denn die Metaphysik bestimmt die Geschichte des abendländischen Weltalters. Das abendländische Menschentum wird in allen seinen Verhältnissen zum Seienden, d. h. auch zu sich selbst, nach allen Hinsichten von der Metaphysik getragen und geleitet."

343. FD, p. 32: "Wir können aber auch von der Unumgänglichkeit eines Fragens überzeugt sein, das alles Bisherige an Tragweite, Tiefgang und Sicherheit noch übertreffen
müsse, weil wir nur so dessen Herr werden, was sonst mit seiner Selbstverständlichkeit
über uns hinwegrast. . . . Wir entscheiden uns für das Fragen, für ein sehr umständliches
und sehr langwieriges Fragen, das auf Jahrzehnte hinaus nur ein Fragen bleibt." See on
the decision that Heidegger's thinking prepares: FD, p. 8: "Indes möchten wir an der Vorbereitung einer Entscheidung mitwerken," and so forth.

344. Cf. FD, p. 31: "Denn die Entscheidungen, die fallen oder nicht fallen, spielen sich
nicht bei der Straßenbahn und beim Motorrad ab, sondern anderswo—nämlich im Bereich
der geschichtlichen Freiheit, d. h. dort, wo ein geschichtliches Dasein sich zu seinem
Grunde entscheidet und wie es sich dazu entscheidet, welche Stufe der Freiheit des Wissens
es sich wählt und was es als Freiheit setzt. Diese Entscheidungen sind zu verschiedenen
Zeiten und bei verschiedenen Völkern verschieden. Sie können nicht erzwungen werden."

345. "Wo aber die Gefahr ist, wächst/ Das Rettende auch." Heidegger quotes this text
many times, for instance in "Die Frage nach der Technik," VA, pp. 32, 39, and in "Wozu
Dichter," HW, p. 273.

346. "Die Frage nach der Technik," VA, p. 28: "Von hier aus bestimmt sich das Wesen
aller Geschichte. Sie ist weder nur der Gegenstand der Historie, noch nur der Vollzug
menschlichen Tuns. Dieses wird geschichtlich erst als ein geschickliches. . . . Das Wesen
der Freiheit ist *ursprünglich* nicht dem Willen oder gar nur der Kausalität des menschlichen
Wollens zugeordnet" (Heidegger's italics); WhD, p. 155: "Das Wesen der Technik ist keine
nur menschliche Machenschaft"; "Der Satz der Identität," ID, pp. 26, 29 ("niemals vom
Menschen allein machbare"); G, p. 19: "diese Mächte sind längst über den Willen und die
Entscheidungsfähigkeit des Menschen hinausgewachsen, weil sie nicht vom Menschen
gemacht sind."

347. "Die Frage nach der Technik," VA, p. 29: "Die Freiheit ist der Bereich des Geschickes, das jeweils eine Entbergung auf ihren Weg bringt."

348. "Überwindung der Metaphysik," § xii, VA, p. 79: "Mit Nietzsches Metaphysik
ist die Philosophie vollendet. Das will sagen: sie hat den Umkreis der vorgezeichneten
Möglichkeiten abgeschritten. Die vollendete Metaphysik, die der Grund der planetarischen
Denkweise ist, gibt das Gerüst für eine vermutlich lange dauernde Ordnung der Erde. Die
Ordnung bedarf der Philosophie nicht mehr, weil sie ihr schon zugrunde liegt. Aber mit
dem Ende der Philosophie ist nicht auch schon das Denken am Ende, sondern im Übergang
zu einem anderen Anfang." Cf. also § x, VA, p. 76, where Heidegger defines "technology"
as the end of metaphysics: "Der Name 'die Technik' ist hier so wesentlich verstanden, daß
er sich in seiner Bedeutung deckt mit dem Titel: die vollendete Metaphysik."

349. Cf. "Brief über den 'Humanismus,' " W, p. 171, where Heidegger observes with
regard to Marx: "Das Wesen des Materialismus besteht nicht in der Behauptung, alles sei
nur Stoff, vielmehr in einer metaphysischen Bestimmung, der gemäß alles Seiende als das
Material der Arbeit erscheint. . . . Das Wesen des Materialismus verbirgt sich im Wesen der
Technik." When Heidegger on p. 170 suggests that his philosophy leads to a "productive
dialogue" with Marxism, he means a dialogue that allegedly shows that Marxism is nothing
but an expression of productionist metaphysics.

350. Safranski (1994), chapter x, p. 205: "Den noch ausstehenden großen zweiten Teil
von *Sein und Zeit*—vorgesehen war die Destruktion exemplarischer Ontologien bei Kant,
Descartes, und Aristoteles—arbeitet Heidegger in den folgenden Jahren zu Einzelschriften
oder Vorlesungen aus: 1929 erscheint *Kant und das Problem der Metaphysik,* 1938 *Die*

Zeit des Weltbildes mit der Kritik des Cartesianismus. . . . In diesem Sinne ist *Sein und Zeit* weitergeführt und auch abgeschlossen worden."

351. SZ, § 6, p. 21: "das Dasein hat . . . die Geneigtheit, an seine Welt, in der es ist, zu verfallen und reluzent aus ihr her sich auszulegen."

352. SZ, § 6, pp. 24–25: "Die res cogitans wird ontologisch bestimmt als ens und der Seinssinn des ens ist für die mittelalterliche Ontologie fixiert im Verständnis des ens als ens creatum. Gott als ens infinitum ist das ens *increatum*. Geschaffenheit aber im weitesten Sinne der Hergestelltheit von etwas ist ein wesentliches Strukturmoment des antiken Seinsbegriffes. Der scheinbare Neuanfang des Philosophierens enthüllt sich als die Pflanzung eines verhängnisvollen Vorurteils" (Heidegger's italics); and p. 25: "Hierbei wird offenbar, daß die antike Auslegung des Seins des Seienden an der 'Welt' bzw. 'Natur' im weitesten Sinne orientiert ist."

353. SZ, § 6, p. 22: "Diese Aufgabe verstehen wir als die *am Leitfaden der Seinsfrage* sich vollziehende *Destruktion* des überlieferten Bestandes der antiken Ontologie auf die ursprünglichen Erfahrungen, in denen die ersten und fortan leitenden Bestimmungen des Seins gewonnen wurden" (Heidegger's italics).

354. SZ, § 15, p. 71: "*Zuhandenheit ist die ontologisch-kategoriale Bestimmung von Seiendem, wie es 'an sich' ist*" (Heidegger's italics). Cf. section 69b. Even natural phenomena show up for us primarily "in the light of natural products" (SZ, § 15, pp. 70–71). However, Heidegger in *Sein und Zeit* also admits of another primary notion of nature: nature that "stirs and strives" (ibid.).

355. VA, p. 38: "Das Wesende der Technik bedroht das Entbergen, droht mit der Möglichkeit, daß alles Entbergen im Bestellen aufgeht und alles sich nur in der Unverborgenheit des Bestandes darstellt. Menschliches Tun kann nie unmittelbar dieser Gefahr begegnen. Menschliche Leistung kann nie allein die Gefahr bannen."

356. SZ, § 5, pp. 16–17: "An dieser sollen nicht beliebige und zufällige, sondern wesenhafte Strukturen herausgestellt werden, die in jeder Seinsart des faktischen Daseins sich als seinsbestimmende durchhalten."

357. SZ, § 6, pp. 20–21: "Hat andererseits das Dasein die in ihm liegende Möglichkeit ergriffen, nicht nur seine Existenz sich durchsichtig zu machen, sondern dem Sinn der Existenzialität selbst . . . nachzufragen, und hat sich in solchem Fragen der Blick für die wesentliche Geschichtlichkeit des Daseins geöffnet, dann ist die Einsicht unumgänglich: das Fragen nach dem Sein . . . ist selbst durch die Geschichtlichkeit charakterisiert. . . . Die Frage nach dem Sinn des Seins ist . . . von ihr selbst dazu gebracht, sich als historische zu verstehen."

358. Cf. Nietzsche, *Vom Nutzen und Nachteil der Historie für das Leben*, in UB.

359. Neither is it possible to argue for a metaphysical framework. Cf. N I, p. 377: "Was sich darstellungsmäßig als Beweis ausgibt, ist nur die Enthüllung der Setzungen, die im Entwurf des Seienden im Ganzen auf das Sein . . . mitgesetzt, und zwar notwendig mitgesetzt sind. Dann ist dieser Beweis nur der zergliedernde Hinweis auf den Zusammenhang des zugleich mit dem Entwurf Mitgesetzten—kurz: Entwurfs-*entfaltung*, aber niemals Entwurfs-errechnung und -begründung" (Heidegger's italics). Cf. "Wer ist Nietzsches Zarathustra?", VA, p. 115: "Aber das Einzige, was jeweils ein Denker zu sagen vermag, läßt sich logisch oder empirisch weder beweisen noch widerlegen"; and p. 117: "Die Geschäftigkeit des Widerlegenwollens gelangt aber nie auf den Weg eines Denkers. Sie gehört in jene Kleingeisterei, deren Auslassungen die Öffentlichkeit zu ihrer Unterhaltung bedarf." On this point, Heidegger's position resembles Carnap's views in "Empiricism, Semantics,

and Ontology," published in Carnap (1956). However, there is an important difference. Whereas Carnap held that the choice between frameworks is pragmatic, Heidegger held that they are "sent" (*geschickt*) to us by Being as our fate (*Geschick*). See section 11, below.

360. Cf. N I, p. 375: "Der Beweisgang für die Wiederkunftslehre untersteht daher an keiner Stelle dem Gerichtshof der Naturwissenschaft, selbst dann nicht, wenn naturwissenschaftliche 'Tatsachen' gegen sein Ergebnis sprechen sollten; denn was sind 'Tatsachen' der Naturwissenschaft und jeder Wissenschaft anderes als bestimmte Erscheinungen, ausgelegt nach ausdrücklichen oder verschwiegenen oder überhaupt ungekannten Grundsätzen einer Metaphysik, d. h. einer Lehre vom Seienden im Ganzen?"

361. Cf. "Vom Wesen des Grundes," § iii, W, p. 60: "Das entwerfend-überwerfende Waltenlassen von Welt ist die Freiheit," and "Vom Wesen der Wahrheit," § 3, W, p. 81: "*Das Wesen der Wahrheit ist die Freiheit*" (Heidegger's italics).

362. Cf. SZ, §§ 72–77.

363. In this sense, Heidegger wrote still in EM (1935): "Es gab doch eine Zeit, da der Mensch nicht war. Aber streng genommen können wir nicht sagen: es gab eine Zeit, da der Mensch nicht *war*. Zu jeder *Zeit* war und ist und wird der Mensch sein, weil Zeit sich nur zeitigt, sofern der Mensch ist. Es gibt keine Zeit, da der Mensch nicht war, nicht weil der Mensch von Ewigkeit her und in alle Ewigkeit hin ist, sondern weil Zeit nicht Ewigkeit ist und Zeit sich nur je zu einer Zeit als menschlich-geschichtliches Dasein zeitigt" (p. 64, Heidegger's italics).

364. Ott (1988), pp. 45–61; cf. Nolte (1992) for a much less critical view of Heidegger's life by the participant in the *Historikerstreit*.

365. Ott (1988), pp. 46–48.

366. Pöggeler in Rockmore and Margolis (1992), p. 119.

367. Ott (1988), pp. 62–66. The GA edition of the early works (FS, GA vol. 1) starts with a piece from 1912 on O. Külpe's solution to the problem of the external world: "Das Realitätsproblem in der modernen Philosophie." GA 13, *Aus der Erfahrung des Denkens*, contains four pieces from 1910–11: three poems and the report on the revelation of a memorial for Abraham-a-Sancta-Clara in Kreenheinstetten, August 1910. But Heidegger published a review of F. W. Förster's *Autorität und Freiheit* (1910) in *Der Akademiker* of May 1910, in which he wholeheartedly endorsed Förster's defense of Catholic authoritarianism against modern influences. Two other publications of Heidegger's hand in *Der Akademiker* (1910, 1911), discussed by Ott reveal the same strictly Catholic and authoritarian attitude.

368. Ott (1988), p. 59.

369. Ott (1988), p. 68.

370. Ott (1988), pp. 90–92. According to Ott, Heidegger was opportunistic in this respect.

371. Cf., again, Ott (1988), p. 96: "es war der entscheidende Schlag. Erinnern wir uns: Abweisung durch die Jesuiten—wegen unzureichender gesundheitlicher Stabilität; Abweisung durch die Erzdiözese Freiburg aus demselben Grund. Jetzt diese Behandlung durch katholische Kreise! Die erste Kehre—nicht eine denkerische!—bahnte sich an: die Abkehr nämlich vom Katholizismus." According to Ott, Heidegger's early resentment explains his later invectives against the Catholic Church. Cf. section 15C, below.

372. This letter, first published by Bernhard Casper in 1980 (see *Freiburger Diözesan-Archiv*, Nr. 100, pp. 534ff.), was quoted in full in a corrected version by Ott (1988),

pp. 106–107. See also Sheehan in Guignon (1993), pp. 71–72. For the influence of Luther on Heidegger's early thought, see Van Buren (1994).

373. We should note, however, that officially Heidegger remained a Catholic during his entire life. See Ott (1988), p. 49.

374. Cf. Van Buren (1994) and Kisiel (1993).

375. FS, p. 406: "Innerhalb des Reichtums der Gestaltungsrichtungen des lebendigen Geistes ist die theoretische Geisteshaltung nur *eine*, weshalb es ein prinzipieller und verhängnisvoller Irrtum der Philosophie . . . genannt werden muß, wenn sie . . .nicht, was ihres eigentlichsten Berufes ist . . . auf einen Durchbruch in die wahre Wirklichkeit und wirkliche Wahrheit abzielt" (Heidegger's italics). Cf. Kisiel (1993), p. 18.

376. For the relation between Scholasticism and mysticism, see also the final chapter of the *Habilitationsschrift*, FS, p. 410: "Scholastik und Mystik gehören für die mittelalterliche Weltanschauung wesentlich zusammen. . . . Philosophie als vom Leben abgelöstes, rationalistisches Gebilde ist *machtlos*, Mystik als irrationalistisches Erleben ist *ziellos*" (Heidegger's italics). Cf. Van Buren (1994), pp. 160–161 and 166; GA 61, p. 7.

377. Cf. Kisiel (1993), pp. 73–74, 101, 111, 228.

378. See Kisiel (1993), pp. 151–217, for a summary of the course, which was published in 1995 in GA 60: *Phänomenologie des religiösen Lebens*. For the *disputatio*, see KM, p. 263: "daß die Philosophie die Aufgabe hat, aus dem faulen Aspekt eines Menschen, der bloß die Werke des Geistes benutzt, gewissermaßen den Menschen zurückzuwerfen in die Härte seines Schicksals"; and the introduction to the present book. Cf. also Jung (1990) on the religious theme in Heidegger's development to *Sein und Zeit*. As Jung argues (pp. 41–62), the religious courses already aimed at a hermeneutics of factical life, leaving undecided the choice for or against Christian faith. Cf. also Sheehan (1979).

379. Heidegger took the term *Destruktion* from Luther's writings. In his Heidelberg *Disputatio*, Luther used the verb *destruere* (to destroy) in translating 1 *Corinthians* 1:19: "I will destroy the wisdom of the wise." The idea is that the wisdom of the Greeks has to be destroyed in order to make room for faith in Christ crucified. Cf. Van Buren (1994), p. 167.

380. Cf. GA 60 and Jung (1990), pp. 56–62.

381. See Thomä (1990), Kisiel (1993), and Greisch (1994), pp. 1–66, for a detailed description of this development.

382. See section 7, above.

383. On Aristotle's influences in *Sein und Zeit*, see the papers by Franco Volpi and Walter Brogan in Kisiel and Van Buren (1994) and Volpi's paper in Macann (1992), vol. 2.

384. Cf. Kisiel (1993), p. 409.

385. "Aus einem Gespräch von der Sprache," *Sprache*, p. 96: "Ohne diese theologische Herkunft wäre ich nie auf den Weg des Denkens gelangt. Herkunft aber bleibt stets Zukunft."

386. Cf. GA 2, p. 264, note 3; p. 243, note vii; GA 20, pp. 418–419 and 302–303; GA 60, p. 349; and GA 61, p. 90.

387. SZ, § 38, first paragraphs. One might argue, however, that St. Paul interpreted the Fall in the very same way as Heidegger's *Verfallen* in *Sein und Zeit*: as a tendency in human life.

388. See on the notion of formal indication: section 8B, above; Kisiel (1993), passim, Oudemans (1990), and Jung (1990), pp. 48, 53, 55, 75, 143–145. Jung explicitly warns against a religious interpretation of SZ (pp. 77–82, 100ff.).

389. PIA, p. 246/15: "Philosophie [ist] als *fragendes* Erkennen, das heißt als *Forschung*, nur der genuine explizite Vollzug der Auslegungstendenz der Grundbewegtheiten des Lebens, in denen es diesem um sich selbst und sein Sein geht . . ., das heißt, [daß] die Philosophie *grundsätzlich atheistisch* ist" (Heidegger's italics); and GA 63, p. 197.

390. PIA, p. 246/15: " 'Atheistisch' nicht im Sinne einer Theorie als Materialismus oder dergleichen. Jede Philosophie, die in dem, was sie ist, sich selbst versteht, muß als das faktische Wie der Lebensauslegung gerade dann, wenn sie dabei noch eine 'Ahnung' von Gott hat, wissen, daß das von ihr vollzogene sich zu sich selbst Zurückreißen des Lebens, religiös gesprochen, eine Handaufhebung gegen Gott ist. Damit allein aber steht sie ehrlich, d. h. gemäß der ihr als solcher verfügbaren Möglichkeit vor Gott; atheistisch besagt hier: sich freihaltend von verführerischer, Religiosität lediglich beredender, Besorgnis."

391. Cf. Jung (1990), part 4, for a study of Bultmann's reception of *Sein und Zeit*, and sections 12C and 13C, below, for a solution to this problem.

392. "Vom Wesen des Grundes," W, p. 55, note 56: "Durch die ontologische Interpretation des Daseins als In-der-Welt-sein ist weder positiv noch negativ über ein mögliches Sein zu Gott entschieden. Wohl aber wird durch die Erhellung der Transzendenz allererst ein *zureichender Begriff* des *Daseins* gewonnen, mit Rücksicht auf welches Seiende nunmehr *gefragt* werden kann, wie es mit dem Gottesverhältnis des Daseins ontologisch bestellt ist" (Heidegger's italics).

393. SZ, § 10, p. 49: "Aber die Idee der 'Transzendenz,' daß der Mensch etwas sei, das über sich hinauslangt, hat ihre Wurzeln in der christlichen Dogmatik, von der man nicht wird sagen wollen, daß sie das Sein des Menschen je ontologisch zum Problematik gemacht hätte."

394. Cf. SZ, § 6, pp. 24–25, and § 20.

395. Recall SZ, § 44c, p. 229, where Heidegger speaks of "längst noch nicht radikal ausgetriebenen Resten von christlicher Theologie innerhalb der philosophischen Problematik."

396. SZ, § 83, p. 436: "Die Herausstellung der Seinsverfassung des Daseins bleibt aber gleichwohl nur *ein Weg*. Das *Ziel* ist die Ausarbeitung der Seinsfrage überhaupt" (Heidegger's italics).

397. However, we can never exclude that the later Heidegger interpreted *Sein und Zeit* in a way very different from the way he intended the book when he was writing it. Indeed, it is obvious that Heidegger reinterpreted the existentialia of *Sein und Zeit* in his later works, as Löwith (1965, pp. 22–38) and Von Herrmann (1964) argued. See sections 12B–C and 13C, below, for discussion.

398. Cf. Löwith (1965), first published in 1953; Gründer (1961); Franzen (1975); and many others.

399. Many early Catholic readers of *Sein und Zeit*, such as Welte (1947) and Lotz (1958), went in this direction. Cf. also Steiner (1978), p. 64: "None the less, the substitution of 'the One'. . . or, simply, of 'God' for *Sein* . . . in many key passages in Heidegger's texts is undeniably plausible"; and Macquarrie (1994), p. 99: "When we were considering the *Letter on Humanism*, it seemed to me that at the time it was written, Being was, for Heideg-

ger, if not God, then a surrogate for God, for the language used in respect to Being was very much like the language of religion. Thus, although Heidegger explicitly says in the *Letter* that Being is not God, one might argue that Being has taken the place of God."

400. Cf. Safranski (1994), p. 492. Cf. "Brief über den 'Humanismus,' " W, p. 162: "Das 'Sein'—das ist nicht Gott."

401. On Heidegger and Eastern religions, see Parkes (1987), and the essay of Zimmerman in Guignon (1993), with many biographical references. On the influence of Eckhart, see Caputo (1986), and his "Meister Eckhart and the Later Heidegger," in Macann II (1992), chapter 21. Macquarrie (1984), pp. 153ff., argues that, broadly speaking, Heidegger stands in the Neo-Platonist tradition. For Heidegger's relation to Christian theology, see Jung (1990), Gethmann-Siefert (1974), Noller (1967), and Robinson and Cobb (1965).

402. Carl Braig, one of Heidegger's professors of theology in Freiburg, wrote *Vom Sein. Abriß der Ontologie* (1896), a book that Heidegger read in 1908–9 during his final year at the Gymnasium. See "Mein Weg in die Phänomenologie," SD, p. 81. Cf. on Carl Braig also the preface that Heidegger wrote to the first edition of *Frühe Schriften* in 1972, FS, pp. x–xi (GA I, pp. 56–57): "Die entscheidende und darum in Worten nicht faßbare Bestimmung für die spätere eigene akademische Lehrtätigkeit ging von zwei Männern aus, die zu Gedächtnis und Dank hier eigens genannt seien: Der eine war der Professor für systematische Theologie Carl Braig, der letzte aus der Überlieferung der Tübinger spekulativen Schule, die durch die Auseinandersetzung mit Hegel und Schelling der katholischen Theologie Rang und Weite gab." Cf. Schaeffler (1988), especially pp. 291–295.

403. The letter was first published in Papenfuss and Pöggeler (1990), vol. 2, pp. 27–32. Cf. Kisiel (1993), pp. 78–79, for extended quotes and comments.

404. Kisiel (1993), p. 77. Cf. Gadamer (1983), "Die religiöse Dimension," p. 142, who comments on the letter to Löwith as follows: "Man geht nicht fehl, wenn man hier die tiefste Motivation für Heideggers Denkweg erkennt: er sieht sich—damals—als einen christlichen Theologen. Das will sagen: alle seine Anstrengungen, mit sich und seinen eigenen Fragen ins Reine zu kommen, sind herausgefordert durch die Aufgabe, sich von der herrschenden Theologie, in der er erzogen war, freizumachen, um ein Christ sein zu können." Cf. ibid., p. 147.

405. Papenfuss and Pöggeler (1991), vol. 2, p. 29: "Ich arbeite konkret faktisch aus meinem 'ich bin'—aus meiner geistigen überhaupt faktischen Herkunft—Milieu—Lebenszusammenhängen, aus dem, was mir von da aus zugänglich ist als lebendige Erfahrung, worin ich lebe. . . . Zu dieser meiner Faktizität gehört—was ich kurz nenne—, daß ich 'christlicher Theo*loge*' bin" (Heidegger's italics). I am using Kisiel's translation in the text, with one minor correction.

406. Kisiel (1993), p. 78; Van Buren (1994), p. 173.

407. Papenfuss and Pöggeler (1991), vol. 2, pp. 29–30: "Sie beide nehmen ein anderes an mir als wesentlich—was ich nicht trenne— . . . das wissenschaftliche, theoretisch begrifflich forschende und das eigene Leben. Die wesentliche Weise der existentiellen Artikulation meiner Faktizität ist die wissenschaftliche Forschung,—so wie ich sie vollziehe. Dabei ist für mich nie Motiv und Ziel des Philosophierens, den Bestand von objektiven Wahrheiten zu vermehren, weil die Objektivität der Philosophie—so weit ich verstehe und wonach ich faktisch gehe—etwas eigenes ist."

408. Cf. GA 60, course of 1920–21, p. 3: "Es besteht ein prinzipieller Unterschied zwischen Wissenschaft und Philosophie"; cf. pp. 7, 9, 15, 62, 64: "Das ist eine Stellungnahme, die der Wissenschaft auf das Äußerste entgegengesetzt ist." For a late text in Hei-

degger's oeuvre, see "Das Ende der Philosophie und die Aufgabe des Denkens" (1964), in which Heidegger pleads for a "thinking" that is neither metaphysics nor science: SD, p. 66: "Ein Denken, das weder Metaphysik noch Wissenschaft sein kann."

409. SZ, § 7C, p. 37: "Sachhaltig genommen ist die Phänomenologie die Wissenschaft vom Sein des Seienden—Ontologie. In der gegebenen Erläuterung der Aufgaben der Ontologie entsprang die Notwendigkeit einer Fundamentalontologie." Accordingly, the fundamental ontology of Dasein and *Sein* is the fundamental science.

410. "Mein bisheriger Weg," B (GA 66), pp. 415–416: "Und wer wollte verkennen, daß auf diesem ganzen bisherigen Weg verschwiegen die Auseinandersetzung mit dem Christentum mitging—eine Auseinandersetzung, die kein aufgegriffenes 'Problem' war und ist, sondern Wahrung der eigensten Herkunft—des Elternhauses, der Heimat und der Jugend—und schmerzliche Ablösung davon in *einem*. Nur wer so verwurzelt ist in einer wirklichen gelebten katholischen Welt, mag etwas von den Notwendigkeiten ahnen, die auf dem bisherigen Weg meines Fragens wie unterirdische Erdstöße wirkten. . . . Es ist nicht schicklich, von diesen innersten Auseinandersetzungen zu reden, die nicht um Fragen der Dogmatik und der Glaubensartikel sich drehen, sondern nur um die Eine Frage, ob der Gott vor uns auf der Flucht ist oder nicht und ob wir selbst dieses noch wahrhaft und d. h. als Schaffende erfahren. Es handelt sich aber auch nicht um einen bloß 'religiösen' Hintergrund der Philosophie, sondern um die Eine Frage nach der Wahrheit des Seins, die allein über die 'Zeit' und den 'Ort' entscheidet, der uns geschichtlich aufbehalten ist innerhalb der Geschichte des Abendlandes und seiner Götter. . . . Aber weil die innersten Erfahrungen und Entscheidungen das Wesentliche bleiben, deshalb müssen sie aus der Öffentlichkeit herausgehalten werden" (Heidegger's italics).

411. Löwith (1965), p. 111: "Was aber allem von Heidegger je Gesagten hintergründig zugrunde liegt und viele aufhorchen und hinhorchen läßt, ist ein Ungesagtes: das *religiöse Motiv*, das sich zwar vom christlichen Glauben abgelöst hat, aber gerade in seiner dogmatisch ungebundenen Unbestimmtheit um so mehr diejenigen anspricht, die nicht mehr gläubige Christen sind, aber doch religiös sein möchten" (Löwith's italics).

412. Guignon (1993), p. 41, note 34; cf. Van Buren (1994) and Jung (1990) on the importance of Luther for Heidegger.

413. Ott (1988), pp. 11, 112ff., 120, 123; Kisiel (1993), passim. Cf. Van Buren (1994).

414. I am quoting an English translation from Luther (1962), p. 470. For the German text of "An den Christlichen Adel deutscher Nation von des Christlichen Standes Besserung," see Luther (1888), vol. 6.

415. Recall that Heidegger's term *Destruktion* was borrowed from Luther's Heidelberg disputation. Cf. Van Buren (1994), pp. 167–168.

416. SZ, § 1, p. 2: "Sie hat das Forschen von *Plato* und *Aristoteles* in Atem gehalten, um freilich auch von da an zu verstummen," and so on (Heidegger's italics). Remember that for Carl Braig, Heidegger's teacher in Catholic dogmatics at the University of Freiburg, the question of Being was also concerned with God as the ground of all beings. Cf. Braig (1896), § 30.

417. SZ, § 6, p. 21: "das Dasein hat nicht nur die Geneigtheit, an seine Welt, in der es ist, zu verfallen und reluzent aus ihr her sich auszulegen, Dasein verfällt in eins damit auch seiner mehr oder minder ausdrücklich ergriffenen Tradition. Diese nimmt ihm die eigene Führung, das Fragen und Wählen ab." In fact, the first kind of "falling" derives from Paul and Luther as well.

418. About Heidegger's early reading of Nietzsche, see the preface that Heidegger wrote for the first edition of *Frühe Schriften* in 1972, GA 1, p. 56: "Was die erregenden Jahre zwischen 1910 und 1914 brachten läßt sich gebührend nicht sagen, sondern nur durch eine Weniges auswählende Aufzählung andeuten: Die zweite um das Doppelte vermehrte Ausgabe von Nietzsches *Willen zur Macht*." There is one reference to Nietzsche in the *Habilitationsschrift* of 1915, GA 1, p. 196 (FS, p. 138): "Zumeist liegt daher jeder philosophischen Konzeption eine persönliche Stellungnahme des betreffenden Philosophen zugrunde. Dieses Bestimmtsein aller Philosophie vom Subjekt her hat Nietzsche in seiner unerbittlich herben Denkart und plastischen Darstellungsfähigkeit auf die bekannte Formel gebracht vom '*Trieb, der philosophiert*' " (Heidegger's italics).

419. Cf. Pöggeler (1990), "Nachwort dur dritten Auflage," pp. 369–370ff., 381, 388.

420. SdU, p. 24: "Im Jahre 1930 war Ernst Jüngers Aufsatz über 'Die totale Mobilmachung' erschienen; in diesem Aufsatz kündigten sich die Grundzüge des 1932 erschienenen Buches *Der Arbeiter* an. In kleinem Kreis habe ich damals mit meinem Assistenten Brock diese Schriften durchgesprochen und zu zeigen versucht, wie sich darin ein wesentliches Verständnis der Metaphysik Nietzsches ausspricht, insofern im Horizont dieser Metaphysik die Geschichte und Gegenwart des Abendlandes gesehen und vorausgesehen wird."

421. SdU, p. 12: "Die nachkommende christlich-theologische Weltdeutung, ebenso wie das spätere mathematisch-technische Denken der Neuzeit haben die Wissenschaft zeitlich und sachlich von ihrem Anfang entfernt." Heidegger quotes Nietzsche on the next page.

422. SdU, p. 12: "die innerst bestimmende Mitte des ganzen volklich-staatlichen Daseins."

423. Heidegger echoes this Lutheran doctrine in ID, p. 70: "Dies ist die Ursache als die Causa sui. So lautet der sachgerechte Name für den Gott in der Philosophie. Zu diesem Gott kann der Mensch weder beten, noch kann er ihm opfern. Vor der Causa sui kann der Mensch weder aus Scheu ins Knie fallen, noch kann er vor diesem Gott musizieren und tanzen."

424. Cf. N II, pp. 347–349, especially: "Wenn aber die Metaphysik als solche das Sein selbst nicht denkt, weil sie das Sein im Sinne des Seienden als solchen denkt, müssen die Ontologie und die Theologie, beide aus der wechselseitigen Angewiesenheit auf einander, das Sein selbst ungedacht lassen" (pp. 348–349); cf. also *Beiträge*, § 52, p. 110: "Die *Seinsverlassenheit* ist am stärksten dort, wo sie sich am entschiedensten versteckt. Das geschieht da, wo das Seiende das Gewöhnlichste und Gewohnteste geworden ist und werden mußte. Das geschah zuerst im *Christentum* und seiner Dogmatik" (Heidegger's italics); § 225, p. 350: "Gerade die vielfach abgewandelte Herrschaft des 'christlichen' Denkens . . . erschwert jeden Versuch . . . aus ursprünglicherer Erfahrung den Grundbezug von Seyn und Wahrheit anfänglich zu denken"; and §§ 81–114.

425. Ott (1988), p. 216.

426. Domarus (1973), vol. 1, p. 17. In his speech of 8 November 1943, Hitler said: "Auch ich bin religiös und zwar tief innerlich religiös, und ich glaube, daß die Vorsehung die Menschen wägt und denjenigen, der vor der Prüfung der Vorsehung nicht bestehen kann, sondern in ihr zerbricht, nicht zu Größerem bestimmt hat"; see Domarus (1973), vol. 2, p. 2057. Like Heidegger, Hitler invented a private religion, according to which human beings are put to the test of fate.

427. That this was one of Heidegger's reasons for his destruction of Christianity is confirmed by Buhr's recollections of a *Wissenschaftslager* in Todtnauberg, 1933. Cf. Ott

(1988), p. 216: "Wenn man das Christentum angreifen wolle, dann genüge es nicht, sich auf den zweiten Artikel dieser Lehre (von Jesus als dem Christus) zu beschränken. Schon der erste Artikel, daß ein Gott die Welt geschaffen habe und erhalte,—daß das Seiende bloß ein Gemachtes sei als von einem Handwerker hergestellt—, das müsse zuerst verworfen werden. Schon da liege der Grund einer falschen Weltentwertung, Weltverachtung und Weltverneinung . . . unwahr gegen das große, noble Wissen um Ungeborgenheit des 'Daseins.' " Only a complete publication of the manuscripts that Heidegger wrote for the conference of the *Amt für Wissenschaft der Deutschen Studentenschaft* in Berlin, 10–11 June 1933, and for his *Wissenschaftslager* will reveal the full extent of his anti-Christian attitude in 1933–34.

428. *Beiträge*, §§ 7, 14, 44, 52, 61, 72, 85, 110, 116, 225, 256, and 259.

429. "Brief über den 'Humanismus,' " W, p. 155: "Die Metaphysik verschließt sich dem einfachen Wesensbestand, daß der Mensch nur in seinem Wesen west, in dem er vom Sein angesprochen wird." Cf. also EM, p. 22: "Das Dasein ist es *selbst* aus seinem wesenhaften *Bezug zum* Sein überhaupt" (Heidegger's italics); p. 156: "Mit der Frage nach dem Wesen des Seins ist die Frage, wer der Mensch sei, innig verknüpft"; cf. EM, pp. 63–64, 106–107, 124, 131, 133–135, and passim in the later works.

430. Letter to the editor, *Die Zeit* (8, no. 39) of 24 September 1953: "Die *Einführung in die Metaphysik* aus dem Sommersemester 1935 wurde als erste unter den schon länger geplanten Vorlesungsveröffentlichungen ausgewählt, weil ich sie ihrer Thematik nach für besonders geeignet halte, eine Strecke des Weges von *Sein und Zeit* (1927) bis zu den letzten Veröffentlichungen sichtbar zu machen," quoted in GA 40, p. 232. EM starts with the question with which WiM ends, the question "why there is something and not rather nothing," and it ends with an eulogy on "questioning": "Fragen können heißt: warten können, sogar ein Leben lang" (p. 157).

431. EM, p. 1: "Jeder wird einmal, vielleicht sogar dann und wann, von der verborgenen Macht dieser Frage gestreift, ohne recht zu fassen, was ihm geschieht. In einer großen Verzweiflung, z. B.," and so on.

432. EM, pp. 2–5, especially p. 4: "Das Fragen dieser Frage ist nur im Sprung und als Sprung und sonst überhaupt nicht." See for Being as *Grund*: EM, pp. 24–25; "Der Satz vom Grund," SvGr; and *Beiträge*, § 5, p. 13: "Die Fragenden haben alle Neugier abgelegt; ihr Suchen liebt den Abgrund, in dem sie den ältesten Grund wissen"; §§ 9, 11, 242, pp. 379–380: "Der Ab-grund ist die ursprüngliche Wesung des Grundes. . . . Der Ur-grund, der gründende, ist das *Seyn*" (Heidegger's italics); and part V, *Die Gründung*.

433. EM, p. 5: "Wem z. B. die Bibel göttliche Offenbarung und Wahrheit ist, der hat vor allem Fragen der Frage 'Warum ist überhaupt Seiendes und nicht vielmehr Nichts?' schon die Antwort."

434. EM, p. 5: "er kann nicht eigentlich fragen, ohne sich selbst als einen Gläubigen aufzugeben mit allen Folgen dieses Schrittes."

435. Paul's first epistle to the Corinthians, 1:18–20, and EM, p. 6: "Was in unserer Frage eigentlich gefragt wird, ist für den Glauben eine Torheit. In dieser Torheit besteht die Philosophie. Eine 'christliche Philosophie' ist ein hölzernes Eisen und ein Mißverständnis."

436. EM, p. 80.

437. Ott (1988), pp. 255–267. Without mentioning the author, Heidegger writes about Haecker's book: "Zwar gibt es jetzt Bücher mit dem Titel: 'Was ist der Mensch?' Aber diese Frage steht nur in Buchstaben auf dem Buchdeckel. Gefragt wird nicht; keineswegs

deshalb, weil man das Fragen bei dem vielen Bücherschreiben nur vergessen hätte, sondern weil man eine Antwort auf die Frage bereits besitzt und zwar eine solche Antwort, mit der zugleich gesagt wird, daß man gar nicht fragen darf. . . . Daß man aber auf den Buchdeckel seiner Bücher die Frage setzt: Was ist der Mensch?, obgleich man *nicht* fragt, weil man *nicht* fragen will und *nicht* kann, das ist ein Verfahren, das von vornherein jedes Recht verwirkt hat, ernst genommen zu werden," and so on (EM, p. 109; Heidegger's italics). As is typical for his later writings (and, incidentally, for Hitler's speeches), Heidegger abuses the author instead of engaging in a real discussion with the book. Only if one reads Haecker (1933), which is a passionate defense of the universal idea of man as an image of God against racism and nationalism, can one understand the enormity of Heidegger's sarcastic dismissal.

438. EM, p. 6: "Alles wesentliche Fragen der Philosophie bleibt notwendig unzeitgemäß."

439. On 18 March 1968, Heidegger wrote in a letter to S. Zemach that "the whole of the lecture series" (of EM) makes clear "daß meine Stellung zum Nationalsozialismus in jener Zeit bereits eindeutig gegnerisch war." The difficulty is, of course, that Heidegger's texts of the time were everything except unambiguous (*eindeutig*). Heidegger's destruction of Christian philosophy could also be seen as his philosophical contribution to the German revolution. Did Heidegger not tell Löwith in 1936 that he still supported Nazism and that he had underestimated the force of the Christian churches? See Löwith (1986), p. 57: "Er ließ auch keinen Zweifel über seinen Glauben an Hitler; nur zwei Dinge habe er unterschätzt: die Lebenskraft der christlichen Kirchen und die Hindernisse für den Anschluß von Österreich. Er war nach wie vor überzeugt, daß der Nationalsozialismus der für Deutschland vorgezeichnete Weg sei; man müsse nur lange genug 'durchhalten.' "

440. *Beiträge*, § 7, p. 26: "Erst wenn wir ermessen, wie einzig notwendig das Sein ist und wie es doch nicht als der Gott selbst west"; pp. 26–27: "Die Wahrheit des Seyns aber als Offenheit des Sichverbergens ist zugleich die Entrückung in die Entscheidung über Ferne und Nähe der Götter und so die Bereitschaft zum Vorbeigang des letzten Gottes." For Heidegger's polemics against Christianity, see *Beiträge*, §§ 7, 14, 44, 52, 61, 72, 85, 110, 116, 225, 256, and 259.

441. Cf. again *Beiträge*, p. 27, where Heidegger says that "Die Wahrheit des Seins . . . ist . . . die Bereitschaft zum Vorbeigang des letzten Gottes."

442. Cf. *Beiträge*, § 126, p. 243: "Einst wurde die Seiendheit zum Seiendsten (. . .), und dieser Meinung zufolge wurde das Seyn zum Wesen des Gottes selbst, wobei der Gott begriffen wurde als die verfertigende Ursache alles Seienden (. . .). Dies bringt den Anschein herauf, als sei damit das Seyn (. . .) am höchsten geschätzt und demnach auch in seinem Wesen getroffen. Und dennoch ist dieses die Verkennung des Seyns.".

443. EM, pp. 14ff., 24ff.

444. Cf. EM, pp. 14–15 (a later addition to the text), and 136ff. Heidegger's interpretation of metaphysics as forgetfulness of being is not as explicit in EM as in later works.

445. EM, p. 29: "Fragen: Wie steht es um das Sein?—das besagt nichts Geringeres als den Anfang unseres geschichtlich-geistigen Daseins *wieder-holen*, um ihn in den anderen Anfang zu verwandeln" (Heidegger's italics).

446. EM, p. 126: "Aber wir müssen an den ursprünglichen Wesenszusammenhang des dichterischen und denkerischen Sagens erinnern; zumal dann, wenn es sich wie hier um das anfängliche dichtend-denkende Gründen und Stiften des geschichtlichen Daseins eines Volkes handelt." Cf. p. 20 and *Beiträge*, part V, *Die Gründung*.

447. EM, p. 152: "Was heute vollends als Philosophie des Nationalsozialismus herumgeboten wird, aber mit der inneren Wahrheit und Größe dieser Bewegung (. . .) nicht das Geringste zu tun hat." Heidegger added something about planetary technology between brackets when he edited the text of EM in 1953. See GA 40, pp. 233–234, and section 14, below. It is interesting to note that Hitler also used the phrase *innere Größe* in relation to Nazism. See, for instance, Hitler's speech to the *Reichstag* on 30 January 1934: "Wenn wir heute rückblickend das Jahr 1933 als das Jahr der nationalsozialistischen Revolution nennen, dann wird dereinst eine objektive Beurteilung seiner Ereignisse und Vorgänge diese Bezeichnung als gerechtfertigt in die Geschichte unseres Volkes übernehmen. Es wird dabei nicht als entscheidend angesehen werden die maßvolle Form, in der sich diese Umwälzung äußerlich vollzog, als vielmehr die innere Größe der Wandlung." See Domarus (1973), vol. 1, p. 352.

448. EM, p. 29: "Unser Volk erfährt als in der Mitte stehend den schärfsten Zangendruck, das nachbarreichste Volk und so das gefährdetste Volk und in all dem das metaphysische Volk," and so on. Cf. p. 32: "Es gilt, das geschichtliche Dasein des Menschen und d. h. immer zugleich unser eigenstes künftiges, im Ganzen der uns bestimmten Geschichte in die Macht des ursprünglich zu eröffnenden Seins zurückzufügen." Heidegger relates the question of being to "dem Schicksal Europas, worin das Schicksal der Erde entschieden wird, wobei für Europa selbst unser geschichtliches Dasein sich als die Mitte erweist." In short, the fate of the earth will be decided by Germany's decision to renew the revelation of Being. Cf. also *Beiträge*, §§ 15, 45, and 251 on *Seyn* and *Volk*.

449. Heidegger rejects the usual translation "Thinking and being are the same," and prefers the following one: "Zusammengehörig sind Vernehmung wechselweise und Sein": EM, pp. 104–111.

450. EM, p. 134: "*Hier*, am Anfang, ist . . . das Menschsein in die Eröffnung des Seins des Seienden gegründet" (Heidegger's italics). Cf. EM, pp. 63–64, 106–107, 124, 133–135, 156.

451. EM, p. 156: "Die Frage nach dem Menschsein ist jetzt in ihrer Richtung und Reichweite *einzig* aus der Frage nach dem *Sein* bestimmt. Das Wesen des Menschen ist innerhalb der Seinsfrage gemäß der verborgenen Anweisung des Anfangs als *die Stätte* zu begreifen und zu begründen, die sich das Sein zur Eröffnung ernötigt. Der Mensch ist das in sich offene Da" (Heidegger's italics).

452. EM, pp. 137–152. Cf. WiPh, p. 15: "Heraklit und Parmenides waren noch keine 'Philosophen.' Warum nicht? Weil sie die größeren Denker waren. . . . Der Schritt zur 'Philosophie' . . . wurde zuerst von Sokrates und Platon vollzogen."

453. "Der Spruch des Anaximander," from 1946, HW, p. 310: "Griechisch . . . ist die Frühe des Geschickes, als welches das Sein selbst sich im Seienden lichtet und ein Wesen des Menschen in seinen Anspruch nimmt." Heidegger lectured already on Anaximander in 1932; see GA 35.

454. HW, p. 310: "Das Sein entzieht sich, indem es sich in das Seiende entbirgt."

455. HW, p. 310: "Doch dieses Verbergen seines Wesens und der Wesensherkunft ist der Zug, in dem das Sein sich anfänglich lichtet, so zwar, daß ihm das Denken gerade *nicht* folgt. Das Seiende selbst tritt nicht in dieses Licht des Seins. Die Unverborgenheit des Seienden, die ihm gewährte Helle, verdunkelt das Licht des Seins. Das Sein entzieht sich, indem es sich in das Seiende entbirgt. Dergestalt beirrt das Sein, es lichtend, das Seiende mit der Irre. Das Seiende ist in die Irre ereignet, in der es das Sein umirrt und so den Irrtum . . . stiftet. Er ist der Wesensraum der Geschichte. In ihm irrt das geschichtlich Wesenhafte

an Seinesgleichen vorbei. Darum wird, was geschichtlich heraufkommt, notwendig mißdeutet." Cf. p. 311: "Ohne die Irre wäre kein Verhältnis von Geschick zu Geschick, wäre
nicht Geschichte."

456. Cf. EM, p. 134: "Im Blickfeld der gewöhnlichen und herrschenden Definitionen,
im Blickfeld der christlich bestimmten neuzeitlichen und heutigen Metaphysik, Erkennt-
nislehre, Anthropologie und Ethik muß unsere Auslegung des Spruches als eine willkür-
liche Umdeutung erscheinen, als ein Hineindeuten von solchem, was eine 'exakte Interpretation' nie feststellen kann. Das ist richtig. Für das übliche und heutige Meinen ist das
Gesagte in der Tat nur ein Ergebnis jener bereits schon sprichwörtlich gewordenen Gewaltsamkeit und Einseitigkeit des Heideggerschen Auslegungsverfahrens"; cf. HW, pp. 197
and 343; N II, pp. 262–263.

457. EM, p. 28: "Liegt es am Sein . . . oder liegt es an uns, daß wir bei allem Betreiben
und Erjagen des Seienden doch aus dem Sein herausgefallen sind? Und liegt dies gar nicht
erst an uns, den Heutigen . . . , sondern an dem, was von Anfang an durch die abendländische Geschichte zieht, ein Geschehnis, zu dem alle Augen aller Historiker nie hin-
reichen werden und das doch geschieht, vormals, heute und künftig?"

458. EM, p. 124: "Die eigentliche Auslegung muß Jenes zeigen, was nicht mehr in
Worten dasteht und doch gesagt ist. Hierbei muß die Auslegung notwendig Gewalt
brauchen. Das Eigentliche ist dort zu suchen, wo die wissenschaftliche Interpretation nichts
mehr findet, die alles, was ihr Gehege übersteigt, als unwissenschaftlich brandmarkt." In
"Aus einem Gespräch von der Sprache," Heidegger claims that his thought is "more Greek
than the Greeks." It aims at elucidating the origin of Greek thought, which the Greeks
could not fathom: "Dieses Lichten selbst bleibt jedoch als Ereignis nach jeder Hinsicht
ungedacht. Sich auf das Denken dieses Ungedachten einlassen, heißt: dem griechisch Gedachten ursprünglicher nachgehen, es in seiner Wesensherkunft erblicken. Dieser Blick ist
auf seine Weise griechisch und ist hinsichtlich des Erblickten doch nicht mehr, nie mehr
griechisch." And he says somewhat earlier: "Unserem heutigen Denken ist es aufgegeben,
das griechisch Gedachte noch griechischer zu denken" (*Sprache*, pp. 134–135).

459. Cf. EM, p. 119: "Die Unerklärbarkeit dieses Anfangs ist kein Mangel und kein
Versagen unserer Erkenntnis der Geschichte. Im Verstehen des Geheimnischarakters dieses
Anfangs liegt vielmehr die Echtheit und Größe geschichtlichen Erkennens. Wissen von
einer Ur-geschichte ist nicht Aufstöbern des Primitiven und Sammeln von Knochen. Es ist
weder halbe noch ganze Naturwissenschaft, sondern, wenn es überhaupt etwas ist, Mytho-
logie." Heidegger later admitted that Being in his sense had manifested itself nowhere in
the history of philosophy, not even in the writings of the pre-Socratics. Cf. "Nietzsches
Wort 'Gott ist tot,' " HW, p. 243: "*Aber nirgends finden wir solches Erfahren des Sein
selbst.* Nirgends begegnet uns ein Denken, das die Wahrheit des Seins selbst und damit die
Wahrheit selbst als das Sein denkt. Sogar dort ist dieses nicht gedacht, wo das vorplato-
nische Denken als der Anfang des abendländischen Denkens die Entfaltung der Metaphysik durch Platon and Aristoteles vorbereitet" (Heidegger's italics).

460. "Überwindung der Metaphysik," VA, p. 88: "Die Welt-Kriege sind die Vorform
der Beseitigung des Unterschiedes von Krieg und Frieden, welche Beseitigung nötig ist,
da die 'Welt' zur Unwelt geworden ist zufolge der Verlassenheit des Seienden von einer
Wahrheit des Seins."

461. See my discussion of Heidegger's lectures of 1927 in section 9C, above.

462. "Die Kehre," TK, p. 42: "Denn das Sein hat nicht Seinesgleichen neben sich."

463. Cf., for instance, *Beiträge*, §§ 257–281; B (GA 66), §§ 16–50.

464. "Wozu Dichter?", HW, p. 286: "Wodurch kann, wenn das Sein das Einzigartige des Seienden ist, das Sein noch übertroffen werden? Nur durch sich selbst, nur durch sein Eigenes und zwar in der Weise, daß es in sein Eigenes eigens einkehrt. Dann wäre das Sein das Einzigartige, das schlechthin sich übertrifft (das transcendens schlechthin). Aber dieses Übersteigen geht nicht hinüber und zu einem anderen hinauf, sondern herüber zu ihm selbst und in das Wesen seiner Wahrheit zurück." Cf. for the expression *transcendens schlechthin*: SZ, § 7C, p. 38, and "Brief über den 'Humanismus,' " W, p. 167.

465. "Brief über den 'Humanismus,' " W, p. 189: "Gleichwohl ist das Sein seiender als jegliches Seiende." Cf. the definition of God in Anselm's *Proslogion*.

466. EM, p. 133: "Wenn gar die Frage nach dem Sein nicht nur das Sein des Seienden sucht, sondern das Sein selbst in *dessen* Wesen" (Heidegger's italics). Cf. WiM, *Nachwort*, 4th ed. of 1943: "dass das Sein wohl west ohne das Seiende" (cf. WiM, p. 46).

467. "Vom Wesen der Wahrheit," W, p. 89: "Nicht ein vereinzeltes Geheimnis über dieses und jenes, sondern nur das Eine, daß überhaupt das Geheimnis (die Verbergung des Verborgenen) als ein solches das Da-sein des Menschen durchwaltet."

468. "Vom Wesen der Wahrheit," W, p. 96: "das sich verbergende Einzige der einmaligen Geschichte der Entbergung des 'Sinnes' dessen, was wir das Sein nennen"; *Beiträge*, §§ 4, 52–74, 217 (p. 342: "Im Sichverbergen west das Seyn"), 242, 245, and passim.

469. "Brief über den 'Humanismus,' " W, p. 162: "Doch das Sein—was ist das Sein? Es ist Es selbst. Dies zu erfahren und zu sagen, muß das künftige Denken lernen. Das 'Sein'—das ist nicht Gott und nicht ein Weltgrund. Das Sein ist weiter denn alles Seiende und ist gleichwohl dem Menschen näher als jedes Seiende. . . . Das Sein ist das Nächste. Doch die Nähe bleibt dem Menschen am weitesten." Cf. WiM, *Nachwort* of 1943, p. 48: "Was jedoch . . . dem Menschen jederzeit schon in einer rätselhaften Unkenntlichkeit näher ist als jedes Seiende." According to the Bible, God is the One who is, and he is always and everywhere near to us. According to *Beiträge*, *Seyn* as Event (*Ereignis*) is always near to us (§§ 7–8); cf. "Die Kehre," TK, p. 43, on "what is": "Das, was eigentlich ist, ist keineswegs dieses oder jenes Seiende. Was eigentlich ist, d. h. eigens im Ist wohnt und west, ist einzig das Sein."

470. "Brief über den 'Humanismus,' " W, p. 163: "Die Lichtung selber aber ist das Sein." Cf. "Vom Wesen der Wahrheit," W, p. 96: "Die Frage nach dem Wesen der Wahrheit entspringt aus der Frage nach der Wahrheit des Wesens. . . . Die Frage nach der Wahrheit des Wesens versteht Wesen verbal und denkt in diesem Wort . . . das Seyn als den waltenden Unterschied von Sein und Seiendem. Wahrheit bedeutet lichtendes Bergen als Grundzug des Seyns." See also WiM, *Nachwort* of 1943, p. 44: "Gesetzt aber, daß nicht nur das Seiende dem Sein entstammt, sondern das auch und anfänglicher noch das Sein selbst in seiner Wahrheit ruht und die Wahrheit des Seins als das Sein der Wahrheit west." Cf. *Beiträge*, §§ 168–247.

471. "Brief über den 'Humanismus,' " W, p. 165: " 'es gibt' das Sein. . . . Denn das 'es' was hier 'gibt,' ist das Sein selbst." What Heidegger says here cannot be translated into English. *Es gibt* means: there is. But this expression does not have "there" as its grammatical subject. Heidegger continues: "Das 'gibt' nennt jedoch das gebende, seine Wahrheit gewährende Wesen des Seins. Das Sichgeben ins Offene mit diesem selbst ist das Sein selber."

472. Cf. *Beiträge*, § 279, p. 509: "Warum Seiendes. . . . Weil Sein west. Warum Seyn? Aus ihm selbst."

473. "Brief über den 'Humanismus,' " W, p. 173: "Weil in diesem Denken etwas Einfaches zu denken ist, deshalb fällt es dem als Philosophie überlieferten Vorstellen so schwer"; cf. p. 164: "etwas Einfaches. Als dieses bleibt das Sein geheimnisvoll, die schlichte Nähe eines unaufdringlichen Waltens"; "Zur Seinsfrage," W, p. 249: "das transcendens, . . . das *Sein des* Seienden . . . das Nicht des Seienden, *jenes* Nichts . . ., das gleichursprünglich das Selbe ist mit dem Sein" (Heidegger's italics); *Beiträge*, § 267, p. 470: "So reich gefügt und bildlos das Seyn west, es ruht doch in ihm selbst und seiner *Einfachheit*" (Heidegger's italics); § 145, p. 266: "Das Nichts ist weder negativ, noch ist es 'Ziel,' sondern die wesentliche Erzitterung des Seyns selbst"; § 269, p. 480: "Das Seyn erinnert an 'nichts,' und deshalb gehört das Nichts zum Seyn."

474. WiM, *Nachwort* of 1943, p. 51: "Das Nichts als das Andere zum Seienden ist der Schleier des Seins."

475. See for *Licht*: "Brief über den 'Humanismus,' " W, p. 191, and for the wholly Other: "Zur Seinsfrage," W, pp. 246–248; *das Unberechenbare*: WiM, pp. 48–50; *das Unzerstörbare*: WiM, p. 50.

476. "Zeit und Sein," SD, p. 4: "Das Wort 'Sache,' 'eine Sache' soll uns jetzt solches bedeuten, worum es sich in einem maßgebenden Sinne handelt, sofern sich darin etwas Unübergehbares verbirgt. Sein—eine Sache, vermutlich *die* Sache des Denkens" (Heidegger's italics). Cf. ID, pp. 41, 59, and passim.

477. *Sprache*, pp. 85–155. A similar list of expressions for Being may be compiled from each of Heidegger's later texts.

478. "Die Spruch des Anaximander," HW, pp. 310–311: "Das Sein entzieht sich, indem es sich in das Seiende entbirgt"; N II, p. 353: "Das Sein selbst west als die Unverborgenheit, in der das Seiende anwest. Die Unverborgenheit selbst jedoch bleibt als diese verborgen"; *Beiträge*, §§ 52–60, § 136, p. 255: "Nur wo das Seyn als das Sichverbergen sich zurückhält, kann das Seiende auftreten"; § 137, and passim.

479. "Brief über den 'Humanismus,' " W, p. 168: "Das Werfende im Entwerfen ist nicht der Mensch, sondern das Sein selbst, das den Menschen in die Ek-sistenz des Daseins als sein Wesen schickt. Dieses Geschick ereignet sich als die Lichtung des Seins, als welche es ist." Cf. p. 167: "so ist das Sein wesenhaft weiter als alles Seiende, weil es die Lichtung selbst ist"; and p. 163: "Die Lichtung selber aber ist das Sein."

480. "Brief über den 'Humanismus,' " W, p. 165: "Das Sichgeben ins Offene mit diesem selbst ist das Sein selber. . . . 'Es ist nämlich Sein.' In diesem Wort verbirgt sich das anfängliche Geheimnis für alles Denken."

481. "Der Spruch des Anaximander," HW, p. 337: "das Einhändigen des Anwesens, welches Einhändigen das Anwesen dem Anwesenden aushändigt und so das Anwesende als ein solches gerade in der Hand behält, d. h. im Anwesen wahrt"; *Beiträge*, § 7, p. 24: "Im Wesen der Wahrheit des Ereignisses entscheidet und gründet sich gleichzeitig alles Wahre, wird Seiendes seiend."

482. WiM, *Nachwort* of 1943, p. 46: "dessen zu erfahren, was jedem Seienden die Gewähr gibt, zu sein. Das ist das Sein selbst. Ohne das Sein, dessen abgründiges, aber noch unentfaltetes Wesen uns das Nichts in der wesenhaften Angst zuschickt, bliebe alles Seiende in der Seinlosigkeit."

483. "Brief über den 'Humanismus,' " W, pp. 165–166: "Denn das 'es,' was hier 'gibt,' ist das Sein selbst. Das 'gibt' nennt jedoch das gebende, seine Wahrheit gewährende Wesen des Seins. Das Sichgeben ins Offene mit diesem selbst ist das Sein selber. . . . Das Geschehen der Geschichte west als das Geschick der Wahrheit des Seins aus diesem. . . . Zum

Geschick kommt das Sein, indem Es, das Sein, sich gibt." Cf. "Der Satz vom Grund," SvGr, p. 205: "So hat denn jedes Seiende, weil vom Sein als dem Grund ins Sein gegeben, unausweichlich die Mitgift eines Grundes. Denn anders wäre es nicht seiend."

484. *Beiträge*, § 43, p. 87: "Von den Göttern gebraucht, durch diese Erhöhung zerschmettert werden, in der Richtung dieses Verborgenen müssen wir das Wesen des Seyns *als solchen* erfragen. Wir können aber dann das Seyn nicht als das scheinbar Nachträgliche erklären, sondern müssen es als den Ursprung begreifen, der erst Götter und Menschen *ent-scheidet* und *er-eignet*" (Heidegger's italics). Cf. B (GA 66), § 70 and § 71, p. 235: "Weder erschaffen die Götter den Menschen noch erfindet der Mensch die Götter. Die Wahrheit des Seyns entscheidet 'über' beide, indem es nicht über ihnen waltet, sondern zwischen ihnen sich und damit erst sie selbst zur Ent-eignung ereignet."

485. Cf. *Beiträge*, § 4, p. 10: "Die Frage nach dem 'Sinn,' d. h. . . . nach der *Wahrheit des Seyns* ist und bleibt *meine* Frage und ist meine *einzige*, denn sie gilt ja dem *Einzigsten*" (Heidegger's italics); § 12, p. 32 ("*Einzigkeit* des Seyns"); § 146, p. 267: "Aus der Einzigkeit des Seyns ergibt sich die Einzigkeit des ihm zugehörigen Nicht"; § 259, p. 429: "Aber das Seyn . . . west als jenes Einzige und Abgründige"; § 267, p. 471: "Das Einfache des Seyns hat in sich das Gepräge der *Einzigkeit*"; § 270, p. 485: "Das Seyn solcher Wesung ist selbst in diesem Wesen einzig" (Heidegger's italics).

486. Cf. Löwith (1965), p. 12: "Wie fern ist dieses [i.e., Heidegger's] eschatologisch-geschichtliche Denken, dem alles nur als Aussaat und Vorbereitung einer ankommenden Zukunft gilt, von der anfänglichen Weisheit der Griechen, für welche die Zeit-Geschichte philosophisch belanglos war."

487. "Der Spruch des Anaximander," HW, p. 311: "Aus der Epoche des Seins kommt das epochale Wesen seines Geschickes, worin die eigentliche Weltgeschichte ist. Jedesmal, wenn das Sein in seinem Geschick an sich hält, ereignet sich jäh und unversehens Welt. . . . Das epochale Wesen des Seins gehört in den verborgenen Zeitcharakter des Seins und kennzeichnet das im Sein gedachte Wesen der Zeit"; and pp. 301–302: "Das bisherige Wesen des Seins geht in seine noch verhüllte Wahrheit unter. Die Geschichte des Seins versammelt sich in diesen Abschied. Die Versammlung in diesen Abschied als die Versammlung (*logos*) des Äußersten (*eschaton*) seines bisherigen Wesens ist die Eschatologie des Seins. Das Sein selbst ist als geschickliches in sich eschatologisch." Cf. "Zeit und Sein," SD, pp. 8–9; *Beiträge*, § 259, p. 433: "Im anderen meint 'Zeit' die erste Anzeige des Wesens der Wahrheit im Sinne der entrückungsmäßig offenen Lichtung des Spielraums, in dem das Seyn sich verbirgt und verbergend sich erstmals eigens in seine Wahrheit verschenkt." Cf. also the notion of *Zeitspielraum*, *Beiträge*, § 6, p. 22 ("die ganze Zeitlichkeit: den Zeit-Spiel-Raum des Da"), and §§ 10, 123, 125, 238–242.

488. "Zeit und Sein," SD, p. 9: "Seinsgeschichte heißt Geschick von Sein, in welchen Schickungen sowohl das Schicken als auch das Es, das schickt, an sich halten mit der Bekundung ihrer selbst"; "Brief über den 'Humanismus,' " W, p. 166: "Das Geschehen der Geschichte west als das Geschick der Wahrheit des Seins aus diesem. (. . .) Zum Geschick kommt das Sein, indem Es, das Sein, sich gibt. Das aber sagt, geschickhaft gedacht: Es gibt sich und versagt sich zumal"; p. 167: "Daß aber das Da, die Lichtung als Wahrheit des Seins selbst, sich ereignet, ist die Schickung des Seins selbst. Dieses ist als das Geschick der Lichtung"; and passim in the later works.

489. "Der Spruch des Anaximander," HW. p. 298: "Der einzige Denker des Abendlandes, der die Geschichte des Denkens denkend erfahren hat, ist Hegel"; N I, p. 450: "Die

Hegelsche Geschichte der Philosophie ist bisher die einzige philosophische geblieben," and so on.

490. "Der Spruch des Anaximander," HW, p. 311: "Jede Epoche der Weltgeschichte ist eine Epoche der Irre"; *Beiträge*, § 263, p. 455: "*Wesensirre* als Geschichte des Menschen"; "Vom Wesen der Wahrheit," W, p. 92: "Die Umgetriebenheit des Menschen weg vom Geheimnis hin zum Gangbaren ... ist das *Irren*. Der Mensch irrt"; "Überwindung der Metaphysik," VA, p. 93: "Die Erde erscheint als die Unwelt der Irrnis. Sie ist seynsgeschichtlich der Irrstern" (Heidegger's italics).

491. See, for instance, WiM, the preface of 1949, pp. 7–8: "Überall hat sich, wenn die Metaphysik das Seiende vorstellt, Sein gelichtet. Sein ist in einer Unverborgenheit (*Alētheia*) angekommen. Ob und wie Sein solche Unverborgenheit mit sich bringt, ob und wie gar Es selbst sich in der Metaphysik und als diese anbringt, bleibt verhüllt. Das Sein wird in seinem entbergenden Wesen, d. h. in seiner Wahrheit nicht gedacht. ... Weil die Metaphysik das Seiende als das Seiende befragt, bleibt sie beim Seienden und kehrt sich nicht an das Sein als Sein," and so on; "Brief über den 'Humanismus,' " W, p. 154: "Die Metaphysik fragt nicht nach der Wahrheit des Seins selbst"; N II, p. 346: "Das Sein bleibt in demjenigen Denken, das als das metaphysische für das Denken schlechthin gilt, ungedacht"; p. 350: "Das Sein selbst bleibt in der Metaphysik wesensnotwendig ungedacht"; *Beiträge*, § 52, p. 112: "Der schärfste Beweis für dieses verborgene Wesen des Seyns ... wird geführt durch die ganze Geschichte der Metaphysik"; §§ 83–114; § 173, p. 297: "Denn die 'Metaphysik' fragt vom Seienden her (...) nach der Seiendheit und läßt die Wahrheit dieser und d. h. die Wahrheit des Seyns notwendig ungefragt"; §§ 207–237; § 258, p. 423: "Der Name 'Metaphysik' wird hier unbedenklich zur Kennzeichnung der ganzen bisherigen Geschichte der Philosophie gebraucht"; §§ 259, 266–273; B (GA 66), §§ 15, 21, 68, 74, 75, 97, and 98–135.

492. "Der Spruch des Anaximander," HW, p. 336: "Die Vergessenheit des Unterschiedes, mit der das Geschick des Seins beginnt, um in ihm sich zu vollenden, ist gleichwohl kein Mangel, sondern das reichste und weiteste Ereignis, in dem die abendländische Weltgeschichte zum Austrag kommt. Es ist das Ereignis der Metaphysik. Was jetzt *ist*, steht im Schatten des schon vorausgegangenen Geschickes der Seinsvergessenheit" (Heidegger's italics). Cf. "Nietzsches Wort 'Gott ist tot,' " HW, p. 244: "Die Metaphysik selbst wäre demgemäß kein bloßes Versäumnis einer noch zu bedenkenden Frage nach dem Sein. Sie wäre vollends kein Irrtum. Die Metaphysik wäre als Geschichte der Wahrheit des Seienden als solchen aus dem Geschick des Seins selbst ereignet." Cf. also "Brief über den 'Humanismus,' " W, p. 166: "Das Geschehen der Geschichte west als das Geschick der Wahrheit des Seins aus diesem. ... Zum Geschick kommt das Sein, indem Es, das Sein, sich gibt. Das aber sagt, geschickhaft gedacht: Es gibt sich und versagt sich zumal." Cf. finally *Beiträge* and B (GA 66), the sections referred to in the previous note.

493. "Der Spruch des Anaximander," HW, p. 336: "Vielmehr wird auch die frühe Spur des Unterschiedes [between Being and beings] dadurch ausgelöscht, daß das Anwesen wie ein Anwesendes erscheint und seine Herkunft in einem höchsten Anwesenden finde."

494. "Die Zeit des Weltbildes," HW, p. 103: "Der Mensch kann dieses Geschick seines neuzeitlichen Wesens nicht von sich aus verlassen oder durch einen Machtspruch abbrechen."

495. "Brief über den 'Humanismus,' " W, p. 158: "Das Da-sein selbst aber west als das 'geworfene.' Es west im Wurf des Seins als des schickend Geschicklichen."

496. "Brief über den 'Humanismus,' " W, p. 162: "Ob und wie es erscheint, ob und wie der Gott und die Götter, die Geschichte und die Natur in die Lichtung des Seins hereinkommen, an- und abwesen, entscheidet nicht der Mensch. Die Ankunft des Seienden beruht im Geschick des Seins"; "Platons Lehre von der Wahrheit," W, pp. 142–143: "Jener Wandel des Wesens der Wahrheit ist gegenwärtig als die längst gefestigte und daher noch unverrückte, alles durchherrschende Grundwirklichkeit der in ihre neueste Neuzeit anrollenden Weltgeschichte des Erdballs. Was immer sich mit dem geschichtlichen Menschen begibt, ergibt sich jeweils aus einer zuvor gefallenen und nie beim Menschen selbst stehenden Entscheidung über das Wesen der Wahrheit."

497. "Der Spruch des Anaximander," HW, p. 303: "das Diktat der Wahrheit des Seins."

498. Cf., for example, EM, pp. 14, 28 ("wir sind . . . aus dem Sein herausgefallen"), 154 ("Metaphysisch gesehen *täumeln wir.* Wir . . . wissen nicht mehr, wie es mit dem Sein steht. Wir wissen erst recht nicht , daß wir es nicht mehr wissen"); WiM, *Einleitung* (1949), p. 19: "unsere Verlassenheit vom Sein"; "Wozu Dichter?", HW, p. 250: "Weil aber das Anwesen sich zugleich verbirgt, ist es schon selbst das Abwesen"; p. 251: "[die] Zeit, die das Sein verbirgt"; "Vom Wesen der Wahrheit," W, p. 90: "Doch dieses Verhältnis zur Verbergung verbirgt sich dabei selbst, indem es einer Vergessenheit des Geheimnisses den Vorrang läßt und in dieser verschwindet"; "Zur Seinsfrage," W, p. 243: "Sein [the word is written with a cross through it] bleibt in einer seltsamen Weise aus. Es verbirgt sich. Es hält sich in einer Verborgenheit, die sich selber verbirgt. In solchem Verbergen beruht jedoch das griechisch erfahrene Wesen der Vergessenheit. . . . Die . . . Vergessenheit . . . gehört zur Sache des Seins selbst, waltet als Geschick seines Wesens,", and so on; cf. *Beiträge*, §§ 209, 217, 227, 242, 254, and passim; B (GA 66), §§ 68 and 97–135.

499. Cf. "Brief über den 'Humanismus,' " W, p. 169: "Die so zu denkende Heimatlosigkeit beruht in der Seinsverlassenheit des Seienden. Sie ist das Zeichen der Seinsvergessenheit. Dieser zufolge bleibt die Wahrheit des Seins ungedacht," and so on.

500. Cf. "Hegels Begriff der Erfahrung," HW, p. 176: "Eine völlig andere Frage ist freilich, ob und inwiefern die Subjektivität ein eigenes Wesensgeschick des Seins ist, darin sich die Unverborgenheit des Seins, nicht die Wahrheit des Seienden, *entzieht* und damit eine eigene Epoche bestimmt" (Heidegger's italics); "Nietzsches Wort 'Gott ist tot,' " HW, p. 196: "daß jedoch die Wahrheit des Seins ungedacht bleibt und als mögliche Erfahrung dem Denken nicht nur verweigert ist, sondern daß das abendländische Denken selbst und zwar in der Gestalt der Metaphysik das Geschehnis dieser Verweigerung eigens, aber gleichwohl unwissend, verhüllt"; "Nietzsches Wort 'Gott ist tot,' " HW, p. 244: "Dann läge es im Wesen des Seins selbst, daß es ungedacht bleibt, weil es sich entzieht. Das Sein selbst entzieht sich in seine Wahrheit. Es birgt sich in diese und verbirgt sich in solchem Bergen"; "Der Spruch des Anaximander," HW, p. 311: "Indem sie Un-Verborgenheit des Seienden bringt, stiftet sie erst Verborgenheit des Seins. Verbergung aber bleibt im Zuge des an sich haltenden Verweigerns"; N II, p. 355: "Das Sein selbst entzieht sich. Der Entzug geschieht," and so on; *Beiträge*, §§ 2, 61, 168, 254, 267, 269; B (GA 66), §§ 68 and 97–135.

501. Cf. "Die Zeit des Weltbildes," HW, p. 104: "In Wahrheit aber ist der Schatten die offenbare, jedoch undurchdringliche Bezeugung des verborgenen Leuchtens. Nach diesem Begriff des Schattens erfahren wir das Unberechenbare als jenes, was, der Vorstellung entzogen, doch im Seienden offenkundig ist und das verborgene Sein anzeigt"; "Hegels Begriff der Erfahrung," HW, p. 143: "in der verborgenen Weise, in der das Sein selbst sich enthüllt und verbirgt." About *die Irre*, see "Vom Wesen der Wahrheit," W, pp. 92–93: "Die

Umgetriebenheit des Menschen weg vom Geheimnis hin zum Gangbaren . . . ist das *Irren*. Der Mensch irrt" (Heidegger's italics); "Der Spruch des Anaximander," HW, p. 310: "Das Sein entzieht sich, indem es sich in das Seiende entbirgt. Dergestalt beirrt das Sein, es lichtend, das Seiende mit der Irre"; "Überwindung der Metaphysik," VA, p. 89: "Die Irrnis kennt keine Wahrheit des Seins." On meaninglesness, see N II, p. 26: "*Das Lichtung-lose des Seins ist die Sinnlosigkeit des Seienden im Ganzen*" (Heidegger's italics).

502. "Wozu Dichter?", HW, p. 254: "Verborgenheit ist, insofern der Bereich ihres Zusammengehörens der Abgrund des Seins ist"; cf. p. 248: "Im folgenden sei jedoch das 'Ab-' als das völlige Abwesen des Grundes gedacht. . . . Das Weltalter, dem der Grund ausbleibt, hängt im Abgrund"; "Der Satz vom Grund," SvGr, p. 205: "So hat denn jedes Seiende, weil vom Sein als dem Grund ins Sein gegeben, unausweichlich die Mitgift eines Grundes. Denn anders wäre es nicht seiend. . . . Grund heißt Sein"; *Beiträge*, § 5, p. 13: "Die Fragenden haben alle Neugier abgelegt; ihr Suchen liebt den Abgrund, in dem sie den ältesten Grund wissen"; § 9, p. 29: "Der Grund gründet als *Ab-grund*: die *Not* als das Offene des Sichverbergens"; § 11, p. 31: "Der gegründete Grund ist zugleich Abgrund"; § 242, pp. 379–380: "Der Ab-grund ist die ursprüngliche Wesung des Grundes. . . . Der Ab-grund ist das Weg-bleiben des Grundes. . . . Der Ab-grund ist die erstwesentliche *lichtende Verbergung*, die Wesung der Wahrheit"; Der Ur-grund, der gründende, ist das *Seyn*" (Heidegger's italics); B (GA 66), §§ 48–50.

503. "Aus einem Gespräch von der Sprache," *Sprache*, p. 148: "Ein Geheimnis ist erst dann ein Geheimnis, wenn nicht einmal dies zum Vorschein kommt, *daß* ein Geheimnis waltet"; "Die Frage nach der Technik," VA, p. 29: "Verborgen aber ist und immer sich verbergend das Befreiende, das Geheimnis" (Heidegger's italics).

504. "Was heißt Denken?", VA, p. 126: "Daß wir noch nicht denken, kommt vielmehr daher, daß dieses zu-Denkende selbst [i.e., Being] sich vom Menschen abwendet, sogar langher sich schon abgewendet hält"; cf. p. 128: "Das zu-Denkende wendet sich vom Menschen ab. Es entzieht sich ihm, indem es sich ihm vorenthält." Cf. also WhD, pp. 4 and 5: "der Mensch denkt noch nicht und zwar deshalb nicht, weil das zu-Denkende sich von ihm abwendet; er denkt keineswegs nur darum nicht, weil der Mensch sich dem Zu-Denkenden nicht hinreichend zu-wendet." Of course, "das Zu-Denkende" is Being; cf. p. 51.

505. "Die Zeit des Weltbildes," HW, p. 89: "Das Fragen der Besinnung fällt jedoch nie ins Grund-und Fraglose, weil es ihm voraus nach dem Sein fragt. Dieses bleibt ihr das Fragwürdigste."

506. Cf. *Beiträge*, §§ 204–237.

507. "Nietzsches Wort 'Gott ist tot,' " HW, p. 243: "Stünde es so, dann müßte die Metaphysik vor Nietzsche das Sein selbst in seiner Wahrheit erfahren und gedacht oder doch wenigstens danach gefragt haben. *Aber nirgends finden wir solches Erfahren des Seins selbst.* Nirgends begegnet uns ein Denken, das die Wahrheit des Seins selbst und damit die Wahrheit selbst als das Sein denkt. . . . Die Geschichte des Seins beginnt und zwar notwendig *mit der Vergessenheit des Seins*" (Heidegger's italics). Cf. B (GA 66), § 68, "Die Seinsvergessenheit."

508. *Beiträge*, § 258, p. 421: " 'Geschichtlich' meint hier: zugehörig der Wesung des Seyns selbst"; cf. § 268, p. 479: "Mit dem Entwurf des Seyns als Ereignis ist erst auch der Grund und damit das Wesen und der Wesensraum der Geschichte geahnt. Die Geschichte ist kein Vorrecht des Menschen, sondern ist das Wesen des Seyns selbst." Cf. B (GA 66), §§ 98–134.

509. *Beiträge*, § 168, p. 293: "Die Seinsverlassenheit ist die erste Dämmerung des Seyns als Sichverbergen aus der Nacht der Metaphysik, durch die das Seiende sich in die Erscheinung und damit die Gegenständlichkeit vordrängte"; §§ 81–114, 204–237, and 258–259; WiM, *Einleitung*, pp. 7–8.

510. WiM, *Einleitung* (1949); *Beiträge*, § 44, p. 94: "Die abendländische Geschichte der abendländischen Metaphysik ist der 'Beweis' dafür, daß die Wahrheit des Seins nicht zur Frage werden konnte," and so on; § 85, p. 173: "Die Metaphysik als das Wissen vom 'Sein' des Seienden mußte zum Ende kommen (siehe Nietzsche), weil sie gar nicht und noch nie nach der Wahrheit des Seyns selbst zu fragen wagte"; "Hegels Begriff der Erfahrung," HW, pp 162–163: "daß schon im Wesensbeginn der Metaphysik die in der Zweideutigkeit des '*on*' waltende Differenz ungedacht bleibt, so zwar, daß dieses Ungedachtbleiben das Wesen der Metaphysik ausmacht"; "Nietzsches Wort 'Gott ist tot,' " HW, p. 193: "Metaphysik ist im folgenden überall als die Wahrheit des Seienden als solchen im Ganzen gedacht. . . . In jeder Phase der Metaphysik wird jeweils ein Stück eines Weges sichtbar, den das Geschick des Seins in jähen Epochen der Wahrheit über das Seiende sich bahnt"; p. 200: "und als Metaphysik ihr eigenes Wesen nie zu denken vermag. Darum bleibt für die Metaphysik und durch sie verborgen, was in ihr und was als sie selbst eigentlich geschieht"; N II, pp. 345–346: "Denkt die Metaphysik das Sein selbst? Nein und niemals"; *Beiträge*, § 52, p. 111: "*Seinsverlassenheit* des Seienden: daß das Seyn vom Seienden sich zurückgezogen und das Seiende zunächst (christlich) nur zu dem von anderen Seienden Gemachten wurde. Das oberste Seiende als Ursache alles Seienden übernahm das Wesen des Seyns"; and passim.

511. Cf. "Die Zeit des Weltbildes," HW, p. 104: "Wie aber, wenn die Verweigerung selbst die höchste und härteste Offenbarung des Seins werden müßte?"; "Der Satz vom Grund," SvGr, p. 210: "Winke sind nur Winke, solange das Denken ihrer Weisung folgt. . . . So gelangt das Denken auf einen Weg, der zu dem führt, was sich in der Überlieferung unseres Denkens von altersher als das Denkwürdige zeigt und sich zugleich verschleiert"; "Hölderlin und das Wesen der Dichtung," EHD, p. 46: "Die Stiftung des Seins ist gebunden an die Winke der Götter"; *Beiträge*, §§ 42, 61, 125 (p. 242: "Das Erste und Lange bleibt: in dieser Lichtung warten zu können, bis die Winke kommen"), § 214 (p. 339: "das Erzittern des Ereignisses im Winken des Sichverbergens"), § 242, p. 385: "Aber die zögernde Versagung selbst hat diese ursprünglich einigende Fügung des Sichversagens *und* des Zögerns aus dem *Wink*. Dieser ist das Sicheröffnen des Sichverbergenden als solchen und zwar das Sicheröffnen für die und als die Er-eignung, als Zuruf in die Zugehörigkeit zum Ereignis selbst" (Heidegger's italics); §§ 255–256.

512. Interpreting metaphysics as *Seinsvergessenheit* means that one has to discover traces of Being in metaphysical texts, which their authors did not perceive. Cf. WhD, pp. 22–24: "Nietzsches Denken, das ganze Denken des Abendlandes wird bei diesem Übergang [the one that Heidegger wants to prepare] in seiner eigentlichen Wahrheit angeeignet. Diese Wahrheit liegt jedoch keineswegs offen am Tag. . . . Aber ein Denker läßt sich niemals dadurch überwinden, daß man ihn widerlegt und eine Widerlegungsliteratur um ihn aufstapelt. Das Gedachte eines Denkers läßt sich nur so verwinden, daß das Ungedachte in seinem Gedachten auf seine anfängliche Wahrheit zurückverlegt wird."

513. Cf. "Nietzsches Wort 'Gott ist tot,' " HW, p. 243: "*Aber nirgends finden wir solches Erfahren des Seins selbst.* Nirgends begegnet uns ein Denken, das die Wahrheit des Seins selbst und damit die Wahrheit selbst als das Sein denkt" (Heidegger's italics).

514. Cf. "Überwindung der Metaphysik," VA, pp. 74–75: "Die Überwindung der Metaphysik wird seinsgeschichtlich gedacht. Sie ist das Vorzeichen der anfänglichen Verwindung der Vergessenheit des Seins. . . . Die Überwindung bleibt nur insofern denkwürdig, als an die Verwindung gedacht wird. Dieses inständige Denken denkt zugleich noch an die Überwindung. Solches Andenken erfährt das einzige Ereignis der Enteignung des Seienden, worin die Not der Wahrheit des Seins und so die Anfängnis der Wahrheit sich lichtet und das Menschenwesen abschiedlich überleuchtet. Die Überwindung ist die Überlieferung der Metaphysik in ihre Wahrheit"; cf. *Beiträge*, part III, *Das Zuspiel*.

515. "Zur Seinsfrage," W, p. 233: "*Allein die Frage nach dem Wesen des Seins stirbt ab, wenn sie die Sprache der Metaphysik nicht aufgibt, weil das metaphysische Vorstellen es verwehrt, die Frage nach dem Wesen des Seins zu denken*" (Heidegger's italics).

516. "Brief über den 'Humanismus,' " W, p. 194: "Das künftige Denken ist nicht mehr Philosophie, weil es ursprünglicher denkt als die Metaphysik," and so on. Cf. also "Das Ende der Philosophie und die Aufgabe des Denkens" (1964), in SD, and *Beiträge*, § 85, p. 173: "Die Metaphysik als das Wissen vom 'Sein' des Seienden mußte zum Ende kommen (siehe Nietzsche), weil sie gar nicht und noch nie nach der Wahrheit des Seins selbst zu fragen wagte."

517. Cf. *Beiträge*, § 82, p. 169: "Das Zuspiel der Geschichte des erstanfänglichen Denkens ist aber keine historische Bei-und Vorgabe zu einem 'neuen' 'System,' sondern in sich die wesentliche, Verwandlung anstoßende Vorbereitung des anderen Anfangs. Daher müssen wir vielleicht noch unscheinbarer und noch entschiedener die geschichtliche Besinnung nur auf die Denker der Geschichte des ersten Anfangs lenken und durch die fragende Zwiesprache mit ihrer Fragehaltung unversehens ein Fragen anpflanzen, das sich einstmals als in einem anderen Anfang gewurzelt eigens findet. Doch weil schon diese geschichtliche Besinnung. . . den Sprung verlangt, unterliegt sie allzusehr der Mißdeutung, die nur historische Betrachtungen vorfindet über denkerische Werke"; cf. § 44, p. 94: "Wohl aber ist die Besinnung darauf, was die Wahrheit des Seyns *nicht* ist, wesentlich als eine *geschichtliche*, sofern sie helfen kann . . ., die Verborgenheit der Seinsgeschichte eindringlicher zu machen" (Heidegger's italics).

518. *Antwort*, p. 100, where Heidegger gives the following answer to the question of *Der Spiegel* as to whether we can help God by thought in coming nearer to us: "Wir können ihn nicht herbeidenken, wir vermögen höchstens die Bereitschaft der Erwartung vorzubereiten."

519. HW, p. 194: "Dem vorbereitenden Denken liegt daran, den Spielraum zu lichten, innerhalb dessen das Sein selbst den Menschen hinsichtlich seines Wesens wieder in einen anfänglichen Bezug nehmen könnte. Vorbereitend zu sein, ist das Wesen solchen Denkens." One should never forget that the term *Wesen* in the later Heidegger, even if used as a substantive, is meant in a verbal sense and linked to *Wesung* (what comes from Being), so that the translation "essence" is misleading. The theme of John the Baptist is ubiquitous in the later Heidegger. See, for instance, EM, p. 152: "Aber auch wenn ein Künftiger sie (i.e. "die eigentliche Mitte der Philosophie") wieder erreichen sollte—wir Heutigen können dem nur vorarbeiten—wird auch er der Verstrickung, nur einer anderen, nicht entgehen"; "Die Zeit des Weltbildes," HW, pp. 89–90: "Die Neuzeit aber verlangt . . . eine Ursprünglichkeit und Tragweite der Besinnung, zu der wir Heutigen vielleicht einiges vorbereiten, die wir aber nie schon bewältigen können"; "Der Spruch des Anaximander," HW, p. 309: "Wohl könnte dagegen der Versuch, unablässig auf die Wirrnis zu achten und ihre zähe Gewalt zu einem Austrag zu bringen, einmal zu einem Anlaß werden, der ein anderes

Geschick des Seins auslöst"; "Wissenschaft und Besinnung," VA, p. 66: "Doch selbst dort, wo einmal durch eine besondere Gunst die höchste Stufe der Besinnung erreicht würde, müßte sie sich dabei genügen, eine Bereitschaft nur vorzubereiten für den Zuspruch, dessen unser heutiges Menschengeschlecht bedarf"; *Beiträge*, §§ 42, 82ff., 248ff., 258–259; and W, pp. 79, 160, 169, 179, 194; B (GA 66), §§ 14–15.

520. Cf. WhD, p. 34: "Aber selbst diese Offenheit für das Sein, die das Denken vorbereiten kann, vermag für sich nichts zur Rettung des Menschen. Für diese ist die eigentliche Offenheit des Bezugs zum Sein zwar notwendige, aber keine hinreichende Bedingung"; *Antwort*, p. 100: "Wir können ihn nicht herbeidenken, wir vermögen höchstens die Bereitschaft der Erwartung vorzubereiten"; *Beiträge*, § 50, p. 107: "Diese Vergessenheit durch eine Erinnerung *als* Vergessenheit zum Vorschein ihrer verborgenen Macht bringen und darin den Anklang des Seyns. Die Anerkenntnis der Not" (Heidegger's italics), and passim.

521. "Brief über den 'Humanismus,' " W, pp. 150–151: "Soll aber der Mensch noch einmal in die Nähe des Seins finden, dann muß er zuvor lernen, im Namenlosen zu existieren. . . . Der Mensch muß, bevor er spricht, erst vom Sein sich wieder ansprechen lassen auf die Gefahr, daß er unter diesem Anspruch wenig oder selten etwas zu sagen hat. Nur so wird dem Wort die Kostbarkeit seines Wesens, dem Menschen aber die Behausung für das Wohnen in der Wahrheit des Seins wiedergeschenkt. Liegt nun aber nicht in diesem Anspruch an den Menschen, liegt nicht in dem *Versuch, den Menschen für diesen Anspruch bereit zu machen*, eine Bemühung um den Menschen?" (my italics); *Beiträge*, § 21, p. 56: "Der Entwurf des Seyns ist nur Antwort auf den Zuruf"; § 27, p. 64: "Sofern aber Da-*sein* erst sich gründet als Zugehörigkeit zum Zuruf in der Kehre des Ereignisses, liegt das Innigste des *In*begriffs im Begreifen der Kehre selbst, in jenem Wissen, das, die Not der Seinsverlassenheit ausstehend, innesteht in der Bereitschaft zum Zuruf" (Heidegger's italics); and §§ 115–167.

522. *Beiträge*, § 45, p. 97: "Dieses Volk ist in seinem Ursprung und seiner Bestimmung einzig gemäß der Einzigkeit des Seyns selbst, dessen Wahrheit es einmalig an einer einzigen Stätte in einem einzigen Augenblick zu gründen hat"; cf. section 251, in which Heidegger says that each *Volk* is a *Volk* only if, by finding its God, it receives its historical mission.

523. "Der Ursprung des Kunstwerkes," HW, p. 65: "Sind wir in unserem Dasein geschichtlich am Ursprung? Wissen wir, d. h. achten wir das Wesen des Ursprungs? Oder berufen wir uns in unserem Verhalten zur Kunst nur noch auf gebildete Kenntnisse des Vergangenen? Für dieses Entweder-Oder und seine Entscheidung gibt es ein untrügliches Zeichen"; "Vom Wesen der Wahrheit," W, p. 93: "Dann ist die Ent-schlossenheit zum Geheimnis unterwegs in die Irre als solche"; *Beiträge*, §§ 43–49, 259; § 8, p. 28: "Diese Notwendigkeit vollzieht sich in der ständigen, alles geschichtliche Menschsein durchherrschenden Entscheidung: ob der Mensch künftig ein Zugehöriger ist zur Wahrheit des Seins," and so on. In fact, Being decides about this, not man. See *Beiträge*, § 43, p. 87: "Wenn da von der Ent-scheidung die Rede ist, denken wir an ein Tun des Menschen. . . . Aber weder das Menschliche eines Aktes noch das Vorgangsmäßige ist hier wesentlich."

524. FD, p. 8: "*Mit unserer Frage möchten wir die Wissenschaften weder ersetzen noch verbessern. Indes möchten wir an der Vorbereitung einer Entscheidung mitwirken. Diese Entscheidung lautet: Ist die Wissenschaft der Maßstab für das Wissen, oder gibt es ein Wissen, in dem erst der Grund und die Grenze der Wissenschaft und damit ihre echte Wirksamkeit sich bestimmen?*" (Heidegger's italics); *Beiträge*, § 16, pp. 44–45: "Und noch kürzer trägt die seit dem Beginn der Neuzeit . . . üblich gewordene Ausrichtung der Philo-

sophie an den 'Wissenschaften.' Diese Fragerichtung . . . muß völlig aufgegeben werden";
§§ 56 and 73–80.

525. Cf. WhD, p. 49: "Insoweit auf unserem Weg die Wissenschaften zur Sprache kommen müssen, sprechen wir nicht gegen die Wissenschaften, sondern für sie, nämlich für die Klarheit über ihr Wesen. . . . Ihr Wesen ist freilich anderer Art, als man sich das heute noch an unseren Universitäten vorstellen möchte. . . . Noch liegt ein Nebel um das Wesen der modernen Wissenschaft. Dieser Nebel . . . ist überhaupt nicht vom Menschen gemacht. Er steigt aus der Gegend jenes Bedenklichsten auf, daß wir noch nicht denken"; cf. *Beiträge*, § 76, lemma 21 on p. 156: "Die vorstehende Kennzeichnung der 'Wissenschaften' entspringt nicht einer Gegnerschaft gegen sie, weil eine solche überhaupt nicht möglich ist."

526. Cf. "Der Spruch des Anaximander," HW, p. 325: "Aber das Denken ist das Denken des Seins. Das Denken entsteht nicht. Es ist, insofern Sein west. Aber der Verfall des Denkens in die Wissenschaften und in das Glauben ist das böse Geschick des Seins"; "Brief über den 'Humanismus,' " W, p. 184: "Im Durchgang durch die so verstandene Philosophie entsteht die Wissenschaft, vergeht das Denken" (see for Heidegger's notion of *Denken*: point 10 in the main text).

527. WiM, *Nachwort* (1943), p. 49: "Das Denken, dessen Gedanken nicht nur nicht rechnen, sondern überhaupt aus dem Anderen des Seienden bestimmt sind, heiße das wesentliche Denken. Statt mit dem Seienden auf das Seiende zu rechnen, verschwendet es sich im Sein für die Wahrheit des Seins. Dieses Denken antwortet dem Anspruch des Seins, indem der Mensch sein geschichtliches Wesen dem Einfachen der einzigen Notwendigkeit überantwortet, die nicht nötigt, indem sie zwingt, sondern die Not schafft, die sich in der Freiheit des Opfers erfüllt. . . . Das Opfer ist die . . . Verschwendung des Menschenwesens in die Wahrung der Wahrheit des Seins für das Seiende. Im Opfer ereignet sich der verborgene Dank, der einzig die Huld würdigt, als welche das Sein sich dem Wesen des Menschen im Denken übereignet hat. . . . Das anfängliche Denken ist der Widerhall der Gunst des Seins, in der sich das Einzige lichtet," and so on. "Das Opfer ist der Abschied vom Seienden auf dem Gang zur Wahrung der Gunst des Seins."

528. B (GA 66), § 13, p. 46: "Die Entscheidung gehört in das Wesen des Seyns selbst und ist kein Gemächte des Menschen, weil dieser selbst jeweilen aus dieser Ent-scheidung und ihrer Versagung das Grund- und Gründerhafte oder das Betriebsame und Flüchtige seines Wesens empfängt," and so on.

529. WiM, *Nachwort* (1943), pp. 49–50: "Das Opfer kann durch das Werken und Leisten im Seienden zwar vorbereitet und bedient, aber durch solches nie erfüllt werden"; N II, p. 367: "Auch eine Überwindung dieses Auslassens könnte von seiten des Menschen nur mittelbar geschehen, nämlich auf die Weise, daß zuvor das Sein selbst unmittelbar dem Wesen des Menschen zumutet, erst einmal *das Ausbleiben* der Unverborgenheit des Seins als solchen *als eine Ankunft* des Seins selbst zu erfahren und das so Erfahrene zu bedenken" (Heidegger's italics).

530. "Die Frage nach der Technik," VA, p. 38: "Menschliches Tun kann nie unmittelbar dieser Gefahr begegnen. Menschliche Leistung kann nie allein die Gefahr bannen." The danger about which Heidegger is writing here is "Die eigentliche Bedrohung des Menschen . . . [which is the] Möglichkeit, daß dem Menschen versagt sein könnte, in ein ursprünglicheres Entbergen einzukehren und so den Zuspruch einer anfänglicheren Wahrheit zu erfahren" (p. 32).

531. WiM, *Nachwort* (1943), p. 50: "Das Opfer ist heimisch im Wesen des Ereignisses, als welches das Sein den Menschen für die Wahrheit des Seins in den Anspruch nimmt. Deshalb duldet das Opfer keine Berechnung. . . . Solches Verrechnen verunstaltet das Wesen des Opfers. Die Sucht nach Zwecken verwirrt die Klarheit der angstbereiteten Scheu des Opfermutes, der sich die Nachbarschaft zum Unzerstörbaren zugemutet hat. Das Denken des Seins sucht im Seienden keinen Anhalt." Cf. on *Ereignis*, *Beiträge*, §§ 1–42, 255, 267, and § 130, p. 248: "Ob diese Umwerfung des bisherigen Menschen . . . glückt, ist nicht zu errechnen, sondern Geschenk oder Entzug der Ereignung selbst."

532. WiM, *Nachwort* (1943), p. 50: "Das wesentliche Denken achtet auf die langsamen Zeichen des Unberechenbaren und erkennt in diesem die unvordenkliche Ankunft des Unabwendbaren. Dies Denken ist aufmerksam auf die Wahrheit des Seins und hilft so dem Sein der Wahrheit, daß es im geschichtlichen Menschentum seine Stätte findet. . . . Das Denken, gehorsam der Stimme des Seins, sucht diesem das Wort, aus dem die Wahrheit des Seins zur Sprache kommt. Erst wenn die Sprache des geschichtlichen Menschen aus dem Wort entspringt, ist sie im Lot. Steht sie aber im Lot, dann winkt ihr Denken die Gewähr der lautlosen Stimme verborgener Quellen"; N II, p. 29: "Das anfängliche Fragen antwortet nie selbst. Ihm bleibt nur das Denken, das den Menschen auf das Hören der Stimme des Seins abstimmt und ihn zur Wächterschaft für die Wahrheit des Seins ge-fügig werden läßt"; *Beiträge*, § 276.

533. Cf. *Beiträge* as a whole.

534. Heidegger generalizes his notion that a philosopher only "thinks one and the same thought," WhD, p. 20: "Jeder Denker denkt nur einen einzigen Gedanken. . . . Und die Schwierigkeit für den Denker ist, diesen einzigen, diesen einen Gedanken als das einzig für ihn zu-Denkende festzuhalten, dieses Eine als das Selbe zu denken und von diesem Selben in der gemäßen Weise zu sagen." What Heidegger says here clearly does not apply to the majority of philosophers, unless one interprets them in a Heideggerian way, imputing to them the concealed intention to articulate a "sense of being." However, the later Heidegger himself had only one thought, the postmonotheist thought (as linked to the Neo-Hegelian leitmotif), which he tried to "say" in many ways.

535. We do not find this notion of thinking in SZ. Heidegger articulated his later conception of thinking for the first time in EM (pp. 88–149). Cf. on *Besinnung*: B (GA 66), § 13, p. 48: "In der Besinnung betritt der Mensch—vor sich her fragend—die Wahrheit des Seyns und nimmt so ihn 'selbst' in die hieraus entspringende Wesenswandlung hinein. . . . Besinnung ist die Überwindung der 'Vernunft,' " and so on; p. 49: "Besinnung ist die Anstimmung der Grundstimmung des Menschen, sofern diese ihn zum Seyn, zur Gründerschaft der Wahrheit des Seyns, bestimmt."

536. WhD, p. 4: "Die Wissenschaft denkt nicht. Das ist ein anstößiger Satz"; cf. p. 57, and "Was heißt Denken?", VA, p. 127: "Es ist nämlich wahr: Das bisher Gesagte und die ganze folgende Erörterung hat nichts mit Wissenschaft zu tun und zwar gerade dann, wenn die Erörterung ein Denken sein dürfte. Der Grund dieses Sachverhaltes liegt darin, daß die Wissenschaft nicht denkt." Cf. *Beiträge*, § 73, p. 143: "der Wahrheitslosigkeit aller Wissenschaft"; § 76, p. 145: "Darnach ist 'die Wissenschaft' selbst *kein Wissen*" (Heidegger's italics); §§ 73–80.

537. WiM, *Nachwort* (1943), p. 43: "Die neuzeitliche Wissenschaft dient weder einem ihr erst angetragenen Zweck, noch sucht sie eine 'Wahrheit an sich.' Sie ist als eine Weise der rechnenden Vergegenständlichung des Seienden eine vom Willen zum Willen selbst gesetzte Bedingung, durch die er die Herrschaft seines Wesens sichert. Weil jedoch alle

Vergegenständlichung des Seienden in der Beischaffung und Sicherung des Seienden aufgeht . . . verharrt die Vergegenständlichung beim Seienden und hält dieses schon für das Sein."

538. Cf. "Der Ursprung des Kunstwerkes," HW, p. 36: "Die Erde läßt so jedes Eindringen in sie an ihr selbst zerschellen. Sie läßt jede nur rechnerische Zudringlichkeit in eine Zerstörung umschlagen"; WiM, *Nachwort* (1943), p. 48: "Alles Rechnen läßt das Zählbare im Gezählten aufgehen, um es für die nächste Rechnung zu gebrauchen. Das Rechnen läßt anderes als das Zählbare nicht aufkommen. . . . Das . . . Zählen . . . verbraucht fortschreitend die Zahlen und ist selbst ein fortgesetztes Sichverzehren," and so on.

539. "Die Zeit des Weltbildes," HW, p. 100: "Nicht das Anwesende waltet, sondern der Angriff herrscht"; G, pp. 17–18: "Diese radikale Revolution der Weltansicht vollzieht sich in der Philosophie der Neuzeit. Daraus erwächst eine völlig neue Stellung des Menschen in der Welt und zur Welt. Jetzt erscheint die Welt wie ein Gegenstand, auf den das rechnende Denken seine Angriffe ansetzt, denen nichts mehr soll widerstehen können. Die Natur wird zu einer einzigen riesenhaften Tankstelle, zur Energiequelle für die moderne Technik und Industrie."

540. "Der Ursprung des Kunstwerkes," HW, p. 64: "Dieses Seiende wurde wieder verwandelt im Beginn und Verlauf der Neuzeit. Das Seiende wurde zum rechnerisch beherrschbaren und durchschaubaren Gegenstand"; "Die Zeit des Weltbildes," HW, p. 80: "Die Forschung verfügt über das Seiende, wenn es dieses entweder in seinem künftigen Verlauf vorausberechnen oder als Vergangenes nachrechnen kann. . . . Nur was dergestalt Gegenstand wird, *ist*, gilt als seiend" (Heidegger's italics); "Wozu Dichter?", HW, p. 270: "An die Stelle dessen, was der einst gewahrte Weltgehalt der Dinge aus sich verschenkte, schiebt sich immer schneller, rücksichtsloser und vollständiger das Gegenständige der technischen Herrschaft über die Erde."

541. "Wozu Dichter?", HW, p. 271: "Indem der Mensch die Welt technisch als Gegenstand aufbaut, verbaut er sich willentlich und vollständig den ohnehin schon gesperrten Weg in das Offene," and so on; "Überwindung der Metaphysik," VA, p. 83: "Im Willen zum Willen kommt erst die Technik (Bestandsicherung) und die unbedingte Besinnungslosigkeit (. . .) zur Herrschaft. Die Technik als die höchste Form der rationalen Bewußtheit, technisch gedeutet, und die Besinnungslosigkeit als das ihr selbst verschlossene eingerichtete Unvermögen, in einen Bezug zum Fragwürdigen zu gelangen, gehören zusammen: sie sind das Selbe"; *Beiträge*, §§ 73–80; "Das Ding," VA, p. 162; EM, pp. 19–20: "Das Nichts bleibt grundsätzlich aller Wissenschaft unzugänglich. Wer vom Nichts wahrhaft reden will, muß notwendig unwissenschaftlich werden."

542. N II, p. 21: "Das Zeitalter der vollendeten Sinnlosigkeit ist daher die Zeit des machtmäßigen Erfindens und Durchsetzens von 'Weltanschauungen,' die alle Rechenhaftigkeit des Vor-und Herstellens ins Äußerste treiben, weil sie ihrem Wesen nach einer auf sich gestellten Selbsteinrichtung des Menschen im Seienden und dessen unbedingter Herrschaft über alle Machtmittel des Erdkreises und über diesen selbst entspringen"; and passim.

543. "Der Ursrpung des Kunstwerkes," HW, p. 50: "Dagegen ist die Wissenschaft kein ursprüngliches Geschehen der Wahrheit." Cf. *Beiträge*, § 16, pp. 44–45, where Heidegger says that the orientation of philosophy toward the sciences has to be cancelled altogether ("muß völlig aufgegeben werden"); § 73, where he speaks of "die Wahrheitslosigkeit aller Wissenschaft"; § 76, in which he says that "die Wissenschaft selbst kein *Wissen* ist"; § 153, in which he says that the science of biology "destroys" life, and that life is inaccessible

for science; and § 273, in which he claims that science is a consequence of the metaphysical oblivion of Being.

544. EM, p. 5: "Wem z. B. die Bibel göttliche Offenbarung und Wahrheit ist, der hat vor allem Fragen der Frage . . . schon die Antwort. . . . Wer auf dem Boden solchen Glaubens steht, . . . der kann nicht eigentlich fragen, ohne sich selbst als einen Gläubigen aufzugeben."

545. "Der Spruch des Anaximander," HW, p. 325: "Aber das Denken ist das Denken des Seins. Das Denken entsteht nicht. Es ist, insofern Sein west. Aber der Verfall des Denkens in die Wissenschaften und in das Glauben ist das böse Geschick des Seins"; according to EM, this "falling" began when thought became autonomous (pp. 91ff., 141ff.).

546. WhD, p. 110: "Die Unbedingtheit des Glaubens und die Fragwürdigkeit des Denkens sind zwei abgründig verschiedene Bereiche."

547. ID, p. 51: "Wer die Theologie, sowohl diejenige des christlichen Glaubens als auch diejenige der Philosophie, aus gewachsener Herkunft erfahren hat, zieht es heute vor, im Bereich des Denkens von Gott zu schweigen." It should be noted that the emotional connotation of Heidegger's pronouncements on Christianity varies with time. They were very negative in 1933–38 (EM, *Beiträge*), became more positive directly after the war, when Heidegger badly needed the support of his old Catholic mentor Dr. Conrad Gröber and tried to cooperate with Romano Guardini (see, for instance, the *Letter on "Humanism"*), and became slightly more negative again in the 1950s, when Heidegger had regained his old self-confidence. Heidegger could easily fit Christianity into his postmonotheist scheme as a "fate" (*Geschick*) sent to us by Being, and he could freely consider the question as to whether Being would send us a new God (or new Gods) to "save us" (*Antwort*, pp. 99–100; *Beiträge*). Whereas originally the postmonotheist leitmotif was a substitute for Christianity, it could incorporate Christianity as a historical destiny sent by Being, simply because all historical epochs are sent to us by Being (cf. *Beiträge*).

548. Already in 1920 Heidegger defined philosophy as a fight against common sense. See GA 60, p. 36: "Aber die Philosophie ist nichts als ein Kampf gegen den gesunden Menschenverstand!"

549. FD, p. 1: "Nimmt man das alltägliche Vorstellen zum einzigen Maßstab aller Dinge, dann ist die Philosophie immer etwas Verrücktes. Diese Verrückung der denkerischen Haltung läßt sich nur in einem Ruck nachvollziehen. Wissenschaftliche Vorlesungen können dagegen unmittelbar mit der Darstellung ihres Gegenstandes beginnen"; "Vom Wesen der Wahrheit," W, pp. 73–74, and p. 94.

550. WhD, p. 69: "Als ob der gesunde Menschenverstand—die Zuflucht jener, die von Natur aus auf das Denken neidisch sind—als ob dieser gesunde, d. h. für keine Fragwürdigkeit anfällige Verstand je schon einmal etwas angefangen, etwas aus seinem Anfang bedacht hätte."

551. WhD, p. 64: "Das, was eigentlich ist, das Sein, das alles Seiende im vorhinein bestimmt, läßt sich jedoch niemals durch die Feststellung von Tatsachen, durch Berufung auf besondere Umstände ausmachen. Der bei solchen Versuchen oft und eifrig 'zitierte' gesunde Menschenverstand ist nicht so gesund und natürlich, wie er sich zu geben pflegt. Er ist vor allem nicht so absolut, wie er auftritt, sondern er ist das abgeflachte Produkt jener Art des Vorstellens, die das Aufklärungszeitalter im 18. Jahrhundert schließlich zeitigte."

552. WhD, p. 48: "Wir versuchen . . . das Denken zu lernen. Der Weg ist weit. Wir wagen nur wenige Schritte. Sie führen, wenn es gut geht, in das Vorgebirge des Denkens. Aber sie führen an Orte, die wir durchwandern müssen, um dorthin zu gelangen, wo nur

noch der Sprung hilft. Er allein bringt uns in die Ortschaft des Denkens." Cf. *Beiträge*, §
4, p. 11: "Die Seinsfrage ist *der* Sprung in das Seyn, den der Mensch als der Sucher des
Seyns vollzieht, sofern er ein denkerisch Schaffender ist"; cf. *Beiträge*, part IV, *Der
Sprung*; "Der Satz der Identität," ID, p. 24: "So wird denn, um das Zusammen*gehören* von
Mensch und Sein eigens zu erfahren, ein Sprung nötig"; SvGr, passim; B (GA 66), § 3,
"Der Sprung"; § 67, p. 212: "*Sein und Zeit* entspringt dem schon vollzogenen Sprung in
diese Zugehörigkeit zum Seyn."

553. *Beiträge*, § 5, p. 13: "In der Philosophie lassen sich niemals Sätze anbeweisen";
§ 76, p. 158: "Sie läßt sich auch nicht durch Tatsachen beweisen, sondern nur aus einem
Wissen von der Geschichte des Seins her erfassen"; § 259, p. 435: "daß jedes Denken des
Seins . . . nie bestätigt werden kann durch die 'Tatsachen,' d. h. durch das Seiende. Das
Sichverständlichmachen ist der Selbstmord der Philosophie"; "Wer ist Nietzsches Zarathustra?", VA, p. 115: "Aber das Einzige, was jeweils ein Denker zu sagen vermag, läßt
sich logisch oder empirisch weder beweisen noch widerlegen. Es ist auch nicht die Sache
eines Glaubens. Es läßt sich nur fragend-denkend zu Gesicht bringen. Das Gesichtete
erscheint dabei stets als das Frag*würdige*"; "Brief über den 'Humanismus,' " W, p. 167:
"Alles Widerlegen im Felde des wesentlichen Denkens ist töricht. Der Streit zwischen den
Denkern ist der 'liebende Streit' der Sache selbst" (i.e., Being); ID, *Vorwort*, p. 10: "Beweisen läßt sich in diesem Bereich nichts, aber weisen manches"; B (GA 66), § 15, p. 75:
"Jeder wesentliche Denker ist unwiderlegbar (der wesentliche Denker ist derjenige, der in
der Seinsgeschichte je eine ursprüngliche und deshalb einzige *Grundstellung* gewonnen
hat). Unwiderlegbarkeit meint hier nicht etwa nur, daß 'einem System' mit Gegengründen
zur Nachweisung einer Falschheit und Unrichtigkeit nicht bei-und durch-zukommen sei,
sondern daß solches *Vorhaben in sich* schon ungemäß ist und somit ein Herausfallen aus
der Philosophie" (Heidegger's italics).

554. "Was heisst Denken?", VA, p. 128: "die Wissenschaft [ist], wie jedes Tun und
Lassen des Menschen, auf das Denken angewiesen. Allein die Beziehung der Wissenschaft
zum Denken ist nur dann eine echte und fruchtbare, wenn die Kluft, die zwischen den
Wissenschaften und dem Denken besteht, sichtbar geworden ist und zwar als eine unüber-
brückbare. Es gibt von den Wissenschaften her zum Denken keine Brücke, sondern nur
den Sprung. Wohin er uns bringt, dort ist nicht nur die andere Seite, sondern eine völlig
andere Ortschaft. Was mit ihr offen wird, läßt sich niemals beweisen . . . (es ist etwas) was
nur offenkundig wird, indem es sich zugleich verbirgt."

555. "Brief über den 'Humanismus,' " W, p. 147: "Die Strenge des Denkens besteht
im Unterschied zu den Wissenschaften nicht bloß in der künstlichen, das heißt technisch-
theoretischen Exaktheit der Begriffe. Sie beruht darin, daß das Sagen rein im Element des
Seins bleibt und das Einfache seiner mannigfaltigen Dimensionen walten läßt"; cf. p. 187:
"daß es ein Denken gibt das strenger ist als das Begriffliche. Das Denken, das in die Wahrheit des Seins vorzudenken versucht"; cf. on the Beginning of thinking, WhD, p. 128: "Das
Denken ist kein Be-greifen. In der hohen Frühe seiner Wesensentfaltung kennt das Denken
nicht den Begriff"; cf. also WiM, *Nachwort* (1943), p. 48: "Niemals ist das exakte Denken
das strengste Denken, wenn anders die Strenge ihr Wesen aus der Art der Anstrengung
empfängt, mit der jeweils das Wissen den Bezug zum Wesenhaften des Seienden innehält."
Cf. *Beiträge*, §§ 28, 146.8, and 265.

556. Cf. *Beiträge*, § 5, p. 12: "Die Wahrheit des Seyns wird nur zur Not durch die
Fragenden. Sie sind die eigentlich Glaubenden"; § 237, p. 369: "Die *Fragenden* dieser Art
sind die ursprünglich und eigentlich Glaubenden" (Heidegger's italics).

557. "Der Satz der Identität," ID, pp. 24–25: "Wohin springt der Absprung, wenn er vom Grund abspringt? . . . Dahin, wohin wir schon eingelassen sind: in das Gehören zum Sein. . . . Der Sprung ist die jähe Einfahrt in den Bereich, aus dem her Mensch und Sein einander je schon in ihrem Wesen erreicht haben. . . . Die Einfahrt in den Bereich dieser Übereignung stimmt und be-stimmt erst die Erfahrung des Denkens"; cf. p. 32: "Ein Sprung, den das Wesen der Identität verlangt, weil es ihn braucht, wenn anders das Zusammen*gehören* von Mensch und Sein in das Wesenslicht des Ereignisses gelangen soll," and so on (Heidegger's italics); and *Beiträge*, §§ 115–167.

558. "Die Frage nach der Technik," VA, p. 40: "Denn das Fragen ist die Frömmigkeit des Denkens." Cf. "Der Ursprung des Kunstwerkes," HW, p. 50: "das Fragen des Denkens, das als Denken des Seins dieses in seiner Frag-würdigkeit nennt"; *Beiträge*, § 5, p. 12: "Die Wahrheit des Seyns wird nur zur Not durch die Fragenden. Sie sind die eigentlich *Glaubenden*" (Heidegger's italics).

559. WhD, p. 128: "das Denken bleibt auf seinem Weg. Das ist der Weg in das Fragwürdige."

560. WhD, p. 73: "die Frage nach dem Sein des Seienden recht zu fragen, d. h. so, daß dieses Fragen unser Wesen in Frage stellt, es dadurch fragwürdig macht in seinem Bezug zum Sein und damit offen für dieses."

561. WiM, *Nachwort* (1943), pp. 46–47, from "Eine Erfahrung des Seins . . . verschenkt die Angst, gesetzt, daß wir nicht aus 'Angst' vor der Angst . . . vor der lautlosen Stimme ausweichen . . ." to "Aber das Sein ist kein Erzeugnis des Denkens. Wohl dagegen ist das wesentliche Denken ein Ereignis des Seins"; N II, p. 29: "Das anfängliche Fragen antwortet nie selbst. Ihm bleibt nur das Denken, das den Menschen auf das Hören der Stimme des Seins abstimmt"; pp. 356–357: "Dagegen gehört das Denken zum Sein selbst, insofern das Denken aus seinem Wesen in das eingelassen bleibt, was . . . *aus* dem Sein selbst und zwar als Es selber herkommt"; "Der Satz vom Grund," SvGr, p. 209: "Im Satz vom Grund spricht der Zuspruch des Wortes vom Sein. . . . Ohne diesen Zuspruch gäbe es nicht das Denken in der Gestalt der Philosophie"; WiPh, pp. 21–23; *Beiträge*, §§ 14–36.

562. WhD, pp. 79ff.

563. *Beiträge*, § 5, p. 17: "Nicht irgend ein Ziel und nicht *das* Ziel überhaupt, sondern das einzige und so einzelne Ziel unserer Geschichte wird gesetzt. Dieses Ziel ist das *Suchen* selbst, das Suchen des Seyns" (Heidegger's italics).

564. WiM, *Nachwort* (1943), pp. 46–50 on *Stimme, Opfer, Dank*, and so on; "Die Zeit des Weltbildes," HW, p. 89: "die Verwandlung des Menschen zu einer dem Sein selbst entspringenden Notwendigkeit werden läßt"; WhD, p. 93: "Also gedenkend und somit als Gedächtnis denkt das Gemüt sich Jenem zu, dem es gehört. Es denkt sich als hörig, nicht im Sinne der bloßen Unterwerfung, sondern hörig aus der hörenden Andacht"; cf. p. 94 on *Dank*; SvGr, pp. 86–91, cf. p. 156: "das denkende Hören erfährt, wenn es recht geschieht, wohin wir immer schon, d. h. eigentlich ge-hören"; ID 22: "Im Menschen waltet ein Gehören zum Sein, welches Gehören auf das Sein hört, weil es diesem übereignet ist"; and *Sprache*, passim.

565. "Was heißt Denken?", VA, p. 133: "Was uns auf solche Weise uns vorenthält und darum ungedacht bleibt, können wir von uns aus nicht in die Ankunft zwingen. . . . So bleibt uns nur eines, nämlich zu warten, bis das zu-Denkende sich uns zuspricht"; EM, p. 156: "Fragen können heißt: warten können, sogar ein Leben lang"; "Spiegel-Gespräch," *Antwort*, p. 100: "Wir können ihn nicht herbeidenken, wir vermögen höchstens die Bereitschaft der Erwartung vorzubereiten."

566. G, p. 24: "Die Gelassenheit zu den Dingen und die Offenheit für das Geheimnis gehören zusammen." This line could well be a quote from Eckhart. Cf. Caputo in Macann II (1992), pp. 144–146.

567. "Der Spruch des Anaximander," HW, p. 343: "Wenn aber das Sein in seinem Wesen das Wesen des Menschen *braucht?*" (Heidegger's italics); "Die Kehre," TK, p. 38: "insofern das Wesen des Seins das Menschenwesen braucht um als Sein nach dem eigenen Wesen inmitten des Seienden *gewahrt* zu bleiben und so *als* das Sein zu wesen" (Heidegger's italics); *Beiträge*, § 133, p. 251: "Das Seyn braucht den Menschen, damit es wese, und der Mensch gehört dem Seyn, auf daß er seine äußerste Bestimmung als Da-sein vollbringe"; "Spiegel-Gespräch," *Antwort*, p. 100: "daß das, was ich mit einem langher überlieferten, vieldeutigen und jetzt abgegriffenen Wort 'das Sein' nenne, den Menschen braucht, daß das Sein nicht Sein ist, ohne daß der Mensch gebraucht wird zu seiner Offenbarung, Wahrung und Gestaltung." As Caputo writes (Macann II, 1992, pp. 147, 145–157): "Eckhart's expressions have fathered a long tradition of the divine 'need' of man in the German tradition."

568. "Brief über den 'Humanismus,' " W, p. 154: "Noch wartet das Sein, daß Es selbst dem Menschen denkwürdig werde."

569. WhD, p. 144: "Der erste Dienst besteht hier darin, daß der Mensch das Sein des Seienden bedenkt, d. h. allererst in die Acht nimmt."

570. "Brief über den 'Humanismus,' " W, pp. 147–148: "Das Denken, schlicht gesagt, ist das Denken des Seins. Der Genitiv sagt ein Zwiefaches. Das Denken ist des Seins, insofern das Denken, vom Sein ereignet, dem Sein gehört. Das Denken ist zugleich Denken des Seins, insofern das Denken, dem Sein gehörend, auf das Sein hört"; B (GA 66), § 14, p. 57: "Die Besinnung der Philosophie auf sich selbst *ist* sie selbst, ist das vom Seyn ereignete Denken"; p. 66: "Das Er-denken des Seyns hat nicht, womit es sich 'beschäftigt,' denn es ist Er-eignung des Seyns selbst—und nichts außer dieser"; § 17, p. 85: "Dieses Fragen ist in sich schon vom Seyn ereignet, will sagen: vollziehbar ist es nur aus der Inständigleit im Da-*sein*" (Heidegger's italics).

571. "Brief über den 'Humanismus,' " W, p. 193: "Das Denken ist in seinem Wesen als Denken des Seins von diesem in den Anspruch genommen. Das Denken ist auf das Sein als das Ankommende (. . .) bezogen. Das Denken ist als Denken in die Ankunft des Seins, in das Sein als die Ankunft gebunden. Das Sein hat sich dem Denken schon zugeschickt. Das Sein *ist* als das Geschick des Denkens. Das Geschick aber ist in sich geschichtlich. Seine Geschichte ist schon im Sagen der Denker zur Sprache gekommen. . . . Darum sagen die wesentlichen Denker stets das Selbe" (Heidegger's italics).

572. N II, "Die Seinsgeschichtliche Bestimmung des Nihilismus," passim.

573. Heidegger derived the idea that Being spreaks to us through hints or signs (*Winke*) from, among others, Hölderlin. Cf., for instance, Hölderlin's poem "Rousseau": "und Winke sind/ Von alters her die Sprache der Götter"; and EHD, pp. 45–46. The notion of a *Wink* plays an important role in *Beiträge*. Cf. also "Mein bisheriger Weg," B (GA 66), p. 417: "und deshalb müssen Einzelne sein, die noch das Eine leisten—was Wenig genug ist ins Große gerechnet—, daß sie die *Winke ins Wesentliche und geschichtlich Notwendige weiterwinken*—durch ihre Versuche—weiter ins übernächste Geschlecht, an dem sich vielleicht das Geschick des Abendlandes im Ganzen entscheidet" (Heidegger's italics).

574. "Platons Lehre von der Wahrheit," W, p. 142: "Der Beginn der Metaphysik im Denken Platons ist zugleich der Beginn des 'Humanismus.' Dieses Wort sei hier wesentlich und deshalb in der weitesten Bedeutung gedacht. Hiernach meint 'Humanismus' den mit

dem Beginn, mit der Entfaltung und mit dem Ende der Metaphysik zusammengeschlossenen Vorgang, daß der Mensch . . . in eine Mitte des Seienden rückt, ohne deshalb schon das höchste Seiende zu sein." Cf. B (GA 66), § 60.

575. "Brief über den 'Humanismus,' " W, pp. 151–153, especially p. 153: "Jeder Humanismus gründet entweder in einer Metaphysik oder er macht sich selbst zum Grund einer solchen."

576. "Brief über den 'Humanismus,' " W, p. 153: "Der Humanismus fragt bei der Bestimmung der Menschlichkeit des Menschen nicht nur nicht nach dem Bezug des Seins zum Menschenwesen. Der Humanismus verhindert sogar diese Frage, da er sie auf Grund seiner Herkunft aus der Metaphysik weder kennt noch versteht."

577. "Brief über den 'Humanismus,' " W, p. 155: "Die Metaphysik verschließt sich dem einfachen Wesensbestand, daß der Mensch nur in seinem Wesen west, in dem er vom Sein angesprochen wird." Cf. B (GA 66), § 52, p. 136: "Der Mensch—die mögliche Ereignung des Seyns (als Da-sein)"; §§ 55–60; p. 154: "Wie aber läßt sich die Vermenschlichung des Menschen überwinden? Nur aus der Entscheidung zur Gründung der Wahrheit des Seins."

578. EM, p. 22: "Das Dasein ist es *selbst* aus seinem wesenhaften *Bezug zum* Sein überhaupt" (Heidegger's italics); cf. p. 38: "unsere ganze Verfassung, die Weise, wie wir selbst im Bezug auf das Sein gefaßt sind"; WhD, p. 45: "was anfänglich zusammengehört . . . das Sein des Seienden und sein Bezug zum Wesen des Menschen"; p. 73: "die Frage nach dem Sein des Seienden recht zu fragen, d. h. so, daß dieses Fragen unser Wesen in Frage stellt, es dadurch fragwürdig macht in seinem Bezug zum Sein und damit offen für dieses"; "Zur Seinsfrage," W, p. 235: "denn schon im Menschenwesen liegt die Beziehung zu dem, was durch den Bezug, das Beziehen im Sinne des Brauchens, als 'Sein' bestimmt"; "Der Satz der Identität," ID, p. 22: "Aber das Auszeichnende des Menschen beruht darin, daß er als das denkende Wesen, offen dem Sein, vor dieses gestellt ist, auf das Sein bezogen bleibt und ihm so entspricht. Der Mensch *ist* eigentlich dieser Bezug der Entsprechung, und er ist nur dies" (Heidegger's italics); and passim in the later works, especially *Beiträge* and B.

579. "Brief über den 'Humanismus,' " W, p. 162: "Der Mensch ist der Hirt des Seins"; p. 172: "Der Mensch ist nicht der Herr des Seienden. Der Mensch ist der Hirt des Seins"; p. 173: " 'Ek-sistenz' ist . . . das ek-statische Wohnen in der Nähe des Seins. Sie ist die Wächterschaft, das heißt die Sorge für das Sein"; p. 176: "Auf diese [die Ek-sistenz] kommt es wesentlich, das heißt vom Sein selber her, an, insofern das Sein den Menschen als den ek-sistierenden zur Wächterschaft für die Wahrheit des Seins in diese selbst ereignet"; p. 173: "Der Mensch ist der Nachbar des Seins"; p. 175: "Bleiben wir auch in den kommenden Tagen auf dem Weg als Wanderer in die Nachbarschaft des Seins."

580. "Brief über den 'Humanismus,' " W, p. 161: "die Weise, wie der Mensch in seinem eigenen Wesen zum Sein anwest, ist das ekstatische Innestehen in der Wahrheit des Seins. Durch diese Wesensbestimmung des Menschen werden die humanistische Auslegungen des Menschen . . . nicht für falsch erklärt und nicht verworfen. Vielmehr ist der einzige Gedanke der, daß die höchsten humanistischen Bestimmungen des Wesens des Menschen die eigentliche Würde des Menschen noch nicht erfahren. Insofern ist das Denken in *Sein und Zeit* gegen den Humanismus."

581. *Beiträge*, §§ 168–203, 271; B (GA 66), § 56, p. 145: "Die *Eigentlichkeit* ist *trotz* alles vordergründlichen *moralischen* Anscheins und *gemäß* dem einzigen Fragen in Sein und Zeit nach der Wahrheit des Seins ausschließlich und je zuvor auf diese hin zu begreifen

als 'Weise,' das 'Da' zu sein, in der sich die Er-eignung des Menschen in die zugehörigkeit zum Sein und seiner Lichtung ('Zeit') ereignet" (Heidegger's italics). Eckhart's writings were the source of inspiration for this conception of a hidden ground or root in man, which is his relatedness to Being.

582. "Brief über den 'Humanismus,' " W, p. 187: "dann ist dasjenige Denken, das die Wahrheit des Seins als das anfängliche Element des Menschen . . . denkt, in sich schon die ursprüngliche Ethik"; and p. 188: "Zum Sein gehörig, weil vom Sein in die Wahrnis seiner Wahrheit geworfen und für sie in den Anspruch genommen, denkt es das Sein. Solches Denken hat kein Ergebnis. Es hat keine Wirkung. Es genügt seinem Wesen, indem es ist."

583. "Brief über den 'Humanismus,' " W, p. 191: "Nur sofern der Mensch, in die Wahrheit des Seins ek-sistierend, diesem gehört, kann aus dem Sein selbst die Zuweisung derjenigen Weisungen kommen, die für den Menschen Gesetz und Regel werden müssen. . . . Nur diese vermag es, den Menschen in das Sein zu verfügen. Nur solche Fügung vermag zu tragen und zu binden. Anders bleibt alles Gesetz nur das Gemächte menschlicher Vernunft."

584. In a very interesting paper, Rabinbach (1994) links Heidegger's *Letter on "Humanism"* to a debate on (or rather against) humanism going on in Nazi Germany during the war. The antihumanist campaign of the Nazis was directed against Allied propaganda which contrasted the democratic humanism of the West with the barbaric violence of the Axis nations.

585. "Brief über den 'Humanismus,' " W, p. 156: "Es könnte doch sein, daß die Natur in der Seite, die sie der technischen Bemächtigung durch den Menschen zukehrt, ihr Wesen gerade verbirgt"; and p. 155: "Aber dadurch wird das Wesen des Menschen zu gering geachtet und nicht seiner Herkunft gedacht, welche Wesensherkunft für das geschichtliche Menschentum stets die Wesenszukunft bleibt."

586. *Beiträge*, § 165, p. 287: "Das 'Wesen' nicht mehr das . . ., sondern Wesung als das Geschehnis der Wahrheit des Seyns"; § 166; § 270, p. 484: "Wesung heißt die Weise, wie das Seyn selbst ist, nämlich das Seyn." Heidegger's term *Wesung* is a neologism, a substantivized gerund from the stem *wes-*, which means "to be."

587. "Brief über den 'Humanismus,' " W, p. 157: "Vermutlich ist für uns von allem Seienden . . . das Lebe-Wesen am schwersten zu denken, weil es uns einerseits in gewisser Weise am nächsten verwandt und andererseits doch zugleich durch einen Abgrund von unserem ek-sistenten Wesen geschieden ist"; *Beiträge*, § 271, p. 488: "Aber der da-seinshaft bestimmte Mensch ist doch wieder gegen alles Seiende ausgezeichnet, sofern sein Wesen auf den Entwurf der Wahrheit des Seins gegründet wird."

588. "Brief über den 'Humanismus,' " W, p. 157: "Weil Gewächs und Getier zwar je in ihre Umgebung verspannt, aber niemals in die Lichtung des Seins . . . frei gestellt sind, deshalb fehlt ihnen die Sprache."

589. In his paper in Guignon (1993), Dreyfus seems to have changed his mind.

590. "Aus einem Gespräch von der Sprache," *Sprache*, p. 96: "Ohne diese theologische Herkunft wäre ich nie auf den Weg des Denkens gelangt. Herkunft aber bleibt stets Zukunft."

591. "Brief über den 'Humanismus,' " W, p. 193: "Diese bleibende und in ihrem Bleiben auf den Menschen wartende Ankunft des Seins je und je zur Sprache zu bringen, ist die einzige Sache des Denkens. Darum sagen die wesentlichen Denker stets das Selbe."

592. See my quote in section 5, above, from HW, p. 197.

593. SvGr, p. 130: "Das gewohnte Vorstellen vermag nicht jenes Einfache und Selbe zu erblicken, das sich zu seiner Zeit zur Sprache bringt und darüber entscheidet, ob an

einer Auslegung etwas ist oder nicht. . . . Die Maßgabe für eine Auslegung kommt aus der Weite des Fragens, in der sie das er-mißt, wovon ihr Fragen angesprochen werden soll."

594. WiM, *Einleitung*, p. 9: "Wohl könnte dagegen das Denken, wenn ihm glückt, in den Grund der Metaphysik zurückzugehen, einen Wandel des Wesens des Menschen mit-veranlassen. . . . Wenn somit bei der Entfaltung der Frage nach der Wahrheit des Seins von einer Überwindung der Metaphysik gesprochen wird, dann bedeutet dies: Andenken an das Sein selbst"; N II, p. 370; *Beiträge*, §§ 81–114.

595. Cf., again, "Brief über den 'Humanismus,' " W, p. 193: "Darum sagen die wesentlichen Denker stets das Selbe"; cf. "Die Bedrohung der Wissenschaft," in Papenfuss and Pöggeler (1991), vol. 1, p. 13: "Im Reich der großen Denker dagegen denken alle dasselbe."

596. WhD, p. 100.

597. Cf. FD, pp. 34–37, 119–122.

598. EM, p. 92: " 'Die Logik' und 'das Logische' sind durchaus nicht ohne weiteres und so, als wäre schlechterdings nichts anderes möglich, *die* Weisen einer Bestimmung des Denkens" (Heidegger's italics); *Beiträge*, § 36, p. 78: "Mit der gewöhnlichen Sprache, die heute immer weitgreifender vernutzt und zerredet wird, läßt sich die Wahrheit des Seyns nicht sagen"; ibid.: "So gilt nur das Eine: die edelste gewachsene Sprache in ihrer Einfachheit und Wesensgewalt, die Sprache des Seienden als Sprache des Seyns sagen. Diese Verwandlung der Sprache dringt in Bereiche, die uns noch verschlossen sind, weil wir die Wahrheit des Seyns nicht wissen"; § 37, p. 79: "Alles Wort und somit alle Logik steht unter der Macht des Seyns"; § 267, p. 473: "Allein, das Sagen . . . sagt das Seyn selbst aus ihm selbst."

599. EM, p. 68: "das aufgeführte Sagen des 'ist' zeigt klar das Eine: in dem 'ist' eröffnet sich uns das Sein in einer vielfältigen Weise"; WhD, p. 107: "Vielleicht beruht in jenem Anschein und in der anscheinenden Gleichgültigkeit des 'ist,' die es mit sich bringt, die einzige Möglichkeit für die Sterblichen, in die Wahrheit zu gelangen"; pp. 141–143: from "Das 'eon' durchspricht die Sprache und hält sie in der Möglichkeit des Sagens" to "Sein gesagtes spricht schon in der Sprache, bevor das Denken dies beachtet und mit einem eigenen Namen benennt. Das Sagen des Denkens bringt dieses Ungesprochene nur eigens in das Wort"; SvGr, p. 204: "Das Wörtchen 'ist' nennt, jeweils vom Seienden gesagt, das *Sein* des Seienden" (Heidegger's italics); N II, p. 394; "Die Kehre," TK, p. 43: "nur im Sein und als Sein ereignet sich, was das 'ist' nennt; das, was ist, ist das Sein aus seinem Wesen."

600. WhD, p. 107: "Jedes menschliche Verhalten zu etwas, jeder menschliche Aufenthalt inmitten von diesem und jenem Bezirk von Seiendem raste unaufhaltsam ins Leere weg, *spräche* nicht das 'ist' " (Heidegger's italics).

601. WhD, p. 107: "Der Satz 'das Seiende ist' hält sich unendlich weit entfernt von einem leeren Gemeinplatz. Er enthält vielmehr das erfüllteste Geheimnis alles Denkens und zwar in einem ersten Wink des Sagens."

602. Cf. "Brief über den 'Humanismus,' " W, p. 146: "Das Sein als das Element des Denkens ist in der technischen Auslegung des Denkens preisgegeben. Die 'Logik' ist die seit der Sophistik und Plato beginnende Sanktion dieser Auslegung," and so on, and pp. 178–179.

603. *Beiträge*, § 265, p. 461: "Die 'Logik' selbst ist mit Bezug auf die Wesensgründung der Wahrheit des Seyns ein Schein"; cf. §§ 44 and 89.

604. Cf. EM, pp. 141–146, cf. p. 130: "als gerade bei Platon und Aristoteles schon der Verfall der Bestimmung des *logos* einsetzt, wodurch die Logik möglich wird"; "Wozu Dichter?", HW, p. 287: "die Logik der Vernunft ist selbst die Organisation der Herrschaft des vorsätzlichen Sichdurchsetzens im Gegenständlichen. . . . Nur innerhalb der Metaphysik gibt es die Logik"; "Nietzsches Wort 'Gott ist tot,' " HW, p. 243: "Jede Metaphysik von der Metaphysik und jede Logik der Philosophie, die in irgendeiner Weise die Metaphysik zu überklettern versuchen, fallen am sichersten unter sie herab, ohne zu erfahren, wohin sie selbst dabei fallen," and so on (this is an implicit reference to Carnap's attempt to overcome metaphysics by logical analysis of language, but clearly Carnap's conception of metaphysics was different from Heidegger's conception). Cf. on Carnap: W, 2nd. ed., pp. 70–71.

605. Logic is a *Geschick* (fate, send to us by Being), cf. WhD, p. 10: "Diese Zernierung ist jedoch keineswegs das Gemächte von Menschen. Vielmehr stehen diese Disziplinen (Logik, Logistik) im Geschick einer Macht, die weither kommt"; "Der Spruch des Anaximander," HW, p. 325: "wohl dagegen hat die Logik, der Metaphysik entsprungen und sie zugleich beherrschend, dahin geführt, daß der in den frühen Grundworten geborgene Wesensreichtum des Seins verschüttet blieb"; "Brief über den 'Humanismus,' " W, pp. 193–194: "Die Schicklichkeit des Sagens von Sein als dem Geschick der Wahrheit ist das erste Gesetz des Denkens, nicht die Regeln der Logik, die erst aus dem Gesetz des Seins zu Regeln werden können." Apparently, Heidegger believes with Descartes that the laws of logic are "created" or "ordained" by transcendent Being.

606. WiM, passim; "Nietzsches Wort 'Gott ist tot,' " HW, p. 247: "Das Denken beginnt erst dann, wenn wir erfahren haben, daß die seit Jahrhunderten verherrlichte Vernunft die hartnäckigste Widersacherin des Denkens ist"; *Beiträge*, §§ 81–114.

607. WhD, p. 100: "Die heute hier Anwesenden können allerdings nicht wissen, daß sich seit der Vorlesung 'Logik' im Sommer 1934 hinter diesem Titel 'Logik' 'die Verwandlung der Logik in die Frage nach dem Wesen der Sprache' verbirgt, welche Frage etwas anderes ist als Sprachphilosophie" (Heidegger's italics); *Beiträge*, § 276.

608. In SZ, the theme of language was of secondary importance. Cf. Franzen (1975), p. 140.

609. *Sprache*, p. 14: "Der Sprache nachdenken heißt: auf eine Weise in das Sprechen der Sprache gelangen, daß es sich als das ereignet, was dem Wesen der Sterblichen den Aufenthalt gewährt."

610. "Die Sprache," *Sprache*, p. 33: "Nichts liegt daran, eine neue Ansicht über die Sprache vorzutragen. Alles beruht darin, das Wohnen im Sprechen der Sprache zu lernen"; cf. WhD, p. 100, and "Brief über den 'Humanismus,' " W, p. 145.

611. "Die Sprache," *Sprache*, pp. 14–19, cf. p. 19: "Die Sprache ist in ihrem Wesen weder Ausdruck, noch eine Betätigung des Menschen. Die Sprache spricht"; "Brief über den 'Humanismus,' " W, p. 158: "Die Sprache ist in ihrem Wesen nicht Äußerung eines Organismus, auch nicht Ausdruck eines Lebewesens. Sie läßt sich daher auch nie vom Zeichencharakter her, vielleicht nicht einmal aus dem Bedeutungscharakter wesensgerecht denken. Sprache ist lichtend-verbergende Ankunft des Seins selbst"; WhD, p. 99: "Die Sprache ist kein Werkzeug"; "Der Ursprung des Kunstwerkes," HW, pp. 60–61; WhD, p. 87; "Der Satz vom Grund," SvGr, p. 203.

612. "Die Sprache," *Sprache*, p. 12: "Der Sprache überlassen wir das Sprechen"; p. 13: "Die Sprache ist: Sprache. Die Sprache spricht. Wenn wir uns in den Abgrund, den dieser Satz nennt, fallen lassen, stürzen wir nicht ins Leere weg. Wir fallen in die Höhe"; p. 19:

"Die Sprache ist in ihrem Wesen weder Ausdruck, noch eine Betätigung des Menschen. Die Sprache spricht"; and *Sprache*, passim. Cf. WhD, p. 87: "Dichten und Denken benutzen nie erst die Sprache . . ., sondern Denken und Dichten sind in sich das anfängliche, wesenhafte und darum zugleich letzte Sprechen, das die Sprache durch den Menschen spricht"; SvGr, p. 161: "Die Sprache spricht, nicht der Mensch. Der Mensch spricht nur, indem er ge-schicklich der Sprache entspricht"; "Die Sprache," *Sprache*, p. 33: "Der Mensch spricht, insofern er der Sprache entspricht."

613. *Beiträge*, § 267, p. 473: "Allein, das Sagen sagt nicht *vom* Seyn etwas ihm allge-mein Zu-kommendes, an ihm vorhandenes aus, sondern sagt das Seyn selbst aus ihm selbst" (Heidegger's italics); § 276, p. 499: "das Seyn und nichts Geringeres als dessen eigenste Wesung könnte gar jenen Grund der Sprache ausmachen, aus dem her sie die Eignung schöpfte"; p. 501: "Die Sprache entspringt dem Seyn und gehört deshalb zu die-sem"; B (GA 66), § 79, p. 299: "Das Sein selbst ist gesagt, als Gesagtes ins 'Wort' gehoben, welches Wort aber hier nicht ein beliebiger sprachlicher Ausdruck, sondern das zur Wahr-heit (Lichtung) gewordene Seyn selbst ist"; § 97, p. 337: "Was ist dann, wenn das Seiende und dessen je nachgetragene Seiendheit (das Apriori) den Vorrang verliert? *Dann ist das Seyn*. Dann wandelt sich das 'ist' und alle Sprache wesentlich" (Heidegger's italics).

614. "Brief über den 'Humanismus,' " W, p. 158: "Sprache ist lichtend-verbergende Ankunft des Seins selbst"; p. 164: "etwas Einfaches. Als dieses bleibt das Sein geheimnis-voll, die schlichte Nähe eines unaufdringlichen Waltens. Diese Nähe west als die Sprache selbst." "Diesem gemäß ist die Sprache das vom Sein ereignete und aus ihm durchfügte Haus des Seins. Daher gilt es, das Wesen der Sprache aus der Entsprechung zum Sein, und zwar als diese Entsprechung, das ist als Behausung des Menschenwesens zu denken"; p. 192: "Das Denken bringt nämlich in seinem Sagen nur das ungesprochene Wort des Seins zur Sprache. Die hier gebrauchte Wendung 'zur Sprache bringen' ist jetzt ganz wörtlich zu nehmen. Das Sein kommt, sich lichtend, zur Sprache. Es ist stets unterwegs zu ihr" (this latter phrase elucidates the title of *Unterwegs zur Sprache*: it is Being itself which is on the way to language); "Der Spruch des Anaximander," HW, p. 336: "Wort des Seins," p. 342: "Die eigentliche geschickliche Begegnung der geschichtlichen Sprachen ist ein stilles Ereignis. In ihm spricht aber das Geschick des Seins"; cf. WhD, p. 89: "das Wesen der Sprache spielt mit uns . . . nicht erst heute, sondern längst und stets"; *Sprache*, p. 30: "Die Sprache spricht, indem das Geheiß des Unter-Schiedes Welt und Dinge in die Einfalt ihrer Innigkeit ruft," and so on; ID, p. 30: "Insofern unser Wesen in die Sprache vereignet ist, wohnen wir im Ereignis"; p. 32: "Im Er-eignis schwingt das Wesen dessen, was als Sprache spricht, die einmal das Haus des Seins genannt wurde"; SvGr, p. 161: "Unsere Sprachen sprechen geschichtlich. Gesetzt, daß an dem Hinweis, die Sprache sei das Haus des Seins, etwas Wahres sein sollte, dann ist das geschichtliche Sprechen der Sprache beschickt und gefügt durch das jeweilige Geschick des Seins. Vom Wesen der Sprache her gedacht, sagt dies: Die Sprache spricht, nicht der Mensch." See for the notion that language is the House of Being: W, p. 150 and passim; *Sprache*, passim.

615. "Brief über den 'Humanismus,' " W, p. 157 (quoted above).

616. "Die Sprache," *Sprache*, pp. 14–15.

617. *Beiträge*, § 276.

618. HW, pp. 25, 45, 46, 50, 62, 64; B (GA 66), § 11, p. 35.

619. SZ, § 44a, p. 218: "Die Bewährung vollzieht sich auf dem Grunde eines Sich-zeigens des Seienden. Das ist nur so möglich, daß das aussagende und sich bewährende

Erkennen seinem ontologischen Sinne nach ein *entdeckendes Sein zum* realen Seienden selbst ist" (Heidegger's italics).

620. SZ, § 44b, p. 220: "Primär 'wahr,' das heißt entdeckend ist das Dasein"; p. 221: "Dasein ist in der Wahrheit"; p. 223: "Das Dasein ist gleichursprünglich in der Wahrheit und Unwahrheit." Heidegger associates "being in the truth" with authenticity, and "being in the untruth" with inauthenticity, but this is highly problematical.

621. *Dichtung* means poetry and prose, but in "Der Ursprung des Kunstwerkes," Heidegger uses the word also in a more general sense, in which all real art is *Dichtung*; see HW, pp. 59–61.

622. "Der Ursprung des Kunstwerkes," HW, p. 59: "Das Wesen der Kunst, worin das Kunstwerk und der Künstler zumal beruhen, ist das Sich-ins-Werk-setzen der Wahrheit. Aus dem dichtenden Wesen der Kunst geschieht es, daß sie inmitten des Seienden eine offene Stelle aufschlägt, in deren Offenheit alles anders ist wie sonst. Kraft des ins Werk gesetzten Entwurfs der sich uns zu-werfenden Unverborgenheit des Seienden," and so on.

623. "Der Ursprung des Kunstwerkes," HW, p. 49: "Mit dem Hinweis auf das Sicheinrichten der Offenheit in das Offene rührt das Denken an einen Bezirk, der hier noch nicht auseinandergelegt werden kann. Nur dieses sei angemerkt, daß, wenn das Wesen der Unverborgenheit des Seienden in irgend einer Weise zum Sein selbst gehört (. . .), dieses aus seinem Wesen her den Spielraum der Offenheit (die Lichtung des Da) geschehen läßt." In the essay, Heidegger enriches his notion of transcendental truth as world (*Welt*) or clearing (*Lichtung*) with the idea that this clearing or world struggles with the earth (*Erde*), which is related with a tendency to conceal things. Truth is now characterized as a struggle (*Streit*, *Urstreit*) between world and earth. Sluga (1993, pp. 219–223) has suggested that Heidegger introduced the notion of Earth into his concept of transcendental truth in order to refute Nazi criticisms of his philosophy to the effect that it would not be able to accommodate the ideology of *Blut und Boden*. Notions such as *Streit* and *Erde* occur also in *Beiträge* and B.

624. Cf. *Beiträge*, § 277, p. 505: "Im Gesichtskreis dieses Wissens hat die Kunst den Bezug zur Kultur verloren; sie offenbart sich hier nur als ein Ereignis des Seins"; B (GA 66), § 11, p. 37, where Heidegger says on the work of art: "Das Werk ist weder sinnbildlicher Gegenstand noch Anlage der Einrichtung des Seienden, sondern Lichtung des Seyns als solchen, welche Lichtung die Entscheidung zu einem anderen Wesen des Menschen enthält." In short, the work of art is meant to transform man in the same manner as divine grace.

625. "Der Ursprung des Kunstwerkes," HW, p. 59: "Alle Kunst ist als Geschehenlassen der Ankunft der Wahrheit des Seienden als eines solchen im Wesen Dichtung." Cf. pp. 60–62.

626. "Der Ursprung des Kunstwerkes," HW, p. 60: "Aber die Poesie ist nur eine Weise des lichtenden Entwerfens der Wahrheit, d. h. des Dichtens in diesem weiteren Sinne."

627. "Der Ursprung des Kunstwerkes," HW, p. 61: "Weil nun aber die Sprache jenes Geschehnis ist, in dem für den Menschen überhaupt erst Seiendes als Seiendes sich erschließt, deshalb ist die Poesie, die Dichtung im engeren Sinne, die ursprünglichste Dichtung im wesentlichen Sinne."

628. *Sprache*, pp. 189ff., 201; WiM, *Nachwort*, pp. 50ff.; WiPh, p. 30, and passim in the later works.

629. Heidegger rejects "traditional" conceptions of poetry: *Sprache*, pp. 37–39; WhD, p. 154; "Dichterisch wohnt der Mensch," VA, pp. 181–198, "Der Ursprung des Kunstwerkes," HW, pp. 60–63; B (GA 66), § 11.

630. B (GA 66), § 14, p. 51: "Weil die Philosophie das Seyn *sagt*, und deshalb nur als Wort im Wort ist, und weil ihr Wort nie das Zusagende nur bedeutet oder bezeichnet, sondern im Sagen das Seyn selbst ist, möchte sie alsbald den Übertritt in die Dichtung als Nothilfe und als Gefäß zumal suchen. Und doch bleibt dies immer eine Verstrickung in die Wurzeln eines Gleichgeordneten, das ob seines aus sich waltenden Eigenwesens von jeher unendlich dem Denken des Seyns ausgewichen. Denn die Dichtung ist auch anderen geschichte-gründenden Wesens; ihre 'Zeiten' decken sich nicht met jenen des Denkens," and so on (Heidegger's italics).

631. "Die Frage nach der Technik," VA, p. 16: "Die Technik ist eine Weise des Entbergens"; cf. pp. 17, 18, 33. Cf. WhD, p. 53: "Denn das Wesen der Technik ist nichts Menschliches. Das Wesen der Technik ist vor allem nichts Technisches," and so on, and B (GA 66), §§ 63–64.

632. "Die onto-theo-logische Verfassung der Metaphysik," ID, p. 48: "Was jetzt *ist*, wird durch die Herrschaft des Wesens der modernen Technik geprägt" (Heidegger's italics).

633. "Die Frage nach der Technik," VA, p. 18: "Das Erdreich entbirgt sich jetzt als Kohlenrevier, der Boden als Erzlagerstätte"; cf. "Spiegel-Gespräch," *Antwort*, p. 98: "Es funktioniert alles. Das ist gerade das Unheimliche, daß es funktioniert und daß das Funktionieren immer weiter treibt zu einem weiteren Funktionieren und daß die Technik den Menschen immer mehr von der Erde losreißt und entwurzelt. . . . Wir brauchen gar keine Atombombe, die Entwurzelung des Menschen ist schon da . . . die Entwurzelung des Menschen, die da vor sich geht, ist das Ende, wenn nicht noch einmal Denken und Dichten zur gewaltlosen Macht gelangen," and so on; "Gelassenheit," G, p. 18: "Die Natur wird zu einer einzigen riesenhaften Tankstelle, zur Energiequelle für die moderne Technik und Industrie"; "Wozu Dichter?", HW, p. 267: "Die Erde und ihre Atmosphäre wird zum Rohstoff. Der Mensch wird zum Menschenmaterial, das auf die vorgesetzten Ziele angesetzt wird."

634. Cf. "Zur Seinsfrage," W, p. 228: "Wenn die Technik die Mobilisierung der Welt durch die Gestalt des Arbeiters ist, geschieht sie durch die prägende Praesenz dieses besonderen menschentümlichen Willens zur Macht. In der Praesenz und der Repraesentation bekundet sich der Grundzug dessen, was sich dem abendländischen Denken als Sein enthüllte," and so on; "Brief über den 'Humanismus,'" W, p. 171: "Als eine Gestalt der Wahrheit gründet die Technik in der Geschichte der Metaphysik"; "Die Zeit des Weltbildes," HW, p. 69: "des Wesens der neuzeitlichen Technik, das mit dem Wesen der neuzeitlichen Metaphysik identisch ist"; B (GA 66), § 63, p. 176: "Die Technik ist der höchste und umfangreichste Triumph der abendländischen Metaphysik, sie ist diese selbst in ihrer Ausbreitung durch das Seiende im Ganzen."

635. *Beiträge*, § 212, p. 336: "Was sich bei Plato, zumal als Vorrang der Seiendheit von der *technē* her ausgelegt, festgemacht, wird jetzt so sehr verschärft und in die Ausschließlichkeit erhoben, daß die Grundbedingung für ein menschliches Zeitalter geschaffen ist, in dem notwendig die 'Technik' . . . die Herrschaft übernimmt."

636. Cf. "Wozu Dichter?", HW, p. 272: "Vor allem aber verhindert die Technik selbst jede Erfahrung ihres Wesens. Denn während sie sich voll entfaltet, entwickelt sie in den Wissenschaften eine Art des Wissens, dem es verwehrt bleibt, jemals in den Wesensbereich

der Technik zu gelangen, geschweige denn in ihre Wesensherkunft zurückzudenken. Das Wesen der Technik kommt nur langsam an den Tag. Dieser Tag ist die zum bloß technischen Tag umgefertigte Weltnacht. . . . Das Heile entzieht sich. Die Welt wird heil-los. Dadurch bleibt nicht nur das Heilige als die Spur zur Gottheit verborgen, sondern sogar die Spur zum Heiligen, das Heile, scheint ausgelöscht zu sein."

637. "Die Frage nach der Technik," VA, p. 32: "Die Bedrohung des Menschen kommt nicht erst von den möglicherweise tödlich wirkenden Maschinen und Apparaturen der Technik. Die eigentliche Bedrohung hat den Menschen bereits in seinem Wesen angegangen. Die Herrschaft des Ge-stells droht mit der Möglichkeit, daß dem Menschen versagt sein könnte, in ein ursprünglicheres Entbergen einzukehren und so den Zuspruch einer anfänglicheren Wahrheit zu erfahren." Cf. "Spiegel-Gespräch," *Antwort*, p. 98: "Wir brauchen gar keine Atombombe, die Entwurzelung des Menschen ist schon da."

638. "Die Frage nach der Technik," VA, p. 32: "Wo aber Gefahr ist, wächst / Das Rettende auch."

639. "Die Frage nach der Technik," VA, p. 34: "Die Entbergung ist jenes Geschick, das sich je und jäh und allem Denken unerklärbar in das hervorbringende und herausfordernde Entbergen verteilt und sich dem Menschen zuteilt"; cf. p. 36; "Gelassenheit," G, p. 19: "Die Mächte, die den Menschen überall und stündlich in irgendeiner Gestalt von technischen Anlagen und Einrichtungen beanspruchen, fesseln, fortziehen und bedrängen— diese Mächte sind längst über den Willen und die Entscheidungsfähigkeit des Menschen hinausgewachsen, weil sie nicht vom Menschen gemacht sind"; "Der Satz der Identität," ID, p. 26: "In dieser Vorstellung befangen, bestärkt man sich selber in der Meinung, die Technik sei nur eine Sache des Menschen. Man überhört den Anspruch des Seins, der im Wesen der Technik spricht."

640. Cf. "Gelassenheit," G, pp. 24–25; "Die Kehre," TK, p. 37: "Das Gestell west als die Gefahr. . . . Aber die Gefahr, nämlich das in der Wahrheit seines Wesens sich gefährdende Sein selbst, bleibt verhüllt und verstellt. Diese Verstellung ist das Gefährlichste der Gefahr."

641. "Die Frage nach der Technik," VA, p. 36: "Das Gewährende, das so oder so in die Entbergung schickt, ist als solches das Rettende"; "Die Kehre," TK, p. 37: "Wenn das Gestell ein Wesensgeschick des Seins selbst ist, dann dürfen wir vermuten, daß sich das Gestell als eine Wesensweise des Seins unter anderen wandelt. Denn das Geschickliche im Geschick ist, daß es sich in die je eine Schickung schickt."

642. Cf. "Die Frage nach der Technik," VA, p. 37: "Dadurch sind wir noch nicht gerettet. Aber wir sind daraufhin angesprochen, im wachsenden Licht des Rettenden zu verhoffen."

643. "Spiegel-Gespräch," *Antwort*, pp. 99–100: "Wenn ich kurz und vielleicht etwas massiv, aber aus langer Besinnung antworten darf: Die Philosophie wird keine unmittelbare Veränderung des jetzigen Weltzustandes bewirken können. Dies gilt nicht nur von der Philosophie, sondern von allem bloß menschlichen Sinnen und Trachten. Nur noch ein Gott kann uns retten"; cf. p. 109.

644. "Spiegel-Gespräch," *Antwort*, p. 104: "Es handelt sich darum . . . aus den kaum gedachten Grundzügen des gegenwärtigen Zeitalters in die kommende Zeit ohne prophetische Ansprüche vorzudenken. Denken ist nicht Untätigkeit, sondern selbst in sich das Handeln, das in der Zwiesprache steht mit dem Weltgeschick."

645. *Beiträge*, § 2, p. 8: "Niemand versteht, was 'ich' hier *denke*: aus der Wahrheit des Seyns (und d. h. aus der Wesung der Wahrheit) das *Da-sein* entspringen lassen . . . Niemand

begreift dieses, weil alle nur historisch 'meinen' "; § 259, p. 435: "Die übergänglichen und dem Wesen nach zweideutigen Denker müssen auch noch *dieses* ausdrücklich wissen, daß ihr Fragen und Sagen unverständlich ist für das in seiner Dauer nicht errechenbare Heute" (Heidegger's italics), and so on.

CHAPTER III
SYNTHESIS

1. Cf. Tietjen (1991). Heidegger ruled that scholars are not allowed to study documents in the Heidegger archives unless these documents have already been published in the *Gesamtausgabe*. As a result, it will not be possible to complete the research needed for such a book until well after the year 2046, for Heidegger died in 1976 and Germany has a seventy-year copyright term.

2. N I, p. 10: "Die Veröffentlichung möchte, als Ganzes nachgedacht, zugleich einen Blick auf den Denkweg verschaffen, den ich seit 1930 bis zum 'Brief über den Humanismus' (1947) gegangen bin."

3. N I, p. 10. The first two texts originated already in 1930–31, whereas the texts on Hölderlin only indirectly show something of this journey ("lassen nur mittelbar etwas vom Weg erkennen").

4. Cf. Kiss (1991).

5. Müller (1949) noted the contradiction for the first time (pp. 75ff.). According to Müller's solution to the problem, Heidegger used *Sein* in 1943 as a term for the ontological difference itself, which has no external relations and which in this sense "acts without beings," whereas in 1949 Heidegger would have used *Sein* in the sense of one of the terms of the ontological difference. The contradiction would be an apparent one only. However, this solution, which was in some sense endorsed by Heidegger's ID, is implausible: the ontological difference cannot "act" without one of its terms. Schulz (1953–54) also argued that the text of 1943 and the text of 1949 do not contradict each other because they "say the same thing" in different ways (pp. 212–213ff.). Schulz's solution was rejected by Löwith (1965), pp. 40–43, who held that the contradiction cannot be removed. Franzen (1975) interpreted the contradiction as the expression of a fundamental difficulty in Heidegger's later thought (pp. 106–107). Whereas *being* in SZ is transcendentally constituted by Dasein, so that it cannot *be* without Dasein, Heidegger hypostatized *Being* in the later works. Being becomes itself a constituting agency, which could in principle exist without beings (the text of 1943). But now the primacy of Being threatens to become a *real* primacy and Being tends to become a transcendent entity or agent, which is the metaphysical position Heidegger wanted to overcome. This is why he would have corrected the text in 1949. For an overview of the corrections that Heidegger made in the postscript of WiM, see W, 2nd ed.

6. Cf. Safranski (1994), p. 382.

7. Cf. Seminar on "Zeit und Sein," SD, p. 56: "Innerhalb des Daß und in seinem Sinne kann das Denken auch so etwas wie Notwendigkeit in der Abfolge, so etwas wie eine Gesetzlichkeit und Logik feststellen. So läßt sich sagen, daß die Seinsgeschichte die Geschichte der sich steigernden Seinsvergessenheit ist"; *Beiträge*, § 152, p. 274: "Jede vorstellungsmäßige und rechnende Ordnung ist hier äußerlich, wesentlich nur die geschichtliche Notwendigkeit in der *Geschichte* der Wahrheit des Seyns" (Heidegger's italics).

8. "Brief über den 'Humanismus,' " W, p. 171: "Als eine Gestalt der Wahrheit gründet die Technik in der Geschichte der Metaphysik." Cf. *Beiträge*, § 212, p. 336: "Was sich bei Plato, zumal als Vorrang der Seiendheit von der *technē* her ausgelegt, festgemacht, wird jetzt so sehr verschärft und in die Ausschließlichkeit erhoben, daß die Grundbedingung für ein menschliches Zeitalter geschaffen ist, in dem notwendig die 'Technik' . . . die Herrschaft übernimmt."

9. Seminar on "Zeit und Sein," SD, p. 55: "Die Frage lautete: Wodurch wird die Abfolge der Epochen bestimmt? Woher bestimmt sich diese freie Folge? Warum ist die Folge gerade diese Folge? Es liegt nahe, an Hegels Geschichte des 'Gedankens' zu denken. Für Hegel waltet in der Geschichte die Notwendigkeit, die zugleich Freiheit ist. Beides ist für ihn eins in dem und durch den dialektischen Gang, als welcher das Wesen des Geistes ist. Bei Heidegger hingegen kann nicht von einem Warum gesprochen werden. Nur Daß—daß die Seinsgeschichte so ist—kann gesagt werden." Cf. *Beiträge*, § 152, p. 275: "Woher aber und welchen Sinnes die Mannigfaltigkeit der *Bergung*? Das läßt sich nicht erklären und im Nachrechnen eines Vorsehungsplanes herleiten" (Heidegger's italics); "Die Kehre," TK, pp. 38–39: "Die Verwindung eines Seinsgeschickes aber, hier und jetzt die Verwindung des Gestells, ereignet sich jedesmal aus der Ankunft eines anderen Geschickes, das sich weder logisch-historisch vorausberechnen noch metaphysisch als Abfolge eines Prozesses der Geschichte konstruieren läßt"; "Zeit und Sein," SD, p. 9: "Die Folge der Epochen im Geschick von Sein ist weder zufällig, noch läßt sie sich als notwendig errechnen"; WiPh, p. 18: "Ich sage: eine freie Folge, weil auf keine Weise einsichtig gemacht werden kann, daß die einzelnen Philosophien und die Epochen der Philosophie im Sinne der Notwendigkeit eines dialektischen Prozesses auseinander hervorgehen."

10. SD, p. 56: "Innerhalb des Daß und in seinem Sinne kann das Denken auch so etwas wie Notwendigkeit in der Abfolge, so etwas wie eine Gesetzlichkeit und Logik feststellen."

11. SD, p. 56: "So läßt sich sagen, daß die Seinsgeschichte die Geschichte der sich steigernden Seinsvergessenheit ist."

12. There is only one possible solution that would save Heidegger from this inconsistency: he might claim that Being did not abandon him, Martin Heidegger, although it abandoned the rest of us. A great many texts suggest that Heidegger saw himself as one of the few privileged prophets of Being. Cf. "Die Kehre," TK, p. 46: "Die Konstellation des Seins sagt sich uns zu"; *Beiträge*, § 5 ("Für die Wenigen—Für die Seltenen"). This explains the curious mixture of modesty and boldness in Heidegger's later writings.

13. WiM, *Einleitung*, p. 13: "Das Denken auf einen Weg zu bringen, durch den es in den Bezug der Wahrheit des Seins zum Wesen des Menschen gelangt, . . . dahin ist das in *Sein und Zeit* versuchte Denken 'unterwegs.' Auf diesem Weg, und das sagt, im Dienst der Frage nach der Wahrheit des Seins, wird eine Besinnung auf das Wesen des Menschen nötig; denn die unausgesprochene, weil erst zu erweisende Erfahrung der Seinsvergessenheit schließt die alles tragende Vermutung ein, gemäß der Unverborgenheit des Seins gehöre der Bezug des Seins zum Menschenwesen gar zum Sein selbst. Doch wie könnte dieses erfahrene Vermuten auch nur zur ausgesprochenen Frage werden, ohne zuvor alle Bemühung darein zu legen, die Wesensbestimmung des Menschen aus der Subjektivität, aber auch aus derjenigen des *animal rationale* herauszunehmen?" Cf. *Beiträge*, §§ 19, pp. 41–44, 81–91, 106, 119, 125, 134, 138, 172, 175–176, 226, 259, 262, and 264.

14. "Brief über den 'Humanismus,' " W, p. 159: "Der zureichende Nach-und Mit-vollzug dieses anderen, die Subjektivität verlassenden Denkens ist allerdings dadurch erschwert, daß bei der Veröffentlichung von *Sein und Zeit* der dritte Abschnitt des ersten

Teiles, 'Zeit und Sein,' zurückgehalten wurde (. . .). Hier kehrt sich das Ganze um . . . die Kehre von 'Sein und Zeit' zu 'Zeit und Sein'. . . . ist nicht eine Änderung des Standpunktes von *Sein und Zeit*, sondern in ihr gelangt das versuchte Denken erst in die Ortschaft der Dimension, aus der *Sein und Zeit* erfahren ist, und zwar erfahren aus der Grunderfahrung der Seinsvergessenheit."

15. Löwith (1965), chapter 1. Löwith's book was first published in 1953.

16. Von Herrmann (1964), p. 9: "daß Heidegger die Probleme aus SuZ nicht mehr aus der Perspektive auslegt, in der sie dort entwickelt sind. . . . Es handelt sich also bei Heidegger um keine bloß erläuternde, sondern um eine *umdeutende Selbstinterpretation*" (Von Herrmann's italics).

17. Cf., for instance, Franzen (1975), p. 153. However, a number of "faithful" commentators, such as Fürstenau, Wiplinger, Pöggeler, Richardson, and Heinrich Ott, endorsed Heidegger's autointerpretations.

18. Cf. Richardson, p. xix: "Wer bereit ist, den einfachen Sachverhalt zu sehen, daß in *Sein und Zeit* der Ansatz des Fragens aus dem Bezirk der Subjektivität abgebaut, daß jede anthropologische Fragestellung ferngehalten, vielmehr einzig die Erfahrung des Daseins aus dem ständigen Vorblick auf die Seinsfrage maßgebend ist, der wird zugleich einsehen, daß das in *Sein und Zeit* erfragte 'Sein' keine Setzung des menschlichen Subjekts bleiben kann."

19. SZ, § 44c, p. 230: "Sein—nicht Seiendes—'gibt es' nur, sofern Wahrheit ist. Und sie *ist* nur, sofern und solange Dasein ist"; cf. § 43c, p. 212: "Allerdings nur solange Dasein *ist*, das heißt die ontische Möglichkeit von Seinsverständnis, 'gibt es' Sein. . . . Die gekennzeichnete Abhängigkeit des Seins, nicht des Seienden, von Seinsverständnis," and so on (Heidegger's italics).

20. SZ, p. 226: "*Wahrheit 'gibt es' nur, sofern und solange Dasein ist*" (Heidegger's italics).

21. Cf. SZ, § 69b, p. 362: "Erst 'im Licht' einer dergestalt entworfenen Natur kann so etwas wie eine 'Tatsache' gefunden und für einen aus dem Entwurf regulativ umgrenzten Versuch angesetzt werden."

22. SZ, § 69c, p. 365: "Sofern Dasein sich zeitigt, *ist* auch eine Welt. . . . Wenn kein *Dasein* existiert, ist auch keine Welt 'da.' "

23. SZ, § 69c, p. 366: "Wenn das 'Subjekt' ontologisch als existierendes Dasein begriffen wird, dessen Sein in der Zeitlichkeit gründet, dann muß gesagt werden: Welt ist 'subjektiv.' Diese 'subjektive' Welt aber ist dann als zeitlich-transzendente 'objektiver' als jedes mögliche 'Objekt.' " The rationale for the latter claim is that the projected world is a transcendental condition of "objectivity," that is, of the fact that objects are manifest.

24. SZ, § 65, pp. 324–325: "Der primäre Entwurf des Verstehens von Sein 'gibt' den Sinn." Cf. §§ 32, 34.

25. SZ, §§ 28, 29, 31, and 69c. See p. 133: "Die ontisch bildliche Rede vom lumen naturale im Menschen meint nichts anderes als die existenzial-ontologische Struktur dieses Seienden, daß es *ist* in der Weise, sein Da zu sein. Es ist 'erleuchtet,' besagt: an ihm selbst *als* In-der-Welt-sein gelichtet, nicht durch ein anderes Seiendes, sondern so, daß es selbst die Lichtung *ist*" (Heidegger's italics).

26. Heidegger developed this interpretation partly in *Beiträge*, §§ 168–186, and partly in *Besinnung*, B (GA 66), §§ 28 (*Sorge*); 36–47, 86–87 (*Wahrheit, Lichtung*); 90 (*Stimmung*); 94 (*Seinsverständnis*); and so on.

27. WiM, *Einleitung*, pp. 7–12.

28. "Brief über den 'Humanismus,' " W, p. 159: "Versteht man den in *Sein und Zeit* genannten 'Entwurf' als ein vorstellendes Setzen, dann nimmt man ihn als Leistung der Subjektivität und denkt ihn nicht so, wie 'das Seinsverständnis' im Bereich der 'existenzialen Analytik' des 'In-der-Welt-seins' allein gedacht werden kann, nämlich als der ekstatische Bezug zur Lichtung des Seins." Cf. *Beiträge*, §§ 181–183.

29. "Brief über den 'Humanismus,' " W, p. 168: "Das Werfende im Entwerfen ist nicht der Mensch, sondern das Sein selbst, das den Menschen in die Ek-sistenz des Da-seins als sein Wesen schickt." Cf. *Beiträge*, § 122, p. 239: "(der geworfene Entwurf) ist der Vollzug des Entwurfs der Wahrheit des Seyns im Sinne der Einrückung in das Offene, dergestalt, daß der Werfer des Entwurfs als geworfener sich erfährt, d. h. er-eignet durch das Seyn"; and § 262, p. 447: "Der Entwurf des Seyns kann nur vom Seyn selbst geworfen werden."

30. Cf. "Brief über den 'Humanismus,' " W, p. 158: "Das Da-sein selbst aber west als das 'geworfene.' Es west im Wurf des Seins als des schickend Geschicklichen"; p. 161: "Der Mensch ist vielmehr vom Sein selbst in die Wahrheit des Seins 'geworfen' "; p. 173: "Dieser Ruf (vom Sein selbst) kommt als der Wurf, dem die Geworfenheit des Daseins entstammt"; and passim. Cf. *Beiträge*, §§ 182–194, especially p. 304: "Der Werfer selbst, das Da-sein, ist geworfen, er-eignet durch das Seyn," and § 262.

31. "Brief über den 'Humanismus,' " W, p. 180: " 'Welt' bedeutet in jener Bestimmung ... die Offenheit des Seins. Der Mensch ... steht in die Offenheit des Seins hinaus, als welche das Sein selber ist." Cf. *Beiträge* on the notion of "Zeitspielraum," §§ 238–242; cf. also B (GA 66), § 31 and passim.

32. "Brief über den 'Humanismus,' " W, p. 180: " 'Welt' ist die Lichtung des Seins, in die der Mensch aus seinem geworfenen Wesen her heraussteht." See WiM, *Einleitung*, for the identification of *Lichtung* and *Wahrheit des Seins*. Cf. *Beiträge*, §§ 204–211, 214, 219, and 220–237.

33. WiM, *Einleitung*, p. 18: " 'Sinn von Sein' und 'Wahrheit des Seins' besagen dasselbe."

34. SZ, §§ 9, 28, and passim.

35. SZ, § 9, p. 42: "Das Sein, *darum* es diesem Seienden in seinem Sein geht, ist je meines" (Heidegger's italics).

36. Cf. already *Beiträge*, §§ 168–203 and §§ 271–272.

37. "Brief über den 'Humanismus,' " W, p. 155: "daß der Mensch nur in seinem Wesen west, in dem er vom Sein angesprochen wird. Nur aus diesem Anspruch 'hat' er das gefunden, worin sein Wesen wohnt. Nur aus diesem Wohnen 'hat' er 'Sprache' als die Behausung, die seinem Wesen das Ekstatische wahrt. Das Stehen in der Lichtung des Seins nenne ich die Ek-sistenz des Menschen." Cf. p. 158: "Ek-sistenz bedeutet inhaltlich Hinausstehen in die Wahrheit des Seins"; *Beiträge*, §§ 168–179 and § 19, p. 51: "Das eigenste 'Sein' des Menschen ist daher gegründet in eine Zugehörigkeit zur Wahrheit des Seins als solchen."

38. "Brief über den 'Humanismus,' " p. 160.

39. "Brief über den 'Humanismus,' " p. 164: "Vielmehr ist die Sprache das Haus des Seins, darin wohnend der Mensch ek-sistiert, indem er der Wahrheit des Seins, sie hütend, gehört. So kommt es denn bei der Bestimmung der Menschlichkeit des Menschen als der Ek-sistenz darauf an, daß nicht der Mensch das Wesentliche ist, sondern das Sein als die Dimension des Ekstatischen der Ek-sistenz"; N II, p. 358: " 'Das Dasein im Menschen' ist das Wesen, das dem Sein selbst gehört," and so on. Heidegger now uses the term "Dasein"

for the deepest level in man, at which he belongs to Being (cf. Augustine, Eckhart). Cf. also *Beiträge*, §§ 168–186.

40. "Brief über den 'Humanismus,' " W, p. 173: " 'Ek-sistenz' ist . . . das ek-statische Wohnen in der Nähe des Seins"; *Beiträge*, § 179, p. 303: "Das Da-*sein* als ex-sistere: Eingerücktsein in und Hinausstehen in die Offenheit des Seins" (Heidegger's italics); B (GA 66), § 92, p. 321: "*Da-sein* nicht Bedingung der Möglichkeit und nicht Bedingungsgrund der Möglichkeit des 'Menschen' als des jetzt vorhandenen, sondern *die ab-gründige Zugehörigkeit in die Lichtung des Seins*" (Heidegger's italics).

41. "Brief über den 'Humanismus,' " W, p. 157: "der Mensch west so, daß er das 'Da', das heißt die Lichtung des Seins, ist," and so on; and p. 167: "Daß aber das Da, die Lichtung als Wahrheit des Seins selbst, sich ereignet, ist die Schickung des Seins selbst. Dieses ist das Geschick der Lichtung." Cf. *Beiträge*, § 151, p. 273: "Das Da ist die geschehende, *ereignete und inständliche* Wendungsaugenblicksstätte für die Lichtung des Seienden in der Ereignung"; § 173, p. 298: "Das Da bedeutet nicht ein irgendwie jeweils bestimmbares Hier und Dort, sondern meint die *Lichtung* des Seyns selbst, deren Offenheit erst den Raum einräumt für jedes mögliche Hier und Dort und die Einrichtung des Seienden in geschichtliches Werk und Tat und Opfer" (Heidegger's italics); § 175, p. 299: "Das Da ist ereignet vom Seyn selbst."

42. WiM, *Einleitung*, pp. 13–14. Cf. *Beiträge*, §§ 168–186.

43. SZ, *Vorbemerkung*, p. v: "Deren Weg bleibt indessen auch heute noch ein notwendiger, wenn die Frage nach dem Sein unser Dasein bewegen soll."

44. Löwith (1965), pp. 24–25: "Heideggers Um-und Weiterdenken der geworfenen Faktizität des Daseins zu einem 'Wurf des Seins' bekundet ein existenzielles Grundmotiv seines ganzen Unterwegsseins: das Verlangen nach dem Verlust von Schwere und Verschlossenheit, zu der die immer wiederkehrende Rede vom Sichöffnen für das Offene in einem direkten Verhältnis steht." For Löwith's list of contradictions, see (1965), pp. 30–32.

45. SZ, § 6, pp. 20–21: "das Fragen nach dem Sein . . . ist selbst durch die Geschichtlichkeit charakterisiert."

46. Heidegger could have derived this motivational link from many religious sources, from Paul to Kierkegaard. But Pascal developed most explicitly an apologetic strategy which, for that reason, I will call the "Pascalian strategy."

47. According to Löwith (1983), p. 517, Heidegger had portraits of Pascal and Dostoyevsky on his desk in his early Freiburg period (1918–23).

48. Feick (1980), p. 120. Cf. also Heidegger's letter to Jaspers of 15 July 1930, Hei/Ja, p. 138: "und wir verlangten gerade das Pascalthema," and GA 61, p. 93.

49. Ott (1988), p. 304.

50. Pascal (1963), p. 514 (*Pensées*, fragment no. 130 in the Lafuma edition; no. 420 in the Brunschvicg edition): "S'il se vante je l'abaisse. S'il s'abaisse je le vante. Et je le contredis toujours. Jusqu'à ce qu'il comprenne, Qu'il est un monstre incompréhensible."

51. And also with Kierkegaard's writings. But the two-stage strategy is clearer in Pascal than in Kierkegaard.

52. SZ, § 3, p. 10: "Die Theologie sucht nach einer ursprünglicheren, aus dem Sinn des Glaubens selbst vorgezeichneten und innerhalb seiner verbleibenden Auslegung des Seins des Menschen zu Gott. Sie beginnt langsam die Einsicht *Luthers* wieder zu verstehen, daß ihre dogmatische Systematik auf einem 'Fundament' ruht, das nicht einem primär

glaubenden Fragen entwachsen ist" (Heidegger's italics). Heidegger means the foundation of Greek philosophy.

53. "Phänomenologie und Theologie," W (2nd ed.), p. 66: "daß der Glaube in seinem innersten Kern als eine spezifische Existenzmöglichkeit gegenüber der wesenhaft zur Philosophie gehörigen. . . . *Existenzform* der Todfeind bleibt." Cf. p. 48 on the struggle between worldviews. See for an analysis of this lecture Jung (1990), part 3.

54. "Phänomenologie und Theologie," W (2nd ed.), p. 65: "die Philosophie als das freie Fragen des rein auf sich gestellten Denkens"; and p. 53: "Der Gläubige . . . kann vielmehr diese Existenzmöglichkeit nur 'glauben' als eine solche, deren das betroffene Dasein von sich aus nicht mächtig, in der das Dasein zum Knecht geworden, vor Gott gebracht und so *wieder*-geboren ist" (Heidegger's italics).

55. "Phänomenologie und Theologie," W (2nd ed.), p. 53: "ein Umgestelltwerden der Existenz in und durch die gläubig ergriffene Barmherzigkeit Gottes."

56. "Phänomenologie und Theologie," W (2nd ed.), p. 49: "daß die Theologie als positive Wissenschaft grundsätzlich der Chemie und der Mathematik näher steht als der Philosophie."

57. "Phänomenologie und Theologie," W (2nd ed.), pp. 51–55. See especially p. 54: "konstituiert sich die Theologie in der Thematisierung des Glaubens und des mit ihm Enthüllten, d. h. hier 'Offenbaren.' "

58. "Phänomenologie und Theologie," W (2nd ed.), pp. 61–67. On the notion of a formal indication, cf. § 8B, above, GA 60, pp 55–65, and Oudemans (1990).

59. SZ, preface to the 7th ed., p. v.

60. Cf. WiM, *Einleitung* (1949): "Das Denken auf einen Weg zu bringen, durch den es in den Bezug der Wahrheit des Seins zum Wesen des Menschen gelangt, dem Denken einen Pfad zu öffnen, damit es das Sein selbst in seiner Wahrheit eigens bedenke, dahin ist das in *Sein und Zeit* versuchte Denken 'unterwegs.' "

61. Cf. B (GA 66), § 34: "*Das Seynsgeschichtliche Wort* ist mehrdeutig. Und zwar 'meint' es nicht zugleich verschiedene 'Gegenstände,' sondern ungegenständlich sagt es das Seyn, das, weil aus-tragendes Er-eignis, zumal und stets mehrfältig west und dennoch von seinem Wort die Einfachheit fordert. Erklärende 'Definitionen' vermögen hier gleichwenig wie unbestimmtes und sinnbildliches Reden in Zeichen. Dieses mehrfältige Sagen der seynsgeschichtlichen Worte schafft im Stillen Zusammenhänge, die eine berechnete Systematik nie trifft, da sie überdies als geschichtliche stets und notwendig ihr Verborgenes und noch Unentschiedenes in sich zurückhalten; dies Unsagbare jedoch ist nicht das Irrationale der 'Metaphysik,' sondern das Erst-zu-Entscheidende der Gründung der Wahrheit des Seins" (Heidegger's italics).

62. *Beiträge*, § 34, p. 74: " 'Zeit' ist in *Sein und Zeit* die Anweisung und der Anklang auf jenes, was als Wahrheit der Wesung des Seyns geschieht in der Einzigkeit der Ereignung"; § 35, p. 76: "Dieser Übergangsbereitung dient *Sein und Zeit*"; §§ 41–43; § 49, p. 103: "Überhaupt: das ganze Menschenwesen, sobald es ins Da-sein gegründet wird, seinsgeschichtlich (aber nicht 'ontologisch') umdenken"; § 91, p. 182: "Dieser übergangliche Doppelcharakter . . . ist durchgängig das Kennzeichen der 'Fundamentalontologie,' d. h. von *Sein und Zeit*"; § 110, p. 217: "*Aber* da nun zugleich Verstehen als geworfener Entwurf gefaßt ist, besagt Transzendenz: in der Wahrheit des Seyns stehen"; § 117, p. 230: "Der Ungewöhnlichkeit des Seyns entspricht im Gründungsbereich seiner Wahrheit, d. h. im Da-sein, die Einzigkeit des Todes"; § 119, p. 234: "*Sein und Zeit* ist der *Übergang* zum Sprung"; §§ 160–163; §§ 172, 175; § 184, p. 305: "Der transzendentale (. . .) Weg nur

vorläufig, um den Umschwung und Einsprung vorzubereiten"; § 202, p. 325: "Der Tod ist als das Äußerste des Da zugleich das Innerste seiner möglichen völligen Verwandlung"; and § 266, p. 468, where Heidegger says that the conceptual structures of *Sein und Zeit* are "nur wie ein erster tastender Schritt auf ein sehr langes Sprungbrett, bei welchem Schritt kaum etwas gespürt wird von der Forderung, die am Ende des Sprungbretts für den Absprung nötig ist" (Heidegger's italics).

63. B (GA 66), § 56, p. 146: "Wie immer—in *Sein und Zeit* ist *von der Wahrheit des Seins her* und *nur* so nach dem Menschen gefragt. Dieses Fragen gehört ganz dem *Erfragen des Fragwürdigsten*—wie aber dieses, das Seyn?"; § 67, p. 212: "*Sein und Zeit* entspringt dem schon vollzogenen Sprung in diese Zugehörigkeit zum Seyn" (Heidegger's italics).

64. W, p. 55, note 56: "Durch die ontologische Interpretation des Daseins als In-der-Welt-sein ist weder positiv noch negativ über ein mögliches Sein zu Gott entschieden. Wohl aber wird durch die Erhellung der Transzendenz allererst ein *zureichender Begriff* des *Daseins* gewonnen, mit Rücksicht auf welches Seiende nunmehr gefragt werden kann, wie es mit dem Gottesverhältnis des Daseins ontologisch bestellt ist" (Heidegger's italics); Heidegger's letter to Elisabeth Blochmann of 12 September 1929, Hei/Blo, pp. 31–32, where Heidegger says: "Denn die Wahrheit unseres Daseins ist kein einfach Ding. Ihr entsprechend hat die innere Wahrhaftigkeit ihre eigene Tiefe und Vielfältigkeit. Sie besteht nicht allein aus den zurechtgelegten rationalen Überlegungen. Sie bedarf ihres Tages und der Stunde, in der wir das Dasein ganz haben [cf. SZ, §§ 45–53, my reference, HP]. Dann erfahren wir, daß unser Herz in allem seinem Wesentlichen sich der Gnade offenhalten muß. Gott—oder wie Sie es nennen—ruft jeden mit anderer Stimme." See for discussion § 13C, below.

65. In *Was ist Metaphysik?* Heidegger first destroys the dominance of reason and logic, which might impede the leap to faith. The lecture ends by stating that philosophy gets under way only by a peculiar insertion (*Einsprung*) of our existence into the fundamental possibilities of Dasein as a whole. Heidegger continues as follows: "Für diesen Einsprung ist entscheidend: einmal das Raumgeben für das Seiende im Ganzen; sodann das Sichloslassen in das Nichts, d. h. das Freiwerden von den Götzen . . . ; zuletzt das Ausschwingenlassen dieses Schwebens, auf daß es ständig zurückschwinge in die Grundfrage der Metaphysik, die das Nichts selbst erzwingt: Warum ist überhaupt Seiendes und nicht vielmehr Nichts?"

66. SdU, p. 13: "Und wenn gar unser eigenstes Dasein selbst vor einer großen Wandlung steht, wenn es wahr ist, was der leidenschaftlich den Gott suchende letzte deutsche Philosoph, Friedrich Nietzsche, sagte: 'Gott ist tot'—wenn wir Ernst machen müssen mit dieser Verlassenheit des heutigen Menschen inmitten des Seienden."

67. *Antwort*, p. 108: "So wenig wie man Gedichte übersetzen kann, kann man ein Denken übersetzen."

68. "Das Wesen der Sprache," *Sprache*, p. 161: "In Erfahrungen, die wir mit der Sprache machen, bringt sich die Sprache selbst zur Sprache."

69. Cf. WhD, p. 107: "Jede Übersetzung ist aber schon Auslegung."

70. Cf. "Der Spruch des Anaximander," HW, p. 342: "Die eigentliche geschickliche Begegnung der geschichtlichen Sprachen ist ein stilles Ereignis. In ihm spricht aber das Geschick des Seins"; cf. WiM, *Nachwort*, p. 49: "Das anfängliche Denken ist der Widerhall der Gunst des Seins, in der sich das Einzige lichtet und sich ereignen läßt. . . . Dieser Widerhall ist die menschliche Antwort auf das Wort der lautlosen Stimme des Seins. Die Antwort des Denkens ist der Ursprung des menschlichen Wortes, welches Wort erst die

Sprache als die Verlautbarung des Wortes in die Wörter entstehen läßt." For a summary of Heidegger's later view on translation, see Von Herrmann (1992).

71. *Beiträge*, § 15; § 45, p. 97: "Dieses Volk ist in seinem Ursprung und seiner Bestimmung einzig gemäß der Einzigkeit des Seyns selbst, dessen Wahrheit es einmalig an einer einzigen Stätte in einem einzigen Augenblick zu gründen hat"; § 196, p. 319: "Das Wesen des Volkes aber ist seine 'Stimme'. . . die *Stimme* des Volkes spricht selten und nur in Wenigen" (Heidegger's italics); and §§ 251–252. Cf. B (GA 66), § 14, p. 61: "Die Besinnung und so auch die Philosophie gehört stets nur den Zukünftigen. . . . Die Zukünftigen freilich sind des harten Geschlechts, das die Deutschen wieder in die Not ihres Wesens rettet. . . . Die Zukünftigen weichen nicht aus in Ersatzwelten und Scheinberuhigungen— sie zerbrechen an dem, was 'ist,' um so das Seyn in das Offene seiner Fragwürdigkeit steigen zu lassen."

72. See Smith (1992).

73. SZ, § 44b, p. 220: "gleichwohl ist es am Ende das Geschäft der Philosophie, die *Kraft der elementarsten Worte*, in denen sich das Dasein ausspricht, davor zu bewahren, daß sie durch den gemeinen Verstand zur Unverständlichkeit nivelliert werden, die ihrerseits als Quelle für Scheinprobleme fungiert" (Heidegger's italics).

74. "Phänomenologie und Theologie," *Anhang* of 1964, W (2nd ed.), p. 70. Heidegger and Carnap allegedly are the "äußersten Gegenpositionen" of modern philosophy.

75. See BT, p. 115, footnote 2 to SZ, p. 84. Macquarrie and Robinson discuss a number of problems for the translator in the translator's preface to BT. See also Macquarrie (1992).

76. Cf., for example, B (GA 66), § 90, p. 320: "Die Stimmung gehört zur Er-eignung; als Stimme des Seyns stimmt sie das Er-eignete (zur Gründung der Wahrheit des Seyns Be-stimmte) in eine Grundstimmung—Stimmung, die zum Grunde wird einer Gründung der Wahrheit des Seyns im Da-sein; Stimmung, die Da-sein als solches stimmend erfügt. Die Grundstimmung aber ist nicht nur nicht Gefühl, . . . sie ist nicht nur 'Grund' aller Verhaltungen," and passim in the later works.

77. Macquarrie (1992), p. 54. Macquarrie promises to answer this question, but he does not do so. However, he argues that *Sein und Zeit* "is not the morass of verbal mystification that it is sometimes said to be. On the contrary, it is a work of quite extraordinary power and originality, expressed in a language which is never lacking in precision, though it may be complex" (p. 57). I have some reservations about Heidegger's gift for "precision"; see sections 17 and 18 of chapter 4.

78. EM, pp. 28–29.

79. "Spiegel-Gespräch," *Antwort*, pp. 107–108: "Ich denke an die besondere innere Verwandtschaft der deutschen Sprache mit der Sprache der Griechen und deren Denken. Das bestätigen mir heute immer wieder die Franzosen. Wenn sie zu denken anfangen, sprechen sie deutsch; sie versichern, sie kämen mit ihrer Sprache nicht durch."

80. Many interpreters who do not succeed in explaining the *Kehre* by an "internal" reconstruction of Heidegger's philosophical career resort to external factors, such as Heidegger's experience of Nazism. According to Habermas (1988), for example, the *Kehre* cannot be explained by an internal reconstruction at all. On p. 185 he writes: "Die Kehre ist wohl tatsächlich das Resultat der Erfahrung mit dem Nationalsozialismus. . . . Erst dieses Moment Wahrheit . . . kann plausibel machen, was aus der internalistischen Sicht einer problemgesteuerten Theorieentwicklung unverständlich bleiben müßte." I do not want to deny the importance of such external factors. But the methodology of interpretation pre-

scribes that one should first try to give an internal reconstruction of the turn, and I reproach Habermas for not having tried hard enough.

81. Löwith saw the turn as a radical rupture, which was then concealed by Heidegger's reinterpretation of the existentialia (1965, ch. 1). Müller (1964), Pugliese (1965), Bretschneider (1965), Van der Meulen (1953), and Fürstenau (1958) stressed the continuity in Heidegger's thought, arguing that one and the same relation between *Sein* and Dasein was described first from the point of view of Dasein and later from the point of view of *Sein*. A third group of commentators has tried to stress both continuity and rupture, trying to discover motives for a radical change in *Sein und Zeit*. To this group belong Schulz (1953–54), Grondin (1987), and Rosales (1984, 1991). None of these interpretations is really satisfactory. To see the turn as a radical rupture is to leave it without an explanation. Interpretations of the second type do not account for the contradictions between *Sein und Zeit* and the later works, nor do they explain why Heidegger concealed these contradictions by an "interpretation" of the existentialia. Finally, finding reasons why the project of *Sein und Zeit* failed does not explain the turn either, for a failure of *Sein und Zeit* might lead to many different conclusions. It may be that *Sein und Zeit* does not describe human finitude in a radical way (Grondin's hypothesis, [1987], pp. 81–127), or that the notion of truth as unconcealedness implies that modes of truth or of being preexist in a totally concealed manner (Rosales' conjecture [1991], p. 134). Indeed, there are many reasons why Heidegger's transcendental philosophy of *Sein und Zeit* failed. But none of these reasons implies Heidegger's later philosophy. As a consequence, they do not really account for the turn.

82. Caputo (1993), pp. 270–288; cf. Ott (1988), pp. 345–346.

83. Cf. Grondin (1987), pp. 12–13: "A la rigueur, il faudrait peut-être dissocier la problématique du tournant de la question de l'évolution de la pensée de Heidegger."

84. *Metaphysische Anfangsgründe der Logik im Ausgang von Leibniz*, lectures of Sommersemester 1928, GA 26, p. 201. Referring to the temporal analytic of being, planned for the third *Abschnitt* of *Sein und Zeit*, Heidegger says: "Diese temporale Analytik ist aber zugleich die *Kehre*, in der die Ontologie selbst in die metaphysische Ontik, in der sie unausdrücklich immer steht, ausdrücklich zurückläuft" (Heidegger's italics). Grondin (1987, p. 75) quotes the text, and concludes that the thought of the turn dates from 1928. However, one should be careful in drawing conclusions about chronology from the *Gesamtausgabe*. According to Heidegger's maxims for producing it, later notes had to be incorporated in the texts, adapting them to the style of the time, in order that the *Gesamtausgabe* would be an edition "aus letzter Hand" (cf. GA 26, p. 288, for a description of this thoroughly uncritical procedure). The quote on *die Kehre* could very well be such a later note. Nevertheless, I will endorse the hypothesis that the notion of a *Kehre* was present in the lectures of 1928, even though the term may have been a later addition.

85. *Beiträge* (GA 65), especially §§ 8–11, 27, 44, 91, 140–142, 190, 202, 226, 233, and 255.

86. For the letter to Buchner, see VA, pp. 176–179. The letter to Richardson is printed as a preface to Richardson (1963).

87. TK, pp. 37–47.

88. Cf. Grondin (1987), pp. 21–22.

89. Heidegger added a reference to *die Kehre* to "Vom Wesen der Wahrheit" in 1949. See the first paragraph of the *Anmerkung*, W, p. 96.

90. "Brief über den 'Humanismus,' " W, p. 159: "Der Vortrag 'Vom Wesen der Wahrheit,' der 1930 gedacht und mitgeteilt, aber erst 1943 gedruckt wurde, gibt einen gewissen

Einblick in das Denken der Kehre von 'Sein und Zeit' zu 'Zeit und Sein.' " An English translation of "Vom Wesen der Wahrheit" is published in BW, entitled "On the Essence of Truth."

91. "Zeit und Sein," SD, pp. 1–25. The text appeared for the first time in a festschrift for Jean Beaufret: *L'endurance de la pensée* (Paris: Plon, 1968).

92. *Richardson*, p. xix: "Die Kehre . . . gehört in den durch die Titel 'Sein und Zeit,' 'Zeit und Sein' genannten Sachverhalt selbst," and so on.

93. "Der Spruch des Anaximander," HW, p. 302: "Das Sein selbst ist als geschickliches in sich eschatologisch. . . . Wir denken die Eschatologie des Seins in dem entsprechenden Sinne, in dem seinsgeschichtlich die Phänomenologie des Geistes zu denken ist."

94. "Der Spruch des Anaximander," HW, pp. 310–311: "Das Sein entzieht sich, indem es sich in das Seiende entbirgt. Dergestalt beirrt das Sein, es lichtend, das Seiende mit der Irre. . . . Dergestalt hält das Sein mit seiner Wahrheit an sich. Dieses Ansichhalten ist die frühe Weise seines Entbergens. . . . Wir können dieses lichtende Ansichhalten mit der Wahrheit seines Wesens die *epoche* des Seins nennen," and so on. See also "Zeit und Sein," SD, pp. 8–9, where Heidegger uses *Sein* in the Neo-Hegelian sense, whereas *Sein* in the postmonotheist sense is called "Es gibt." He then says: "Im Beginn des abendländischen Denkens wird das Sein gedacht, aber nicht das 'Es gibt' als solches. Dieses entzieht sich zugunsten der Gabe, die Es gibt." He goes on to make his usual puns on *schicken, Geschichte*, and *epoche*; *Beiträge*, § 2, p. 8: "Wenn aber das Ereignis zur Weigerung und Verweigerung wird, ist dies nur der Entzug des Seyns"; § 61, p. 128: "das Seyn selbst entzieht sich"; § 123, p. 241: "*daß die Verweigerung die erste höchste Schenkung des Seyns, ja dessen anfängliche Wesung selbst ist.* Sie ereignet sich als der Entzug" (Heidegger's italics); §§ 168; 267, and 269.

95. For the term *Abfall*, see EM, pp. 139–141ff.

96. Cf., for instance, "Überwindung der Metaphysik," VA, especially sections iii, x, xix, xxvi, and xxviii.

97. During the depression of 1929, Heidegger wrote in his lecture course *Die Grundbegriffe der Metaphysik*, GA 29/30, p. 244: "Nicht dieses soziale Elend . . . nicht das ist die Not, daß diese oder jene Not so oder so bedrängt, sondern das zutiefst und verborgen Bedrängende ist vielmehr: *das Ausbleiben einer wesenhaften Bedrängnis unseres Daseins im Ganzen*" (Heidegger's italics). In his later writings, Heidegger set himself the task of awakening our awareness of this hidden but essential distress: that we are abandoned by Being. Cf. *Beiträge*, § 4, p. 11: "Im Zeitalter des endlosen Bedürfens aus der verborgenen Not der *Notlosigkeit* muß diese Frage notwendig als das nutzloseste Gerede erscheinen"; §§ 17, 45, 53, 56 (p. 119, no 14: "Die Seinsverlassenheit ist der innerste Grund für die Not der Notlosigkeit"); § 119, p. 234: "zuvor muß die Not der Notlosigkeit, die Seinsverlassenheit, erfahren werden"; § 216, p. 341: "in der Not, die so tief wurzelt, daß sie für jedermann *keine* ist: daß wir die Frage nach der Wahrheit des Wahren gar nicht als Frage in ihrer Notwendigkeit erfahren und begreifen"; and § 259, p. 429: "dergestalt, daß sie sich als die Not, die sie ist, entzieht und die Notlosigkeit (hinsichtlich des Seins und der Seinsfrage) zum herrschenden Zustand werden läßt. In Wahrheit ist aber die Notlosigkeit das äußerste dieser Not, die zuerst als die Verlassenheit des Seienden vom Sein erkennbar wird" (Heidegger's italics).

98. "Die Frage nach der Technik," VA, pp. 30–32ff.

99. "Die Frage nach der Technik," VA, pp. 32 and 39: "Wo aber Gefahr ist, wächst / Das Rettende auch." Cf. "Wozu Dichter?", HW, p. 273, and passim in the later works.

100. "Die Kehre," TK, p. 38: "Wir stellen die Geschichte in den Bereich des Geschehens, statt die Geschichte nach ihrer Wesensherkunft aus dem Geschick zu denken. Geschick aber ist wesenhaft Geschick des Seins, so zwar, daß das Sein selber sich schickt und je als ein Geschick west und demgemäß sich geschicklich wandelt.... Weil jedoch das Sein sich als Wesen der Technik in das Gestell geschickt hat, zum Wesen des Seins aber das Menschenwesen gehört, insofern das Wesen des Seins das Menschenwesen braucht, um als Sein nach dem eigenen Wesen inmitten des Seienden *gewahrt* zu bleiben und so *als* das Sein zu wesen, deshalb kann das Wesen der Technik nicht ohne die Mithilfe des Menschenwesens in den Wandel seines Geschickes geleitet werden" (Heidegger's italics). Cf. also p. 40: "Das Wesen des Gestells ist die Gefahr. Als die Gefahr kehrt sich das Sein in die Vergessenheit seines Wesens von diesem Wesen weg und kehrt sich so zugleich gegen die Wahrheit seines Wesens. In der Gefahr waltet dieses noch nicht bedachte Sichkehren. Im Wesen der Gefahr *verbirgt* sich darum die Möglichkeit einer Kehre, in der die Vergessenheit des Wesens des Seins sich so wendet, daß mit *dieser* Kehre die Wahrheit des Wesens des Seins in das Seiende eigens einkehrt" (Heidegger's italics). Cf. B (GA 66), § 55, p. 139: "Das Seyn ist vom Menschen abhängig; das will sagen: Das Wesen des Seyns erreicht sich selbst und gerät in den Wesensverlust, je nach dem das *Wesen* des Menschen— der Seinsbezug des Menschen—für den Menschen wesentlich und der Grund der 'Menschlichkeit' ist. Das Seyn ist darnach dem Menschen—der jeweiligen Wesentlichkeit des Menschen—ausgeliefert" (Heidegger's italics).

101. *Beiträge*, §§ 8, 10, 11, 27, 44 (p. 95: "der *Kehre*, die im Seyn selbst west"); § 91, p. 184: "Jetzt aber ist not die *große Umkehrung* . . . in der nicht das Seiende vom Menschen her, sondern das Menschsein aus dem Seyn gegründet wird"; p. 185: "als Seyn der Wahrheit, d. h. als das *in sich kehrige Ereignis*"; § 140, p. 261: "Eine, ja die Kehre, die eben das Wesen des Seins selbst als das in sich gegenschwingende Ereignis anzeigt"; §§ 141– 142; § 190, p. 311: "*Das tiefste Wesen der Geschichte ruht mit darin, daß die erklüftende (Wahrheit gründende) Ereignung erst Jene entspringen läßt, die, einander brauchend, erst im Ereignis der Kehre einander sich zu-und abkehren*"; § 202, p. 325: "ist der Widerschein der Kehre im Wesen des Seins selbst"; § 226, p. 351: "Die Lichtung für die Verbergung ist schon die Schwingung des Gegenschwunges der Kehre des Ereignisses"; § 233, pp. 360–361: "Das Sichverbergen muß ins Wissen kommen als Wesung des Seyns selbst als Ereignis. Der innigste Bezug von Seyn und Dasein in seiner Kehre wird sichbar" (here the turn is said to occur in the relation [*Bezug*] between Being and Dasein); and § 255, p. 407: "Die im Ereignis wesende Kehre ist der verborgene Grund aller anderen.... Kehren" (Heidegger's italics).

102. *Beiträge*, § 255, p. 407: "Was ist diese ursprüngliche Kehre im Ereignis? Nur der Anfall des Seyns als Ereignung des Da bringt das Da-*sein* zu ihm selbst," and so on; § 198, p. 320: "Sofern das Da-sein *sich* zu-ge-eignet wird als zugehörig zum Ereignis, kommt es zu sich *selbst*" (Heidegger's italics); B (GA 66), § 94, p. 324: "Die Eigentlichkeit aber meint entsprechend nicht eine besondere Existenzauslegung im Sinne eines moralischen Ideals, sondern wieder nur enthält sie den Wink in die Selbstheit des Da-seins, in die Entschlossenheit, als Fügung in die Wahrheit des Seins. Eigentlichkeit und Uneigentlichkeit sind als 'Existenzialien' nicht Titel einer 'neuen' Anthropologie und dergleichen, sondern die Hinweise darauf, daß die Wesung des Seyns selbst das Da-sein ab-stimmt auf Aneignung der Wahrheit des Seyns und auf Verlust."

103. On *Augenblick* (Luther's translation of the Greek *kairos*), see *Beiträge*, §§ 5, 58, 189, 190, 200, 217, 225, 227, 238, 242, 245, 255 (p. 409: "dem *Augenblick* als dem Erblitzen des Seyns aus dem Beständnis des einfachen und nie errechenbaren Ereignisses").

104. *Richardson*, p. xvii: "das Durchdenken eines so entscheidenden Sachverhalts"; "der unter dem Namen 'Kehre' gedachte Sachverhalt." On p. xix, Heidegger says: "Die Kehre spielt im Sachverhalt selbst."

105. "Zeit und Sein," SD, p. 4: "Das Wort 'Sache,' 'eine Sache' soll uns jetzt solches bedeuten, worum es sich in einem maßgebenden Sinne handelt, sofern sich darin etwas Unübergehbares verbirgt. Sein—eine Sache, vermutlich *die* Sache des Denkens" (Heidegger's italics). The term *Sache* in this context might also be translated as "topic" or "matter," or perhaps as "what is at stake."

106. "Zeit und Sein," SD, pp. 7–8: "Die Entfaltung der Wandlungsfülle des Seins sieht zunächst aus wie eine Geschichte des Seins," and passim; *Beiträge*, § 2, p. 7: "Unausmeßbar ist der Reichtum des kehrigen Bezugs des Seyns zu dem ihm ereigneten Da-sein, unerrechenbar die Fülle der Ereignung"; § 267, p. 476: "Das Seyn west als das Zwischen für den Gott und den Menschen . . . , in deren Lichtung Welten sich fügen und versinken, Erden sich erschließen und die Zerstörung dulden."

107. Cf. *Beiträge*, § 5, p. 14: "In der philosophischen Erkenntnis dagegen beginnt mit dem ersten Schritt eine Verwandlung des verstehenden Menschen und zwar nicht im moralisch-'existenziellen' Sinne, sondern da-seinsmäßig. Das will sagen: der Bezug zum Seyn und zuvor immer zur Wahrheit des Seyns wandelt sich in der Weise der Verrückung in das Da-sein selbst"; and §§ 81–114, *Das Zuspiel*.

108. Cf. WiM, *Einleitung*, p. 9: "Wandel des Wesens des Menschen"; *Beiträge*, § 5, p. 14 ("Verwandlung des verstehenden Menschen"); §§ 42, 44, 53 (p. 113: "völlige Verwandlung des Menschen"), § 259 (p. 440: "Verwandlung des Menschen"). Cf. also §§ 168–203.

109. "Brief über den 'Humanismus,' " W, p. 159: "Kehre von 'Sein und Zeit' zu 'Zeit und Sein' "; *Richardson*, p. xix: "Die Kehre ist in erster Linie nicht ein Vorgang im fragenden Denken; sie gehört in den durch die Titel 'Sein und Zeit,' 'Zeit und Sein' genannten Sachverhalt selbst."

110. "Zeit und Sein," SD, pp. 5–10. Cf. especially p. 6: "Das Sein eigens denken, verlangt, das Sein als den Grund des Seienden fahren zu lassen zugunsten des im Entbergen verborgen spielenden Gebens, d. h. des Es gibt. Sein gehört als die Gabe dieses Es gibt in das Geben"; and p. 8: "Im Beginn des abendländischen Denkens wird das Sein gedacht, aber nicht das 'Es gibt' als solches. Dieses entzieht sich zugunsten der Gabe, die Es gibt." In *Beiträge*, *Sein* in this second sense (*Es gibt*) is written as "das Seyn."

111. "Zeit und Sein," SD, p. 6: "gewaltigsten Denken der neueren Zeit." Heidegger rejects Hegel and yet is close to him, as this quote shows. The Neo-Hegelian theme explains why this is the case. Cf. *Beiträge*, § 119, p. 232: "bei Hegel vollzieht sich erstmals ein philosophischer Versuch einer Geschichte der Frage nach dem Seienden."

112. "Zeit und Sein," SD, pp. 10–17. See especially pp. 15–16: "Vielmehr beruht die Einheit der drei Zeitdimensionen in dem Zuspiel jeder für jede. Dieses Zuspiel erweist sich als das eigentliche, im Eigenen der Zeit spielende Reichen, also gleichsam als die vierte Dimension—nicht nur gleichsam, sondern aus der Sache. Die eigentliche Zeit ist vierdimensional." Cf. also p. 18: "Denn die Zeit bleibt selber die Gabe eines Es gibt, dessen Geben den Bereich verwahrt, in dem Anwesenheit gereicht wird. So bleibt das Es weiterhin unbestimmt, rätselhaft, und wir selber bleiben ratlos." It is interesting to note that the verb

reichen is also used for the ritual of administering the Last Supper in the Catholic Mass. Cf. on *Zuspiel, Beiträge,* §§ 81–114.

113. "Zeit und Sein," SD, pp. 17–25. See especially p. 17: "Das Geben im 'Es gibt Sein' zeigte sich als Schicken und als Geschick von Anwesenheit in ihren epochalen Wandlungen. Das Geben im 'Es gibt Zeit' zeigte sich als lichtendes Reichen des vierdimensionalen Bereiches"; and p. 20: "Demnach bezeugt sich das Es, das gibt, im 'Es gibt Sein,' 'Es gibt Zeit,' als das Ereignis," and "der Sach-Verhalt . . . ist das Ereignis. . . . Der Sach-Verhalt ereignet erst Sein und Zeit aus ihrem Verhältnis in ihr Eigenes."

114. "Zeit und Sein," SD, p. 22: "Allein die einzige Absicht dieses Vortrages geht dahin, das Sein selbst als das Ereignis in den Blick zu bringen. . . . Sein verschwindet im Ereignis."

115. Cf. *Beiträge,* § 125, p. 242: "Die 'Zeit' sollte erfahrbar werden als der 'ekstatische' Spielraum der Wahrheit des Seins"; cf. § 12, p. 32: "Geschichte hier nicht gefaßt als ein Bereich des Seienden unter anderen, sondern einzig im Blick auf die Wesung des Seyns selbst"; § 25, p. 61: "Die Geschichtlichkeit hier begriffen als *eine* Wahrheit, lichtende Verbergung des Seins als solchen"; § 42; § 268, p. 479: "Mit dem Entwurf des Seyns als Ereignis ist erst auch der Grund und damit das Wesen und der Wesensraum der Geschichte geahnt"; § 273, p. 494: "*Das Seyn als Er-eignis ist die Geschichte*"; and § 276, p. 501: "Unsere Geschichte—nicht als der historisch bekannte Ablauf unserer Geschicke und Leistungen, sondern wir selbst im Augenblick unseres Bezugs zum Seyn" (Heidegger's italics). Cf. also WiM, *Einleitung* (1949), p. 17: "im Anwesen waltet ungedacht und verborgen Gegenwart und Andauern, west Zeit. Sein als solches ist demnach unverborgen aus Zeit. So verweist Zeit auf die Unverborgenheit, d. h. die Wahrheit von Sein."

116. *Richardson,* p. xix: "Die Kehre . . . gehört in den durch die Titel 'Sein und Zeit,' 'Zeit und Sein' genannten Sachverhalt selbst."

117. *Beiträge,* §§ 81–114; and § 44, p. 94: "Die abendländische Geschichte der abendländischen Metaphysik ist der 'Beweis' dafür, daß die Wahrheit des Seyns nicht zur Frage werden konnte"; § 52, p. 112: "Der schärfste Beweis für dieses verborgene Wesen des Seyns (für das Sichverbergen in der Offenheit des Seienden) . . . wird geführt durch die ganze Geschichte der Metaphysik"; § 173, p. 297: "Denn die 'Metaphysik' fragt vom Seienden her . . . und läßt die Wahrheit dieser und d. h. die Wahrheit des Seyns notwendig ungefragt"; § 207, p. 330: "Das Sichverbergen aber, das ist die Grundlehre des ersten Anfangs und seiner Geschichte (der Metaphysik als solcher)"; §§ 258, 259, and 266.

118. Cf. SZ, § 5, p. 18; KM, § 44; GA 26, § 10, pp. 181–187.

119. *Richardson,* p. xvii: "Das Denken der Kehre ergibt sich daraus, daß ich bei der zu denkenden Sache 'Sein und Zeit' geblieben bin, d. h. nach der Hinsicht gefragt habe, die schon in *Sein und Zeit* (S. 39) unter dem Titel 'Zeit und Sein' angezeigt wurde." Cf. "Brief über den 'Humanismus,' " W, p. 159.

120. *Richardson,* p. xvii: "daß der unter dem Namen 'Kehre' gedachte Sachverhalt mein Denken schon ein Jahrzehnt vor 1947 bewegte."

121. In fact, we find this Lutheran notion of faith already in the religion courses of 1920–21 (cf. GA 60). As Van Buren (1994) writes (p. 163): "This Coming will arrive in the Kairos as 'the fullness of time.' However, the time and content of this arrival are not objectively available in advance to be awaited, expected (*erwartet*), represented, and calculated, but rather are to be determined only out of the Kairos itself"; cf. SZ, § 3, p. 10.

122. TK, p. 41: "Vielleicht stehen wir bereits im vorausgeworfenen Schatten der Ankunft *dieser* Kehre. Wann und wie sie sich geschicklich ereignet, weiß niemand."

123. "Ein Brief an einen jungen Studenten," VA, p. 177: "um einen Anspruch des Seins zu hören. Aber gerade dabei kann es sich verhören. Die Möglichkeit des Irrgangs ist bei diesem Denken die größte." Cf. *Beiträge*, § 42, p. 85: "Weil im Denken des Seyns alles sich auf das Einzige zu hält, sind hier die Umstürze gleichsam die Regel!" and so on, and "Deshalb wird allerdings der *Weg* selbst immer wesentlicher, nicht als 'persönliche Entwicklung,' sondern als die völlig unbiographisch gemeinte Anstrengung des Menschen, das Seyn selbst im Seienden zu seiner Wahrheit zu bringen" (Heidegger's italics).

124. "Brief über den 'Humanismus,' " W, p. 159: "Der fragliche Abschnitt wurde zurückgehalten, weil das Denken im zureichenden Sagen dieser Kehre versagte und mit Hilfe der Sprache der Metaphysik nicht durchkam." Cf. *Beiträge*, § 262, p. 451: "Daher galt es, an der entscheidenden Stelle die Krisis der notwendig so zunächst angelegten Seinsfrage zu überwinden und vor allem eine Vergegenständlichung des Seyns zu vermeiden, einmal durch das *Zurückhalten* der 'temporalen' Auslegung des Seyns," and so on (Heidegger's italics).

125. In *Beiträge*, Heidegger endorses the Pascalian interpretation of *Sein und Zeit*: cf. § 34, p. 74: " 'Zeit' ist in *Sein und Zeit* die *Anweisung* und der *Anklang* auf jenes, was als Wahrheit der Wesung des Seyns geschieht in der Einzigkeit der Er-eignung"; p. 76: "Dieser Übergangsbereitung dient *Sein und Zeit*, d. h. es steht eigentlich schon in der Grundfrage, ohne diese rein aus sich anfänglich zu entfalten"; §§ 42, 43, 49; § 91, p. 182: "Dieser übergängliche Doppelcharakter, der die 'Metaphysik' zugleich ursprünglicher faßt und damit überwindet, ist durchgängig das Kennzeichen der 'Fundamentalontologie,' d. h. von *Sein und Zeit*"; § 110, no. 20c; § 117, p. 230: "Der Ungewöhnlichkeit des Seyns entspricht im Gründungsbereich seiner Wahrheit, d. h. im Da-sein, die Einzigkeit des Todes"; § 119, p. 234: "*Sein und Zeit* ist der Übergang zum Sprung"; §§ 160–163, 172, 175; § 184, p. 305: "Der *transzendentale*. . . . Weg nur vorläufig, um den Umschwung und Einsprung vorzubereiten"; §§ 189, 202, 226, 266, and 276.

126. Richardson, p. xvii: "daß ein Durchdenken eines so entscheidenden Sachverhalts viele Jahre benötigt, um ins Klare zu kommen." The text refers to the years 1937–47. According to my hypothesis, it also applies to the years 1927–37.

127. "Brief über den 'Humanismus,' " W, p. 159: "Diese Kehre (von 'Sein und Zeit' zu 'Zeit und Sein') ist nicht eine Änderung des Standpunktes von *Sein und Zeit*, sondern in ihr gelangt das versuchte Denken erst in die Ortschaft der Dimension, aus der *Sein und Zeit* erfahren ist, und zwar erfahren aus der Grunderfahrung der Seinsvergessenheit." Cf. WiM, *Einleitung* (1949), pp. 9–10 and *Beiträge*, the texts listed in the one but previous note. Cf. also B (GA 66), § 56.

128. "Vom Wesen des Grundes," footnote 56, W, p. 55: "Durch die ontologische Interpretation des Daseins als In-der-Welt-sein ist weder positiv noch negativ über ein mögliches Sein zu Gott entschieden. Wohl aber wird durch die Erhellung der Transzendenz allererst ein *zureichender Begriff* des Daseins gewonnen, mit Rücksicht auf welches Seiende nunmehr *gefragt* werden kann, wie es mit dem Gottesverhältnis des Daseins ontologisch bestellt ist" (Heidegger's italics).

129. Cf. GA 26, p. 177: "Der existenzielle Einsatz der Fundamentalontologie führt mit sich den Schein eines extrem individualistischen, radikalen Atheismus. . . . Gleichwohl darf man nicht aus dem Blick verlieren, daß mit einer solchen fundamentalontologischen Klärung noch nichts entschieden wird, vielmehr ja gerade gezeigt werden soll, daß so nichts entscheidbar ist." This text of 1928 also points to the notion of faith as grace.

130. One might substantiate this interpretation further by interpreting important texts that Heidegger wrote between 1922 and 1927, such as the conference on the notion of time in historical research "Der Zeitbegriff in der Geschichtswissenschaft," given in July 1924 for the *Theologenschaft* in Marburg. See FS, pp. 415–433.

131. *Metaphysische Anfangsgründe der Logik im Ausgang von Leibniz*, GA 26, p. 201.

132. GA 26, pp. 174–175 (*transzendentale Zerstreuung*).

133. Many other passages in § 10 point to a religious turn. See, for instance, GA 26, p. 176: "Denn gerade der metaphysische Entwurf selbst enthüllt die wesenhafte Endlichkeit der Existenz des Daseins, die existenziell nur verstanden wird in der Unwesentlichkeit des Selbst, die konkret nur wird . . . durch den Dienst und im Dienst des je möglichen Ganzen," a quote that reminds us of Eckhart. Cf. also the passage on atheism on p. 177.

134. Heidegger does not draw the parallel, but he was clearly inspired by Kant. See the first *Critique*, third chapter of the transcendental doctrine of method, "Die Architektonik der reinen Vernunft," KdrV, A 832–851.

135. GA 26, p. 202: "Fundamentalontologie und Metontologie in ihrer Einheit bilden den Begriff der Metaphysik."

136. The term "metontology" was inspired by Scheler, who used terms such as "metanthropology" for the metaphysical basis of anthropology.

137. GA 26, p. 199: "Mit anderen Worten: die Möglichkeit, daß es Sein im Verstehen gibt, hat zur Voraussetzung die faktische Existenz des Daseins, und diese wiederum das faktische Vorhandensein der Natur. Gerade im Horizont des radikal gestellten Seinsproblems zeigt sich, daß all das nur sichtbar ist und als Sein verstanden werden kann, wenn eine mögliche Totalität von Seiendem schon da ist."

138. GA 26, p. 201: "Diese temporale Analytik ist aber zugleich die *Kehre*, in der die Ontologie selbst in die metaphysische Ontik, in der sie unausdrücklich immer steht, ausdrücklich zurückläuft" (Heidegger's italics). There is a formal parallelism with Husserl's later philosophy (1913–38) at this point, for according to Husserl, eidetic phenomenology (ontology) is ultimately grounded in an ontic or factual metaphysics.

139. GA 26, p. 202: "Aber darin kommt nur zum Ausdruck die Verwandlung des einen Grundproblems der Philosophie selbst, das schon oben . . . berührt wurde mit dem Doppelbegriff von Philosophie als *protē philosophia* und *theologia*."

140. This is also the point of *Was ist Metaphysik?* of 1929.

141. There is yet another possible unification. It could be that Heidegger's notion of *Sinn* in § 32 of SZ as the "for-the-sake-of" of projection (*das Woraufhin des Entwurfs*) has a religious connotation: Being would be the ultimate sense or "for-the-sake-of" of all our projections.

142. Hei/Blo, p. 31; cf. Safranski (1994), pp. 215–216.

143. Hei/Blo, pp. 31–32: "Denn die Wahrheit unseres Daseins ist kein einfach Ding. Ihr entsprechend hat die innere Wahrhaftigkeit ihre eigene Tiefe und Vielfältigkeit. Sie besteht nicht allein aus den zurechtgelegten rationalen Überlegungen. Sie bedarf ihres Tages und der Stunde, in der wir das Dasein ganz haben. Dann erfahren wir, daß unser Herz in allem seinem Wesentlichen sich der Gnade offenhalten muß. Gott—oder wie Sie es nennen—ruft jeden mit anderer Stimme."

144. WiM, p. 42: "Die Philosophie kommt nur in Gang durch einen eigentümlichen Einsprung der eigenen Existenz in die Grundmöglichkeiten des Daseins im Ganzen . . . das Sichloslassen in das Nichts."

145. Hei/Blo, p. 32: "So muß uns der heutige Katholizismus u. all dergleichen, der Protestantismus nicht minder, ein Greuel bleiben."

146. Hei/Blo, p. 32: "So ist Ihnen die Complet zum Symbol geworden des Hineingehaltenseins der Existenz in die Nacht u. der inneren Notwendigkeit der täglichen Bereitschaft für Sie. . . . Entscheidend ist dieses urgewaltige *Negative: nichts* in den Weg legen der Tiefe des Daseins" (Heidegger's italics). Cf. WiM, p. 35: "Da-sein heißt: Hineingehaltenheit in das Nichts."

147. "Brief über den 'Humanismus,' " W, p. 159.

148. Hei/Ja, p. 157: "Bei mir ist es . . . ein mühsames Tasten . . . und sonst sind ja auch zwei Pfähle—die Auseinandersetzung mit dem Glauben der Herkunft und das Mißlingen des Rektorats—gerade genug an solchem, was wirklich überwunden sein möchte." Cf. for the expression "Pfahl im Fleisch" Paul's second letter to the *Corinthians*, 12:7: "And to keep me from being too elated by the abundance of revelations, a thorn was given me in the flesh, a messenger of Satan, to harass me, to keep me from being too elated." Heidegger surely suffered from an abundance of revelations, hence he received two thorns instead of one.

149. "Brief über den 'Humanismus,' " W, p. 159: "Der Vortrag 'Vom Wesen der Wahrheit,' der 1930 gedacht und mitgeteilt, aber erst 1943 gedruckt wurde, gibt einen gewissen Einblick in das Denken der Kehre von 'Sein und Zeit' zu 'Zeit und Sein.' "

150. Rosales (1991, § 4) discusses some crucial differences between the original draft and the published text, which show that the draft of 1930 was still near to "Vom Wesen des Grundes" (1929) and to Heidegger's course of the summer of 1928 (GA 26, § 9).

151. Cf. *Beiträge*, § 44, p. 95: "*Die Wahrheit des Seyns ist das Seyn der Wahrheit*—so gesagt klingt es wie eine gekünstelte und verzwungene Umkehrung und, wenn es hoch kommt, wie eine Verleitung zu einem dialektischen Spiel. Während doch diese Umkehrung nur ein flüchtig-äußeres Zeichen ist der *Kehre*, die im Seyn selbst west" (Heidegger's italics).

152. "Vom Wesen der Wahrheit," W, p. 81: "*Das Wesen der Wahrheit ist die Freiheit*" (Heidegger's italics).

153. "Vom Wesen des Grundes," part III, W, pp. 59–71. At the end of this text, it is clear that Heidegger prepares for a turn, for freedom as the ground (*Grund*) of projecting reveals itself as an Abyss (*Abgrund*).

154. "Vom Wesen der Wahrheit," W, p. 83: "daß wir zu einer Wandlung des Denkens bereit sind."

155. "Vom Wesen der Wahrheit," § 4, W, p. 86: "Die so verstandene Freiheit als das Sein-lassen des Seienden erfüllt und vollzieht das Wesen der Wahrheit im Sinne der Entbergung von Seiendem."

156. "Vom Wesen der Wahrheit," § 4, W, p. 85: "Der Mensch 'besitzt' die Freiheit nicht als Eigenschaft, sondern höchstens gilt das Umgekehrte: die Freiheit, das ek-sistente, entbergende Da-sein besitzt den Menschen," and so on, and p. 86: "Der Mensch ek-sistiert, heißt jetzt: die Geschichte der Wesensmöglichkeiten eines geschichtlichen Menschentums ist ihm verwahrt in der Entbergung des Seienden im Ganzen." Cf. N II, p. 398: "Das Sein west, indem es—die Freiheit des Freien selbst—alles Seiende zu ihm selbst befreit und dem Denken das zu Denkende bleibt."

157. "Vom Wesen der Wahrheit," § 6, W, pp. 89–91, especially p. 90: "Für den Wissenden allerdings deutet das 'Un-' des anfänglichen Un-wesens der Wahrheit als der

Un-wahrheit in den noch nicht erfahrenen Bereich der Wahrheit des Seins (nicht erst des Seienden)."

158. "Vom Wesen der Wahrheit," § 7, W, pp. 91–94; especially pp. 93–94: "Dann ist die Ent-schlossenheit zum Geheimnis unterwegs in die Irre als solche. Dann wird die Frage nach dem Wesen der Wahrheit ursprünglicher gefragt. Dann enthüllt sich der Grund der Verflechtung des Wesens der Wahrheit mit der Wahrheit des Wesens. . . . Das Denken des Seins."

159. "Vom Wesen der Wahrheit," W, p. 96: "ob die Frage nach dem Wesen der Wahrheit zugleich und zuerst die Frage nach der Wahrheit des Wesens sein muß. Im Begriff des 'Wesens' aber denkt die Philosophie das Sein."

160. "Vom Wesen der Wahrheit," § 9, *Anmerkung*, W, pp. 96–97.

161. *Beiträge*, § 29, p. 66: "Der Grundsatz des anfänglichen Denkens lautet daher ge-doppelt: alles Wesen ist Wesung"; § 164, p. 286: "Aber hier in diesem Äußersten muß das Wort Gewalt brauchen, und *Wesung* soll nicht etwas nennen, was noch über das Seyn wieder *hinaus* liegt, sondern was sein Innerstes zum Wort bringt, das Er-eignis, jenen Gegenschwung von Seyn und Da-sein"; § 276; and § 270, p. 484: "Wesung heißt die Weise, wie das Seyn selbst ist, nämlich das Seyn" (Heidegger's italics).

162. Cf. "Vom Wesen der Wahrheit," W, p. 97: "Weil zu ihm [viz. das Seyn] lichtendes Bergen gehört, erscheint Seyn anfänglich im Licht des verbergenden Entzugs. Der name dieser Lichtung ist *alētheia*."

163. Ott (1988), pp. 131–246.

164. "Das Rektorat 1933/34: Tatsachen und Gedanken," SdU, p. 22, where Heidegger says that he repeated his course on the Greek conception of truth and Plato's simile of the cave in the winter semester of 1933–34. According to Rockmore (1992), p. 54, "Heideg-ger's approach to politics in his speech [i.e., the rectoral address] is quasi-Platonic, in fact a form of right-wing Platonism." Rockmore substantiates this interpretation by an extensive analysis of the rectoral address (pp. 54–72).

165. SdU, p. 10: "Die Selbstbehauptung der deutschen Universität ist der ursprüngliche, gemeinsame Wille zu ihrem Wesen. Die deutsche Universität gilt uns als die hohe Schule, die aus Wissenschaft und durch Wissenschaft die Führer und Hüter des Schicksals des deutschen Volkes in die Erziehung und Zucht nimmt," and so on.

166. SdU, p. 24: "Auf diese Weise hoffte ich, dem Vordringen ungeeigneter Personen und der drohenden Vormacht des Parteiapparates und der Parteidoktrin begegnen zu kön-nen"; and p. 26: "Mit der Übernahme des Rektorats hatte ich den Versuch gewagt, das Positive zu retten und zu läutern und zu festigen." See also Heidegger's letter of 15 Decem-ber 1945 to Professor Constantin von Dietze, published in Martin (1989), pp. 207–211.

167. SdU, p. 15: "Die vielbesungene 'akademische Freiheit' wird aus der deutschen Universität verstoßen. . . . Der Begriff der Freiheit des deutschen Studenten wird jetzt zu seiner Wahrheit zurückgebracht. Aus ihr entfalten sich künftig Bindung und Dienst der deutschen Studentenschaft," and so on. We may reject Heidegger's views without morally condemning him for holding them in 1933, and it is not my primary aim in this section to judge Heidegger's behavior from a moral point of view. However, the reason for this atti-tude is not that, "as members of a later generation who cannot know how we would have acted under conditions of a political dictatorship, we do well to refrain from moral judg-ments," as Habermas says (in Dreyfus and Hall [1992], p. 187). On the contrary, we should try to form our moral judgment, and we should condemn ourselves if we think that we would have behaved badly in such conditions. The reason is rather that it is very difficult

to reconstruct in detail the context in which Heidegger acted and formed his opinions at the time. We should note, for instance, that Karl Jaspers in 1933 proposed a much more radical version of the *Führerprinzip* for the universities than Heidegger was prepared to endorse. In Jaspers' version, the right to select new staff would be transferred to the state. See Tietjen (1991), p. 122; and Martin (1989), pp. 188 and 213–219.

168. "Die Universität im nationalsozialistischen Staat," *Tübinger Chronik* of 1 December 1933, published in Martin 1989, pp. 178–183. This seems to be a reliable account of Heidegger's speech. See especially p. 183: "Wir heutigen stehen in der Erkämpfung der neuen Wirklichkeit. Wir sind nur ein Übergang, nur ein Opfer. Als Kämpfer dieses Kampfes müssen wir ein hartes Geschlecht haben, das an nichts Eigenem mehr hängt, das sich festlegt auf den Grund des Volkes." For the notion of present man as a transition, see Nietzsche, *Also Sprach Zarathustra, Z, Vorrede*, § 3.

169. "Der Einzelne, wo er auch stehe, gilt nichts. Das Schicksal unseres Volkes in seinem Staat gilt alles." Quoted by Ott (1988), p. 229.

170. After 1934, Heidegger did not give up his claim that he was preordained to lead the Germans. Cf. *Beiträge*, § 15, pp. 42–43: "Die Besinnung auf das Volkhafte ist ein wesentlicher Durchgang. So wenig wir dies verkennen dürfen, so sehr gilt es zu wissen, daß ein höchster Rang des Seyns errungen sein muß, wenn ein 'völkisches Prinzip' als maßgebend für das geschichtliche Da-sein gemeistert ins Spiel gebracht werden soll. Das Volk wird erst Volk, wenn seine Einzigsten kommen, und wenn diese zu ahnen beginnen." That Heidegger considered himself as one of these "Einzigsten" is clear from many passages in *Beiträge*, such as on pp. 11, 28, 398 (§ 251), 414, and in *Besinnung* (GA 66). Cf. on Heidegger's attitude in 1945, Farias (1987), p. 286.

171. SdU, p. 21. Cf. Ott (1988), pp. 131–145 and Aly's letter to the ministry of 9 April 1933, published in Martin (1989), pp. 165–166. According to Habermas, Heidegger wrote a letter to Carl Schmitt on 22 August 1932, expressing his hope that he could count on Schmitt in rebuilding the law faculty and signed with *Heil Hitler*. Quoted by Habermas (1992), p. 206, note 34. But Ott (1988) dates this letter 22 August 1933, which is more plausible (p. 226). Hermann Mörchen noted in his diary after a visit to Heidegger's hut on New Year's Eve 1931 that the Heidegger family had become National Socialist, and that Heidegger thought that only a dictatorship that eliminated its opponents would be able to prevent communism. Quoted by Pöggeler (1989), p. 84. Cf. Mörchen, *Der Zauberer von Messkirch* (Westdeutsches Fernsehen, 1989). Ott's reconstruction of the beginning of the rectorate has been contested by Tietjen (1991), p. 112.

172. SdU, pp. 26–27, 33.

173. See for the telegram: Ott (1988), p. 187, and Martin (1989), p. 200; for Heidegger's role in military trainings: Ott (1988), p. 148, and Schneeberger (1962), texts no. 77, 88, 89, 117, 144; for the address to the German students of 3 November 1933: Martin (1989), p. 177; for the address of 11 November: Ott (1988), p. 196, and Schneeberger (1962), nos. 129 and 132; and for the Staudinger case: Ott (1988), pp. 201–213. Most documents relevant to the rectorate have been published for the first time clandestinely by Schneeberger (1962). Even "loyal" Heidegger scholars such as Pöggeler have not been able to deny these facts. Some of them typically resort to "interpretations," which are supposed to shed a more favorable light on Heidegger's Nazi actions. Vietta (1989) argues, for instance, that we should see Heidegger's denunciation of Staudinger against the background of his critique of technology and the technical conception of science, of which Staudinger would have been a proponent (pp. 22–23). However, this does not make things better: it would

prove that Heidegger was prepared to denounce his colleagues for philosophical reasons. Tietjen (1991) stresses correctly that Hitler's propaganda in 1933 presented his regime as a champion of a peaceful coexistence of nations (p. 113). But this propaganda did not cohere well with the violent practices of the Nazis.

174. SdU, pp. 40–43.

175. See on the project for the academy: Farias (1987), pp. 213ff. and Ott (1988), pp. 244–246; on Heidegger's attitude concerning the *Habilitation* of Siewerth and Müller: Ott (1988), pp. 261–265 and the interview with Müller in Martin (1989), pp. 107–108; on Heidegger's fame as a National Socialist in 1938 and 1945: Ott (1988), pp. 275, 295; Farias (1987), pp. 178ff., 215ff., 229ff., 248ff., 262–267, 273, 284–290; and Martin (1989), p. 169; and on Heidegger's lecture in 1942: Ott (1988), p. 287, and Heidegger, *Hölderlins Hymne "Der Ister,"* GA 53, pp. 98 and 106. The passage on p. 98 reads: "Dieser Übereifer der Gelehrten scheint gar nicht zu merken, daß er mit solchen 'Ergebnissen' dem National-sozialismus und seiner geschichtlichen Einzigartigkeit durchaus keinen Dienst erweist, den dieser außerdem gar nicht benötigt." Ott also describes how within Nazi circles opposition to Heidegger arose as early as 1934, and of course Heidegger made much of this after the war. Farias discovered Heidegger's membership booklet of the NSDAP in the Berlin archives, from which it is clear that Heidegger paid his contribution until the end of the war. See Farias (1987), p. 97.

176. SdU, p. 14: "Denn das Entscheidende im Führen ist nicht das bloße Vorangehen, sondern die Kraft zum Alleingehenkönnen."

177. "Das Rektorat 1933/34. Tatsachen und Gedanken," SdU, p. 30: "Man kann so vorgehen, . . . wenn man nur genug Maß von Böswilligkeit aufbringt."

178. "Das Rektorat 1933/34. Tatsachen und Gedanken," SdU, p. 27: "Den 'Wehrdienst' aber habe ich weder in einem militaristischen, noch in einem aggressiven Sinne genannt, sondern als Wehr in der Notwehr gedacht."

179. "Das Rektorat 1933/34. Tatsachen und Gedanken," SdU, p. 28. We should not forget that Hitler also quoted Heraclitus's dictum that "Struggle is the father of all things," for instance, in his speech at Kulmbach on 5 February 1928. See Bullock (1955), p. 353.

180. SdU, p. 15: "Die *zweite* Bindung ist die an die Ehre und das Geschick der Nation inmitten der anderen Völker. Sie verlangt die in Wissen und Können gesicherte und durch Zucht gestraffte Bereitschaft zum Einsatz bis ins Letzte. Diese Bindung umgreift und durchdringt künftig das ganze studentische Dasein als *Wehrdienst*" (Heidegger's italics).

181. SdU, p. 16: "Die Fragwürdigkeit des Seins überhaupt zwingt dem Volk Arbeit und Kampf ab und zwingt es in seinen Staat, dem die Berufe gehören"; p. 18: "Alle willent-lichen und denkerischen Vermögen, alle Kräfte des Herzens und alle Fähigkeiten des Leibes müssen *durch* Kampf entfaltet, *im* Kampf gesteigert und *als* Kampf bewahrt bleiben" (Heidegger's italics). The word *Kampf* occurs frequently in most official speeches that Heidegger gave as a rector. In a lecture on the university in the new *Reich*, given on 30 June 1933, Heidegger said for instance: "Dagegen ist ein *scharfer Kampf* zu führen im nationalsozialistischen Geist, der nicht ersticken darf durch humanisierende, christliche Vorstellungen, die seine Unbedingtheit niederhalten. . . . Wer den Kampf nicht besteht, bleibt liegen. . . . Der neue Mut . . . wird gekämpft aus den Kräften des neuen Reichs, das der Volkskanzler Hitler zur Wirklichkeit bringen wird." See Schneeberger (1962), no. 69, pp. 74–75.

182. Carl von Clausewitz (1780–1831) is the most influential German writer on military strategy, and he was widely read in Germany during the interbellum. He wrote, among

many other works, the celebrated book *Vom Kriege* (*On War*), in which he argued that "war is nothing but a continuation of political intercourse with the admixture of different means." Although he also argued that defensive warfare is both militarily and politically the stronger position, German readers in the 1930s tended to forget this warning. That Heidegger advocated Hitler's pan-German policies is clear from Schneeberger (1962), pp. 200, 121, and 214. In February 1934, Heidegger said at a meeting for political education in the house of the student corps Suevia, that "unser Endziel sei, unser deutsches Volk wieder zu einem Gesamtvolk zusammenzuschmieden, auch über die Staatsgrenzen hinaus" (ibid., p. 214).

183. Moreover, Heidegger omitted his references to Nazism and the war in his 1961 edition of his courses on Nietzsche.

184. EM, p. 152: "Was heute vollends als Philosophie des Nationalsozialismus herumgeboten wird, aber mit der inneren Wahrheit und Größe dieser Bewegung (nämlich mit der Begegnung der planetarisch bestimmten Technik und des neuzeitlichen Menschen) nicht das Geringste zu tun hat, das macht seine Fischzüge in diesen trüben Gewässern der 'Werte' und der 'Ganzheiten' " (this passage is the end of a critique of the philosophy of values prevalent in Heidegger's days).

185. Cf. Franzen (1975), p. 93. In the interview with *Der Spiegel*, Heidegger stressed again that the passage between parentheses belonged to the original manuscript. See *Antwort*, p. 96: "Das stand in meinem Manuskript drin."

186. Pöggeler, *Nachwort* to the 1983 edition of (1963), pp. 340ff.; see also Ott (1988), p. 277.

187. Cf. Petra Jaeger in GA 40, p. 233.

188. This hypothesis is confirmed by two of the three proofreaders of 1953, H. Buchner and R. Marten. See Buchner (1977), p. 49; and Marten (1987). Cf. also Ebeling (1991), pp. 145–147.

189. Christian E. Lewalter, *Die Zeit*, 13 August 1953. Lewalter's interpretation has been endorsed by Heidegger scholars such as, for instance, Vietta (1989), p. 92.

190. See for an account of this episode Habermas (1992), pp. 200–201.

191. M. Heidegger, *Schelling*. Cf. the letter from Karl Ulmer to *Der Spiegel*, 21 May 1977; and GA 42, § 3a, pp. 40–41: "Es ist überdies bekannt, daß die beiden Männer, die in Europa von der politischen Gestaltung der Nation bzw. des Volkes her—und zwar in je verschiedener Weise—Gegenbewegungen eingeleitet haben, daß sowohl Mussolini wie Hitler von Nietzsche wiederum in verschiedener Hinsicht wesentlich bestimmt sind, und dieses, ohne daß dabei der eigentliche metaphysische Bereich des Nietzscheschen Denkens unmittelbar zur Geltung käme."

192. Schneeberger (1962), pp. 135–136; Martin (1989), p. 177: "Jeder muß jede Begabung und Bevorzugung erst bewähren und ins Recht setzen. Das geschieht durch die Macht des kämpferischen Einsatzes im Ringen des ganzen Volkes um sich selbst. Täglich und stündlich festige sich die Treue des Gefolgschaftwillens. Unaufhörlich wachse Euch der Mut zum Opfer für die Rettung des Wesens und für die Erhöhung der innersten Kraft unseres Volkes in seinem Staat. Nicht Lehrsätze und 'Ideen' seien die Regeln Eures Seins. Der Führer selbst und allein *ist* die heutige und künftige deutsche Wirklichkeit und ihr Gesetz" (Heidegger's italics).

193. It was only in the interview with *Der Spiegel* of 1966, which was published posthumously in 1976, that Heidegger said of the sentence I just quoted that he would not write it anymore today. See *Antwort*, p. 86: "Die angeführten Sätze würde ich heute nicht mehr

schreiben." The wording of this *retractatio* is exasperatingly mild, even ambiguous, compared to the clarity and disastrous intent of the original phrases.

194. We have seen that in the "Brief über den 'Humanismus' " he substituted Being for Hitler as a moral authority (W, p. 187). But this is a minor change, because in 1933 Heidegger thought that Hitler was justified by Being.

195. Marcuse's letters are published in Martin (1989), pp. 155–157. In his letter of 28 August 1947, Marcuse writes: "Aber die Tatsache bleibt bestehen, daß Sie heute noch in den Augen vieler als einer der unbedingtesten geistigen Stützen des Regimes gelten. Ihre eigenen Reden, Schriften und Handlungen aus dieser Zeit sind der Beweis. Sie haben sie niemals öffentlich widerrufen—auch nicht nach 1945. Sie haben niemals öffentlich erklärt, daß Sie zu anderen Erkenntnissen gekommen sind als denen, die Sie 1933–34 ausgesprochen und in ihren Handlungen verwirklicht haben. Sie sind nach 1934 in Deutschland geblieben, obwohl Sie überall im Ausland eine Wirkungsstätte gefunden hätten. Sie haben keine einzige der Taten und Ideologien des Regimes öffentlich denunziert. Unter diesen Umständen sind Sie auch heute noch mit dem Nazi-Regime identifiziert."

196. Marcuse, letter to Heidegger of May 1948; Martin (1989), p. 157: "Sie schreiben, daß alles, was ich über die Ausrottung der Juden sage, genauso für die Alliierten gilt, wenn statt 'Juden' 'Ostdeutsche' steht. Stehen Sie nicht mit diesem Satz außerhalb der Dimension, in der überhaupt noch ein Gespräch zwischen Menschen möglich ist—außerhalb des Logos?", and so on.

197. Safranski (1994), p. 484: "Daß er sich, wie von der Öffentlichkeit verlangt, von dem millionenfachen Mord an den Juden distanzieren sollte, diese Forderung empfand Heidegger zu Recht als eine Ungeheuerlichkeit. Er hätte nämlich dabei implizit ein öffentliches Urteil anerkennen müssen, das ihm die Komplizenschaft mit dem Mord zutraute."

198. The earliest book on Heidegger's political philosophy is Schwan (1965). Rockmore (1992) offers the most extensive discussion of Heidegger's Nazism and its relation to Heidegger's philosophy in the English language, whereas Rockmore (1995) discusses the reception of Heidegger by postwar French philosophy.

199. See Rockmore (1992), pp. 21–24, on the negative influences of the predominance of expert commentators in Heidegger scholarship.

200. Löwith (1986), p. 57, quoted in my introduction. Yet the fact that Heidegger told this to Löwith, a former pupil and friend and a Jewish refugee in Rome, probably implies that Heidegger meant sincerely what he said.

201. Sluga (1993), p. 8, and passim; SdU, p. 40; cf. Ott (1988), pp. 241–244; cf. also Haug (1989) and Laugstien (1990).

202. Schmidt (1989), p. 57: "Heideggers Philosophie hat mit dem Nationalsozialismus keinerlei Gemeinsamkeit, wie sogar Heideggers Feinde eingestehen mußten. Heidegger war gar kein Nationalsozialist, sondern Hitlerist." This is a curious argument: as if Hitler was not the leader (*Führer*) of the National Socialist movement. Even though Hitler in his propaganda sometimes distanced himself for tactical reasons from acts of violence committed by the Party, the Party was primarily Hitler's Party, because the *Führerprinzip* was fundamental.

203. Chamberlain (1855–1927) argued in his 1899 work that the so-called Aryan element in European cultures was both racially and culturally superior, whereas the Jewish influence had been primarily negative. These ideas inspired pan-German and German nationalist thought, particularly Adolf Hitler's National Socialist movement.

204. Rockmore (1992), p. 24 and passim (my italics).

205. For a short history of German ideology, see Vermeil (1955), who concludes: "The Nazi doctrine, with the help of anti-Semitism, revives and popularises the current themes of the Pangermanic tradition. If it is guilty of any originality at all, it is in using anti-Semitism as a jumping-off ground for its attack on Western humanism and for its active policy in Germany. . . . Hitler could never have established the totalitarian dictatorship he did establish in January 1933 if his Party, so to speak under the mantle of the Weimar Republic, had not revived the essential themes of Pangermanic imperialism, reinforcing them with an extremely powerful propaganda machine" (p. 111). Cf. also Mosse (1964) and Bracher (1972).

206. Rockmore (1992), p. 48. I should add, however, that I nearly agree with Rockmore that "with the exception of biologism, [Heidegger] evidently held all the views of the ordinary Nazi" (p. 71). I nearly agree because it is unclear whether Heidegger endorsed Hitler's anti-Semitism. We do not find anti-Semitic statements in his philosophical writings, but Elfride Heidegger clearly was an anti-Semite and Heidegger himself also showed anti-Semite sentiments. Cf. Ott (1988), pp. 178–186, 316–318. Rockmore drew my attention to a clearly anti-Semite letter by Heidegger published by Ulrich Sieg in *Die Zeit* of 22 December 1989, p. 50.

207. Rockmore (1992), p. 42: "Now it is difficult to describe a philosophical position adequately. In virtue of its original character, no simple description is adequate to the complex nature of Heidegger's thought. It is also not possible to attempt anything like a full description of Heidegger's position. Fortunately, that is not necessary for our purposes here. Since the present discussion is concerned with the relation of Heidegger's thought to Nazism, we can restrict our account . . . merely to those concepts which form the background of his turn to practical politics." However, if one selects the elements of Heidegger's thought one wants to discuss on the basis of their relevance to Nazism, the argument that Heidegger's philosophy is *centrally* related to Nazism tends to become a *petitio principii*. The same holds, of course, for attempts to argue that Heidegger's philosophy is in fundamental opposition to Nazism, such as Young's (1997). Young discusses in detail a great many attempts to relate Heidegger's philosophy to Nazism, and he rejects all of them. But because his rejection is not based on a thorough interpretation of the philosophy of Being, many of Young's arguments are ad hoc.

208. Cf. SZ, § 5, pp. 16–17: "An dieser sollen nicht beliebige und zufällige, sondern wesenhafte Strukturen herausgestellt werden, die in jeder Seinsart des faktischen Daseins sich als seinsbestimmende durchhalten." According to the transcendental theme, the distinction between the ontological and the ontical is the distinction between "existential conditions for the possibility" of specific human phenomena such as worries or dedication, and these factical phenomena themselves; see SZ, § 42, p. 199. According to the phenomenologico-hermeneutical theme, the distinction is one between the essential constitution of being of entities and their individual factual traits.

209. See, again, Rockmore (1992), p. 48: "Rather, the concern with 'Being' is itself intrinsically political."

210. Such as Pierre Aubenque and François Fédier.

211. Bourdieu (1988), pp. 78–79: "Il suffit de penser par référence à la logique du champ universitaire ou du champ politique les prises de positions philosophiques de Heidegger et celles de ses interlocuteurs théoriques pour apercevoir les implications proprement politiques de ses choix les plus purement théoriques. Ces significations secondaires n'ont pas besoin d'être voulues comme telles, puisqu'elles se dégagent automatique-

ment des correspondances *métaphoriques*, des doubles sens et des sousentendus qui, du fait de l'homologie entre des champs, surgissent" (Bourdieu's italics).

212. Bourdieu correctly tries to avoid two extremes in the interpretation of Heidegger's philosophy: on the one hand the extreme of a purely internal reading, which is blind to possible political connotations, and on the other hand a Marxist reduction of a philosophical text to the material and political conditions of its author. Yet there is a marked reductionist tendency in his book (1988). He argues that there is a structural resemblance (homology) between the socio-economical-political field and the philosophical domain, and that, for this reason only, Heidegger's philosophical texts have a secondary political meaning, which is hidden from view by the logic of the philosophical domain. As is the case with the arguments of many French philosophers and social scientists, Bourdieu's argument is never made precise. For instance, what does it mean to claim that "les produits culturels doivent donc leurs propriétés les plus spécifiques aux conditions sociales de leur production" (p. 84)? Which *specific* properties of, say, Gödel's work, are due to the social conditions of its production, and which specific social conditions does Bourdieu have in mind? The reader can only guess.

213. Löwith (1946), Lukacs (1949), and Krockow (1958) were among the first to take this line. Habermas and many others followed.

214. SZ, § 75, pp. 390–391.

215. SZ, § 60, p. 298: "Die Entschlossenheit ist ihrem ontologischen Wesen nach je die eines jeweiligen faktischen Daseins. . . . Aber woraufhin erschließt sich das Dasein in der Entschlossenheit? Wozu soll es sich entschließen? Die Antwort vermag *nur* der Entschluß selbst zu geben" (Heidegger's italics).

216. SZ, § 61, p. 303: "Sie wird zur interpretierenden Befreiung des Daseins *für* seine äußerste Existenzmöglichkeit" (Heidegger's italics).

217. Cf. § 8B, above, and GA 60, pp. 55–65. Cf. also Kisiel (1993), pp. 121, 129, 142, 146–148, 149–152, 164–170, and passim; Oudemans (1990).

218. GbM, GA 29/30, pp. 428–429.

219. The entry "formale Anzeige" is lacking in Hildegard Feick's *Index zu Heideggers "Sein und Zeit"* (Feick [1980]), but the term is used in the book without explanation. Cf., for instance, SZ, pp. 114, 116, 231, 313, 315.

220. GA 60, p. 8: "Faßt man dies Problem radikal, so findet man, daß die Philosophie der faktischen Lebenserfahrung entspringt. Und dann springt sie in der faktischen Lebenserfahrung in diese selbst zurück." Cf. Kisiel (1993), p. 153.

221. SZ, § 7, p. 38: "Philosophie ist universale phänomenologische Ontologie, ausgehend von der Hermeneutik des Daseins, die als Analytik der Existenz das Ende des Leitfadens alles philosophischen Fragens dort festgemacht hat, woraus es *entspringt* und wohin es *zurückschlägt*" (Heidegger's italics).

222. Rockmore (1992), pp. 40–41.

223. Rockmore (1992), p. 48.

224. SZ, p. 263: "Der Tod ist *eigenste* Möglichkeit des Daseins. Das Sein zu ihr erschließt dem Dasein sein *eigenstes* Seinkönnen, darin es um das Sein des Daseins schlechthin geht. Darin kann dem Dasein offenbar werden, daß es in der ausgezeichneten Möglichkeit seiner selbst dem Man entrissen bleibt, das heißt vorlaufend sich je schon ihm entreißen kann. Das Verstehen dieses 'Könnens' enthüllt aber erst die faktische Verlorenheit in die Alltäglichkeit des Man-selbst" (Heidegger's italics).

225. SZ, p. 299: "Die Entschlossenheit bedeutet Sich-aufrufenlassen aus der Verloren-heit in das Man."

226. SZ, § 40, p. 187: "Die Angst vereinzelt das Dasein auf sein eigenstes In-der-Welt-sein, das als verstehendes wesenhaft auf Möglichkeiten sich entwirft," and p. 188: "Die Angst vereinzelt und erschließt so das Dasein als 'solus ipse.' "

227. SZ, § 53, p. 263: "Der Tod 'gehört' nicht indifferent nur dem eigenen Dasein zu, sondern er *beansprucht* dieses *als einzelnes*. Die im Vorlaufen verstandene Unbezüglich-keit des Todes vereinzelt das Dasein auf es selbst" (Heidegger's italics).

228. SZ, § 60, pp. 295–296: "Das Rufverstehen erschließt das eigene Dasein in der Unheimlichkeit seiner Vereinzelung."

229. SZ, § 62, p. 307: "Der Ruf des Gewissens übergeht im Anruf alles 'weltliche' Ansehen und Können des Daseins. Unnachsichtig vereinzelt er das Dasein auf sein Schul-digseinkönnen, das eigentlich zu sein er ihm zumutet."

230. SZ, § 62, pp. 307–308: "Die Gewißheit des Entschlusses bedeutet: *Sichfreihalten für* seine mögliche und je faktisch notwendige *Zurücknahme*" (Heidegger's italics).

231. Cf. Dreyfus (1991), pp. 283–340 for an extensive analysis of these two notions.

232. This is not to deny that for Kierkegaard a revolutionary age disposes one more to authenticity and faith than "the present age" of leveling and indifference. See *The Present Age* (1846) in Kierkegaard (1962).

233. Löwith (1986), p. 57.

234. SZ, § 74, p. 383: "Trotzdem muß gefragt werden, woher *überhaupt* die Möglich-keiten geschöpft werden können, auf die sich das Dasein faktisch entwirft" (Heidegger's italics).

235. SZ, § 74, p. 383: "Die Entschlossenheit, in der das Dasein auf sich selbst zurück-kommt, erschließt die jeweiligen faktischen Möglichkeiten eigentlichen Existierens *aus dem Erbe*, das sie als geworfene *übernimmt*" (Heidegger's italics).

236. SZ, § 74, p. 384: "Nur das Freisein *für* den Tod gibt dem Dasein das Ziel schlecht-hin und stößt die Existenz in ihre Endlichkeit"; and p. 385: "Die *Wiederholung ist die ausdrückliche Überlieferung*, das heißt der Rückgang in Möglichkeiten des dagewesenen Daseins. Die eigentliche Wiederholung einer gewesenen Existenzmöglichkeit—daß das Dasein sich seinen Helden wählt—" (Heidegger's italics).

237. SZ, § 74, p. 384: "Die ergriffene Endlichkeit der Existenz reißt aus der endlosen Mannigfaltigkeit der sich anbietenden nächsten Möglichkeiten des Behagens, Leichtneh-mens, Sichdrückens zurück und bringt das Dasein in die Einfachheit seines *Schicksals*" (Heidegger's italics).

238. SZ, § 74, p. 384: "Wenn aber das schicksalhafte Dasein als In-der-Welt-sein we-senhaft im Mitsein mit Anderen existiert, ist sein Geschehen ein Mitgeschehen und be-stimmt als *Geschick*. Damit bezeichnen wir das Geschehen der Gemeinschaft, des Volkes. Das Geschick setzt sich nicht aus einzelnen Schicksalen zusammen, sowenig als das Mitein-andersein als ein Zusammenvorkommen mehrerer Subjekte begriffen werden kann. Im Miteinandersein in derselben Welt und in der Entschlossenheit für bestimmte Möglich-keiten sind die Schicksale im vorhinein schon geleitet. In der Mitteilung und im Kampf wird die Macht des Geschickes erst frei. Das Schicksalhafte Geschick des Daseins in und mit seiner 'Generation' macht das volle, eigentliche Geschehen des Daseins aus" (Heideg-ger's italics). In the main text I am quoting BT, p. 463, with some modifications.

239. Farias (1987), pp. 72–76, concludes that "cette philosophie [*Sein und Zeit*] met en place, positivement, des éléments proprement fascistes, qui se trouveront en parfaite

continuité aves les événements historiques ultérieurs" (p. 76). Cf. Rockmore (1992), who claims that plausibly "the work [SZ] as a whole culminates in this passage, in the account of the transition from a manifold account of forms of human authenticity and inauthenticity to the concrete authentic person or group" (p. 47). And he concludes (p. 47): "In a deep sense, for Heidegger to be authentic is to embrace or to repeat the past in one's own life through a reinstantiation of the tradition. Since Nazism claimed to embody the values of the authentic German, of the German *Volk* as German, there is, then, a profound parallel, providing for an easy transition without any compromise of basic philosophical principles, between Heidegger's conception of authenticity through resoluteness and National Socialism." See for the notion of *völkisch* ideology: Mosse (1964), and Herf (1984).

240. Rockmore (1992), p. 48.

241. Farias (1987), p. 76 (quoted above). For a critique of Farias, see Janicaud (1992), pp. 107–109.

242. SZ, § 60, p. 298: "Die Entschlossenheit zu sich selbst bringt das Dasein erst in die Möglichkeit, die mitseienden Anderen 'sein' zu lassen in ihrem eigensten Seinkönnen. . . . Das entschlossene Dasein kann zum 'Gewissen' der Anderen werden. Aus dem eigentlichen Selbstsein der Entschlossenheit entspringt allererst das eigentliche Miteinander, nicht aber aus . . . den redseligen Verbrüderungen im Man und dem, was man unternehmen will." Cf. § 26, p. 122.

243. SZ, § 27, p. 129: "Zunächst ist das Dasein Man und zumeist bleibt es so."

244. SZ, § 27, p. 129: "*Zunächst* 'bin' nicht 'ich' im Sinne des eigenen Selbst, sondern die Anderen in der Weise des Man" (Heidegger's italics).

245. SZ, § 60, p. 298: "Die Antwort vermag *nur* der Entschluß selbst zu geben" (Heidegger's italics).

246. Cf. SZ, § 74, pp. 384–385.

247. SZ, § 62, p. 307.

248. One finds this view in many writers, from Löwith (1949) and Krockow (1958) to Habermas (1992) and Janicaud (1992), pp. 110–113. For a critique of decisionist interpretations, see Young (1997), chapter 3. But Young's critique is based on construals of decisionism in SZ that are somewhat different from mine. He assumes, for example, erroneously, that "Being and Time is an unmistakably post-death-of-God work" (p. 82), and supposes that it might contain Nietzschean nihilism, and so on. Furthermore, he argues that Heidegger's delegation of conventional morality to the domain of Everyman is limited to "a degenerate form of moral life" (p. 88), "moral legalism" (p. 87). But this interpretation is not supported by the texts.

249. SZ, § 74, p. 384: "Wenn das Dasein vorlaufend den Tod in sich mächtig werden läßt, versteht es sich, frei für ihn, in der eigenen *Übermacht* seiner endlichen Freiheit" (Heidegger's italics).

250. SZ, § 74, p. 384: "die *Ohnmacht* der Überlassenheit an es selbst" (Heidegger's italics). I assume that "es selbst" refers to Dasein, and not, as the translation of BT has it, to Dasein's having chosen (see BT, p. 436).

251. Cf. SZ, § 27, p. 127: "Das Man *entlastet* so das jeweilige Dasein in seiner Alltäglichkeit" (Heidegger's italics); cf. for Dasein as a burden: SZ, pp. 134f., and 284.

252. SZ, § 74, p. 384: "für die Zufälle der erschlossenen Situation hellsichtig zu werden." The German word *Zufall* means "accident" or "chance." But the verb *zufallen* may mean "to be awarded to someone," "to pass to someone as a heritage." I am supposing that Heidegger uses the word *Zufall* here in both senses.

253. Cf. SZ, § 74, pp. 384–385.

254. "Aufruf an die Deutschen Studenten," *Freiburger Studentenzeitung* 1933–1, p. 1; reprinted in Martin (1989), p. 177 and in Schneeberger (1962), pp. 135–136.

255. The answer is No, unless this faith is *völkisch* itself, so that a political revolution is *eo ipso* a religious conversion. See below for discussion of this possibility.

256. WiM, p. 42: "Für diesen Einsprung ist entscheidend:. . . das Sichloslassen in das Nichts, d. h. das Freiwerden von den Götzen, die jeder hat . . .; zuletzt das Ausschwingenlassen dieses Schwebens, auf daß es ständig zurückschwinge in die Grundfrage der Metaphysik, die das Nichts selbst erzwingt: Warum ist überhaupt Seiendes und nicht vielmehr Nichts?"

257. Letter of 12 September 1929, Hei/Blo, p. 33: "ich fühle mich ungewöhnlich frisch—d. h. innerlich sicher für die Arbeit u. entsprechend aufgeregt. Mit meiner Metaphysikvorlesung im Winter soll mir ein ganz neuer Anfang gelingen."

258. GbM, GA 29/30, pp. 511–512: "*aufgrund einer Verwandlung des Daseins selbst.* Zu dieser Verwandlung und ihrer Vorbereitung sind wir *zwei Wege* gegangen," and so on (Heidegger's italics). Cf. p. 116: "Oder sollen wir uns so finden, daß wir uns dabei selbst *zurückgegeben* werden?" (Heidegger's italics).

259. GbM, GA, 29/30, pp. 244–245: "Das *Geheimnis* fehlt in unserem Dasein, und damit bleibt der innere Schrecken aus, den jedes Geheimnis bei sich trägt und der dem Dasein seine Größe gibt. Das Ausbleiben der Bedrängnis ist das im Grunde Bedrängende und zutiefst Leerlassende, d. h. die *im Grunde langweilende Leere.* . . . Die tiefste, wesenhafte Not im Dasein ist nicht, daß eine bestimmte wirkliche Not uns bedrängt, sondern daß eine wesenhafte Bedrängnis sich versagt, daß wir dieses Sichversagen der Bedrängnis im Ganzen kaum vernehmen und vernehmen können. Und das darum, weil das unhörbar bleibt, was in solchem Versagen *sich ansagt*" (Heidegger's italics).

260. Franzen (1988). Rockmore (1992), pp. 50–53, relies heavily on Franzen's article in his interpretation of the 1929–30 lectures.

261. GbM, GA 29/30, p. 243: "Diese zappelnde Notwehr gegen die Nöte *läßt gerade eine Not im Ganzen nicht aufkommen*"; and p. 247: "Wozu also hat sich das Dasein zu entschließen? Dazu, daß es sich selbst erst wieder *das echte Wissen um das verschafft, worin das eigentlich Ermöglichende seiner selbst besteht*" (Heidegger's italics).

262. GbM, GA 29/30, p. 240: "daß es aber schwer ist, einer *tiefen Langeweile nicht entgegen zu sein, von ihrem Stimmen sich durchstimmen zu lassen, um von ihr Wesentliches zu hören*"; and "das *Ansichhalten des Daseins*, was ein *Warten* ist" (Heidegger's italics).

263. "Brief über den 'Humanismus,' " W, p. 159.

264. SdU, pp. 13–14.

265. SdU, p. 24: "Wie ich die geschichtliche Lage schon damals sah, möge durch einen Hinweis angedeutet sein. Im Jahre 1930," and so on, to p. 25: "die universale Herrschaft des Willens zur Macht innerhalb der planetarisch gesehenen Geschichte. In dieser Wirklichkeit steht heute Alles, mag es Kommunismus heißen oder Faschismus oder Weltdemokratie."

266. Hei/Ja, p. 157: "und sonst sind ja auch zwei Pfähle—die Auseinandersetzung mit dem Glauben der Herkunft und das Mißlingen des Rektorats—gerade genug an solchem, was wirklich überwunden sein möchte." Paul says in 2 *Corinthians* 12:7 that "to keep me from being too elated by the abundance of revelations, a thorn was given me in the flesh, a messenger of Satan, to harass me, to keep me from being too elated." Cf. section 13C, above, *in finem*.

267. *Beiträge*, § 7, p. 26: "Erst wenn wir ermessen, wie einzig notwendig das Sein ist und wie es doch nicht als der Gott selbst west, erst wenn wir unser Wesen gestimmt haben auf diese Abgründe zwischen dem Menschen und dem Seyn und dem Seyn und den Göttern, erst dann beginnen wieder 'Voraussetzungen' für eine 'Geschichte' wirklich zu werden. Darum gilt denkerisch allein die Besinnung auf das 'Ereignis.' "

268. This is a very common interpretation. Cf., for example, Tietjen (1991), p. 110: "Die ab 1936 erreichte Grundstellung des seynsgeschichtlichen Denkens und—damit verbunden—die Kritik der Technik begründen vielmehr ein gewandeltes, jetzt umfassend und grundsätzlich kritisches Verhältnis zum Nationalsozialismus." Cf. also Pöggeler (1992), p. 134: "In the years 1936 through 1938, in total seclusion, Heidegger wrote his main work, *Contributions to Philosophy* [= *Beiträge*]—a final attempt, in the company of Nietzsche and Hölderlin, to search for a 'revolution'; it offers a sharp criticism of National Socialism, and of 'Liberalism' and Bolshevism as well." However, *Beiträge* does not contain an unambiguous and sharp criticism of Nazism at all.

269. Cf. Stern (1961), pp. 35–70, in particular pp. 51 and 61.

270. Stern (1961), p. 87.

271. Stern (1961), p. 92. On Lagarde's anti-Semitism, cf. Mosse (1964). Because Lagarde saw the unity of Germany as a spiritual one, the "Jewish problem" became urgent for him. He advocated "the extermination of the Jews like bacillae" (p. 39).

272. Vermeil (1955), p. 95. Cf. Mosse (1964), p. 34: "Lagarde's *Völkisch* precepts extolled the process whereby an inner religious dynamic led each Volk to its own peculiar destiny"; and p. 43: "In Langbehn's theology, duplicated in other Germanic religions, the Volk and the God of the Universe participate in a direct relationship."

273. Cf. Zaradar (1990).

274. *Antwort*, pp. 107–108: "Ich denke an die besondere innere Verwandtschaft der deutschen Sprache mit der Sprache der Griechen. Das bestätigen mir heute immer wieder die Franzosen. Wenn sie zu denken anfangen, sprechen sie deutsch; sie versichern, sie kämen mir ihrer Sprache nicht durch."

275. Rauschning (1940), p. 212.

276. See for this topic and the quotes: Steiner (1983).

277. *Beiträge*, § 45, p. 97: "Dieses Volk ist in seinem Ursprung und seiner Bestimmung einzig gemäß der Einzigkeit des Seyns selbst." Cf. EM, pp. 28–29, where Heidegger says that, whereas Russia and America are metaphysically the same (*metaphysisch gesehen, dasselbe*), the Germans are the "metaphysical people" and most in danger (*das gefährdeste Volk und in all dem das metaphysische Volk*). They have a unique historical mission which, however, can be carried out only if they place themselves in "the original domain of the powers of Being" (*Mächte des Seins*). Clearly, Heidegger saw it as his task to place the Germans in this domain.

278. Pöggeler (1990), p. 381: "Zugleich ist dieses Werk sein letzter Versuch, die Revolution retten zu helfen." The word *letzter* should not be taken to mean that Heidegger gave up this attempt later, because, as Pöggeler admits, *Beiträge* informs Heidegger's later works. It is still an unanswered question to what extent Heidegger's concept of the Nazi revolution differed from the official Party line—if any. Surely there is no explicit critique of Nazism in *Beiträge*, contrary to what Pöggeler suggests (p. 382), and Heidegger nowhere argues that his conception of the revolution is *incompatible* with the Nazi conception, as Pöggeler says (ibid.).

279. Ott (1988), p. 229: "Der Einzelne, wo er auch stehe, gilt nichts. Das Schicksal unseres Volkes in seinem Staat gilt alles."

280. See "Das Rektorat 1933/34. Tatsachen und Gedanken," written in 1945 and published in SdU, pp. 24–25: "Was Ernst Jünger in den Gedanken von Herrschaft und Gestalt des Arbeiters denkt und im Lichte dieses Gedankens sieht, ist die universale Herrschaft des Willens zur Macht innerhalb der planetarisch gesehenen Geschichte. In dieser Wirklichkeit steht heute Alles, mag es Kommunismus heißen oder Faschismus oder Weltdemokratie." The word *heute* refers to 1945.

281. GA 42, § 3a.

282. Course of the second trimester of 1940 on *Nietzsche: der europäische Nihilismus*, GA 48, pp. 4, 13–14, 100–102, 138–139, 168. Cf. Losurdo (1992). Losurdo overinterprets this course, and is not very careful in his quotations.

283. GA 48, p. 205: "In diesen Tagen sind wir selbst die Zeugen eines geheimnisvollen Gesetzes der Geschichte, daß ein Volk eines Tages der Metaphysik, die aus seiner eigenen Geschichte entsprungen, nicht mehr gewachsen ist in dem Augenblick, da diese Metaphysik sich in das Unbedingte gewandelt hat. Jetzt zeigt sich, was Nietzsche bereits metaphysisch erkannte, daß die neuzeitliche 'machinale Ökonomie' . . . in ihrer unbedingten Gestalt ein neues Menschentum fordert, das über den bisherigen Menschen hinausgeht. Mit anderen Worten: Es genügt nicht, daß man Panzerwagen, Flugzeuge und Nachrichtengeräte besitzt; . . . Es bedarf eines Menschentums, das von Grund aus dem einzigartigen Grundwesen der neuzeitlichen Technik und ihrer metaphysischen Wahrheit gemäß ist, d. h. vom Wesen der Technik sich ganz beherrschen läßt, um so gerade selbst die einzelnen technischen Vorgänge und Möglichkeiten zu lenken und zu nützen. Der unbedingten 'machinalen Ökonomie' ist nur der Übermensch gemäß, und umgekehrt: Dieser bedarf jener zur Einrichtung der unbedingten Herrschaft über die Erde."

284. GA 48, pp. 332–333, especially p. 333: "die vollständige, d. h. hier von Grund auf grundsätzliche 'Motorisierung' der Wehrmacht . . . ist . . . ein metaphysischer Akt, der an Tiefgang sicherlich etwa die Abschaffung der 'Philosophie' übertrifft."

285. Course of summer semester 1942, on *Hölderlins Hymne "Der Ister,"* GA 53, p. 68: "Wir wissen heute, daß die angelsächsische Welt des Amerikanismus entschlossen ist, Europa, und d. h. die Heimat, und d. h. den Anfang des Abendländischen, zu vernichten. Anfängliches ist unzerstörbar. Der Eintritt Amerikas in diesen planetarischen Krieg ist nicht der Eintritt in die Geschichte, sondern ist bereits schon der letzte amerikanische Akt der amerikanischen Geschichtslosigkeit und Selbstverwüstung. . . . Der verborgene Geist des Anfänglichen im Abendland wird für diesen Prozeß der Selbstverwüstung des Anfangslosen nicht einmal den Blick der Verachtung übrig haben, sondern aus der Gelassenheit der Ruhe des Anfänglichen auf seine Sternstunde warten."

286. Course of the winter semester 1942–43 on *Parmenides*, GA 54, p. 241: "Wie soll Seiendes gerettet und in das Freie seins Wesens geborgen werden, wenn das Wesen des Seins unentschieden, ungefragt und gar vergessen ist?"

287. Losurdo (1992), p. 154.

288. WiM, p. 47: "Der klare Mut zur wesenhaften Angst verbürgt die geheimnisvolle Möglichkeit der Erfahrung des Seins. . . . Die Tapferkeit erkennt im Abgrund des Schreckens den kaum betretenen Raum des Seins."

289. WiM, p. 49: "Das Opfer ist der Abschied vom Seienden auf dem Gang zur Wahrung der Gunst des Seins."

290. WiM, *Nachwort*, edition of 1943: "dass das Sein wohl west ohne das Seiende."
Cf. § 12A, above, for discussion of this passage.

291. In his last lecture of the summer semester 1943, on "Der Anfang des abendländischen Denkens," Heidegger said (GA 55, *Heraklit*, pp. 180–181): "Das Wort, worin sich das Wesen des geschichtlichen Menschen übereignet, ist das Wort des Seyns. Dieses anfängliche Wort wird verwahrt im Dichten und Denken. Was immer und wie immer das äußere Geschick des Abendlandes gefügt werden mag, die größte und die eigentliche Prüfung der Deutschen steht noch bevor, jene Prüfung, in der sie vielleicht von den Nichtwissenden gegen deren Willen geprüft werden, ob sie, die Deutschen, im Einvernehmen sind mit der Wahrheit des Seyns, ob sie über die Bereitschaft zum Tode hinaus stark genug sind, gegen die Kleingeisterei der Modernen Welt das Anfängliche in seine unscheinbare Zier zu retten."

292. EM, p. 152.

293. Cf. Herf (1993).

294. SdU, pp. 24–25 (see quote above).

295. *Antwort*, p. 96: "Es ist für mich heute eine entscheidende Frage, wie dem heutigen technischen Zeitalter überhaupt ein—und welches—politisches System zugeordnet werden kann. Auf diese Frage weiß ich keine Antwort. Ich bin nicht überzeugt, daß es die Demokratie ist." Cf. Heidegger's course of the winter semester 1936–37 on *Nietzsche: Der Wille zur Macht als Kunst*, GA 43, p. 193: "Europa will sich immer noch an die 'Demokratie' klammern und will nicht sehen lernen, daß diese sein geschichtlicher Tod würde. Denn die Demokratie ist, wie Nietzsche klar sah, nur eine Abart des Nihilismus." Here, Heidegger uses his Neo-Hegelian theme in order to condemn democracy. Cf. Pöggeler (1990), who argues that Heidegger never after 1933 saw other political options than Nazism. In distancing himself from Nazism between 1937 and 1950, he opted out of the political domain altogether (pp. 386–387).

296. Tietjen (1991) protests against such an interpretation: "Die Zuordnung des Nationalsozialismus zum Nihilismus des Willens zur Macht und dann zur machenschaftlichen Herrschaft der Technik im seynsgeschichtlichen Denken ab 1936 bedeutet *nicht* dessen Rechtfertigung oder Bestreitung einer geschichtlichen Verantwortung" (p. 117, Tietjen's italics). I would say that it does not imply an unambiguous rejection of Nazism either, because Nazism is accepted as an unescapable Destiny. Surely this view is an attempt to deny the historical responsibility of individuals. Cf. "Überwindung der Metaphysik," § xxvi, VA, p. 89: "Man meint, die Führer hätten von sich aus, in der blinden Raserei einer selbstischen Eigensucht, alles sich angemaßt und nach ihrem Eigensinn sich eingerichtet. In Wahrheit sind sie die notwendigen Folgen dessen, daß das Seiende in die Weise der Irrnis übergegangen ist." Probably, Heidegger wrote these lines in 1946; did he include himself in the category of *Führer*?

297. WhD, p. 65: "Was hat der zweite Weltkrieg eigentlich entschieden, um von seinen furchtbaren Folgen für unser Vaterland, im besonderen vom Riß durch seine Mitte, zu schweigen? Dieser Weltkrieg hat nichts entschieden, wenn wir hier die Entscheidung so hoch und so weit nehmen, daß sie einzig das Wesensgeschick des Menschen auf dieser Erde angeht. . . . Allein auch hier steigt erneut die Gefahr . . . daß dieses zu-Entscheidende noch einmal in die überall zu kurz tragenden und zu engbrüstigen politisch-sozialen und moralischen Kategorien hineingezwängt und dadurch aus einer möglichen und hinreichenden Besinnung abgedrängt wird."

298. In 1935, Heidegger argued that Russia and America are metaphysically the same (EM, pp. 28 and 34–35), but he held that the Germans, as the "metaphysical people," were different (EM, p. 29). After the Second World War, it seemed to Heidegger that the age of leveling had come to its completion.

299. SZ, § 74, pp. 384–385: "In der Mitteilung und im Kampf wird die Macht des Geschickes erst frei. Das schicksalhafte Geschick des Daseins in und mit seiner 'Generation' macht das volle, eigentliche Geschehen des Daseins aus."

300. Hei/Blo, p. 60.

301. Cf. also Pöggeler (1990), pp. 366–370ff.

302. Cf. Nietzsche, FW, § 108.

303. N I, p. 10: "Die Veröffentlichung möchte, als Ganzes nachgedacht, zugleich einen Blick auf den Denkweg verschaffen, den ich seit 1930 bis zum 'Brief über den Humanismus' (1947) gegangen bin. . . . Die *Erläuterungen zu Hölderlins Dichtung* (1951), die eine Abhandlung und Vorträge aus der Zeit zwischen 1936 und 1943 enthalten, lassen nur mittelbar etwas vom Weg erkennen." Cf. Haar (1994), who says about Heidegger's confrontation with Nietzsche on p. 190: "C'est de loin, la plus longue, la plus patiente, la plus insistante lecture jamais menée par un grand philosophe vis-à-vis d'un prédécesseur."

304. Cf. Pöggeler (1990), p. 371: "Die Edition von 1961 (und ihre Übersetzungen) lassen Heideggers Distanzierung zur fatalen Option von 1933 sehen, also den Weg von Hitler zu Nietzsche; daß Heideggers Weg zuerst von Nietzsche zu Hitler geführt hatte, war nicht mehr sichtbar."

305. This is overlooked in Michel Haar's scrupulous analysis of Heidegger's interpretation of Nietzsche. Cf. Haar (1994), chapter 8.

306. Janicaud (1992), p. 104.

307. N I, p. 258: "wenn wir nach Nietzsches metaphysische Grundstellung im abendländischen Denken *fragen*. . . . Schließlich muß angesichts dieser metaphysischen Grundstellung Nietzsches als der letzten, die das abendländische Denken erreicht hat, gefragt werden, ob und wie in ihr die eigentliche Frage der Philosophie gefragt ist oder ob sie ungefragt bleibt, und wenn ja, warum" (Heidegger's italics). Cf. "Nietzsches Wort 'Gott ist tot,' " HW, p. 193.

308. Cf. "Nietzsches Wort 'Gott ist tot,' " HW, p. 193: "In jeder Phase der Metaphysik wird jeweils ein Stück eines Weges sichtbar, den das Geschick des Seins in jähen Epochen der Wahrheit über das Seiende sich bahnt"; cf. § 11, above.

309. N I, pp. 13, 16, 17, 28–41, 255, 258ff., 373, 425ff., 438, 448–472, and N II, passim.

310. N I, pp. 26–41, 54, 160, 263, 369, 416–418, 425, 427ff., 463ff. Cf. "Nietzsches Wort 'Gott ist tot,' " HW, p. 219: "Die beiden Grundworte der Metaphysik Nietzsches, 'Wille zur Macht' und 'ewige Wiederkunft des Gleichen,' bestimmen das Seiende in seinem Sein nach den Hinsichten, die von altersher für die Metaphysik leitend bleiben, das ens qua ens im Sinne von essentia und existentia."

311. For critical comments on Heidegger's interpretation, see Haar (1992).

312. Cf. N I, p. 375: "Der Beweisgang für die Wiederkunftslehre untersteht daher an keiner Stelle dem Gerichtshof der Naturwissenschaft, selbst dann nicht, wenn naturwissenschaftliche 'Tatsachen' gegen sein Ergebnis sprechen sollten; denn was sind 'Tatsachen' der Naturwissenschaft und jeder Wissenschaft anderes als bestimmte Erscheinungen, ausgelegt nach ausdrücklichen oder verschwiegenen oder überhaupt ungekannten Grundsätzen einer Metaphysik, d. h. einer Lehre vom Seienden im Ganzen?"

313. See Baeumler in Nietzsche, WM, p. 699: "Der Wille zur Macht ist das philosophische Hauptwerk Nietzsches"; and Heidegger, N I, pp. 15–26.

314. Cf. N I, pp. 365–403, especially p. 377: "Wenn es so steht, dann ist der vermeintliche Beweis kein Beweis, der seine Kraft in der Geschlossenheit und Schlüssigkeit der Folgerungsschritte haben könnte. Was sich darstellungsmäßig als Beweis ausgibt, ist nur die Enthüllung der Setzungen, die im Entwurf des Seienden im Ganzen auf das Sein als ewig wiederkehrend im Gleichen mitgesetzt, und zwar notwendig mitgesetzt sind. Dann ist dieser Beweis nur der zergliedernde Hinweis auf den Zusammenhang des zugleich mit dem Entwurf Mitgesetzten—kurz: Entwurfs-*entfaltung*, aber niemals Entwurfs-errechnung und—begründung" (Heidegger's italics).

315. Heidegger, "Wer ist Nietzsches Zarathustra?", VA, p. 114–115: "Wir Heutigen sind durch die eigentümliche Vorherrschaft der neuzeitlichen Wissenschaften in den seltsamen Irrtum verstrickt, der meint, das Wissen lasse sich aus der Wissenschaft gewinnen und das Denken unterstehe der Gerichtsbarkeit der Wissenschaft. Aber das Einzige, was jeweils ein Denker zu sagen vermag, läßt sich logisch oder empirisch weder beweisen noch widerlegen. Es ist auch nicht die Sache eines Glaubens. Es läßt sich nur fragend-denkend zu Gesicht bringen." Cf. WhD, pp. 23–24: "Aber ein Denker läßt sich niemals dadurch überwinden, daß man ihn widerlegt und eine Widerlegungsliteratur um ihn aufstapelt. Das Gedachte eines Denkers läßt sich nur so verwinden, daß das Ungedachte in seinem Gedachten auf seine anfängliche Wahrheit zurückverlegt wird."

316. Nietzsche, WM, §§ 1–13.

317. Nietzsche, JGB, Vorrede: "Aber der Kampf gegen Plato, oder um es verständlicher und fürs 'Volk' zu sagen, der Kampf gegen den christlich-kirchlichen Druck von Jahrtausenden—denn Christentum ist Platonismus fürs 'Volk'—hat in Europa eine prachtvolle Spannung des Geistes geschaffen, wie sie auf Erden noch nicht da war."

318. Nietzsche, note written in 1870–71: "Meine Philosophie umgedrehter Platonismus," published in UW, I, § 79. Cf. Heidegger, N I, pp. 33ff., 180ff., 242, 469.

319. Cf. "Das Ende der Philosophie und die Aufgabe des Denkens" (1964), SD, pp. 62–63: "Was meint die Rede vom Ende der Philosophie? Zu leicht verstehen wir das Ende von etwas im negativen Sinn als das bloße Aufhören, als das Ausbleiben eines Fortgangs, wenn nicht gar als Verfall und Unvermögen. Dem entgegen bedeutet die Rede vom Ende der Philosophie die Vollendung der Metaphysik. Indes meint Vollendung nicht Vollkommenheit, derzufolge die Philosophie mit ihrem Ende die höchste Vollkommenheit erreicht haben müßte. . . . Jede Epoche der Philosophie hat ihre eigene Notwendigkeit. Daß eine Philosophie ist, wie sie ist, müssen wir einfach anerkennen. . . . Die alte Bedeutung unseres Wortes 'Ende' bedeutet dasselbe wie Ort: 'von einem Ende zum anderen' heißt: von einem Ort zum anderen. Das Ende der Philosophie ist der Ort, dasjenige worin sich das Ganze ihrer Geschichte in seine äußerste Möglichkeit sammelt. Ende als Vollendung meint diese Versammlung." Cf. B (GA 66), § 10.

320. N I, p. 469: "Nietzsche selbst bezeichnet schon früh seine Philosophie als umgekehrten Platonismus. Die Umkehrung beseitigt die Platonische Grundstellung nicht, sondern verfestigt sie gerade durch den Anschein, als sei sie beseitigt." Cf. "Nietzsches Wort 'Gott ist tot,' " HW, p. 200: "Als bloße Gegenbewegung bleibt sie jedoch notwendig, wie alles Anti- im Wesen dessen verhaftet, wogegen sie angeht. Nietzsches Gegenbewegung gegen die Metaphysik ist als die bloße Umstülpung dieser die ausweglose Verstrickung in die Metaphysik." Cf. also "Überwindung der Metaphysik," § ix, VA, p. 75; and "Das Ende der Metaphysik und die Aufgabe des Denkens," SD, p. 63: "Nietzsche kenn-

zeichnet seine Philosophie als umgekehrten Platonismus. Mit der Umkehrung der Metaphysik . . . ist die äußerste Möglichkeit der Philosophie erreicht. Sie ist in ihr Ende eingegangen. Soweit philosophisches Denken noch versucht wird, gelangt es nur noch zu epigonalen Renaissancen und deren Spielarten."

321. N II, p. 201: "Was meint aber dann 'Ende der Metaphysik'? Antwort: den geschichtlichen Augenblick, in dem die *Wesensmöglichkeiten* der Metaphysik erschöpft sind. Die letzte dieser Möglichkeiten muß diejenige Form der Metaphysik sein, in der ihr Wesen umgekehrt wird" (Heidegger's italics).

322. N I, pp. 464–468, especially p. 468: "Nietzsche schließt in seinem wesentlichsten Gedanken von der ewigen Wiederkehr des Gleichen die beiden Grundbestimmungen des Seienden aus dem Anfang der abendländischen Philosophie—das Seiende als Werden und das Seiende als Beständigkeit—in Eins zusammen." Cf. EuPh, pp. 39–40: "die Sackgasse der Lehre von der ewigen Wiederkunft. Das ist ein gewaltiger Versuch, Seyn und Werden gleich wesentlich in eins zu denken. Aber ein Versuch, der sich in den bodenlos gewordenen Kategorien des 19. Jahrhunderts bewegt und nicht zurückfindet in das ursprüngliche Wiederfragen der ersten Frage nach dem Seyn."

323. N II, p. 18: "Dieses umkehrende Auslöschen des Gegensatzes von Sein und Werden macht die eigentliche Vollendung aus. Denn jetzt ist kein Ausweg mehr, weder in die Zertrennung noch in eine gemäßere Verschmelzung."

324. N II, pp. 141–240 (course of 1940); Cf. "Wozu Dichter?", HW, pp. 268–269, and passim in the later works.

325. Cf. "Die Zeit des Weltbildes" (1938) in HW; "Überwindung der Metaphysik," §§ ix–xxvi, in VA; "Die Frage nach der Technik," VA; and "Nietzsches Wort 'Gott ist tot,' " HW, especially pp. 234–237; "Wozu Dichter?", HW, pp. 267–273. Heidegger derived the notion that Nietzsche's metaphysics expresses the fundamental stance of technology from Ernst Jünger.

326. Cf. N II, p. 202: "Allerdings bleibt die Frage zu entscheiden, ob denn überhaupt und wie alle Wesensmöglichkeiten der Metaphysik geschlossen übersehbar sind."

327. He did so already in EM (1935), pp. 137–149.

328. Cf. "Nietzsches Wort 'Gott ist tot,' " HW, p. 238: "Wenn das Sein des Seienden zum Wert gestempelt und wenn damit sein Wesen besiegelt ist, dann ist innerhalb dieser Metaphysik . . . jeder Weg zur Erfahrung des Seins selbst ausgelöscht."

329. Cf. "Wozu Dichter?", HW, p. 272: "Das Wesen der Technik kommt nur langsam an den Tag. Dieser Tag ist die zum bloß technischen Tag umgefertigte Weltnacht. . . . Das Heile entzieht sich. Die Welt wird heil-los. Dadurch bleibt nicht nur das Heilige als die Spur zur Gottheit verborgen, sondern sogar die Spur zum Heiligen, das Heile, scheint ausgelöscht zu sein." It should be noted that the postmonotheist interpretation of these texts resolves a problem that Rorty was unable so solve in his essay "Heidegger, Contingency, and Pragmatism" (Dreyfus and Hall [1992], p. 220; Rorty [1991], pp. 42–43), the problem of the tension between "contingency" and "nostalgia." On the one hand, Heidegger claims that all fundamental metaphysical stances are on a par: "Jede Epoche der Philosophie hat ihre eigene Notwendigkeit. Daß eine Philosophie ist, wie sie ist, müssen wir einfach anerkennen. Es steht uns jedoch nicht zu, eine gegenüber der anderen vorzuziehen" ("Das Ende der Philosophie und die Aufgabe des Denkens," SD, pp. 62–63). On the other hand, Heidegger claims that real history, that is, the sequence of metaphysical stances, is a history of decline and fall (*Abfall*). As Rorty says, it is a "downward escalator." How should we reconcile these opposite claims? The postmonotheist interpretation solves the

problem as follows. All metaphysical stances are on a par because they are destinies (*Geschicke*), sent (*geschickt*) by Being. In this sense they are "necessary." But they are also radically contingent, because Being sends them freely. Nevertheless, the last metaphysical stance, called the reign of technology, is worse than the others because in it no trace of Being is left. Even the trace that consits of Being's reification, God, is wiped out.

330. *Beiträge*, § 110.18, p. 216: "Alles weit entfernt von der Aufgabe. . . dem Seyn selbst in die Frage zu stellen."

331. Nietzsche, FW, § 125.

332. "Nietzsches Wort 'Gott ist tot,' " HW, pp. 242–243: "Aber wie ist es mit dem Wertsetzen selbst, wenn dieses . . . aus dem Hinblick auf das Sein gedacht wird? Dann ist das Denken in Werten das radikale Töten. Es . . . bringt das Sein gänzlich auf die Seite. Dieses kann, wo es noch benötigt wird, nur als ein Wert gelten. Das Wertdenken der Metaphysik des Willens zur Macht ist in einem äußersten Sinne tödlich, weil es überhaupt das Sein selbst nicht in den Aufgang und d. h. in die Lebendigkeit seines Wesens kommen läßt. Das Denken nach Werten läßt im vorhinein das Sein selbst nicht dahin gelangen, in seiner Wahrheit zu wesen."

333. "Nietzsches Wort 'Gott ist tot,' " HW, p. 193: "Die Absetzung des Übersinnlichen . . . endet im Sinnlosen"; "Überwindung der Metaphysik," § xxviii, VA, p. 95: "Die unbedingte Gleichförmigkeit aller Menschentümer der Erde unter der Herrschaft des Willens zum Willen macht die Sinnlosigkeit des absolut gesetzten menschlichen Handelns deutlich."

334. "Überwindung der Metaphysik," §§ xi–xxvii, VA, pp. 77–94, especially p. 83: "Die Technik als die höchste Form der rationalen Bewußtheit, technisch gedeutet, und die Besinnungslosigkeit als das ihr selbst verschlossene eingerichtete Unvermögen, in einen Bezug zum Fragwürdigen zu gelangen, gehören zusammen: sie sind das Selbe."

335. N I, pp. 365, 469; N II, pp. 337–338: "Nietzsche anerkennt das Seiende als solches. Doch anerkennt er in solcher Anerkenntnis auch schon das Sein des Seienden, und zwar Es selbst, *das Sein*, nämlich *als das Sein*? Keineswegs. Das Sein wird als Wert bestimmt und damit als eine vom Willen zur Macht, vom 'Seienden' als solchem gesetzte Bedingung aus dem Seienden erklärt. Das Sein ist nicht als das Sein anerkannt. Dieses 'anerkennen' heißt: Sein aus dem Hinblick auf seine Wesensherkunft in aller Fragwürdigkeit walten lassen; es heißt: die Seinsfrage aushalten" (Heidegger's italics). Cf. N II, passim; "Nietzsches Wort 'Gott ist tot,' " in HW; and *Beiträge*, § 88, p. 176: "mit Nietzsche die Auseinandersetzung wagen als dem Nächsten und doch erkennen, daß er der Seinsfrage am fernsten steht"; § 110, p. 215: "Obzwar Nietzsche das Seiende als Werden erfährt, bleibt er mit dieser Auslegung als *Gegner* innerhalb des überlieferten Rahmens, das Seiende wird nur anders ausgelegt, aber die Seinsfrage als solche nie gestellt" (Heidegger's italics); § 110.21, pp. 218–219: "Auch da, wo Nietzsche als übergehender Denker zuletzt aus dem Platonismus und seiner Umkehrung herausgedreht wird, kommt es nicht zu einer ursprünglich-überwindenden Fragestellung nach der Wahrheit des Seyns und nach dem Wesen der Wahrheit."

336. N II, pp. 338–356, and passim.

337. Remember that in *Beiträge*, Heidegger explains Wesen as *Wesung*: what happens as the truth of Being: § 165, p. 287: "Das 'Wesen'. . . (ist) Wesung als das Geschehnis der Wahrheit des Seyns"; cf. pp. 66, 474ff., 484.

338. "Nietzsches Wort 'Gott ist tot,' " HW, pp. 243–244: "Das Wesen des Nihilismus beruht in der Geschichte, der gemäß es im Erscheinen des Seienden als solchen im Ganzen

mit dem Sein selbst und seiner Wahrheit nichts ist, so zwar, daß die Wahrheit des Seienden als solchen für das Sein gilt, weil die Wahrheit des Seins ausbleibt. . . . Nietzsche hat . . . das *Wesen* des Nihilismus nie erkannt, so wenig wie je eine Metaphysik vor ihm. Wenn jedoch das Wesen des Nihilismus in der Geschichte beruht, daß im Erscheinen des Seienden als solchen im Ganzen die Wahrheit des Seins ausbleibt, und es demgemäß mit dem Sein selbst und seiner Wahrheit nichts ist, dann ist die Metaphysik als die Geschichte der Wahrheit des Seienden als solchen in ihrem Wesen Nihilismus" (Heidegger's italics). Cf. N II, p. 338: "Das Wesen des Nihilismus ist die Geschichte, in der es mit dem Sein selbst nichts ist"; pp. 345–346: "Denkt die Metaphysik das Sein selbst? Nein und niemals. . . . Das Sein bleibt in demjenigen Denken, das als das metaphysische für das Denken schlecht- hin gilt, ungedacht"; and p. 350: "Das Sein selbst bleibt in der Metaphysik wesensnot- wendig ungedacht. Die Metaphysik ist die Geschichte, in der es mit dem Sein selbst wesen- haft nichts ist: *Die Metaphysik ist als solche der eigentliche Nihilismus*" (Heidegger's italics); *Beiträge*, § 72, p. 138: "In der Absicht auf den anderen Anfang muß der Nihilismus gründlicher als Wesensfolge der Seinsverlassenheit begriffen werden"; cf. § 55, p. 115: "Was Nietzsche erstmals . . . als Nihilismus erkennt, ist in Wahrheit . . . nur der Vorder- grund des weit tieferen Geschehens der Seinsvergessenheit. . . . Aber selbst die Seinsver- gessenheit (. . .) ist nicht das ursprünglichste Geschick des ersten Anfangs, sondern die Seinsverlassenheit, die vielleicht am meisten verhüllt und verneint wurde durch das Chris- tentum"; and § 59, p. 119.

339. N II, pp. 336–398; "Ueberwindung der Metaphysik," VA, p. 75: "Diese Art der Überwindung der Metaphysik . . . ist . . . nur die endgültige Verstrickung in die Metaphy- sik"; "Nietzsches Wort 'Gott ist tot,' " HW, p. 200: "Nietzsches Gegenbewegung gegen die Metaphysik ist als die bloße Umstülpung dieser die auswegslose Verstrickung in die Metaphysik, zo zwar, daß diese sich gegen ihr Wesen abschnürt und als Metaphysik ihr eigenes Wesen nie zu denken vermag"; ibid., p. 214: "Nietzsche hält diese Umkehrung für die Überwindung der Metaphysik. Allein jede Umkehrung dieser Art bleibt nur die sich selbst blendende Verstrickung in das unkennbar gewordene Selbe."

340. Cf. what Nietzsche says on "Hinterweltlerei" in Z, first part, "Von den Hinterweltlern."

341. "Brief über den 'Humanismus,' " W, p. 191: "Nur sofern der Mensch, in die Wahr- heit des Seins ek-sistierend, diesem gehört, kann aus dem Sein selbst die Zuweisung derje- nigen Weisungen kommen, die für den Menschen Gesetz und Regel werden müssen."

342. Cf. *Beiträge*, § 87, p. 175: "um erfahren zu lassen (für die anfangenden Fragen- den), daß zum Wesen des Seyns die Verweigerung gehört. Dieses Wissen ist, weil es den Nihilismus noch ursprünglicher in die Seinsverlassenheit hinabdenkt, die eigentliche Über- windung des Nihilismus . . . jetzt erst kommt das große Leuchten über alles bisherige denkerische Werk."

343. In "Nietzsches Wort 'Gott ist tot,' " HW, p. 193: "Die folgende Erläuterung," and so on; and p. 196: "Die folgenden Überlegungen versuchen, das Wort Nietzsches nach einigen wesentlichen Hinsichten zu erläutern." It is preposterous that authors such as Rorty assume that they may derive from Heidegger's biased interpretations a license to practice this genre of "violent" interpretation themselves. Rorty brazenly writes: "In this paper I have been reading Heidegger by my own, Deweyan lights. But to read Heidegger in this way is just to do to him what he did to everybody else, and to do that what no reader of anybody can help doing." See "Heidegger, Contingency, and Pragmatism," in Dreyfus and Hall (1992), p. 225, and in Rorty (1991), p. 49. In fact, Rorty is projecting his pragmatist

views onto Heidegger. If his projections clearly conflict with what Heidegger says, Rorty criticizes Heidegger for being inconsistent, instead of rejecting his own interpretation. If this is what philosophers can contribute to the "conversation of mankind," it would be better to abolish philosophy altogether.

344. HW, p. 197; cf. N II, pp. 262–263.

345. Cf. *Beiträge*, §§ 81–114.

346. In *Beiträge*, Heidegger calls Nietzsche his "nearest" (Nächsten): § 88, p. 176. Cf. for Heidegger's reinterpretation of Nietzschean nihilism: *Beiträge*, § 55, p. 115: "Was Nietzsche erstmals und zwar in der Ausrichtung auf Platonismus als *Nihilismus* erkennt, ist in Wahrheit von der ihm fremden Grundfrage aus gesehen nur der Vordergrund des weit tieferen Geschehens der Seinsvergessenheit," and so on (Heidegger's italics); § 57, p. 119: "Die Seinsverlassenheit ist der Grund und damit zugleich die ursprünglichere Wesensbe-stimmung dessen, was Nietzsche erstmals als Nihilismus erkannt hat"; § 72, p. 138: "In der Absicht auf den anderen Anfang muß der Nihilismus gründlicher als Wesensfolge der Seinsverlassenheit begriffen werden." Cf. Heidegger's later texts on Nietzsche, in which he developed this "more profound" understanding of nihilism, but also presented it mis-leadingly as an elucidation of what Nietzsche himself said.

347. Heidegger admits this in *Beiträge*, but not in his published works. Cf. *Beiträge*, § 88, p. 176: "mit Nietzsche die Auseinandersetzung wagen als dem Nächsten und doch erkennen, daß er der Seinsfrage am fernsten steht."

348. N I, p. 17: "Die eigentliche Philosophie bleibt als 'Nachlaß' zurück."

349. Cf. Nietzsche, JGB, § 23, which ends with the telling remark that psychology becomes again the route to the fundamental problems ("Denn Psychologie ist nunmehr wieder den Weg zu den Grundproblemen").

350. Luther used to say that he was a farmer's son, and Nietzsche believed him. In fact, Luther was the son of a miner. Cf. Friedenthal (1967), p. 15.

351. Cf. Heidegger's letter to Jaspers of 1 July 1935, Hei/Ja, p. 157: "und sonst sind ja auch zwei Pfähle—die Auseinandersetzung mit dem Glauben der Herkunft und das Miß-lingen des Rektorats"; "Aus einem Gespräch von der Sprache," *Sprache*, p. 96: "Ohne diese theologische Herkunft wäre ich nie auf den Weg des Denkens gelangt. Herkunft aber bleibt stets Zukunft"; "Mein bisheriger Weg," B (GA 66), pp. 415–416.

352. Cf. Ott (1990), p. 14.

353. Heidegger, quoted by Ott (1990), p. 20: "für den geistigen Kampf der Zukunft um das christlich-katholische Lebensideal."

354. Hugo Ott stressed this biographical fact for the first time in his writings on Heidegger.

355. Hei/Blo, p. 52: "Kommunismus u. a. ist vielleicht grauenhaft, aber eine klare Sache—Jesuitismus aber ist—verzeihen Sie—teuflisch."

356. Such as EM, p. 6: "Eine 'christliche Philosophie' ist ein hölzernes Eisen und ein Mißverständnis." Cf. *Beiträge*, § 14, p. 41: "Daß nun aber der totale politische Glaube und der ebenso totale christliche Glaube bei ihrer Unvereinbarkeit dennoch auf den Ausgleich und die Taktik sich einlassen, darf nicht verwundern. Denn sie sind desselben Wesens. . . . Ihr Kampf ist kein schöpferischer Kampf, sondern 'Propaganda' und 'Apologetik' " (an interesting text, because it is critical of actual Nazism as well); § 52, p. 110: "Die Seinsver-lassenheit ist am stärksten dort, wo sie sich am entschiedensten versteckt. . . . Das geschah zuerst im *Christentum* und seiner Dogmatik"; § 55, p. 115: "die Seinsverlassenheit, die vielleicht am meisten verhüllt und verneint wurde durch das Christentum"; § 72, p. 139:

"Der verhängnisvollste Nihilismus besteht darin, daß man sich als Beschützer des Christentums ausgibt"; § 103, p. 203: "Die Verirrung dieses deutschen Idealismus . . . liegt darin, daß er . . . ganz und völlig in der Bahn des. . . . Christentums sich bewegte, statt über das 'Seiende' hinweg die Seinsfrage zu stellen"; § 116, p. 228: "die christliche Verkennung aller Wahrheit des Seyns"; § 225, p. 350: "Gerade die . . . Herrschaft des 'christlichen' Denkens in der nach-und *gegen*christlichen Zeit erschwert jeden Versuch, von diesem Boden wegzurücken und aus ursprünglicher Erfahrung den Grundbezug von Seyn und Wahrheit anfänglich zu denken"; part VII, p. 403: "Der letzte Gott. Der ganz Andere gegen die Gewesenen, zumal gegen den christlichen"; and § 256 (Heidegger's italics). All these texts confirm my "Lutheran" interpretation, that Heidegger saw the God of Christianity as a transcendent entity that obstructed the access to transcendent Being. In *Beiträge*, Heidegger's postmonotheism is staged as a *rival* of Christianity, and this is explained by the hypothesis that Heidegger wanted to develop an authentic German (Nazi?) and anti-Christian religion (see § 14B, above).

357. Schneeberger (1962), no. 176, pp. 205–206: "Dieser öffentliche Sieg des Katholizismus gerade hier darf in keinem Falle bleiben. Es ist das eine Schädigung der ganzen Arbeit, wie sie zur Zeit *größer nicht gedacht werden kann*. Ich kenne die hiesigen Verhältnisse und Kräfte seit Jahren bis ins Kleinste. . . . Über die Aufhebung des konfessionellen Prinzips läßt sich verschieden denken. Man kennt katholische Taktik *immer noch nicht*. Und eines Tages wird sich das schwer rächen" (Heidegger's italics).

CHAPTER IV
CRITIQUE

1. *Beiträge*, § 259, p. 435: "Das Sichverständlichmachen ist Selbstmord der Philosophie."

2. "Mein bisheriger Weg," B (GA 66), p. 416: "Aber weil die innersten Erfahrungen und Entscheidungen das Wesentliche bleiben, deshalb müssen sie aus der Öffentlichkeit herausgehalten werden." These experiences and decisions are concerned with religion and Heidegger's relation to Christianity: "Und wer wollte verkennen, das auf diesem ganzen bisherigen Weg verschwiegen die Auseinandersetzung mit dem Christentum mitging" (p. 415). Heidegger adds: "Es ist nicht schicklich, von diesen innersten Auseinandersetzungen zu reden, die nicht um Fragen der Dogmatik und der Glaubensartikel sich drehen, sondern nur um die Eine Frage, ob der Gott vor uns auf der Flucht ist oder nicht und ob wir selbst dieses noch wahrhaft und d. h. als Schaffende erfahren" (p. 415; see § 11, above, for discussion).

3. "Beilage zu Wunsch und Wille. Über die Bewahrung des Versuchten," B (GA 66), p. 421: "Die Vorlesungen sind alle *geschichtlich*, geschichtegründend, aber nie historisch. Wer sie *unmittelbar* nur liest und hört als eine historische Darstellung irgend eines Werkes und wer dann die Auffassung vergleicht und verrechnet mit schon bestehenden oder sie ausnutzt, um diese zu 'verbessern,' *der hat noch nichts begriffen*" (Heidegger's italics).

4. "Beilage zu Wunsch und Wille. Über die Bewahrung des Versuchten," B (GA 66), p. 420: "Die Vorlesungen. . . . Sie sind alle meist das in ein anderes Denken verhüllte Tasten nach der Wahrheit des Seyns und ihrer Gründung im Da-sein."

5. "Mein bisheriger Weg," B (GA 66), pp. 415–416: "sondern um die Eine Frage, ob der Gott vor uns auf der Flucht ist oder nicht . . . die Eine Frage nach der Wahrheit des Seins."

6. Kaufmann (1963), § 4.

7. Quoted by Kaufmann (1963), in § 10.

8. Cf. "Brief über den 'Humanismus,' " W, p. 167: "Alles Widerlegen im Felde des wesentlichen Denkens ist töricht"; and "Wer ist Nietzsches Zarathustra?", VA, p. 117: "Die Geschäftigkeit des Widerlegenwollens gelangt aber nie auf den Weg eines Denkers. Sie gehört in jene Kleingeisterei, deren Auslassungen die Öffentlichkeit zu ihrer Unterhaltung bedarf."

9. Cf. "Brief über den 'Humanismus,' " W, p. 193: "Darum sagen die wesentlichen Denker stets dasselbe."

10. On 29 September 1949 Hannah Arendt wrote to Karl Jaspers concerning Heidegger's postwar publications: "And then, of course, this whole intricate and childish dishonesty has quickly crept into his philosophizing" (Arendt and Jaspers [1992], p. 142).

11. FD, § A.3, p. 8; *Beiträge*, pp. 28, 44, 87ff., 470, 482.

12. Cf. "Brief über den 'Humanismus,' " W, p. 156: "Daß die Physiologie und die physiologische Chemie den Menschen als Organismus naturwissenschaftlich untersuchen kann, ist kein Beweis dafür, daß in diesem 'Organischen,' das heißt in dem wissenschaftlich erklärten Leib, das Wesen des Menschen beruht. . . . Es könnte doch sein, daß die Natur in der Seite, die sie der technischen Bemächtigung durch den Menschen zukehrt, ihr Wesen gerade verbirgt."

13. SZ, § 53, p. 263: "Der Tod ist *eigenste* Möglichkeit des Daseins" (Heidegger's italics).

14. Caputo (1992), pp. 148–164. Cf. also Schürmann (1972) and Caputo (1986).

15. Cf. "Der Satz der Identität," ID, pp. 13–34.

16. SZ, § 7C, p. 35: "Was aber in einem ausnehmenden Sinne *verborgen* bleibt oder wieder in die *Verdeckung* zurückfällt oder nur '*verstellt*' sich zeigt, ist nicht dieses oder jenes Seiende, sondern, wie die voranstehenden Betrachtungen gezeigt haben, das *Sein* des Seienden. Es kann so weitgehend verdeckt sein, daß es vergessen wird und die Frage nach ihm und seinem Sinn ausbleibt" (Heidegger's italics). Passages like this one cannot be sufficiently understood from a Husserlian or transcendental point of view. I suggest that Eckhartian impulses are operative here, as they are in that other passage in § 7C, where Heidegger says: "Das Sein als Grundthema der Philosophie ist keine Gattung eines Seienden, und doch betrifft es jedes Seiende. Seine 'Universalität' ist höher zu suchen. Sein und Seinsstruktur liegen über jedes Seiende und jede mögliche seiende Bestimmung eines Seienden hinaus. *Sein ist das transcendens schlechthin*" (p. 38; Heidegger's italics).

17. Caputo (1992), pp. 164–172.

18. Caputo (1992), pp. 164–167.

19. Caputo (1992), p. 167.

20. Caputo (1992), p. 168.

21. Caputo (1992), p. 169.

22. Caputo (1992), p. 163.

23. Caputo (1992), p. 168.

24. Caputo (1992), p. 168.

25. Caputo (1992), p. 169.

26. Cf. *Beiträge*, § 237, p. 369: "Die *Fragenden* dieser Art sind die ursprünglich und eigentlich Glaubenden" (Heidegger's italics).

27. ID, p. 10: "Beweisen läßt sich in diesem Bereich nichts, aber weisen manches"; "Das Ding," *Nachwort*, VA, p. 177: "Die Möglichkeit des Irrgangs ist bei diesem Denken

die größte. Dieses Denken kann sich nie ausweisen wie das mathematische Wissen. Aber es ist ebensowenig Willkür, sondern gebunden an das Wesensgeschick des Seins, selber jedoch nie verbindlich als Aussage, vielmehr nur möglicher Anlaß, den Weg des Entsprechens zu gehen"; "Wer ist Nietzsches Zarathustra," VA, p. 115: "Aber das Einzige, was jeweils ein Denker zu sagen vermag, läßt sich logisch oder empirisch weder beweisen noch widerlegen"; "Was heisst Denken," VA, p. 128: "Es gibt von den Wissenschaften her zum Denken keine Brücke, sondern nur den Sprung," and so on; "Zeit und Sein," SD, p. 2: "Es gilt, einiges von dem Versuch zu sagen, der das Sein ohne die Rücksicht auf eine Begründung des Seins aus dem Seiende denkt."

28. In particular, Catholicism is incompatible with Heideggerian postmonotheism. The Catholic Church will not endorse Heidegger's statement that Being is never a characteristic of God, or that gods are only gods in mutual struggle. Cf. *Beiträge*, § 123, p. 240: "Denn niemals ist das Seyn eine Bestimmung des Gottes selbst"; and § 127, p. 244: "Vielmehr müssen wir die Zerklüftung zu denken versuchen aus jenem Grundwesen des Seyns, kraft dessen es das Entscheidungsbereich für den Kampf der Götter ist. Dieser Kampf spielt um ihre Ankunft und Flucht, in welchem Kampf die Götter erst göttern und ihren Gott zur Entscheidung stellen."

29. *Beiträge*, § 27, p. 64: "Niemals läßt sich das herrschaftliche Wissen dieses Denkens in einem Satz sagen"; *Richardson*, p. ix: "Jeder Versuch, Gedachtes der herrschenden Vorstellungsweise näherzubringen, muß selber das zu Denkende diesen Vorstellungen angleichen und dadurch die Sache notwendig verunstalten"; "Zeit und Sein," SD, p. 25: "Es sagt auch nichts, solange wir das Gesagte als einen bloßen Satz hören und ihn dem Verhör durch die Logik ausliefern"; cf. p. 19 and SvGr, p. 20.

30. The best known argument is given by Davidson, "On the Very Idea of a Conceptual Scheme," in Davidson (1984). But Davidson's argument is marred by misconceptions about language and about the notion of truth. See Hacker (1996), pp. 289–307.

31. Quine (1960), §§ 1–6; cf. Quine (1990), §§ 1–9.

32. Cf. Hacker (1996).

33. Quine (1960), § 1, p. 1: "Physical things generally, however remote, become known to us only through the effects which they help to induce at our sensory surfaces." Cf. Quine (1990), § 1, p. 1: "From impacts on our sensory surfaces, we in our collective and cumulative creativity down the generations have projected our systematic theory of the external world."

34. SZ, § 31, p. 147: "Dadurch, daß gezeigt wird, wie alle Sicht primär im Verstehen gründet . . ., ist dem puren Anschauen sein Vorrang genommen."

35. This does not imply, of course, that we *first* perceive things in a culturally neutral way and *then* interpret them within the framework of our culture. For instance, when we have learned a language, we do not first perceive the words of this language as sounds or ink-marks that require an interpretation. We immediately grasp them as meaningful. However, it does not follow, contrary to what Heidegger claims, that *perceiving as* is more fundamental than, or as fundamental as, simply perceiving. For we could only learn the language because we perceived its words first. Cf. on this topic Mulhall (1990).

36. SZ, § 69b; FD, pp. 33, 38, 50, 52, 74; "Die Zeit des Weltbildes," HW, p. 69: "Die Metaphysik begründet ein Zeitalter, indem sie ihm durch eine bestimmte Auslegung des Seienden und durch eine bestimmte Auffassung der Wahrheit den Grund seiner Wesensgestalt gibt. Dieser Grund durchherrscht alle Erscheinungen, die das Zeitalter auszeichnen";

"Wissenschaft und Besinnung," VA, p. 41: "Die Wissenschaft ist eine und zwar entscheidende Weise, in der sich uns alles, was ist, darstellt."

37. Cf. Dreyfus (1991), p. 279: "Kuhn argues persuasively in his Sherman lectures that a given scientific lexicon of natural kind terms determines what can count as true, so that for Aristotle, for example, it was true that the sun was a planet and that there could not be a void, while for us Aristotle's assertions are neither true nor false because 'planet' and 'void' have different meanings in the lexicon of modern science." This is slightly confused. We should accept the statement that the sun is a "planet" in Aristotle's sense of the word "planet" (a heavenly object that, seen from the earth, moves in relation to the background of the stars) and reject the very different statement that the sun is a planet in our usual sense of the word (a large satellite of a star).

38. Relativism concerning truth has disastrous consequences for science and culture in general, because it destroys the notion of truth altogether. According to Bloom (1987), "Heidegger's teachings are the most powerful intellectual force in our times," and Bloom thinks that they are largely responsible for "the closing of the American mind" (pp. 311–312).

39. "Die Frage nach der Technik" in VA and passim in the later works.

40. *Richardson*, p. xxiii: "Wer für das Erblicken des Gebens einer solchen Gabe an den Menschen, für das Schicken eines so Geschickten keinen Sinn hat, wird die Rede vom Seinsgeschick nie verstehen, so wenig wie der von Natur Blinde je erfahren kann, was Licht und Farbe sind."

41. Cf. "Nietzsches Wort 'Gott ist tot,' " HW, p. 193: "In jeder Phase der Metaphysik wird jeweils ein Stück eines Weges sichtbar, den das Geschick des Seins in jähen Epochen der Wahrheit über das Seiende sich bahnt."

42. Franzen (1975) defends this thesis also concerning SZ. See his chapter 1.3, p. 47: "Statt einen Beitrag zur Wiedergewinnung des Geschichtsproblems zu leisten, fordert sie [i.e., Heidegger's analysis of historicity] dessen Verdrängung," and p. 50: "die Verlegung der Geschichte ins 'Innere'—und zwar in das Innere eines aufs private Sein-zum-Tode reduzierten, monadischen Subjekts—hält die reale, 'nur' äußere Geschichte als ein vermeintlich Sekundäres in sicherem Abstand von sich fern." On the later works, see Franzen (1975), chapter 4.1.3, p. 124: "Enthält Heidegger's Spätphilosophie wirklich eine Geschichtstheorie? Oder ist sie vielleicht eher ein Unternehmen zum Zwecke der Geschichts-*vermeidung*?"; p. 129: "Als Verfallstheorie ist Heideggers Geschichtsphilosophie an einem ideal orientiert, durch welches Geschichte außer Kraft gesetzt würde"; and passim (Franzen's italics).

43. For instance, in "Das Rektorat 1933/34," SdU, p. 39: "Die verschiedenen Beurteilungen dieses Rektorats . . . mögen in ihrer Weise richtig und im Recht sein, sie treffen das Wesentliche doch nie. . . . Das Wesentliche ist, daß wir mitten in der Vollendung des Nihilismus stehen, daß Gott 'todt' ist und jeder Zeit-Raum für die Gottheit verschüttet," and so on. In other words, moral criteria for evaluating what Heidegger did during his rectorate are not "essential" because they can never be used to evaluate the "fate" that Being sends to us. Cf. WhD, p. 65: "Was hat der zweite Weltkrieg eigentlich entschieden, um von seinen furchtbaren Folgen für unser Vaterland, im besonderen vom Riß durch seine Mitte, zu schweigen? Dieser Weltkrieg hat nichts entschieden, wenn wir die Entscheidung so hoch und so weit nehmen, daß sie einzig das Wesensgeschick des Menschen auf dieser Erde angeht. . . . Allein auch hier steigt erneut die Gefahr, daß . . . dieses zu Entscheidende noch einmal in die überall zu kurz tragenden und zu engbrüstigen politisch-sozialen und

moralischen Kategorien hineingezwängt und dadurch aus einer möglichen und hinreichenden Besinnung abgedrängt wird."

44. "Aufruf an die Deutschen Studenten" of 3 November 1933, *Freiburger Studentenzeitung* VIII, no. 1 (1933), p. 1. See Schneeberger (1962), pp. 135ff. and Martin (1989), p. 177.

45. GA 53, *Hölderlins Hymne "Der Ister,"* pp. 98, 106, 118.

46. One might argue on empirical grounds that no political or technological action will be able to avert destruction of our ecosystem by overpopulation and technology, and I think that there is a very strong case for this conclusion. However, this is not at all Heidegger's argument. The empirical argument does not lead to quietism, because we might try even if it is improbable that we will succeed.

47. Heidegger's argument is that man will never be able to master the "essence" of technology, because this is sent to us by Being as our destiny. Cf. "Die Frage nach der Technik," VA, p. 21: "Der Mensch kann zwar dieses oder jenes so oder so vorstellen, gestalten und betreiben. Allein, über die Unverborgenheit, worin sich jeweils das Wirkliche zeigt oder entzieht, verfügt der Mensch nicht." Cf. "Spiegel-Gespräch," *Antwort*, p. 97: "Zunächst bitte ich Sie zu sagen, wo ich über Demokratie und was Sie weiter anführen gesprochen habe. Als Halbheiten würde ich sie auch bezeichnen, weil ich darin keine wirkliche Auseinandersetzung mit der technischen Welt sehe, weil dahinter immer noch, nach meiner Ansicht, die Auffasung steht, daß die Technik in ihrem Wesen etwas sei, was der Mensch in der Hand hat. Das ist nach meiner Meinung nicht möglich. Die Technik in ihrem Wesen ist etwas, was der Mensch von sich aus nicht bewältigt."

48. Cf. on *Irre*: "Der Spruch des Anaximander," HW, p. 310: "Das Sein entzieht sich, indem es sich in das Seiende entbirgt. Dergestalt beirrt das Sein, es lichtend, das Seiende mit der Irre. Das Seiende ist in die Irre ereignet, in der es das Sein umirrt und so den Irrtum (zu sagen wie Fürsten-und Dichtertum) stiftet." Cf. "Vom Wesen der Wahrheit," W, p. 92: "Die Umgetriebenheit des Menschen weg vom Geheimnis hin zum Gangbaren, fort von einem Gängigen, fort zum nächsten und vorbei am Geheimnis, ist das *Irren*. Der Mensch irrt. Der Mensch geht nicht erst in die Irre," and so on (Heidegger's italics).

49. "Das Rektorat 1933/34," SdU, p. 25: "die universale Herrschaft des Willens zur Macht innerhalb der planetarisch gesehenen Geschichte. In dieser Wirklichkeit steht heute Alles, mag es Kommunismus heißen oder Faschismus oder Weltdemokratie."

50. Quoted with approval by Schirmacher (1983), p. 25: "Ackerbau ist jetzt motorisierte Ernährungsindustrie, im Wesen das Selbe wie die Fabrikation von Leichen in Gaskammern und Vernichtungslagern, das Selbe wie die Blockade und die Aushungerung von Ländern, das Selbe wie die Fabrikation von Wasserstoffbomben." By referring to bomb and blockade, Heidegger is insinuating that Western countries such as the United States are not any better than Nazi Germany.

51. "Das Rektorat 1933/34," SdU, p. 25, where Heidegger says that world democracy belongs to the metaphysical reality of the will to power (see previous quote from SdU).

52. Cf. § 11B.11, above, and "Brief über den 'Humanismus,' " W, p. 191: "Nur sofern der Mensch, in die Wahrheit des Seins ek-sistierend, diesem gehört, kann aus dem Sein selbst die Zuweisung derjenigen Weisungen kommen, die für den Menschen Gesetz und Regel werden müssen. . . . Nur diese vermag es, den Menschen in das Sein zu verfügen. Nur solche Fügung vermag zu tragen und zu binden. Anders bleibt alles Gesetz nur das Gemächte menschlicher Vernunft."

53. AED, p. 17: "Wer groß denkt muß groß irren."

54. This subsection is nearly identical with section IV of Philipse (1994a).

55. Cf. EM, p. 19: "Es könnte umgekehrt sein, daß die gesamte uns bekannte und wie ein Himmelgeschenk behandelte Logik in einer ganz bestimmten Antwort auf die Frage nach dem Seienden gründet, daß mithin alles Denken, das lediglich die Denkgesetze der herkömmlichen Logik befolgt, von vornherein außerstande ist, von sich aus überhaupt die Frage nach dem Seienden auch nur zu verstehen."

56. E.g., Richardson, p. ix: "Jeder Versuch, Gedachtes der herrschenden Vorstellungsweise näherzubringen, muß selber das zu Denkende diesen Vorstellungen angleichen und dadurch die Sache notwendig verunstalten"; "Spiegel-Gespräch," *Antwort*, p. 111: "Aber die größte Not des Denkens besteht darin, daß heute, soweit ich sehen kann, noch kein Denker spricht, der 'groß' genug wäre, das Denken unmittelbar und in geprägter Gestalt vor seine Sache und damit auf seinen Weg zu bringen."

57. Cf., for instance, Schirmacher in *Technik und Gelassenheit* (1983), p. 11: "Zeitkritik wird niemals radikal genug sein, wenn sie die Schärfe des Nichts scheut. Heideggers Denken läßt sich auch in größter Not von der Zeit nicht vorschreiben, welche Phänomene es zu berücksichtigen hat. Denn eine umstandslose Analyse der gesellschäftlichen Verhältnisse und ausgeklügelte Lösungen nach deren Machart bleiben dem technischen Vorstellen auch dort verhaftet, wo sie Wissenschaft und Technik leidenschäftlich bekämpfen." Schirmacher's entire oeuvre offers fine instances of the rhetorical strategems that I am discussing.

58. EM, p. 34: "Rußland und Amerika, die metaphysisch dasselbe sind"; "Das Rektorat 1933/34," SdU, p. 25: "In dieser Wirklichkeit [of the will to power] steht heute Alles, mag es Kommunismus heißen oder Faschismus oder Weltdemokratie"; "Das Ge-Stell" (unpublished), quoted by Schirmacher (1983), p. 25.

59. Cf. Kaufman (1963), p. 118.

60. SZ, § 44a, p. 218: "Die Aussage *ist wahr*, bedeutet: sie entdeckt das Seiende an ihm selbst. . . . *Wahrsein* (*Wahrheit*) der Aussage muß verstanden werden als *entdeckend-sein*. Wahrheit hat also gar nicht die Struktur einer Übereinstimmung zwischen Erkennen und Gegenstand"; § 44b, p. 220: "Wahrsein als entdeckend-sein ist eine Seinsweise des Daseins. . . . Primär 'wahr,' das heißt entdeckend ist das Dasein. . . . daher wird erst mit der *Erschlossenheit* des Daseins das *ursprünglichste* Phänomen der Wahrheit erreicht"; p. 223: "Wahrheit im ursprünglichsten Sinne ist die Erschlossenheit des Daseins" (Heidegger's italics).

61. SZ, § 44b, p. 220: "gleichwohl ist es am Ende das Geschäft der Philosophie, die *Kraft der elementarsten Worte*, in denen sich das Dasein ausspricht, davor zu bewahren, daß sie durch den gemeinen Verstand zur Unverständlichkeit nivelliert werden, die ihrerseits als Quelle für Scheinprobleme fungiert"; "Die 'Definition' der Wahrheit als Entdeckheit und Entdeckendsein ist auch keine bloße Worterklärung, sondern sie erwächst aus der Analyse der Verhaltungen des Daseins, die wir zunächst 'wahre' zu nennen pflegen" (Heidegger's italics). Aristotle also uses the Greek word for "true" in this "existential" sense, but he does not claim that this sense is "more fundamental" than that of propositional truth.

62. SZ, § 44b, p. 221: "Diese *eigentliche* Erschlossenheit zeigt das Phänomen der ursprünglichsten Wahrheit im Modus der Eigentlichkeit. Die ursprünglichste und zwar eigentlichste Erschlossenheit, in der das Dasein als Seinkönnen sein kann, ist die *Wahrheit der Existenz*" (Heidegger's italics).

63. "Wer ist Nietzsches Zarathustra?", VA, p. 117: "Die Geschäftigkeit des Widerlegen-wollens gelangt aber nie auf den Weg eines Denkers. Sie gehört in jene Kleingeisterei, deren Auslassungen die Öffentlichkeit zu ihrer Unterhaltung bedarf."

64. "Brief über den 'Humanismus,' " W, p. 167: "Alles Widerlegen im Felde des wesentlichen Denkens ist töricht"; WhD, p. 56: "Das immer weiter und in verschiedenen Formen um sich greifende eingleisige Denken ist eine jener erwähnten unvermuteten und unauffälligen Herrschaftsformen des Wesens der Technik, welches Wesen nämlich die unbedingte Eindeutigkeit will und sie deshalb braucht." Cf. "Vom Wesen der Wahrheit," W, p. 74: "Die Philosophie jedoch kann den gemeinen Verstand nie widerlegen, weil er für ihre Sprache taub ist"; p. 94: "Aber was die Philosophie nach der Schätzung des gesunden und in seinem Bezirk wohlberechtigten Verstandes ist, trifft nicht ihr Wesen"; "Nietzsches Wort 'Gott ist tot,' " HW, p. 247: "Das Denken beginnt erst dann, wenn wir erfahren haben, daß die seit Jahrhunderten verherrlichte Vernunft die hartnäckigste Widersacherin des Denkens ist"; VA, pp. 115; and WhD, p. 49: "Jede Art von Polemik verfehlt im voraus die Haltung des Denkens. Die Rolle eines Widersachers ist nicht die Rolle des Denkens. Denn ein Denken denkt nur dann, wenn es dem nachgeht, was *für* eine Sache spricht" (Heidegger's italics).

65. Cf. Ott (1988), pp. 162–164.

66. Cf. *Richardson*, p. xix: "Die Kehre ist in erster Linie nicht ein Vorgang im fragenden Denken; sie gehört in den durch die Titel 'Sein und Zeit,' 'Zeit und Sein' genannten Sachverhalt selbst." Cf. postscript to *Was ist Metaphysik?*, WiM, p. 50: "Das wesentliche Denken achtet auf die langsamen Zeichen des Unberechenbaren und erkennt in diesem die unvordenkliche Ankunft des Unabwendbaren."

67. "Zur Seinsfrage," W, p. 217: "Wer in solcher Weise beteiligt bleibt, dessen Verantwortung muß sich in derjenigen Ant-wort versammeln, die aus einem unentwegten Fragen innerhalb der größtmöglichen Fragwürdigkeit des Nihilismus entspringt und als die Entsprechung zu dieser übernommen und ausgetragen wird." What "Antwort" means here is clarified in other texts, such as "Zeit und Sein," SD, p. 20: "Antworten meint das Sagen, das dem hier zu denkenden Sach-Verhalt, d. h. dem Ereignis entspricht."

68. Cf. *Beiträge*, § 270.

69. GA 60, p. 36: "Philosophie ist nichts als eine Kampf gegen den gesunden Menschenverstand."

70. WhD, p. 64: "Das, was eigentlich ist, das Sein, das alles Seiende im vorhinein bestimmt, läßt sich jedoch niemals durch die Feststellung von Tatsachen, durch Berufung auf besondere Umstände ausmachen. Der bei solche Versuchen oft und eifrig 'zitierte' gesunde Menschenverstand ist nicht so gesund und natürlich, wie er sich zu geben pflegt. Er ist vor allem nicht so absolut, wie er auftritt, sondern er ist das abgeflachte Produkt jener Art des Vorstellens, die das Aufklärungszeitalter im 18. Jahrhundert schließlich zeitigte"; p. 69: "Als ob der gesunde Menschenverstand—die Zuflucht jener, die von Natur aus auf das Denken neidisch sind—als ob dieser gesunde, d. h. für keine Fragwürdigkeit anfällige Verstand je schon einmal etwas angefangen, etwas aus seinem Anfang bedacht hätte."

71. *Beiträge*, § 5, p. 11: "*Für die Wenigen—Für die Seltenen* . . . die den höchsten Mut zur Einsamkeit mitbringen, um den Adel des Seyns zu denken und zu sagen von seiner Einzigkeit" (Heidegger's italics).

72. *Beiträge*, § 8, p. 28: "Nur Wenige stehen immer in der Helle dieses Blitzes."

73. *Beiträge*, § 15, pp. 42–43: "Die Besinnung auf das Volkhafte ist ein wesentlicher Durchgang. So wenig wir dies verkennen dürfen, so sehr gilt es zu wissen, daß ein höchster

Rang des Seyns errungen sein muß, wenn ein 'völkisches Prinzip' als maßgebend für das geschichtliche Da-sein gemeistert ins Spiel gebracht werden soll. Das Volk wird erst Volk, wenn seine Einzigsten kommen, und wenn diese zu ahnen beginnen."

74. *Beiträge*, § 251, p. 398: "Ein Volk ist *nur* Volk, wenn es in der Findung seines Gottes seine Geschichte zugeteilt erhält. . . . Aber wie soll es den Gott finden, wenn nicht jene sind, die *für* es verschwiegen *suchen* und als diese Sucher sogar dem Anschein nach *gegen* das *noch nicht* volkhafte 'Volk' stehen müssen" (Heidegger's italics).

75. Cf. *Beiträge*, § 256, p. 414: "Nur die großen und verborgenen Einzelnen werden dem Vorbeigang des Gottes die Stille schaffen und unter sich den verschwiegenen Einklang der Bereiten"; B (GA 66), § 57, p. 147: "*Grunderfahrung*: . . . wird nicht von *Beliebigen* vollzogen, sondern von 'Einzelnen,' Aus-gezeichneten. Diese 'Einzelnen' aber gehören als die Gezeichneten dem Seyn" (Heidegger's italics).

76. SZ, § 7, p. 38: "Ontologie und Phänomenologie sind nicht zwei verschiedene Disziplinen neben anderen zur Philosophie gehörigen. Die beiden Titel charakterisieren die Philosophie selbst nach Gegenstand und Behandlungsart. Philosophie ist universale phänomenologische Ontologie, ausgehend von der Hermeneutik des Daseins, die als Analytik der Existenz das Ende des Leitfadens alles philosophischen Fragens dort festgemacht hat, woraus es *entspringt* und wohin es *zurückschlägt*" (Heidegger's italics).

77. See Philipse (1995) for a rational reconstruction of Husserl's transcendental idealism.

78. Cf. Philipse (1994) and sections 3 and 9A, above.

79. SZ, § 4, p. 13: "Daher muß die *Fundamentalontologie*, aus der alle andern erst entspringen können, in der *existenzialen Analytik des Daseins* gesucht werden" (Heidegger's italics).

80. SZ, § 69, p. 350: "Die ekstatische Einheit der Zeitlichkeit . . . ist die Bedingung der Möglichkeit dafür, daß ein Seiendes sein kann, das als sein 'Da' existiert."

81. SZ, § 1, p. 2: "Sie [i.e., the question of being] hat das Forschen von *Plato* und *Aristoteles* in Atem gehalten, um freilich auch von da an zu verstummen—*als thematische Frage wirklicher Untersuchung.* Was die beiden gewonnen, hat sich in mannigfachen Verschiebungen und 'Übermalungen' bis in die 'Logik' *Hegels* durchgehalten. Und was ehemals in der höchsten Anstrengung des Denkens den Phänomenen abgerungen wurde, wenngleich bruchstückhaft und in ersten Anläufen, ist längst trivialisiert" (Heidegger's italics).

82. SZ, § 6, p. 24: "Geschaffenheit aber im weitesten Sinne der Hergestelltheit von etwas ist ein wesentliches Strukturmoment des antiken Seinsbegriffes."

83. Cf. SZ, §§ 3, 6, and 9.

84. Cf. SZ, § 3.

85. *Genesis* 1:27.

86. See Philipse (1990) for a detailed critique of Churchland's eliminative materialism.

87. Cf., for instance, SZ, § 18, p. 85: "Dieses, woraufhin umweltlich Zuhandenes freigegeben ist, so zwar, daß dieses allererst *als* innerweltliches Seiendes zugänglich wird, kann selbst nicht als Seiendes dieser entdeckten Seinsart begriffen werden" (Heidegger's italics); and p. 88: "Innerhalb des jetzigen Untersuchungsfeldes sind die wiederholt markierten Unterschiede der Strukturen und Dimensionen der ontologischen Problematik grundsätzlich auseinanderzuhalten: 1. das Sein des zunächst begegnenden innerweltlichen Seienden (Zuhandenheit); . . . 3. das Sein der ontischen Bedingung der Möglichkeit der Entdeckbar-

keit von innerweltlichem Seienden überhaupt, die Weltlichkeit von Welt. Das letztgenannte Sein ist eine existenziale Bestimmung des In-der-Welt-seins, das heißt des Daseins."

88. SZ, § 15, p. 71: "*Zuhandenheit ist die ontologisch-kategoriale Bestimmung von Seiendem, wie es 'an sich' ist*"; § 18, p. 87: "*Das Dasein ist in seiner Vertrautheit mit der Bedeutsamkeit die ontische Bedingung der Möglichkeit der Entdeckbarkeit von Seiendem, das in der Seinsart der Bewandtnis (Zuhandenheit) in einer Welt begegnet und sich so in seinem An-sich bekunden kann*"; cf. § 23, p. 106: "*Das umsichtige Ent-fernen der Alltäglichkeit des Daseins entdeckt das An-sich-sein der 'wahren Welt', des Seienden, bei dem Dasein als existierendes je schon ist.*" The fact that Heidegger italicized all these passages proves their importance.

89. SZ, § 18.

90. SZ, § 69b, p. 362: "Erst 'im Licht' einer dergestalt entworfenen Natur kann so etwas wie eine 'Tatsache' gefunden und für einen aus dem Entwurf regulativ umgrenzten Versuch ausgesetzt werden. Die 'Begründung' der 'Tatsachenwissenschaft' wurde nur dadurch möglich, daß die Forscher verstanden: es gibt grundsätzlich keine 'bloßen Tatsachen.' Am mathematischen Entwurf der Natur ist wiederum nicht primär das Mathematische als solches entscheidend, sondern daß er ein *Apriori erschließt*" (Heidegger's italics). Cf. FD, § B.I.5.e.

91. In *Beiträge*, Heidegger interprets his earlier analysis of Kant's transcendental philosophy (KM) as a preparation for raising the question of Being in the postmonotheist sense. Cf. *Beiträge*, § 44, pp. 93–94: "Weil all dies bei Kant am reinsten vollzogen wird, deshalb *kann* an seinem Werk versucht werden, ein noch Ursprünglicheres und deshalb von ihm her nicht Ableitbares, ganz Anderes sichtbar zu machen"; § 134, p. 253: "bietet sich da nicht eine Gelegenheit . . . an der . . . jener Bezug von Da-sein und Seyn den Heutigen aus dem Bisherigen erstmals näher gebracht werden kann? Allerdings. Und das ist versucht im 'Kantbuch' " (Heidegger's italics).

92. SZ, § 40, p. 186: "Die innerweltlich entdeckte Bewandtnisganzheit des Zuhandenen und Vorhandenen ist als solche überhaupt ohne Belang. Sie sinkt in sich zusammen. Die Welt hat den Charakter völliger Unbedeutsamkeit."

93. SZ, § 18, p. 86: "*Das Worin des sichverweisenden Verstehen als Woraufhin des Begegnenlassens von Seiendem in der Seinsart der Bewandtnis ist das Phänomen der Welt.* Und die Struktur dessen, woraufhin das Dasein sich verweist, ist das, was die *Weltlichkeit* der Welt ausmacht" (Heidegger's italics).

94. Cf. SZ, § 40, p. 187: "Was beengt, ist nicht dieses oder jenes, aber auch nicht alles Vorhandene zusammen als Summe, sondern die *Möglichkeit* von Zuhandenem überhaupt, das heißt die Welt selbst. . . . Wenn sich demnach als das Wovor der Angst das Nichts, das heißt die Welt als solche herausstellt, dann besagt das: *wovor die Angst sich ängstet, ist das In-der-Welt-sein selbst*" (Heidegger's italics).

95. SZ, § 43c, p. 212: "Allerdings nur solange Dasein *ist*, das heißt die ontische Möglichkeit von Seinsverständnis, 'gibt es' Sein. Wenn Dasein nicht existiert, dann 'ist' auch nicht 'Unabhängigkeit' und 'ist' auch nicht 'An-sich' " (Heidegger's italics).

96. SZ, § 13, p. 61: "Damit Erkennen als betrachtendes Bestimmen des Vorhandenen möglich sei, bedarf es vorgängig einer *Defizienz* des besorgenden Zu-tun-habens mit der Welt" (Heidegger's italics).

97. Dreyfus (1991), chapter 15 and passim.

98. SZ, § 44c, p. 230: "Sein—nicht Seiendes—'gibt es' nur, sofern Wahrheit ist. Und sie *ist* nur, sofern und solange Dasein ist" (Heidegger's italics). Cf. SZ, § 43c, pp. 211–212.

99. This is also true if one endorses other interpretations of Heidegger's claims that (a) entities do not depend on Dasein whereas (b) *being* depends on Dasein. Claim (a) might be taken as *internal* to the framework of presence-at-hand (*Vorhandenheit*); hence Heidegger supposedly is an *empirical* realist as far as science is concerned. He is also a transcendental idealist, because the transcendental framework on which scientific facts depend is a projection of Dasein (SZ, § 69b) and because the transcendental temporality of Dasein is more basic than the time of physics (SZ, §§ 69c and 78–81). If one now asks what the status of entities is from the *transcendental* point of view, one might either reply that this question is illegitimate, because questions about entities can only be raised within a projected transcendental framework. However, if transcendental questions about entities are illegitimate, the very notion of a transcendental framework that organizes or sytetizes *something else* becomes incomprehensible, because the notion of "something else" drops out of the picture. This is precisely my critique. Or one might reply that Heidegger is also a *transcendental* realist concerning entities after all. But in that case he cannot argue that the notion of purely present things is only valid within the framework of *Vorhandenheit*, and his antinaturalism collapses. The inconsistencies in Heidegger's transcendental theory are similar to the traditional problem of the *Ding an sich* that was raised with regard to Kant's transcendentalism, and there is no satisfactory solution to these problems.

100. Cf. also SZ, § 68a, p. 337: "Das Verstehen ist als Existieren im wie immer entworfenen Seinkönnen *primär* zukünftig" (Heidegger's italics).

101. SZ, § 31, p. 145; cf. § 69b.

102. SZ, § 69b, p. 362: "Erst 'im Licht' einer dergestalt entworfenen Natur kann so etwas wie eine 'Tatsache' gefunden . . . werden. Die 'Begründung' der 'Tatsachenwissenschaft' wurde nur dadurch möglich, daß die Forscher verstanden: es gibt grundsätzlich keine 'bloße Tatsachen.' Am mathematischen Entwurf der Natur is wiederum nicht primär das Mathematische als solche entscheidend, sondern daß er ein *Apriori erschließt*" (Heidegger's italics).

103. Cf. Philipse (1990).

104. SZ, § 44c, pp. 226–227: "*Wahrheit 'gibt es' nur, sofern und solange Dasein ist.* . . . Die Gesetze *Newtons,* der Satz vom Widerspruch, jede Wahrheit überhaupt sind nur solange wahr, als Dasein *ist.* . . . Bevor die Gesetze *Newtons* entdeckt wurden, waren sie nicht 'wahr,' " and so on; "Die Gesetze *Newtons* waren vor ihm weder wahr noch falsch, kann nicht bedeuten, das Seiende, das sie entdeckend aufzeigen, sei vordem nicht gewesen. Die Gesetze wurden durch *Newton* wahr, mit ihnen wurde für das Dasein Seiendes an ihm selbst zugänglich," and so on (Heidegger's italics).

105. Cf. SZ, § 44c, p. 227: "Die Gesetze wurden durch *Newton* wahr."

106. Okrent (1988), pp. 97–107, gives a rational reconstruction of Heidegger's statement that is somewhat more complex. But to the extent that the reconstruction yields a plausible philosophical view, it boils down to the trivial point that there are no (formulated) truths without the system of social practices that constitutes a language. The further point that there is no objective perception of extant (present-at-hand) entities without a language is very dubious.

107. Instead of pointing out incoherencies in Heidegger's text, one might attempt to give a rational reconstruction of what Heidegger should have meant. Cf., again, Okrent

(1988), pp. 280–297, who ends up with the view, derived from Carnap's "Empiricism, Semantics, and Ontology," that according to Heidegger ontic truths are relative to a semantic scheme only in the innocuous sense that the semantic scheme fixes the determinate meanings of the relevant sentences. Once that meaning is fixed, the evaluation of the sentence as true or false is not affected by the relativity to the language. Yet the choice of the linguistic scheme itself supposedly is relative to the pragmatic aims of Dasein. This reconstruction depends ultimately on a questionable distinction between internal and external questions, that is, between scheme and content, which I have rejected above.

108. SZ, §§ 66–68.

109. Cf. the notion of *Zuwendung* in KM, § 16, p. 69: "Wohl aber drängt das Wesen der Endlichkeit unausweichlich zu der Frage nach den Bedingungen der Möglichkeit eines vorgängigen Gewendetseins zum Objekt, d. h. nach dem Wesen der hierzu notwendigen ontologischen Zuwendung zum Gegenständ überhaupt"; § 24, p. 113: "damit ein Gegenstand sich soll geben können, muß im vorhinein schon eine Zuwendung zu solchem geschehen sein"; p. 114: "daß das sichzuwendende Gegenstehenlassen als solches den Horizont der Gegenständlichkeit überhaupt bildet"; § 31, p. 159: "Die Gegenständlichkeit bildet sich aber im sich zuwendenden Gegenstehenlassen, das im reinem Subjekt als solchem geschieht"; and passim.

110. SZ, § 7C, p. 35: "Was aber in einem ausnehmenden Sinne *verborgen* bleibt oder wieder in die *Verdeckung* zurückfällt . . . ist . . . das *Sein* des Seienden" (Heidegger's italics).

111. SZ, § 7A, p. 31: "Dieser vulgäre ist aber nicht der phänomenologische Begriff von Phänomen. Im Horizont der Kantischen Problematik kann das, was phänomenologisch unter Phänomen begriffen wird . . . so illustriert werden, daß wir sagen: was in den Erscheinungen, dem vulgär verstandenen Phänomenen je vorgängig und mitgängig, obzwar unthematisch, sich schon zeigt . . . sind Phänomene der Phänomenologie."

112. SZ, § 3, second paragraph of p. 10.

113. SZ, § 5, pp. 16–17: "An dieser sollen nicht beliebige und zufällige, sondern wesenhafte Strukturen herausgestellt werden, die in jeder Seinsart des faktischen Daseins sich als bestimmende durchhalten"; § 11, p. 52: "Das synkretistische Allesvergleichen und Typisieren gibt nicht schon von selbst echte Wesenserkenntnis"; § 42, p. 199: "Die existenzial-ontologische Interpretation ist der ontischen Auslegung gegenüber nicht etwa nur eine theoretisch-ontische Verallgemeinerung. . . . Die 'Verallgemeinerung' ist eine *apriorisch-ontologische*"; § 45, p. 231: "wesenhafte Strukturen" (Heidegger's italics).

114. Husserl, PhdA, chapters 1–4.

115. LU II, fourth investigation, § 9, p. 305: "Wollen wir uns die Bedeutung des Wortes *und* klarmachen, so müssen wir irgendeinen Kollektionsakt wirklich vollziehen und in dem so zu eigentlicher Vorstellung kommenden Inbegriff eine Bedeutung der Form *a und b* zur Erfüllung bringen" (Husserl's italics). Cf. Tugendhat (1976), lectures 9 and 10.

116. Quine (1960), § 27, p. 131: "There are philosophers who stoutly maintain that 'exists' said of numbers, classes, and the like and 'exists' said of material objects are two usages of an ambiguous term 'exists.' What mainly baffles me is the stoutness of their maintenance. What can they possibly count as evidence?" Cf. also § 49, pp. 241–242.

117. SZ, § 7C, p. 35: "Was ist es, was in einem ausgezeichneten Sinne 'Phänomen' genannt werden muß? . . . Offenbar solches, was sich zunächst und zumeist gerade *nicht* zeigt, was gegenüber dem, was sich zunächst und zumeist zeigt, *verborgen* ist" (Heidegger's italics).

118. SZ, § 3, p. 10: "Sofern aber jedes dieser Gebiete aus dem Bezirk des Seienden selbst gewonnen wird, bedeutet solche vorgängige und Grundbegriffe schöpfende Forschung nichts anderes als Auslegung dieses Seienden auf die Grundverfassung seines Seins."

119. LU II, pp. 106–221; PhPs, *Husserliana* IX, § 9; EU, § 87.

120. Cf. section 7A, above, and PIA, p. 248/18: "In der Idee der Faktizität liegt es, daß je nur die eigentliche—im Wortsinne verstanden: die eigene—die der eigenen Zeit und Generation der genuine Gegenstand der Forschung ist." Heidegger means: one's understanding of life and world.

121. SZ, § 7C, pp. 34–35: "Phänomenologie sagt dann. . . . Das was sich zeigt, so wie es sich von ihm selbst her zeigt, von ihm selbst her sehen lassen"; " 'Phänomenologie' nennt weder den Gegenstand ihrer Forschungen, noch charakterisiert der Titel deren Sachhaltigkeit. Das Wort gibt nur Aufschluß über das *Wie* der Aufweisung und Behandlungsart dessen, *was* in dieser Wissenschaft abgehandelt werden soll," and so on (Heidegger's italics).

122. SZ, § 7C, p. 35: "Wissenschaft 'von' den Phänomenen besagt: eine solche Erfassung ihrer Gegenstände, daß alles, was über sie zur Erörterung steht, in direkter Aufweisung und direkter Ausweisung abgehandelt werden muß. Denselben Sinn hat der im Grunde tautologische Ausdruck 'deskriptive Phänomenologie.' Deskription bedeutet hier nicht ein Verfahren nach Art etwa der botanischen Morphologie—der Titel hat wieder einen prohibitiven Sinn: Fernhaltung alles nichtausweisenden Bestimmens."

123. SZ, § 4, p. 12: "Diesem Seienden eignet, daß mit und durch sein Sein dieses ihm selbst erschlossen ist. *Seinsverständnis ist selbst eine Seinsbestimmtheit des Daseins.* Die ontische Auszeichnung des Daseins liegt darin, daß es ontologisch *ist*" (Heidegger's italics).

124. LU II, second investigation, introduction *in finem*, pp. 107–108.

125. PGZ, § 7. According to Heidegger, Husserl's phenomenology had shown that a priori structures are to be found everywhere and not only in the knowing subject, and that a priori structures may be grasped on the basis of intuition. He says, for instance, misusing Husserl's terminology of "schlichte Anschauung": "Sofern das Apriori jeweils in den Sach- und Seinsgebieten gründet, wird es in einer schlichten Anschauung an ihm selbst aufweisbar. Es wird nicht indirekt erschlossen. . . . Das Apriori ist an ihm selbst vielmehr direkt erfaßbar" (pp. 101–102).

126. Cf. Hacker (1986), chapter 7.

127. Cf., for instance, Strawson (1970) for discussion. I have borrowed some insights from this paper.

128. Cf. SZ, § 9, pp. 44–45.

129. Strawson (1970), p. 194. A priori in the sense that no empirical research is needed for justifying the rejection of either the affirmation or the denial.

130. Strawson (1970), p. 199.

131. Cf. Strawson (1970), pp. 202–203 for a general account of categorial predicates.

132. My argument here has been inspired by P. M. S. Hacker's writings on Wittgenstein. Cf. also Hacker (1996).

133. SZ, division 1, chapter 4, p. 114: "mit der Frage: *wer* ist es, der in der Alltäglichkeit das Dasein ist?" (Heidegger's italics). Cf. § 25, p. 114: "wer dieses Seiende (das Dasein) je ist"; § 26, p. 117: "die Frage nach dem Wer des alltäglichen Daseins."

134. SZ, § 26, pp. 117–118.

135. SZ, § 26, p. 120: "Fehlen kann der Andere nur *in* einem und *für* ein Mitsein" (Heidegger's italics).

136. Dreyfus (1991), p. 151. Cf. also Okrent (1988), pp. 44–51.

137. SZ, § 26, p. 125: "Das Dasein ist im Aufgehen in der besorgten Welt, das heißt zugleich im Mitsein zu den Anderen, nicht es selbst." The italics in the main text are mine.

138. Cf. the last sentence of SZ, § 26, p. 125: "*Wer* ist es denn, der das Sein als alltägliches Miteinandersein übernommen hat?"(Heidegger's italics).

139. SZ, § 27, p. 126: "Nicht es selbst *ist*, die Anderen haben ihm das Sein abgenommen" (Heidegger's italics).

140. SZ, § 27, p. 126: "Entscheidend ist nur die unauffällige, vom Dasein als Mitsein unversehens schon übernommene Herrschaft der Anderen." Macquarrie and Robinson mistranslate vom as "from": BT, p. 164.

141. SZ, § 27, p. 126: "Dieses Miteinandersein löst das eigene Dasein völlig in die Seinsart 'der Anderen' auf."

142. Cf. SZ, § 27, p. 127: "Weil das Man jedoch alles Urteilen und Entscheiden vorgibt, nimmt es dem jeweiligen Dasein die Verantwortlichkeit ab"; p. 128: "Man ist in der Weise der Unselbstständigkeit und Uneigentlichkeit"; p. 129: "*Zunächst* 'bin' nicht 'ich' im Sinne des eigenen Selbst, sondern die Anderen in der Weise des Man"; cf. p. 128: "Jeder ist der Andere und Keiner er selbst" (Heidegger's italics).

143. Dreyfus (1991), pp. 151–152. Cf. Okrent (1988), p. 48: "The others with whom I share a world are those who are like me." Okrent attempts to integrate Heidegger's theses about "the They" into his pragmatist account: as my personal ends are typically standardized ends within a community (e.g., writing a book), and as these ends typically perform instrumental roles for others within that community (e.g., the readers of my book), it would be correct to say that "as Dasein I am for the sake of the 'they' " (p. 51). However, Okrent's *tour de force* is not convincing as an interpretation of *Sein und Zeit* because he leaves out the passages on inauthenticity.

144. Cf. Carey (1992) on intellectuals and the masses between 1880 and 1939.

145. Dreyfus (1991), p. 154.

146. Dreyfus (1991), pp. 143 and 154.

147. Dreyfus (1991), pp. 156–157.

148. Dreyfus (1991), p. 157.

149. Dreyfus wrote an interesting appendix on Kierkegaard and Heidegger to his 1991 work, in cooperation with Jane Rubin.

150. SZ, §§ 38 and 68c. The notion of *Verfallen* is a complex one and I will not analyze it here.

151. SZ, § 62, p. 310: "Die vorlaufende Entschlossenheit . . . entspringt dem nüchternen Verstehen faktischer Grundmöglichkeiten des Daseins. Met der nüchternen Angst, die vor das vereinzelte Seinkönnen bringt, geht die gerüstete Freude an dieser Möglichkeit zusammen."

152. Dreyfus (1991), p. 333.

153. I discussed the dimension of resoluteness in section 14A. Apart from resoluteness and being-toward-death, there are the dimensions of conscience and guilt (SZ, §§ 54–60), constancy (SZ, §§ 65, 74–75), and authentic historicality (SZ, § 74). Furthermore, authenticity is related to fundamental moods such as anxiety and joy.

154. SZ, § 53, p. 263: "Der Tod ist *eigenste* Möglichkeit des Daseins. Das Sein zu ihr erschließt dem Dasein sein *eigenstes* Seinkönnen"; p. 265: "Tod ist je nur eigener"; § 50,

p. 250: "Der Tod ist eine Seinsmöglichkeit, die je das Dasein selbst zu übernehmen hat. Mit dem Tod steht sich das Dasein selbst in seinem *eigensten* Seinkönnen bevor"; § 53, p. 261: "zu einer ausgezeichneten Möglichkeit des Daseins selbst" (Heidegger's italics).

155. SZ, § 47, p. 240: "Indes scheitert diese Vertretungsmöglichkeit völlig, wenn es um die Vertretung der Seinsmöglichkeit geht, die das Zu-Ende-kommen des Daseins ausmacht.... *Keiner kann dem Anderen sein Sterben abnehmen*"; "Das Sterben muß jedes Dasein jeweilig selbst auf sich nehmen" (Heidegger's italics).

156. Cf. SZ, § 49, p. 248: "wie es (das Phänomen des Todes) als Seinsmöglichkeit des jeweiligen Daseins *in dieses hereinsteht*" (Heidegger's italics).

157. SZ, § 49, p. 247: "*Sterben* aber gelte als Titel für die *Seinsweise*, in der das Dasein zu seinem Tode *ist*"; from this it follows "daß das Dasein nicht erst stirbt oder gar nicht eigentlich stirbt bei und in einem Erleben des faktischen Ablebens" (p. 247), but that "Das Dasein stirbt faktisch, solange es existiert" (p. 251). Cf. § 52, p. 259: "Als geworfenes In-der-Welt-sein ist das Dasein je schon seinem Tode überantwortet. Seiend zu seinem Tode, stirbt es faktisch und zwar ständig, solange es nicht zu seinem Ableben gekommen ist" (Heidegger's italics).

158. SZ, §§ 51–52.

159. SZ, § 52, p. 258: "So verdeckt das Man das Eigentümliche der Gewißheit des Todes, *daß er jeden Augenblick möglich ist*" (Heidegger's italics).

160. Cf. SZ, § 53, p. 261: "Im Sein zum Tode dagegen, wenn anders es die charakterisierte Möglichkeit als *solche* verstehend zu erschließen hat, muß die Möglichkeit ungeschwächt *als Möglichkeit* verstanden, *als Möglichkeit* ausgebildet und im Verhalten zu ihr *als Möglichkeit ausgehalten* werden" (Heidegger's italics).

161. SZ, § 52: "einer Seinsart des Daseins, in der es *als Dasein ganz* sein kann"; § 53, p. 264: "Weil das Vorlaufen in die unüberholbare Möglichkeit alle ihr vorgelagerten Möglichkeiten mit erschließt, liegt in ihm die Möglichkeit eines existenziellen Vorwegnehmens des *ganzen* Daseins, das heißt die Möglichkeit, als *ganzes Seinkönnen* zu existieren" (Heidegger's italics); p. 265: "Im Vorlaufen kann sich das Dasein erst seines eigensten Seins in seiner unüberholbaren Ganzheit vergewissern." Heidegger's analysis of being-toward-death was meant from the start as the solution to the problem of how we are able to grasp Dasein as a whole. Cf. SZ, §§ 45–47.

162. SZ, § 53, pp. 265–266: "Im Vorlaufen zum unbestimmt gewissen Tode öffnet sich das Dasein für eine aus seinem selbst entspringende ständige *Bedrohung*.... *Die Befindlichkeit aber, welche die ständige und schlechthinnige, aus dem eigensten vereinzelten Sein des Daseins aufsteigende Bedrohung seiner selbst offen zu halten vermag, ist die Angst*" (Heidegger's italics).

163. SZ, § 53, p. 263: "Darin kann dem Dasein offenbar werden, daß es in der ausgezeichneten Möglichkeit seiner selbst dem Man entrissen bleibt, das heißt vorlaufend sich je schon ihm entreißen kann," and so on; "Die im Vorlaufen verstandene Unbezüglichkeit des Todes vereinzelt das Dasein auf es selbst"; p. 264: "Das vorlaufende Freiwerden für den eigenen Tod befreit von der Verlorenheit"; and p. 266.

164. SZ, § 53, p. 262: "im verstehenden Näherkommen wird die Möglichkeit des Möglichen nur 'größer' "; "um so reiner dringt das Verstehen vor in die Möglichkeit *als die der Unmöglichkeit der Existenz überhaupt*"; "Der Tod als Möglichkeit gibt dem Dasein nichts zu 'Verwirklichendes'.... Er ist die Möglichkeit der Unmöglichkeit jeglichen Verhaltens zu . . ., jedes Existierens," and so on (Heidegger's italics).

165. SZ, § 49, p. 248: "Mit Sinn und Recht kann überhaupt erst dann methodisch sicher auch nur *gefragt* werden, *was nach dem Tode sei,* wenn dieser in seinem vollen ontologischen Wesen begriffen ist" (Heidegger's italics). Cf. p. 247: "Die ontologische Analyse des Seins zum Ende greift andererseits keiner existenziellen Stellungnahme zum Tode vor," and so on.

166. Edwards (1979).

167. SZ, § 50, p. 250: "Wenn das Dasein als diese Möglichkeit seiner selbst sich bevorsteht, ist es völlig auf sein eigenstes Seinkönnen verwiesen. So sich bevorstehend sind in ihm alle Bezüge zu anderem Dasein gelöst"; § 53, p. 263: "Die . . . Unbezüglichkeit des Todes vereinzelt das Dasein auf es selbst."

168. SZ, § 53, p. 263: "Der Tod ist eigenste Möglichkeit des Daseins. . . . Darin kann dem Dasein offenbar werden, daß es in der ausgezeichneten Möglichkeit seiner selbst dem Man entrissen bleibt, das heißt, vorlaufend sich je schon ihm entreißen kann."

169. SZ, § 49, p. 248: "Die Analyse des Todes bleibt aber insofern rein 'diesseitig,' als sie das Phänomen lediglich daraufhin interpretiert, wie es als Seinsmöglichkeit des jeweiligen Daseins *in dieses hereinsteht*" (Heidegger's italics).

170. See, for instance, SZ § 53, p. 261: "Zunächst gilt es, das Sein zum Tode als ein Sein *zu einer Möglichkeit* und zwar zu einer ausgezeichneten Möglichkeit des Daseins selbst zu kennzeichnen"; § 51, p. 252: "Im Sein zum Tode verhält sich das Dasein *zu ihm selbst* als einem ausgezeichneten Seinkönnen" (Heidegger's italics).

171. Cf. for quotes: Edwards (1979), pp. 26–26.

172. SZ, § 53, p. 261: "Wenn also mit dem Sein zum Tode nicht eine 'Verwirklichung' seiner gemeint ist, dann kann es nicht besagen: sich aufhalten bei dem Ende in seiner Möglichkeit. Eine solche Verhaltung läge im 'Denken an den Tod.' " Edwards (1979), p. 30, found a case in which one might perhaps say that someone's crowning achievement occurred while he was dying, the story of Karl Fiala in *Der Tod des Kleinbürgers* by Franz Werfel. But what may be called Fiala's crowning achievement is rather that he *refused* to die before a specific day.

173. SZ, § 47, p. 239: "Zu den Seinsmöglichkeiten des Miteinanderseins in der Welt gehört unstreitig die *Vertretbarkeit* des einen Daseins durch ein anderes," and so on (Heidegger's italics).

174. SZ, § 47, pp. 239–240: "Bezüglich dieses Seins, des alltäglichen Miteinanderaufgehens bei der besorgten 'Welt,' ist Vertretbarkeit nicht nur überhaupt möglich, sie gehört sogar als Konstitutivum zum Miteinander. *Hier* kann und muß sogar das eine Dasein in gewissen Grenzen das andere *'sein'* " (Heidegger's italics).

175. I am using here a generalized notion of substitutivity, because one must distinguish between the general sense in which anyone else may follow the rule that I am following (anyone else may, in principle, follow the rules for English usage) and "representation" in the much more specific sense in which the word is used in legal contexts, for instance. In this specific sense, it is not true that we may represent each other in all social or legal roles. Quite often, representation is ruled out explicitly. Heidegger does not bother about these distinctions, which in fact violate his argument.

176. SZ, § 47, p. 240: "Indes scheitert diese Vertretungsmöglichkeit völlig, wenn es um die Vertretung der Seinsmöglichkeit geht, die das Zu-Ende-kommen des Daseins ausmacht."

177. SZ, § 47, p. 240: "*Keiner kann dem Anderen sein Sterben abnehmen*" (Heidegger's italics).

178. SZ, § 47, p. 240: "Jemand kann wohl 'für einen Anderen in den Tod gehen.' Das besagt jedoch immer: für den Anderen sich opfern '*in einer bestimmten Sache*,' " and so on (Heidegger's italics).

179. SZ, § 47, p. 240: "Der Tod ist, sofern er 'ist,' wesensmäßig je der meine."

180. There are a few exceptions, such as SZ, § 23 (on the specific spatiality of Dasein), pp. 108–109. Dreyfus (1991) mistakenly infers "that Dasein is not necessarily embodied" (p. 41) from SZ, § 12, p. 54: "In-sein dagegen meint eine Seinsverfassung des Daseins und ist ein *Existenzial*. Dann kann damit aber nicht gedacht werden an das Vorhandensein eines Körperdinges (Menschenleib) 'in' einem vorhandenen Seienden" (Heidegger's italics). If Heidegger says that the analysis of Dasein "must be carried out prior to every factual concretion" (Dreyfus, p. 41), he does not mean that Dasein is not necessarily embodied but rather that the analysis of Dasein in SZ is meant as an *ontological* analysis that has essential generality, and is independent of the *ontical* peculiarities of individual Daseins. And the passage on *In-sein* in SZ, § 12, means that there is a categorial difference between on the one hand the notion of one extant thing being "in" another extant thing and on the other hand the notion of Dasein's being "in" the world.

181. SZ, § 27, p. 126: "sie *sind*, was sie betreiben"; § 47, p. 239: " 'Man *ist*' das was man betreibt" (Heidegger's italics).

182. SZ, § 53, p. 262: "Der Tod als Möglichkeit gibt dem Dasein nichts zu 'Verwirklichendes' und nichts, was es als Wirkliches selbst *sein* könnte. Er ist die Möglichkeit der Unmöglichkeit jeglichen Verhaltens zu . . . , jedes Existierens" (Heidegger's italics).

183. Dreyfus (1991), p. 311.

184. SZ, § 48, p. 245: "Das mit dem Tod gemeinte Enden bedeutet kein Zu-Ende-sein des Daseins, sondern ein *Sein zum Ende* dieses Seienden" (Heidegger's italics).

185. SZ, § 48, p. 245: "Sobald ein Mensch zum Leben kommt, sogleich ist er alt genug zu sterben"; § 49, p. 247: "*Sterben* aber gelte als Titel für die *Seinsweise*, in der das Dasein zu seinem Tode *ist*," and so on; § 50, p. 251: "Das Dasein stirbt faktisch, solange es existiert"; cf. § 52, p. 259 (Heidegger's italics).

186. SZ, § 48, p. 244: "*in welchem Sinne überhaupt der Tod als Enden des Daseins begriffen werden muß*" (Heidegger's italics).

187. SZ, § 48, p. 245: "*Durch keinen dieser Modi des Endens läßt sich der Tod als Ende des Daseins angemessen charakterisieren*" (Heidegger's italics).

188. SZ, § 48, first three paragraphs on pp. 241–242. Cf. p. 245: "Würde das Sterben als Zu-Ende-sein im Sinne eines Endens der besprochenen Art verstanden, dann wäre das Dasein hiermit als Vorhandenes bzw. Zuhandenes gesetzt."

189. SZ, § 31, passim. Cf. p. 145: "weil es *ist*, was es wird bzw. nicht wird, kann es verstehend ihm selbst sagen: 'werde, was du bist!' " (Heidegger's italics).

190. SZ, § 48, p. 245: "So wie das Dasein vielmehr ständig, solange es ist, schon sein Noch-nicht *ist*, so *ist* es auch schon immer sein Ende. Das mit dem Tod gemeinte Enden bedeutet kein Zu-Ende-sein des Daseins, sondern ein *Sein zum Ende* dieses Seienden. Der Tod ist eine Weise zu sein, die das Dasein übernimmt, sobald es ist" (Heidegger's italics).

191. Edwards (1979), p. 22.

192. SZ, § 48, p. 245: "Das mit dem Tod gemeinte Enden bedeutet kein Zu-Ende-sein des Daseins, sondern ein *Sein zum Ende* dieses Seienden" (Heidegger's italics).

193. SZ, § 53, p. 261: "Das fragliche Sein zum Tode kann offenbar nicht den Charakter des besorgenden Aus-seins auf seine Verwirklichung haben," and so on.

194. SZ, § 7C, pp. 34–35.

195. SZ, § 47, p. 237: "Das Erreichen der Gänze des Daseins im Tode ist zugleich Verlust des Seins des Da. Der Übergang zum Nichtmehrdasein hebt das Dasein gerade aus der Möglichkeit, diesen Übergang zu erfahren und als erfahrenen zu verstehen."

196. SZ, § 47, pp. 238–239: "Je angemessener das Nichtmehrdasein des Verstorbenen phänomenal gefaßt wird, um so deutlicher zeigt sich, daß solches Mitsein mit dem Toten gerade *nicht* das eigentliche Zuendegekommensein des Verstorbenen erfährt. Der Tod enthüllt sich zwar als Verlust, aber mehr als solcher, den die Verbleibenden erfahren. Im Erleiden des Verlustes wird jedoch nicht der Seinsverlust als solcher zugänglich, den der Sterbende 'erleidet' " (Heidegger's italics). I have translated *eigentliche* as "actual" and not as "authentic" (cf. BT, p. 282), because I do not think that in this context the word has Heidegger's technical meaning of authenticity.

197. SZ, § 47, p. 239: "Die Frage steht nach dem ontologischen Sinn des Sterbens des Sterbenden als einer Seinsmöglichkeit *seines* Seins" (Heidegger's italics).

198. SZ, §§ 52–53; pp. 258 and 261 (for quotes, see above).

199. SZ, § 53, p. 261: "Damit entzöge sich aber das Dasein gerade den Boden für ein existierendes Sein zum Tode."

200. SZ, § 53, p. 262: "im verstehenden Näherkommen wird die Möglichkeit des Möglichen nur 'größer' "; "Im Vorlaufen in diese Möglichkeit wird sie 'immer größer,' das heißt sie enthüllt sich als solche, die überhaupt kein Maß, kein mehr oder minder kennt." Of course, when we approach something, it does not increase in size, nor does it even look larger: it just occludes more. And it need not look more impressive from close up. Clearly, even Heidegger's image as such is confused.

201. SZ, § 53, p. 262: "*Die nächste Nähe des Seins zum Tode als Möglichkeit ist einem Wirklichen so fern als möglich*" (Heidegger's italics).

202. SZ, § 53, p. 262: "Je unverhüllter diese Möglichkeit verstanden wird, um so reiner dringt das Verstehen vor in die Möglichkeit *als die der Unmöglichkeit der Existenz überhaupt.* Der Tod als Möglichkeit gibt dem Dasein nichts zu 'Verwirklichendes' und nichts, was es als Wirkliches selbst *sein* könnte. Er ist die Möglichkeit der Unmöglichkeit jeglichen Verhaltens zu . . ., jedes Existierens" (Heidegger's italics).

203. Edwards (1979), p. 33.

204. SZ, § 45, p. 232: "Eine *ursprüngliche* ontologische Interpretation . . . muß sich ausdrücklich dessen versichern, ob sie das Ganze des thematischen Seienden in die Vorhabe gebracht hat" (Heidegger's italics).

205. SZ, § 45, p. 233: "Seiendes, dessen Essenz die Existenz ausmacht, widersetzt sich wesenhaft der möglichen Erfassung seiner als ganzes Seiendes."

206. Heidegger's argument in SZ, § 45, is the more remarkable because he defines the problem of wholeness in section 41 as one of structural wholeness—it is concerned with "Die formal existenziale Ganzheit des ontologischen Strukturganzen des Daseins" (p. 192)—and because he solves this problem of structural wholeness by means of his notion of concern (*Sorge*). As the global argument of SZ does not require the problem of diachronic wholeness at all, we must suppose that its presence in the text should be explained by "external," Pascalian motives.

207. SZ, § 53, p. 264: "Weil das Vorlaufen in die unüberholbare Möglichkeit alle ihr vorgelagerten Möglichkeiten mit erschließt, liegt in ihm die Möglichkeit eines existenziellen Vorwegnehmens des *ganzen* Daseins, das heißt die Möglichkeit, als *ganzes Seinkönnen* zu existieren" (Heidegger's italics).

208. SZ, § 53, p. 262: "Der Tod als Möglichkeit gibt dem Dasein nichts zu 'Verwirklichendes' und nichts, was es als Wirkliches selbst *sein* könnte" (Heidegger's italics).

209. SZ, § 49, p. 248: "Den Fragen einer Biologie, Psychologie, Theodizee und Theologie des Todes ist die existenziale Analyse methodisch vorgeordnet."

210. SZ, § 49, pp. 247–248: "Wenn der Tod als 'Ende' des Daseins, das heißt des In-der-Welt-seins bestimmt wird, dann fällt damit keine ontische Entscheidung darüber, ob 'nach dem Tode' noch ein anderes, höheres oder niedrigeres Sein möglich ist, ob das Dasein 'fortlebt' oder gar, sich 'überdauernd,' 'unsterblich' ist."

211. SZ, § 53, p. 262: "Der Tod . . . gibt dem Dasein nichts zu 'Verwirklichendes' und nichts, was es als Wirkliches selbst *sein* könnte," and so on (Heidegger's italics).

212. Dreyfus (1991), p. 333.

213. We might say something like "Richard is himself again," but not "these last six months I have really been myself," let alone "finally I have become myself."

214. Edwards (1979), p. 45.

215. SZ, § 49, p. 248: "Mit Sinn und Recht kann überhaupt erst dann methodisch sicher auch nur *gefragt* werden, was *nach dem Tode sei*, wenn dieser in seinem vollen ontologischen Wesen begriffen ist" (Heidegger's italics).

BIBLIOGRAPHY

A. HEIDEGGER BIBLIOGRAPHIES

Gerber, Rudolph (1968). "Focal Points in Recent Heidegger Scholarship." *New Scholasticism* 42: 560–577.

Haar, Michel, ed. (1983). *Martin Heidegger. Les Cahiers de l'Herne*. Paris: Éditions de l'Herne.

Lübbe, Hermann (1957). "Bibliographie der Heidegger-Literatur 1917–1955." *Zeitschrift für philosophische Forschung* 11: 401–452.

Nordquist, Joan, ed. (1990). *Martin Heidegger. A Bibliography*. Santa Cruz, Calif.: Reference & Research Service.

Paumen, Jean (1960). "Eléments de bibliographie Heideggérienne." *Revue Internationale de Philosophie* 14: 263–268.

Pereboom, Dirk (1969). "Heidegger Bibliographie 1917–1966." *Freiburger Zeitschrift für Philosophie und Theologie* 16: 100–161.

Sass, Hans-Martin (1968). *Heidegger-Bibliographie*. Meisenheim am Glan: Hain.

———(1975). *Materialien zur Heidegger-Bibliographie 1917–1972*. Meisenheim am Glan: Hain.

———(1982). *Martin Heidegger. Bibliography and Glossary*. Bowling Green: Philosophy Documentation Center.

Schneeberber, Guido (1960). *Ergänzungen zu einer Heidegger-Bibliographie*. Bern: Suhr.

B. WORKS BY HEIDEGGER

Works by Heidegger that I used in writing this book are specified in the list of abbreviations that precede the Notes, with the exception of volumes of the *Gesamtausgabe* that I quoted only a few times. For a list of Heidegger's lectures and works in chronological order, see: Richardson (1963), pp. 663–680; Biemel (1973), pp. 159–163; and Kisiel (1993), pp. 461–476. No published list of Heidegger's publications is complete. Schneeberger (1960 and 1962) discovered a number of new items, as did Farias (1987).

The program of the *Gesamtausgabe* of November 1991 is reprinted in Guignon (1993), which also contains a selective bibliography. As the program is updated regularly, one should consult the latest edition.

C. ENGLISH TRANSLATIONS OF HEIDEGGER

For lists of English translations of Heidegger, see: Sheehan (1981), pp. 281–292; and Guignon (1993), pp. 363–365. All translations in the main text are mine, although in translating *Sein und Zeit* I tried to remain close to the translation of Macquarrie and Robinson (BT).

D. OTHER WORKS CITED IN THE TEXT

Ackrill, J. L. (1963). *Aristotle's "Categories" and "De Interpretatione."* Translated with notes and glossary. Oxford: Oxford University Press, 1963. Reprint 1979.

Arendt, Hannah, and Karl Jaspers (1992). *Correspondence 1926–1969.* Translated and edited by L. Kohler and H. Saner. New York: Harcourt, Brace.

Aristotle (An. Post.). *Posterior Analytics.* Loeb Classical Library, vol. 391. Cambridge, Mass.: Harvard University Press, 1976.

Aristotle (Cat.). *Categories.* Loeb Classical Library, vol. 325. Cambridge, Mass.: Harvard University Press, 1973.

Aristotle (Met.). *Metaphysics.* Loeb Classical Library, vols. 271 and 287. Cambridge, Mass.: Harvard University Press, 1975 and 1969.

Aristotle (Top.). *Topica.* Loeb Classical Library, vol. 391. Cambridge, Mass.: Harvard University Press, 1976.

Barash, Jeffrey A. (1988). *Martin Heidegger and the Problem of Historical Meaning.* Dordrecht: Nijhoff.

Bast, Rainer A. (1986a). "Ist Heideggers *Sein und Zeit* ein Patchwork?" *Information Philosophie* 4: 18–30.

———(1986b). *Der Wissenschaftsbegriff Martin Heideggers im Zusammenhang seiner Philosophie.* Stuttgart-Bad Cannstatt: Fromann-Holzberg.

Beaufret, Jean (1984). *Entretiens avec Frédéric de Towarnicki.* Paris: Presses Universitaires de France.

Biemel, Walter (1973). *Martin Heidegger in Selbstzeugnissen und Bilddokumenten.* Reinbek bei Hamburg: Rowohlt Taschenbuch Verlag.

Blattner, William D. (1994). "Is Heidegger a Kantian Idealist?" *Inquiry* 37: 185–201.

Bloom, Allan (1987). *The Closing of the American Mind.* New York: Simon & Schuster.

Borgmann, Albert (1978). "Heidegger and Symbolic Logic." In Murray (1978), pp. 3–22.

Bourdieu, Pierre (1988). *L'Ontologie politique de Martin Heidegger.* Paris: Les Éditions de Minuit.

Bracher, Karl Dietrich (1972). *Die deutsche Diktatur. Entstehung, Struktur, Folgen des National Sozialismus.* 4th ed. Köln: Verlag Kiepenheuer & Witsch.

Bracher, Karl Dietrich, Manfred Funke, and Hans-Adolf Jacobsen, eds. (1983). *Nationalsozialistische Diktatur 1933–1945. Eine Bilanz.* Düsseldorf: Droste Verlag.

Braig, Carl (1896). *Vom Sein. Abriß der Ontologie.* Freiburg im Breisgau: Herdersche Verlagshandlung.

Brentano, Franz (1862). *Von der mannigfachen Bedeutung des Seienden nach Aristoteles.* Freiburg im Breisgau: Verlag Herder; Reprint Hildesheim: Georg Olms, 1960.

Bretschneider, W. (1965). *Sein und Wahrheit.* Meisenheim am Glan: Anton Hain.

Buchner, Hartmut (1977). "Fragmentarisches." In Neske, ed. (1977), pp. 47–51.

Bullock, Alan (1955). "The Political Ideas of Adolf Hitler." In *The Third Reich,* pp. 350–378.

Caputo, John D. (1986). *The Mystical Element in Heidegger's Thought.* New York: Fordham University Press.

———(1992). "Meister Eckhart and the Later Heidegger: The Mystical Element in Heidegger's Thought." In Macann (1992), vol. 2, chapter 21.

———(1993). "Heidegger and Theology." In Guignon (1993), pp. 270–288.

Carey, John (1992). *The Intellectuals and the Masses. Pride and Prejudice among the Literary Intelligentsia 1880–1939*. London and Boston: Faber & Faber.

Carnap, Rudolf (1928). *Scheinprobleme in der Philosophie. Das Fremdpsychische und der Realismusstreit*. Berlin, 1928. Translated by Rolf A. George in Rudolf Carnap, *The Logical Structure of the World: Pseudoproblems in Philosophy*. Berkeley and Los Angeles: University of California Press, 1967.

———(1931). "Überwindung der Metaphysik durch logische Analyse der Sprache." *Erkenntnis* 2: 219–241.

———(1956). *Meaning and Necessity. A Study in Semantics and Modal Logic*. Enlarged edition. Chicago and London: University of Chicago Press.

Cerbone, David R. (1995). "World, World-Entry, and Realism in Early Heidegger." *Inquiry* 38: 401–421.

Chamberlain, Houston Stewart (1898). *Die Grundlagen des neunzehnten Jahrhunderts*. München: Bruckmann, 1900.

Davidson, Donald (1984). *Inquiries into Truth and Interpretation*. Oxford: Oxford University Press.

De Rijk, Lambertus M. (1980). "On Ancient and Mediaeval Semantics and Metaphysics (3)." *Vivarium* 18: 1–62.

———(1988). "Categorization as a Key Notion in Ancient and Medieval Semantics." *Vivarium* 26: 1–18.

Dewey, John (1929). *The Quest for Certainty*. New York: Capricorn, 1960.

Dilthey, Wilhelm (1914–). *Gesammelte Schriften*. Stuttgart: B. G. Teubner Verlagsgesellschaft.

Domarus, Max (1973). Hitler, *Reden und Proklamationen 1932–1945*. Wiesbaden: R. Löwit.

Dreyfus, Hubert L. (1991). *Being-in-the-World. A Commentary on Heidegger's "Being and Time," Division I*. Cambridge, Mass.: MIT, 1992.

Dreyfus, Hubert L., and Harrison Hall, eds. (1992). *Heidegger: A Critical Reader*. Oxford: Blackwell.

Dreyfus, Hubert L., and Harrison Hall (1992a). Introduction to Dreyfus and Hall (1992).

Ebeling, Hans (1991). *Martin Heidegger. Philosophie und Ideologie*. Hamburg: Rowohlt Taschenbuch Verlag.

Edwards, Paul (1979). *Heidegger on Death. A Critical Evaluation*. Monist Monograph, 1. La Salle, Ill.: The Hegeler Institute.

Ettinger, Elzbieta (1994). *Hannah Arendt-Martin Heidegger*. New Haven, Conn., and London: Yale University Press.

Ezrahi, Y., E. Mendelsohn, and H. Segal, eds. (1993). *Technology, Pessimism, and Postmodernism*. Dordrecht: Kluwer.

Farias, Victor (1987). *Heidegger et le nazisme*. Lagrasse: Verdier.

Fay, Thomas A. (1977). *Heidegger. The Critique of Logic*. Den Haag: Martinus Nijhoff.

Fehér, Istrán M. (1991). *Wege und Irrwege des neueren Umganges mit Heideggers Werk*. Berlin: Duncker & Humblot.

Feick, Hildegard (1980). *Index zu Heideggers 'Sein und Zeit.'* 3rd ed. Tübingen: Niemeyer.

Franzen, Winfried (1975). *Von der Existenzialontologie zur Seinsgeschichte. Eine Untersuchung über die Entwicklung der Philosophie Martin Heideggers*. Meisenheim am Glan: Anton Hain.

Franzen, Winfried (1988). "Die Sehnsucht nach Härte und Schwere." In Gethmann-Siefert (1988), pp. 78–92.

Frede, Dorothea (1986). "Heidegger and the Scandal of Philosophy." In A. Donovan, A. N. Perovich, and M. V. Wedin, eds., *Human Nature and Natural Knowledge.* Dordrecht: Reidel, 1986.

Frege, Gottlob (1892). "Über Sinn und Bedeutung." *Zeitschrift für Philosophie und philos. Kritik, NF* 100: 25–50. Also in Patzig (1975).

Friedenthal, Richard (1967). *Luther. Sein Leben und seine Zeit.* München: Piper Verlag.

Fürstenau, P. (1958). *Heidegger. Das Gefüge seines Denkens.* Frankfurt a/M.: Klostermann.

Gadamer, Hans-Georg (1975). *Wahrheit und Methode. Grundzüge einer philosophischen Hermeneutik.* 4th ed. Tübingen: J. C. B. Mohr.

———(1983). *Heideggers Wege. Studien zum Spätwerk.* Tübingen: J. C. B. Mohr.

———(1989). "Heideggers 'theologische' Jugendschrift." *Dilthey-Jahrbuch für Philosophie der Geisteswissenschaften* 6: 229–234 (introduction to Heidegger, PIA).

Gethmann-Siefert, Annemarie (1974). *Das Verhältnis von Philosophie und Theologie im Denken Martin Heideggers.* Freiburg and München: Alber Verlag.

Gethmann-Siefert, Annemarie, and Otto Pöggeler (1988). *Heidegger und die praktische Philosophie.* Frankfurt a/M.: Suhrkamp Verlag.

Greisch, Jean (1994). *Ontologie et temporalité. Esquisse d'une interprétation intégrale de 'Sein und Zeit.'* Paris: Presses Universitaires de France.

Grondin, Jean (1987). *Le tournant dans la pensée de Martin Heidegger.* Paris: Presses Universitaires de France.

Gründer, Karlfried (1961). "M. Heideggers Wissenschaftskritik in ihren geschichtlichen Zusammenhängen." *Archiv für Philosophie* 11: 312–335.

Guignon, Charles B., ed. (1993). *The Cambridge Companion to Heidegger.* Cambridge and New York: Cambridge University Press.

Haar, Michel (1994). *La fracture de l'Histoire. Douze essais sur Heidegger.* Grenoble: Millon.

———(1992). "Critical Remarks on the Heideggerian Reading of Nietzsche." In Macann (1992), vol. 2, chapter 27.

Habermas, Jürgen (1971). *Philosophisch-politische Profile.* Frankfurt a/M.: Suhrkamp Verlag.

———(1988). *Der philosophische Diskurs der Moderne.* Frankfurt a/M.: Suhrkamp Verlag.

———(1992). "Work and *Weltanschauung.* The Heidegger Controversy from a German Perspective." In Dreyfus and Hall (1992), pp. 186–208.

Hacker, P. M. S. (1986). *Insight and Illusion. Themes in the Philosophy of Wittgenstein.* Rev. ed. Oxford: Oxford University Press.

———(1996). "On Davidson's Idea of a Conceptual Scheme." *The Philosophical Quarterly* 46: 289–307.

Haecker, Theodor (1933). *Was ist der Mensch?* Leipzig: Jakob Hegner.

Haug, W. F., ed. (1989). *Deutsche Philosophen 1933.* Berlin and Hamburg: Argument.

Heath, Sir Thomas L. (1925). *The Thirteen Books of Euclid's "Elements."* Translation and commentary. Vol. 1. 2nd ed. New York: Dover reprint, 1956.

Hegel, Georg Wilhelm Friedrich (1955). *Grundlinien der Philosophie des Rechts* (1821). Hamburg: Felix Meiner Verlag.

Herf, Jeffrey (1984). *Reactionary Modernism. Technology, Culture, and Politics in Weimar and the Third Reich.* New York: Cambridge University Press.

———(1993). "Belated Pessimism: Technology and Twentieth-Century German Conservative Intellectuals." In Y. Ezrahi, E. Mendelsohn, and H. Segal, eds. (1993), pp. 115–136.

Hirsch, E. D. (1967). *Validity in Interpretation.* New Haven, Conn., and London: Yale University Press.

Hühnerfeld, Paul (1961). *In Sachen Heidegger. Versuch über ein deutsches Genie.* München: Paul List Verlag.

Husserl, Edmund (PhdA, 1891). *Philosophie der Arithmetik.* Husserliana XII. Den Haag: M. Nijhoff, 1970.

———(LU, 1900, 1901). *Logische Untersuchungen.* Halle a.S.: Niemeyer, 1900, 1901.

———(*Ideen* I, 1913). *Ideen zu einer reinen Phänomenologie und phänomenologischen Philosophie.* Erstes Buch, Husserliana III/1. Den Haag: M. Nijhoff, 1976.

———(PhPs, 1925). *Phänomenologische Psychologie.* Husserliana IX. Den Haag: M. Nijhoff, 1968.

———(*Krisis,* 1936). *Die Krisis der europäischen Wissenschaften und die transzendentale Phänomenologie.* Husserliana VI. Den Haag: M. Nijhoff, 1954.

———(EU, 1939). *Erfahrung und Urteil. Untersuchungen zur Genealogie der Logik.* Hamburg: Felix Meiner Verlag, 1972.

———(1968). *Briefe an Ingarden.* Den Haag: M. Nijhoff.

Jaeger, Werner W. (1923). *Aristoteles. Grundlegung einer Geschichte seiner Entwicklung.* Berlin: Weidmann.

Janicaud, Dominique (1992). "The Shadow of This Thinking." In Macann (1992), vol. 4, chapter 52.

Jünger, Ernst (1930). "Die totale Mobilmachung." In *Krieg und Krieger.* Berlin: Junker & Dünnhaupt.

———(1932). *Der Arbeiter. Herrschaft und Gestalt.* Hamburg: Hanseatische Verlags-Anstalt.

Jung, Matthias (1990). *Das Denken des Seins und der Glaube an Gott. Zum Verhältnis von Philosophie und Theologie bei Martin Heidegger.* Würzburg: Königshausen & Neumann.

Kant, Immanuel (KdrV, 1781, 1787). *Kritik der reinen Vernunft.* Hamburg: Felix Meiner Verlag, 1976.

———(1786). *Metaphysische Anfangsgründe der Naturwissenschaft.* Darmstadt: Wissenschaftliche Buchgesellschaft, 1968.

Kaufmann, Walter (1963). *The Faith of a Heretic.* Garden City, N.Y.: Doubleday.

Kemper, Peter, ed. (1990). *Martin Heidegger—Faszination und Erschrecken. Die politische Dimension einer Philosophie.* Frankfurt a/M.: Campus Verlag.

Kierkegaard, Søren (1962). *The Present Age.* Translated by Alexander Dru; introduction by Walter Kaufmann. New York: Harper & Row.

Kisiel, Theodore (1992). "Edition und Übersetzung. Unterwegs von Tatsachen zu Gedanken, von Werken zu Wegen." In Papenfuss and Pöggeler (1992), vol. 3, pp. 89–107.

———(1993). *The Genesis of Heidegger's "Being and Time."* Berkeley and Los Angeles: University of California Press.

———, and John Van Buren (1994). *Reading Heidegger from the Start.* Albany: State University of New York Press.

Kiss, Endre (1991). "Die Stellung der Nietzsche-Deutung bei der Beurteilung der Rolle und des Schicksals Martin Heideggers im Dritten Reich." In Papenfuss and Pöggeler (1991), vol. 1, pp. 425–440.

Kockelmans, Joseph J. (1984). *On the Truth of Being. Reflections on Heidegger's Later Philosophy.* Bloomington: Indiana University Press.

Krockow, Christian von (1958). *Die Entscheidung. Eine Untersuchung über Ernst Jünger, Carl Schmitt, und Martin Heidegger.* Stuttgart: Enke Verlag.

Kuhn, Thomas S. (1970). *The Structure of Scientific Revolutions.* 2nd Enlarged Edition. Chicago: University of Chicago Press.

Laugstien, Thomas, ed. (1990). *Philosophieverhältnisse im deutschen Faschismus.* Hamburg: Argument.

Löwith, Karl (1949). "Les implications politiques de la philosophie de l'existence chez Heidegger." *Les Temps Modernes* 2: 343–360.

———(1965). *Heidegger. Denker in dürftiger Zeit.* 3rd ed. Göttingen: Vandenhoeck & Ruprecht.

———(1983). *Der europäische Nihilismus. Sämtliche Schriften.* Vol. 2. Stuttgart: J. B. Metzler.

———(1986). *Mein Leben in Deutschland vor und nach 1933. Ein Bericht.* Stuttgart: J .B. Metzler.

Losurdo, Domenico (1992). "Heidegger and Hitler's War." In Rockmore and Margolis (1992), pp. 141–166.

Lotz, Johannes B. (1958). "Denken und Sein nach den jüngsten Veröffentlichungen von M. Heidegger." *Scholastik* 33: 81–97.

Lukacs, Georg (1949). "Heidegger redivivus." *Sinn und Form* 1: 37–62.

Luther, Martin (1888). *Martin Luthers Werke. Kritische Gesamtausgabe.* Weimar, 1888.

———(1962). *Martin Luther. Selections from His Writings.* Edited with an introduction by John Dillenberger. New York: Doubleday.

Macann, Christopher (1992). *Martin Heidegger. Critical Assessments.* 4 vols. London and New York: Routledge.

Macquarrie, John (1984). *In Search of Deity.* London: SCM and Crossroad.

———(1992). "Heidegger's Language and the Problem of Translation." In Macann (1992), pp. 50–57.

———(1994). *Heidegger and Christianity.* New York: Continuum.

Margolis, Joseph (1983). "Pragmatism, Transcendental Arguments, and the Technological." In *Philosophy and Technology.* Edited by Paul T. Durbin and Friedrich Rapp. Boston: D. Reidel.

Marten, R. (1987). "Ein rassistisches Konzept von Humanität." *Badische Zeitung,* 19–20 December 1987.

Martin, Bernd (1989). *Martin Heidegger und das "Dritte Reich." Ein Kompendium.* Darmstadt: Wissenschaftliche Buchgesellschaft.

McDowell, John (1994). *Mind and World.* Cambridge, Mass.: Harvard University Press.

McGuinness, Brian, ed. (1979). *Wittgenstein and the Vienna Circle. Conversations Recorded by Friedrich Waismann.* Oxford: Blackwell.

Mohanty, J. N. (1992). "Heidegger on Logic." In Macann (1992), vol. 3, chapter 37.

Mosse, George L. (1964). *The Crisis of German Ideology. Intellectual Origins of the Third Reich.* New York: Schocken, 1981.

Mulhall, Stephen (1990). *On Being in the World. Wittgenstein and Heidegger on Seeing Aspects.* London: Routledge.

Müller, Max (1949). *Existenzphilosophie im geistigen Leben der Gegenwart.* 3rd ed. Heidelberg: Kerle Verlag, 1964.

Murray, Michael (1978). *Heidegger and Modern Philosophy. Critical Essays.* New Haven and London: Yale University Press.

Natorp, Paul (1888). "Thema und Disposition der aristotelischen Metaphysik." *Philosophische Monatshefte* 24: 37–65 and 540–574.

Neske, G. (1977). *Erinnerung an Martin Heidegger.* Pfullingen: Neske Verlag.

Nietzsche, Friedrich (UB, 1873–76). *Unzeitgemäße Betrachtungen.* Stuttgart: Kröner, 1964.

———(M, 1881). *Morgenröte. Gedanken über die moralischen Vorurteile.* Stuttgart: Kröner, 1964.

———(FW, 1882). *Die fröhliche Wissenschaft.* Stuttgart: Kröner, 1965.

———(Z, 1883–85). *Also sprach Zarathustra.* Leipzig: Kröner, 1930.

———(JGB, 1886). *Jenseits von Gut und Böse.* Leipzig: Kröner, 1930.

———(GM, 1887). *Zur Genealogie der Moral.* Leipzig: Kröner, 1930.

———(WM, 1906). *Der Wille zur Macht. Versuch einer Umwertung aller Werte.* Edited by Peter Gast and Elisabeth Förster-Nietzsche. Stuttgart: Kröner, 1964.

———(UW, 1931), *Die Unschuld des Werdens. Der Nachlaß.* Edited by Alfred Baeumler. 2 vols. Stuttgart: Kröner, 1978.

Noller, G., ed. (1967). *Heidegger und die Theologie.* München: Kaiser Verlag.

Nolte, Ernst (1992). *Heidegger, Politiek und Geschichte im Leben und Denken.* Berlin and Frankfurt a/M.: Propyläen.

Nuchelmans, Gabriel (1990). "Pleidooi voor een ingetogen hermeneutiek." In Nuchelmans et al., *Tekstinterpretatie.* Mededelingen van de Koninklijke Nederlandse Akademie van Wetenschappen, afd. letterkunde, Nieuwe Reeks, Deel 53, no. 6. Amsterdam: Noord-Hollandsche.

Okrent, Mark (1988). *Heidegger's Pragmatism. Understanding, Being, and the Critique of Metaphysics.* Ithaca, N.Y., and London: Cornell University Press.

Ott, Hugo (1988). *Martin Heidegger: unterwegs zu seiner Biographie.* Frankfurt a/M. and New York: Campus Verlag.

———(1990). "Biographische Gründe für Heideggers 'Mentalität der Zerrissenheit.' " In Kemper (1990), pp. 13–29.

Oudemans, Th. C. W. (1990). "Heideggers *logische Untersuchungen.*" *Heidegger Studies* 6: 85–105.

Papenfuss, Dietrich, and Otto Pöggeler (1991, 1992). *Zur philosophischen Aktualität Heideggers.* 3 vols. Frankfurt a/M.: Klostermann.

Parkes, Graham, ed. (1987). *Heidegger and Asian Thought.* Honolulu: University of Hawaii Press.

Pascal, Blaise (1963). *Oeuvres complètes.* Edited by Louis Lafuma. Paris: Seuil.

Patzig, Günther (1960–61). "Theologie und Ontologie in der 'Metaphysik' des Aristoteles." *Kant-Studien* 52: 185–187.

———ed. (1975). Gottlob Frege, *Funktion, Begriff, Bedeutung. Fünf logische Studien.* Göttingen: Vandenhoeck & Ruprecht.

Patzig, Günther (1979). "Logical Aspects of Some Arguments in Aristotle's 'Metaphysics.' " In P. Aubenque, ed., *Études sur la Métaphysique d'Aristote. Actes du VIe symposium Aristotelicum.* Paris: Vrin.

Philipse, Herman (1983). *De fundering van de logica in Husserls "Logische Untersuchungen."* Leiden: Labor Vincit.

———(1990). "The Absolute Network Theory of Language and Traditional Epistemology." *Inquiry* 33: 127–178.

———(1992). "Heidegger's Question of Being and the 'Augustinian Picture' of Language." *Philosophy and Phenomenological Research* 52: 251–287.

———(1994). "Towards a Postmodern Conception of Metaphysics: On the Genealogy and Successor Disciplines of Modern Philosophy." *Metaphilosophy* 25: 1–44.

———(1994a). "Heidegger's Question of Being: A Critical Interpretation." In Barry Smith, ed., *European Philosophy and the American Academy.* La Salle, Ill.: The Monist Library of Philosophy, pp. 99–122.

———(1994b). "Husserl and the Origins of Analytical Philosophy." *The European Journal of Philosophy* 2: 165–184.

———(1995). "Transcendental Idealism." In Barry Smith and David W. Smith, eds., *The Cambridge Companion to Husserl.* New York: Cambridge University Press, pp. 239–322.

Pöggeler, Otto (1963). *Der Denkweg Martin Heideggers.* Pfullingen: Neske.

———(1983). Idem. Second edition, with a postscript.

———(1990). Idem. Third edition, with a postscript.

———(1986–87). "Heideggers Begegnung mit Dilthey." *Dilthey-Jahrbuch für Philosophie der Geisteswissenschaften* 4: 121–160.

———(1989). " 'Praktische Philosophie' als Antwort an Heidegger." In Martin (1989), pp. 62–92.

———(1990a). "Nietzsche, Hölderlin und Heidegger." In Kemper (1990), pp. 178–195.

———(1992). "Heidegger, Nietzsche, and Politics." In Rockmore and Margolis (1992), pp. 114–140.

Pugliese, Orlando (1965). *Vermittlung und Kehre.* Freiburg im Breisgau: Alber Verlag.

Quine, Willard V. O. (1960). *Word and Object.* Cambridge, Mass.: MIT.

———(1990). *Pursuit of Truth.* Cambridge, Mass.: Harvard University Press.

Rabinbach, Anson (1994). "Heidegger's Letter on Humanism as Text and Event." *New German Critique* 62: 3–38.

Rauschning, Herrmann (1940). *Gespräche mit Hitler.* Zürich: Europa Verlag.

Reiner, Hans (1954). "Die Entstehung und ursprüngliche Bedeutung des Namens Metaphysik." *Zeitschrift für philosophische Forschung* 8: 210–237.

Richardson, William J. (1963). *Heidegger. Through Phenomenology to Thought.* Den Haag: Martinus Nijhoff.

Robinson, J. M., and J. B. Cobb, eds. (1965). *Der späte Heidegger und die Theologie.* Zürich and Stuttgart: Zwingli Verlag.

Rockmore, Tom (1992). *On Heidegger's Nazism and Philosophy.* Berkeley and Los Angeles: University of California Press.

———(1995). *Heidegger and French Philosophy. Humanism, Antihumanism, and Being.* London and New York: Routledge.

Rockmore, Tom, and Joseph Margolis (1992). *The Heidegger Case. On Philosophy and Politics*. Philadelphia: Temple University Press.

Rorty, Richard (1980). *Philosophy and the Mirror of Nature*. Princeton, N.J.: Princeton University Press.

———(1991). *Essays on Heidegger and Others, Philosophical Papers*. Vol 2. Cambridge: Cambridge University Press.

Rosales, Alberto (1984). "Zum Problem der Kehre im Denken Heideggers." *Zeitschrift für philosophische Forschung* 38: 241–262.

———(1991). "Heideggers Kehre im Lichte ihrer Interpretationen." In Papenfuss and Pöggeler (1991), vol. 1, pp. 118–140.

Routila, L. (1969). *Die aristotelische Idee der ersten Philosophie. Untersuchungen zur onto-theologischen Verfassung der Metaphysik des Aristoteles*. Amsterdam: North Holland.

Russell, Bertrand (1937). *The Principles of Mathematics*. 2nd ed. London: Allen & Unwin.

———(1962). *An Inquiry into Meaning and Truth*. Harmondsworth: Penguin.

Safranski, Rüdinger (1994). *Ein Meister aus Deutschland. Heidegger und seine Zeit*. München: Carl Hanser Verlag.

Schaeffler, Richard (1988). "Heidegger und die Theologie." In Gethmann-Siefert and Pöggeler (1988), pp. 286–309.

Schatzki, Theodore R. (1992). "Early Heidegger on Being. The Clearing and Realism." In Dreyfus and Hall (1992), pp. 81–98.

Schirmacher, Wolfgang (1983). *Technik und Gelassenheit: Zeitkritik nach Heidegger*. Freiburg and München: Karl Alber.

Schmidt, Gerhart (1989). "Heideggers philosophische Politik." In Martin (1989), pp. 51–61.

Schneeberger, Guido (1962). *Nachlese zu Heidegger. Dokumente zu seinem Leben und Denken*. Bern: private edition.

Scholz, G. (1967). "Sprung. Zur Geschichte eines philosophischen Begriffs." *Archiv für Begriffsgeschichte* 11: 206–237.

Schulz, Walter (1953–54). "Über den philosophiegeschichtlichen Ort Martin Heideggers." *Philosophische Rundschau* 1: 65–93; 211–232.

Schürmann, Reiner (1972). *Maître Eckhart ou la joie errante. Sermons allemands traduits et commentés*. Paris: Éditions Planète.

Schwan, Alexander (1965). *Politische Philosophie im Denken Heideggers*. Köln and Opladen: Westdeutscher Verlag.

Searle, John R. (1992). *The Rediscovery of the Mind*. Cambridge, Mass., and London: MIT.

Sheehan, Thomas (1979). "Heidegger's 'Introduction to the Phenomenology of Religion.'" *The Personalist* 60: 312–324.

———ed. (1981). *Heidegger, The Man and the Thinker*. Chicago: Precedent.

———(1981a). "Introduction: Heidegger, the Project and the Fulfillment." In Sheehan (1981), pp. vii–xx.

———(1981b). "Heidegger's Early Years: Fragments for a Philosophical Biography." In Sheehan (1981), pp. 3–19.

Sluga, Hans (1993). *Heidegger's Crisis. Philosophy and Politics in Nazi Germany*. Cambridge, Mass.: Harvard University Press.

Smith, Barry (1992). "Zur Nichtübersetzbarkeit der deutschen Philosophie." In Papenfuss and Pöggeler (1992), pp. 125–147.

Steiner, George (1978). *Heidegger*. Glasgow: Fontana/Collins.

Steiner, John M. (1983). "Über das Glaubensbekenntnis der SS." In Bracher, Funke, and Jacobsen (1983), pp. 206–222.

Stern, Fritz (1961). *The Politics of Cultural Despair. A Study in the Rise of the Germanic Ideology*. Berkeley: University of California Press.

Strawson, Sir Peter (1970). Categories. In *Ryle. A Collection of Critical Essays*. Edited by Oscar P. Wood and George Pitcher. London and Basingstoke: Macmillan, 1971, pp. 181–211.

Stroud, Barry (1968). "Transcendental Arguments." *Journal of Philosophy* 65: 241–256.

The Third Reich (1955). An inquiry into the methods and procedures of Fascism and Nazism, agreed to by the General Conference of UNESCO in 1948. London: Weidenfeld & Nicolson.

Thomä, Dieter (1990). *Die Zeit des Selbst und die Zeit danach. Zur Kritik der Textgeschichte Martin Heideggers 1910–1976*. Frankfurt a/M.: Suhrkamp.

Tietjen, Hartmut (1991). "Martin Heideggers Auseinandersetzung mit der nationalsozialistischen Hochschulpolitik und Wissenschaftsidee (1933–1938)." In Fehér (1991), pp. 109–128.

Tugendhat, Ernst (1967). *Der Wahrheitsbegriff bei Husserl und Heidegger*. Berlin: Walter de Gruyter.

———(1970). "Das Sein und das Nichts." In *Durchblicke. Martin Heidegger zum 80. Geburtstag*. Frankfurt a/M.: Klostermann, 1970, pp. 132–160.

———(1976). *Vorlesungen zur Einführung in die Sprachanalytische Philosophie*. Frankfurt a/M.: Suhrkamp Verlag.

Van Buren, John (1994). "Martin Heidegger, Martin Luther." In Kisiel and Van Buren (1994), pp. 159–174.

———(1994a). *The Young Heidegger. Rumor of the Hidden King*. Bloomington and Indianapolis: Indiana University Press.

Van der Meulen, J. (1953). *Heidegger und Hegel oder Widerstreit und Widerspruch*. Meisenheim am Glan: Westkultur Verlag. Anton Hain.

Vermeil, Edmond (1955). "The Origin, Nature and Development of German Nationalist Ideology in the 19th and 20th Centuries." In *The Third Reich*.

Vietta, Silvio (1989). *Heideggers Kritik am Nationalsozialismus und an der Technik*. Tübingen: Niemeyer.

Von Herrmann, Friedrich Wilhelm (1964). *Die Selbstinterpretation Martin Heideggers*. Meisenheim am Glan: Verlag Anton Hain.

———(1992). "Übersetzung als philosophisches Problem." In Papenfuß und Pöggeler (1992), vol. 3, pp. 108–124.

Welte, Bernhard (1947). "Remarques sur l'ontologie de Heidegger." *Revue des Sciences Philosophiques Théologiques* 31: 379–393.

Wittgenstein, Ludwig (1921, *Tractatus*). *Tractatus Logico-Philosophicus*. German text with a new edition of the translation by D. F. Pears and B. F. McGuinness. London: Routledge, 1971.

———(1965). "A Lecture on Ethics." *Philosophical Review* 74: 3–12.

———(1979). *Wittgenstein and the Vienna Circle. Conversations Recorded by Friedrich Waismann*. Edited by Brian McGuinness. Oxford: Blackwell.

Young, Julian (1997). *Heidegger, Philosophy, Nazism*. Cambridge: Cambridge University Press.

Zarader, Marlène (1990). *La dette impensée. Heidegger et l'héritage hébraïque*. Paris: Éditions du Seuil.

Zimmerman, Michael E. (1990). *Heidegger's Confrontation with Modernity. Technology, Politics, Art*. Bloomington and Indianapolis: Indiana University Press.